# THE
# PROBATE RECORDS

OF

# ESSEX COUNTY

MASSACHUSETTS

VOLUME I
1635 - 1664

Southern Historical Press, Inc.
Greenville, South Carolina

This volume was reproduced
from a personal copy located in
the Publishers private library

All rights reserved. No part of this publication may be reproduced,
stored in a retrieval system, transmitted in any form, posted
on the web in any form or by any means without the
prior written permission of the publisher.

Please direct all correspondence and book orders to:
**SOUTHERN HISTORICAL PRESS, Inc.**
**1071 Park West Blvd.**
**Greenville, SC 29611**

Published 1916 by:
 The Essex Institute
ISBN #978-1-63914-649-9
*Printed in the United States of America*

THE COUNTY COMMISSIONERS FOR THE COUNTY OF ESSEX BY THEIR SUBSTANTIAL SUPPORT AND THE REGISTER OF PROBATE BY HIS CORDIAL CO-OPERATION HAVE MADE POSSIBLE THE PUBLICATION OF THESE IMPORTANT RECORDS.

# LIST OF ESTATES.

| | |
|---|---:|
| Abbott, George, Rowley (1647) | 84 |
| Thomas, Rowley (1659) | 301 |
| Adams, William, Ipswich (1662) | 366 |
| William, Jr., Ipswich (1659) | 278 |
| Ager, William, Salem (1654) | 184 |
| Alderman, John, Salem (1657) | 256 |
| Anard, John (1662) | 362 |
| Anderson, Arzbell, Lynn (1661) | 358 |
| Andrews, John, Corp., Ipswich (1662) | 378 |
| Robert, Ipswich (1644) | 27 |
| Annable, John, Ipswich (1664) | 454 |
| Antrum, Thomas, Salem (1663) | 413 |
| Averill, Abigail, Mrs., Ipswich (1655) | 201 |
| William, Ipswich (1653) | 151 |
| Avery, Joseph, Rev., Newbury (1635) | 3 |
| Babson, Isabel, Mrs., Gloucester (1661) | 343 |
| Bacon, Rebecca, Mrs., Salem (1655) | 227 |
| William, Salem (1653) | 161 |
| Badger, Giles, Newbury (1647) | 78 |
| Bailey, John, Newbury (1652) | 145 |
| Richard, Rowley (1648) | 92 |
| Baker, Robert, Salem (1640-41) | 13 |
| Sarah, Ipswich (1651) | 138 |
| Balch, Agnes, Salem (1657) | 263 |
| John, Salem (1648) | 96 |
| John, Salem (1662) | 365 |
| Ballard, William, Lynn (1643) | 24 |
| Barker, Thomas, Rowley (1651) | 128 |
| Barnes, Thomas, Salem (1664) | 432 |
| Barrett, Richard, Lynn(?), (1651) | 136 |
| Bartholomew, Richard, Salem (1646) | 51 |

## LIST OF ESTATES.

| | |
|---|---:|
| Bartlett, Richard, Newbury (1647) | 86 |
| Bartoll, John, Marblehead (1664) | 456 |
| Batchelder, Joseph, Wenham (1657) | 252 |
| Beadle, Samuel, Salem (1664) | 452 |
| Beard, William (1664) | 435 |
| Beckes, Tobiah (1662) | 363 |
| Belflower, Benjamin, Salem (1661) | 351 |
| Belknap, Abraham, Lynn (1643) | 26 |
| Bellingham, William, Rowley (1650) | 120 |
| Bennet, John, Marblehead (1663) | 415 |
| Birdsall, Henry, Salem (1651) | 143 |
| Blaisdell, Ralph, Salisbury (1651) | 130 |
| Blumfield, John, Newbury (1639-40) | 12 |
| Boovey, Joseph, Lynn (1655) | 225 |
| Bowtwell, James, Lynn (1651) | 143 |
| Brabrooke, John, Newbury (1662) | 391 |
| Bradley, John, Salem (1642) | 18 |
| Bradstreet, Humphrey, Ipswich (1655) | 217 |
|     John, Marblehead (1660) | 317 |
|     Rebecca, Ipswich (guardianship, 1657) | 258 |
| Bridgman, John, Salem (1655) | 226 |
| Browne, Edward, Ipswich (1660) | 306 |
|     George, Newbury (1643) | 22 |
|     Richard, Newbury (1661) | 339 |
|     William, Gloucester (1662) | 386 |
| Bullock, Henry, Salem (1664) | 450 |
|     Henry, Jr., Salem(?), (1657) | 255 |
| Bunker, George, Topsfield (1658) | 267 |
| Burrill, George, Sr., Lynn (1654) | 177 |
| Burt, Hugh, Lynn (1661) | 355 |
|     Hugh, Jr., Lynn (1650) | 122 |
| Butcher, Walter (1660) | 323 |
| Buxton, Thomas, Salem (1654) | 182 |
| Byley, Henry, Salisbury (1649) | 102 |
| Calie, John, Newbury (1663) | 422 |
| Call, Philip, Ipswich (1662) | 392 |

# LIST OF ESTATES.

| | |
|---|---|
| Candall, Edward, Salem (1646) | 58 |
| Cantlebury, William, Salem (1663) | 420 |
| Carthrick, Michael, Ipswich (1647) | 62 |
| Cartwright, Bethiah, Salem (1640) | 12 |
| Chamberlin, ——, Mrs., Ipswich(?), (1647) | 62 |
|     Samuel, Ipswich(?), (1649) | 103 |
| Chandler, Abiel, Newbury (guardianship, 1652) | 150 |
| Chaplin, Hugh, Rowley (1657) | 250 |
| Chin, George, Marblehead (1653-4) | 162 |
| Churchman, Hugh, Lynn (1644) | 32 |
| Chute, Lionel, Ipswich (1645) | 46 |
| Clarke, William, Salem (1647) | 65 |
| Clements, John, Haverhill (1659) | 290 |
|     Robert, Haverhill (1658) | 272 |
| Cock, Sifforye (1662) | 362 |
| Cockerell, Elizabeth, Mrs., Salem (1664) | 444 |
|     William, Salem (1661) | 357 |
| Codner, Christopher, Marblehead(?), (1660) | 325 |
| Cogswell, John, Jr., Ipswich (1653) | 156, 458 |
| Colby, Anthony, Salisbury (1661) | 407 |
| Cole, George, Lynn (1653) | 154 |
| Conant, Joshua, Salem (1659) | 303 |
| Cooke, Henry, Salem (1662) | 383 |
|     Thomas, Ipswich(?), (1650) | 119 |
| Cooley, John, Ipswich (1654) | 173 |
| Cooper, Timothy, Lynn (1659) | 276 |
| Corwithy, Samuel, Marblehead(?), (1659) | 276 |
| Creeke, Andrew, Topsfield (1658) | 271 |
| Crimp, William, Isle of Shoals(?), (1653) | 152 |
| Cromwell, Thomas, Newbury (1646) | 53 |
| Cross, John, Ipswich (1651) | 125 |
| Cummings, Joanna, Salem (1644) | 34 |
|     John, Salem (1663) | 419 |
| Cutting, John, Newbury (1660) | 308 |
| Davis, Jenkin, Lynn (1662) | 357 |
| Deale, William, Haverhill (1664) | 442 |

## LIST OF ESTATES.

| | |
|---|---|
| Dent, Francis, Lynn (1638-9) | 11 |
| Dickinson, Thomas, Rowley (1662) | 372 |
| Dillingham, Sarah, Mrs., Ipswich (1636) | 3 |
| Dorman, John, Topsfield (1662) | 367 |
| Dow, Thomas, Haverhill (1656) | 239 |
| Eaborne, Thomas, Salem (1643) | 24 |
| Elie, John, Marblehead(?), (1653-4) | 162 |
| Elithorp, Thomas, Rowley (1654) | 174 |
| Elliott, Richard (1662) | 364 |
|     William, Salem (?), (1660) | 326 |
| Ellitt, Richard (1664) | 449 |
| Eyers, John, Sr., Haverhill (1657) | 260 |
| Fairfield, Benjamin, et al. (guardianship, 1660) | 325 |
|     John, Wenham (1647) | 73 |
| Farr, George, Lynn (1662) | 402 |
| Fay, Henry, Newbury (1655) | 214 |
| Firman, Thomas, Ipswich (1648) | 95 |
| Fiske, William, Wenham (1654) | 188 |
| Flint, Thomas, Salem (1663) | 416 |
| Fowler, Philip, Ipswich (adoption, 1651) | 132 |
| Fraile, George, Lynn (1664) | 434 |
| French, Susan, Ipswich (1658) | 272 |
| Friend, John, Salem (1656) | 238 |
| Frithy, Richard, Salem(?), (1659) | 289 |
| Fuller, Anne, Mrs., Salem(?), (1662) | 389 |
| Gaines, Jane, Mrs., Lynn (1645) | 44 |
| Gardner, William (1663) | 423 |
| Garven, John (1662) | 364 |
| Gilbert, Humphrey, Ipswich (1658) | 264 |
| Goffe, John, Newbury (1641) | 13 |
| Golt, William, Salem (1660) | 316 |
| Goodale, Elizabeth, Mrs., Newbury (1647) | 65 |
| Goodridge, William, Watertown (1656) | 230 |
| Goog, William, Lynn (1646) | 50 |
| Goose, William, Salem (1664) | 435 |

## LIST OF ESTATES.

| | |
|---|---|
| Goyte, John, Marblehead (1662) | 358 |
| Gray, Robert, Salem (1662) | 384 |
| Griffin, Humphrey, Ipswich (1661) | 353 |
| Haffield, Richard, Ipswich (1652) | 144 |
| Hardy, Elizabeth, Mrs., Salem (1654) | 200 |
| John, Salem (1652) | 146 |
| Harker, William, Lynn (1662) | 368 |
| Hart, John, Marblehead (1656) | 243 |
| John (1662) | 362 |
| Harwood, Henry, Salem (1664) | 446 |
| Hauxworth, Thomas, Salisbury (1651) | 140 |
| Hawes, Frances, Mrs., Salem (1645) | 46 |
| Heard, Luke, Ipswich (1647) | 81 |
| Hersome, Mary, Mrs., Wenham (1646) | 57 |
| Hobson, William, Rowley (1659) | 294 |
| Hollingsworth, Richard, Salem (1654) | 171 |
| Holman, Richard (1662) | 362 |
| Holyoke, Edward, Lynn (1660) | 312 |
| Homan, William (1662) | 361 |
| Hooke, William, Salisbury (1653) | 158 |
| Hopkinson, Jonathan, Rowley (guardianship, 1662) | 390 |
| Michael, Rowley (1657) | 253 |
| How, Joseph, Lynn (1651) | 130 |
| Howe, Edward, Lynn (1639) | 12 |
| Huckstable, Macklin, Marblehead (1656) | 245 |
| Humphries, John (1661) | 345 |
| Hunter, Robert, Rowley (1647) | 80 |
| Ingalls, Edmund, Lynn (1648) | 99 |
| Ingersoll, Richard, Salem (1644-5) | 43, 458 |
| Ivory, William, Lynn (1653) | 152 |
| Jackson, John, Ipswich (1648) | 97 |
| John, Sr., Salem (1656) | 240 |
| James, Erasmus, Marblehead (1660) | 314 |
| Jarrat, John, Rowley (1648) | 98 |
| Jewett, Ann, Mrs., Rowley (1661) | 338 |

## LIST OF ESTATES.

| | |
|---|---|
| Jewett, Joseph, Rowley (1661) | 327 |
| Nehemiah, Rowley (guardianship, 1661) | 329 |
| Patience, Rowley (guardianship, 1661) | 330 |
| Jiggles, William, Salem (1659) | 287 |
| Johnson, Caleb, Andover (1656) | 244 |
| Robert, Rowley (1650) | 116 |
| Keniston, Allen, Salem (1648) | 101 |
| Kenning, Jane, Ipswich (1654) | 165 |
| Kent, Richard, Sr., Newbury (1654) | 186 |
| King, Richard, Salem(?), (1635) | 3 |
| William, Salem (1650) | 117 |
| Kirtland, Philip, Lynn (1661) | 343 |
| Knight, Alexander, Ipswich (1664) | 439 |
| William, Lynn (1655) | 213 |
| Knowlton, John, Ipswich (1654) | 163 |
| Margery, Mrs., Ipswich (1654) | 163 |
| William, Ipswich(?), (1655) | 219 |
| Lambert, Francis, Rowley (1648) | 94 |
| Gershom, Rowley (1664) | 436 |
| Jane, Mrs., Rowley (1659) | 300 |
| Jonathan, Rowley(?), (1664) | 443 |
| Lamson, William, Ipswich (1659) | 282 |
| Lane, Aniball (1662) | 361 |
| Laskin, Hugh, Salem (1659) | 280 |
| Leach, John, Sr., Salem (1659) | 288 |
| Lawrence, Salem (1662) | 388 |
| Lee, Thomas, Ipswich (1662) | 373 |
| Lewis, David, Salem (1662) | 381 |
| Edmund, Lynn (1650) | 123 |
| Robert, Newbury (1644) | 34 |
| Lightfoot, Francis, Lynn (1646) | 55 |
| Littlehale, Richard, Haverhill (1663-4) | 431 |
| Lookman, John (1662) | 361 |
| Nicholas (1662) | 362 |
| Lowell, Elizabeth, Mrs., Newbury (1651) | 138 |
| John, Newbury (1647) | 67 |

## LIST OF ESTATES.

| | |
|---|---|
| Lume, Ann, Mrs., Rowley (1662) | 371 |
| Lumpkyn, Richard, Ipswich (1645) | 43 |
| Lunt, Henry, Newbury (1662) | 393 |
| Mason, Emme, Mrs., Salem (1646) | 57 |
| Mattox, John, Salem (1644) | 36 |
| Merrill, Nathaniel, Newbury (1655) | 204 |
| Mighill, Thomas, Rowley (1655) | 206 |
| Millard, Thomas, Newbury (1653) | 160 |
| Miller, Mary, Mrs., Newbury (1664) | 437 |
| Mitchell, William, Newbury (1654) | 189 |
| Moores, James, Lynn (1659) | 305 |
| Morrill, Abraham, Salisbury (1662) | 399 |
| Morse, Joseph, Ipswich (1646) | 53 |
| Moulton, Robert, Sr., Salem (1655) | 210 |
| Mountjoy, Benjamin, Salem (1659) | 287 |
| Muddle, Henry, Gloucester(?), (1662) | 359 |
| Mudge, James (1662) | 361 |
| Muzzey, Robert, Ipswich (1644) | 28 |
| Nelson, Thomas, Rowley (1649) | 109 |
|     Thomas, Rowley (guardianship, 1657) | 250 |
| Nevill, William, Ipswich (1643) | 25 |
| Newhall, Anthony, Lynn (1657) | 247 |
| Nicholson, Edmund, Marblehead (1660) | 324 |
| Norington, Robert, Salem(?), (1650) | 117 |
| Norris, Edward, Rev., Salem (1660) | 320 |
| Norton, George, Salem (1659) | 304 |
| Noyes, James, Rev., Newbury (1656) | 245 |
| Odry, William (1661) | 330 |
| Oliver, John, Newbury (1642) | 15 |
| Osgood, Christopher, Ipswich (1650) | 121 |
|     John, Andover (1651) | 141 |
| Park, George, Marblehead(?), (1653-4) | 162 |
| Parrot, Francis, Rowley (1656) | 244 |
| Partridge, John, Olney, Eng. (1652) | 150 |
|     Sarah (guardianship, 1663) | 407 |

# LIST OF ESTATES.

| | |
|---|---|
| Partridge, William, Salisbury (1654) | 192 |
| Patch, James, Salem (1658) | 269 |
| Payne, Thomas, Salem (1644) | 37 |
| Pease, Margaret, Mrs., Salem (1644) | 40 |
|     Robert, Salem (1644) | 42 |
| Peasley, Joseph, Salisbury (1661) | 336 |
| Perkins, John, Jr., Ipswich (1659) | 284 |
|     John, Sr., Ipswich (1654) | 190 |
|     William, et al., Topsfield (guardianship, 1660) | 324 |
| Philbrick, Robert, Ipswich(?), (1654) | 192 |
| Pickering, John, Salem (1657) | 254 |
| Pickworth, John, Manchester (1663) | 428 |
| Pike, John, Sr., Salisbury (1654) | 193 |
| Pitford, Peter, Marblehead (1659) | 289 |
| Pittice, John, Ipswich(?), (1653) | 155 |
| Plasse, William, Salem (1646) | 49 |
| Pollard, George, Marblehead (1646) | 59 |
| Pomeroy, John, Gloucester(?), (1662) | 361 |
| Porter, Samuel, Wenham (1659) | 306 |
| Pride, John, Salem (1647) | 91 |
| Priest, James, Salem (1664) | 452 |
| Quilter, Mark, Ipswich (1654) | 167 |
| Rea, Daniel, Salem (1662) | 375 |
| Read, Thomas, Col., Salem(?), (1663) | 415 |
| Redverne, Isabel, Mrs., Ipswich (1650) | 117 |
| Reyner, Humphrey, Rowley (1660) | 320 |
| Richardson, William, Newbury (1657) | 247 |
| Ring, Daniel, Ipswich (1662) | 368 |
| Roberts, Robert, Ipswich (1663) | 422 |
| Robinson, Abraham, Gloucester (1648) | 102 |
|     John, Salem (1653) | 159 |
|     John, Ipswich (1658) | 267 |
| Rogers, Ezekiel, Rev., Rowley (1661) | 331 |
|     Nathaniel, Rev., Ipswich (1655) | 222 |
|     Robert, Newbury (1664) | 433 |
| Rolfe, Daniel, Ipswich (1654) | 176 |

## LIST OF ESTATES. xiii

| | |
|---|---:|
| Rolfe, Ezra, Ipswich (1652) | 149 |
| Henry, Newbury (1643) | 21 |
| Honor, Newbury (1651) | 137 |
| John, Newbury (1664) | 438 |
| Thomas, Ipswich (1657) | 258 |
| Rooten, Richard, Lynn (1663) | 429 |
| Row, John, Gloucester (1662) | 380 |
| Rowell, Thomas, Andover (1662) | 395 |
| Valentine, Salisbury (1662) | 401 |
| Sadler, Anthony, Salisbury (1650) | 121 |
| Sallows, Grace, Mrs., Salem(?), (1664) | 444 |
| Michael, Salem (1646) | 58 |
| Robert, Salem (1663) | 418 |
| Thomas, Salem (1663) | 418 |
| Sanders, John, Salem (1643) | 26 |
| Sandie, John, Marblehead (1654) | 176 |
| Scarlet, Anne, Mrs., Salem (1643) | 24 |
| Scott, Thomas, Ipswich (1654) | 168 |
| Thomas, Ipswich (1657) | 258 |
| Scruggs, Thomas, Salem (1654) | 185 |
| Scudder, Thomas, Salem (1658) | 268 |
| Scullard, Samuel, Newbury (1647) | 82 |
| Seers, Thomas, Newbury (1661) | 342 |
| Sewall, Henry, Sr., Rowley (1656) | 232 |
| Shatswell, John, Ipswich (1647) | 60 |
| Theophilus, Haverhill (1663) | 424 |
| Sherman, Samuel, Ipswich (1662) | 375 |
| Sibly, John, Manchester (1661) | 347 |
| Skelton, Samuel, Rev., Salem (1638) | 10 |
| Smith, Edith (1647) | 78 |
| George, Salem (1662) | 364 |
| Hannah, Rowley (guardianship, 1664) | 453 |
| Henry, Rowley (1655) | 202 |
| Hugh, Rowley (1656) | 235 |
| James, Marblehead (1661) | 348 |
| John, Rowley (1661) | 351 |

## LIST OF ESTATES.

| | |
|---|---|
| Smith, Martha, Rowley(?), (guardianship, 1664) | 443 |
| Mary, Mrs., Marblehead (1663) | 410 |
| Nathaniel (1651) | 133 |
| Samuel, Wenham (1642) | 18 |
| Sarah, Rowley(?), (guardianship, 1664) | 435 |
| Thomas (1660) | 323 |
| Thomas, Salem (1662) | 363 |
| Somerby, Henry, Newbury (1652) | 150 |
| Southmead, William, Gloucester (1648) | 101 |
| Southwick, Lawrence, Salem (1660) | 318 |
| Spencer, John, Newbury (1649) | 107 |
| Michael, Lynn (1653) | 159 |
| Spooner, Thomas, Salem (1664) | 455 |
| Stevens, John, Andover (1662) | 377 |
| William, Newbury (1653) | 153 |
| Stileman, Elias, Salem (1662) | 390 |
| Stuart, William, Lynn (1664) | 449 |
| Symonds, Mark, Ipswich (1659) | 285 |
| Samuel, Jr., Ipswich (1654) | 170 |
| Talbey, John, Salem (1644) | 39 |
| Thorne, John, Salem (1646) | 50 |
| Tibbott, Walter, Gloucester (1651) | 132 |
| Tilton, Daniel, Lynn (guardianship, 1662) | 370 |
| William, Lynn (1653) | 155 |
| Travers, Henry, Newbury (1659) | 292 |
| Tresler, Elinor, Mrs., Salem (1655) | 211 |
| True, Henry, Salisbury (1660) | 311 |
| Trumble, John, Rowley (1657) | 259 |
| Joseph, Rowley (1664) | 432 |
| Judah, et al., Rowley (guardianship, 1660) | 312 |
| Trusler, Thomas, Salem (1654) | 183 |
| Tucker, Nicholas, Marblehead (1664) | 454 |
| Roger, Salem (1660) | 323 |
| Turner, Charles, Salem (1643) | 26 |
| Tuttle, John, Ipswich (1659) | 277 |

| | |
|---|---|
| Varnam, George, Ipswich (1649) | 108 |
| Varney, William, Ipswich (1654) | 173 |
| Verin, Philip, Salem (1650) | 123 |
| Wake, William, Salem (1654) | 181 |
| Waklye, Isaac, Gloucester (1662) | 359 |
| Walcott, William, Salem (1643) | 25 |
| Waldridge, William, Salem(?), (1658) | 275 |
| War, Abraham, Ipswich (1654) | 175 |
| Ward, Alice, Mrs., Ipswich (1655) | 203 |
|     John, Ipswich (1656) | 234 |
|     Miles, Salem (1650) | 118 |
| Waters, Stephen, Marblehead(?), (1657) | 254 |
| Wathen, Margery, Mrs., Salem (1644) | 38 |
|     Thomas, Gloucester (1652) | 148 |
|     Thomas, Gloucester (1657) | 263 |
| Watkins, John, Salem (1641) | 13 |
| Webster, Israel, et al., Ipswich (guardianship, 1662) | 402 |
|     John, Ipswich (1646) | 52 |
| West, Isabel, Salem (1644) | 41 |
| Whipple, Matthew, Ipswich (1647) | 87 |
|     Matthew, Ipswich (1658) | 274 |
|     Matthew, Ipswich (1663) | 417 |
| White, William, Salem (1658) | 268 |
| Whittingham, John, Ipswich 1649) | 103 |
| Wickam, Richard, Rowley (1664) | 441 |
| Wickes, Thomas, Salem (1656) | 241 |
| Wild, William, Ipswich (1662) | 397 |
| Wilkes, Thomas, Salem (1662) | 381 |
| Williams, George, Salem (1654) | 195 |
|     Mary, Mrs., Salem (1654) | 199 |
| Willix, Belshazzar, Salisbury (1651) | 130 |
|     Mary, Mrs., Salisbury (guardianship, 1664) | 442 |
| Winsley, Samuel, Salisbury (1663) | 424 |
| Wise, Humphrey, Ipswich (1638-9) | 11 |
| Witter, William, Lynn (1661) | 350 |
| Wood, Daniel, Ipswich (1649) | 106 |

Woodbury, John, Salem (1642) . . . . . . 21
Woodis, John, Salem (1659) . . . . . . . 289
Woodman, Richard, Lynn (1647) . . . . . . 91
Worcester, Moses, Salisbury (guardianship, 1663) . . 410
    William, Rev., Salisbury (1662) . . . . . 403
Wright, John, Newbury (1658) . . . . . . 275

Yoe, Samuel, Salem(?), (1657) . . . . . . . 263
Yongs, Christopher, Wenham (1647) . . . . . 76

# INTRODUCTION.

The charter of "The Governor and Company of Massachusetts Bay in New England," granted March 4, 1628-9, provided that a "Greate and Generall Court" should be held four times each year. This court, sitting in Boston, exercised the entire judicial powers of the Colony until March 3, 1635-6, when quarterly courts were ordered to be kept in several of the larger towns, and Salem and Ipswich were the towns selected within what is now the county of Essex. These courts also exercised probate jurisdiction and proved wills and granted administrations, although probate business for a long time after was brought before the Great and General Court, from time to time, seemingly as a matter of personal convenience. The colony was divided into shires or counties in 1643, and each county had its own courts. Haverhill, Amesbury and Salisbury, lying north of the Merrimac river and which now are included within the limits of Essex County, were then placed in old Norfolk County and so remained until Feb. 4, 1679-80, when new boundary lines were established. The probate records of the southern jurisdiction of old Norfolk County which relate to these three towns are therefore here included. Essex County probate business sometimes was taken to Suffolk County. This was especially the case during the administration of Governor Andros, when, for the centralization of business for the obtaining of fees, all save a few unimportant estates were probated in Boston. Under the new charter probate courts were established in each county by an order in council adopted June 18, 1692, and Bartholomew Gedney was appointed the first judge in this county. This court has had a continuous existence to the present day.

After the Quarterly courts were instituted the probate records were entered by the clerk in the same books of record which contained the civil and criminal business. This continued until 1671, when the probate matter was first recorded in separate volumes. The original papers accompanying the records of the Quarterly courts of Essex County contain many of the early probate papers, but many early wills are preserved in the custody of the Probate court, where they are docketed in an alphabetical order first arranged about 1885, each estate having its separate docket number. Copies of all the wills in the Quarterly courts files are also preserved in three volumes in the probate registry.

In assembling the material for the following pages an effort has been made to include probate records from every available original source, viz:—

Records of the Massachusetts Bay Colony (Shurtleff), Boston, 1854, 6 vols.

Massachusetts Archives.

Records and files of the Quarterly Courts of Essex County and old Norfolk County.

Old Norfolk County Deeds.

Ipswich Deeds.

Ipswich Town Records.

Suffolk County Probate Records.

Records and Docket of the Probate Court of Essex County.

It must not be assumed that all estates were administered by the courts in the early days. From the records of the Massachusetts Bay Colony for the session of October 18, 1649, it appears that " whereas itt is found by often experience that some men dying and making wills, the said wills are concealed, and not prooved and recorded, and others dying intestate, no administration is sought for nor granted ... it is ordered ... if any nominated executors, knowing thereof ... shall not within thirty days after the decease of the partye, ... make probate of any will ... they shall be liable to be sued, and shall be bound to pay all such debts as the deceased partye owed ... and shall forfeite to the common weale so many somes of five pounds as shall happen to be moneths betweene the next Courte ... after the death of the deceased partye and the prooving of such will."

The wills are printed in full, with the exception only of that part of the preamble which states no material fact. Such omissions are indicated by an ellipsis. Each will is followed in chronological order by abstracts of all documents relating to the settlement of the estate, in which every essential particular is retained, so that the lawyer, genealogist and sociologist may be assured that nothing of value has been omitted. Names are spelled exactly as they appear in the original papers.

GEORGE FRANCIS DOW,<br>
Editor.

# THE PROBATE RECORDS OF ESSEX COUNTY, MASSACHUSETTS.

### ESTATE OF RICHARD KING OF (SALEM?).

"There is administration granted [June 2, 1635] to Richard Bishopp (in the behalf of his wife) of the goods & chattells of Richard King, desceased." *Mass. Bay Colony Records, vol. 1, page* 151.

### ESTATE OF REV. JOSEPH AVERY OF NEWBURY.

"There is administration granted [Sept. 1, 1635] to M$^r$ Anthony Thacher of the goods & chattells of M$^r$ Joseph Avery, disceased, w$^{ch}$ hee is to inventory, & returne the same into the nexte Court; & the said goods are to remaine in his hands till further order be taken therein.

"An Inventory of the Goods and chattells of Joseph Avery, desceased.

|  | li | s | d |
|---|---|---|---|
| Due to him from John Emery, carpenter, | 07 | 00 | 00 |
| It: from Robte Andrewes, of Ipswich, w$^{ch}$ he confesseth to be due, & to be p$^d$ forthw$^{th}$, | 02 | 00 | 00 |
| It: from M$^r$ Willm Hilton, | 02 | 16 | 00 |

or a sowe & piggs to that valewe. Testis, Rich: Kent.
From Rich: Kent, of Ipsw$^{ch}$, ten bushels of Indian corne, which hee acknowledgeth.

"John Emery denyes his debt; but Richard Knight, Nicholas Holte, & John Knight, all three of Newberry, can & will testify & prove it to be due, onely hee was, by condition, to pay the 7$^{li}$ in his worke, w$^{ch}$ he was to doe so soon as M$^r$ Auery did call vpon him for it; out of w$^{ch}$ said 7$^{li}$ there is something paide in lab$^r$ already, as hee can make to appeare.

"p me, Anthon$^y$ Thacher."
*Mass. Bay Colony Records, vol.* 1, *page* 154.

### ESTATE OF SARAH DILLINGHAM OF IPSWICH.

"This is the last will and testament of mee Sarah Dillingham of Ipswich widowe ffor my soule I commend it into ye hands of God in ye mediacon of Jesus Crist: ffor my temporall estate: I give to my onely child Sarah Dillingham my whole estate in lands and goods (except such pticular legacyes as heerafter are named): and if my child Dye before it shall be marryed or attain to ye age of one and twenty years, then my will is that the same shalbe devyded equally between my mother Thomasine Caly, my brothers Abraham Caly and Jacob Caly, my sister Bull and my sister Bast, the wyves of John Bull and John Bast, and my sisters Rebecca Caly and emme Caly, or such of them as shalbe lyving at ye tyme of ye death of such child, all w$^{ch}$ my mother brethren & sisters are now lyving in England: also I give to m$^r$ ward Pastor of ye Church at Ipswich ffyve pounds and to Richard Saltonstall esqr ten pounds and to m$^{rs}$ Saltonstall his wife a silver bowle, To m$^r$ Samuell Appleton ffyve pounds and to his wife a silver porringer: and of this my will I make executors ye said m$^r$ Saltonstall and m$^r$ Appleton, committing ye educacion and government of my said child and ye estate I leave her unto their faithfull ordering intreating them in the bonds of Christian love to see this my will fulfilled my due debts paid, my body decently buyried and my child religiously educated if God give it life, and that they will order the estate as they would doe their owne. In wytnes that this is my true will made in my pfect memory though my body be weake & sick I publish it after it had been read unto me in the presenc of those whose names are under wrytten this xiiijth Day of July 1636." Sarah Dillingham

Witness: Tho: Dudley, Robert Lord, Phillip P his mark ffowler. *Mass. Archives, vol.* 15B, *leaf* 59.

Inventory taken by John Tuttell, John Perkines, John Crosse, Thomas Howlett and Robert Mottley: Towe steers & tow heffers, 47li.; One mare, 25li.; One Cowe calfe of a moneth olde, 6li.; Towe piggs, 16s.; Towe piggs, 8s.; ffower Acres of Corne, 15li.; The house wth thapurtenances viz. fenceinge aple trees wth other fruits in the gardens wth 30 acres of Uplands, 60 acres of meadowe & 6 acres of planting ground neare the house, 130li.; Towe bull Calves & one Cowe Calfe weaned all verye power, 10li.; Three Cowes, 67li.; Towe bedsteds in the parlour, 1li. 6s. 8d.; a large neste of boxes, 2li.; a Smale neste of boxes, 3s.; a Cubert, 10s.; a Sea chest, 10s.; towe Joynd Chaires, 5s.; a rounde table, 7s.; a deske, 4s.; a band boxe, 2s. [The child hath it: *in margin.*]; a Coverlet, 1li.; a fether bed a boulster & 2 pillows, 1li. 5s.; a fether bed boulster & one pillow, 1li. 5s.; a rug, a coverlet & a blanket, 1li.; a bed sted, 3s.; Sundrye pcells of wearinge lynine, 4li. 5s. 6d.; pcells of wearing clothes, 5li. 8s. 4d.; 6 paire of flaxen Sheets, 6li.; 6 paire of Course sheets, 2li. 12s.; Table clothes, 14s.; napkins, 7s.; a yd. of Canvis, 1s.; yarne, 4s.; 2 paire of bodyes, 6s. 8d.; 2 Cushions, 6s.; a Remnnte of woollen Cloth, 1s. 6d.; a towell & table cloth, 1s. 6d.; a bag & wallet, 1s. 6d.; 1 Rend of cloth, 4s.; kniues, 5s.; 10: paire of stockings, 1li.; 10: Ells 1-4 of Canvis att 15d. p ell, 12s.; 6 yds. of blew linine, 6s.; 8 yds. of Lynsi-wollsi, 10s.; poynts & showstrings, 3s.; 2 steels & Cinamon, 2s.; a carde of lace, 1s.; 2 ells of Holland, 8s.; a peece of tufted Holland, 6s.; 6 yds. of Loomworke, 5s.; in a box: in money, 2li. 5s. 4d.; in another box, 1li. 12s. 6d.; in her purse, 1li. 2s. 2d.; in wampompege, 4d.; in a boxe, 10s. 4d.; a case of bottles, 2s. 6d.; 3 hatts, 1li.; 2 boxes, 1s. 6d.; a broken warmeige pan, 2s. 6d.; 2 firkins & halfe of butter, 3li. 15s.; 6 chesemots 2 Jugs 3 pans one tray, 15s.; 21 cheeses new, 2li. 16s.; halfe a bushell of malte, 3s. 6d.; 2 basketts, 1s. 2d.; Taps and smale things, 1s.; 1 paire of stireipe hose leather, 1s.; 25 Sawcers, 5s.; 6 porringers, 6s.; 2 chamber potts, 1s. 6d.; 40li. & a halfe of pewter, 2li. 14s.; 7 spoones, 1s. 9d,; a treavett a fier shovell & tongs gredIron potthookes, 13s. 4d.; a paire [Goodma Perkings: *in margin.*] of bellowes & one old darke lanthorne, 2s.; a brase pott, 18s.; a morter, 5s.; an Iron pott & a frying pan both haue holes in them, 3s. 4d.; [2 ketls: *in margin.*] 2 kettles 2 skelletts & an Iron ladle, 1li. 6s. 8d.; bulletts hinges & other smale things, 6s. 8d.; a box, 3s. 4d.; a chiste, 8s.; a paire of stockings, 2s.; 1 paire of stockings, 2s. 6d.; 1 paire of stockings, 2s. 6d; a coate, 6s.; a old suite & cloake, 1li. 2s.; a paire of drawers, 1s. 8d.; a Coate w$^{th}$ silver buttons, 1li.; [Jo. Andr. *in margin.*] a suite of searge, 12s.; a blacke suite of searge Unmaide, 10s.; a Jackett of cloth, 3s. 4d,; a graite, 1s. 6d.; a pcell of nailes, 1s. 4d.; 6li. of Raisins, 2s.; 7 bushells of Rye, 2li. 16s.; towe beare Vessells, 5s.; 3 cushions, 9s.; some spice, 2s.; a read waistecoote, 3s. 4d.; a bedd pan, 5s.; 2 old hooes: 1 old hatchett: 1 old sythe, 5s.; 2 wayne bodys, 16s.; 1 olde paire of wheeles, 12s.; 2 borded Canow, 1li.; John Andrews tyme, 16li.; a lader, 3s. 4d.; total, 385li. 14s. 5d.

"When we Valued John Andrewes tyme at 16li we heard not of these demands that now he makes after his time is expired, but in Case you bringe him to the Courte, we desier they would heare his demands and value his time as they thinke meete, els the former Rate muste stand till further Consideration."

*Mass. Archives, vol.* 15B, *leaf* 61.

Ordered, 6:7:1636, that Mr. Dudley, Mr. Endecot and Mr. Bradstreete, or any two of them, should examine the accounts between Mr. Richard Saltonstall and Edward Dillingam, and report on the estate of John Dillingam and his wife, deceased. *Mass. Bay Colony Records, vol. 1, page* 177.

Rich$^r$d Saltonstall is debtor to ye estate of Jno. Dillingham, deceased : for land, 230li., oxen, 100li., a bull, 10li., corne, 24li., 364li. ; 2 steeres & 2 heifers valued in the inventory at 47li., to me at 63li.; one cowe calfe valued in the inventory at 6li., to me at 9li. 10s. ; one mare 24li ; allowed upon several accounts, 13li. 8s., 10li. 2s., 13li. 10s. 8d., 61li. 8d. ; for Levies, 4li. 18s., for severall disbursmts concerning cattle, 8li., 2li., 1li., 3li., 2li., 10s., 21li. 8s.; Bord of Mr. Bracy, 1li. 15s., of Mr. Gardner, 1li. 6s. 6d., Hoggs, 8li. 10s., 11li. 11s. 6d.; abated out of Thom. Wells account, 5li. 5s. 7d. ; note yt Wm. Giles of Salem oweth ye estate of Jno. Dillingham 3li. in pt. Rcd of his wifes passage unless he pve it hath bene pd Mr Appletones selfe, 3li. ; recd in an inventory (saving to my selfe ye liberty of some exceptions in respect of some pticulers), 385li. 14s. 5d.; for halfe ye ship Kettle not mentioned in ye Inventory, 1li. 10s.; a cradle, 12s., bord of goodman Pinder, 6li., 6li. 12s. ; 2 Cowes —— of ther increase for 3 years now past & one yong cowe & a cow, 1—; total 932li. 12s. 9d. Richard Saltonstall is Creditor : due to mee & alowed by certeine Comissioners apptd by ye court, 424li. 13s. 2d. ; alowed by ye said comissiours, 120li. 13s. 8d., more 11li. 2s. 6d., rates 5li. 15s., 137li. 1—s. 2d. ; alowed mee by ye comissioners in respect of servants, 24li. 2s. ; pd. Jno. Andrews, 12s. 6d. for ye ship at Graves End, 1li. 10s. ; for ye Calves, 12s., 2li. 14s. 6d. ; alowed mee wn ye Cowes were pted, 1li., for Keeping of ye Corne, 12s. ; Tho. Sherman, 12s., 2li. 4s. ; pd at sevrall times about ye Cowes, 1li. 4s., for beefe, 2li. 11s. 3d., for Caske, 3s. 3d., 3li. 18s. 6d. ; for bisket, 8li., for Robrt Crane, 10s., Recd for frait of goods, 3li., 11li. 10s. ; pd. Tho. Downes, wch was due to him, 2li., Mr. Bachiler, 10s., Mrs. Dillingham lent 3li., 5li. 10s. ; pd Ann ffowle, servant, 2li. 8s., for Ann ffowles passage, 5li., to Satchell in bea$^r$, 1li. 9s., 8li. 17s. ; pd Edwa. Dillingham 3 bls. rye at 8s. p bl. at Saugust, gn. Brazor jorny to Sandwich, 1li. 17s. ; for Proctor looking to a sicke calfe, 3s. 10d., to Kent of Newberry, 2li. 16s. 8d., due Mr. Dillingham, 3li. 6d. ; note for 2li. 16s. 8d. was paid as aforesaid by Mr. Nowells direction (being one of ye commissioners) upon a letter he recd from ye said Kent wch gave him satisfaction concerning his demand; to Mr. Cartwright due from Mr. Dillingham, 20s.; 1li. pd. Edwa. Dillingham, 23li. 11s. 8d. in pt. of wt. was given, 24li. 11s. 8d.; by order of ye commissioners Ed. Dillingham recd out of ye Inventory aforesaid ye pcels wch he challenged as his owne pp goods, a featherbed, boulster & 2 pillowes, 1li. 5s.; 2 coverlets, 1li. 10s., 6 pr flaxen sheets, 6li., 6 pr corse sheets, 2li. 12s., 5 table cloaths, 10li. 2s.; napkins, 7s., 2 quishions, 6s., 13s.; pd. Mr. Satchwell for 8 years boarding of Sara Dillingham, 69li. 18s. 2d.; note yt was pd by order of an arbitration, 34d. p weeke in ye sume aforesaid Wm. Satchwell hath recd 11s. 6d. more yn his due for wch he is countable; pd Jno. Andrewes for Sara Dillingnam as an addition to his wages, 1li.; pd. for Mrs. Dillingham to Mr. ffirman due to him from Mr. Parker of Roxbry & for Comodities, 2li. 19s. 2d.; pd. for Sara Dillingham to Mr. Ward wch was given to him by her mothers will, 5li.; pd. for Sara Dillingham to my Cousen Apleton, 3li. 2s. 8d.; pd. in Cattle out of ye Inventory according to ye order of ye Commissioners as may app by ption, 149li.; abated in ye sale of ye house & land (wth Edwa. Dillinghams consent) being over prized, 20li.; abated Wm. Cartwright in ye price of Jno. Andrews time, 4li.; to be abated out of ye inventory for pigs killed by ye wolves at Plum Iland, 1li. 4s.; pd. Sara Dillingham out of ye inventory sundry pcels of wearing linnen wch shee hath & are reserved for her, 4li. 5s. 6d.; pd. for a pr of bodies, 2s. 6d., for her schooling to good. Symonds, 1li., 1li. 2s. 6d.; one stuffe petticoat & waskote, 4 shifts wth shewes dd to good. Satchwell for Sara Dillingham; for Sara Dillingham daughter of Jno. Dillingham, 2 Cowes & 2-3 of thir increase for 3y more, one heifer & a lowance for her peculiar for milk, 4li.; Mr. Saltonstall gave back wt. her mother gave him, 13li.; for a bible, 4s.; for a goune, 2li. 10s.; to be abated out of this for wintering cattle, 4li.; & rest in Mr. Saltonstalls hand, 8li. 10s. 1d.; a heifer in Mr. Saltonstalls hand, 2 cowes & 2-3 of ther increase, Perkins works. *Mass. Archives, vol.* 15B, *page* 66.

Upon the 9: 4: 1637 the Commissioners found due to me from the estate of John Dillingham, 67li. 13s. 9½d., and besides they allowed me 5li. 15s. for rates paid by me for Mr. Dillingham, also 7li. 16s. 8d. and I have a bill under Edward Dillingham's hand, dated June 29, 1637 that whenever the commissioners should see cause to allow the said sum it should be paid in goods. In satisfaction of the aforesaid debts I received 2 stears, 30li.; a brown hefer, 16li.; a branded heffer, 17li.; a white faced yearling, 9li., wth a very pore cow Calfe, 6li. [so prized by Mr. Appleton and not worth so much as I conceive.] This cow-calfe being paid to myself. Sarah Dillingham hath not received so much in cattle for her part as Edward Dillingham did for his by 6li. 10s. Paid out of her cattle to satisfy Mr. Downing whereof Edward Dillingham is to repay his proportion, 8li. 6s. 8d. Sarah Dillingham hath received [besides her part in cattle] money paide Mrs. Dillingham, 3li.; pd. for a sick calfe, 3s. 10d.; her boarding at Gm. Satchells, 69li. 18s. 2d.; John Andrews, 1li.; To Parker of Roxbury, 2li. 19s. 2d.; Mr. Ward [by will], 5li.; Mr. Apleton, 3li. 2s. 8d.; out of the inventory, 4li. 5s. 6d.; bodyes, 2s. 6d.; To Goody Symonds, 1li.; she hath in my hand, which I will make good with advantage, 8li. 10s. 1d.      Richard Saltonstall.

If Edward Dillingham deny that he received the courser sheets mentioned in the inventory & will take his oath before the present commissioners I shall rest satisfied therewith.

*Mass. Archives, vol.* 15B, *page* 67.

"To the honrd Generall Court Having thought [if God will] of going for England by the next passage; & beeing desirous [in the meanetime] that all accompts concerning myselfe may bee concluded & especially those that fall vpon mee as Executor to the estate of John Dillingham deceased; in respect of which estate; for the ordering & issuing of all accompts or differences concerning the same; M$^r$ Nowell & M$^r$ Mahur by order of the Quarter Court were made Comissioners:

"My humble request is that in the roome of M$^r$ Mahur [who is now absent & not of like respect & creditt in the country as when he was first joyned with M$^r$ Nowell in this Comission]: This Court would bee pleased to appoynt an an other; who may joyne with M$^r$ Nowell to examine such accompts as I am ready to tender: & that these Comissioners may have power to end & determine the same unless there bee some other course that may seeme more meete unto the Court which I shall bee willing to attend according to your order.

Y$^{rs}$ in all christian observance

"Dat 15$^{th}$ 8$^{th}$ 1645      Richard Saltonstall

" The peticon is graunted & M$^r$ Hibbins is by the magistrate appoynted Commissioner in stead of M$^r$ Mahew

Tho: Dudley Gov$^r$

Consented to by y$^e$ Deputy
    Edward Rawson."

*Mass. Archives, vol.* 15B, *page* 60.

"Worthily honrd for my accompt presented to yourselves there is an article wherin I make Goodman Satchwell debtor to Sarah Dillingham ———, 11s. 6d. as I remember wherunto I was ledd by my booke; & that very rightly as I yet conceive. But because Goodman Satchell doth affirme the contrary; & I would not differ with a neighbour but had much rather buy my peace then contend in such a case; I will take the debt upon myselfe & soe much I thought meete to certify.
"Yrs unfaynedly to love & serve you
"12th Decr 1645. Richard Saltonstall."

"Sarah Dillingham hath these books in my hands and Mr Nath: Rogers: viz. Perkins works in 3 vollums, Seaven Treatises [2 severall bookes], the Spowse Royall the bruised reade, A little new testament."

*Mass. Archives, vol.* 15B, *page* 63.

"A note of whate Edward Dillingham have received of Mr. Saltonstall of the third pt. of my brother John Dillingham's estate, which he gave to my wife and children, appointed to me by the commissioners: on mare, 18li.; on Cowe, 22li.; in my account, 4li. 2s. 1d.; paid for me to William Spawforth, 3li.; Jhon Bell his time, 5li.; John Butler his time, 5li.; on sewte of old Clothes, 1li.; on hat & other small thinges, 1li. 5s.; rec'd of Mr. Wade, 5s.; rec'd of Mr. Paine, 5li.; rec'd of Mr. Paine, 5li.; received of Mr. Paine more, 3li. 6s. 8d.; the remainder of my brothers inventory, 8li.; rec'd of Mr. Borman, 5li.; total, 82li. 12s. 1d. Also received of goodman Pinder 3li. in discharge of 6li. of our third pt. of that det in his hand. Rec'd as by my booke: in rye at Saugus 3bl at 8s. which was then the prise currant, 1li. 4s. Jorney to Sadwich concerning Mr. Downing, 0."

On reverse. "Mr. Saltonstall hath one cow which he hath had for years for which he will allow, and Mr. Apleton hath one Cowe, two Oxen & one heifer.

"The Commissioners to consider that John Bells and Butlers time are much under prised, whereby Sarah Dillingham is damnifyed in her proportion."

*Mass. Archives, vol.* 15B, *page* 63.

"The particulars formerly questioned by Edward Dillingham are these: 1st, for fraight of goods, 3li., which is utterly denied, therefore in reason to be recharged to the estate. 2d, the 2li. paid Tho. Downes, he hath been a good servant and his master hath not kept covenant with him, in which respect, we the executors saw fit to discharge him and pay him the 2li. for satisfaction. 3d, for the 5li. paid to An

Fowle, she hath been a faithful servant and though she was discharged by her mistress a little before her time was out, yet it may be borne by the estate, considering her diligence. 4th, for the cow calfe [contained in the inventory] which I received at 6li., no executor can be liable for the worst goods expressed in an inventory, if the best goods be taken out of his hands and 2dly the calf was then very pore and as I conceive not worth the money. 3dly, I took the calf at 6li. with Mr. Appletons consent who being executor might justly dispose of it as he then did. Mem. Edward Dillingham hath received 6li. of goodman Pinder, without the knowledge or consent of the executors, he covenanted with him to abate the said Pinder 6li. in lieu of that which he received in ready money and this he did when he could not but know that he had already received beyond his proportion.

"Richard Saltonstall."
*Mass. Archives, vol.* 15B, *page* 61.

Richard Saltonstall, of Ipswich, Esq., executor to the estate of John Dillingham, having tendered his account concerning sd estate unto Increase Nowell and William Hibbins, being by order of the General Ct. appointed commissioners to settle the same, do find that the said Richard hath received of the estate of John Dillingham to the value of 932li. 12s. 2d. Also we find said estate doth owe the said Richard 924li. 2s. 1d. He was allowed for his disbursement and adventure in the ship Seaflower, upon a former commission granted by the Quarterly Court, the sum of 604li. 3s. 11d. The rest of the 924li. 2s. 1d. is demanded for several sums paid out by said Richard as executor. The court ordered him to be allowed the full sum of 924li. 2s. 1d. out of the estate. *Mass. Bay Colony Records, vol.* 2, *page* 144.

Wills of John and Sarah Dillingham with the inventory shall be kept by Mr. Nowell and Hibbins and Richard Saltonstall discharged. *Mass. Bay Colony Records, vol.* 2, *page* 145.

### ESTATE OF REV. SAMUEL SKELTON OF SALEM.

The Court of Assistants held at Cambridge, 5 : 4: 1638, being a quarterly court, ordered, with the consent of Mrs. Baggerly, that the increase of Mr. Skelton's cattle should be divided according to his will, and that the goods and household stuff which belongs to the 3 eldest children should be divided by some of the church in Salem and committed to the church of Salem. *Mass. Bay Colony Records, vol.* 1, *page* 232.

## Estate of Francis Dent of Lynn.

The Quarterly Court held at Boston 5 : 1 : 1638-9, granted to Edmond Audeley administration on the goods of Francis Dent, deceased, upon the testimony of John Winge and Sergeant Davies. *Mass. Bay Colony Records, vol.* 1, *page* 249.

## Estate of Humfry Wise of Ipswich.

The General Court held at Boston, 13 : 1 : 1638-9, ordered the court at Ipswich to examine and settle all things belonging to the estate of Humfrey Wisse, including the land, sold and unsold. *Mass. Bay Colony Records, vol.* 1, *page* 254.

Humfry Wise of Ipswich, died intestate, and Samuel Greenfeild late of Salem married his widow and took into his possession the lands and goods of the said Humfry, without legal order. The Court held at Ipswich 26 : 1 : 1639, caused them to deliver an inventory of the estate which amounted to about 140li. Wise left a wife and five children, Beniamyn, Joseph, Em., Sarah and Ann, besides some that were married and had received their portions. Samuel Greenfeild was appointed administrator, and with his consent the Court sold the house, and house lot of an acre & a planting lot of six acres with the appurtenances to William ffellowes for 20li., also the farm of about 120 acres to Thomas Emerson for four score pounds, and such other sales of cattle & goods that the said Samuel had made the Court allowed. The money was given to Samuel Greenfeild, he giving bond for 120 li., to bring up the five children, until the sons were twenty one years, and the daughters eighteen, at which time each to receive a certain portion of the estate. If any die before such time the said portions to be equally devided among the survivors. George Gittings and Richard Lumpkyn were chosen overseers for the children. As there was yet 30li., being part of the money for which the farm was sold, remaining in the hands of Thomas Emerson, at his request and with the consent of Samuel, it was ordered that it should remain in his hands until 1 : 3 : 1640, then he to pay the money to the overseers and to give such recompence to Samuel Greenfeild as he shall think equal. It was further agreed that with the consent of Samuel Greenfield and Susan his wife that Benjamin Wise, eldest son of Humfry Wise, should be with Abraham Perkins of Hampton as an apprentice to him for seven years from Sept. 29 last past. *Ipswich Deeds, Vol.* 1, *leaf* 1.

### Estate of Edward Howe of Lynn.

The General Court held at Boston May 22, 1639, granted administration on the estate of Mr. Edward Howe (of Linn, deceased), to his wife Elisabeth. *Mass. Bay Colony Records, vol. 1, page* 259.

### Estate of John Blumfield of Newbury.

The Court of Assistants, held at Boston, a quarter court, 3 : 1 : 1629-40, appointed Thom. Blumfeild administrator to his father, John Blumfeild, deceased, and to have the house and ground; the lame daughter to have the overplus of the goods not disposed of. *Mass. Bay Colony Records, vol.* 1, *page* 286.

### Estate of Bethia Cartwright of Salem.

"I Bethia Cortwrite of Salem being in pfect memory doe make and ordaine this my last will and testament, first I give and bequeath my bed, my bolster and two pillow-beres with a blancet and a coverlet unto Elizabeth Capon my sister in walderswick in Suff item I give unto Mary Norton the wife of Georg Norton in Salem my best coat, item I giue unto my sister above said thre peuter platters and a double saltseller, item I giue vnto John Jackson the son of John Jackson half a dozen spoones and a porrenger, item I give unto Margret Jackson the wife of John Jackson of Salem my box of linning, with a payre of shetes, item I will that fower payer of sheets be sold to pay pt of my debts, item I give unto Elizabeth Kellem a surg wascot, Item I give unto John Jackson aforesaid my bible, item I will that my two best cloath wascotes to be sold as my shets aforesaid, Item I give unto Elezabeth Nicksone my payer of Anderens, item I will that my napkins and bord cloaths to be sold as my wascots aforesaid. In witnes whereof I have hereunto set my hand this second day of May Anno Dom : 1640."

her mark<br>Elizabeth E Cartwrit

Witness : Elizabeth Nickson, Thomas Warren.

*Salem Quarterlg Court Files, vol.* 1, *leaf* 5.

Proved June 30, 1640. No executor being named, John Jackson is appointed administrator. Georg Norton had expended about 5li. under the deacons' hands during her sickness, which is to be paid him, the coat mentioned in the will to be made a part of it. Norton's man attended her. *Salem Quarterly Court Records, vol.* 1, *page* 39.

## ESTATE OF ROBERT BAKER OF SALEM.

The court held at Boston, 2:1:1640-41, fined Richard Hollingworth, 10li., to be paid to the wife and children of Robert Baker, his negligence being the occasion of the said Robert's death. *Mass. Bay Colony Records, vol. 1, page* 314.

Accounts of widow Baker and Nathaniel Pittman, and depositions relating to them, examined 30:1:1641. *Salem Quarterly Court Records, vol. 1, page* 50.

## ESTATE OF JOHN WATKINS OF SALEM.

Mr. Walter Price brought in an invoice of clothing, 29:4:1641, that was left by his servant John Watkins, who died within six or seven weeks after landing. Mr. Price was ordered to keep the goods as he had been at charge for Watkins' passage, and had no service of him of value. *Salem Quarterly Court Records, vol. 1, page* 53.

Price brought Watkins with him from England and had paid 5li. for his passage. His clothing was appraised by James Cary and Abell Kelly, as follows: Piece of leather, 6s. 8d.; pair of gloves, 6d.; an old suit, 8s.; a suit of clothes, 1li. 5s.; 2 pair drawers, 4s.; 6 pair stockings, 7s. 6d.; 2 cots, 1li. 2s.; 3 pair new shoes and 2 old, 12s. 4d.; 1-2li. thread and a little hemp, 2s.; 3 shirts, 10s. and 3 ragged ones, 2s. 6d., 12s. 6d.; a chest and a few nails, 2s. 6d.; an old hat, 10d.; 3 old bands; total, 5li. 4s. 10d. *Salem Quarterly Court Records, vol. 2, page* 90.

## ESTATE OF JOHN GOFFE OF NEWBURY.

"The last will & testament of John Goffe of Newbury, being weake in body but in perfect senses and knowledge Dec. 4, 1641.

My will is that whatsoever lands and housing and cattel and moveables shall appear that my estate consisteth of that it shall be divided into two parts equally and the one halfe I doe give to my wife Amy Goffe and the other halfe I doe give unto my two children Susan Goffe and Hanna Goffe in equall portions betwixt them as it shall amount, my debts & other charges being paid and for performance of this my will I have desired and doe give power to these parties named, Edward Woodman, Henry Short, Richard Kent junior and John Cheney all of Newbury to see my estate divided between my wife & children and to take care of my children's portions that they may be improved to their maintenance and best advantage & I have desired these brethren to advise and counsell my wife for her good according as God shall direct them, & if either of these my children decease this life, my will is that the other shall injoye her portions. Also my will is that if the children should both decease this life that my wife shall injoye their portions. Also my will is that if my children shall live to marriage or to the age of 18 years that then they shall have power to dispose of their portions according to their own pleasures."

his<br>Jno. I Goffe.<br>marke

Witness: Thomas Browne, William White.
Proved [Dec.] 28, 1641.

*Ipswich Town Records.*

Inventory of estate of John Goffe, late of Newbury, deceased, Dec. 4, 1641, taken by Edward Raw——, Richard ——, Tho. H—— and John ——, Dec. 16, 1641 :—Wearing apparel, 1 purple cloth sute, dublett and 2 hose, 1li. 4s. ; 1 short cote, 9s. ; 1 longe blew coat, 14s. ; 1 longe white coat, 4s. ; 1 pr. lead Coll. breeches, 11s. ; another same, 3s. 4d. ; 1 pr. drawers, 1s. 6d. ; 1 greene dublet, 4s. ; 1 cloth dublet, 7s. ; 1 leather dublet, 8s. 6d. ; 1 pr. shoes, 3s. 8d. ; 1 pr. leather stockins, 2s. ; 1 pr. cloth stockins, 1s. 2d. ; 1 pr. wollen stockins, 1s. 6d. ; 2 hatts, 2s. 6d. ; 1 cloth capp, 1s. ; total, 5li. 5s. In the hall, 3 bedsteeds, 1li. ; 1 pr. curtens, 3 rodds, 18s. ; one greene rugg, 1li. 6s. ; 2 blanketts, 15s. ; 1 bed, bolster, 4 pillows, 4li. 10s. ; 1 Coverlet, 10s. ; 1 bed matt, 2s. ; 5 wedges and 2 rings waighing 27li., 11s. 3d. ; 3 peck axes, 3s. 6d. ; 1 gouge, 4 chissels, one pr. gimboles and 2 wimble trees, 6s. ; old Iron waighing 23li., 7s. 8d. ; same waighing 18li., 3s. ; one hand bill, ——; 1 chafing dish, ——; 2 old axes, ——; 24li. of waights, ——; one trevet, a tramell chayne, 5s.; one pitch fork, beaving bill, ——; 1 spade, 3s. ; 2 musketts, 1 sword, bandeleers and rest, 2li. ; one spitt and slice, 3s. ; 1 pr. bellows, 1s. ; longe sawe, 4s. ; 1 shovell and 1 pick ax, 3s. ; 2 pitchforks & a sith, 4s. ; 1-2 of the boat, 12s. ; 1 wheele barrow, 5s. ; 1 wimshete, 5s. ; 1 peece of leather, 4s. ; 1 Chest, 5s. ; a trunke, 6s. ; 4 hogsheads, 8s. ; 2 old boxes, 2s. ; 2 sackes and one bagg, 6s. 8d. ; 1 old cloth, 5s.; total, ——. In provitions, 160 waight of pork, 2li. ; 7 bushells indian corne, ——; 1 bushell of english wheat, 4s. ; 1 bushell mault, 4s. ; 1 bushell meale, 2s. ; 12li. butter, 6s. ; carretts and cabbidges, 12s. ; total, 4li. 8s. Cattle, 2 cowes, 11li. ; 1 steere, 4li. 10s. ; 2 cow calves, 3li. ; 1 steere, 3li. ; 4 piggs, 1li. ; total, 22li. 16s. 3d. ; house and land, a farme of

80 acres, 9li.; a house with 6 acres upland and 6 acres marsh, ———; a hooke, hatchet and old kettle, ———; a peece of wooden ———; tubbs, platters, spoo———. *Ipswich Town Records.*

### ESTATE OF JOHN OLLIVER OF NEWBURY.

Mr. ———on Olliver, late of Newberry, died intestate, and 29: 1: 1642, John ——— is appointed administrator. Mr. John Woodbridg mentioned. *Ipswich Town Records.*

John Oliver, Newbury, dyed intestate, leaving a wife and one only daughter, aged about two years, and an estate of about 420li., and upon petition of Joane Oliver his wife, the court held June 14, 1642, ordered that she possess the entire estate and to bring up the child. To give her 100li. at her mariage or when she is eighteen years and 100li. when she is twenty-one years, and to give bond to the next Ipswich court for security. She also hath power to free her servant for the year desired. *Mass. Bay Colony Records, vol. 2, page* 11.

Copy of power of attorney from Walter Stephens of Bristoll, mercer, to my "Cosen Christopher Olliver of the said citty Merchant" to recover of the executors or administrators of John Olliver, heretofore of the city of Bristoll, mercer and late of New England, deceased, all demands whatsoever which are due or owing to me by the said John Olliver; signed Jan. 10, 1642[-3], by Walter Stephens, and witnessed by ffrancis Brewster, Richard Stephens, Walter Stephens, jr. and Abell Kelly.

Certificate that this power of attorney was a true copy of the original; signed by Jno. Lowle and Christopher Olliver. Acknowledged in court held at Ipswich, 24: 7: 1644, by Christopher Olliver.

By virtue of above described power of attorney Christopher Olliver of Bristoll, merchant, received of Mrs. Johan Olliver certain cattell in full of all accounts betwixt the above Walter Stephens and John Olliver, and acquitted "ye said Johan Olliver from all debts duties or demands of the said walter Stephens pvided that the sume of nineteene pounds ten shillings be paid in Bristoll according vnto the above Johan Olliver her order vnto the said Walter Stephens or assignes otherwise the said Johan Olliver to stand indebted vnto the above Walter Stephens or assignes for the sume of nineteene pounds ten shillings." Signed Sept. 3, 1644, by Christopher Olliver, and witnessed by Jno. Lowle. Acknowledged to be a true copy in court held at Ipswich, 24: 7: 1644.

*Ipswich Deeds, vol.* 1, *leaf* 17.

Copy of a power of attorney from George Batherne of Bristoll, sopemaker, to my "brother in lawe Christopher Olliver of the said Citty mrchant," to receive of the executors or administrators of John Olliver, heretofore of Bristol, mercer, and late of New England, deceased, what may be due to me from said estate; dated Jan. 10, 1642[-3]; signed by George Batherne and witnessed by Richard Newman and James Birkin.

Certificate as to this power of attorney being a true copy of the original, by Christopher Olliver and Jno. Lowle; and acknowledged in Court holden at Ipswich, 24 : 7 : 1644, by Christopher Olliver.

By virtue of above described power of attorney, Christopher Olliver of Bristol, merchant, received of Mrs. Johan Olliver, executrix of Mr. John Olliver, late of Newbury in New England, deceased, 19li., and acquits "the aforesaid Johan Olliver from the said George Batherne his debts or demands from the begining of the world to this day." Signed Nov. 4, 1644, by Christopher Olliver and witnessed by Roger Daniel and John Lowle.

John Lowle testified 30 : 7 : 1646, that the abovesaid writing was the act of the abovesaid Christopher Olliver, before John Endicot and Richard Saltonstall.

*Ipswich Deeds, vol. 1, leaf 18.*

Upon consideration of the petition of Mr. Gerish the General Court held at Boston 7 : 8 : 1646, judge it equall that the 100li. debt and overprizall should be taken out of the whole estate of John Oliver, intestate, and the daughter shall have an equall moyety of the remainder at the time appointed in the former order. *Mass. Bay Colony Records, vol. 2, page 164.*

Inventory taken 3m : 1649, by Edmond Grenlefe, John Saunders and Richard Knight: one Dwelling Howse & barne, 16li.; one orchard, 15li.; 4 Acers of Land, 7li.; 20 Acers of fresh medow, 17li. 10s.; 12 Acers of Salt marsh, 7li. 10s.; 7 Acers of land sould, 3li. 3s.; 40 rod of ffence, 1li. 10s.; total, 67li. 13s.; more in ffence aboute the meddow & Land, 10li.; in bookes, 7li. 15s.; two little Howses, 1li. 10s.; losses in debts & catle allowed ℈ the Generall Court, 14li. 10s.; loss in the Howse & lands, 45li. 7s., one halfe allowed ℈ the Generall Court being 22li. 13s. 6d.; 2 Oxen, 16li.; 2 Cowes, 9li. 18s. 6d.; total, 150li. *Mass. Archives, vol. 15B, page 143.*

Upon the petition of Mr. Wm. Gerish the Court, May 2, 1649, grants the following: 1, that 14li. 10s. be abated out of the 150li. due to the child; 2, that the remainder of the 150li. be paid for the use of the child, in the house that John Oliver dwelt in at Newbury, together with the lands belonging thereunto, if this is not sufficient to discharge the sum, then to be supplied out of the estate of Mr. Gerish, and that an apprizall be made, to include a dwelling house, barn and cow house purchased by Mr. Gerish of Mr. Lowle; 3, that the child should stand to the advance or loss of the value of the estate; 4, that the Court may authorize Mr. Gerish, John Saundrs and Mr. Edward Woodman, or such of them as they think meet, to be intrusted with the estate, for the benefit of the child, giving an account of their proceedings; that Mr. Gerish should have competent allowance from the profits, for her education and maintenance, to be determined by the Court.

John Sanders, Richard Knight and Mr. Greenleife authorized to apprize the estate of John Oliver and to make return to the next sessions of the General Court, and then to determine what allowance to be made for the child's education and maintenance.

*Mass. Bay Colony Records, vol. 2, page* 275.

In answer to the petition of Mr. Wm. Gerrish, the Court, May 16, 1649, grants the following: that 14li. 10s. be abated out of the 150li. due to the child, and the remainder be paid for the child's use, in the house that John Oliver lately dwelt in, at Newbury, together with the lands appertaining thereunto. If this be not sufficient then to be supplied out of the estate of Mr. Gerish; that the child should stand to the advance or loss of the value of the estate; that the Court may authorize Mr. Gerrish, John Saunders and Mr. Edward Woodman, or such of them as they think meet, to be intrusted with the estate of the child for the benefit of the child; that Mr. Gerrish shall have competent allowance from the profits of the estate of the child, for his education and maintenance.

John Saunders, Richard Knight and Mr. Greenleafe ordered to apprize the houses and lands, which was the estate of John Oliver, and what other shall be tendered for the daughter's portion, and return made to the next session of the General Court, and then to determine what allowance to be made for the child's education and maintenance and if the houses and lands shall be sold who shall keep the portion and when to be paid the child.

*Mass. Bay Colony Records, vol. 3, page* 165.

Upon the petition of Lt. Willi. Gerrish to the Generall Court held at Boston, 17 : 8 : 1649, ordered that he should have the portion of Mary Oliver, the daughter of John Oliver, deceased, in his own hands to his own use, he to give sufficient security to pay her at the age of fourteen years, 135li. 10s. in corn or cattle, at current price, as the late order of this Court provides for. *Mass. Bay Colony Records, vol. 2, page* 282.

Petition of Lt. Wm. Gerrish of Newbury, that he may have the estate of Mary Oliver as it is valued. Granted by the Court, Oct. 19, 1649, he to give security to pay her 135li. 10s., in corn or cattle, at fourteen years of age, and in the meantime to maintain and educate her.
*Mass. Bay Colony Records, vol. 3, page* 176.

### Estate of John Bradley of Salem.

"The last [will] & Testament of John Bradley of Salem deceased the fourth month 1642 as he related to us while he was of pfect memory. Ursly Greenoway deposed saith, that John Bradley of Salem deceased being asked in the time of his sicknes what was his will, & perswaded to make a will, did aske why he should make his will, he had nobody to give his estate but his wife, only some of his cloths & tooles he gave to his brother in lawe william Allen." 29 (5) 1642. Testifyed before the Governo<sup>r</sup> & Court. *Suffolk Co. Probate Records, vol. 1, page* 21(16).

Inventory taken 21: 4: 1642, by Will Hathorne and Thomas Putman : A ten acre lot on Capt An side, 4 acres therof broken & 6 unbroken, 7li.; 2 acres of Corne upon the same, 3li.; 25 acres at Jaffrys Creeke, 6li. 5s.; an acre of Corne at Towne, 1li. 3s. 6d.; for 3 goats & 3 kids, 1li. 15s.; for 3 Swine, 1li. 6s.; 7 bushills of Indian Corne, 1li. 3s. 4d.; 2 Iron Pots, a paire of pothooks, on old frying pan, 1li.; a musket, bandlers and rest, 1li. ; —— axes, 2 hows and som old Iron, 10s. 6d.; —— Chaires and a Tub, 4s. 6d.; —— a halfe headed bedstead, 8s.; —— old bed a bolster 2 —— bears, 1li. 10s.; ——ests, 12s.; ——t a kit ——, 1li.; ——nes ——; —— of Pen——; ——owbea——; —— in Lan ——; ——; total, ——. —— oweing by him to others. *Suffolk Co. Probate Files, docket* 24.

### Estate of Samuel Smith of Wenham.

"This 5th of ocktober : 1642 : This my last will and testament of Samewell Smith of Enon being in perfect memorey first I will and bequeath vnto my wife Sarah Smith my farme in Enon with all the housen vpon it as allsoe all the frutes vpon it as corne hemp and the like: for har owne proper vse for the tearme of har life vpon consideration that she shall discharg me of that promise vpon maridge; which is vnto my sunn: william Browne fiftie pounds: as allsoe that she shall giue vnto his two children william and ‖ by ‖ Browne ‖ 20¹ between y^m ‖ : all which shall be paid John my exequetors hearafter named: my will further is to giue vnto Sarah my wif all my Cattell nowe vpon the farme young and owld as neat bests horse bests and swine in full consideration of that hundred pounds that I stand bound vnto har by A bond obligatore in lue of A former Joynter payabell after my dissease which shall be parformed by my Exsequetors as allsoe further my will is that my farme with all the medowe and upland belongine thearvnto my sunn Thomas Smith shall haue it to himself and his heairs for euer vpon this consideration that he shall pay vnto his sister Mare if then liuing fiftie pownds in thre years after the entrie of it that is to say sixtene pounds and A mark A yeare and for the parformance hearof he is to lay in good securitye vnto the Exsequetors if the lord take har away by death this payment is to be made vnto the Children of the aforesaid william Browne and Thomas Smith that then shall be liuing Equally deuided among them further my will is that if my sunn: Thomas shall die without issue that my land and housen vpon it shall com to my daughter mare and har heaires foreuer: and after har to william Browne and his haaires for ever all wich debts and legasies and ‖ other ‖ parformances are to be parformed by my two Exsequetors which I haue Apointed which is my Louing wife and my trustie sun william Browne: & my will further is that if Sarah my wif shall marey that then the first gift of my farme shall stand voyd and my will is that she shall then resigne it vp into my other exequetors hand with A Just accounte of all those goods and whatsoever belong to the manadgine of the farme ‖ and proffitt ‖ except that hundred pounds which har due which is to be paide har in Cattell by the Judgment of men: and all my houshould stufe within dores whatsoeuer it be I give to my wife: and my will is that my excequetor william Browne and my sunn Thomas Smith to Joyne with him to leat the farme: or improue it to the best advantage for the good of my daughter mare and to be accounted with and prouided for by my excequetor william Browne in that particquler: Item with ‖ this ‖ consideration that if my wif marey that then the farme is to be leat as aboue said untill thear be gathered for ‖ my ‖ A portion ‖ of ‖ A hundred and fiftie pounds to be paid vnto the excequetor william Browne and he to pay that hundred & fiftie pounds at har day of maredg & if har mother leave har then the excequetor william Browne to se ye bringing of har vp. allsoe my sunn Thomas Smith is to be Aquitted of that fiftie pounds he stand ingadged to pay vnto har : and all the ouerplush of A hundred and fiftie pounds if the lord give longer life vnto my wif Arising out of ye farme is to be left in my sun browns hand and improved to the best vse and after har dissease to be equally parted betwixt my daughter mare and all the grand children I shall haue then living further my will is that my sunn Thomas Smith whome I fear not : will be truly faithfull to me shall be thearfore my Suprevisor of this my last will :

Samwell Smyth ". [seal]

Witness: Richard S (his marke) Pettingall, William Sawyer.

*Salem Quarterly Court Files, vol. 1, leaf 12.*

Proved 27 : 10 : 1642. Wit : Jno. Thorndike, who deposed that he had his senses ; Georg Emerey. that " he had a fitt of a feaver ye day before and the vapors in his stomake caused paine in his head, and did cause sleep troubld sleep & ye Last day till toward 2 of the Clock was very sensible." Mr. Jno. Fiske, Mrs. Fisk, and the two witnesses to the will, Richard Pettingell and William Sawyer, also deposed. *Salem Quarterly Court Records, vol. 2, page* 127.

Inventory taken 18 : 9 : 1642, by Lawrence Leach, Jefferie Massey and Will. Howard : Dwelling house, barn, etc., 40li. ; farm of 234 acres, 33 broken up, 177 in common and 24 meadow, 99li. 8s. ; 6 calves, 7li. ; 3 heffers, 10li. 10s. ; 4 oxen, 24li. ; mear and coult, 20li. 10s. ; 2 young stears, 9li. ; 7 cowes, 36li. 10s. ; 9 swine, 14li. ; Inglish and indian Corne, 28li. ; hempe, 2li. 10s. ; hay, etc., 12li. 6s. ; carte, plow, harrow, etc., 3li. 15s. ; silver beacker, and 2 spounes, 2li. 15s. ; peauter, brasse, Iron potts, 8li. 5s. ; 2 muskitts, 1 birding pese & 1 pr. bandelerers, 1li. 10s. ; sword and belt, 12s. ; in cellar, 3li. 10s. ; corne & hemp sed, 3li. 10s. ; severall towles, 1li. 16s. ; bed, boulster & blanckits, 2li. ; bed & bedstead, 4li. 2s. ; bed in chamber, 12s. ; bed, blanckits & Ceverlet, 7li. 8s. ; another, 9li. 3s. 6d. ; bed teek, 2li.; bed, bedstead & furniture, 4li. 14s. ; wearing aparell of his, 7li. 6s. ; A 11 Cushings, 2li. 15s. ; one carpitt, 15s. ; Cobbard Clothes, 1li. ; 3 Chists & A whele, 11i.; napkins & bord lining, 4li. 18s.; pillow bears, 3li.; sheets, 7li. 16s.; bookes, 15s.; wood worke, viz., 1 tabell & standard, warming pann & stooles, 3li. 3s.; 1 grinstone, a brake, tuter & Iron Rake. Total, 395li. 9s. 2d. Goods not seen by appraisers but reported to them: Hand carte, 5s.; 2 towe comes, 5s.; a small cowe hide, 8s.; total, 18s. " the boyes time Prised at three pownds intending the boyes Covenant to be performed as it is in the indenter," 3li. *Salem Quarterly Court Files. vol.* 1, *leaf* 12.

### Estate of John Woodbury of Salem.

Court ordered 27 : 10 : 1642, that widow Woodbury bring in her husband's will and inventory of his estate.

Will of John Woodbury, deceased, proved 27 : 4, 1643. His widow Ann Woodbury, executrix, ordered to bring in inventory.

Inventory of estate of John Woodbury, deceased, sworn to by his widow, 20 : 12 : 1643.

*Salem Quarterly Court Records, vol.* 2, *pp.* 128, 142, 150.

### Estate of Henry Roffe of Newbury.

" The 15th 12th month 1642 I desire to comend my sonle into the hands of the lord Jesus Christ. I desire my goods may be equally divided to my wife & all my children, only my sonne John Roffe must have the howse & land more then all the rest of my children and that their porcons shalbe divided when they be 21 yeares of age if they marry not before In case my wife dye or marry then the goods shalbe divided; otherwise not till my eldest childe come to be 21 yeares of age But still to remayne in their mothers hands with the rest till that either of them are 21 yeares of age or marry If any of my children dye then that porcon shalbe equally divided betweene my wife & the rest of my children. I doe give vnto my wife one great brasse pott and one great brasse pann, and a great brasse posnett and a chafing dish and five pewter platters I doe give vnto my Kinsman Thomas whittear a swarme of bees. I desire my brother John Roffe and my Cosen John Saunders of Sallisbery and william Mondy of Newberry to oversee my will & order it to my desire & accordinge to my will."

Henry Roffe.

Witness : Thomas Hale, Thomas Cowllman, william Mose. Proved 28 : 1 : 1643.

*Ipswich Deeds, vol.* 1, *leaf* 2.

Inventory taken 1 : 1 : 1642, by John Woodbridg, Henry Short and Richard Knight : howse & land, 30li.; Six kowes, 30li.; foure oxen, 24li.; one bull & one steere, 3 yeare old, 7li. 10s.; three beasts, two years old, 8li.; two beasts, one yeare old, 2li. 10s.; three Calves, 1li. 4s.; three hoggs, 1li. 4s.; Bees, 7li. 10s.; haye, 4li.; Soyle, 1li.; Cart, Slead & 3 Yoaks, 1li. 6s.; within the howse : one fetherbed & flockbed, 3li. 10s.; Six fether pillowes, 18s.; 4 Coverleds, 2li.; 5 blanketts, 1li. 10s.; 3 paier of Sheets, 1li. 8s.; 2li. and a halfe of bee wax, 2s. 6d.; bowlster Case & pillow & napkins, 10s.; porke, 2li. 7s.; butter & Cheese, 12s.; barrells & butte[r] Cherne & other lumb., 18s.; Pewter, 1li. 7s. 6d.; Brasse, 3li. 13s.; a Brasse pott, 1li.; iron potts, 1li. 6s.; A chafing dish & a posnet, 5s.; 12 bushells of indian corne, 2li. 2s.; 9 bushells of wheate, 2li. 6d.; 2 bushells of pease, 9s.; hogsheads & howes & other lumber, 16s.; in apparrell, stockins & shoes, 3li.; muskett & fowling peeces & 2 Swords & bandileers, 1li. 19s.; working Tooles & lanthorne, 15s.; bookes, 1li.; spining wheeles, 10s.; a chest & chaiers & other lumb., 16s.; harrow tines, 10s.; total, 153li. 8s. 6d. *Ipswich Deeds, vol.* 1, *leaf* 3.

### Estate of George Browne of Newbury.

" The last will & Testament of George Browne May 26th 1642 In the name of God amen I George Browne being sick & weake in body but pfect in minde &c doe make my last will & Testament in mann & forme as followeth Impr I bequeath my soule into the hands of god and my body to the earth to be buried It I give to my beloved wife my howse & land with all my howshehold goods except my muskett & sword my wearing clothes & Tooles. Item I give unto her my kow It I give to my brother Richard Browne my wearing clothes & Tooles It I give vnto Richard Littleale Twenty shillings to be paid out of the rent of the Mill Item : I give vnto my father & to my brother Michael Twenty shillings a peece to be paid out of the Mill, but if god by his pvidence bring them into this land then my will is to give them six pounds a peece or if but one of them ||come over|| then he shall receive twelve pounds & if afterward the other come then he shall repay to him six pounds Item I give to all my brethren & sisters besides Twelve pence a peece my will is that all this shalbe paid out of my Mill after all my debts are discharged It I give vnto Joseph Browne sonne of my brother Richard Browne my share in the Mill ||at|| Salisbury with the land belonging to it, to be assigned vnto him when he come to be eighteene yeares of age & in the meane tyme the revenew of it to be imployed for his use & at the Terme aforesaid Provided that my debts be first paid out of it & then those legacies before mentioned before any of the revenew goe to him It I make my brother Richard Browne executor of this my will & Testament And I desire my two frends Richard Knight & Thomas Macye to se that this my will be pformed according to my plaine intent and meaning pvided that they shalbe sattisfied for whatsoever trouble or charge may come to them about the same ffurthermore my will is that if my wife be with child that then my former will shalbe voyde. I then give vnto my wife my howse & lande & all the rest of my estate to my child to be deliued to it when it come to be eighteene yeares old and that my wife in the meane tyme shall have the vse of it toward the bringing vp of the child and all charges that doe or shall arise whatsoever to be paid out of the child's porcon This alsoe I desire my two frends aforenamed to oversee Item I give vnto my wife the swyne and my shirts except one and my bands except three & a hatt & a paire of shoes and my will is that my wife shall pay these debts that which I owe to Richard Littleale & John Bishopp & to Henry ffay & to John Lowle & m^{ris} Goodale & m^{ris} Olliver Item I give to my wife my bible Item my will is that if my father & my brother michael come not then my two Nephews Margery & Josua shall have that which my father & brother should have."

George Browne.

Witness: Richard Knight, Thomas Macy.
Proved by Richard Knight, Mar. 28, 1643.

*Ipswich Deeds. vol. 1., leaf 4.*

Inventory of estate of George Browne, Newbury, deceased Aug. 1, 1642, taken by Thomas Blanchar, Thomas Hale, Tho. Macie and Richard Knight: A howse & four acres of ground with an acre & halfe of corne on it, 12li.; A Kowe, 5li. 10s.; a yearling heifer, 2li. 6s. 8d.; 2 Swyne, 1li. 4s.; goat, 10s.; a Table & frame & forme, 7s.; 2 Cushens, 3s. 4d.; Halfe a mault mill, 13s. 4d.; Tooles, 5s.; frying pan, a paire potthooks & a skillet, 3s. 6d.; pewter & other goods, 17s.; A Bedstead, 2 Chests & a Box, 15s.; a Bed & bedinge, 2s.; his wearing clothes, 4li.; his share in a mill at Salisbury, 20li. a muskett, 12s.; a Bible, 5s.; a paire of Bootes, 5s.: total, 52li. 6s. 10d.

*Ipswich Deeds, vol. 1, leaf 5.*

### Estate of Thomas Eaborne of Salem.

Will of Thomas Eaborne proved 27 : 4 : 1643, and inventory presented. Amount, 21li. 16s. 5d. *Salem Quarterly Court Records, vol. 2, page* 142.

### Estate of William Ballard of Lynn.

Inventory of William Ballard of Lynn, deceased, filed 27 : 4 : 1643. *Salem Quarterly Court Records, vol. 2, page* 142.

Timothie Tomlins and Thomas Erington were appointed guardians of the children of William Ballard, deceased; and Timothie Tomlins having since deceased, Nicolas Batty of Lin was appointed in his place 28 : 10 : 1647. Thomas Putnum of Lin and Thomas Laughton were appointed to divide the lands between the mother and children according to the will. *Salem Quarterly Court Records, vol. 2, page* 224.

### Estate of Anne Scarlet of Salem.

Will of Anne Scarlet, who died " the last day of the 12th month," dated 2 : 1 : 1639. " I doe Desire to have some order taken for the payinge my brother Samuell . . . in old England the some of Tenne pownds w$^{ch}$ he layd out for mee. And also my brother D[avid's] Children twelve shillings a peece to buy them a [w$^{th}$all.] And for the rest of my goods & moveables, & lynnen & wollin I desire they shall be equallie Devided to my three children, Mary Margaret & Joseph equally alike to them : Also I Doe give unto my sister Dennis my blew gowne further I give to my brother James Hindes tenne shillings. And alsoe my three Children to be wholy executo$^{rs}$ & my brother Browning & his wiefe advisers. And also my brother Joseph Grafton I desire him to advise in the ordering of my goods & my things as are abovewritten. And that my children may equallie devide such of my goods as shall remayne after these things be discharged that are abovenamed equallie amonge them."

Anne Scarlet.

Witness : James Hinds, James Moulton.

Mr. Endecott, Dep. Gov., delivered the will to Court 11m : 1642; proved 30 : 4 : 1643.

*Salem Quarterly Court Files, vol.* 1, *leaf* 16.

### Estate of William Nevill of Ipswich.

"I william Nevill of Ipswich singleman being weake of body but of pfect memory & vnderstanding doe make this my last will & Testament as followeth I comit my soule to god that gave it & my body to the earth when I shall depart this life and for my worldly goods I thus dispose of them first that Phisitian & other debts that I owe shalbe paid Alsoe I give Mary whipple my bible and I give to her & to the rest of my m$^r$ children that which my master oweth me alsoe I give that which my dame oweth me; and 18$^d$ which Philip ffowler oweth me to william Robinson alsoe I give to william Gooderson my interest in the Teame hired of m$^r$ Bradstreet and in the ground hired of m$^r$ Carner being ptner with william Robinson as alsoe in an other bargaine and agreement wherein william Robinson & I are ptners and my will is that william Gooderson shall have halfe the profitt past & to come & to beare halfe the charges that are past & are yet to pay for & that shalbe hereafter to be done Alsoe I give to Goody Langton the feed wheat alsoe I give to Mary Langton that which goodman Horton oweth me alsoe I give to Joseph Langton my fowling peece also I give to Sarah Langton my barly Alsoe I give John wooddam one bushell of Barly as is at Goodman Quilters & a little debt which John doth owe me And lastly I make Roger Langton my only executor & overseer of this last will & Testament Alsoe I give Ann whipple my chest wittnes my hand the 2 month the 15$^{th}$ day 1643."

william Nevell

Witness: Joseph Morse, Thomas Dorman.
Proved 7m: 1643.

*Ipswich Deeds, vol. 1, leaf 5.*

### Estate of William Walcott of Salem.

Willia Walcott's wife, children and estate committed to Richard Inkersell, his father-in-law, 27 : 10 : 1643, to be disposed of "according to God; and the said Wm. Walcott to bee & Remaine as his servant." *Salem Quarterly Court Records, vol. 2, page* 146.

### Estate of Charles Turner of Salem.

Creditors of widow of Charles Turner, deceased, ordered 27 : 10 : 1643, to prove claims. Inventory of his estate to be brought in, " for y^e more peacable & comfortable subsistance of the widdow." *Salem Quarterly Court Records, vol. 2, page 149.*

Widow Rachell Turner brought in inventory ult : 12m : 1643 of estate, of her husband, Charles Turner. Estate to be paid to creditors by Ralph Fogg, for the court. *Salem Quarterly Court Records, vol. 2, page 158.*

### Estate of John Sanders of Salem.

" The Last wil & testament of John Sanders, inhabytant of the Towne of Salem, I bequeath unto my sonn John Sandars my Tenn Aker lot with my hous new built on the Commons side right over a gainst it when he Come to the age of one & twentie yeers or at the death of his mother with the Aker And halfe of middow ground adioyning to it and I do be trust my father Joseph Graften & goodman Hardie to see this my wil & ded performed mad in the yeere 1643 y^e 28 of October." [no signature.]

Witness: Nathaniell Porter, Henrye Birdsall.

" Testified upon oaths in Court & also y^t the sd Jn^o Sand^rs Left all the Rest of his Estate to his wyfe."

Proved 28 : 10 : 1643.

*Salem Quarterly Court Files, vol. I, leaf 18.*

### Estate of Abraham Belknap of Lynn.

Will of Abram Belknap sworn to, 20 : 12 : 1643. *Salem Quarterly Court Records, vol. 2, page 150.*

Inventory of estate of Abraham Belknap of Lynn, who deceased the beginning of the 7 mo. 1643, taken by William (his mark) Tilton and Edward Tomlins, 16 : 12 : 1643 : Sheep, 4 yewes, 5li.; 2 wethers, 1li. 6s. 8d.; 7 yerlinge calfes, 3li. 10d.; 2 cowes and calfes, 8li. 10s.; 2 yerlinge calfes, 3li. 15s.; 4 yow gotes, 1li. 6s. 8d.; 1 kidd, 4s.; 1 sow and piggs, 1li.; 4 shottes, 1li. 10s.; the houses and 5 akres of land, 7li.; 2 akers of planting Land, 1li. 10s.; 2 akers salt marsh, 1li.; 6 akers salt marsh at fox hill, 2li.; 30 akers at the village, 2li.; 1 braspitt, 10s.; 1 iron cettle, 6s. 8d.; 1 brascettle, 3s. 4d.; 3 ould skillets, 3s.; 1 friing pan, 1s.; pot hookes and pot hangers, 2s. 6d.; 1 spitt, 1s. 6d.; 7 pewtor platters, 14s.; 1 bras pestill & morter, 2s. 6d.; 1 candle stick and dripping pan, 2s.; 1 ould warming pan, 3s. 4d.; 1 payre of tongs, 1s.; 1 payre andirons, 2s.; 1 table, 3s.; 1 Chyer, 2s. 6d.; 1 chest, 1 box, 4s.; 1 chest, 1s.; 2 flock beds, 1 boulster, 13s. 4d.; 1 fether bed & boulster, 1li.; 3 coverlettes, 1li. 6s. 8d.; 4 blankits, 13s. 4d.; 3 pillowes, 6s.; 3 prs. sheetes, 1li.; 1 sheete, 2s. 6d.; 2 payre pillow beres, 6s.; 2 table clothes, 4s.; 1 doos. of napkins, 3s.; ould iron, 4 wedges, 4s.; 1 ould ax, 1s.; 1 ould hatchett, 8d.; 1 mattock, 1s. 6d.; total, 53li. 10s. 3d. Signed by Mary (her mark) Belknapp. The estate owed Joseph Armytage, Francis Ingalls, Goodman Phillipes, Rich. Rowton, Tho. Laighton, Ed. Farington, Jerard Spencer, Mr. Kinge and John Person, amounting to 5li. 13s. 3d. *Salem Quarterly Court Files, vol. 1, leaf 18.*

### ESTATE OF ROBERT ANDREWS OF IPSWICH.

" the first of March 1643. In the name of god amen I Robert Andrewes of Ipsw<sup>ch</sup> in New England being of pfect vnderstanding & memory doe make this my last will & Testament Imprimis I comend my soule into the hands of my mercifull Creator & redeemer & I doe comitt my body after my departure out of this world to be buried in seemly manner by my frends &c concerning my estate Imprimis I doe make my eldest sonne John Andrewes my executor Item I give vnto my wife Elizabeth Andrews forty pounds and to John Griffin the sonne of Humfry Griffin sixteene pounds to be paid vnto him when he shalbe Twenty one yeares of age, & if he shall dye before he comes to that age it shall returne to my two sonnes John & Thomas Andrewes Item concerning my sonne Thomas Andrews my will is that he shall live with his brother John Andrews three yeares two of which he shalbe helpfull to his brother John Andrewes in his husbandry and the last of the three yeares he shall goe to schoole to recover his learning and if he shall goe to the vniversity or shall set himselfe vpon some other way of living his brother John shall allow him ten pounds by the yeare for foure yeares & then fifteene pounds by the yeare for two yeares succeeding after. Item concerning the fourescore pounds which is to be paid vnto my sonne in lawe ffrancklins daughter Elizabeth ffrancklin my grandchild my will is that if she die before the debt is due it shalbe thus disposed ten pounds of it shall goe to my sonne Daniell Hovies Child Daniell Hovey my grand child and the other seav[en]ty pounds shalbe divided betweene my Two sonnes John & Thomas Andrews and if those my Two sonnes should dye then thirty pounds should be divided betweene my kinsmen John Thomas & Robert Burnum by equall porcons. & Twenty more should goe to Humphry Gryffins Two other sonnes & the other Twenty shall goe to Daniell Hovey. And because my sonne John Andrewes is yet vnder age I doe comend him vnto Thomas Howlet as his Guardian vntill he shall come of age."

Robert Andrews.

Witness: William Knight, John whipple, Thomas Scot and Joseph Metcalfe.

Proved 26: 1: 1644.

*Ipswich Deeds, vol. 1, leaf 6.*

### Estate of Robert Muzzey of Ipswich.

" Januarij 5° AD 1642 I Robert Mussy of the Towne of Ipswich in New England expecting my change approaching though at p<sup>r</sup>sent of firme memory & vnderstanding And desiring seasonably to sett in order my estate of earthly goods that the lord hath gratiously given me doe thus dispose thereof in particulars as follow: ffirst I give & bequeath vnto Bridgett my wife the howse & howslott that lyes in the west street of the Towne neare ioyning to the howse of John Dane the elder w<sup>th</sup> the out howsen ptainyng vnto it during her life, and she to keepe it in sufficient repayring But the commonage ptayning to my howse & land I leave to be divided betwixt my wife & children according to the discretion of my overseers Alsoe the free vse of a peece of land that I bought latly of John Newman which of the quantity of six acres whether more or lesse ioyning to my farme on the south side of it at Egipt River and this for the terme of her widdowes estate. Likewise I give vnto her one of the bedds that I lye vpon (which she shall like best) the rugg one paire of blanketts and one paire of sheets one pillow & bowlster & two pillowbeeres to inioye them for the tyme of her widdowhood. I likewise give vnto my wife a morter bell mettle skillett an iron pott & pott hangers a Coltrell or tramell & a brasse kettle during her widdowhood moreover I give her two Ewe goates only willing if they prosp she give two Ewegoates to my daughter Mary   I alsoe give her the biggest chest but not to be carried out of my howse   alsoe the table but both to be standing in the howse for my daughter Mary afterward :   And as for such things as she brought with her I leave them wholly w^{th}out any intermeddling therewith. Item I bequeath to Joseph my eldest sonne my farme w^{th} all the app^{r}tuncs belonging vnto it lying on the other side of Egipt river only reserving a peece of land called the Cowleas and a peece of meadow adioyning to it called the rocky meadowes all which may containe Twenty acres Alsoe I give to him my muskett and what belongs to it   Alsoe I give to him foure pewter platters And a felling axe two dubble hookes and my biggest fowling peece alsoe a firepan & tongs. And one bed & a paire of sheets a couerlett & a blankett the second biggest chest alsoe a paire of cobirons and a plow chaine & a spitt & three wedges & a warming pan two narrow howes & one silver spoone   Alsoe I give vnto him my dun mare, one diap napkin & two hollan napkins one of the best hollan pillowbeeres all which I give to him & his heires for ever   Item I give vnto my sonne Beniamin the Cowleas & the Rocky meadowe both adioyning to my farme alsoe a peece of land which was foremenconed to be my wives during the tyme of her widdowes estate & noe longer that I bought of John Newman containyng the quantity of six acres whether more or lesse that I give to my sonne Beniamin after her widdowhood likewise two silu spoones alsoe a Cowple of young steeres and one flockbed a paire of sheets a coverlett alsoe two hollan napkins & one hollan pillowbeere four pewters platters & a felling axe. Item I give to my daughter Mary the howse & howlott that lyes in the west street of the Towne neare adioyning to the house of John Dane the elder with the out howsen ptaining vnto it after the death of my wife. Alsoe I give vnto her foure cowes p^{r}sently after my decease alsoe a bull & a Cow calfe & foure ewe goates all these p^{r}sently after my decease to be imployed for her best benefit   I give her alsoe my best bible a great brasse pan to be reserved for her till she comes to yeares also a silver spoone alsoe a paire of the best sheets & two diap napkins foure peuter platters the broad box with all her mothers wearing linen. Item I give to my daughter Ellen a dripping pan a brasse candlestick a brasse skillet & a spitt. Alsoe I give vnto my daughter Ellen one yoak of oxen   Item I give to the vse of the poore one Ewe goate to be disposed of by the overseers of my will to such as are godly onely the first yeares vse I appoynt to my brother Dane the elder if she brings kidds or else longer and when the goat growes old I will that one of the yonge ones be reserved for such a vse. I likewise intreete & appoynt m^r Bradstreet m^r Dumer m^r Rogers & m^r Norton to be overseers of this my will to see the same faithfully pformed & leave what is doubtfull & defective by them to be ordered & disposed moreover I desire m^r Dumer to take Joseph m^r Norton to take Beniamine & my daughter Mary if it pleaseth him when the overseers shall ioyntly see meet to take them from my wife my will likewise & meaning is that the stock which I give to my children seually shalbe in the hands & vse of each of those freinds that take them into their governm^t giving assurance for the payment thereof vnto my children when they shall come to convenient age as to my two sonnes when they come to the age of one & twenty yeares & my daughter Mary at the age of eighteene yeares and for any addicon to be made to the p^rsent stock I leave it to the good will of those my frends on whom I repose the trust of their educacon. ffineally I appoynt Bridgett my wife the sole executrix of this my last will & testament And after all this what ever my overseers shall see remaining meet to be diuided I will that they dispose thereof equally amonge my three least children

"In wittnes hereof I sett my hande & seale the day & yeare above written."
(his mark)
Robert Muzzall

Witness: John Daine, Humphry Bradstreet, William Norton and ffrancis Dane.

"Item I give & bequeath vnto Joseph my eldest sonne one yoake of two yearling steers with my best yoake & a chaine with my cart & plough Alsoe I give vnto him my dun mare Alsoe I give vnto him my grug axe alsoe I give to my sonne Joseph one spade & shovell Alsoe I give vnto him three bills alsoe I give vnto him one yoake & a chayne alsoe I give vnto him my hand sawe a long saw alsoe I give vnto him the practice of piety alsoe I give vnto him my little hamer Alsoe I give vnto him my pisterill shot tmould. alsoe a pitchforke alsoe a draught shave and a hatchett alsoe a sword & a fowling peece. Alsoe I give vnto my sonne Joseph m^r Prestons works I alsoe give to him my best hammer alsoe I give vnto my sonne Joseph 2 S bullett moulds Alsoe I give to him my horse booke alsoe a pitchforke alsoe I give to him my phizike booke alsoe I give to him my broad axe & frow alsoe I give to him a sword & a fowling peece alsoe I give to my daughter Mary m^r Downhams works & m^r Dods works  Alsoe I give to her my great butter churne  alsoe I give vnto her the second best gowne & a green wastcote with all her owne mothers wearing linen And I give to my daughter Mary foure of the best ewe goats & a ram.  Alsoe I give to my wife Bridget one of my form^r wives best gownes and two of the best petticotes.

" And I give vnto my two sonnes Joseph & Beniamin all my wearing cloathes & my bootes & stockins and shoes.

" 18^th of this first month 1643.  My will is that whereas I gave vnto my wife two ewe goates that now she shall have in the lieu of them one milch cowe vntill the tyme of her death and after her decease to returne to my daughter Mary Item my will is that whereas I gave to my two sonnes Joseph & Beniamin either of them a pillow-beere now my will is that my daughter Mary should have them  Item whereas I gave to my daughter Ellen a yoke oxen now my will is that my eldest sonne Joseph should have them & that he in consideracon of them after the terme of seaven yeares after my decease shall pay vnto my daughter Ellen sixteene pounds in Cuntry paye  Item whereas I gave vnto my daughter Mary foure Cowes & a Bull now my will is that she shall have two cowes one bull & three yearling heffers and one two yearling heffer.

" These alteracons vnder the date of the 18^th of y^e first month 1643 were made & written by the appoyntment of Robert Mussy being of pfect memory."

Witness:  Robert Payne, John whipple.

" Proved by Robert Payne and John Whipple, May 16, 1644, except that clause concerning the ewe goat given to the poore & the vse to John Dane for the first yeare; otherwise by word of mouth disposed of viz: to the widdow Vernham for that yeare."

*Ipswich Deeds, vol. 1, leaf 40.*

Inventory taken 2 : 2 : 1644, by Robert Payne and John Whipple : in the hall : one small ioynd table, 5s. ; one ioyned chest, 5s. ; 2 small fowling peeces, 16s. ; 12 pewter dishes, one chamb. pott with some other small peeces of pewter, 1li. 10s. ; 3 kettles, one old caldron, one brasse pan, 2 skilletts, one warming pan, 2li. 5s. ; one iron pott, one brasse pott, 6s. ; 3 payles, one Cowle, one firkin, two charnes, one beere vessell, 10s. ; 4 silu. spoones, 1li. 6s. 8d. ; 3 bibles with other bookes, 1li. ; one paire cobirons, one paire tongs, one fire pan, 6s. 8d. ; 2 spitts, one paire tramells & one gridiron, 5s. ; 2 swords, 6s. 8d. ; 2 fether bedds, 2 fether boulsters & 2 pillowes, 3li. 10s. ; one paire blanketts, one rugg, 10s. ; one flockbed, one other featherbed, 2 paire blanketts & 2 coverletts, 1li.; one great chest, one small chest, one box, one trunk, 16s.; one table cloth, 5 napkins, 3 diap. napkins, 3 paire pillowbeeres, 18s.; 5 paire sheets, 2 towells, 1li. 5s.; all his wearing apparrell, 5li.; 2 candlesticks, one pestle & morter with other implements, 5s.; 3 axes, 2 howes, 2 sawes with other working tooles, 15s.; 2 plow chaynes, one cowlter, one share, one wayne, 2 yoaks, 1li. 5s.; 3 Cowes, 12li., 2 oxen, 12li.; 2 steers, 6li.; one heffer, 3li.; one bull, 3li.; 3 yearlings, 4li. 10s.; one mare, 7li.; 7 gotes, 7 kidds, 3li. 7s.; 3 calves, 1li. 16s.; 3 piggs, one sowe, 1li.; one cow hide, 12s.; 2 calves skins, 4 goat skins, 4s.; in mony, 13s.; a debt due from Joseph Jewett, 2li. 15s.; total, 82li. 19s. 4d.

Inventory taken May 16, 1644, by Tho. Scott, Thomas Howlett and John (his mark) Gage: one silu. whissell & a Corall, 2s. 6d.; corne upon the ground, 3li.; corne upon the chamb., 18s.; 4 hogsheads & some old trayes & a peece of an old heire, 7s. 6d.; some other small things, 2s. memord. one blankett was sett downe on the other side more then was.

This addition together with the rest of the inventory sworn to by Brigitt, wife of Thomas Rowlison, late wife of Robert Mussey, 17 : 2 : 1648. She had been instructed by the Court to go to such members of the Court as should be together in the meeting house of Ipswich on April 17th and perfect the first inventory.

*Ipswich Deeds, vol. 1, leaf 42.*

27 : 1 : 1649, Joseph Mussye judged to be twenty-one years old, and his portion to be paid him. *Ipswich Quarterly Court Records, vol. 2, leaf 16.*

Mary Muzye, "being of age," according to her father's will, on 25 : 1 : 1651, chose Mr. John Norton for her guardian and gave him power to dispose of her in marriage. *Ipswich Quarterly Court Records, vol. 2, leaf 23.*

### Estate of Hugh Churchman of Lynn.

"I heugh Churchman of Len do macke this my last will as foloeth: first, I give my howse and Lot ||in Len|| w$^{th}$ ale my march and ale other the apurtenances tharevnto belonging to wilyam wenter tel his son Josias shale atayen the age of twenty one yeares and then to his son Josias and his Ayeres for ever: w$^{th}$ this Condicon that he shale paye to his sister hanna winter ten poundes w$^{th}$ in one hole year after the aforsayed Josias winter shale atayen the age of twenty one yeares and if he shale Refeuse to paye to his sister hana winter ten poundes of Corant money then my will is that hanna winter shale have the howse and lot w^th ale and singeler the apurtenances to her and her ayeres for ever and she shall paye to her brother Josias ten poundes: and my will is that if the aforesaid Josias shale dy before he shale atayen the age of twenty & one yeares that then the aforsayed hanna shale have it w^thout paying aney thing out of it: and my will is further that if the aforsayed Josias and hanna shale booth dy before that theye shale atayen the age of twenty one yeres that then wilyam winter or his now wif or the longer liver of them shale have it to them and thar Ayeres for ever: I do give to the widow Androes that thre shilinges that she oethe me and further I do giv her one buchel of Ingen Coren to be payed w^thin one moneth after my death: I do give gorge far one buchel ale so to be payed at the same tyem: I do ale so give to edward burt ten shilinges to be payed w^thin one hole yer after *after* my death: I ale so give to m^r whiten and m^r Cobet: five shilinges apece to be payed w^thin one hole year after my death: ale the Rest of my goodes or Chateles vnbequeaved I give to wilyam winter whom I do macke sole exeter to this my will in witnese whar of I have her vnto put my hand the fourth daye of the fourth mounth in the sixtenth year of the Rayen of ower soveran lord Charles by the grace of god Kyng of Ingland scotland ffrance and Irland &c 1640."

hegh Churchman.

*Salem Quarterly Court Files, vol. 1, leaf 20.*

Witness: Zacheus Gould.

Proved 9: 5: 1644, by Zacheus Gould. *Salem Quarterly Court Records, vol. 2, page 154.*

Inventory taken 4: 6 mo: 1644, by Nathaniel Tiler, Hugh Burtt and Robert Driver: Wearing aparrill, 2li.; straw bed, two blankits, tow pillows, three shetes, 1li.; little iron pot, little bras cettle & a friing pan, 10s.; puter pint pot & 2 sponns, 2s.; grediron, pot hookes and bellowes, 2s.; one trofe with a cover and a little kneding trof, one tra, and other woden dishes & trenchers, 6s. 8d.; 2 emti cask, a pale, a peck and a halfe peck, 4s. 6d.; 2 chestes, 4s.; shers and presing iron and yard & a qushing, 1s. 6d.; betle and wedgis, 2 axis, 2 sawes, 2 hows and other working towls, 16s.; a flich of bacon, 6s.; puter Chamber pot, 1s.; a bed cradle, with other lumber,3s.; 20 bushels wheat,4li.: 4 bushils Indian,12s.; 2 bushils barly veri cors & musti, 4s. 6d.; 3 bags, 1s. 6d.; a bible with another booke, 4s.; corne one the ground, 2li. 10s.; debts due, 1li.; 4 scins, 6s.; total, 14li. 14s. 8d. Atendance in his siknes & chargis at his buriall, 1li. 15s. 6d. Debts owing by him, 26s. 3d. House, lot and marsh appraised at 6li. *Salem Quarterly Court Files, vol. 1, leaf 20.*

### ESTATE OF ROBERT LEWIS OF NEWBURY.

Inventory of estate of Robert Lewis, deceased, brought in 10 : 5 : 1644, and referred to the Governor to take oath. John Croxen swore that the deceased made Goody Jackson, wife of John, his executrix to pay his debts and give the remainder to his wife and child. *Salem Quarterly Court Records, vol. 2, page 157.*

Inventory of estate of Robert Lewis, deceased May 4, 1643, taken 6: 5: 1644, by Goodman Edwards and Goodman Prince: Mr. Fowles bill, 7li.; bill of John Bond, 3li. 20s.; Richard Hollingsworths bill, 1li. 7s.; his best clothes, 16s.; 2 yards 1/2 ell of kersie, 9s.; ould hat, 7s.; ould stuffe dublett, 3s.; a cotten wasecoate, 3s.; cotten paire of breeches and wasecoate, and a paire of Cotten stockeings, 3s.; paire stockings, 2s.; 2 shertts, 7s.; cotten sheete, 5s.; 10 yards of lockrum, 11s. 8d.; 4 bands, 2s. 6d.; a chist, 5s.; a bible, 8s.; hatte, 7s.; paire shewes, 4s.; one pillow, 2s.; total, 26li. 12s. 8d. *Salem Quarterly Court Files, vol. 1, leaf 21.*

### ESTATE OF JOANNA CUMMINGS OF SALEM.

"I Jone Comins: dow give vnto my sonn John after my death my house & ground & my gote: & my sow & he shall give vnto gooman Cornish a hog pig of tow months ould: m$^r$:es noris shall have my mufe. I dow give my Cow to m[y] gran Child mary Bourne: [I dow give ||all|| my best Apparil & Beding & bed to my Gran Child Johanah to by a heafer of tow yere ould to bee put forth for hir good & that wich *ken a parte* of that to my sonn John to Buery mee with all.*]

"I will have my debtes to bee payed out of the pipe staves & that wich Remaynes to bee giuen the one halfe to my granchild mary borne & the other halfe to Johanah borne my gran Child.

"I will haue all my best Apparel bed & bedding & all my housould goods sould: & out of that a heafer of tow yere ould to bee bought for Johanah Bourne & ||*erefr*|| to burie mee|| I give to m$^r$ Noris Twenty shilings & to the Church twenty shilings: desiring y$^m$ to Exsept so smal a gift I giue to goody Cotta my Blew petticote & a wast Cote. My trunck & Cloth vpon it Goodye wathin shall haue it for tenn shilings & the feet to bare it vp with & Goody ||wathin|| shall bee

*The words enclosed in brackets are crossed out in the original.

payed what I owe hir & the Rest to the deacons for them to giue wher Is appoynted Goody ffeld shall haue my Iorn pot at 4$^d$ a pound to bee payed that I owe hir & that w$^{ch}$ Remaines to the dacuns I giue to goody Beacham a petticot with 3 laces about & a green savegard & an ould wast Cote & an ould linin Change I giue to Ann shiply Tow linin Changes. I give goodman boyce an ould blanckit wc [is] vp in the Chamber & a pilow wich he hath a Redie what so euer is vnder my bed I giue to goody Corning & goody wathin to bee Equally deuided I giue John brownes wife a whit Cutworke Coyfe: I giue goody wathin a black Coyfe w$^{th}$ a lace: a grograne Coyfe: I giue my whit llas wast Cot & ould hat to Deborah wathin I giue goody ffeld one of my lase han carchefes wi$^{ch}$ is at good bornes

"I desire That ‖the‖ Tow deacons m$^r$ Got: & goodman horne: that they shall haue the ordring & desposing of these things in my will to Improve for the Childrens good: y$^t$ it may not bee bangled away The 11 of the : 3d : month Caled may beeing the last day of the week."

Jone Comins

her mark      her mark

Witness: Mary 8 Beacham, Elizabeth VI Corning,
her mark
Elnor M Wathin.

Proved 10 : 5 : 1644.

On the same paper upon which the will is written the testatrix gives a list of her debts, viz: "I owe to John Mattstone, 25s., upon his covenant concerning my house; M$^{ris}$. Goose for a pound of sugar ; Goody Feld, 3s. 6d.; Mr. Cocall, 1s. 6d.; Good Masse, 6d.; ould Knight, 3s. 6d.; yong Goody Lech, 8d.; something to Goodman Salace, let him tell it, and the deacon will pay it; Goodman Salace, 5s; and Goody Sharman in the Bay, 6d."

Inventory taken 17 : 3 : 1644, by Gervase Garford, Jefferie Massey and Georg Emery : House and quarter acre of ground, with the corn upon it, 3li; ewe goat, 7s.; spotted sowe, 18s.; milch cowe, 5li. 10s.; fether bed and flocke boulster, 1li. 15s.; 1 green rugge, 10s.; 1 litle fether pillow, 1s. 6d.; 3 blankits whitt, 14s.; one littell Darnix curtayn. 3s.; 2200 pipe stavs of whitt oake, 8li. 16s.; one sad collored Carsy gowen and hud sutable, 1li.; 1 stamill Carsy peetty coot mitered about the scirts with vellvit, 1li. 6s. 8d.; 1 green Carsy petticot, 3 laces, 10s.; 1 blew petticote, 7s.; 1 stufe petticoot, 7s.; 1 blacke wastcoat, 1s.; 1 red cotton shage wastcot, 3s.; 1 whit shagg wastcoot, 5s.; 1 blacke cloake, 1s.; 1

blacke grogerane Goune, 1li. 6s.; 1 wastcoot and petticoote, 12s.; 1 tauny seay appron, 2s.; 1 green say appron, 1s.; 5 Corse sheets, 1li.; 1 blacke hatt, 4s.; 2 callico approns lased about, 5s.; 9 Crostcloths, last and playn, 4s. 6d.; 2 Coyfes, one Cutworke, one blacke worke, 2s. 6d.; 4 hancherifs, more playn, 1s.; 2 payer stockins, 2s.; 1 brass morter & pestell, 3s. 4d.; shifs ould, 7s.; 1 lining pillabear, 2s.; looking glass, 3s.; blew apron, 6d.; payer of shoos, 1s. 6d.; trunke with a foot, 14s. 6d.; littell Box with locke & key, 1s. 6d.; carpitt and tabell, 7s. 8d.; one mufe, 2s.; Chamber pott, 6d.; 2 syves, 2s.; tubs and paylls, 8s.; littel barrill, 1s.; pare bellows, 1s.; Iron pott and hanger, 8s.; bras kettell and scellit, 6s.; whell, 4s.; Candell sticke, 4d.; total. 33li. *Salem Quarterly Court Files, vol. 1, leaf 22.*

Inventory taken "divers years agoe" by Henry Skerry and Georg Emery, but received 14:11:1646: The house & lot at home & the tenn Aker lot & the corne upon them both, 22li.; halfe an aker of salte marsh, 1li. 10s.; 1 heafer of 2 yeares old & vantage, 3li. 10s.; 2 swine, 1li. 10s.; 1-2 a canowe, 5s.; 2 fethar bedes, 4 bolsters, 3 pillowes, 3li.; 5 blankets, 1 ruge & one covering, 10s.; 6 dieper napkines & 2 tow towalles, 7s.; 3 par of sheetes, 1li. 4s.; 1 warminge pan, 6s. 8d.; 1 trunke & 2 chaistes, 15s.; 9 peeces of putor, 15s.; 3 boxes for lining, 4s.; 1 bedstead, 4s.; 1 brase kettell & a skellet & 2 skimmers, 6s. 8d.; 2 chayers & a forme, 4s.; 1 Iron pott, 6s.; 1 payer of sheetes more, 10s.; glasses, trayes & earth weare & other old lumber, 6s.; total, 39li. 3s. 4d. *Salem Quarterly Court Files, vol. 1, leaf 66.*

### Estate of John Mattox of Salem.

Will of John Mattox proved 10: 5: 1644, by Thomas Pickton and inventory brought in. *Salem Quarterly Court Records, vol. 2, page 157.*

Inventory of estate of John Mattackes, deceased Apr. 22, 1643, taken 6:5 mo: 1644, by Goodman Edwards and Goodman Prince: bill of Mr. Fowles, 5li.; John Buds bill, 2li. 7s.; bill of John Bonds, 2li. 16s. 9d.; best shute, 1li. 10s.; ould shute of truckinge Clothe, 4s.; cotten shute, 6s. 6d.; ould Cloth shute, 10s.; ould graye shorte Coate, 2s.; paire of knitt stockings, 2s.; 4 bands, 5s.; paire of Cloth stockings, 2s.; paire of Russitt bootes, 11s.; paire of Canvis sheetes, 20s.; 2 shertes, 7s.; Chistle, 4s.; ould blanckitt, 2s.; paire of shewes, 4s.; ould hatt, 4s.; 4 Raile hoockes, 4s.; an old pillow, 2s. 6d.; paire of shewes, 4s. Total, 14li. 13s. 9d. *Salem Quarterly Court Files, vol. 1, leaf 21.*

## Estate of Thomas Payne of Salem.

"Touching the outward estate & goods of this life god hath ben pleased to lend me, I Thomas Payne doe in this my last will & testam$^t$ thus bequeath them as followeth: ffirst unto my wife I give my house I now live in, gardens & houcefitting with my two acre lotte with the pfitts accrewing therefrom during her life; commending unto my Son Thomas the care of his mother, & the diligent improvem$^t$ of the sayd ground, to his mothers use; during her life, in consideration whereof, he to have his dwelling with his mother, & ||the|| forth pte of the pfitts of the lott, & the third pte of the pfitts of the garden so improued by him during the sayd terme of time. It, I give unto my wife the bedstead Beding & there appurtenances as they now stand in the hall. Item I bequeath my pte of the Ship Mary-Anne of Salem, to be sold, & my debts to be payd, And the residue of the monies with the rest of my goods to be devided as followeth. Item I giue Thomas my Son my Loomes & Sluices with there appurtenances concerning his trade of a weaver. Item I give the s$^d$ Thomas one Coffer wch was his grandfathers. Item I give unto my three Sons my ten Acre lott & my one Acre of meddow to be equally shared amongst them. Item concerning the residue of the monies arising from my pte in the Ship, & the rest of my goods I bequeath them to be valued reasonably, & equaley devided to my wife & my Children, my wife to haue the choise of the first pte excepted: & my Children to share in the rest as their ptes fall, pvided alwaies & reserved out of the sayd goods one fetherbed lying on the trundle bed with coverlett & blankett, one bolster & pillow, w$^{ch}$ I give & bequeath unto mary my daughter. Item I giue my house wherein my wife should live, with the goods remaining of hers, to be sold after her decease, & the monies to be equally divided amongst my children. It my mill left in the hands of Henery Blomfeild my kinsman, I bequeath to be sold, & the monies thereof returned into my executo$^r$s hand, & so to be equally divided to my wife & children. Item I Constitute & appoynt Thomas my Son executo$^r$ to this my will & m$^r$ John fiske of Salem Suprevisor. in witnes wherof I have heereunto sett my hand & seale the 10$^{th}$ of this p$^r$sent 2$^d$ month in the yeere 1638."

Thomas Payne.

Witness: John ffiske, John Thurston,
           her mark
    Mary X Beechum

Will brought into court 10m : 1642; proved 10 : 5 : 1644, by John Thurston.

*Salem Quarterly Court Files, vol. 1, leaf 23.*

### Estate of Margery Wathin of Salem.

Inventory of estate of widow Wathen brought into court 27 : 6 : 1644. The two deacons of Salem, Mr. Charles Gott and John Horne, appointed executors. Nathaniel Porter took oath in court. *Salem Quarterly Court Records, vol. 2, page 163.*

Inventory taken 20 : 5 : 1645, by Peeter Palfray, William Alford and Nathaniel Porter : One greene rugge, 15s. ; white blanket, 5s. 6d. ; one white blanket, 2s. 6d. ; 1 white course ould rugge, 1s. ; 1 mixt color Coverlett, 7s. ; 1 pare of grene say curtaines & vallences, 12s. ; 1 stripte carpet & cubberd cloth, 12s. ; 1 red bearing blanket with 2 gr : Laces, 10s. ; 1 flock bed, 2 flock boulsters & one feather pillow & one boulster tike, 1li. 5s. 6d. ; one ould stockbed & Cradlebed, 5s. ; 1 purple goune of cloth lined with gr : say, 1li. 4s. ; one purple wastcloth laced, 7s. ; 1 red petecote & wastcloath, 18s. ; 1 tawny cloake cloth, 5s. 6d. ; one ould mixt color cloth gowne, 5s. ; one russet gowne of cloth ript open, 16s. ; one pr. petuana hoods, 3s. ; one ould purple petecoate & wastcloth cloth, 6s. ; 1 pr. of white blankets, 1 being litle, 8s. ; 1 tawny dublet & portingal cap, 5s. ; 1 ruset pr. aprons, 4s. 6d. ; 2 pr. aprons 1 say & 1 linsy wolsey, 5s. 2d. ; 1 holland white wastcloth, 6s. ; 1 holland aprone, 6s. 8d. ; apron of fleecy holland, 3s. ; 4 necke handkerchiefes laced, 5s. 4d. ; 1 neck handcherchief, 8d; 3 plaine neck handkerchefes, 3s. ; 3 pocket handkerchiefs, 1s. ; 3 pocket handkerchiefes & 1 long neckcloth, 6d. ; 3 laced neckclothes at 18d. pr. & 2 at 6d. pr., 5s. 6d. ; 2 plaine crosclothes at 3d. pr., 6d. ; 1 white wrought coife, 1s. 6d. ; 4 white stuff coyfes, 6d. pr., 2s. ; 3 ould coyfes, 2d. pr., 6d. ; 2 holland coyfes and an ould one, 2s. 6d. ; 3 white stuff stomachers, 6d. ; 3 white wrought stomachers, 2s. 2d. ; 1 pr. white knit thrid gloves, 1s. 4d. ; 1 pr. handcuffs & 1 yd. seaming lace, 5d. ; white & colored thrid, 3d. ; 1 silke girdle, 1s. 8d. ; 1 yd. of stript callico, 1s. ; 1 bundle of smal linen in a corse cloth, 6s. ; 1 holland sheet with a seaming lace, ——— ; 1 pr. ould flaxen sheets, ——— ; 10 sheetes, 1 course one, 2li. ; 2 flaxen tablecloathes, 3s. 6d. ; 1 wrought towell, ould fushion, 2s. 4d. ; 2 boulster cases, 5s. ; 1 pr. pillowbeares, 8s. ; 1 pr. Scotch cloth pillowbeares, 4s. ; 1 pillowbeare with tossells, 2s. 6d. ; 1 pr. flaxen pillowbeares, 4s. 6d. ; 1 fringed & 1 diap. napkin, 1s. 4d. ; 4 short napkins, 3s. ; 6 flaxen napkins, 6s. ; 4 napkins, 2 towels, 3s. 4d. ; 5 childs beds, 9d. ;

5 woomen's shiftes, 16s. 6d.; 1 pr. cotten gloves & 1 straddle band, 1s. 6d.; 1 rema$^t$ painted 1 imbroyderd girdle, 1s. 8d.; 1 pr. ould shooes, 2s. 6d.; 1 white apron, 3d.; 1 blew apron, 1 necke handkerchief, 16d. delivred to Deborah for Mrs. Traske to pay for, 8s. 2d.; 1 bed cord, 1s. 8d.; 1 pr. ould wosted stockings, 10d.; 1 flannel neckcloth, 9d.; 6 bags, 4s. 7d.; 2 hatts, 4s.; bible & one testament, 9s.; 24 ould books, 8s.; 4 chests, a settle & a box, 1li.; 1 pr. whalebone bodyes, 1 cotton wastcoate & 2 cloake buttons, 7s.; 34li. pewter at 9d., 11i. 5s. 6d.; 12li. kettle brass at 12d., 12s.; 2 skimmers, 1s.; ould iron & tooles, 1li.; 2 brass candlesticks, 2s. 4d.; 1 box, smothing iron, 1s. 4d.; 1 whipsaw, 1 ould gun, 1 spit, nailes, etc., 12s.; 2 brass potts, 1li. 15s.; 1 case with 5 bottells, 2s.; 1 glew pott, 1s. & 1 looking glass, 1s., 2s.; 2 earthern potts & yarne, 2s.; chaires, woodden dishes, 10s.; wood & timber, 6s. 8d.; corne, 6s. 6d.; 5 barrells, 4s.; 1 house, 7li. 10s.; halfe a heifer at Goodman Southwickes, 15s.; one heifer at Mr. Batters farme, 3li. 5s.; total, 39li. 13s. 5d. Order of court, 3:11: 1644, for disposal of goods for settlement of estate signed by Jo. Endecott, Govr. *Salem Quarterly Court Files, vol. 1, leaf 25.*

Court ordered (signed by Jo. Endecott, govr.), 3:11 mo: 1644, that the estate of Widow Margery Wathen to be disposed of according to her will by the two deacons of Salem, Mr. Charles Gott and John Horne. p. curia, Raph Fogg. *Salem Quarterly Court Files, vol. 1, leaf 25.*

Ezekiell Wathen, a boy of about eight years and a half, committed to Tho. Abre, 27:6: 1644, as an apprentice until he is twenty years old, if his master live so long. *Salem Quarterly Court Records, vol. 2, page 163.*

Court ordered, 30: 10: 1647, that Thomas Abree of Salem have one quarter of that house, sometime of the widow Wathen, deceased, and one quarter of one year's rent of the same for the use of Ezekiell Wathen, who is committed to him. *Salem Quarterly Court Records, vol. 2, page 226.*

### Estate of John Talbey of Salem.

Inventory of estate of John Talbey, taken 11m: 1644, by Peter Palfrey and William Lord: 20 bushels Indian Corne, 2li. 13s. 4d.; 3 pekes oates, 7s.; apparrell and beding, 10s.; a Cannoe, 1li.; a Ten acre lott, 3li.; brasse kettels, 14s.; one Barrel & one Tub, 5s.; one old axe, etc., 3s. 6d.; one axe more, 4s.; spookshave, 1s.; one wheele to spin with, 4s.; rakes and rake hedds, 7s. 8d.; 2 Chares, 1s. Debts due unto him: from William Bayley, 1li. 15s.; Richard Singeltarie of Salesberie, 1li. 6s.; Richard Edwards, 8s.; Mr. ——man, 3s. 11d. Anne, Stephen and their elder brother John Talby to have certain parts of the estate. *Salem Quarterly Court Files, vol. 1, leaf 26.*

### Estate of Margaret Pease of Salem.

" the first day : 7 : munth 1644. This is the last will off margit pease. That is that her grane childe John pease the sonne off Robert pease shall with the rest of her goods be put ouer to Thomas : wadsson off sallme to be as her true feffeye off trust to despoes off her estate as she dereckteth : at this tyme beinge in parfite memory fist yt as before Tht the sed John pease shall be give frely to the sed Thomas wadsson that he shall desposse off him as his one child and : seconly : yt the housse she liff in & with the ground beloninge ther to shall be give to the sed John pease all soe haffe an acker off Indon corne all soe he is to have my heffer all soe y$^t$ John shell have my bede and all yt belonges to it all soe that her grane childern the childern off Robert peasse her sonne she givth to the rest off them the tow gottes & kids to be equally despossed a monge them and all her mouffeabell goods are to be at thomas wadsho despoes for the good off John. all soe her grane childe Robert pease shell have : her lesser chist and y$^t$ if yt the sed John pease die then his brother Robert pease must have the rest off the estatte and all yt doughter pease the wiffe off Robert pease is to have my best cloth gowne and all partiqlers are not set dun the same mst Thomas wadson is to desposse off it for the good off John her grane childe." [No signature.]

Witness: John Barbor, Obadiah (his mark) Huellme.

Proved 1 : 11 : 1644, by the witnesses.

Petition of Robert Pease, son of Robert Pease, who had been allowed 6li. out of his father's estate by the court; he now desires to know how the money shall be paid, and having remained twelve months with his mother, now wishes to be free to choose a master and to have sufficient clothing to fit him out. Ann, wife of Robert Isbell, testified that after widow Margaret Pease had made a written will, she gave to Faith Barber her best red petticoat; also that Susan, wife of Henry Bullock, deceased, was present when bequest was made. *Salem Quarterly Court Files, vol. 1, leaf 35.*

Inventory taken by John Alderman and John Bulfinche: 1 fether bed, 2 Bolsters, 4 pillowes, 2 blanketts, one coverlid,

2li.; 4 courtaynes & 4 rods of Iron, 11s.; one Payr of fine sheets, 12s.; two Pilcovrs and two Payer of course sheets, 10s.; one cloth gowne, 10s.; one stuffe gowne, 12s.; one red Petticote, 13s. 4d.; two old Putticoats, 6s.; two old wascoats, 4s.; one red wastcoat, 5s.; two hoods, 5s.; one Cloake, 5s.; one greene apron an a hatt, 4s.; 14 peeces of Small and great Pewter, 10s.; one small brasse morter and Pestle, 1s. 6d.; tow Cettles and an old Cettle, 12s.; one brasse Pott, 7s.; one frying pan and an old warming Pan with a paire of tongs and an old fire shovell, 3s. 4d.; on pair of bellows and a payr of doges and a pott hanger and a skillett, 5s.; one whele, 2s. 5d.; two chests, 5s. 5d.; tow old chayres and a old Barrel and a Payle with all other things that are not seene, 2s.; tow bushells of corne and tow busshels of Indian corne, 13s. 4d.; half acre of Indian corne, 16s.; som rye that is betwine Goodman Suthweeks and Goodwiffe Pease, 4s.; one earlinge heifer, 2li. 10s.; for Pte of a sowe and one Pig, 12s. 3d.; the howse and 3 quarters of an acre of ground, 1li. 10s.; two goats and a kid, 18s.; Marie Pease oweth her mother Pease, 1li.; Mr. Bacon owth Megerett Pease, 10s.; Goodman Barbour oweth me a bushell of corne, 2s. 8d. Total, 19li. 2s. 8d. Note of charges layed out by Thomas Wattson for wid. Margaret Pease: To Mr. Rucke for bread and beere and wyne, 16s. 8d.; to Goodwife Bullocke for fyve days attendance in sickness, 7s. 6d.; to Goodman Burcham for her Coffine, 6s.; for making her grave, 1s.; to William Woodbery for keeping a heifer and for some part of wyntering her, 7s. 6d.; to the ferryman to bring her over the water, 10d.; for writinge, 1s.; total, 2li. 6d. *Salem Quarterly Court Files, vol.* 1, *leaf* 36.

Inventory was brought in 1 : 11 : 1644, and sworn to by Obadiah Holme and Jno. Barber. Upon request of An, wife of Robt. Isbell, Goodwife Watson must allow her for her pains, or else the court will. *Salem Quarterly Court Records, vol.* 2, *page* 171.

On 30 : 4 : 1652, Robert Pease and his brother John Pease, both of Salem, acknowledged a bill, dated 6 : 11 : 1651, to Tho. Watson, in regard to the estate of their grandmother, Margaret Pease, of whom said Watson was a feoffee. *Salem Quarterly Court Records, vol.* 3, *leaf* 40.

## Estate of Isabel West of Salem.

Inventory of estate of Isabel West, taken 30 : 10 : 1644, by Henr. Skerry, Robert Cotta and George Ropes, brought into court 2 : 11 : 1644: House and tow acres of ground,

4li.; 10 acre lot in North Feld, 7li.; 10 acre lot on dabyfort side, 2li. 10s.; foure gotes, 1li. 8s.; one sowe, 1li. 6s.; sawes, 10s.; playnes, Ackes & sawes & other smale toules, 1li. 14s.; an Iorne persters & 6 bites belonging to it, 5s.; 16 bushels of Indian corne, 2li. 8s.; 5 bushels pease, 1li.; a grinding stone & the iron of it, 14s.; Three ould howes, 2s. 6d.; an ould spad & a matock, 2s. 6d.; one Joynt Chest, 10s.; one sea chest, 5s.; one fether bed & tow boulsters, 2li.; one ould fether bed & two boulsters, 1li.; one rugge & 2 ould blanketts, 1li. 10s.; pare of sheetes & a bedsted, 1li. 5s.; old pare of sheetes, table cloth & a pilabere, 5s.; 2 ould Jerkines, 10s.; one hat, 10s.; a whele, 8s.; one iorne pot, 10s.; ould iron pot & an Iron skelet, 13s.; puter plates & dishes, 16s.; bras Cetel & a bras skelet & 2 brase Candelsticks, 16s.; tow Cheares & tow Cushenes, 6s.; fringpan pot hokes & pot hangers, pare of trays, 10s.; chest, 3s.; pales, trayes, dishes & spoones, 10s.; 2 peeces of bacon, 10s.; debts due from Nathaniel Vering, 3li.; John Thore, 2li.; John Whitlock, 3li.; Thomas Smith, 30s., and James Smith, 20s., 2li. 10s.; Philip Udale, 1li.; other small debts, 1li. 7s.; a spit & a sawe, 10s.; other debts, 2li. 8s.; total, 54li. 12s.—*Salem Quarterly Court Files, vol. 1, leaf 24.*

### ESTATE OF ROBERT PEASE OF SALEM.

Robt. Peas died intestate, and his son Robt. Pease was committed to his mother, Marie Pease, who was appointed administratrix of the estate. Inventory brought in 3 : 11mo : 1644. *Salem Quarterly Court Records, vol. 2, page 172.*

Inventory of estate of Robert Pease of Salem, late deceased, taken 3 : 11 mo : 1644, by Jo. Alderman and Myhill Shaflinge (also Michaell Shaflen): ffyve ewe goats and three lambs, 3li. 6s.; iron pott and iron kettle, a posnett and tow Pewter dishes, with other small things of pewter, 1li.; one Conell, tube, three trays and one paile, 7s.; one flockbede, a teike, one Cowhide and a little ruge, 1li. 10s.; one sheet, one Pilowbere, 3s. 4d.; one stone hammer, two trowells, one lathing hammer & axe, 6s.; one Barrall and a Pecke, 2s. 6d.; one Chest and a little table board, 5s.; an acre of wheat, one of Barly, an acre of Pease, 2li.; 2 acres Indian Corne, 10li.; one muskett with Bandileers and the sword, 16s.; one house and a Barne and 11 acres of ground, 14li.; 2 shuts of aparell and a Coate, 3li. 10s.; one hatte, one Payr of stockins, one payre of shoos, two shirts, 2 bands, 10s.; a sack, 1s.; swyne, 1li. 6s. 8d.; a Cannew, 10s.; total, 39li. 12s. 6d. Indebted to several persons, 6li. Widow Marie Pease appointed administratrix 3 : 11 mo : 1644. Robert Pease was the eldest son of the deceased, and John Pease the second son. There were other young children. The deceased's mother is mentioned. "Abraham" is also mentioned. *Salem Quarterly Court Files, vol. 1, leaf 24.*

### ESTATE OF RICHARD INGERSOLL OF SALEM.

"July 21, 1644. I Richard Ingersoll of Salem in the County of Essex in New England being weak in body, but through God's mercy in perfect memory, doe make this my last will and testament as followeth viz. I give to Ann my wife all my estate of land, goods & chattels whatsoever except as followeth viz. I give to George Ingersoll my son six acres of meadow lying in the great meadow. Item I give to Nathaniel Ingersoll, my youngest son a parcell of ground with a little frame thereon, which I bought of John P[ease?] but if the said Nathaniel dy without issue of his body lawfully begotten then the land aforesaid to be equally shared between John Ingersoll my son, & Richard Pettingell & William Haines my sons in law. I give to Bathsheba my youngest daughter two cowes. I give to my youngest daughter Alice Walcott my house at town with 10 acres of upland & meadow after my wife's decease." R (his mark V) I.

"I read this will to Richard Ingersoll & he acknowledged it to be his will. Jo. Endecott."

Witness: Townsend Bishop.

Proved Jan. 2, 1644-5. Inventory taken Oct. 4, 1644.

*Probate papers in the Quarterly Court Records copied by Joshua Coffin and now in the Probate Registry, vol. 1, page 29.*

### ESTATE OF RICHARD LUMPKYN OF IPSWICH.

Inventory of estate of Richard Lumpkyn, late deceased, taken 23 : 9 : 1642, by Robert Payne and John Whipple : in the hall : one longe Table, one stoole, two formes, 15s.; three chaiers & six cushins, 4s.; Bookes, 2li. 10s.; one paire Cobirons, one fire pan, one gridiron & two paire of tramells & one paire of bellowes, 10s.; one muskett, one fowling peece, 1li. 10s. In the Parlor : one table with six ioyned stooles, 1li. 5s.; 3 chaiers & 8 cushins, 14s.; one bedstead, one trundlebed with curtins. 1li. 10s.; one paier cobirons, 1 fire pan, 4s. 6d.; one chest, 4s.; one fetherbed, two bowlsters, two pillowes, two flock beds, 5 blanketts, one rugg, one coverlett, 8li.; one warming pan wth other implements, 6s. In the chamber over the Parlor : one bedstead, one Trundlebedd, 10s.; 2 flockbedds, one featherbed, one feather bolster, 4 blanketts, 2 pillowes, 2 coverletts, 4li.; 4 chests, 2 boxes, 1li. 5s.; one table, 3s.; one corslett, 1li. 10s.; one feather bed tike, 1li. 10s. In the leanto: 7 brasse kettles, one iron kettle, 4li. 10s.; one small copper, 1li.; one iron pott, 4 posnetts wth other implem[en]ts, 1li.; 10 pewter dishes, 2 chamb. potts, 2li.; Butter & Cheese, 2li.; 30 bushells corne, 4li. 10s.; plate, 4li.; 5 Cowes, 2 steers, 3 heffers, 4 yearlings, 36li.; his wearing apparell, 10li.; linen, 5li.; debts, 200li.; total, 296li. 19s. 6d. Received and allowed 26 : 1 : 1645. *Ipswich Deeds, vol. 1, leaf 7.*

### ESTATE OF JANE GAINES OF LYNN.

Thomas Laighton brought in a nuncupative will of Jane Gaines, deceased, 9 : 5 : 1645. Court appointed Thomas Layghton and Nathaneell Hanforth overseers to see the will fulfilled for the good of the children. *Salem Quarterly Court Records, vol. 2, page 178.*

Jane Gaines, widow, who deceased at Lin, and whose nuncupative will was proved 10 : 5 : 1645, left three children, viz: John, Danyell and Samuell, and an estate of 37li. 11s. 10d. Ordered 2m : 1649, that John, the eldest, aged about thirteen years, have 19li. 12s. 8d. in possession of Mr. Thomas Leighton and Nathaniell Handforth, who are to improve it for him; and to be apprenticed to Fransis Dowse of Boston, shoemaker, for seven years, to learn the shoemaker's trade. Danyell, the second son, aged about eleven years, to have 9li. 16s. 4d. in the hands of said Leighton and Handforth, who are to improve it for him; and he is apprenticed to Luke Potter of Concord for eight years from 1 : 1 : last, to learn the "skill and mistery" of a tailor. Samuell, the youngest son, aged six or seven years, to have 9li. 16s. 4d.; and he is apprenticed, until he is twenty-one years old, to Nathaniell Handforth, who is to educate him and give him 10li. as his portion. If any of the children die before reaching the age of twenty-one, the others are to have the share of the deceased one, except Samuel's, which, if he dies within four years, is to go to Mr. Handforth. *Salem Quarterly Court Records, vol. 3, leaf 8.*

Inventory taken by Nicholas Brown and Edmund Needham, 14 : 11 : 1644, and sworn to by Thomas Leighton and Nathaneell Hanforth, 10 : 5 mo : 1645: One house and lote of upland containinge 6 acres with a smale parcel of salt marsh lyinge before the door & 2 acres of salt marsh lyinge in Rumley marsh, 8li.; 30 bushill of Indian corn, 4li.; one fetherbed and a feather bolster, 2s.; one flockebed & one flock bolster & 6 flock pillows, 16s.; three feather pillows 8s. 6d.; curtains & valance, 17s.; one bolster ticke, 2s. 6d.; one covering for a bed, 1li. 2s.; one blankett for a bed, 10s.; another, 6s. 6d.; another, 4s.; another, 3s.; another, 5s. 6d.; one covering for a bed, 3s,; one trundell bed, 2s. 6d.; one man's coat & breeches, 1li. 4s.; one man's dublett, 12s.; one weascoat for a man, 3s.; one Gowen for a woman, 1li. 14s.; one weascoat for a woman, 3s.; one man's coat, 6s.; two weascoats for a woman, 9s. 6d.; one cloake & hoode for a woman, 13s.; one petycoat, 14s.; one petycoatt, 5s.; too petycoats, 3s. 6d.; one hatt for a woman, 2s. 6d.; one blankett for a child, 3s.; one paire sheets, 11s.; another, 8s.; another, 4s. 6d.; another, 4s. 6d.; one sheet, 8s.; another, 6s.; another, 4s.; too pillowbears, 9s.; too pillowbears, 5s.; one bord cloath, 1s. 8d.; three napkins, 1s. 6d.; too Diaper Napkins & one linnen skirt for a shift, 2s. 4d.; too shifts for a woman and too skirts for shifts, 6s. 10d.; one old peece of linnen cloath & a whit apron, 5s. 6d.; tenn Handkerchers, 9s. 4d.; twelve coyfes, 6s.; twelve croscloaths, 3s.; one parcell of blackstuff, 1s. 6d.; too croscloaths, 3s. 6d.; three headcloaths & 4 neck cloaths & too bands, 3s. 10d.; a parcell of childbed linnen, 6s.; too coshens & a chaire, 3s.; too silver nippls, 1s. 10d.; bonelass & thread & a pinn coshen, 1s.; a sword, 5s.; one trunke, 2s.; too boxes, 2s. 6d.; too old weascoats, —; straw hatt and brush, 2s.; one brass pann, 10s.; one warming pann, 2s.; one Kettell, 1s. 7d.; another, 5s.; another, 4s. 6d.; foure pewter dishes with other pewter, 12s.; one little skellett & one fryinge pann, 2s. 1d.; 3 wegges & 2 beetle ringes, 4s. 6d.; one daubinge truell & a parcell of old Iron, 2s. 6d.; one gouge & a chisle & a wimble, 1s.; one handsaw, 1s.; a paire of bellows, 1s.; one spade, 2s.; one Iron pott, 6s.; one drawinge knife & an old Hatchet, —; three old & narrow axes, 4s.; one spitt and a gridiron, 1s. 4d.; a stocking hooe, 1s. 6d.; too pott rackes, 4s 8d.; paire tonges & paire pott hooks, 1s. 9d.; a pitchfork and one gimlet, 1s.; three spoons, a ladel and an earthern pott, 1s. 4d.; one pair choos, 1s. 6d.; a tub & chirne, 6d.; too leather Bottls, 4s.; a flick of bakon, 8s.; too piggs, 1s. 5d.; an old Chest & foure trayes, 1s.; an old barrell & an old hogshead, 2s.; a pair of glovs, 1s.; a Apron & a paire of stockinges, 4s. 8d.; 3 pair of bodys, 10s.; two bibles, 10s. 6d.; a baskett & a sife, 1s. 4d.; a parcell of books, 3s. 6d.; a barrell & bedcord, 1s. 4d.; a parcell of Hay, 3s.; a barrell with some oats in it & sife, 4s.; a parcell of white pease & beans & hempe & flax, 3s.; a locke for a doore, 10s. 6d.; a sieth & a sneath & a peece of sieth, 4e.; two paire of hinges & too hookes & a cheafendish, 2s. 2d.; foure old hooes & a piece of old Iron, 4s.; a little table, 1s. 8d.; too meal baggs, 2s. 6d.; debt due from Will. Patridge, 9s.; due from Samuell Bennett, 1s.; 1 pinte pott, 1s. 4d.; one paire pattens, 1s.; one paire sheers, 10d.; one old sith, 1s.; total, 43li. 5s. 7d. *Salem Quarterly Court Files, vol. 1, leaf 30.*

### Estate of Frances Hawes of Salem.

"We whose names are vnderwriten were present w$^{th}$ the wife of Rob$^t$ Hawes when she lay vpon her deth bed on the 12$^{th}$ of June who did will to be given to pticuler people as followeth.

"Itim to the little Child w$^{ch}$ she had by Rob$^t$ Hawes she bequethed twentie pownd and to her two sons Robert Edwards & mathew Edwards. & her young Child Thomas Hawes to bring them vp in lerning her sayd Husband Robert Hawes is to pay into the Hands of sume honest man ten pownds to see them brought vp in leringe & to his daughter she did will to be given (Alis Haws) her worst plilp & Cheny gown & two petticoat & a wast coat & two Aporns w$^{th}$ all smale linnin sutable to it & a siluer bodkine & a payre of pillowbeers & to Robert & mathew Hawes she Did will to be giuen to Each of them a payre of sheets & each of them a payre of pilowbears & each of them half a duson of napkins & two siluer spoons & a gould ring to thomas Hawes & to Elin Hilles her sister in owld England she wiled to be sent two yerde of lawn & a bible. Alsoe to the tow mayds that kept her in her sicknes. she did will to be giuen to them namly Kathrin Dorlow & Sarah bartlett each of them a new handkerchor a Coyf & Croscloth & to Katurne Dorlow half an ell of lase: morouer in the presens of Katrin Dorlow & Sarah Bartlett she Did will fowre pound w$^{ch}$ her husband pmised to send to owld England to a Child ther & a pewter dish: this is a trew testimony as near as we are able to remember vnto wch we have sett ower hands this 24 of July 1641."

Witness: Wm. Goose, Katerine (her mark C) Dorlow, Sarah barttlet.

Sworne to 10:7:1645, by Mr. Wm. Goose.

*Salem Quarterly Court Files, vol. 1, leaf 32.*

### Estate of Lionell Chute of Ipswich.

"The fourth day of the seaventh month Anno Dm 1644 I Lionell Chute of the Towne of Ipsw$^{ch}$ in New England Schoolmaster doe make & ordayne this my last will & Testament revoking all form$^r$ wills by me made. Item I give vnto Rose my wife for terme of her naturall life all this my dwelling howse with the Barne & all the edifices: the two chambers over the howse & entry only excepted which I will that James my sonne shall have to his only vse for the Terme of one yeare next after my decease with free ingresse, egresse, & regresse & w$^{th}$ the yards, gardens, the home-lott & planting lott purchassed of m$^r$ Bartlemew with the Comonage and appurtenances therevnto belonging. And after my wives decease: I give the said howse, barne, lotts & p$^r$emisses with all thappurtnances vnto James Chute my sonne & to his heires. Item I give vnto my said sonne James Chute & to his heires for ever all & singular my other lands, lotts, meadow grounds marishes, with all & singuler their appurtnances & pfitts whatsoever ymdiatly after my decease. And I giue more vnto James Chute my sonne (over & above all things before given him) my heffer that is now at goodman whites farme, & my yonge steere. Item I give him all my books, with all things in my chest and white box *my* deepe box with the lock & key; one chaire: foure hogsheads: two Coombsacks two flockbedds two flock bolsters two feather pillows: one rugg two Coverlets: two blanketts: my casting nett: my silver spoone: all my owne wearing apparrell, and that which was his brother Nathaniells: and three paire of sheets, three pillow beeres two table clothes: foure towells: six table napkins: and the one halfe of the brasse & pewter, & working tooles: & five bushells of english wheat. Item I give vnto my frend Joseph Mosse five shillings Item I give vnto the poore of the Church of Ipswich Twenty shillings to be distributed by the Deacons Item my meaning is that my wife shall haue my chest after that James hath empted it. Item all the rest of my goods howshold stuff, Cattell, & chattells whatsoever vnbequeathed (my debts & legacies being discharged & paid) I will that Rose my wife shall have the free vse of them for terme of her life: but the remainder of them at the tyme of her decease over & above the valewe of five pounds sterling I giue vnto James Chute my sonne & to his heires & assignes Item I make Rose my wife executrix of this my last will & Testament. And in witnesse that this is my deed I have herevnto sett my hand and seale in the p$^r$sence of these witnesses herevnder written."

Lionell Chute

Witness: Marke Simonds, Joseph Morse.
Proved 7 : 9 : 1645, by the witnesses.

*Ipswich Deeds, vol. 1, leaf 15.*

Inventory taken 25 : 4 : 1645, by Marke Symonds and Robert Lord : one Cowe, 5li. ; one yearling heffer, 1li. 10s. ; one two yearling heffer, 3li. ; one yearling steere, 1li. 10s. ; one calfe, 15s. ; 5 gotes, 2li. 5s. ; 3 hoggs & piggs, 3li. 16s. ; 40 bushells of wheat, 7li. 6s. 8d. ; 8 bushells of Rie, 1li. 6s. ; 40 bushells of Indian corne, 5li. 15s. ; one casting nett, 13s. 4d. ; 3 paire of bootes & 4 paire of shoes, 1li. 10s. ; hempe drest & undrest, 1li. 4s. ; 2 bushells of mault, 8s. ; 12 sacks & baggs, 1li. 10s. ; 8 yards of linsy woolsy, 16s. 8d. ; a helbert, 6s. 8d. ; two haire lines & 3 sives, 4s. 6d. ; 6 hogsheads, 8s. ; one rope, 5s. ; 3 chests & 3 boxes, 1li. 2s. ; fether bed & bolster, 3li. 10s. ; 5 fether pillows, 1li. 5s.; one flockbed & one flock pillow, 13s. 4d. ; one paire blanketts, 9s. ; 2 coverletts & an old rugg, 2li. ; one old paire of Curtains & rodds, 10s. ; bedstead matt & cord, 14s. ; 2 flockbedds & 2 flock boulsters, 1li. ; fether pillow, 5s. ; one paire of blanketts & one Coverlett, 1li. ; bedstead & line, 4s. ; 4 yards of yard wide tyking, 16s. ; 12 paire of sheets, 10li. ; 6 pillow beers, 1li. ; 4 table clothes, 1li. 10s. ; one dozen of napkins, 12s. ; 5 towells & one yard kerchife, 10s. ; one short Course Table cloth, 1s. 6d. ; shirts, 10s. ; his wearing apparell, 12li. ; books, parchment & other things in a chest, 2li. ; 3 yards of holland, 7s. ; one old danakell Coverlett, 5s. ; pewter dishes small & great, 14, salts, sausers, poringers 11, chamber potts 2, one ele pot, 2li. ; dozen alcamy spoones, 3s. 4d. ; 2 great kettells, 2 smaller kettells & one brasse pan, 3li. ; 4 skilletts, one scumer & a ladle, 6s. ; two iron potts old ons, 8s. ; frying panns, 4s. ; one trevitt, 2 paire of cobirons, tongs & firepan, 2 tramells, 2 paire of pott hooks, one spit, 1li. 12s. ; one Silver Spoone, 6s. ; 2 broad howes & 2 narrow howes, 8s. ; one broad ax, three narrow axes, one hatchett & 2 froos, 13s. ; 2 augars, one gowge, 2 chissells, one shave, one sickle, 5s. ; one betle & six wedges, 10s. ; one spade, one morter & pestle, 9s. ; 2 paire of bellows, 2s. 6d. ; one bible & other books in the hall, 1li. ; one great boarded chest, 10s. ; 3 chaires & other lumber. 6s. ; two pewter candlesticks, one pewter bottle, 8s. ; one powdering tubb, 2 beere vessells, one Cowle, 8s. ; one flockbed, 3 flockbolsters, 1li. ; one rugg, 2 blanketts, 2 coverletts, 1li. 10s. ; one bedstead matt & cord, 10s. ; 3 ladders & pitchforke, 5s. Owing to several persons out of the estate, 10li. ; Taking out the debts, total, 84li. 11s. 4d. *Ipswich Deeds, vol. 1, leaf 15.*

## Estate of William Plasse of Salem.

Inventory of estate of William Plasse, deceased, at the house of Thomas Weekes (also Wickes and Wikes), 15 : 2 : 1646 (perhaps date of death), brought in 20 : 2 : 1646 : One fetherbedd, twoe fether bolsters, one great Bible, one psalme booke, one ould Chest, tooles that Richard Walters hath that he must give accompt of. " And whereas ffyve pownds was given to the sd Plasse by the Towne which I gathered up in Corne for him, I did thus Discharge it, viz. : Imprimis By so [much] unto my self for dyett & elce yt I had Laid out befor y$^e$ Towne granted him 5li. y$^e$ some of 2li. & out of the 3li. Left I pd fo$^r$ 1 pr shoes, 6s. ; cloth to make him a Capp, 3s. 6d.; a pair of stockings, 2s. 4d. ; for steele Iron & Cole, 4s. ; total, 2li. 15s. 10d. ; spent in dyett, 2li. 4s. 2d. ; total, 5li." In hands of Richard Walters : One chere & stoole, one anvile, 2 vices, one smale beakhorne, 2 hamers, one smale and one great ; one old pair of Bellows, 18 files, 1 pr. vice Tongs, 1 pr. snuffers with a bras chayne & 3 kegs, 2 storne plates, 2 pr. & 1-2 of forging tongs, 2 match Locks, 2 stock nail tooles, 2 brok Iron bolsters & a drill boxe, 7 forging hott punches, 2 Iron wrenches, 1 brass Lampe, 1 litle hack-hamer, 2 pan bores & galloes, 25 smale Could punches, 1 burnishyng steele & a harth staff, 3 hartopps prt. brok, 1 old pr. mittins, 1 turne vice, 5 fil hafts & a flatt bord, 10li.; 8 oz. of old bushell Iron, 1li., 8 oz. of Lead, one wrench for breech pl. Charges of Thomas Weekes for William Plass in his sickness : For Veale & Fowle, 5s. 2d. ; sugar, 4s. 9d. ; Bread, 1s. 2d. ; beare, 1s. 7d. ; more for egges, 6d. ; spices, 6d. ; 2 weekes board before he fell sick, 9s. ; for a debt that I am ingaged to Goodman Rumball before he fell sick, 3s. 6d. ; coffin, 6s. ; bread and beare att his buryinge, 5s. ; for Goodwife Ager, 1s. ; for the Grave makinge, 1s. ; for wood & aleven dayes tendance as you maye thinke meete, 2li. 10s. 2d. more the towne is willing to allowe him for buriall & atendance of him, 9s. 10d. ; total, 3li. *Salem Quarterly Court Files, vol. I, leaf* 45.

## Estate of William Goog of Lynn.

Inventory of William Goog brought in 30 : 4: 1646, and his widow Ann Goog (also Gouge) appointed administratrix. Court gave her the goods for the bringing up of her three small children. *Salem Quarterly Court Records, vol. 2, page 197.*

Inventory taken 28 : 8 : 1645, by Nathaniell Handforth, Francis Lightfoote and Francs Ingols: His purse and apparrill, 1li. 4s.; 1 house & lott & 2 ackers of medow and one ten acker lott, 8li.; 4 hoges, 2li. 10s.; 5 bushels of wheate 1li.; ten bushels of indian Coren, 1li. 10s.; the beddinge, 1l, 18s. 8d.; Flax in the bun[dle], 14s.; one cheste & a chaier 13s. 4d.; 3 wheles, 7s. 6d.; one handsaw & one wharte saw, 5s.; one sword & a belte, 5s.; one muskett & bandeleares, 1li.; one warming pan, 3s.; one payer of bellis, 1s.; one Friinge pan, 4s.; one gridiron & recke hookes, 3s. 6d.; one peice of steele, 8d.; soume ould Ieren, 2s.; too ould howes, 2s.; one reappinge hooke & a sith, 4s.; gunpouder, 2s. 6d.; hay, 10s.; a pece of wolen Cloth, 5s.; a pece of lininge Cloth, 14s.; aleven pott hookes, 7s.; one scellitt & posnitt, 3s. 6d.; earthen pott, 1s. 8d.; 6 spoones, 1s.; 3 wood trayes & 3 wood boules & 3 wood dishes, 1s. 9d.; one runlitt, 1s.; paieles & tube, 3s.; 2 bages, 2s.; one ould chaier & stoole & trunke, 2s. 6d.; one old axe & other small thinges, 2s. 6d.; one Cow, 4li. 10s. Debts to be paid out of this, 4li. 9s. 7d.; total, 28li. 11s. 7d. *Salem Quarterly Court Files, vol. I, leaf 49.*

## Estate of John Thorne of Salem.

"Salem the 27 of July : 1646 : wee whouse names are heare vnderwritten being present with John Thorne in the time of his Sicknes and at that time when the sayd John was in his perfect memory doe testifie that wee heard him say thease woards vinsit that hee did giue unto Ann : Pallgraue all his Estate of mony. goods. aparell. & debtts out of which sayd aparell it was the will of the sayd John that John Jackson Junio<sup>r</sup> : should haue his best Hatt and further moure it was his will that James Thomas should haue som-thinge out of his Estate if the said Ann Paulgraue so pleaseth."

                  her mark                 her mark
Witness: Elisabeth H Harwod, Margaret V Jackson,
    her mark
Elisabeth E Esticke.

Sworn to 4 : 6 : 1646, by the witnesses.

Inventory taken Aug. 1, 1646, by Jefforie Massey, George Emery and John Harbert, and sworn to before Jo. Endecott: 20li. of Indico at 3s. 6d. per li., 3li. 10s.; 1 Roule of Tobacco, containing 73li., at 4d. per li., 1li. 4s. 4d.; 1 Roule of tobacco containing 79li. at 4d. per li., 1li. 6s. 4d.; 8li. of tobacco in a Runlet at 4d. per li., 2s. 8d.; 1 Greate Coate, 1li.; 1 Cloth Shute, 12s.; 1 Stufe Shute, 1li. 2s.; 1 Cloth Shute, 1li.; 2 Hatts, 12s.; 2 shurts, 3 bands, 2 HandCarshers, 10s.; 1 pr. of mille stockings, 4s.; 1 pare of yarne Stockings, 2s.; 2 pare of Shues, 5s.; 1 wast coate, 1s. 6d.; Carpenters tooules, 16s.; in monny, 3li. 17s. 6d.; 1 Sea bed and pillo, 7s. 6d.; 1 bible and 1 Cap, 4s.; 1 Musket, Bandileas, soard & rest, 1li. 6s.; one aker and 3 quarters of Land, 1li.; debts owing, 8li. 3s. 4d.; total, 27li. 16s. 2d.

*Salem Quarterly Court Files, vol. 1, leaf 53.*

ESTATE OF RICHARD BARTHOLOMEW OF SALEM.

Will of Richard Bartholomew, in the form of a letter, and addressed " To my Louinge Brother Henry Bartholomew ":—

"Boston the 6$^{th}$ : 11$^{mo}$ : 45

Brother Henry heare in Clossed is anotte of whatt estatte I have shippt w$^{th}$ mee & whatt is here oweinge to mee: w$^{th}$ whatt estatte I have shippt w$^{th}$ mee & whatt is here oweinge to mee: w$^{th}$ what I owe in England w$^{ch}$ is all I owe in the world as I know off: these things only the bills of ex$^{c}$ I have Consigned to m$^{r}$ Edward Shrimpton in London hee is y$^{e}$ brassiers bro at Boston: to him I haue wrighte y$^{t}$ in Case god should not bringe mee to London y$^{t}$ hee would vs these goods [to] pay my debts & returne y$^{e}$ Remaynder to you: I should have bine glad to have seene you before I went, butt if god should not returne mee againe but take me away by death: my desier is if the returns of these goods Come to yo$^{r}$ hand: that they may be thus disposed of: viz To yo$^{r}$ two children 40$^{li}$ apeece to my bro willms 3 Children 20$^{li}$ apeece to my mother if liveinge 10$^{li}$ to my m$^{r}$ Gearringe beinge very poore: 10$^{li}$ & the remaynder of my estatte bee it whatt will more or lesse all that is mine I dessier may be equally devided between o^r bro Thomas: Abraham & Sister Sara, only what Jacob Barney owes to mee I giue it to him, butt for any other debts house ground &c devide as before, this is my desier & that I would haue done if god shall please to take mee away: I desier to Cast my self only uppo him & to rest myself only in the armes of his mercy in Christ Jesus intreatinge of him to stay my soule there in the worst howers even in death itself, vnto him I leaue you with yo^rs to gather w^th myself & all his and rest: yo^r faythfull and Lovinge Brother:

Richard Bartholmew."

Proved 4 : 6 : 1646.

Inventory taken 27 : 5 : 1646, by William Hathorne and Jefferie Massey: Parsell linen cloth, 50li. 12s. 11d,; parsell wollon cloth and stockins, 30li. 9s. 6d.; parsell of hatts, 10li. 12s.; parsell of boddis, 3li. 17s. 9d.; parsell of shott, 3li. 12s. 7d.; lead, 9li. 9s. 10d.; parsell of stuffes and yearne, 30li. 5s.; parsell of heaire bottoms, 3li. 4s.; 4 chests of glass, 7li.; 8 ferkins of sope, 4li. 8s.; advance upon these goods, the executor bearing the charge, 22li. 10s.; 100 bushels of malt, 14li. 16s.; 2 trunkes, 6s.; 3 ould sheetes with some ould linen and other smale thinges in the ould trunke, 1li. 3s. 4d.; an old flockbedd, 10s.; 2 feather pillowes, 10s.; 2 old blanketts, 2s. 6d.; one old hatchett, 1s.; a paire of bootes and a paire of shooes, 14s.; a house and one acre and halfe of lande, 5li.; ten acre lott, 6li.; a Carbine, 18s.; brass ketle and scillett, 9s.; a fire shouell and pott hangers, 3s.; a howe, a frow, 4 wedges, a hammer and shoe horne, 5s.; total, 206li. 19s. 5d. Debts owing to him, 79li. 1s. 9d. Total, 286li. 9s. 1d.

*Salem Quarterly Court Files, vol. 1, leaf 54.*

### Estate of John Webster of Ipswich.

Inventory of John Webster's lands and goods sworn to 29 : 7 : 1646, by his widow, Mary Webster, who is appointed administratrix. *Ipswich Quarterly Court Records, vol. 2, leaf 5.*

Petition of Mary, widow of John Webster, that her eldest son, John, should have the land called the farm, of about 32 acres, which lyeth between Mr. Rogers oxe pasture and Thom. Bishop's farm, when he is twenty-one years, he to pay Nathan, the youngest child, 5li. at fourteen years, or if he refuse, then the 1-4 part of that land in kind or worth; that Mary, Stephen and Hannah may have the island bought of the widow Androws, in equal portions, when they shall be twenty-one;

that Elisabeth, Abigail and Israell have 20 nobles each, when twenty-one; the dwelling house and 6 acres of land tied to make it good. The Court, Nov. 4, 1646, granted that the estate be ordered as the widow desired and appointed her administratrix, to give bond for security in such sum as the next Ipswich court shall approve and receive of her the inventory amounting to 147li. 5s. *Mass. Bay Colony Records, vol. 2, page* 184.

John Emery of Newbury married Mary, widow of John Webster, late of Ipswich, and she had power from the Court to administer and dispose of his goods to his children. Some of the children now grown, almost ready to receive their portions, John Emery petitions for liberty to sell the Island which is devided to three of the children, and also the house and 6 acres of land which was bound to make good the 20li. to the other three, and upon grant of this, binds himself to pay the children the full price he shall sell it at, and to the other three children, who are to have 20 nobles, to make good to them the 8li. apiece and to pay the daughters their portions at eighteen and the sons at twenty-one years. *Mass. Archives, vol.* 15B, *page* 147.

The above petition was granted Oct. 14, 1651. *Mass. Bay Colony Records, vol.* 3, *page* 254.

### ESTATE OF THOMAS CROMWELL OF NEWBURY.

Will of Thomas Croomwell brought in 29 : 7 : 1646 to be proved, Gyles Croomwell objecting to it, court ordered Mr. John Lowell and Mr. Edward Woodman to take an inventory of the estate. *Ipswich Quarterly Court Records, vol.* 2, *leaf* 6.

The court held 6 : 5 : 1647, addressed Mr. Woodman, saying that the Ipswich court ordered Mr. John Loule and himself to take into custody the goods of Thomas Cromlom of Newbury, deceased, that were in the hands of Samuel Scullard, deceased. Not having done so, they are now ordered to answer next court, and this order to be published next lecture day. *Salem Quarterly Court Records, vol.* 2, *page* 217.

### ESTATE OF JOSEPH MORSE OF IPSWICH.

"The foure & twentith day of the second month Anno Dm 1646 I Joseph Morse of Ipswich in New Engl: Planter doe make & ordayne this my last will & Testament revoking all other form wills by me made: Item I give vnto Dorothy my loving wife my howse & lott & out howses bought of Thomas Dorman. alsoe ‖ my howse ‖ & lott of about six acres bought of the widdow Perkins, one Cow, and alsoe the wholl bed & bedding that I lye vpon standing in the hall. Item I give vnto my sonne Joseph Morse my best cloake Item I give to my daughter Hannah my great bible which I vse. Item I give to my wife Docter Prestons works and m^r Dykes besides her owne bibles the one greater and the other smaller & one felling axe & one broad howe. Item I give vnto my sonne John Morse my other howse & out howsing with the lott containing about two acres, and alsoe to John my sonne a lott of six acres butting vpon an end of the fore named lott of two acres toward *toward* the North west and to my sonne John my lott of ten acres neare Egipt River & to John one yearling heiffer. Item I give vnto John Morse all my apparrell vngiven & one yard of musk coloured broad cloth Item I give to John Morse the ‖wholl‖ bed and all the bedding he lyeth on standing in the parlour and one paire of sheets & a pillow beere Item I give all my Tooles vn-given to my sonne John Morse. Item I give to my sonne John my barne with the ground thereto belonging bought of ffrancis Jordan. Item I give to my sonne John all my marsh containyng about five acres onely allowing vnto my wife the one halfe of the grasse growing vpon it from yeare to yeare during her life My will is alsoe that John shall have halfe of the grasse from yeare to yeare that may be mowen vpon the lott given to my wife onely pviding that this shall not hinder her either from felling or breaking it vp Alsoe my will is likewise that the Cropp that shall arise of all my ground planted or sowen this year shalbe equally divided betweene my wife & my sonne John the charges of the same equally borne by them Item I give to my wife the two first payments for keeping the herd Item I give to my sonne John the last pay for the herd keeping I appoint Dorothy my wife to be sole executrix to this my last will And in witnesse that this is my deed I have herevnto set my hand & seale in the p^rsence of these witnesses here vnder written."

Joseph Morse

    Witness: Roger Lanckton, william (his mark) Gudderson, James Chute.

    Proved 29:7:1646. *Ipswich Deeds, vol. 1, leaf 18.*

    Inventory taken 28:7:1646, by Robert Lord and Thomas Dorman: a howse, 22li.; in the hall: one table and a short forme, 4 chaires, 6s. ; 5 bibles & some other bookes, 2li. ; 2 kettles, one brasse pot, 1li. ; 2 iron potts, 10s. ; 2 little posnetts, 3s. ; 9 peeces of pewter, 1li. ; one skim[mer], one chafing dish, 2s. 6d. ; old frying pane & 1 gridiron, 5s. ; one chirne, one barrell & keeler, 6s. ; one powdering tubb, 2 barrells & earthen pans, 10s. ; in the chamb. : 20 bushell of Indian corne, 2li. 10s. ; 2 bushells mault, 8s. ; halfe bushell of hemp seed, 2s. ; 6 small cheeses, 2s. ; 20li. butter, 10s. ; hempe drest & undrest, 10s. ; an old bedstead, a flock bed, coverlett & blanketts, 2li. 10s. ; in the little roome : one bedsteed, a fetherbed, a rugg, one coverlett & 3 blanketts, 6li. ; a warming pan, 4s. ; 7 paire of sheets, 3li. ; 7 pillow beers, 2 short table clothes, 2 table napkins, 1li. ; 2 chests & one old trunke, 1li. ; one small table & 3 chaiers, 12s. ; 4 Cushens, 6s. ; one yard brodcloth, 10s. ; his wearing apparrell, 4li. ; one sowe & two piggs, 1li. 13s. 4d. ; one Cowe & a heiffer, 6li. 10s. ; 4 load of haye, 2li. ; about 6 bushells of wheat not thresht, 18s. ; a howse & ground bought of widdow Perkins, 9li. ; one other old howse & 8 acres of ground & a barne, 8li. 10s. ; 10 acre of upland & 5 of marsh, 10li. ; his axes & tooles, 2li. ; a muskett, bandaleers & rest, 1li. 4s. ; total, 83li. 1s. 10d. *Ipswich Deeds, vol.* 1, *leaf* 19.

ESTATE OF FRANCIS LIGHTFOOT OF LYNN.

"Dat : Linn Decemb : 10 : 1646 The last will & testimone off ffrancis Lightfoote in pfect memory though weake in bodye. I Doe bequeathe vnto my Brother John Lightfoote, off London, in case hee bee Livinge, or his children Lawffullye begotten off his bodye, y$^e$ sum off one pounde when ever it shall bee Demanded, & I Desyre yt all good meanes maye be vsed to giue them Know Lidge off it. 2lye : I Bequeath to my sister Isebell Lightffoote Liuing in Linckhornshire in ffrestone neare ouLde Bostone, one pounde, & Doe Desyer shee maye haue notis off it, as soone as conveniently maye bee. 3lye : I Bequeath to mye Brother Pell, one pounde. 4lye : I Bequeath to Samuell Cocket ffiue shillings. 5lye : I Bequeath to Hannah Pell : ffiue shillings. 6lye : I Bequeath to Darytye whiting, one Lambe. 7lye : I Bequeath to ELisabeth whiting, one Lambe. 8lye : I Bequeath to Samuell Cobit, one Lambe. My will is to make my wife Executo$^r$ off all my Lands, & goods vndesposed off I Owe to James Axe ffor tending mye sheepe y$^e$ Sumer tyme : with y$^e$ month Octob, & one weeke : in November, onelye in pte off payment I haue payed vnto him nineteen groats : &

eLeven pence, I owe him alsoe ffor y<sup>e</sup> winter Beffore Ite: To M<sup>r</sup> George Burrell, 00—09—06. Ite: To Goodm: Mansfeilde when hee hath Careyed three Loades off wood more ffor mee 00—10—00. Ite: To Allinn Bread I owe: 0—05—2. Dew to mee ffrom Samuell Bennit 0—19—4 Ite: ffrom Hugh Alley 0—2—, one peck off indian corne. Ite: ffrom Edward Iresonn 0—3—0. It: ffrom John witt Dew to mee in p<sup>r</sup>sent monye —0—4—0."

francis lightfoote.

Witness: Nathaniel Handforth, Francis Borrell, Andrew Mansfeild.

"I Likewise Doe Depute my Brother Handforth and my Brother Pell as overseers.

Andrew Mansfeild."

Proved Dec. 29, 1646, by Nathaniell Handforth and Francis Borrell.

The Court confirmed Anue Lightfoot to be executrix of her deceased husband's will.

*Salem Quarterly Court Files, vol. 1, leaf 57.*

Inventory taken 21: 10: 1646, by Edward Burcham, Francis (his mark) Ingalles and *Wm.* (his mark) Tilton: His purse and apparell, 2li. 12s.; his house & 2 ackers of ground it stands on, with 3 ackers of medow, 6li. 13s. 4d.; too kowes with Calfe, 9li.; two yearlinge steares, 3li. 13s. 4d.; to this yeare Calves, 2li.; 5 Sheepe, 5li. 5s.; 2 Iorn potes and kettell, one war[m]ingpan, 1li. 1s.; one kettell & a littell pan, 5s.; pewter prised at 18s.; one spitt & a smoothinge Ieron, 2s.; one hogesheade, 2 tubes, 7s. 6d.; one lanthoren, 1s. 4d.; one tube & one ould Chiste, 3s. 6d.; one Ioyne box & a littel trunke, 5s.; one Joynt Chiste & a Chayer, 14s.; one trundell bed & a Foot path, 3s. 4d.; one payell & 4 trayes, 4s.; 2 barrells, 2s.; one axe, 2 howes & one spaide, 5s. 6d.; one wascote, 4s.; too hoges, 3li.; in butter & Eages, 12s.; one Chane, 2s. 6d.; in earthern ware, 5s. 4d.; one hand saw, one trauell, one pr. of tonges & frying pan, & a broylinge Ieren, 6s. 4d.; in Corn, English & indian, 2li. 10s.; flax in the bund[le], 10s.; in bever, 5s.; a weuers loame & furniture belonging to it, 1li. 13s.; 3 ould sithes & 2 Ieren wedges & a Ringe, 4s.; linse yarn & Cotten yarn & tow, 12s.; flax seed & a bage & flax & yarn, 6s. 4d.; hay, 2li.; one littell gune, 8s.; one bed & furniture, 3li.; one box & one Chayer, 2s.; linse, 1li. 2s. 6d.; one payer of stockings, 3s. 4d.; total, 51li. 2d. Debts due to estate, 1li. 8s. 4d. Money owing wife, 1li. *Salem Quarterly Court Files, vol. 1, leaf 58.*

### Estate of Mary Hersome of Wenham.

Inventory of estate of widow Mary Hersome of Wenham, deceased, taken 2 : 7 : 1646, by Esdras Reade, John Fairefilde, William Fiske and George Norton, presented 29 : 10 : 1646 : A house and three Acres of ground Joyning to it, Two Acres and halfe of it broken up or theree abouts, 4li. 5s. ; Halfe of the Corne growinge upon that two Acres an halfe, with the other fruits, 2li. 10s. ; Ten Acres of upland more with two Acres of middow lyinge Remotte, 1li. 5s. ; a Cowe, 4li. ; A Swine, 18s. ; Three sheets & a halfe, 15s. ; one Bedsack, with two Boulsters, one Pillow, 10s. ; one old Coverlett and one Old Blankett, 6s. 8d. ; two shifts, two Aporns, a litle box with other small lininge, 1li. 2s. ; three Peticots, 16s. ; three old doublits, with one old shortt Cote, 5s. ; 2 wheles & a reele, 6s. ; a Brass Candlestick, 1s. 4d. ; payre of Cards, 1s. ; a parsell of tow, 2s. ; two hatts, 6s. ; tower Bushels of Endian corne, 10s. 8d. ; three pecks of wheat, 2s. 9d. ; three Baggs, 2s. 6d.; one peuter Plater, two spons, 2s. ; an old Brass Pott and a skillett, 5s.; two bibles and two small books with an Inkhorn, 10s. ; one fryinge pan, 3s.; one old Chest with a hammer with other old Iron, 2s. 6d.; a matcuke and two old Howes, 3s. ; a Muskitt and a barrel of a litle burden peece, 16s. ; three pots with butter and one Earthing Pott, 11s. ; two trayes, two Panns with a litle suit, 1s. 8d. ; two payre of shoos and Stockings, 5s. 4d. ; one Rundlitt, 10d. ; a parsell of small Cheeses, 1s. 8d. ; one Bundell of lyning yarne, 5s. ; ladder, a forme, a Cooke & hine & a payre of bodyes, 4s. 6d. *Salem Quarterly Court Files, vol. 1, leaf 63.*

### Estate of Emme Mason of Salem.

Inventory of estate of widow Emme Mazon. deceased, 26 : 3 : 1646, taken by Georg Corwin and Walter Price. Sworn in court, 30 : 10 : 1646 : All the lyning smalle & great, 2li. ; 1 boulster & 1 pillow, 13s. 8d. ; 1 fether bed, 3li. 5d. ; 1 bedsteed matt, and Cord, 7s. ; 1 Red Rugg, 8s. & blanket, 4s. 6d., 12s. 6d. ; 1 blankett, 13s. ; 3 ould Curtens, 18d., 14s. 6d. ; 1 settle, 4s. 6d. ; a Chest, 5s., 1 box, 18d., 11s.; a table boord, 4s., 2 payles, 2s. 4d., 6s. 4d. ; one trunk, 8d., a linsy woolsy sutte, 10s., 10s. 8d. ; one carsy waskott, 12s., one pettycott, 12s., 1li. 4s. ; one sarfe, 16s. ; 2 ould wascots, 18d., 7s. 6d. ; 1 ould bodes, 8d., 1 stuff wascott, 2s. 6d., 3s. 2d. ; a Carsy whood, 2s. 6d., a hatt, 11s., 13s. 6d. ; in pewter, 9s. 7d., more in pewter, 4s., 13s. 7d.; one brass cansteeke, 4s., a pestle & morter, 3s., 7s.; one ould warming pann, 3s. 6d., 1 hatchell, 2s. 6d., 6s.; 1 ould chafiug dish, 10d., ladle, 6d., 1s. 4d.; a sift, 15d., one skimer, 6d., 1s. 9d.; one hake, 3s. 6d.; tongs, 4d.; grd. iron, 18d., 5s. 4d.; one baking Iron, 2s. 6d., one brass kytle, 16s., 18s. 6d.; one Iron kytle, 10s. 10d., an Iron pott, 2s., 12s. 10d.; one brass skillett, 4s. 6d., another skillett, 8d., 5s. 2d.; one Iron Dogg., 2s., 9 books, 13s., 15s.; 2 books, 4s., one byble, 9s., 13s.; oue salme booke, 16d., & a sermon booke, 6d., 1s. 10d.; one lining wheele, ———; one Cotten wheele, 2s., a halfe pek, 6d., 2s. 6d.; 6 boules, 2s., and 2 payles, 14d., 3s. 2d.; 2 trayes, 6d., 3 platters, 2 wooden dishes, 16d., 1s. 10d.; one erthen pann, 6d., 1 pot, 4d., a brush, 8d., 1s. 6d.; in yaron, 16s. 8d., 16s. 8d.; 2 cushings, 16d., 1s. 4d.; one house and an Acre of ground, 2li. 10s.; one smalle kow, 3li. 15s.; in new fensing stuff, 12s.; total, 25li. 16s. Court disposed of these goods according to law, to the elder brother a double portion and the remainder to be equally divided among the rest of the children. *Salem Quarterly Court Files, vol. 1, leaf* 59.

### ESTATE OF EDWARD CANDALL OF SALEM.

Inventory of goods of Edward Candall, deceased Nov. 15, 1646, taken by John Bourne, William Ager and Peter Palfrey: 19 Bushell of Indian Corne which I bought of him before his Departure at 2s. per bushel, 1li. 18s.; his close being prised at 13s.; total, 2li. 11s. Payd to severall men for him before & after his Departure: to Mr. Price for Shugr for him, 2s. 4d.; Mr. Feald & Phillip Cromwell, 6s. 6d.; William Willemore, 7s. 6d.; Henry True, 3s.; myself for Logein and Diet, 1li. 8s. 2d.; Buriall and Coffing, 13s. 6d.; total, 3li. 1s. Due to Mr. Emry for him, 3s.; due to me for him, 10s. *Salem Quarterly Court Files, vol. 1, leaf* 60.

### ESTATE OF MICHAEL SALLOWES OF SALEM.

"The last will and testam$^t$ of michall Sallowes of Salem bearing date the 14$^{th}$ day of the nienth month Anno: 1646 I michall Sallowes sicke in bodie but in pfect memorie do make this my last will and testam$^t$ in manner and form following viz. my debts paid and my funerall expences discharged doe out of those goods w$^{ch}$ god hath gyuen vnto [me?] dispose of them after this manner fist I gyue vnto micha Sallowes my youngest sonne the sume of eight pounds for & towards the education of the said micha and doe desyre that Georg Emerie John Jacksonne and Jefferie Massey will dispose of the said micha and of the some afforsaid for the welfarr of the aforesaid micha Sallowes. Itm I gyue and bequeath vnto Martha Sallowes my daughter the some of six pounds twoo pillow beeres a morter & a Jug pott w$^{th}$ my ernest desyer that the said John Jacksonne shall bring vp the said martha and improue the said six pounds for my said daughters best advantage. Itm for the remainder of my estate my will is it be equallie divided amongst the rest of my Children viz. Thomas Sallowes, Robert Sallowes & John Sallowes & Samuell Sallowes my sonnes and to Edward wilsone my sonne in law, by equall porcons And for the better pformance of this my will & testam$^t$ I doe apoint for my executo$^r$ Edward wilson my said sonne in law & Robt Sallowes my sonne & for ouerseers of this my will I doe desyre the aboue said Georg Emerie John Jackson & Jefferie massey in witnes whereof I haue herevnto put my hand the day & yeare aboue writen."

his mark michaell ᛉ Sallowes

his mark
Witness: Georg ᛉ Williams, John Tucker, Jefferie massey, Georg Emery.

Proved 31 : 10 : 1646, by Georg Emery, Jeffery Massie, Jno. Tucker. *Salem Quarterly Court Files, vol. 1, leaf 61.*

The executors declined to serve, and Jeffery Massey, John Jackson and George Emerie were appointed in their place. 28 : 10 : 1647, Mr. George Emorie and Jefferie Massie were discharged upon request, and their account, under the hands of Capt. Hathorne and Mr. Curwin, approved by the court. John Jackson, the other executor, was continued, two of the children being with him. *Salem Quarterly Court Records vol. 2, page 225.*

### Estate of George Pollard of Marblehead.

" 3 month 13$^{day}$ 1646. I George Pollard of Marblehead weake in body yet in perfect memory doe make this my last will & testament first I bequeath my soule to God y$^t$ gaue it & my body to be interred according to ye discretion of my frends and for my temporal estate I dispose of it as followeth Imprimis I giue to Goodman Tiler of linne the summe of tenne pounds Also to John Hart y$^e$ younger the summe of fiue pounds & to Christopher Nicolson the sonne of Edmund Nicolson, the summe of fiue pounds, lastly to see this my will performed I doe appoint Wm Walton of Marblehead my executor *to see my* debts payd the remainder of my whole estate I give vnto y<sup>e</sup> sayd executor & also I doe intreat m<sup>r</sup> Mauerick & William Charles to be assisting & helpefull to my sayd executor for ye recovering of my debts  In witnes heerof I haue heervnto set my hand ye day & yeere aboue written."

his mark<br>
George ✸ Pollard

Witness : Moses Mavericke, John I Hart (his mark), william W Charles (his mark).

Proved 31 : 10 : 1646, by Moses Maverik. *Salem Quarterly Court Files, vol. 1, leaf* 64.

Inventory, all credits :  Due from Willm. Walton, Moses Mauerick, John Deuereux, Wm. Charles, David Carwithin, Nicholas Merit, Ephm. Keene, Ralph Parker, George Vicary, John Coit, Abraham Whitehear, George Chin, Richard Norman, Richard Curtis, Edmund Nicholson, John Peach, sr., John Peach, jr., John Bartol, Thomas Pitman, John Hart, Samuel Gatchel, John Gatchel, Thomas Sams, Arthur Sandin, John Legg, Mary Hill, Nicolas Lisson, John Lyon, Wm. Chichester, John Northy, Richard Cooke, Samuel Delabar ; total, 60li. 4s. 3d.  Due to John Deuereux for diet for two years and a quarter, 17li. 12s. ; and to John Bartol for his boy, 6li. *Salem Quarterly Court Files, vol. 1, leaf* 65.

### ESTATE OF JOHN SATCHWELL OF IPSWICH.

"ffebruary ii<sup>th</sup> 1646. The last will & Testament of me John Satchwell of Ipswich though weake in body yet in pfect sence & memory doe comend my soule to god who gave it & my body to the dust whence it was at first till the resurreccon which I doe expect. And for my estate I give to my sonne Richard all my howses and land w<sup>th</sup> their app<sup>rt</sup>e<sup>n</sup>a<sup>n</sup>ces except that pt of the 25 acre lott from the vper end of the plowd land & soe downward to the sea, & sixteene acres of pasture beyond muddy river pt of the ox pasture towards Rowley which pcells of land I give to Johan my wife during her naturall life and to her Issue if she have any and for want of such yssue then to returne to Richard my sonne his heires & Assignes : further it is hereby pvided & my will is that Johan my wife shall have the vse of my howses barne Cowhowse orchard halfe of my particular during her naturall life, or vntill she can conveniently pvid otherwise for her selfe.  And my will is that if Richard shall not marry w<sup>th</sup> Rebecca Tuttle which is now intended then my wife shall have her being in the howse as is before mentioned during her life vnlesse she see good to dispose of her selfe otherwise. But in case my sonne Richard should decease w$^{th}$out issue lawfully begotten of his body then my will is that all that estate that is not given to his wife by ioynture shall returne to Johan my wife if then living and if both dept this life without issue then my will is that such estate of land as remayne should be equally divided betweene my brother & sisters' children that are here in New England. I doe hereby give to my brother Theophilus Satchwell my best cloth sute & coate  To my brother Curwin my stuff sute  To my sister webster about seaven yards of stuff to make her a sute and alsoe a yonge heiffer thought to be w$^{th}$ calfe ffurther I doe hereby make my wife sole executrix & to receive what is due to me & alsoe to pay if I doe owe any thinge to any that is iustly due  In wittnesse of this my last will & Testament I doe hereto sett my hand the daye & yeare first above written. Those words (of land as remaynes) were interlined before the subscripcon hereof."

John Satchwell.

Witness: Jonathan wade, James Howe.
Proved Mar. 30, 1647, by the witnesses.

Inventory taken by Jonathan Wade and Thomas Howlett: one dwelling howse & home stall, with barne, cowhowse, orchard yard wth the apprtnancs, 100li.; several pcells of land, meadow & upland, 207li.; 6 oxen, 36li.; 5 cowes, 25li.; one yearling, 1li. 10s.; 3 calves, 1li. 10s.; one heiffer, 2li. 15s.; corne, not threshed, 5li.; several pcells of corne, 10li.; sithes, 12s.; carts & wheeles & irons belonging to them, 4li. 10s.; plowes & plow irons, 2li.; yoaks & chaines, 2li. 5s.; guns & swords, 5li. 12s.; a swarme of bees, 1li.; several bed steeds, 2li. 6s.; a sett of curtaines, 1li.; a fetherbed & bolster, 2li. 10s.; a Coverlit, 1li. 16s. 8d.; several blanketts, 1li. 10s.; a fether bed & pillowes, 1li. 12s.; a Coverlit, 1li. 5s.; a Coverlit, 1li. 5s.; In stuff, 2li. 8s.; Two blanketts, 18s.; A fether bed & bolster, 1li. 9s.; Curtaines, valance & carpit, 2li. 5s.; matts & cords, 15s.; sheets, pillowbeeres & several lynen, 8li.; Cushens, 12s.; a Chest, 14s.; a Chest, 8s.; a case of bottles, 6s. 8d.; a Table, 10s.; several chaires, 8s.; a Table & stoole, 13s.; In brasse & iron potts, 8li.; pewter & brasse, 1li. 15s.; a frying pan, 7s.; In England upon band, 18li.; swyne, 6li.; dunge, 2li.; powder, 8s.; fire shovell, tongs, spit, 6s.; silver spoones, 15s.; sawes, 10s.; 4 bibles, 1li.; several bookes, 15s.; hatts, 1li.; Tramell & pott hooks, 6s.; flax seed & flax, 1li. 4s.; ropes, 16s.; Tubbs, churne, barrell, 1li.; other caske, 7s.; a pistoll, 8s.; In debts, 5li.

*Ipswich Deeds, vol. 1, leaf 22.*

### Estate of Mrs. Chamberline of (Ipswich?).

Mrs. Chamberline dying intestate, an inventory of her estate, amounting to 32li. 4s. 5d. was filed 30 : 1 : 1647. Ordered to be divided, two parts to the son and one part to the daughter. *Ipswich Quarterly Court Records, vol. 1, page 7.*

Mr. Whitingham and Joseph Medcalfe to be administrators. Marke Symonds and Edward Browne to help divide the goods. *Ipswich Quarterly Court Records, vol. 2, leaf 7.*

### Estate of Michael Carthrick of Ipswich.

" I Michael Carthrick of Ipswich in New England Carpenter being weake in body but of good memory thanks be to the lord doe make & ordaine this my last will & Testament in mann & forme following first I comitt my body vnto the earth there to be interred decently according to the discretion of myne executrix and my soule into the hands of god that gave it and as for my outward estate as followeth Imprimis I leave my wholl estate of which I am now possessed in the hands of my wife to be improved by her for her owne & my childrens good vntill my sonne John shall accomplish the age of 21 years alsoe I give vnto my sonne John my howse wherein I now dwell with the barne out howses fences & howslott w$^{th}$ all thapp$^r$ten$^a$ncs to them belonging and alsoe all other my lands & meadow of which I am now possessed to him & his heires for ever when he shall accomplish the age of one & Twenty yeares to be deliv$^r$ed vnto him in good condicon & repaire fitt for habitacon & vse alsoe my minde & will is That my two childen John & Mildred shalbe brought vp by my wife vntill the tyme of the putting forth of my sonne or at his full age & vntill the tyme of marriage or full age of my daughter Alsoe my will is that my sonne John shalbe by my wife kept at schoole pvided there be a schoole in the Towne where she liveth vntill the age of 14 or 15 yeares yet foe as that at tymes his mother shall have power as the condicon of the family & her necesseties shall require to take him off to be helpfull to her in her businesse as the overseers & his mother shall see cause further my will is that my sonne John at the age of 14 or 15 yeares as the overseers shall thinke good shalbe put out to some trade and that his mother shall then furnish him with dubble apparrell & pay vnto the overseers six$^{li}$ to be imployed for his best advantage either for his putting forth or otherwise according to the discretion of the overseers further I giue vnto my daughter Mildred ten pounds to be paid vnto her out of the movable goods according to the appoyntm$^t$ of the overseers when she shall have accomplished the full age of 21 yeares or at the day of her marriage she marrying with the consent of the overseers & her mother: further in case my wife shall marry whilst my children or either of them be vnder age my will is that my wife & her husband shall both stand bound to fulfill my will vnto my children according to the true intent thereof and that her husband shall agree with my overseers for the fulfilling of the same in defect whereof or of the due vsage of my children or either of them my overseers shall have power to dispose of them by removing of them or otherwise soe as they may see them supplied & educated according to the true intent of this my last will & Testam$^t$ he or she paying according to the pporcon of the charge that shall soe arise about the children And further my will is that my wife shall not remove both or either of my children out of this Jurisdiccon without the consent of my overseers ffineally I doe make Sarah my loving wife sole executrix of this my last will & Testam$^t$ desiring her to see all things therein to be pformed according to my Intent & meaning therein specified as alsoe I doe appoynt our reverend & faithfull Teacher m$^r$ John Norton & Robert Payne oversers of this my last will & Testam$^t$ and in case of the decease or departure of either or both of them I give either or both of them power to appoynt an other or others in his or their place or places In wittnesse to this my last will & Testam$^t$ I have herevnto sett my hand & seale the 16$^{th}$ day of the eleventh month 1646."

Michael Carthrick.

Witness: Robert Lord, Edward Browne. *Ipswich Deeds, vol. 1, leaf 30.*

Proved 30 : 1 : 1647, by the witnesses. *Ipswich Quarterly Court Records, vol. 1, page 7.*

Inventory taken 25 : 11 : 1646, by Marke Symonds, Edward Browne and Robert Lord: one great cubberd, 1li.; an old little table & 3 chaires, 4s. 6d.; two wheeles, 6s.; one paire of tongs, one firepan, one andiron, 2 tramells, 1 spitt & one gridiron & one paire of bellowes, 13s.; a fowling peece, one muskett, 2 swords, 2 paire of bandeleeres & 2li & halfe of powder, 3li. 3s.; 10 pewter dishes, 2 quart potts, one pint pott, one beaker, a little pewter cupp, one chamb. pott, 1li. 8s.; a pewter salt, a brasse candlestick, a brasse pann, a morter & pestle, 12s. 6d.; a little kettle & two posnetts, 12s.;

a great bible, psalme booke & an other booke, 10s.; 3 gally dishes, an iron candlestick, 2 old lamps, 2s.; 3 iron potts, 1 iron kettle & two paire of pott hooks, 2li. 4s.; one powdering tubb, 2 keelers, a kneeding trough & other lumber, 1li. 3s.; one bushell of mault & 20 bushells of indian corne, 3li. 4s.; one flock bedd & bolster, 2 blanketts, matt & bedsteed, 1li. 15s.; hempseed, hopps & flax seed & leather, 8s.; 10li. of hempe undrest, 4s. 2d.; 12 li. of linen yarne, 1li.; two old hogsheads, 2s.; one bedsted in the parlor, 1li. 4s.; one fether bed waying 58 li. at 14d. & 3 pound of fethers, 3li. 10s.; one fetherbed and two boulsters weying 64li. at 12d., 3li. 4s.; one paire of blankets and two coverlets, 2li.; curtaines, valents and hangings, 2li.; 5 payer of sheettes, 1li. 15s.; 4 tablecloaths, 8s.; one cupboard cloth, 5s.; 1 short diaper table cloth, 6s. 8d., 11s. 8d.; two paire of pillow beeres, 9s.; 6 old napkins and one towell, 7s.; 3 shirts, 10s.; his weareing apparell, shooes, stockings & hatt, 4li. 10s.; a warmeing pan and a payer of tongs, 11s.; one chaire & 3 joyned stooles, 10s.; 2 chests & 3 boxes, 1li.; a hatchett, 12s.; a looking glasse & halfe houre glasse, 2s. 6d.; 2000 of nailes, 10s.; a lanthorne, 2 beere vessells & beerestall, 6s.; 200 of clapboards, 7s.; 3 pitchforks & 2 rakes, 4s.; one spade & shovell, 3s.; several tooles sold to Jo: Catcham, 17s.; one large handsaw, 6s., 7 axes, 22s., 1li. 8s.; one twibill, 5s., one long saw, 5s., one hand saw, 3s., 13s.; 5 augers, 3s. 4d., 4 augers, 6s., 9s. 4d.; 2 ham[mer]s & a holdfast & 16 planes, 1li. 1s.; 9 chissells, 7s., several small chissells, 3s., 10s.; a shave, a little square, a little sawe & a hatchett, 4s.; an auger & a frame sawe & hand saw, 4s. 4d.; a frow, a mattock & a square, 6s. 6d.; a beetle ring & 4 wedges, 5s.; Tooles laid by for willm Addams, 4s.; two cowes, 9li.; one steere, 2li., one calfe, 20s., 12li.; 5 piggs, 7li. 10s.; 12 acres of land, within the fence, 12li.; 26 acres of land, 4li.; a grindstone, winch & trough, 5s.; the howse, barne, yards, garden & the apprtences, 20li.; total, 99li. 2s. 6d. *Ipswich Deeds, vol. 1, leaf 31.*

Michaell Carthricke by his will gave his son John all his houses and land, and the said John dying after he was twenty years, Thomas Brigden, in right of Mildred, his wife, only sister of John, and by whom Brigden hath children, petitioned the court for due aud just relief. May 28, 1659, ordered that Mildred, the only daughter of Michael Carthrick, and sister and heir to John, should have the estate given to her brother, and to pay the widow of Carthricke 10li. *Mass. Bay Colony Records, vol. 4, page 377.*

### Estate of Mrs. Elizabeth Goodale of Newbury.

Mr. Edward Rawson, Richard Kent and Henry Short of Newbury appointed 6 : 5 : 1647, administrators of the estate of Mrs. Goodale until the General Court takes further order. *Salem Quarterly Court Records, vol. 2, page* 217.

Petition of Abraham Toppan, in right of Susan, his wife, and Thomas Milward and Richard Lowle, overseers to the will of Elizabeth Lowle, and on her behalf, that as this court, on their petition in 1647, granted unto Abraham Toppan, in right of Susan, his wife, and to Elizabeth Loule, executrix to the estate of her husband, John Loule, power of administration to the estate of Elizabeth Goodale, their mother, amounting to 191li. in money and about 30li. in goods, and reserved liberty to John Goodall anytime within three years to make challenge thereunto, now the time being expired, and no record found of the court's grant, desire that it may be entered on the records. Ordered May 27, 1652, that the former grant be recorded. *Mass. Bay Colony Records, vol.* 4, *page* 92.

### Estate of William Clarke of Salem.

Cp. Wm. Hathorne, Mr. Georg Corwin and his widow Katherine Clerk, all of Salem, appointed 6 : 5 : 1647, administrators of estate of William Clerk, late of Salem, deceased. *Salem Quarterly Court Records, vol. 2, page* 219.

Inventory taken 25 : 4 : 1647, by William Hathorne and sworn to by Mrs. Katherin Clerk, 9 : 5 : 1647 : An eight pte of a barke in Robert Lemmon his hands, 10li. 10s. ; an eight pte of a barke in Mr. Gooses hand, 20li.; twoo thirds of a shallop att marblehead in the hands of John Keagle, 7li. ; a house & land neere Mr. Johnsons & 200 acres of land neere Mr. Humfryes farme, 20li. ; a third of 9 acres of corne upon the ground, 3li. ; the houses & an acre of land neere Mr. Brownes, 28li. ; three Cowes, 13li. 10s. ; 12 small swine, 6li. ; pte of a bagg of Cotten, containing $1\frac{1}{4}$ hundred weight, 6li. 15s. ; 40li. of ginger at 9d. per li., 1li. 10s. ; 500 waight of Tobacco in Mr. Peeters seller at 4d. per li., 8li. 6s. 8d. ; in Mr. Downing's seller, 1000li. of Tobacco at 4d. per li., 16li. 13s. 4d. ; one hogshead & pt. of 2 hogsheads of suger, being about 700li. waight, 26li. 5s. In the Hall : One long table & frame, 4 Joynt stooles & a bench, 1li. 13s. ; 1 Court cubberd & old cloth, 14s. ; 3 red Leather chaires, 13s. 4d. ; 1 short forme, 2s. In the Parlor: 1 Table, 3 formes & a stoole,

14s. 6d.; 1 halfe headed bedstead, 7s.; 1 curtaine & vallance, 5s.; 1 feather bed & bolster, 2li.; 1 straw bed & flocke bolster, 7s.; 1 white blanckett, 3s.; 1 pr. of sheetes, 7s.; 1 greene rugg, 14s.; 1 other bedstead & mat, 7s.; 1 Curtaine & valance, 2s.; 1 canvas flocke bed, 10s.; 1 Feather bolster, 14s.; 1 pr. of old sheetes, 4s.; 2 old blancketts, 4s.; 1 Red Rugg, 8s. In the great Chamber: In a Deske in silver, 4li. 11s. 3d.; in Wampon about 3li. worth, 3li.; his deske, 1li.; 3 Joynt stooles, 5s.; 3 Leather stooles, 5s.; 1 old Turky carpet, 8s.; in the Closett in Endico, 5li.; trenchers & other small things, 14s. In the hall Chamber: 1 table & forme, 10s.; one old carpett, 3s.; one Joyned bedstead, 14d.; Cartines & vallances, 16s.; 1 feather bed, 3li.; 1 feather boulster, 15s.; four feather pillowes, 1li.; 1 matt, 2s. 6d., 1 Tapestry covering, 1li. 10s., 1li. 12s. 6d.; 1 Round Table, 7s.; 1 Cubberd cuishion, 2s.; 1 greate blacke Truncke with locke & key, 10s.; 1 great cuishion wrought with wosted with a chaire covering, 1li.; one sempiternum cubbord cloth with silke frenge, 1li.; 2 Cubberd cuishions of dammaske & one needle worke one, 1li.; 1 phylaselle cloake lined with plush, 3li.; for 1li. of silke frenge, 10s.; 3 say curtaines & a peece of vallance, 15s.; 3 red capps, 3s.; 6 silver spoones & 2 small peeces of plate, 3li.; one small Truncke, 6s.; one dussen of diaper napkins & a table cloth, 1li. 4s.; 1 dussen of lockrum napkins & a table cloth, 1li.; 1 dussen & ½ of Holland napkins wrought & a table cloth, 1li. 14s.; a paire of holland sheetes wth seaming lace, 1li.; a dussen of towells, 2s.; 1 close stoole, 6s. In the Chamber over the kitchin: 1 great truncke, 2s.; 10 pr. of sheetes, 5li.; 2 dussen of flaxen napkins & 2 table cloths, 1li. 4s.; 3 dussen of old napkins, 10s.; 3 old Table clothes, 10s.; 1 great chest, 14s.; 1 Turkey Carpitt, 1li.; 1 old Carpitt, 8s.; 1 great truncke with some small things in the same, 12s.; 1 bedstead, 5s.; curtaines & vallance, 7s., 12s.; a feather bed and boulster, 4li.; a covering & a blanckett, 8s.; a fire shovell, tongs & a pr. of andirons, 10s.; in a low bedstead, 1 feather bed & boulster, 2li.; a blanckett Rugg & a curtaine, 6s.; a Cutlas & a leather belt, 14s. 4d.; 1 old quilt, 3s. 4d.; a warming pan, 4s. In the Garrett: 2 flocke beds & a boulster, 14s.; a quilt & a Rugg, 4s.; some old tubs & Lumber, 1li.; 3 bushells of indian corne, 8s.; 15 bushells of wheat at 8d. per li., 2li. 15s.; 35 bushells of mault at 4s. per bushell, 7li. In the kitchin: 20 pewter platters, 2li. 10s.; 2 great plates & 10 little ones, 12s.; 1 great pewter pott, 1 flagon, 1 pottle, 1 quart, 3 pints, 4 ale qrts., 1 pint, 6 beare cups, 4 wine cups, 4 Candlestickes,

5 Chamber potts, 2 pewter lamps, 1 tunnill, 6 sawcers & old pewter, 3li. 18s.; China dishes, 12s.; 1 great brasse Copper, 1 small Copper kittle, a great kettle, 1 brasse pan, 1 brasse pott, 1 little kettle, 6li. 19s.; Iron, 1 great pott, 3 hangers, 2 spitts, 1 treevett, a paire of tongs, 1 fire shovell, 1 peele, 1 Jacke with some old Iron & tubs in the kitchin, 3li. 2s. 6d.; in the seller, hogsheads & old lumber, 1li.; a bible & Purchas Pilgrimage, 1li.; his wearing apparell, 6li.; owing to him per book, 310li. 13s. 5d., but what debts he oweth doth not to us appeare; total, 586li. 2s. 2d. *Salem Quarterly Court Files, vol. 1, leaf 81.*

Mrs. Katherine Clarke of Salem, widow, petitioned the General Court about the settlement of her husband's estate and it was referred to this court. Ordered 30: 10: 1647, that the widow have 150li. and the four younger children have 110li., 40li. to be allowed toward their education, and the remainder to be paid when of age or upon marriage. "The elder son to have a double pchon and his eldest son by his former wife to have 20li., the oth$^r$ 10li. and shee that was married in his life time, 5li." *Salem Quarterly Court Records, vol. 2, page 226.*

### Estate of John Lowell of Newbury.

Mr. Willia Gerish, Richard Lowle, Nicholas Noyse, John Saunders and Richard Knight appointed 6: 5: 1647, administrators of the estate of Mr. John Lowle, late of Newbury, deceased, until the General Court takes further order. *Salem Quarterly Court Records, vol. 2, page 217.*

"The Last will & Testament of John Lowle Late of Newberry deceased made this nine & twentieth of the fowrth mounth 1647

"That I John Lowle of Newberry beeing in Pfect vnderstanding knowing my ffrailty doe declare this to bee my last will & Testa[m]ent: stedfastly beleiveing that when I goe hence I shall rest in Glory through my Saviour the Lord Jesus Ch$^t$. As for the Estate the Lord hath given me heare I thus dispose of it: I give vnto my wife Elizabeth Lowle one halfe of my Estate whether it Consists in Goods within or without Land Howses Cattell Howshowld stuffe meddoes land brocken or vnbrockne or what else Alsoe my said wife to Chuse Twenty pownds out of the residewe of that Estate w$^{ch}$ Came by her mother fformerly or latter. The rest of my Estate to be devided Equally betweene my Sonn John Lowle Mary Lowle Peter Lowle James Lowle Joseph Lowle

Beniamine Lowle & Elizabeth Lowle. Alsoe I doe Humbly intreate these fiue my Christian deare Loving ffreinds & bretherne my brother william Gerrish Richard Lowle John Sanders Richard Knight & Nicholas Noice to be my Exec and Adm of this my last will & testament as alsoe to be the ouerseers of my wife and Children in A ffreindly Christian way towards them and that yo$^u$ five showld take the advise of our Elders; in Cace any one of my first wifes Children dye before theie have their portion in their hands that it be equally devided amongst the rest that are Living the same I say Concerning my second wifes Children Beniamine & Elizabeth these portions for my Children to be paid them when the Court Judge them wise, and able to manage an Estate as theie shall receive information from sixe of the wise Godly men of the Towne with the Elders. Alsoe I will that before the Goods be devided that my daughter Elizabeth shall take tenn pownds worth of her owne mothers Clothers for her vse; Alsoe that my daughter mary take Twenty pownds worth of her owne mothers Clothers, Alsoe if my wife marry I will that my daughter mary then shall Live with my Sister Johan Gerrish if my Sister please; if my daughter mary Chuse to Live with my sister before my wife; And that my two daughters shall have their Thirty pownds worth of Clothers taken out before the Estate be devided dated as above writne. In witnes wherevnto I have put my hand this day and yeare above writne."

Jn° Lowle.

Witness: Edmond Grenleife, Will: Gerrish, Robert Long. Proved 27: 8: 1647, by Edm. Greenleife and Willi. Gerish.

Inventory taken the last of June, 1647, by Edward Rawson, Thomas Miller (signed Milward) and Abraham Toppan: his Wearing Apparell: 1 bl. wat grogrin Suite, 1li.; a leather Suite, 1li. 6s. 8d.; a leather Jackett, 4s.; a bl. cloth Coate, 18s.; an old bl. Cloake & suite, 1li. 1s. 4d.; a freeze Jackett, 4s.; a lin coll Cloth Cloake, 18s.; a lin coll Coate old, 7s.; a Red wascoate & old dublet, 6s. 8d.; a lin coll Jackett & hose, 15s.; 2 hatts, 12s.; a pr. of bootes, 10s.; 4 pr. of shooes, 10s.; 4 p old stockings, 1 new pr., 12s. 6d.; 4 shirts worne, 15s.; 5 night Capps, 3s. 6d.; 11 day Capps, 1li. 3s.; 6 bands, 1 pr. of bootstopp, 7s. 6d.; 6 old handcherkess, 2s.; 2 Swords, 1 pr. of bandaleeres, 1 muskett, 1 pistoll, 1 feather, 1 ponyard, 2li. 4s. 6d.; total, 10li. 19s. 8d. In a little chamber: 1 pr. of greene Curtaines & valiants wrought, 2li. 15s.; a faire Cuppboard Cloth, 1li.; 2 wrought Cushions, 1 chaire, 1 Case for a chaire, 1li. 10s.; 1 Carpett, 1li.; 1 peece of greene searge, 8s.; another pr of green Curtains & valiants, 13s. 4d.; a pcell of bookes, 3li. 7s.; total, 10li. 13s. 4d. Lynnen: a tufted holland wascoatt, 4s.; an old holland shift, 2s. 6d.; 2 old Linn. wascoats, 3s. 6d.; a lardge diapr table Cloth, 10s.; on doz: of diapr napkins, 12s.; one pr. of fyne canvas sheets, 12s.; 3 pr. of Canvas sheets, 18s.; 3 odd sheets old, 5s. 4d.; 2 pr. of old sheetes, 4s.; 2 Course towells, 1s. 4d.; 1 Callico pillowby, 3s. 4d.; on pr. of pillowbyes, 6s.; a pr. of doulas pillowbyes, 4s.; 9 course napkins, 4s.; 14 Course napkins, 7s.; 5 other napkins, 3s.; 17 quoifes, 1 ruffe, 11s. 6d.; 8 forehead clothes, 10s.; a pcell of child bed linnen, biggins, head bands, &c, 9li.; one odd sheete, 1s. 10d.; 4 napkins, 1 Towell, Table cloth, 7s. 4d.; a Table cloth & 3 broken peeces 2s.; an old od sheet & 2 chese clouts, 1s.; a pillowby, 2s.; an old tablcloth & 2 napkins, 1s.; 2 old bands, 6d.; 9 pls of yarne & a seive, 9s. 6d.; 2 old Carpetts, ———— 6d.; 6 drinking napkins, 2s.; 1 pr. of holland sheets, 1li. 2s.; ———— of ————; ———— of Cou ————; fine old od she[et], ———— 8s.—; a pr. of fine litle sheets, 13s. 4d.; 2 p. of sheets, 1li. 12s. ————; a Table cloth & 12 napkins, 1li.; a diap Table cloth, 7 napkins & one damask, 1li.; a Table cloth, 2s.; 18 napkins, 15s.; 6 napkins, 3s.; 12 napkins, 4s.; pr. of Scotches pillowb., 4s.; 2 pr of holl pillowbyes, 16s.; 5 smale pillowbyes, 10s.; 1 pr. of cours pillowbyes, 4s.; one half sheete, 4s.; 2 Towells, 3s.; a fine Cuppboard cloth, 8s.; a fine plane Cupboard cloth, 6s. 8d.; a long Towell, 2s.; a pr. of [pill]owbyes, 4s.; a ———— [s]heete, 6d.; ———— colld Cloake, 5s. ————; 2 pinn cushions, 2s.; 3 *sk* of bl. woorsteed, 2s.; a flaring waskoate, 3s.; a pr. of course sheets, 6s.; a pr. of pillowbyes, 3s. 4d.; a pr. of pillowbyes, 6s.; an od sheete, 4s.; an od old sheete, 1s. 6d.; a pcell of old linnen, 2s.; an old table cloth, 1s.; 3 peeces of Cloth, 1s.; an old wascoate, 1s. 6d.; total, 23li. 9s. 8d. Bedding: a featherbed, 4li.; a greene Rugge, 1li. 10s.; a flocke bed, 18s. ————; 2 feather bolsters & one pillow, 1li. 10s.; 2 pillowes & a bolster, 1li.; a bolster Case, 6s.; a pr. of blancketts, 14s.; a pr. of fine blan., 1li. 2s.; a pr. of blancketts, 10s.; an od blanckett, 4s.; 6 Cushions, 1li.; a blew Rugge, 6s. 8d.; a feather bed & two pillowes, 4li.; a pillow & pillowby, ———— 2s.; a flocke bed & boulster & 3 old Coverleeds, 1li. ————; one grene Coverleed & 2 old Coverleed & 2 blankts, 16s.; a Red Rugge, 13s. 4d.; a feather bed, 3li.; a flocke bed, 13s. 4d.; 2 *som$^{este}$* mantles, 6s. 8d.; total, 24li. 3s. Other Apparrell: on grogd kertle & goune, 3li.; payer goune kertle, 2li.; a stamell bear: whitle,

18s.; a Red p[a]yer peticoat, 1li.; a Red Cloth peticoat, 1li.; a Red mantle, 8s.; 2 Swathing bands, 2s.; a Coate & hoode, 12s.; total, 9li. In pewter & brasse wth other necessary [ut]ensills, &c: 21 peuter platters, 3 butter dishes, 7 porringrs, 12 sasers, 1 flagon, 1 peuter Cupp, one salt celler, 2 Canstickes, 3li. 7s.; 1 grt pott, 1 p—— po— & 1 –innger, 5s.; 3 brasse candsticks & one chamber pott, 6s. 6d.; 2 brasse scales & beames & on pr of sheres, 4s. 10d.; 1 p of brasse Snuffers, 1s. 2d.; 2 iron candsticks, chafing dish, 2 skimers, 5s.; 2 steeling irons, a woodpress & brush, 6s.; one boule, 2 latt—— kiver, 1s. 6d.; one pr of bellowes, 2s.; one Case of boxes, 8s.; one file, one draft shave, 2 hand Sawes, one Augure, one plaine, 2 hamers, 2 chessell, one gouge, 3 aules, a gimblett & 2 Rings, 13s.; one pr. of Iron Andirns, one fender, one Iron pott, pr of hangers & Hookes, tonnes & firepanne, a litle Crooke, 1li. 10s.; on brasse ketle, 2 brasse skilletts, 6s.; 2 sithes & a Cutting knife, 3s.; a Carte Roape, 5s.; a brasse Copper, 2li. 10s.; one Iron pott, 3 brasse potts, one bellmetle skillett, on litle bell skillet, 3li. 4s.; one grt pr. of Iron doggs, 4 Spitts, 3 p of pott hangers, one grt grid Iron, 2 frying panns & one dripping pann, 1li. 13s. 4d.; one pessell & morter, one pr. of bellowes, pott hookes, 2 brasse ketles, one Iron with stake & yarmo knife, 1li. 17s.; a boxe wth several pcells of smale things, 5s.; Indian baskett & some Smale things in it, 2s.; a long brush & 2 other brushes, 2s. 6d.; a deske, 1s.; 3 trunkes, 18s.; a haire line, 1s.; a Canne & powder & 6li. of bulletts & 5li. of shott, 6s.; 3 lockes & a key, 3s.; a boxe, 6d.; a barrell & 5li. of brimston, 1s.; a boxe —4 papers of needles, 4s.; a litle trunke, 2s.; a Lampe & Iron Candsticke, 1s.; a sell drink Cupp & a glasse, 1s.; a chest, 15s.; a pr of doggs, 5s.; a brasse chaser, 5s.; a warming panne, 3s. 4d.; several peeces of leather, 3s. 4d.; Several peeces of Iron & a hooke, 10s.; 13 bushells of malte, 2li. 12s.; a pcell of flaxe & hemp, 7s.; 1200li. of nailes, 6s.; a bedsteed & 2 Joynt stooles, 5s.; a search & a boxe, 1s. 6d.; a flaskett, 1s.; a Casement Iron fendr, hookes, staples, old Iron, nailes, boxes, 15s.; 4 hogsheads & 3 barells, 11s.; a seve, 8d.; a Calves skin, 1s.; 2 old sithes, nibs & Rings, 3s. 6d.; a bedsteed & 1 doz. half last, 6s. 8d.; a pcell of orang & yellow silk, 8s.; 9 pr. of childrs gloves, 3s.; a bundle of lists, 3d.; a looking glasse, 3s. 4d.; 9 doz. of bl: button, a swath, a pcell of cruell, threed & Silke, 8s.; a tunell, grater & 3 Juggs, 3s.; one Iron hooke, one grater, one ——, one do —— forke, —— 6d. ——; a liske chaine, 2 old Rings, a garden rake, 2 —— peuter one muskett, 3li. 2s. ——; one pashall, one iron fire fork, 3s. ———; one chare, one bedsteed, on frame of a table, on flaskett, one Toe comb, Augur, pr of sheres & peeces of Iron, 13s. ———; 2 beere barrells, on hand barr, one powdring tub & kiver, 2 churnes & other old tubbs, wooden boule, 3 earthen potts, one Tunnrell, 3 chese vatts, one wood Cupp, 1 pecke & a halfe pecke, 1li. 9s.; 1 froe, a peece of lead, one table chaire together, 7s.; one kneading trough, a beacke, 5s.; one salt boxe, 1s.; one hedghooke, 2 Reaphookes, one pitchfork, one Spade & one Shovell, 10s.; one doz & a half of trenchers, 1s.; one bedsteed, one Cradle, 3 trayes, one kiver, 10s.; one wooden plough, one axe & a ladder, 5s.; one slidde & 3 yoakes, one 2 hand Ed sawe, a chayne, one Carte & wheeles, Ringg pinns, lince pins & bands wth a hatchett, 2li. 10s. ———; a pitchforke, 2 hogsheads & a butt, 8s.; a winne sheete & some flaxe, 4s.; a Still porringer & Saser, 13s. 6d.; 4 Sackes, 8s.; 5 leather baggs, 6s. 4d.; a little bagge, 1s. 6d.; a Grindstone, 6s. 8d.; 3 howes, one wedge, 2 ladders & a frame ——— 14s. 6d.; one plowe, one share, 10s.; on harrowe, 12s.; total, 40li. 1s. 11d. Catle: 2 Cowes, 10li.; 2 oxen, 11li.; 2 3yers steres, 9li.; a 2 yeere steere, 2li. 10s.; a yeere steere, 1li. 10s.; 2 bull calves, 2li.; 4 Swyne, 2li. 10s.; total, 38li. 10s. House & lands: his dwelling howse & 4 acr of Land, 26li.; ye Corne on ye 4 acrs, 5li. 10s.; another howse & two acrs of land, 7li.; ye Cropp of it, 3li. 10s.; a barne wth halfe an acr & ye Cropp, 10li.; 6 Acr of ground at 26s., 7li. 16s.; The Cropp of it, 7li. 4s.; 18 acrs at 10s. p acr., 9li.; fence to it, 6li.; 9 acrs of land, 1li. 16s.; 6 acrs of meadowe, 7li. 10s.; 8 acrs of marsh, 2li. 13s. 4d.; 13 acrs of marish, 3li. 1s. 8d.; 4 acrs of meadow, 1li. 10s.; total, 88li. 11s. Sum total, 245li. A bill of chardge & expenses for ye funerall, advise, Counsell & physicke & proving ye will come to 5li.

*Suffolk Co. Probate Files, Docket 61.*

Petition of Wm. Gerrish, Richard Lowle, John Saunders, Richard Knight and Nicolas Noyes shewing that the estate of John Lowle, deceased, was divided by them and Elizabeth Lowle, widow, between the widow and the children, only 10li. worth of clothes which were given in the will to Elizabeth Lowle, daughter to the widow, as is the will of the widow, but the genuine interpretation of the will is that the father intended his daughter to have the legacy out of her grandmother's clothes, which by this court was given to Elizabeth Lowle, widow, and Susanna Toppan, daughter to Elizabeth Goodale, deceased, who died intestate, and now the petitioners wish to know to which the court inclines and their order shall be observed. Further that the two sons may be called to know whom they will choose for guardians.

The court [May 13, 1648] decided that the clothes mentioned as given to Elizabeth Lowle (of her mother's clothes, now living), is to be understood as the clothes of her grandmother, Elizabeth Goodale, and out of them she should be satisfied. Richard Lowle appointed guardian to the children and the petitioners at their request discharged. *Mass. Archives, vol.* 15B, *page* 68.

Petition of Edmond Mores requesting the court that on condition of the payment of the sum agreed upon to the executors and overseers of John Lowle, deceased, as guardians to the children, the inheritance of the lands sold him with the liberties mentioned in the sale, be confirmed to him. Oct. 18, 1648, the petition was granted. *Mass. Bay Colony Records, vol.* 2, *page* 254.

Mary Lowle, about seventeen years of age, daughter of John Lowle, of Newbury, deceased, desiring to go to England to some near friends of hers, from whom she received her education, petitioned the court that a legacy of 10li. due unto her from Richard Lowle, her uncle, either at the age of twenty one or as this court shall determine, be paid unto her. Oct. 15, 1650, the petition was granted. *Mass. Bay Colony Records, vol.* 3, *page* 213.

Upon a motion made by Richard Lowle of Newbury, brother to John, deceased, the court, 1 : 4 : 1653, gave full power to either of the county courts, to appoint some person to be guardian of James and Joseph Lowle, sons of John Lowle, the said Richard by reason of sickness being incapable of looking after them further. *Mass. Archives, vol.* 15B, *page* 24.

Acquittance of Phillip Nellson of Rowley, to Richard Lowle and others, overseers of the will of John Lowle, deceased, and Elizabeth Lowle, of all demands. Dated Feb. 20, 1666. Wit: Ezekiell Northend, John Pickard. Sworn to Sept. 30, 1673, by John Pickard, and Sept. 29, 1674, by Ezekiel Northend. *Ipswich Deeds, vol.* 3, *page* 326.

## Estate of John Fairfield of Wenham.

"The 11th day of the 10mo December 1646: To god be the prayse, I John ffayrefeild beinge in perfect memory though weake in Boddy doe make this my last will and Testament in manner & forme as followeth. . . . I doe Give and Bequeath to Elizabeth my beloued wife my pte of house & ground which I haue in Coptnershipe with Joseph [Bat]chelder to her & to her Heires foreuer Item: I doe giue vnto my wife all my moueables within dores and without as namely my Cowes Cattle Swine Corne Housall Implyments and vtensels Bed bedinge Lininge Woollinge Brass Peuter mony Debts and whatsoeuer is mine either in Possession or accruinge or belonginge to me for her the said Elizabeth to haue and inioy the same as her owne fee Simple to disposs of at her pleasure without Interruption or molestation from any other, and also my will is that my said wife shall haue the vse and occupation of the house I now liue in and the ground Appertayninge thereunto and of my fearme had from Salem; vntill such time as Beniamen my yongest sonne shall Come to twenty yeeres of Age; And then my minde and will is that this house & Land & my moueable Goods ‖ then remaininge ‖ shall all be equally in the proportion devided, betwine my wife, and three Children ‖ soe many of them as shall then *survive* ‖. And further this is my will that my wife shall see the bringinge vp of my Children Christian Like and Honestly and alsoe the due disposall of them vnto such honest occupations or lawefull Callings or Conditions of life as she in her wisedom *with* the *advice* of the *supervisors of this my will shall esteem most meete, this her said* Care of them to extend towards my said Children vntill my yongest son Beniamine Comes to twenty yeeres of age And Likewise my will and pleasure is my sonne Walter shallrset himself satisfyed with what I heere haue done as Concerninge him and to take it as my minde and advice that he would approue himselfe dutifull vnto his Mother vpon whose Curtisy he shall depend for ought elce he might expect; Alsoe my minde is my said wife shall make no estripp or wast of Timber fensinge, and shall keepe my said houses in good & sufficient Reperrations and my ground sutably fenced and inclosed accordinge as she finds the same duringe the same space of Tearme, and in Cause she shall disposs her selfe in marryage that then she shall before the solemnisinge of the same enter into sufficyent bond & security for the fulfillment of this my will vnto the Supervisors, further my minde and will is that for my gunes and swordes : my Chrildrne shall haue the vse of them as need require Item I giue vnto Mathew Edwards my Cossen Twenty Acres of vpland lyinge within my fearme had from Salem with two acres of middow to be laid out most indifferently by my supvisors to injoy it at one and twenty yeeres of Age. Item I Constitute And ordayne Elizabeth my wife sole Executrix And my Louinge and well approued freinds Mr. Henery Bartholomew of Salem and Robertt Hawes of Salem these two Supvisars to this my last will and Testament. In witnes where of I haue set to my hand and Seale."

his mark<br>John ⌒ Fairefild.

Witness: Jo. Fiske, William Fiske, Robert Hawes.

Proved 7 : 5 : 1647, by William Fiske and Robert Hawes, and 8 : 5 : 1647, by Jo. Fiske. *Essex County Quarterly Court Files, vol.* 1, *leaf* 77.

Inventory taken 23 : 10 : 1646, and sworn to by widow Elizabeth Fairfield, 7 : 5 : 1647: One dwelling house, 7li. 10s.; seventie five Acres of upland and seven acres of meddow, 21li. 16s.; fearme of Eightie Acres of upland and eight acres of meddow, 6li.; a Joynte purchase with Joseph Bachelder, containing fortie eight Acres of upland and three Acres of meddow & a dwelling house and a Cowhouse & Corne sowed upon it, 10li.; wheat unthrashed, 1li.; Rye unthrashed, 1li.; Indian corne, 8li. 15s.; five loads of hay, 2li. 10s.; three cowes, 13li. 10s.; three yeereling Calves, 4li. 16s.; one sucking calfe, 8s.; one fatt Hogge, 2li. 10s.; one sow, 1li. 15s.; one hogg, 1li. 8s.; two shotts, 1li. 4s.; three piggs, 1li. 4s.; one feather bed & Bolster & five feather pillowes, 3li.; under bed, one greene rugge and one blankett, 1li. 12s. 6d.; one feather bed, one feather boulster and one flock boulster, 2li.

5s.; two coverlits, one pillow and two under Blankets, 16s. 6d.; Greene lincye woolsie curtaynes and a darnick Vallience, 1li.; one Bedstead and cord, 5s. 6d.; fowre payre of old sheets, 1li. 4s.; two sheets and a halfe of fine flax, 1li. 8s.; fowre pillowbeeres, 8s.; two diaper boord clothes and one little playne boord clothes, 10s.; two diaper napkins and three playne napkins, 4s.; two hand towells & one old boord Cloth, 4s.; one great brass Kettle, 18s.; one middle brass kittle, 12s.; one lesser brass kittle, 7s.; one brass bakinge pann with a Cover to it, 7s.; three brass skillitts and a brass scommer, 5s.; one small iron pott, 2s.; five peuter dishes, 9s.; two fruitt dishes and two sawcers, 3s. 6d.; fowre peuter porringers, 2s. 4d.; one pinte pott of peuter, 2s.; one double salt of pewter, 1s. 6d.; one peuter Candlestick, 1s. 8d.; six pewter spoones, 6d.; a chamber pott of pewter, 2s.; two chests, 10s.; three boxes, 3s.; one cubbortt, 5s. 6d.; two payles, 2s.; one beere barrell, 5s.; one spitt, 2s.; a payre of andyrons, 3s.; a gridiron, 1s. 6d.; a frying pan, 1s.; a payre of tongs & fyre shovell, 1s. 6d.; a warming pan, 2s. 6d.; a muskett with a fyrelock, 14s.; an old Fowlinge peece, 14s.; a pistoll dag, 5s.; a sword and bandlears, 8s.; a beetle & fowre wedges, 4s.; two old axes, 3s.; a crosscutt saw, 8s.; a hand saw & two old shovells and payre of pinsons, 4s.; twenty-three harrow tines, 4s. 9d.; three hanginge locks, 2s.; an iron foot, 1s.; two payre of hookes & eyes for a gatte, 2s.; a browne bill, 2s.; an iron spade, 4s.; twenty pounds of leadinge weights, 5s.; old iron, 5s.; three sickles, 2s.; a Bible with Bezes notes, 10s.; a smoothing iron, 2s.; a black stuff sute, 1li.; an old jerkin and bretches of silke russet cloth, 12s.; an old full coate and whood, 1li.; an old Black hatt, 2s.; a payre of boots, 1s. 6d.; a wicker fan, 4s.; a halfe bushell and halfe peck measure, 2s. 6d.; two old hoggs heads, 4s.; a barrell with a cover, 3s.; hempe, 5s.; two baggs, 2s.; fower trayes, 3s.; a trundle bed, 5s.; a broad box, 6d.; a wheele barrow, 1s. 6d.; fower old howes and an old garden rake, 3s.; a pitchfork and a dung forke, 2s.; a woollinge wheele and a lingeinge wheele, 6s. 8d.; a brason morter & pestell, 3s.; eighten pound of drest hempe, 12s.; three old chayres, 3s.; two pott racks & a payre of bellowes, 5s.; a lether sack and an iron peele & some other old iron, 3s.; a mattocke, 2s. 6d.; total, 113li. 3s. 7d. *Essex County Quarterly Court Files, vol.* 1, *leaf* 78.

2 cowes, 9li.; 3 steers and heighfers of 2 years old, 7li. 10s.; 1 calfe under one yeere, 10s.; 1 hogge, 2li.; a sowe and a smale pigge, 1li. 4s.; a bush. of Indian Corne, 3 bush. of

wheate; total, 20li. 4s.; for the keeping of the two Children, the one 2 years & 5 months & the other 2 yeare, 10li.; the rent of the Farme & stock, per yeare, 8li.; the wife's pte., 4li.; 1 child 5 monethe, 1li.; the estate being devided into 4 pts is to each, 9li. 12s. 10d. *Essex County Quarterly Court Files, vol. 1, leaf 79.*

### Estate of Christopher Yongs of Wenham.

"9th of 4th 1647. I Christopher yongs of wenham in the County of Essex in New England being at the day of the date hereof in good & pfect memory (although weak in body) blessing Almighty God therefore, doe make this my last will & Testam$^t$ in manner as followeth Imp$^r$imis I committ myselfe & mine into the hand of my gracious God & father in Jesus Christ, to be disposed according to his good pleasure, beseeching him for pdon of my sins, & relying on the merits of Christ my Savior for a glorious resurection at the last day. It. as concerning the outward goods of this life I bequeath them as followeth as first of all that there be made out of my Cloath, linin &c. two suits ||of Appel|| a peece for each of my three Children ||to be sent into England w$^{th}$ them|| & then the rest of my Estate moveable and Immoveable to be sold or disposed of according to the discretion of my executors, in pte towards the pviding for my Children whilest heere remayning in this land, & the seasonable transportation of them ouer Sea into o$^r$ Native County vnto Greate yarmouth in Norfk in old England, & the Residue that shall remayne to be sent over vnto my feoffoes of Trust there, to be imployed by them to the vse of my sd Children. It. my will & mind is to bequeath my two daughters vnto my deere mother in Law m$^{ris}$ Elvin in Greate yarmouth entreating her, & my *lov*ing father in law m$^r$ Elvin her Husband, to take care of them, at what time the providence of god shall bring them ouer, when I due also hearby constitute my feofes of trust together with m$^r$ John Philips of wenham or any one of these at that time surviving to see to the dispose of these my s$^d$ Children, & of what estate shall remaine to be distributed betwene them. And I doe bequeath my Son in Special vnto the care of the sd m$^r$ John Philips if he shall then liue to be disposed of by him as his owne: these my children to be sent ouer vnto yarmouth aforesd. to be disposed of as specifyed. It. my will & desire is, that my children during the time of there abode in this County shall remayne with my two Sisters, the wife of Joseph Yongs, &

the wife of Thomas Moore of Salem, they to be allowed for the time by my executors what may be *convenient*. It. I giue my greate Bible to my daughter Sarah, and my lesser bible to my daughter mary & a booke entitled Of Gods alsufficiency vnto Christopher my Son, to be carefully p^rserved for them & to there use, to enjoy as a remembrance of my affection & welwishing towards them. & I giue my booke entitled the Deceitfulness of mans Heart to my deere freind Ezdras Read as a testimony of my love towards him. lastly I doe heereby constitute & ordeyne my trusty & welbeloued freind m^r William Browne of Salem, Ezdras Read of Wenham, & the wife of Joseph yongs of Salem executors to this my last will to see to the dispose & transportation of my children, ‖towards my buryall & paym^t of my debts‖ & to the Sale & dispose of my estate as heerein is specifyed. & for ther paynes & expences thereabouts my will & mind is, they should haue reasonable satisfaction out of my s^d goods, giueing an accompt heereof vnto my Supvisor & finally I doe heereby make my beloved freind M^r Hennery Bartholmew Supvisor of this my will."

Christopher Yongs [seal]

Witness: John ffiske, Edward spouldyng.

Proved 7:5:1647, by Edward Spouldyng, and 8:5:1647 by John ffiske. *Essex County Quarterly Court Files, vol. 1, leaf 82.*

Inventory taken July 5, 1647, by Phinehas Fiske, William Fiske and Edward Spolding. Sworn to 7:5:1647, by Esdras Read, executor: A dwelling House wth five acres of ground Joyning to it & ten acres more Remote, 8li. 10s.; one acre & Quarter of Corne on the ground, 1li. 10s.; Two Cowes, 9li. 10s.; One Swine, 10s.; One Lome wth ye Gares belonging to it & seven Reeds, fowre beinge Hernest & two brassen Reeds hernest, 3li. 10s.; One Bedstead & Cords, 12s.; Curtains & Valliants, 5s.; One fetherbed & Boulster & three fether Pillows, 3li. 10s.; One old Rugg, 9s.; Two old Chests, 4s.; Three Iron Potts & two payre of pothooks & a brass Skillett, 1li.; One Postiron, a hale & a how, 5s.; Two old axes wth some old Iron, 2s.; One Muskett & Rest, 16s.; One Pewter basen, a drinkinge pott, three platters, three old saucers, a salt & an old Porringer, 10s.; One Bakinge Pan, 6d.; Two Lamps, 2s.; Spoons, Trenchers & Dishes & pipking, 1s. 6d.; a Box with some Salt, 6d.; Two Chayres, 1s. 6d.; a Settle, 3s. 4d.; a Spade, 3s. 4d.; Three trayes, two payles & a boule, 3s. 2d.; a Table & Minginge trough, 3s. 4d.; a Looking Glass, 6d.; a Smoothing Iron & three knives, 3s.; **two** bibles & some other old bookes, 13s. 4d.; one Hogshead wth Certaine hempe & flax, 5s.; two Boxes with some other old things, 5s. 9d.; Corne, 4s.; a hammer, 6s.; a pichforke, 1s.; two payer of sheets wth other Lininge, 19s.; five yards & halfe of serge & lace, 1li.; a payer of gloves & some hoss yarne, 5s. 4d.; line sowinge thrid & a Ruff, 2s.; Fower bredthes of old stuff, 5s.; one payer of upper bodyes, 1s.; Cartine Tape, 1s. 6d.; a bearinge Cloth, 10s.; Three Peticots, fowre wescots, a whood & an Apren, 2li. 13s.; Three black wrought Coifes, three Cut worke Coifes, a silke Cap, seven Cross Clothes, two handkerchiefe, three Aperns, a stuff Cap, 1li. 5s.; a Diaper Boordcloth & halfe a dozen diaper napkins, 1li.; two yards of Holland & five other psels of new lininge, 12s.; Certaine Lininge for a Child, 16s.; Three Sheets & a peece of new cloth, 1li. 5s.; Certaine other Lininge, 2s.; Black thrid & Gray, 1s. 6d.; a weskott, 1s. 6d.; Two hatts, 10s.; Fowre yards of Carsy, 1li.; a yard & halfe of Carsy, 7s. 6d.; a payre of stuff Briches and a peece of Stuff of the same, 1li.; Silke & Buttons, 1s.; a Gowne, 15s.; a Doublett, Briches & Cott and two payre of Lynings and some other old Clothes, 14s.; a payre of Stockings, 1s.; an old Straw bed and Creadle Rugg with an old Bed Rugg, 6s.; a Shurtt, 2s. 6d.; a Butter Pott, 1s.; a persell of Goods sent over this yeere from Ingland, 2s. 5d.; a Ringe of a beetle, 1s.; an old Coat, 1s.; Poultry, 3s.; total, 51li. 11s. *Essex County Quarterly Court Files, vol. 1, leaf 83.*

The petition of the executors of Christopher Yonge, late deceased, to have liberty to place the children in this country and not to send them to old England as expressed in the will, was granted 26 : 10 : 1648. *Salem Quarterly Court Records, vol. 3, leaf 3.*

### Estate of Edith Smith.

Will of Edith Smith, made 3 : 12mo : 1642, proved 9 : 5mo : 1647, by oath of John Robinson. *Salem Quarterly Court Records, vol. 2, page 218.*

### Estate of Giles Badger of Newbury.

"The 29th day of June in the yeare of our Lord 1647 I Giles Badger of Newbury being sick in body but of pfect memory thankes be given to god And I doe ordaine & make my last will & Testamt in mann & forme as followeth first I give & bequeath my soule to god & my body to the earth to be buried in hope to be raised againe in the resurrection by Jesus Christ my saviour   secondly I give & bequeath to my wife two parts of my estate if she remaine vnmarried & my will is that my child should have one part the which part my will is should be paid to my sonne when he is 18 yeares of age the benefitt of it to be improved for bringing vp vntill he be 18 yeares of age   Likewise my will is that if my wife doe marry againe that then my wife shall have the one halfe & my sonne the other halfe to be paid to him when he is 18 yeares of age and soe likewise the benefit of it to be improved for his maintenance.   Likwise I doe desire my christian frends my father Greenleff Daniel Perce & Henry Short & Richard Knight to diuide my estate betweene my wife & child." Giles Badger

Witness : Richard Knight, william Ilesley, Henry Somerbe.

Proved 28 : 7 : 1647, by Richard Knight. *Ipswich Deeds, vol. 1, leaf 33.*

On 27 : 1 : 1649, Mr. Symonds ordered to take the oath of the other witness. *Ipswich Quarterly Court Records, vol. 1, page 15.*

Inventory taken Sept. 12, 1647, by Lt. Edmund Greenleff, Henry Short, Daniel Pearce and Richard Knight: Two Coates, 1li. ; one short coat, 10s. ; one cloth sute, 1li. 4s. ; one stuff sute, 1li. ; one paire of cloth hose, 13s. ; one leather sute, 1li. 10s. ; one leather jackett, 1li. ; one blew wastcote, 10s. ; a paire of drawers, 3s. ; 2 paire of bootes, one paire of shoes, 18s. ; 4 paire of stockins, 10s. ; 2 sutes, 2 hatts, one cap, 1li. ; a muskett, sword, bandaleeres, 1li. 8s.   In the Chamb : one bed, one bowlster, 2 pillowes, a paire of blanketts, a paire of sheets, one coverlet & curtins, 7li. 5s. ; one paire of sheets, 1li. ; one sheet, 5s. ; 2 chests, 1li. 4s. ; a warming pan, 7d. ; a Cubberd, 2 boxes, 1li. ; a little wheele, 4s. ; 2 pillow beeres, 10s. ; the board cloth, 3 napkins, 10s. ; a diap. board cloth, 8s. ; in linen yarne 12li., 1li. 4s.   In the loff :   12li. of cotten wooll, 12s. ; a Pcell of hempe & flax undrest, 6s. ; a peece of sole leather, 9s. ; a churne, halfe bushell & a peck, 6s. ; 3 barrells, 2 firkins, 7s. ; 3 little vessells, 5s. ; 2 sives, a chest & other lumb., 5s. ; 8li. shott, 2s. 8d. ; 5 sacks, 12s. ; a great bagg, 6s. ; a bushell of mault, 4s.   In the fire roome : a table, 4 chaires, 9s. ; a cushen stoole, 3s. ; two stooles, 2s. ; two kettles, 1li. 16s. ; two skilletts, 5s. ; an iron pott & pott irons, 10s. ; a glasse bowle, beaker, Jugg, 3s. ; Three silu. spoones, 1li. ; a morter & pestle, a scum., 5s. ; 6 porringers, 3 saucers, 7s. ; 3 platters, a bason, 9s.; a chamb. pott, 2 candlesticks, 6s.; 2 beakers & a bowle, 5s.; a quart pott & a pint pott, 7s.; 3 little dishes, 6 spoones, 3s.; a salt seller, a tunell, a great dowrubb, 1s.; 6 wooden dishes, 2 ladles, 4s.; 2 wooden platters, a peele, 4 earthen panns, a frying pan, 2 bellowes, other lumb., a fire pan & tongs, 7s.; 3li. of powder, 6s.; 4 axes & other tooles & 4 sawes, 3li.; a spade & a shovell, 4s.; 3 pitchforks, 3 rakes, 4s.; 3 yoaks, a chayne, 2 plowes, 19s.; a cart & wheeles, 16s.; 2 Sithes, 5s.; 2 oxen, 15li.; a Cowe, 2 yearlings, a calfe, 19li.; 3 piggs, 1li. 15s.; In powltry, 5s.; Corne in the barne, 16li. 10s.; In land & howsing, 60li.; 5 caske, 17s.; one mattock, one holdfast, 4s.; a tow combe & pessell, 5s.; 3 sives, 3s.; hay, 5li.; In the seller in barrells & other lumb., 1li.; dung, 10s.; 2 wedges & a betle ringed, 6s.; bookes & gloves, 11s.; total, 153li. 9s. 8d. Soe that all recknings on his books being cleare remaines owing 24li. 9s. 8d., which being taken out of the 153li. 9s. 8d., there remaines in estate to be divided 129li. *Ipswich Deeds, vol. 1, leaf 33.*

Richard Browne's bond, dated Mar. 27, 1655, to pay his wife's son, John Bager, 34li. at eighteen years of age, besides the half of the land left by the latter's father. *Ipswich Quarterly Court Records, vol. 1, page 49.*

### Estate of Robert Hunter of Rowley.

"this 5th of the 6th month 1647. I Robert Hunter weake of body but of pfect memory praysed be god doe make & ordayne this to be my last will & Testament. first all my debts being paid I leave my howse & lott to my wife Mary Hunter for Terme of her life. Item all my goods within the howse I give to my wife Item I give vnto Thomas Birkby one little browne heffer that coms two yeares and my shop geare. Item I give vnto some poore in the Church of Rowley ten pounds to be paid out of two mares of which ten pounds ten shillings I give to Richard Clarke Ite ten shillings to John Dresser Item to John Burbant 10s. Item to willm Jackson 10s. Item to Jane Grant I give 10s. Item to Sisly wood 10s. Item to Margaret Crosse 10s. Item I give to william Stickne 20s. & all my workiday clothes Item to Thomas Elethorp 10s. Item I give to mris Shove 40s. which I desire may be for helping her sonne when he is to ||goe|| [to] Cambridg Item I give to John Trumbell 20s. Item to Edward Sawier 10s. Ite to Thomas Tenny I give 10s. and the remainyng 20s of the 10l I give to mris Shove Item as for all the rest of my goods & Chattells I leave vnto my wife Mary Hunter whom I make sole executrix of this my last will & Testament." Robert Hunter.

Witness: Humfry Rayner, Maximilian (his mark) Jawet.

"Memorand for the Inheritance of my howse & lott In case Abell Langley settle here & carry well towards his Dame my minde is that he shall have the Inheritance of them, but if not then I leave it to be disposed of by the Church for the vse of the poore of Rowley Item it is the will of the said testator that if the abovesaid Abell Langley have a call to goe for England to settle any estate he hath there that then he shall have libty to goe and returne but in case he goe & doe not returne to live here in such convenient tyme as may be thought fitt by the Church then the said Abell Langley shall not have power to sell or dispose of the Lott or howse but they shall fall into the hands of the Church at Rowley to be disposed of as abovesaid."

Proved 28 : 7 : 1647. *Ipswich Deeds, vol. 1, leaf 25.*

### Estate of Luke Heard of Ipswich.

" The last will of Luke Herd Latly deceased about the Imprimis I give vnto my eldest sonne John Herd ten pounds to be paid him at the age of 21 yeares Item I doe give vnto my sonne Edmund five pounds to be paid him at the Age of 21 yeares Item I give my bookes vnto my two sonnes to be equally parted betweene them Alsoe this is my will y$^t$ my two sonnes be brought vp to writing & to reading & then when they shalbe fitt to be putt forth to such trades as they shall Choose. Alsoe I make my loving wife Sarah Herd my sole executrix. Thus much as abovesaid was exprest by the above named Luke Herd in the p$^r$sence of vs."

[no signature.]

Witness: John (his mark) Wyatt, Simon Tompson.

Proved 28: 7: 1647, by the witnesses. *Essex County Quarterly Court Files, vol. 1, leaf 94.*

Inventory taken by James How, Thomas Howlett and John Wyatt: shopp Tooles, 6li.; all kinde of iron tooles, 4li. 14s. 6d.; iron potts, a posnett & a kettle, 1li. 2s.; a brasse kettle, 15s.; 12 pewter dishes & other pewter, 2li. 11s. 6d.; wooden ware, 6s.; fether bedds & bolsters, 6li. 10s.; a rugg, coverlett & curtins, 1li. 14s.; apparrell, 6li. 16s.; bookes, 4li. 10s.; linen, 2li. 9s.; cotten wooll, 6s.; a great chest, 2 boxes & chaires, 1li. 1s.; a muskett & pistolett, sword, bandaleers & powder, 1li. 16s. 8d.; scales & waites, 1li.; sackes a half bushell & a peck, 10s.; three Cowes & three steeres of 3 yeare old & two steeres of 2 yeare old & a heffer, 36li. 15s.; swine, 1li.; corne, wheate & indian, 5li. 1s.; total, 84li. 17s. 8d.  *Ipswich Deeds, vol. 1, leaf 33.*

Bond of Joseph Bexby (also Bigsby) of Ipswich, husbandman, and Sarah (her mark) Heard (also Herde), widow, to Ipswich court, for 30li., dated 15 : 10 : 1647. Wit: Margaret Rogers and John Rogers. Condition: Parties intend to marry each other; the two children (sons) of said Sarah and her late husband Luke Heard of Ipswich, linen weaver, to be well brought up, be taught to read and write, at the age of thirteen at the furthest to be apprenticed to such trades as Mr. Nathaneel Rogers, their grandfather Wyat and Ensigne Howlet ordain, and that they be paid at the age of twenty-one the 15li. given to them by the will of their father, viz: 10li. to the elder and 5li. to the younger, and the books bequeathed them by their father; that 5li. be paid to the children of said Sarah if living, she to divide it according to her discretion, equally, or to give the whole to the younger, if the elder be better provided for; and that the land in Asington, in Suffolk, England, which was to be Sarah's after the decease of her mother, the tenure of which was not certainly known by them, if the land was not entailed, to be Sarah's solely, the said Joseph Bigsby to have no right in it on account of marriage. *Essex County Quarterly Court Files, vol. 1, leaf 95.*

Petition of Nathaniel Rogers and John Wiatt, under the will of Luke Heard and above bond, requesting General Court to fulfil will of deceased, Joseph Bigsby being gone out of the country without giving notice of his return. Ordered, attachment of estate of Joseph Bigsby to the amount of the children's legacies, his estate being so weakened that the petitioners fear for the security of the children's property. *Essex County Quarterly Court Files, vol. 1, leaf 96.*

### ESTATE OF SAMUEL SCULLARD OF NEWBURY.

"In the name of god amen In the Twenty seaventh day of March in the yeare of our lord 1647 I Samuell Scullard being sick in body but of pfect memory thanks be given to god; And I doe ordaine & make my last will & Testament as followeth first I bequeath my soule to god & my body to the earth in hope to be raised againe in the resurreccon by Jesus Christ my saviour   Secondly I give & bequeath all my estate to my wife & children that is to say one halfe to my wife & the other half to my two Children Mary & Sarah by equall porcons and my will is y^t if my wife be now with child & bring forth a sonne then my will is that my estate be diuided into three parts and my sonne to have one part my wife one part & my two daughters one part to be equally divided betweene them   But if my wife bring forth a daughter then my will is that my estate yet should be diuided into three pts my wife to have one part & my two daughters to have two parts to be equally diuided betweene them   Now my will is that my childrens porcons should be improved for the bringing vp of my children vntill they be twelve yeares of age and after the Twelve yeares to be improved to their advantage vntill they be eighteene yeares of age the two daughters or three before, if they be married and the sonne at one & Twenty and then to be paid to they themselves. And for that forty pounds which I am to have of my wives father Richard Kent at his decease of my wives porcon my will is that my wife should have Thirty pounds of it her selfe besides.   And I doe not account yt w^th my other estate and for the other ten pounds of it to be equally diuided betweene the Children.   Likwise my will is that if any one of my children die that then that porcon is to be diuided equally betweene my wife & children.   Likewise I doe desire my three frends Henry Short Richard Kent Jun & Richard Knight to see that this my will & Testament be pformed."

[No signature.]

Witness: John Sweett, w^m Moneday.
Proved 28 : 7 : 1647, by Henry Short and Richard Knight.

Inventory taken Apr. 7, 1647, by Stephen Kent, John Merrell and John Emery: 5 oxen at 6li. 10s., 32li. 10s.; 2 cowes at 4li. 10s., 9li.; 1 steere, 3li. 15s.; a bull & heffer, 4li. 10s.; 4 yearlings, 5li. 10s.; 2 calves, 1li. 16s.; 14 bushells of corne at 3s. 6d., 2li. 9s. 10d.; a cart & irons, 1li. 10s.; a plow & cart Irons, 1li.; 2 sithes, 2s.; 15 acres of land at the New Towne, 10li.; 6 acres of salt marsh, 3li.; debts due to him, 2li. 8s.; 2 Cowes at 4li. 10s., 9li.; 3 hoggs, 5li.; 5 shotes with five piggs, 5li.; a hogg of bacon, 2li. 10s.; a fetherbed & two boulsters, 2li. 10s.; a rugg & hangings, 1li.; 3 sheets & 2 pillowties, 1li.; a Iron kettle, 1li. 5s.; a brasse pott & potsnet & hookes, 14s.; 4 pewter dishes & 3 small ones, 12s.; a frying pan, 2s.; a muskett, sword & bandeleers, 18s.; wooden vessels, 12s.; leather, 1li. 6s.; a howse

& barne & orchard, 9li.; 12 acres of ground with the fencing, 15li.; 9 acres of ground, 4li. 10s.; 13 acres of ground, 9li. 10s.; 6 acres of meadow at the little river, 8li.; 20 acres of salt marsh, 5li.; total, 99li. 19s.; due unto her from her father at his decease whereof 10li. is due unto the children, 40li.; total, 139li. 19s.; debts that are owing from him, 10li. 18s. 4d.

*Ipswich Deeds, vol. 1, leaf 27.*

Administration granted 28: 7: 1647, to John (his mark) Bishop and Rebecca (her mark) Bishop, his wife. The houses and lands to be divided between said John and his wife and the two children. The cattle and the rest of the stock for John and his wife to take as they were appraised. Henrye Short, Rich. Knight and Rich. Kent were ordered to dispose of half of the houses and lands of Samuel Scullard for the good of the children. *Ipswich Quarterly Court Records, vol. 1, page 11.*

Samuell Denise of Woodbridge in the province of New Jersey acknowledged the receipt from John Bishop, sr., sometime of the Island of Nantucket, of " fortie od pounds," in behalf of his wife Sarah Dennis, formerly Sarah Scullard, it being her share given unto her by her father Samuel Scullar. The 5li. given her by her grandfather Richard Kent included in the value. Dated Sept. 19, 1670. Witness: Richard Dole, Wm. Chandler.

Jno. Roffe of the Island of Nantucket acknowledged the receipt from Jno. Bishop, sr., sometime of the Island of Nantucket, of " forty od pounds," in behalf of his wife Mary Rolfe, formerly Mary Sculler, it being her share given unto her by her father, Samuell Sculler. The 5li. given her by her grandfather Richard Kent included in the value. Dated Sept. 19, 1670. Witness: Wm. Chandler, Nathaniell Clark, Richard Dole.

*Ipswich Deeds, vol. 3, page 162.*

ESTATE OF GEORGE ABBOT OF ROWLEY.

Marke Symonds appointed 28: 7: 1647, administrator of the estate of George Abott, late of Rowley. The will referred to General Court. *Ipswich Quarterly Court Records, vol. 1, page 10.*

Nuncupative will of George Abbott of Rowley sent here from General Court, 28: 10: 1647, ordered that it shall stand; and after paying legacies to the children, the remainder shall remain in hands of Marke Simons of Ipswich, according to the will, to be disposed of to the children, who are to choose their guardians, etc. Marke Simons to have 4d. and the wintering of two cows. *Salem Quarterly Court Records, vol. 2, page* 224.

Inventory taken Aug. 30, 1647, by Sebastan Brigham, Thomas Barker, Mathew Boyes and James (his mark C) Barker: all his aparell, 1li. 10s.; in silver, 1li. 3s.; one Gold Ringe, 10s.; two greene Coverings, 16s.; one featherbed & two pillows & one Bolster, 1li. 9s.; three flock bolsters, one Coverlett & one Blankett, 11s.; two flocke beds, 6s.; seaven Sheets, two tablecloths, Seven pillowbers, nine napkins, two Aprons, 4 handkerchifes with other small linen, 4li. 6s.; fower Course Sheetes, 7s.; one Trunke, 5s.; two hogsheads & one Barrell, 5s.; one keiler, 1s.; one kilne haire, 4s.; one whip saw & one Croscutt saw, 8s.; two black Gownes, 12s.; one Satten Capp & white thred, 4s.; one pillowbeere & other lininge, 5s.; one Steele mill, 1li. 10s.; one Steele Trape, 10s.; three brand Irons, fower wedges, one fire shovell & other Iron, 1li.; two tramels, one bar of Iron & one Gridiron, 8s.; thirty eight pound of pewter, 1li. 12s.; one silver ringe & spoone, 5s.; two friing pans, 4s.; one brasse pott & one Iron pott, 15s.; three kettles, 1li. 2s.; one Skillet & two Chafing dishes, 3s.; one warming pan, 3s.; three paire of Scales & weights, 9s.; one brasse morter & pestle, 5s.; one Skimer, 1s.; one paire of horse bits with buckles & furrells, 3s. 6d.; one nest of boxes with things in them, 5s.; one Little Gun with bandelers, 5s.; one Spitt & one brush bill, 3s.; one head peice & one axe with some other things, 5s.; one bushell & half of oatemeale and one Tub, 7s.; one Chest & one Churne, 3s. 6d.; one bowle, fowre trayes & one tunnell, 4s.; one flockbed, two Curtains & one pillow, 10s.; one drinking pott & one Jugg, 3s.; three Leather bottles, 5s.; thirty bookes, 1li. 10s.; the dwelling house & land with the Apurtenances, 30li.; two black Steeres, 9li.; two younger Steeres, 6li.; one yearling Steere, 2li.; one Calfe, 1li.; two Cowes, 9li.; all the Corne & hay, 8li.; one Sow & three piggs, 1li. 10s.; Some Land at Newbery, 2li.; one yoake & chaine, 4s.; one brasse Ladle, 8d.; all the ffowle aboute the house, 1s.; all the hops & flaxe, 7s. 6d.; one Chaire & two Cushions, 3s.; one Short Sithe & old Iron, 2s. 6d.; total, 95li. 2s. 8d. Debt owing to the deceased, of Steven Kent of Newbery, 7s. *Ipswich Deeds, vol.* 1, *leaf* 61.

Humphry Rayner (also Reiner) and Thomas Mighill were chosen guardians by the children of Georg Abott, late of Rowly, 28 : 1 : 1648. The overplus of Georg Abbot's children's estate is left in the hands of Marke Symonds, executor of Georg Abott. *Ipswich Quarterly Court Records, vol. 1, page 13.*

Guardians, Humfrey Reyner and Thomas Mighell, confirmed by Salem and this court. They acknowledged the receipt of 53li., the children's portions, divided as follows: George, 16li., Nehemyah, 21li., Thomas, jr., 16li. *Ipswich Quarterly Court Records, vol. 2, leaf 12.*

On Mar. 28, 1654, Mr. Reyner presented Nehemiah Abbott and Thomas Abbott, jr., who acknowledged that they had received satisfaction from Mr. Humphry Reyner and Thomas Mighill, guardians to the children of Georg Abbott, for their portions. Thomas Abbott, sr., and Nehemiah Abbott testified that their brother, George Abbott, had satisfaction also. The guardians were discharged. *Ipswich Quarterly Court Records, vol. 1, page 45.*

### ESTATE OF RICHARD BARTLETT OF NEWBURY.

" The testimony of william Titcombe & Anthony Somersby concerning the last will & testament of Richard Bartlett sen of Newbury deceased the 20[th] of May 1647 About a month before he deceased we being with him & two of his sonnes being p[r]sent he being very ill & had bene weake all the spring finding in himselfe that he was not like to continew he desired vs to take notice what his mind was concerning that small estate he had how he would dispose of it. As for his sonne John Bartlett he had done for him more then for the rest of his children & at that tyme did not dispose any to him. To his sonne Christofer Bartlett he did bequeath the debt which latly he had borrowed of him which was five bushells of wheat if soe be it should please the lord to take him away at this sicknesse or ells if he should lye longe vizitted his necessity would require that he should pay it againe. To his daughter Johan wife of william Titcombe he bequeathed one paire of new shoes for herselfe & her foure daughters each one a paire of shoes And all the rest of his goods & chattells that were not disposed of he bequeathed wholly to his sonne Richard Bartlett whom he made his sole heire & executor. I Anthony Somersby the next day Pswaded him to give somthing to his sonne John Bartlett his answere was that he had bene with his sonne Richard Batlet this twelve month & all that he had was to little for to give him seing he had bene weake & ill & could doe little but lay vpon his sonnes charges; besides said he if I should lye longe sick I shalbe chargable to Richard & not to any of the rest and for John I have done more form$^r$ly yet I will give him the warming pan and vpon his sonnes request he gaue him a great bible: this he spake being in pfect memory & soe continewed to the last breath.

"I Edward Rawson wittnes to the last pt of the will that I often heard the said Richard Bartlett sen (the tyme of his sicknesse) say he would & did give all to his sonne Richard Bartlett 29$^{th}$ Septemb 1647. This was before the witness

Edward Rawson."

The first part of this will proved 28: 7: 1647, by Mr. Rawson, the whole by Anthony Somersby. *Ipswich Deeds, vol. 1, leaf 25.*

Inventory of estate of Richard Bartlett of Newbury, shoemaker, deceased May 21, 1647, taken by William (his mark) Titcombe, John Batlett & Anthony Somersby: in leather, 2li. 15s.; his wearing apparrell, 1li. 4s.; 2 paire of canvas sheets, 1li. 1s.; one old shirt & a napkin, 2s. 1d.; one old coverlet & a blanket, 1li.; one old flock bed & a bolster, 1li.; one old great kettle, 12s.; one paire of pott hangers, 1s. 4d.; one brasse pott, 10s.; two little kettles, 5s.; one small brasse morter, 7s. 6d.; one warming pan, 6s.; one great bible, 12s.; some other small books, 7s.; one Cow, 4li. 5s.; one heiffer, 1li. 15s.; his working geare and lasts, 4s.; old pewter platters and an old pint pott, 2s.; one spit & frying pan, 3s. 6d.; one small muskett, 9s.; one paire of bellowes, 1s.; bushell bagg, 2 old chests, a stone bottle & a halfe bushell bagg, 5s.; his debts, 4li. 19s.; in silv., 2li. 5s. *Ipswich Deeds, vol. 1, leaf 26.*

### Estate of Matthew Whipple of Ipswich.

"Month 3: day 7: 1645. In the name of god amen. I Mathew whipple of Ipswich in New England being by reason of p$^r$sent sicknesse much increasing vpon me seriously admonished of my mortality yet through the mercy of god inioying pfect memory & good vnderstanding after humble acknowledgm$^t$ of the great pacience & rich mercy of god to me a most vnworthy siner all my life longe and the Comending of my spirit to his grace in Jesus Christ my body after my decease to Comly buriall in the earth out of which it was

taken in hope of resurreccon vnto eternall life and my deare
children to the everlasting blessing of their heavenly father
I doe hereby dispose of that estate which the lord hath gra-
tiously given vnto me as followeth vnto my eldest sonne
John Thre score pounds to my sonne Mathew forty pounds
To my sonne Joseph forty pounds vnto my daughter Mary
Twenty pounds vnto my daughter Anna Twenty pounds
vnto my daughter Elizabeth Twenty pounds vnto our rev
Elders m$^r$ Nathaniel Rogers and m$^r$ John Norton to either of
them forty shillings To the poore of Ipsw$^{ch}$ forty shillings.
In case my estate be found to exceed these sumes the one
halfe thereof I give to my eldest sonne John the other halfe
to my two yonger sonnes. In case my estate fall short of the
aforesaid sumes the de*cuct* shalbe out of the porcons of all my
children equally my will is that none of my children shalbe
disposed of in marriage or service but by the approbacon &
consent of the p$^r$sent Elders & my deare brother John whipple I leave the disposing of my three sonnes to the care of
my executors whom I name & desire to be m$^r$ Nathan: Rogers
m$^r$ Norton m$^r$ Robert Payne & my brother John Whipple.
In wittnes hereof I have set to my hande the day & yeare
above written."  Mathew whipple

Witness: John Norton, John whipple.

"Month the 9$^{th}$ 13$^{th}$ day 1646 I having by the pvidence
of god changed my estate by marriage since the making of
the writing above I doe give vnto my wife Rose the sume of
ten pounds to be paid her p$^r$sently after my decease leaving
vnto her all the goods or estate that she had before marriage
And this being done I will that the writing above should
stand in full force & vertue as my last will & Testament;
further declaring my meaning to be that the porcons of my
sonnes be paid at the age of one & Twenty yeares and my
daughters at the age of Twenty: and the mann$^r$ of the disposing my estate for the best accomplishment of the intent
of my will I comitt vnto my above-named executo$^{rs}$ or any
other matter that may be forgotten to be by them ordered
and because they may be removed or diminished by death or
any other departure I hereby give them power that the remayning numb shall choose a supply in that case to fill vp
the numb except he that is removed shall appoynt an other
in his roome. And this whole writing to wit that part that
was write the 7$^{th}$ day of the 3 month 1645 and this addicon
I make & declare to be my last will & Testament being of

THE PROBATE RECORDS OF ESSEX COUNTY. 89

good vnderstanding & memory setting herevnto my hand."
his mark<br>Mathew whipple
Witness: Theophilus wilson, Thomas Knowlton.
Proved 28 : 7 : 1647, by Theophilus Wilson and Thomas Knowlton.

Inventory taken the 24 : 9 : 1646, by Robert Payne and John Whipple: In the hall: three musketts, three paire of bandaleeres, three swords, two rests, 3li.; one fowling peece, 1li.; a costlett, pike & sword, 1li.; one rapier, 5s.; one halberd and one bill, 4s.; thre brasse potts waying 68li. at 9d., 2li. 11s.; one old brasse pott, 2s. 6d.; 5 kettels and a potlid, waying 58li. at 16d., 3li. 17s. 4d.; one copper waying 40li., 2li.; 5 posnetts, 12s.; 85 peeces of pewter waying 147li. at 16d., 9li. 16s.; 4 pewter candlesticks, 10s.; 2 pewter salts, 5s.; 2 pewter potts, one cupp and a bottle, 4s. 6d.; one pewter flagon, 7s.; 21 brasse alchimic spoones att 2d. ob [4s. 4d. ob. *in margin*] the spoone, 4li. 4s. of.; 9 pewter spoones at 18d. p dosen, 1s. 1d.; one pestel & morter, 5s.; 5 chaffeing dishes and a skimmer, 14s.; 7 peeces of latten, 7s.; 2 paire of cobirons, one fire pan, 2 paire of tongs, one fire forke & one fire iron, wayeing 58 at 4d., 19s. 4d.; 4 spitts waying 20li. at 6d., 10s.; 2 warming panns, 14s.; 2 iron dripping panns, 6s.; one silv. bowle & 2 silv. spoones, 3li. 3s.; one paire cobirons with brasses, 6s.; 71li. of new iron at 5d. a li., 1li. 12s. 6d.; 38li. in wedges & one hare at 4d. a li., 14s. 3d.; 4 hoops 24li. at 5d. 10s.; 55 li. of old iron at 3d., 13s. 9d.; 7 howes & 2 spades, 10s.; 29 bookes, 4li. 8s. 6d.; 6 dozen of trenchers, 3s.; 4 trayes & a platter, 5s.; 3 Juggs, 3s. 6d.; one earthen salt & 1 pan & potts, 3s.; 3 cheese mootes & two cheese breads, 3s.; one Cowle, one paile, two bowles, 4 dishes, 5s. 6d.; one halfe bushell, peck & halfe peck, 4s. 6d.; one bowle & 3 sives, 4s. 6d.; 3 barrells, 7s.; 2 firkins, one chirne, 4s.; 2 frying panns & one trevitt, 11s. 8d.; 2 bottles & 2 jacks, 4s.; 2 spades, 8s.; 2 brode axes & 4 narrow axes, 18s.; 2 mattocks, one spitt & a spoone, 10s.; 4 brode hatchetts, 2 bills & a beetle & a masons ham., 13s.; 2 iron dibbles, a trowel and shovel tippe, 2s. 6d.; 3 payer of tramels, one iron barre, 12s.; one paire of bellowes, one grediron, one paire of sheers & one smoothing iron wth one heater, 6s.; 2 paire of pott hooks, 1 brasse ladill, 3s. 4d.; 2 keilers, 4s.; 2 formes, one dresser, 2 chaires, one long boarded chest, 11s. 6d.; one crow, one andiron, one mathook, one fireforke waying 24li. at 4d., 8s. In the parlor: one joyned table, 3 chests, 1li. 12s.;

one chest with glasse, 2li.; one paire of cobirons wth fire pann & tongs, 12s.; one clock, 1li.; 4 chest locks & 4 box locks & 6 paire of joints, 7s. 6d.; one stamell bearing cloth, 1li.; one baies bearing cloth, 8s.; two cloakes, 3li.; one old coate, 10s.; one sute, 1li.; one dublett & jackett, 1li. 4s.; one leather sute, 1li. 6s. 8d.; one leather dublett, 14s.; 2 hatts, 7s.; 2 paire of gloves, 2s. 4d.; 2 p of stockins, 4s.; 3 paire of sheetes, 3li. 10s.; 2 paire of sheetes, 1li. 4s.; 3 paire of sheetes, 1li. 2s.; one diap. table cloth & 2 dozen diap. napkins, 2li. 6s. 8d.; 2 table clothes, 1li.; one little table cloth, 7s. 6d.; two old table clothes, 4s.; 21 napkins at 9s. p doz., 15s. 9d.; one paire pillow beeres, 6s. 8d.; 2 paire of pillow beeres, 8s.; one laced cubbord cloth & one fringed, 8s.; one laced cubbord cloth, 6s.; 4 towells, 6s.; 3 shirts, 1li.; 4 remnants of holland & sackcloth, 12s. 6d.; one silke girdle, 2s. 6d.; one feather bedd, one bolster, 9 pillows, waying 106li. at 22d., 5li. 6s.; one paire blanketts, one coverlett, 2li. 10s.; 3 flockbedds & 3 flock bolsters, 5li. 8s.; one flockbedd & bedstead and one bolster, 1li.; one paire of sheets & one pe. pillow beeres, 6s. In the chamb. over the parlor: 3 flock bedds & 3 bolsters, 4li. 6s.; 5 blanketts, 1li.; 4 old coverletts, 1li. 10s.; one rugg, 1li.; one paire of curtins & vallence, 1li. 5s.; one cupboard cloth, 4s.; 4 cushens, 3s.; one paire of curtins, 12s.; 7 Childrens blanketts, 7s.; one pillion cloth & foot stoole, 6s. 8d; 6 sithes, 6s.; 5 crosse cutt sawes, 18s.; 4 stock locks, 6s. 8d.; 3 garden rakes, 4s.; 2 adds, 2 hand sawes, a mattock, one ax & a spade, 18s.; 4 howes, 5s. 4d.; one vise, 10s.; one frow, one bill & a joyners saw, 6s.; 6 iron candlesticks, 12 chissells, 6 sickles & one dozen of augurrs & 3 shaves, 1li. 5s. 6d.; 3 old axes, 6 pitchforks, one iron peele wth other implements, 1li.; 2 bedsteeds & 2 bed lines, 14s.; 20 empty hoggsheads, 2li.; 2 linen wheeles & one cotton wheele & a baskett, 9s.; one bed line, one haire line & one cart rope, 6s.; one paire of great scales & 15 leaden waites, 1li. 4s.; 6 window curtaines, 1li.; 2 stooles & thre cushens, one paire of bellowes, cradle rugg, 16s.; one seller with glasses, 5s.; one trunk and 2 boxes, 8s.; 2 grindstones, 10s.; one plow, one cart, 1 slead, 1li. 12s.; 3 chaines, 2 shares, one coulter, 1li. 7s.; 3 yoakes, 9s.; six bullocks, 36li.; 3 cowes, 14li. 10s.; 4 heffers, 12li. 10s.; in corne, 11li. 7s. 6d.; his dwelling howse wth 4 acres of ground with a barne & other out howses, 36li.; a six acre lott, one 4 acre lott and six acres of marsh, 17li.; his farme contayning 160 acres of upland with meadow belonging to the same, contayning about

30 acres with a frame upon it, 36li. 10s.; six acres of marsh, with other wast ground adjoining thereunto, in all about 20 acres, 2li.; a harrow, 6s. 8d.; total, 287li. 2s. 1d.
*Ipswich Deeds, vol. 1, leaf* 28.

ESTATE OF RICHARD WOODMAN OF LYNN.

"The will of Richard woodman of the Towne of Lynn deseced as followeth Being spoken to by Nicholas ||Potter|| to make his will [he] said that hee would make his will and being asked by John Gillow too whome hee would giue his goods said that hee would giue fower pounds to the Elders of lynn fortie shilings apeece, and ||all|| the rest of his goods hee would giue to Joseph Redknap Richard moore and ||to|| his master John Gillowe, equally to either of them alike and y$^t$ Joseph Redknap he did make his exequtor. Witnesses to this will John Gillow & Richard moore witness that Joseph Redknap is the executor. John Gillow."

Order of court, allowing the will, signed by Henry Bartholomew. *Essex County Quarterly Court Files, vol. 1, leaf* 89.

Proved 30: 10: 1647, by John Gillo and Rich. Moore. Joseph Redknap swore to the inventory. *Salem Quarterly Court Records, vol. 2, page* 226.

ESTATE OF JOHN PRIDE OF SALEM.

John Pride of Salem died intestate, and his widow brought in an inventory of his estate, the last, 12m: 1647.

Court ordered distribution to his son, under twenty-one years, 8li., and two daughters, under eighteen years, 4li. each. The mother was to bring them up. House and land bought of Mr. Holgrave security. *Salem Quarterly Court Records, vol. 2, page* 225.

Inventory: One dwellinge house, one barne and worke house with foure Akers of land adjoyninge to it, 16li.; marsh and uplande grounde uppon the necke beinge the one halfe of that sometime belonginge to Mr. Holgraue, 8li. 15s.; one halfe aker of marsh and halfe an aker of upland, 1li. 10s.; two Cowes and one heighfer of two yeares old, 13li.; three Calves of this yeare, 3li.; one hogge and two shotts, 2li. 17s. 6d.; foure ewe gotes and 2 lambes, 2li.; one fether bed, one bolster, foure pillowes, one Rugge, one pr. blanketts, 5li.; two old Rugges, two course beds, one blanket and one bolster, 12s.; three pr. of sheetes, 1li. 13s. 4d.; for other smale lenen in the same chest, 1li. 10s.; bands and capps, 10s.;

wearinge apparrell, 6li.; one brass kettle, 1 lettle brass pott and one Iron pott, 1li. 4s.; thirtie and seaven dozzen of earthen ware, 4li. 12s. 6d.; warminge pann and three pewter cupps, 6s. 8d.; leade and other earthen ware, 1li. 7s.; a bible and other books and a glass, 12s.; two fryinge panns, 7s.; one Fowlinge peece, one muskett rest and sword, 2li. 10s.; a pr. of pot hookes and hangers, 7s.; foure Axes, a spade and a picke Axe, 14s.; two table boords, two chests, two boxes with chaires and stoole, 1li. 18d.; one bed steed and a trundle bedsteed, 10s.; fifteene Akers of Lande on Cape An side, 9li.; for wheate, barly, Pease and Indian Corne, 3li,; total, 88li. 16s. *Essex County Quarterly Court Files, vol. 1, leaf 88.*

### ESTATE OF RICHARD BAILEY OF ROWLEY.

" Rowley 15 of the last 1647. I Richard Baly sick in body but of perfect memory praysed be God doe ordeine and make this my last will and Testament first I comende my soule into the hands of God in faith of a ioyfull resurrection throw our Lord Jesus Christ And as concerning my outward estate ffrst my minde and || will is that all my || lawfull debts be paid and discharged. Ite my will is that fforty and tow pounds I giue vnto my sonn Joseph Baly but in case my wife should be with Child then my will is that the said sum of tow and forty pounds be deuided, and one third part thereof my other child shall haue it Item my will is that my Child shall haue a fether bedd in part of the saide portion also one Great Bible and Practicall Catachisme Ite my will and minde is that if my wife Edna Baly marry againe and hir husbande proue vnlouing to the Child or Children or wastefull then I giue power to my Brother James Baly and Micael Hobkinson with my wife hir Consent to take the Child with his portion from him and so to dispose of it for the Best behoofe of the children with my wifes consent Ite I giue my house and lott vnto my son Joseph Baly after my wife hir dissease Ite I giue to my Son tow stuffe Sutes of Cloaths and my best Coate, and a Cloath sute and my best hatt, and I giue to my Brother James Baly a great Coate one paire of buck lether Breches and a paire of Bootes one little Booke I giue to my nephew John Baly I giue vnto Thomas Palmer one Gray hatt one Cloath dublit and an old Jackit and a paire of Gray Breeches Ite I make my wife Edna Baly executrix of this my last will and Testament Memoradad and I giue eleuen shillings which is owing to me from Mr Rogers Ipswich and mr Johnson vnto the poore of the Towne." Rich baly.

Witness: Humfrey Reyner, willem Cavis.

Proved 28: 1: 1648, by Humphry Reynor, and 29: 1: 1648, by Jeames Bayley.

Inventory taken 23: 6: 1648, by Joseph Jewitt, Maxemillean Jewett and Mathew Boyes, allowed 27: 7: 1648: In monyes, 2li. 12s.; one Box and small things in it, 1li.; two stuffe sutes of Cloathes, 1li. 10s.; one Gray hatt, 10s.; one Cloath Suite, 1li. 10s.; one peece of fustian, 6s.; one Cloath Coate, 1li. 6s.; two Childes Mantles, 15s.; ticking for two boulsters, 10s.; one paire of Brasse Scales and weights, 6s. 6d.; two Couerletts & two Ruggs, 2li. 15s.; fiue Blanketts, 1li. 11s.; fiue Pillowes, 11s.; one feather bed tick, 7s.; one Brasse Pott & a Still, 1li. 19s.; a Parcell of old Cloathes, 1li.; a Bagg wt some Cotten woole, 12s.; a Bagg wt. Inke stuffe, 7s.; foure Cushings & a leather girdle, 5s.; an old Coate, 3s.; two Basketts wth six pounds of Cotton yarne, 15s.; in little stone potts, 4s.; two Bed Coords, 2s.; one Barrell, 1s.; one trough wt. Leather satchels & baggs, 14s.; one sword, 5s.; one Muskett wt. bandiliers, 1li.; one Brasse Morter & Pestill, 3s. 4d.; one Lanterne, 1s.; in Brasse, 3li. 12s.; one Iron Pott, 12s.; one Fouleing peece, 15s.; in Puter, 1li. 18s.; one Case of Bottles, 5s.; a Parcell of Bookes, 2li. 12s. 6d.; two Chests, 11s.; fiue Cushings, 7s.; in Iron tooles, 1li. 14s.; in milke vessell, 9s. 6d.; a paire of Bellowes, 6d.; a stoole, a Box and a Dreaping Pan, 10s.; one dwelling house, 10li.; one Barne, 5li.; broken up land, meadows & Comons, 14li.; in Corne and hay, 8li.; in Cattle, 22li. 10s.; in Swine, 1li. 10s.; in Linen, 3li. 15s.; three Temses, 3s.; one feather bed wt. boulsters & other bedding, 4li. 5s.; a Churne and Iron Pott wt. some Puter, and two wheeles, 17s.; total, 106li. 8s. 10d.

*Essex County Quarterly Court Files, vol. 1, leaf 98.*

For explanation of the order given by the court Oct. 27, 1648, in answer to a petition received of Edney Bayly, widow, of Rowley, and final determination of the case, it is ordered May 3, 1649, that the 46li. given by Wm. Halsteed to her son, Joseph Bayly, by Richard Bayly, deceased, remain in the hands of Ezekiell Northin, her present husband, until he shall be twenty one, and then so much be paid him as the will of Wm. Halsteed appoints; that Joseph's portion out of his father's estate shall be 41li., which is two thirds of the estate, and shall also remain in the hands of Ezekiel Northin until he is fourteen years. Ezekiel Northin to give security to the next Ipswich court. *Mass. Bay Colony Records, vol. 3, page* 148.

Joseph Bayly of Rowley acknowledges the receipt from Ezekiell Northend of Rowley, his father-in-law, of " all my whole portion given me by the will of my ffather Richard Bayly which portion was ordered by the Generall Court & apoynted to be forty one pound or there abouts which was two thirds of the estate, and alsoe of a legasie of nyne pounds foure shillings, given by my unckle william Halsted, also all rents of my whole portion and of the aforesayd legasie since I was of the age of forteene years." Dated Nov. 14, 1667. Witness: Phillip Nellson, Elizabeth Nellson, ffrancis Tildisleg. *Ipswich Deeds, vol.* 3, *page* 78.

### ESTATE OF FRANCIS LAMBERT OF ROWLEY.

" The last will of ffranciss Lambertt of Rowley made upon the 20th day of september: 1647: Ips I giue my soule and bodye to the allmightye god: tt I giue vnto my wife my house; and land ioyneinge therevnto with six acers of land lately bought of Joseph Juitt: as alsoe all the meadowes and gates which doth belonge vnto the sayd house; all which I giue vnto hir dureing hir naturall life tt I giue vnto my eldest sonne all the aforesayd house and land with gates and meadowes after the death of Jane my wife: provided that my eldest sonn John doe pay vnto Ann Lambert Jonathan and Gersome Lambert (all beinge my Childeren) fiue pounds to bee equally devided amongest them tt: It is my will that Jane my wife and Thomas Barker shalbe the executers of the rest of my estate as alsoe to haue the ordering and disposeinge of my childeren : except my sonne Thomas which I freely giue vnto my Brother Thomas Barker to order and dispose of tt I giue vnto my daughter Ann fortye shillings to be payed by my executers ether att marriage or when shee is att eighteene yeeres of age: tt: In Case my sonne John should dye before the time come wherein he should be possessed of my house and land then it is my will : that my sonne Jonathan shall haue it; but if by providence it be soe ordered that my sonne Jonathan be brought vp att schoole and soe pceed to be a scholler then my house and land with gates and meadowes shall be my sonne Gersomes."

[No signature.]

Witness: Edwarde Carlton, Thomas Barker.

Proved 28 : 1 : 1648, by Edward Carlton and Thomas Barker. *Essex County Probate Files, Docket* 16,178.

## Estate of Thomas Firman of Ipswich.

Inventory of Mr. Thomas Firman, deceased, received April 13, 1648, and his widow Sarah Firman appointed administratrix. *Ipswich Quarterly Court Records, vol.* 1, *page* 13.

Inventory taken 10 : 2 : 1648, by Edward Browne, Thomas Byshop and Rob[er]t Lord : In the Chamber : one Bedsted, curtaynes & Vallans, 1li. 10s. ; A small fetherbed & boulster & one pillowe, 2li. ; a Coverlett & Rugg & Matt, 1li. 10s. ; A Trundlebed fflockbed & boulster, 2 blankets & an ould rugg, 1li. 10s. ; a payre of darnicle Curtaines & Vallens, 12s. ; A small Trunke, 4s. ; A Baskett, 1s. ; one ould Trunke & 2 ould boxes, 4s ; one halfheaded Beadsteed & Coarde, 6s. ; one ffetherbed & Coverlett, 4li. ; one Trunke, 12s. ; one Chest of boxes & an ould box, 12s. ; hookes and Eyes, 3s. In the Parlor : A Table & 3 Joyne stooles, 9s. ; 6 Cushions, 12s. ; 2 Chayres, 4s. ; A paire of Brasse Scales & Brasse wayghts & 14li. Lead waight, 17s. ; 6 Pewter platters, one bason & other pewter, in all aboute 38li., 2li. 4s. ; eleven bookes, 1li. 15s. ; A paire of Andirons, 10s. ; 2 greate Chests, 1li. ; A remnant of stuffe, 6 boxes & 8 thred lases & some small things, 8s. ; 7 silver Spoones & 2 broken ones, 2li. 5s. ; Seven fflaxen Sheetes at 15s. p paire, 2li. 12s. 6d. ; one paire of Sheetes, 1li. ; 2 paire ould Sheetes, 14s. ; 2 paire Pillowbeeres, 15s. ; one Course Pillowbeere, 2s. ; 3 Table Clothes, 1li. 2s. ; 2 dozen & twoe napkins, 1li. 4s. ; 3 dozen of Trenchers, 1s. 8d. In the kitchinge : A Copper bakeing pan & a fish plate, 16s. ; 2 fryinge pans, 5s. ; A dripping pan, 5s. ; 5 Brasse Panns, 1li. 13s. 4d. ; A Brasse Pott & 3 kettles, 3li. ; one Iron Pott & 2 p pothookes & 2 Tramells, 1li. ; An ould warmeing pan, 4s. ; A Brasse Skimer & Ladle, 2s. ; 3 Posnetts, 10s. ; A Morter & Pestle, 4s. ; 2 Iron Candlesticks, 1s. ; A paire Andyrons, fire pan & tonges, 15s. ; Earthen ware & wooden dishes, 7s. ; one Iron peele & Iron spade, 4s. ; Powder blew. 3s. ; one Spitt & Gridiron, 3s. 6d. ; 2 barrells, a Powdering Tub & other Lumber, 16s. ; A wheele & 5 ould Chaires, 7s. ; 2 Smoothing Irons, 2s. ; 2 haire Syves & a tiffeny sive, 3s. ; an Axe & an Iron Beame & wooden Scales, 10s. ; An ould Sawe, 1s. 6d. ; A Blacke Cowe, 4li. 5s. The Dwelling House, 15li. The howse yt was Goodman Procter's, 18li. 10s. ; one Hogge, 13s. 4d. ; 2 Pyllows & a cradle Rugg, 6s. 8d. In Debts to be gathered up aboute 9li.; total, 89li. 15s. 6d. *Ipswich Deeds, vol.* 1, *leaf* 46.

### Estate of John Balch of Salem.

"The last will & tesem$^t$ of John Balch of salem bearing date the 15$^{th}$ day of may 1648  I John Balch sicke in bodie but in pfect memorie doe make this my last will & testam$^t$ in manner & forme following my debts paid & funeral expences discharged those goods w$^{ch}$ god hath gyven me it is my will to dispose of them as followeth: Imprimis I gyve vnto Annis Balch my loveing wife the Roome newly built w$^{th}$ twentie Akrs of land of w$^{ch}$ 4 akres to be in till and also 4 Akres of meadowe w$^{th}$ some pt of the barne to lay in her fruits and halfe of the great fruit trees for & during the life of the said Annis  Itm I gyve vnto my said wife my best bed w$^{th}$ all Conuenienc furniture there vnto belonging & one fourth pt of all my houshould goods except the rest of my beding & alsoe 2 Cowes by name Reddie & Cherie & one yearling heaffer  ffurther my will is that soe long as my said wife shall liue my said sonnes shall sowe or plant 2 akres of the afforesaid 4 akers for my said wife for the term of 7 years and after thatt my sonne Beniamin shall doe all himselfe  Item I gyue & bequeth to benimin Balch my oldest sonne one halfe of my farme to him & his heires for euer as also twoe yoake of oxen 1 Cowe one third of my yong Cattall & of the mare Coalt w$^{th}$ one fourth pt of my houshould goods & halfe the great fruit trees & after the decease of my said wyfe my will is that the said Beniamin shall haue them all w$^{th}$ all those he hath planted himselfe.

Item my will is thatt all my Corne growing vpon the ground shall be equallie deuided into 4 equally pts amongst my wife & Children  Itm I gyve vnto John Balch my second sonne one fourth pt of my farme and one yoake of oxen one third of my yong Cattell & mare Coalt one fourth of my houshould goods & halfe of all the yong aple trees vndispost of and one Cowe  I gyve to Freeborne Balch my yongest sonne one fourth pt of my ffarme one youke of oxen & one Cow I bred vp for him  one third of the yong Cattell ‖ & one third of the mare ‖ & one fourth of my houshould goods & halfe the yong Aple trees betwixt him & his brother John equallie to be diuided & further my will is that Annis my wife & Beniamin my sonne shall be executo$^{rs}$ to this my last will & testamt & my loveing frends John Portor & william woodberie shall be ouerseers of the same  in wittnes herof I haue herevnto put my hand the day and year aboue written."  Jo. Balch.

Witness: Peter Palfrey, Nicholas Patch and Jefferie Massey.

Proved 28: 4: 1648 by Peter Palfree and Jefferie Massey. *Essex Co. Quarterly Court Files, vol. 1, leaf 99.*

Inventory taken by John Porter, Peter Palfrey, Jefferie Massey and Nicholas Patch: [Ap]parell, 51li. 10s.; dwelling house & barne, 16li.; one farme of medow & upland containege 210 Ackers, 56li.; 9 Ackers of whete, 9li.; 6 Ackers of indian, 6li.; one Acker of ——, 1li.; 2 Ackers of barley, 2li.; 5 yoaks of oxen at 10, 11 & 12 each yoke, 33li.; a yoke of Steares, 8li. 10s.; 3 cowes & 2 heffers, 22li.; 2 yearelinge heffers, 4li.; a yearlinge mare fole, 5li.; wheles, chaines & yokes wth other implements of husbantry, 3li.; Frute trees in the Orchad, 10li.; 5 yeards & ½ of broadcloth, 3li. 6s.; 11 yeards of sarge, 2li. 15s.; 22 yeards of linin, 1li. 2s.; 13 yeards of cotten cloth, 1li. 14s. 8d.; 2 fether beads, 2 bolsters & 2 pilloes, 5li. 5s.; 1 paire of sheats, 8s.; 2 bead couerings, 16s.; one Rugg, 10s.; one bead & bolster, 1li. 10s.; one blankett & coveringe, 8s.; one paire of shees, 5s.; 4 shetes & ½, 1li. 10s.; 2 pillobeares, 4s.; 6 napkins, 6s.; 2 beadsteads, 12s.; 2 tables, 7s.; 2 tronks, 6s.; one chest, 5s.; one warmeinge pan, 6s.; yearne, flakes & hempe, 1li. 4s.; chares & stoles, 3s.; 12 bushells of indian corne, 1li. 16s.; 4 bushells of malte, 16s.; one winopett & 3 bages, 14s.; tubes & 6 barells & other wooden ware, 1li.; 3 hides, 15s.; 2 old chestes, 2s.; tooles & old ireron, 1li.; one bras pan & 2 bras cettles, 1li.; a littell bras pott, 2 ireron pottes, 1li.; peuter, 10s.; 2 muskets, one fowllinge peace with other armes, 2li.; 2 ——, 4s.; one ——, 10s.; ——, 10s.; ——, 5s.; one cannoe, 10s.; chease & chease pres, 1li.; one hog, 1li. 6s. 8d.; severall books, 12s.; one calfe, 1li.; total, 220li. 13s. 4d. Benjamin Balch, executor, 22: 2: 1679, added five acres of meddow to the inventory. *Essex Co. Quarterly Court Files, vol. 1, leaf* 100.

### ESTATE OF JOHN JACKSON OF IPSWICH.

Administration on the estate of John Jackson granted 26: 7: 1648, to his widow, Kathren Jackson. To pay her son, John Jackson, 14li. at the age of twenty-one, and to the five daughters 6li. each at the age of twenty years or at marriage. The widow to have the remainder for the education of the children, and "hir husband to be posesed of the whole estate presently to bring up the children," giving security for payment of the children's portions in corn or cattle. *Ipswich Quarterly Court Records, vol. 1, leaf 14.*

Copy of inventory taken 18: 7: 1648, by Theophilus Wilson

and John Knowlton: A howse & barne & the ground neare about it, 25li.; a planting lott all broke up contayning 6 acres, 10li.; 26 acres of upland at Egipt River, 6li. 10s.; 6 acres of meadow at west meadowes, 2li.; 6 or 8 acres of meadow by Chebaccoe, 1li.; 3 Cowes, 12li. 10s.; one yearling heiffer, 2li.; one hogg, 1li.; 2 flockbeds wth 2 bowlsters, 2li.; 3 fether pillowes, 12s.; one flockbed & bowlster, 12s.; 3 old blanketts & an old dornix coverlett, 16s.; 2 old greene ruggs, 1li. 5s.; one bedsteed and Cord, 16s.; 3 curtens & valence, 10s.; 2 paire of of fine sheets, 2li. 18s.; 3 paire of course sheets, 1li. 8s.; 4 pillowbeers, 1li.; one table cloth & eleven napkins, 1li. 8s.; 2 pillowbeers, 3s.; one halfe headed bedstead, 6s.; 4 chests, 1li.; 7s.; 2 boxes, one glasse case, 8s.; one cubbard, 8s.; one side bed for a child, 2s.; one table, 5s.; 5 chaires & a stoole, 7s.; 30li. of pewter, 1li. 10s.; one brasse pott, 10s.; one warming pan, a skillet, chaffing dish & scum., 9s.; a kettle, 7s.; a frying pan & morter, 4s.; an iron pott & kettle, 1li.; 2 pott hangers, one paire pott hooks, 4s.; one paire of andirons, one paire of tongs, one fire shovell, spitt, dripping pan, 11s.; 3 keelers, 5 trayes, 13s.; a bucking tubb, a powdering tubb & a buckett, 7s.; one longe saw, a hand saw, a drawing knife, 6s. 6d.; 2 axes, 2 augers, one paire sheers, a pressing iron, 7s. 6d.; a copper pott, 2s.; one trevett, one wedge, 3s.; total, 83li. 6s. 6d. *Ipswich Deeds, vol. 1, leaf 43.*

### ESTATE OF JOHN JARRAT OF ROWLEY.

"Rowley 11th 1647 I John Jarrat sicke in body but of perfect memory (praysed be God) doe ordaine and make this my last will and Testament: ffirst I comit my soule vnto God through Jesus Christ: As concerning my outward estate my will and minde is that ffirst all my debts being discharged and paide I giue vnto my Daugter Elisabeth Ten pounds out of my Goods and Lande and in Case my wife marry againe, I giue my Daughter three pounds six shillings eight pence more Ite if my wife Susanna Jarrat be now with Child I giue vnto my Child ten pounds but in case my wife marry againe three pounds six shillings eight pence more Ite all the rest of my Lande Goods and Cattel I giue vnto my wife Susanna Jarrat whom I make executrix of this my last will and Testament dated the eleuenth day of the ii month 1647."

his hand<br>John *John* Jarrat

Witness: Humfrey Reyner, Thomas mighell.
Proved in Ipswich court 27: 7: 1648 by the witnesses. *Essex Co. Probate Files, Docket* 14,789.

Inventory taken 12mo: 1647, by Edward Carlton, Humfrey Reyner and Thomas Mighill: His apparill, 5li.; Corne of the Grounde, 1li. 10s.; one paire of oxen, 12li.; two Cowes, 8li. 10s.; one stare, 4li.; two heffers, 7li.; one hog, 16s.; pewther, 36 peices, 2li. 10s.; 2 brass pots, 1li. 6s. 8d.; 3 brasse ketles, 2li.; 3 brasse skellits, 6s.; one Iron ketle, 6s.; one warming pan, 6s.; brasse Candelsticks, one morter, 8s.; 2 fether Beds, 3 boulsters, 6li.; five pillows, 1li.; a bed, two boulsters, 13s. 4d.; 3 bed Coverings, one Rug, 3li. 10s.; two paire blankits, 1li. 6s. 8d.; one paire Curtaines, 14s.; 10 paire of sheets, 5li.; 12 table napkins, 12s.; 4 pillow beares, 2 Towels, one Table Cloath, 13s. 4d.; tow Chists, 16s. 6d.; one trunke, 3s. 4d.; one table, 13s. 4d.; two Beds ticks, 10s.; 4 Chares, 5s.; one paire Hande Irons, 5s.; one paire tongs & fire shovels, 5s.; the Recken hooks & some small things, 4s.; 4 silver spoones, one Jug tipt with silver and one pott, 6s.; total, 69li. 16s. 2d. *Essex Quarterly Court Files, vol. 1, leaf* 102.

### Estate of Edmund Ingalls of Lynn.

"August 28. Anno Dom: 1648. I Edmund Ingalls of Linne being of perfect memory comit my soule to God, my body to the grave, and dispose of my Earthly goods in this wise, ffirstly I make my wife Ann Ingalls sole Exectrix: leauing my house & houslot together with ye Stock of Cattle & Corne w$^{th}$ her. Likewise I leaue Kathrine Skipper w$^{th}$ my wife. Item. I bequeath to Robert my sonne & heire, foure pound to be payd in two yeers time by my wife either in Cattle, or Corne; likewise I bequeath to him || or his heires || my house & houslot after the decease of my wife. Likewise I bequeath to Elizabeth my daughter twenty shillings to be payd by my wife in a heifer calf in two yeers time after my decease. Likewise to my daughter Faith wife to Andrew Allin I bequeath two yeerling calues, and injoyne my wife to pay to him forty shillings debt in a yeers time after my decease. Likewise to my Sonne John I bequeath the house & ground that was Jerimy fitts lying by the Meeting house only out of it the sd John is to pay w$^{th}$in foure yeers foure pound to my sonne Samuel and the ground to be his security: further I leaue w$^{th}$ the sd John that three Acres land he hath in England fully to possesse & Enjoy. Likewise I giue to Sarah my daughter, wife to william Bitnar my two Ewes. Likewise to Henry my sonne I giue the house that I bought of Goodman west, & Six acres of ground lying to it, & three acres of marsh ‖ ground ‖ lying at Rumly Marsh, and this the sd Henry shall possesse in two yeers after my decease, Only out of this the sd Henry Shall pay to Samuel my Sonne foure pound w$^{th}$in two yeers after he Enters upon it. Likewise I bequeath to Samuel my Sonne Eight pound w$^{ch}$ is to be discharged as above in the proomisses. Lastly I leaue w$^{th}$ mary the heifer Calfe that formerly she enjoyed and leaue her to my wife for future dowry. Finally I appoint Francis Ingalls my brother, & Francis Dane my sonne in Law overseers of my will, and order that those things that haue no particular Exemption in the will mentioned be taken away presently after my decease: I intreat my overseers to be helpful to my wife for ordering these matters."

his mark<br>Edmund X Ingalls.<br>his mark

Witness: William Morton, Francis Dane, Francis 6 Ingols.

Proved 14: 9: 1648 by Francis Ingalls, and 27: 4: 1649 by William Morton. *Essex Co. Quarterly Court Files, vol. 1, leaf* 103.

Inventory taken by Edward Burchum, Henry Collins and Francis (his mark) Ingils: One payer of oxen, 12li.; too Steares, 8li.; one oxe, 5li.; thre Cowes, 11li.; fouer yearlings & advantage, 5li. 10s.; one calfe, 1li.; one mare, 10li.; too ewe Sheepe, 3li.; too hoges & too piges, 2li.; hay, 4li.; Coren, 6li.; plow yoke & cheanes, 1li.; hempe & flax in the bune, 1li.; one bede with the furnituer, 4li.; one bed with the furnituer, 1li.; one trundell bed, 3s. 4d.; one bed in the chamber, 1li. 10s.; thre payer of Shetes, 1li. 4s.; a tabele cloth & too napkines, 4s.; one chiste, 6s.; thre lininge wheles, 5s.; one tube, 1s.; one carpette, 10s.; purse & aparell, 1li. 10s.; pote hooks & keckines, 10s.; thre brase kettels, 10s.; puter, 16s.; wooden ware, 4s.; two gunes, 1li.; spite, tonges & dripinge pan, 5s.; table, chare & stooles, 10s.; a broylinge Ieren, 6d.; an ax & ould Ieron & a too hand saw, 15s.; thre bibels, 10s.; one beare barill & other hushellments, 5s.; house & lands, 50li.; total, 135li. 8s. 10d. Debts and legacies to be paid out of the estate: To Mr. Leader, 1li. 16s.; to Mr. Sauage, 1li. 12s; to the kow keeper, 1li. 5s.; to Kather Skeper, 50li.; to John Hud, 10s.; to marke graues, 8s.; to Robert Driuer, 5s.; to Mr. Emery, 15s.; to Mr. Whightinge, 8s.; att Ipswitch, 11s.; to Joseph Armatage, 14s. 4d.; a Shoomaker, 12s.; to Mr. *Jobitt*, 1li. 2s.; to Mr. Kinge, 1li.; total, 60li. 18s. 4d. Legacies: To Roborte Ingols, his sonne, 4li.; to Elizabeth, his daughter, 1li.; to Faith, his daughter, 3li.; to John Ingols, his sone, 13li. 10s.; to Sarah, his daughter, 3li.; to Henry Ingols, 8li.; to Samwell Ingols, 8li.; Mary Ingols lefte to her mother the executrix for her porchon; total, 40li. 10s. *Essex Co. Quarterly Court Files, vol. 1, leaf 104.*

### ESTATE OF ALLEN KENISTON OF SALEM.

"The 10$^{th}$ 9. 1648 I Alin Keniston of Salem, being weake in body, but of sound mind, doe make and ordaine this my last will & Testament in manner and forme following, that is to saye, ffirst I bequeath my soule into the hands of Almighty God trusting for saluation alone throught Jesus Christ, And my body to Christian Buriall. Item I giue vnto Cap$^t$ Hathorn fiue pounds. Item I giue vnto Cap$^t$ Dauenport three pounds, Item I giue vnto John Bayley either, a heifer or a Cow, Item I giue vnto m$^r$ Curwin, & m$^r$ Price twenty Shillings apeece in money, Item all the rest of my estate not here bequeathed I giue vnto Dorathy my wife whome I make and ordayne sole Executrix of this my last will and Testament Witness my hand the day & yeare aboue Written."

Witness: W$^m$ Hathorne, Anna Hathorne.

"Item I giue vnto m$^r$ Norris fifty shillings to m$^r$ Sharpe forty Shilling, & to mr Bartholmew 40 Shilling these three guifts were exprest before the signing hereof."

his mark<br>Alin A Keniston

Witness: Wm. Hathorne, Anna Hathorne.

Proved 27: 10: 1648 by Capt. Hathorne. *Essex Co. Quarterly Court Files, vol. 1, leaf 105.*

Mrs. Dorothie Keniston presented the will of her husband, Mr. Allin Keniston, 26: 10: 1648, also an inventory of his estate. *Salem Quarterly Court Records, vol. 3, leaf 3.*

### ESTATE OF WILLIAM SOUTHMEAD OF GLOUCESTER.

Millissent Southmate, presented for not returning inventory of the estate of her deceased husband, Will. Southmate. Mr. Addis brought one in for her, 22: 12: 1648, and she was appointed administratrix and discharged from the presentment. She was ordered to bring up the children. *Salem Quarterly Court Records, vol. 3, leaf 7.*

Inventory of estate of William Southmead of Gloster, deceased, taken 16: 12: 1648, by William Addiss (also Adies) and Christofer Averye: His apparrell, 2li.; his Bedsteed & feather bed & the apptenc., 8li.; one flockbedd & pillers, 1li. 10s.; one dussen of napkins & one table cloth & two towells & one pare of sheits, 3li.; one pare pillibeers, 10s.; in pewter & tining vessells, 1li. 10s.; two Brass kittles, one brass pott, two skilletts, 3li.; his chests, 1li.; two swords & a pare of Bandolers, one fowling piece, 2li.; one pare augers & tooles, with other Instrumts, 2li.; his timber vessels, 10s.; five Gots, 2li.; three piggs, 3li.; his house & land, 8li.; debts due to him, 4li.; a part in a boat, 1li. 10s.; in desperate debts, 25li. 16s. 4d.; total, 43li. 10s. His debts which he owed we found but 6li. More forgoten and some remembred in glloues & other thinges, 10s. *Essex Co. Quarterly Court Files, vol. 1, leaf 107.*

### ESTATE OF ABRAHAM ROBINSON OF GLOUCESTER.

William Vinson brought in inventory of estate of Abraham Robinson of Gloster, 23: 12: 1648. Amount, 18li. 11s. William Browne, who married the widow, was appointed executor. *Salem Quarterly Court Records, vol. 3, leaf 7.*

### ESTATE OF HENRY BYLEY OF SALISBURY.

Rebeckah Hall, widow, of Salisbury was possessed of a house and lands in Salisbury by the death of her former husband, Mr. Henry Bylye, which at the time of her marriage with Mr. John Hall she made sure to her two children Henry and Rebekah and hath lately sold to Henry Ambross, the and Rebekah Bylye as part of their portion, and hath lately sold to Henry Ambross, the house, situated between the houses of John Sanders on the north, and Andrew Greely on the south, with 10 acres of land adjoining, and 10 acres of planting ground lying within Mr. Hookes fence, also a — acre lot of meadow lying between the meadows of Mr. William Worcester on the west, and Richard Wells on the east, with 6 acres of salt marsh lying at the north end of Willi Worcester's farther meadow, together with his commons and all town privilidges thereto belonging, the deed bearing date 18 Nov., 1647. This sale having been made for the future good of the children and present help to her for their education, she petitioned the General Court to confirm the sale and to appoint some [person?] to take care of this part of the children's portion which amounted to 40li. that it might be improved to the best advantage until they be of age. In answer the court gave power to the Norfolk County court, held at Hampton, 1648, both to confirm the sale and provide for the children's good. This power was not made use of at the time and upon the renewing of the petition they gave the same power to the court held at Salisbury. The court 24: 2: 1649, confirmed the sale to Henry Ambross and ordered that Mrs. Hall should, if she pleased, upon bond keep one half of the 40li. in her own hands, during the time of her widowhood. Mr. Cri[sto]pher Batt and Lt. Robert Pike made overseers, to see that the said sum is paid to the two children when they are of age, Henry Bylie's part when he is twenty one years and Rebekah Bylie when she is seventeen years, or at the time of marriage; also to see to the disposing of the other 20li. in a safe way upon good security, which security they shall present to ye next county court held at Salisbury. The court reserves power to themselves to supply other overseers if these should die, or to change them if they see reason for it. *Norfolk Deeds, vol. 1, leaf* 1.

On 24: 2: 1649, Willi. Partridge acknowledged that he had 12li. 14s., Mr. Sam Dudley, 7li. 6s., and Mrs. Hall, 20li. of Mrs. Hall's children's portions, and they petitioned the court as to the disposal of the money. Mrs. Hall bound in thirty pounds. *Salisbury Quarterly Court Records, vol. 1, leaf* 11.

The court 1: 8: 1650 ordered Mr. Worcester to give bond to the country for 20li. of his wife's children's portion, and to give satisfactory security for the other 20li. to Mr. Batt and Mr. Bradbury until next Salisbury court. *Hampton Quarterly Court Records, vol. 1, leaf* 22.

ESTATE OF SAMUEL CHAMBERLIN OF (IPSWICH?).

Richard Betts, who married Joana Chamberlin, allowed 27: 1: 1649, as administrator of the estate of Samuell Chamberlin, brother to said Joana, who was heir to the estate. *Ipswich Quarterly Court Records, vol. 1, page* 15.

ESTATE OF JOHN WHITTINGHAM OF IPSWICH.

"Anno 48. In the Name of God Amen. I John Whittingham of Ipswich in New England Sick in body but of perfect understanding & memory, haveing Comended my Spirit unto God & my body to decent buriall in hope of Resurrection unto eternall Life. I say I doe in Case of death dispose of y^t outward Estate which y^e Lord hath Graciously giuen me as followeth. I Giue vnto Martha my dearly beloued wife, the House wherein I now dwell, w^th the Land belonging unto it, & the moueables: After her Death my sone John to haue the house & Land, the moueables to be equally diuided amongst all my Children. Also I giue unto her fforty pownds by the yeare dureing her Life out of my Lands in England. I giue to my twoe youngest Sonnes Richard, and William, to them & to their heyres for euer, all y^t Land together with the howses, messages, tenements, and other Appertinences now in the occupation of George Beckwell and John Randall, their heires Executors or Assignes Lieing in the parish of Southerton neere Boston in Lynkolnshire to be equally diuided betweene them, if eyther of them die before the Age of one & Twentie, the suruiuer shalbe heire vnto the deceased. My minde & will is that my twoe sonnes Richard & william shall enjoy their seuerall portions of howses & Lands at the Age of one & twentie. I giue all the rest of my Lands Lyinge in the Parish of Southerton with the howses, messages, Tenements, & other Appertinances thereunto belonging unto John my eldest Sonne. to him & to his heires for euer, to enter upon the same at the Age of one & Twentie. I giue unto my Three Daughters Martha, Elizabeth & Judith y^t hundred & fifty pounds dewe unto me from M^r Pendleton for my ffarme Lately sould unto him as also all y^t I haue in the tradinge stock of the Company of Ipswich the arrearages of all my rents in England & all the reuenues of my Lands their untill my Sonnes shalbe of Age that is accomplish their Seuerall Ages of one & Twenty yeares. all necessary Charges for the Conuenient education of my Children being deducted out of the same. my Daughters shall haue their portions payed unto them at twenty yeares of Age or the time of their Lawfull Marriage. my minde & will is that the portions of my daughters shalbe equall & if any of them die before the time whereat they are to enjoye their portions the suruiuers to be heires to the deceased. In Case of my Wifes marriage my will is y^t her husband shall put in suffitient Securyty to keepe the house in repayre & to make good the moueables accordinge as they are bequeathed to my Children. I ordaine & make my ffather in Law M^r William Hubbard & my brother M^r Samuell Haugh & Martha my wife Executors, and Executrixe of this my Last will & Testament. I Appoynt the present Elders of Ipswich, M^r Nathaniell Rogers and m^r John Norton ouerseers of this my will.

"Mʳ whittingham also at the same time gaue in Legacies vnto the executors twenty Pounds apiece vnto the ouerseers ten pounds apiece. to Mʳˢ Smith twenty Shillings, to Hanniell Bosworth Twenty Shillings. testifyed by William Hubbard, John Norton.

"Subscribed by me the day and yeare aboue written."
                                            John Whittingham.

Witness: John Norton, William Hubbard, Junior, James How, Haniell Bosworth. *Copy of will, Ipswich Deeds, vol. 1, leaf* 48.

Proved 27: 1: 1649, and upon petition, time given until 7: 1650, to bring in an inventory. *Ipswich Quarterly Court Records, vol.* 2, *leaf* 16.

On 24: 7: 1650, Mr. Hubard given more time on Mr. John Whitingham's inventory.

Mr. Willm. Hubard perfected the inventory 30: 7: 1651. Amount, 981li. 16s. 1d.

*Ipswich Quarterly Court Records, vol.* 1, *pp.* 21, 26.

Copy of inventory taken Dec. 25, 1648, by William Payne, Robert Payne and John Whipple: In the Parlour: one Joyne Table with five Chaires & one ould Carpet, 10s.; one fetherbed, one flockbed, two boulsters, one pillow, one p blankets, one Rugge, Curtaines & valients and bedsted, 12li.; one cupbord and Cloth, 10s.; two paire Cobirons, 15s.; two window Curtaines and Curtaine rods, 6s.; one case of Bottles, 5s.; Bookes, 6li. 5s.; Eleven Cushions, 1li. 10s.; one Still, 5s. In the Kitchin: one Copper, 3li. 10s.; one Brasse Pott, 15s.; one Brasse Pan, 1li. 5s.; fowre kettles, 3li.; fowre Brasse Skillets & one Chafeing dish, 12s.; 117li. of Pewter at 12d. p. li., 5li. 17s.; one Pewter fflaggon & 2 candlesticks, 12s.; 3 Iron potts, 18s.; 2 Iron kettles, 8s.; Brasse potts, 16s.; 4 Brasse candlesticks, 4s.; one frying pan & one warming pan, 7s.; two Musketts, 2 ffowling peeces, 2li. 10s.; one table, one Dresser, 3 tubs & 2 formes, 1li. 1s.; 2 payre of Cobirons, one fire pan & Tonges, one driping pan & spitt, 2 tramells, 1li. 4s.; one pestle and Morter, 10s. In the Chamber over ye Parlour: one Bedsteed, 2 fetherbeds, one p of blankets, one Rugge, 2 pillows & Curtaines & vallents, 2 Boulsters, 13li.; one ffetherbed, one boulster, 2 Quilts, two p blanketts, one coverlett & Trundlebed, 6li.; 4 Trunkes, one Chest, one boxe, 2 Chaires, 4 stooles, two Small Trunks, 3li. 5s.; 9 peeces of Plate & 11 spoones, 25li.; Tenn paire of Sheetes, 8li. & tenn other paire, 4li., 12li.; 3 paire pillowbeers at 8s. p paire, 1li. 4s.; 3 paire pillowbeers at 5s. p paire, 15s.; 4 Table Clothes, 2li. 10s.; 1 Duz: Diap. & 2 duz: fflaxen napkins, 1li. 10s.; twoe Duzen of napkins, 12s.; the Hangings in the Chamber, 2li. 10s.; Three holland Cupbord Cloathes, 1li. 4s.; Twoe half Sheets, 1li. 10s.; 1 Diap. & 1 Damaske Cupbord Cloth, 1li.; one Screene, 10s.; Twoe paire of Cobirons, 1 p tongs, 15s.; one Carpett, 3li. 10s.; 6li. of Hose yarne, 1li.; 1 paire Curtains & vallents, 5li.; 1 blew Coverlett, 1li. In the Chamber over the Kitchin: Bedsted, 2 ffeatherbeds, 2 boulsters, one pillow, 5 blanketts, 2 Coverlets, one Trundlebed, 8li.; one Saddle, 1li.; 3 Chests, 1li. 13s.; 7 yds. Canvas at 12d. & ells at 2s. p, 1li. 1s.; 16 yds. Canvas at 20d. p yd., 1li. 6s. 8d.; 16 yds. Canvas at 18d., 1li. 4s.; 10 yds. ffrench Serge, 3li.; 6 yds. Carpeting, 1li. 4s.; one ffeatherbed, 4 blanketts, 1 boulster, 4li.; Remants of Holland, 1li. 10s.; his weareing Apparrell, 22li.; in Mony, 25s., 1li. 5s.; 6 oxen, 2 Bulls, one yeare ould Heifer, 48li.; 8 Cowes, 32li.; 2 Mares, one Geldinge, 30li.; in Rent, 14li.; The Corne in the Barne, 6li.; in Debts ffrom Mr. Pendleton, 150li.; in Debts, 60li.; Imployed in way of Trade, —; for arears of rent in England as by his accounts appears, ——; A Debt for part of the Shipp Sarah in Portue or not knowne, ——; in Cartes, Plowes & Chaines, together with other Implements for husbandry, 3li.; A House & Barne & Cowehouse & 44 Acres of Lande, 100li.; 3 Hogges, 3li.; A rem[n]ant of Holland, 1li.; one Stock of Bees, 1li. *Ipswich Deeds, vol. 1, leaf 49.*

ESTATE OF DANIEL WOOD OF IPSWICH.

Inventory of the estate of Daniell Wood of Ipswich, deceased, amounting to 37li. 16s., filed, and his widow Marye Wood appointed administratrix 27: 1: 1649. She was to bring up the two children, the whole estate being left to her for that purpose. *Ipswich Quarterly Court Records, vol. 1, page 15.*

Copy of inventory taken Mar. 23, 1648, by Robert Lord and Thomas Wells: House and the Ground about it with 6 Acres at Hart breake hill & 10 Acres beyond Chebacco river, 21li.; 40 bushells of Indian Corne, 6li.; A Sute & Coate, 1li. 16s.; one fflockbed & fether Boulster & 2 Pillows, 1li. 6s. 8d.; one Rugg and one Coverlet, 1li.; 2 payer of Sheetes, 1li.; 1 Table Cloth & 2 Napkins, 7s.; 2 payer of Pillowbeeres, 16s.; 1 payre of ould Sheetes, 3s.; Child bed Linen

& 2 Towells, 1li.; 2 Chests & 2 Boxes, 10s.; 5 Pewter Dishes & one Plate, 15s.; A pint pott & 1 dozen of Spoones & other Small porringers, 10s.; A Hogshead with ffethers in it, 15s.; An ould Bedsted, 2 kneading Troughs & other Lumbar, 8s.; one Bedsted & a Little Table, 3 Chaires & a fforme, 15s.; A Powdering Tub & A Charne & other Lumbar, 8s.; 3 Axes, 1 Howe & 1 handsawe with other Tooles, 15s.; one iron Pott, A ffrying pan, tongs & fire Shovell, 12s.; 4 boards & 2 working Benches, 8s.; 3 kettles, 1 Postnet & one warmeing pan, 2li.; one Cowe & one Heifer, 7li.; 2 Piggs, 1li. 4s.; A Linen wheele, 2s. 6d.; 4li. & ½ of Cotton yarne & 4li. & ½ of fflaxen yarne, 16s.; 7li. of Hempe, 5s. 6d.; About 14 Gallons of oyle, 1li. 3s. 4d.; total, 52li. 16s. Owing out of this estate to Mr. Webb, Mr. Will. Payne & others, 15li. *Ipswich Deeds, vol. 1, leaf 46.*

ESTATE OF JOHN SPENCER OF NEWBURY.

"Know all men by these p$^r$sents that If God be pleased to Call me out of this life in this single Condition It is my full purpose & will that John Spenser shall inherit all my Lands and Goods which God hath giuen unto me in this Country of Newengland, to pay out of the same within three years after my discease to his reuerent instructer in Christ m$^r$ Cotton, ten pounds to euery household Seruant which is so at the time of my discease fiue pounds a peece, to the Children of my Cosen Ann Knight of Newbery fiue pounds a peece, and to her self fiue pound, And vnto euery Child of my brother Thomas Spenser Twenty pounds a peece, To Thomas Theacher fiue pounds, And to mine honoured freind m$^r$ Vane. m$^r$ Richard Dumer, m$^r$ Nicholas Eston. m$^r$ ffoster of Ipswich and Goodman Motte, of Hingham, doe I comitte the ouersight & execution of this my will & Testament, and do Comend the said John Spenser my nephew together with his estate hereby giuen him, to be Managed & ordered for his good, & him selfe for his education to be by their Care in the knowledge of the Lord Jesus Christ, and that if mony be not in their hands to defraye the seuerall Legacies heere bequeathed that then they take as many Cowes or heyfors out of the Stocke & Share them betweene them at Twenty pounds the Beast till euery portion be satisfyed. And my will is y$^t$ mine honoured and louinge ffreinds should in their accompt unto myne heire make abatement for all their paines and Charges in the following any busynes theirin Contayned, whome I desire the Lord to blesse, that the worke may prosper in thire hands. Dated this first of the sixt month 1637, and signed with mine owne hand."

P<sup>r</sup> Jo: Spenser.

"My will & intent is that if John Spencer my Nephew should die with out heires of his body Lawfully begotten that then my brother Thomas Spencer & his Children shall share the same, A Sonne to haue three times as a Daughter: & if they should faile by death That then the Children of my brother Nicholas Kidwel & the Children of my Sister Rachell Kidwel to them halfe theirof, & the next of my blood & whole Kindred that shall first come ouer to reside in this Country to haue thother halfe: More ouer I giue to my Cosen Gardnars Children twenty Shillings the peece."

Jo: Spenser.

Witness: Robert Jeoffreys, Thomas Thatcher. *Copy of will, Ipswich Deeds, vol. 1, leaf 55.*

Will brought into court Mar. 29, 1649, and Mr. Rich. Dumer swore that it was delivered into his hands before Mr. Spencer's going to England. *Ipswich Quarterly Court Records, vol. 1, page 15.*

Left at Newbury 11 Cowes, 3 Heyfors, 4 oxen, 1 Steere, 4 Cowe Calves, 1 Bull, 7 Steer Calves, 1 Mare, 3 Mare Colts, besides Swine and Powltry, Corne, Cloaths, Cloathes Apparell, Howshould stuffe. In land granted by the Town of Newbury in 1635: one house lot of about 4 acres, in breadth eight rods, in length four score rods, bounded south by the street next the great river, north by a lot of William Franckling's, east by a lot of William Sergeant's and west by Merrimack Street; a farm lot of about 400 acres of upland and meadow, bounded north by Mr. Woodbridge, south by Mr. Parker, west by the street of eight rods in breadth, next Merrimack River on the east and the common on the west end; about 150 acres on the left hand of Merrimack ridge the same in breadth as that on the right hand of the ridge and in length six score rods; 30 acres of salt marsh beyond Pyne Island and about 3 acres of upland on the Neck over the Great River. *Ipswich Deeds, vol. 1, leaves 55, 56.*

### ESTATE OF GEORGE VARNAM OF IPSWICH.

"The 21<sup>th</sup> of the 2<sup>th</sup> mounth, 1649 I George Varnam of

Ipswich being in pfect memorye, doe ordayne this my last will and testament as followeth. first I Giue my house and barne & lands and goods and chattells to my wife for hir life, And after hir decease Two pts of all my estate to my sonne Samuell Varnam and the third pt to my daughter Hannah to be equally deuided. And my meaneing is if my sonn dye without Isue, my whole estate is to returne to my daughter Hannah, and further soe long as she remayne vnmaried is to enioye a chamber in my house; and I doe apoynte Thomas Scott and my sonn Samuell to be my Executors." [no signature]

Inventory taken 12: 8: 1649: Halfe the dwelling howse and barne and all the ground, 52li. 15s.; Three Cowes, 14li.; Two oxen and a shott, 12li. 15s.; Half a Cart, a Chene and a yook, half a share, 12s.; fouer puter Dishes and a friing pan and the trammels, 16s.; for Beding and som of his clothes and other things, 1li. 6s.; for Iron and Chayres and other things, 1li. 16s.; for a mortor and Churne and wedges and other things, 1li. 6s.; total, 85li. 16s. Things that was forgot: A matock, meale and salt and some things alse wich all come to 8s.; in seed corne, 13s. 6d. Debts oweing to severall men to the value of 7li. 11s. *Essex Co. Quarterly Court Files, vol. 1, leaf 110.*

## Estate of Thomas Nelson of Rowley.*

"I Thomas Nelson of Rowley in the Countie of Essex (in New England) beeing by pudence Called now to make a uoyage into old England, not knowing what may be fall me there in (vpon seuerall Considerations) dispose of & settle the estate which god hath giuen mee (by way of will) in manner and forme following. Inprimis I giue vnto my beloued wife Joane for her naturall life, my Mill, mill house with the appurtenances scituate & being within the limits of Rowley: & all that ground (neere unto the said mill) which was lately in the occupation of Joseph wormehill, & all that my vpland & meadow (or other ground) which lyeth betweene Rowley Oxe-Pasture on one pte, the Comon on another pte, & the mill river, & the brooke that goeth

---

*For additional matter, see Records and Files of the Quarterly Courts of Essex Co. Mass., vol. I (1911), p. 424; vol. II (1912), pp. 12-21, 42, 44-46, 233, 234; Ipswich Deeds, vol. 1, leaves 221, 222; vol. 4, p. 190; vol. 5, pp. 148, 257, 484; Mass. Archives, vol. 15B, p. 216.

from the towne on the other pte thereof, all which land or ground Conteineth by estimation fiftie acres be it more or lesse. puided she make no other Claime to any other parte of my howses, lands, tenements, heriditaments and appurtinances. Item I giue her two acres of ground during her naturall life in the pond feild next m$^r$ Rogers leaueing out the pond to build her an house on. The remainder or reuersion of which mill land and premises & all other my houses, lands, tenements, and heriditaments I giue amongst my Children & to their heires as well that Child which my wife is with all, as the reft. Item I giue & bequeath to my eldest sonne Phillip Nelson a double portion, & to my sonne Thomas Nellson, & my Daughter mercie nelson & the Child or Children she is withall there equall pts. puided if any of them die before they Come to the age of twentie & one yeers, or marriage, then there pts to be equally deuided amongst the suruiueing Children. Item my will is that Richard Bellingham Esquire, & my honored Vncle Richard Dumer Gent. shall haue the education of my sonne Phillip nelson & Thomas nelson & the proportion of their estates both of lands & goods for their education & maintenance till they Come to Twentie one yeers, & then they to receiue their estates, & the ouerplus aboue their maintenance giueing a sufficient discharge. Item that my will is that my wife & my vncle Richard Dumer shall haue the education of my daughter Mercie Nelson, & the other child my wife is withall, & the proportion of their estates both of lands & goods for their education & maintenance till they marry & then they to receiue their estates & the ouerplusse aboue their maintenance giueing a sufficient discharge. Item I giue & bequeath to my wife (Joane) foure Choise Cowes, one Choise mare, & ten pounds to build her a house, Item I giue to my sone Phillip Nelson ten pownds which was giuen him by my aunt Katherin Withars, & is in my hands, & his plate marked with his owne name P. N. & to my second sone Thomas Nelson a wine bowle, & one spoone, all the rest of my psonall estate my debts being paid I giue vnto my Children to be deuided as aboue onely my eldest sone Phillip to haue a double portion. Item I make m$^r$ Richard Bellingham & my vncle Richard Dumer my executors of this my last will & testament. & my desire is, & I wold intreate m$^r$ Ezekiell Rogers of Rowley, & m$^r$ John Norton of Ipswich to be my ouerseers, & my mind further is if any differances arise Concerning this my last will & testament my ouerseers shall haue the heareing & deciding of the same. Item I giue unto my wife all her apparrell, her Chest, boxe, A Bed and ffurniture, & a Siluer Beaker. December 24: 1645. Sealed Signed & deliuered"

Tho: Nelson

Witness: Jeremy Howchin, Ezekiell Northene.
Proved 26: 10: 1649 by Jerymy Howchin and 26: 1: 1650 by Ezekiell Northen before the court.

"A Schedule to be Annexed to the will of T. Nelson.
"These are to Certify all whom it anyways may Concerne, that I Thomas Nelson, about to returne to Rowland in New England, being at present sick in body but enjoying vnderstanding & memory, as formerly, doe by these presents testify my confiring of my last will & testament which I made & left in Newengland with my wiues vncle m$^r$ Richard Dumer; onely with addition of these puiso's. first that my yongest child Samuell Nelson, being borne since that will was made, & if my wife be now with Child, & shall bring forth a Child: that Samuell, & this then, (my will is,) may enjoy A Childs portion pportionable to the rest of my Children. my eldest enioying a double portion as is mentioned in that will; or if there can be more done for her.

"Also I ernestly desire of o$^r$ reuerend Pastor, & Elder m$^r$ Rogers, & of that whole Church of Rowley, that they may not mistake themselues Concerning the Eleuen pounds, & the Seuenteene pownds which I paid to Goodman Seathcwell, for his farme; & I did not giue these in with other monies that I laid out for the Plantation: Least this being a wrong to mee, be to their greefe at the Day of Jesus Christ, as also fifteene pownd paid to m$^r$ Carletons hundred pound which I ought not to pay. This I entreate them seriously to lay to hart, & righting me in all these pticulars. witnes my hand, the sixt Day of psextilis here Caled August, 1648."

Tho: Nelson
his mark

Witness: Henry Jacie alias Jesse, Daniell D Elly and
her mark
Sarah N Appleyard. *Copy of will, Ipswich Deeds, vol. 1, leaf 72.*

Copy of inventory taken Feb. 23, 1648, by Edward Carlton, Sebastian Brigham, Thomas Barker and Joseph Jewett: his Apparell, 3li. 11s. 6d.; his silver plate, 12li. 13s.; the Pewter, 3li. 10s.; one Carpett, 1li.; one Long Cushing, 6s.; one Carpett, 17s. 6d.; one bed teaster & vallance, 17s. 6d.;

one peice of stuffe, 10s.; one peice of stuffe, 5s.; three pillowbers, 7s. 6d.; one vallance for a Cupbord, 6s.; two petticoats, 2li. 10s.; one old black Gowne, 10s.; one peice of stuffe, 2li. 10s.; three Sheets, 1li.; three towells, 10s.; one Diap. table Cloth, 6s. 8d.; one bed & boulster, 2li.; six bedsteeds, 1li. 10s.; one Presse, 10s.; one Chest & two trunkes, 1li.; one Corslett, 1li.; one Chest & old Iron, 8s.; eight Casements of Iron, 1li. 14s.; one Jack of Iron, 8s.; three marking Irons, 1s. 6d.; one Clock, 2li.; one Table & one buffett, 3s.; two hay spades, one hay crooke, one horse Combe, 3s.; one great copp, 10li.; fower Sawes, 1li.; two Saddles, 6s. 8d.; three old Sickles, 1s.; one steele mill, 1li.; one grinding stone, two old ropes, 2s.; one timber Chaine, 17s.; tow Coulters, two shares & other old Iron, 1li. 13s. 3d.; five Chaines & one paire of hooks, 1li.; two wainehead yoakes, 5s.; two sling yoakes, 3s. 4d.; one spitt, 3s. 4d.; two brass potts, 1li. 13s. 4d.; one Driping pan, 2s.; two old ketles, 8s.; one paire of stilyards, 3s. 4d.; one Beckor balke, two hayles & two p of tongs, 10s.; one frying pan, 1s. 4d.; one brass Candlestick, 8d.; three waights of lead, 11s. 8d.; one table & two formes, 3s.; one matteris, one pillow & other beding, 1li.; one Chaine, 3s.; one payre of Racks, 14s.; thre fowling peices, one Corbyne & two swords, 4li.; all the bookes, 9li.; one Cart & two plowes, 1li. 3s. 4d.; two harrows, 16s.; one ladder & som saw timbr, 2s. 6d.; three Iron forkes, 4s.; five yong Cattell, 2 yere old, 15li.; one black Cowe, 5li.; one black heiffer, x; two steeres, 4 yere old, 10li.; two steers, 3 yere old, 8li.; one black heifer, 3li. 13s. 4d.; one browne oxe, 9li.; 6 oxen, 42li.; fower Cowes, 17li.; one bay mare, 12li.; one sorrild mare & Colt, 12li.; one Dun mare & Colt, 13li.; one Gray mare, 6li. 13s. 4d.; one sorrild mare, 8li.; one water mill & other implements belonging to her & 10 acres of land, 120li.; one dwelling howse & barne with other howses & one orchard, 50li.; all the broken & unbroken up land & meadow lying over against the howse, 55li.; all the broken upland lying in the ware howse field, 48li.; all the upland lying at Sachells meadow, 1li.; all the upland lying at sandy bridge, 1li.; all the upland lying by the oxe pasture, 8li.; all the upland lying at Mr. Dumers ffarme, 10li.; all the meadow lying in Satchwells medow, 15li.; all the meadow on the south side of Sandy bridg, 9li.; all the salt marsh lying at Mr Dumers ffarme, 16li.; all the rough marsh pt. lying at Mr. Dumers ffarme & pt. at Sandy bridge & pt. Joyning upon the oxe pasture & pt. at the ends of the Salt marsh, 10li.; all the meadow lying in the straits meadow, 1li. 5s.; all the comon Pasture & comons upon the oxe Pasture, 25li.; all the upland at the mill, 2li. 10s.; all the land at the warehouse, 10li.; one brasse morter & an Iron pestle, 1li. 6s.; one old bed & other beding, 1li. 13s. 4d.; one brasse ladle, 1s.; 2 Acres of upland in manings ffarme, 1li. 6s. 8d.; one pitchforke, 1s; one brass Candle sticke, 1s. 4d.; one planke & a stoole, 5s. 6d.; total, 527li. 12s. 7d. Sworne to 26:1:1650. *Ipswich Deeds, vol. 1, leaf 73.*

Contract of marriage between Thomas Nelson of Rowley and Joane Dumer, dated 15:12:1641.

"Know all men by these p<sup>r</sup>sents, that whereas there is a Contract of marriage betwixt Thomas Nelson of Rowley in New-England Gent: & Joane Dumer Spint<sup>r</sup> y<sup>e</sup> daughter of Thomas Dumer of Badgeth in old England Gent: and whereas alsoe Richard Dumer of Newbery in New-England Gent hath engaged & bound himselfe for y<sup>e</sup> payment of two hundred pownds for or towards y<sup>e</sup> marriage portion of the said Joane, as by his bond bearing euen date w<sup>th</sup> these p<sup>r</sup>sents appeareth, Now the said Thomas Nelson (In Consideracion of his marriage w<sup>th</sup> the said Joane) doth hereby bind himselfe his heires Execu<sup>rs</sup>: Administrato<sup>rs</sup> & assignes & euery of them vnto y<sup>e</sup> said Richard Dumer his executo<sup>rs</sup> admin<sup>rs</sup> & assignes & to euery of them, in y<sup>e</sup> summe of fower hundred pownds, to be paid vnto them or some one of them, in case therebe a faileing to pforme the Condicons Following: Viz<sup>t</sup>. That if after the Compleating of the marriage Contract above mentioned, the said Joane doe survive the said Thomas Nelson then (Imediately upon the death of the said Thomas) the summe or uallue of two hundred pownds & Likewise soe much more as the said Thomas Dumer shall ad unto the said porcon of two hundred pownds (together alsoe w<sup>th</sup> what else the said Thomas Nelson shall thinke fitt) shall be allowed payed or deliuered unto y<sup>e</sup> said Joane for her owne use behoofe & benefitt, And further that as y<sup>e</sup> Eldest sonn of the said Thomas Nelson shall have a double porcon out of his estate, soe the remainder of his estate shalbe equally deuided amongst ye rest of the children, as well those as shall be ye Joynt issue of them y<sup>e</sup> s<sup>d</sup> thomas & Joane (if any such be) as y<sup>e</sup> other: w<sup>ch</sup> condicons being performed according to y<sup>e</sup> true intent & meaning of these p<sup>r</sup>sents, Then the bond in these p<sup>r</sup>sents conteined shalbe utterly void or els it shall stand remaine & be in full force & vertue; Dated y^e fifteenth day of y^e Twelfth month 1641"

Tho Nelson

Witness: Richard Saltenstall, Ez: Rogers, Wm: Wakefeild.

"M^d: that befor y^e ensealing & deliuery of y^e p^rsent Writing, it was agreed that the whole porcon that shalbe Rece^d by the aboue named Thomas Nelson shall (upon y^e Requirey & according to y^e aduise of y^e Friends of his p^rsent Contracted wife) be disposed & assured for the maintenance of his s^d wife during her life (in case she suruive the said Thomas) & afterward to be equally devided amongst there Children, but while they both Live it is to be for there Joynt maintenance, Alsoe it is agreed that y^e s^d porcon shalbe Receiued & disposed of from time to time by the aduise of y^e friends indifferently of the said Thomas & his said wife; ec." *Salem Quarterly Court Records, vol. 3, leaf 67.*

Upon the petition of Richard Bellingham and Rich. Dumer to the General Court, May 2, 1649, ordered that Mr. Richard Dumer shall give an accounting to Mr. Rich. Saltonstall and Mr. Sam. Symonds, that he may have his discharge as attorney, and with the other executor may enter upon the estate of Mr. Nelson and dispose of the same in behalf of Mrs. Nelson, widow, and her children, and the children of Mr. Nelson by a former wife. *Mass. Bay Colony Records, vol. 2, page 272.*

Mr. Richard Saltonstall intending to go to England, Capt. Robert Bridges was chosen 18: 8: 1649 to join with Mr. Simonds to receive the account of Mr. Nelson's estate. *Mass. Bay Colony Records, vol. 3, page 171.*

Petition to the Court at Boston, 14: 3: 1656, of Richard Dumer, executor, for power to sell some of the land, in order to pay several legacies to the wife and children some of the children being in England; and also for direction for the dividing of the whole estate as one of the children was of age to receive his portion, and the executor wished to be freed from the care of the estate. *Mass. Archives, vol. 15B, page 155.*

In answer to the petition the court May 30, 1656 impowered the executor to sell so much of the estate as of right belonged to the two youngest children now in England, provided the two oldest sons that are in this country have such a part of the estate as doth fulfil the will of their father; if the sons dislike the distribution then the overseers named in the will to settle the difference, but if they refuse, then the difference to be determined by law. *Mass. Archives, vol.* 15B, *page* 156.

Letter from Mr. Ezekiel Rogers dated Rowley 26: 3: 1656, to the "Secretary and my deare Cousin," in which he answers questions propounded to him by order of the court: 1st, whether he had allowed the sale of Mr. Nelson's lands and 2d whether he now allows the sale, and the answer to both is in the negative. *Mass. Archives, vol.* 15B, *page* 157.

Philip Nelson's reasons why Mr. Dummer should not sell the lands of the children of Mr. Thomas Nelson:

1st, he can make no good assurance to them the inheritance being settled on the four children and the eldest having a double portion is of age to dispose of his own. The second son being near twenty years of age, Mr. Dumer ought not to have power to disinherit the children of that which is given them by their father; 2d. it is the only way of subsistence for the two oldest sons; 3d, they will be able to improve all of most of the lands and houses and be able to pay 2-5 to their youngest sister who is about eleven or twelve years and to their youngest brother who is about eight or nine years, both being in England; 4th, the estate is not indebted but large, neither hath Mr. Dummer been at much charge for the children; 5th, the land is more valuable now than it was ten years ago and no better thing could be returned to the children than their own land; 6th, what Mr. Dummer calls legacies should be called portions, as both goods and lands are to be divided equally into five parts, which your petitioner hopes the next Salem court will expedite; 7th, Mr. Dummer hath agreed to sell half the mill which is the best estate and I hope this court will make no alteration of my father's will; 8th, if he finds it so much trouble to keep the estate of these four children the petitioner hopes to find friends enough to take it out of his hands. *Mass. Archives, vol.* 15B, page 158.

Richard Dummer's answer to Philip Nelson: 1st, it is not only the executor's power by will but the faithful discharge of his trust to sell the lands that each child may have their full due; 2d, it is not their only means of subsistence, one of them being a student at the College and they are not to expect to have the command of that which belongs to the other children; 3d, they are not fit trustees to take the power out of the executor's hands; 4th, this objection is needless as I have rendered an account from time to time and the second son is with me and receives wages. There was no estate in England left with the widow to educate the children for he had not enough to pay his debts and the education of the children has been at my charge; 5th, if the land is worth so much more there ought to be a new valuation or sale that each may have just right; 6th, there were legacies remaining in Mr. Nelson's hands which were gifts of others and therefore debts from Mr. Nelson; 7th, the sale of the mill is not an alteration of the will, but produces a double advantage to the estate. The objection that I cannot sell the mill because it is given to the widow I grant, if I have not liberty from her and therefore I desire the sale to be confirmed by the next court at Salem if I make it clear that I have legal power from her to do for her as I see good. *Mass. Archives, vol.* 15B, *page* 159.

Richard Dummer of Newbury, executor, having had much trouble from the estate, inasmuch as a considerable part belongs to Mercie Nellson, daughter of Thomas Nellson, whose abode is in England, and as she has not taken any effectual course for the payment of her portion remaining in his hands, though she hath been of age about two years since, and that he may not be any longer exposed to damage by keeping the same, hath set apart for her use certain cattle as by schedule hereto annexed, which tender of payment he desires to be recorded. The valuation of certain cattle for the use of Mercie Nelson, made by Richard Kent and Henry Short: two great Red oxen, 17li.; fower black steers, foure years old, 20li.; three black cowes, two about 7 years, one 4 years ould, 14li. 5s.; one heifer, three year old, black, 3li. 10s.; 5 steeres of three years old come next winter, 21li. 5s.; 3 cowes, one of them haveing a white foote, 14li. 10s.; A bay mare & colt comg two years old, 11li.

Witnessed June 14, 1667 by Joseph Hills, Daniell Lunt.

The Ipswich court Sept. 24, 1667 ordered the above to be recorded. *Ipswich Deeds, vol.* 3, *page* 44.

### ESTATE OF ROBERT JOHNSON OF ROWLEY.

"The last will & Testament of Robert Johnson Sick & weake of Body But of perfect memory (praysed be God)

"Imp my will and minde is that all my Debts be paide, & all my lawfull debts being paid my will is that out of the

remaynder of my goods something be distributed vnto the pore of Rowley according vnto the Discression of my Cosen Thomas Barker & Humfrey Reyner. Ite that which || may || remayne of my Goods after the aforesaid things be done I doe Assigne it to be returned unto my ffather Robert Johnson at the new hauen. Item I make Thomas Barker & Humfrey Reyner my Executors of this my last will & Testament. In witnesse whereof I the said Robert Johnson Junior haue subscribed my hand this 13. of the 7$^{th}$ mo: 1649."
                                                    Robert Johnson.
Witness: John Brocke, Thomas Barker, Humfrey Reyner.
Proved 26: 1: 1650.

Inventory taken Dec. 14, 1649, by Sebastian Brigham and Thomas Mighell: his Apparell, 9li. 12s.; thre blacke hatts, 1li. 2s.; one silver Seale, 5s.; two paire of Gloves, 3s.; fower payre of stockins, 10s.; one payre of bootes, two p shooes 12s.; one Shirt, fower Caps, 7s. 4d.; six bands, fower handkerchefs with some other small things, 6s.; one Claspe, one Inkhorne, one knife, 1s. 8d.; one houre glasse, one lampe, 2s.; one Covering, one blankett with some peeces of stuffe, 14s.; thre Chests, one Combe, 16s. 8d.; his Bookes, 12li. 13s. 3d.; total, 27li. 4s. 11d.

*Copy of will and inventory, Ipswich Deeds, vol. 1, leaf 85.*

### ESTATE OF ROBERT NORINGTON OF (SALEM?).

Administration on the estate of Robert Norington, who was drowned near Marblehead, granted 26: 1: 1650, to Henry Bartholomew of Salem. *Ipswich Quarterly Court Records, vol. 1, page 18.*

### ESTATE OF MRS. ISABEL REDVERNE OF IPSWICH.

The will of Mrs. Isable Redverne of Ipswich brought in 25: 4: 1650. Proved by Robert Lord and Thomas Lovell. *Salem Quarterly Court Records, vol. 3, leaf 24.*

### ESTATE OF WILLIAM KING OF SALEM.

Dorathie Kinge, widow, brought in inventory of estate of William Kinge, her late husband, 27: 4: 1650. Amount 141li. 18s. Four cows were adjudged to be her own estate.
William Kinge dying intestate, his widow Dorothie Kinge and his eldest son William (to whom is given 14li. for two

oxen to teach his brothers his father's trade) were ordered by the court held last 3d day: 12: 1650, to dispose of the estate, which amounted to 112li. 10s., as follows: To William Kinge, eldest son, double portion, 20li.; Samuell, second son, aged eighteen years, 10li.; John, third son, aged thirteen, 10li.; Mary, his daughter, wife of John Scuddr, 5li.; Katherine, wife of John Swaysy, his second daughter, 5li.; Hannah, his third daughter 10li.; Mehitabell, his fourth daughter, aged fifteen, 10li.; and Deliverance, his fifth daughter, aged nine, 10li. John is to serve his brother William seven years and to have 16li. at the end of his time; Sam. to serve him three years and to have 12li.; and William to allow his mother, Dorathie Kinge, two shillings per week for her son John's service, beginning 1: 1: 1653. The two younger daughters, Mehitabell and Deliverance, are to remain with their mother. Mr. Battar and Sergiant Palfree to divide the estate.

William Kinge agreed with his mother, Dorothie Kinge, to be relieved from his brother John Kinge, and that said John be apprenticed to his mother. The court 28: 9: 1651, consented to the agreement.

*Salem Quarterly Court Records, vol. 3, leaves 24, 30, 38.*

### ESTATE OF MILES WARD OF SALEM.*

Margret Rix, sometime wife of Miles Ward, deceased, brought in 17: 7: 1650, a writing of his subscribed by Jo. Browne and Joseph Grafton; and also an inventory of 108li. 3s. 6d., subscribed by Edmund Battar and Jeffery Massy. She was appointed administratrix. The estate was to be divided as follows: To the eldest son, 10li., to the eldest daughter, 10li., and 10li. each to the two younger, the parents to have the use of that of the two youngest for their bringing up until they are of age. *Salem Quarterly Court Records, vol. 3, leaf 25.*

Inventory of the estate of Miles Ward of Salem, with debts receivable and payable, related by himself in Virginia, 3: 1: 1650:—to Joseph Grafton and John Browne.

Debtors in Virginia to Mils Ward.

| | |
|---|---|
| Thomas Tenny, tob. | 0100 |
| Goody Hamond, tob. | 0200 |
| John ——ton, tob. wt. Cask | 0300 |

*See also Records and Files of the Quarterly Courts of Essex Co., Mass., vol. 3 (1913), p. 458.

|  |  | g. | st. |
|---|---|---|---|
| [Deb]tors at yᵉ mauadus | | | |
| Rich. —— to pay in pound beavor | | 68 | 15 |
| ditto is debtor in pound beavor | | 52 | 00 |
| ditto is dr 4 light beavors or 3 heavy ones | | | |
| ditto is dr to a lock & pʳ of shoos | | 04 | 00 |
| ditto is dr to a bible beaver 1 li. ¼ | | | |
| good Steevens is dr | | 46 | 00 |
| at New Haven | | s. | |
| John Bishop is dr in peage | | 11 | 00 |
| at Boston | li. | s. | |
| John Wilks is dr | 02 | 10 | 00 |
| Mils Ward is Dr. at Boston | | | |
| To goo Clark yᵉ Smith | 03 | 00 | 00 |
| To goo Shrimpton | 01 | 02 | 06 |
| of which goo Becket to pay 4s. 6d. | | | |
| To Mr. Butten as ℔ accs. | | | |
| To Mr. Sheaffe according to his book | | | |
| To Mr. Walker acording to his booke | | | |
| To goo Buttall about | 01 | 10 | 00 |
| To Mr. Usher | 00 | 05 | 00 |
| At Charlton | | | |
| To Mr. Burt for shooes | 01 | 06 | 00 |
| To James Browne | 01 | 05 | 00 |
| at Salem | | | |
| To Mr. Curwin according to his book | | | |
| To Mr. Price according to his book | | | |
| To Mr. Browne for sope | 03 | 00 | 00 |

In England, 40li. given by his father as a legacy to be paid to said Miles Ward by his brother, which he bequeathed to his four children. The proceeds of two hds. of tob. shipped aboard Mr. Fenn's vessel, to return to his wife at Salem, and three hds. of tob. shipped by John Browne and Rich. More to New England for his wife to dispose of; also three bags of tob. and two sides of pork, four sides and five roles of tob. from Goo Hamond and Tho. Tally, all to his wife, to whose care he committed all things. *Essex Co. Quarterly Court Files, vol. 1, leaf 115.*

### ESTATE OF THOMAS COOKE OF (IPSWICH?).

Rachell, wife of Thomas Cooke, deceased, sometime "inhabiting" at Ipswich, brought in 17: 7: 1650 an inventory of the estate of her late husband. He left no will and she was appointed administratrix. *Salem Quarterly Court Records, vol. 3, leaf 26.*

Inventory taken by William Bartholmew and William Varny. Debt from Mr. Batter of Boston, 20li.; a cow, 5li.; in goods, 5li.; total, 30li.; debt of John Gorames at the Iron Works, 5li. 8s.; more found since in goods, 5li. *Essex Co. Quarterly Court Files, vol. 1, leaf 116.*

### ESTATE OF WILLIAM BELLINGHAM OF ROWLEY.*

"I william Bellingham being at this time very weake in body, but of perfect memory doe thus make my last will & Testament. ffirst I doe Comitt my soule into the hands of God through the alone merritts of Jesus Christ Item for my outward estate, I doe will that my Debts be paide, as I haue formerly ordered, that is to say that John Smith haue the little heifer at merimacke; & the rest in Corne; for John Aslet, if it appeare vpon reckoning that I doe owe him any thing I will that it be paid in Corne according to o$^r$ agreement. ffor Hugh Smith that he be paid partly by the hire of his Cowe, & the rest in Corne accordinge as we agreed, Mychaell Hopkinson in beading & Corne. Richard Holmes for Merimacke ffence, is to be paid in Corne, for fencing the vpper lott he is to be paid in Corne & beading. M$^r$ Broughtons father in law Demandeth three pounds of me, but he must make it appeare to my Executor before it be paid, ffor M$^r$ Rogers he hath my filly & her fole for Seuen pounds which I ought him, & nine pounds more which I owe him, he is to be paid out of my Cattle. Item I will that whatsoeuer is due to me from the Towne shalbe remitted, & is giuen by me, Toward a Comon Stock for the Towne. Item I doe freely giue to my Seruant Jeremy Northende fowre pounds whatsoeuer other Small debts doe really appeare to be due from me to any man, I will to be paide out of the rest of my goods. Item whatsoeuer time my man Jerimy is to serue I will that he shall Serue that time wholly to m$^r$ Rogers, to whom I doe giue him ouer, & his Care, Item I doe giue to my loueing ffreinde m$^r$ Thomas Nelson my Smallest byble which was my wiues, Item I doe giue to m$^r$ Rogers my golde ringe which was my wiues, Item I doe giue to Jeremy my man two Cloth Suites, a white one & a browne, Item I giue to Marget Crosse my ould w$^t$ Cloth Coate. Item I giue Eliz: Jackson m$^r$ Rogers maide twenty Shillings. Item to william Hobson fiue shillings & as much to Hannah Grant.

* See also Records and Files of the Quarterly Courts of Essex Co., Mass., vol. 2 (1912), pp. 360-362, 367, 395-401.

Item I will that after all my Debts be paide the whole remainder of my goods, Lands & whole estate be giuen, & I doe giue it to my loueing Nephew m^r Samuell Bellingham, & this my last will & Testament I doe Confirme with my owne hand & Seale."

William Bellingham.

Witness: Ez: Rogers( who writt this), Tho: Nulson. *Copy of will, Ipswich Deeds, vol. 1, leaf 83.*

Proved 24: 7: 1650. *Ipswich Quarterly Court Records, vol. 1, page 21.*

ESTATE OF ANTHONY SADLER OF SALISBURY.*

Administration on the estate of Anthony Sadler granted 1: 8: 1650 to his wife Martha Sadler. Ordered that ten pounds be reserved out of the estate for the use of the child she was with, she to use it for the bringing up of said child. John Cheiney, sr., surety. *Hampton Quarterly Court Records, vol. 1, leaf 22.*

Inventory of estate of Anthonie Sadler, Sallisburi, taken 20: 4: 1650, by Edward ffrench, John Cheney and Sam. Winsley: his wearing apparrell, 4li. 10s.; a musket, bandelers and sword, 1li. 10s.; a great and a small bible, 15s.; 1 bed bowlster, 1 pillow, 1 rugg, 1 coverlett, 3 sheets, 1 blankett, 4li. 5s.; 1 small table, 6s.; 2 chests, 8s.; 1 bedstead, 8s.; 1 Iron pott, 6s.; 1 frying pann, 2s. 8d.; 1 brass skillett, 4s.; 4 peces of pewter, 10s.; 4 trayes, 2 payles, 1 seive, 5s.; 1 axe, 1 how and other Lumber, 6s.; 2 cowes, 10li.; 2 twoe yerelings, 5li.; 1 calfe, 16s.; 1 sowe, 8s.; 1 pcell of land, 5li.; debts due 21li. 10s.; towe and cotten wooles and 2 yards l[i]ninge, 1li.; total, 57li. 9s. 8d. *Essex Co. Probate Files, Docket 24,489.*

ESTATE OF CHRISTOPHER OSGOOD OF IPSWICH.

"I Christopher Osgood of Ipswich beinge weake in body but of perfect vnderstandinge & memory doe Comitt my soule into the hands of my redeemer, & Concerning that little Estate the Lord hath lent mee this is my last will & testament, first I give unto my eldest Daughter Mary Osgood ten pounds to be paid her or her assignes at her day of marriage, and to my other three Daughters Abigail Elisabeth & Deborah,

* See also Records and Files of the Quarterly Courts of Essex Co., Mass., vol. 1 (1911), p. 279.

five pounds to each of them to be paid to them and euery of them at or upon their respectiue dayes of marriage. And to my Sonne Christopher Osgood I doe give my house and lands to haue & enioy the same at the age of two & twentie yeares, And my will is that my beloued wife Margery Osgood shalbe the sole executrix of this my will & to enioy the pffit & benefitt of my estate duringe the minority of my Children as abouesaid. And lastly I doe request and desire M<sup>r</sup> John Norton, and my ffather Phillip ffowler to be ouerseers that this my will be performed according to the true intent thereof. in witness heereof I haue subscribed my hand the nineteenth day of Aprill 1650." Christopher Osgood.

"I doe also desire our respected Major to a Joyne with M<sup>r</sup> Norton & my ffather."

Witness: Nathaneel Mather, Joseph Rowlandson, Daniell Rolfe.

"memorandum which was forgotten my will is that my eldest Daughter marry not without the aduice of my wife & the Consent of my ouerseers, & that my younger Daughters marry not without the Consent of their mother & the advice of the ouerseers if it may be had, and that their seuerall portions be paid unto them when they shall attaine the age of twenty yeares if they be not marryed before that age."

Christopher Osgood.

Proved 10: 8: 1650, by Daniell Rolfe. *Copy of will, Ipswich Deeds, vol. 1, leaf 76.*

Petition of Margery Osgood, widow, of Ipswich for a greater portion of the estate of her husband, than by will is given to her. Oct. 16, 1650, ordered that the business concerning the estate be referred to Mr. Samuel Symonds, Maj. Denison and Mr. John Norton, and to put an issue thereunto, keeping as near to the will as may be. *Mass. Bay Colony Records, vol. 3, page 217.*

Samuel Symonds, John Norton and Daniel Denison having considered the case, make the following alterations in the will: the eldest daughter instead of 10li. mentioned in the will, to have 8li.; the second daughter instead of 5li., to have 4li.; the eldest son to have the house and land and pay the two younger children when they shall be eighteen years, 4li. each. Dated Dec. 15, 1650. *Ipswich Deeds, vol. 1, leaf 104.*

ESTATE OF HUGH BURT, JR. OF LYNN.

"Memar Random I Hew Bort doe freeley make my wife

full exseckter. and I giue vnto hear my holle estat and I giue all soe my *my* House and land to my wife During hear life and after hear Deseese the house and land to falle to hear 2 Chilldren and all soe I freely lefe my tow Chilldren to my wifes Disposing acording to hear Discresion all soe if my wife be with Chilld y$^t$ Chilld to haue a Equll porsion with the other tow all soe I giue to my 2 Chilldren the holle estat that is left mee by my vnkell in Eingland after my ants deseese and for the seeing to hit to be parformed I haue mayd Choise of 4 to ouer see hit for the youse of my Chilldren my father Bort and Nathanell Hanfort and John Deakin and Edward Bort theese 4 I haue mayd Choise of to ouer see this estat wich is in Eingland for the youse of my 2 Chilldren." [No signature.]

Proved 31: 10: 1650, by Hugh Burt, sr. and John Deacon. *Essex Co. Quarterly Court Files, vol. 1, leaf* 118.

Inventory of estate of Hugh Burtt, jr., of Line, taken 8: 8: 1650, by Nathaniell Handforth and Robert Pepper: House and land belonging, 22li.; one hefar & to yearlinges year & vantag, 5li.; one Cowe, 5li.; to hoges & to pidges, 2li. 8s.; his beeding, blanketes belonging thereunto, 3li. 8s. 6d.; in whearing aparell, 6li. 8s.; in lienin, 2li. 16s.; in putar & poutes, 2li. 4s. 9d.; muskete, sword, cerbine & other armes, 2li.; powdar, boulates & snapsake, 3s. 6d.; 2 Chestes, to bokes & tabell, 1li. 11s. 8d.; Cheares & stoulles, 4s.; trayes, tubes, akes, spade & other toules, 1li. 3s. 2d.; one ladar, 3s. 4d.; old ireren, 6d.; in fleekes, 5s.; 8 load of hay, 4li.; in Corne, wheat & other Englesh grane, 1li. 1s.; 30 bushelles of ingen Corne, 4li. 10s.; oeing to hem the sume of 18s. 6d.; to bibelles, 10s.; total, 65li. 15s. Debts owed, 20li. 8s. Laid out for his burying, 1li. 10s. 9d. *Essex Co. Quarterly Court Files, vol. 1, leaf* 119.

### Estate of Philip Verin of Salem.

The will of Phillip Verin of Salem, deceased, not proved by witnesses, but with consent of all legatees in the country whose names were subscribed to it, it was allowed 2: 11: 1650. *Salem Quarterly Court Records, vol. 3, leaf* 29.

### Estate of Edmund Lewis of Lynn.

"Line the 13$^{th}$ of the 11$^{mo}$ 1650 memorandum that Edmund Lewis beinge sicke & weake but of perfecte remembrance doe make & Confirme this my laste will and testy-mente as foloweth firste my will Is that my land att watertowen shall be sould & thatt my eldeste sone John Lewis shall have A double portyon & yt the reste of my Children namly the fiue youngeste to haue euery one of them A licke portyon of my estate. Secondly my deare & Louinge wife to have the thirds of All my whole estate 3 I desier that my wife may have A cow over & aboue towards the bringine vpe of my youngeste Children 4 my desires Is my wife to be my whole Executor to dispose of my body & goods ackordinge to my will 5 my requeste to my sone John Is to giue his mother a Cow to hellpe her towards the bringine vpe of my youngeste Children 6 my requeste to my sone Thomas Lewis Is to giue his mother halfe of his sheepe to helpe her as Aforesaide 7 my desire & meninge is that the Cow I aske of John & the sheepe I aske of Thomas Is of them that they now have in theare possesion. Allso my requeste is to Thomas Austines to be my supervisor to assiste my Lovinge wife."

Edmund Lewes.

Witness: John Deakin, Edward Burchum.

Proved 25: 12: 1650, by Edward Burcham and ordered that the children shall have their portions paid them at the age of twenty one years. *Essex Co. Quarterly Court Files, vol. 1, leaf* 120.

Inventory taken 12: 12: 1650, by John Deakin, James Axey, Edward Burchum and William (his |×| mark) Tilton: One payer of oxen, 13li.; one payer of oxen, 14li.; fouer workinge Steares, 24li.; one too year ould heffer, 3li.; six shots, 3li.; one heffer, 2li.; too milch kine & a Calfe, 9li.; thre yearlings, 5li.; fouer wether sheepe, 2li. 16s.; fouer ewe sheepe, 6li.; thre lames of this yeare, 1li. 6s.; hay, 2li. 10s.; too littell harrowes, 10s.; one plow wth coulter & share, 6s.; one cheane, 2s. 6d.; one payer of ould wheles, 10s.; A carte & draughts, 1li.; the waine, 1li. 10s.; an ould plow, 2s. 6d.; too yockes, 6s.; one bede with the Furniter, 3li. 3s.; one bed with the Furnituer, 1li. 1s.; purse and aparell, 2li.; five pilow coverings & five napkins, 18s. 6d.; a table cloth, 2s.; a bedsteade, 5s.; a chiste, 3s. 4d.; thre wheles & too litell Chayers, 10s.; In yaren, flax & wooll, 1li. 17s.; In wheate, 10 bushels, 2li.; In Oats, 1li. 7s.; a fan, 3s. 4d.; too sithes & fouer hooks, 9s.; thre score bushels of Indyan Coren, 9li.; a sword, belte & bandelears, 12s.; too muskets & too rests, 1li. 16s.; A foulinge pece, 1li. 6s.; too small gunes, 16s.; A Cettell & too Iern pots, 14s. 8d.; A grid Ieren & a Iern kettell & a ould postnett, 6s.; peuter, 10s.; a frying pan &

a hooke, 7s.; too trayes & a meale sive & other lumber, 11s.; thre axes, too wedges & a drawinge knife, augers & a handsaw, 11s. 8d.; too drinke barells, 3s.; a bibell, 8s.; A churen, a bottell & a littell tube, 5s.; A pece of Lether, 6s.; too tubes, a brake & a crackell, 7s.; total, 122li. 7s. 6d. Debts to be payd that is owinge, 7li. 6s. 1d. *Essex Co. Quarterly Court Files, vol. 1, leaf 121.*

### ESTATE OF JOHN CROSS OF IPSWICH.

"To All vnto whom these p$^r$sents may Com: Know yee: That I John Crose of Ipswich Being in pfect memory doe make this my last will & bequest: first I bequeath my body vnto the earth vnto Christian buriall, & my soule vnto God, by & through the Lord Jesus Christ: in whom I doe Confidently expect saluation: Secondly I doe bequeath of my estate as ffolloweth: As first I bequeath vnto Anne my loueing wife my gray meare, & one horse of twoe yeare old & vpwards of a ronesh Culler with a whitesh face & wall-eyes, And also one brind Collered Cowe of three yeare old, & also an other Cowe that Marke Symens shall leaue: (hee haueing taken his two Cowes out) & also two black steeres of a yeare old & vpwards: & also two bull Calfes of this yeare: And Also I giue vnto my said wife all my household stuffe (excepting onely the second best bed, with what doe belong vnto it) & also I giue vnto my said wife the Income & benifitt of one hundred pounds for time & terme of her life: Secondly I giue vnto my Daughter Hanna my second-best bed with what doe belong unto it (excepted as abousaid) And also I giue unto my said Daughter one horse of a sanded graye Coller of two yeare old & vpwards: & also one meare Coult of this yeare: & one black horse Coult of this yeare: & Also two Cowes now in the hands of m$^r$ Coffen: & Also two heifers of a yeare old & vpwards in my owne hands: And also I giue unto my saide Daughter my feirme with all my other ground & nine Cattle now in the hands of Thomas Ellethrop as Appeareth by an Indenture beareing date the one & thirtie day of the eight m$^o$ one thousand six hundred & fifty, (excepting onely for what is to be paid for building & repations of the said feirme) And also I giue unto my said Daughter after my wifes Decease one hundred pounds (the which my said wife is to haue the benefitte of for terme of her life as is aboue said) But in Case my said Daughter doth depart this life with out Issue leaueing behind her, then my will is to giue the saide hundred pounds to the Towne of Ipswich to be & remaine towards the maintenance of a free schoole for euer: the which is to be ordered & dissposed by the officers of the Church of Ipswich for the saide worke as is aforesaid. And my will further is to make my loueing wife, & my loueing frend william Inglish my executors: moreouer my will is Concerneinge the farme & stock now in the hands of Thomas Ellethrop: bequested to my said Daughter as aforesaid: that if my said Daughter should Depart this life before she be married, Then my will is that my said wife shall haue the benifitt of the said farme & stock for terme of her life: & then my said wife shall haue powre to giue & bequeath the one halfe of the said farme & stock, & the other halfe I then giue to the Towne of Ipswich towards the maintenance of a free Schoole, Answerable as is the hndred pounds aforesaid: & my will further is to make my loueing & trustie ffreinds m$^r$ william Paine & william Howard my superuisers & feffees in trust to this my last will & Testament whom I doe inuest with powre for the dissposeinge of my estate Answerable to this my said will: And I doe hereby intreate my welbeloued & much honered ffrend m$^r$ John Norton to aford his aduice & Counsell in the dissposall of my said Daughter in a way of marryage: unto this my last will & testament I doe heereunto sett my hand & seale the first Day of Nouemb$^r$ 1650."

John Cross

Witness: Beniamin Muzzie, Elisabeth (her mark) How.

"memorand that I John Crosse of Ipswich Doe by these presents Confirme this my last will & bequest, as it is on the other side expressed; onely with this addition or Alteration: as followeth (first) that when the lord shall please in mercie to take me vnto himselfe, I doe bequeath my said Daughter Hanna Crosse vnto the Care & trust of my said executors & superuisers to be disposed of as the Lord shall direct them or the mager p$^t$ of them: for her well-being. And also for the disposeing of her said estate, to her nessesary use Answerable to her degree: & not otherwise That soe the saide estate with the income thereof may be kept together for the further benifitt of my said Daughter, to be deliuered vp unto her, & her husband at her day of marriage. (Secondly) I doe hereby request my said executors & supuisers that they will aforde their aduice & Ceare vnto my said Daughter in her dissposall in a way of marriage: & that my said Daughter shall not Joyne her selfe in a way of marriage without the Councell & Consent of the said m$^r$ John Norton of Ipswich Aforesaid whose faithfullnes I doe not in any measure question: vnto which, as an addision vnto my said Will I do heere unto sett my hand: Dated the 30$^{th}$ Day 9$^{th}$ m°: 1650."

John Cross

Witness: Robert Lord, Marke Simonds.

"memorand that wheras I John Crosse of Ipswich haue made this my last will & Testament and disposed of my estate as is therein expressed: & least that my said estate should Come short in respect of Charges & expence growing And some small debts which I was not priuie vnto, my will therefore is that when the seuerall legacies be taken out of my said estate, & what there will be then wanting to pay such Debts as shall be Justly Due: the same shall be taken out of the Cattle giuen & bequeathed to my said wife & daughter (an equall proportion) to pay such debt as shall be then due as is aforesaid, witnesse my hand Dated 18$^{th}$ Day 10$^{th}$: m° 1650."

his mark<br>John Cross.

Witness: Robert Lord.

Proved 25: 1: 1651, by Benjamin Muzye, Elisabeth How, Robert Lord. *Copy of will, Ipswich Deeds, vol. 1, leaf 112.*

Inventory taken Dec. 10, 1650, by Richard (his mark) Kemball, sr., and Robert Lord: Wearing apparell, 4li.; a featherbed & boulster & an ould coverlet, 5li.; a flockbed, 1li.; a bed floks & feathers together, a fether bolster and a tike, 2li. 14s.; 2 prs. of Red blanketts, 2li. 14s.; 1 large yarne couerlett, 1li. 8s.; 3 feather pillows, 12s. 9d.; 3 Curtaynes, 1li. 4s.; 3 Chests, an ould trunke & ould bordcloth, 1li. 8s.; in pewter, 2li. 10s.; in Gally potts & drinking pots, and holand juggs, 10s.; 3 silluer spoones, 1li.; 3 dozen & one silver butons, at 5s. per oz., 6s.; 31 yards of cotton & lenen at 16d., 2li. 1s. 4d.; a Cubord cushen, 6s. 8d.; musket, sword & bandeleors, 1li. 2s.; 5 ould axes, a wedg & other ould Iron, 1li.; a pr. of Andirons, 12s.; 2 pr. of tonges, 3s.; a tosting Iron, 2s.; a paniell and bridle, 7s.; an ould Joyne chayre with a couer, 4s.; 2 hoggsheds, a bucking tub, 2 keelars, too ould poudering tubs & 1 ould tub, 16s.; a saw, a spit, a garden rake & an ager, 6s. 8d.; a chirne, a payle & 2 lether bottells, 7s.; 2 kettells, 2 candell sticks & a chafendish, a skimer & a basting ladell, 3 spoones, 1li. 15s.; 2 little brase potts, 2 posnetts, 1li.; a diping pan, 2 sives, 4 boothauches & 1 lanthorne, a glas case, 12s.; 2 spades, a pillion, a basket, 6s. 8d.; 3 cushens, 6s.; 2 pitchforkes, 4li.; leadwayte, a grinston, 3s. 6d.; 5 pr. of sheets, 2li. 5s.; a diap. short board cloth, 3s. 4d.; a pr. of ould holand pillowbeers, 5s.; 3 corse pillowbeeres, 4s. 6d.; 6 ould corse napkins, 4s.; Corse board cloth, 4s.; a bedsted & a trundle bed & bedlyne, 16s.; 2 trayes & a stocklock & a battelor, a runlet & dressor kneding trough, 10s.; a linen wheele, a flasket & a paile, woole & hempe, 8s.; a pr. of shoes & a pr. of bootes, 12s.; 7 cheeses about 40li., 3 quarters of a firkin of buttar, 1li. 18s. 6d.; a warming pan, 6s.; a sadell, 10s.; a syd & halfe of porke, 10s.; 1 graye mare & a colt of almost 3 y: of a ronish coular, 26li.; 2 cowes, 10li., 2 steeres, 1 year & vantag, 15li.; 1 horse sanded graye of 2 yea., 2 colts, 24li.; 2 cowes & 2 heifers, yea. & vantage, 15li.; 7 cowes & 2 steers of 3 & vantage, 45li.; the farme, 100li.; in debts, 111li.; 2 small hogs, 1li. 12s.; total, 382li. 5s. 2d. Severall debts oweing wch. yet appeares not. *Essex Co. Quarterly Court Files, vol. 2, leaf 41.*

The court 28: 7: 1652, interprets words in John Crose's will, about paying debts between mother and daughter, to mean that they shall be shared equally. *Ipswich Quarterly Court Records, vol. 1, page 31.*

### Estate of Thomas Barker of Rowley.

"I Thomas Barker of Rowley, in Newenglande though at p$^r$sent weake of body, yet of good vnderstanding, doe ordaine & make this my Last will & Testament. ffirst I doe Comfortably giue up my Soule into the hands of God through Jesus Christ in whom I doe trust that I shall haue a Joyfull resurrection. And I doe abhorre all the errors & Blasphemies that doe abounde in these dayes, against the said resurrection & the holy Scriptures. Inprimis for the blessings of this life which God hath giuen me I doe giue to o$^r$ reuerend Pastor, m$^r$ Ezekiel Rogers, my young mare, he paying out of it A Cowe to the Stock of the Towne of Rowley to be disposed of by the Elders & Deacons. Item I giue to my Deare Sister Jane Lambert one Ewe Sheepe. Item I giue to Thomas Leauer & his wife one Ewe sheepe. Item I giue to John Johnson two pounds: To Elizabeth Johnson one pounde. Item I giue to Thomas Lambert Sixty pounds or the one halfe of my Lande, w$^{th}$ ten pounds: whether of these my wife seeth meete: And my meaning is that if he haue the halfe of the Lande, that the dwellinge howse & Barnes & other housing are excepted, with all the yards & lands betweene the Streete & the Brooke. Item I doe giue to my wellbeloued wife Mary Barker my Dwellinge house, Barnes all the rest of the housinge & yards as before excepted. Item I doe giue to my saide wife, Mary All my Lands & priuiledges therto belonging in Rowley. Item I giue to mary my saide wife all my Goods, houshold Stuffe, Cattell, money or whatsoeuer is mine my Legacies & debts being discharged. Item for the time when Thomas Lambert his aforesaide portion is to be paid, my meaning is, that it be paide him at the Age of one & Twenty yeeres. but if he the saide Thomas Die before the Age of one & twenty yeeres, my will is that the portion to him bequeathed shallbe diuided among all his brothers & sisters, Jonathan haueing a double share, & the rest equall. Item I doe giue to my beloued Brethren Thomas Mighill, & mathewe Boyes, each of them forty shillings. I doe make my Deare wife mary my sole Executrix of this my last will & testament. And o$^r$ Loueing Pastor, Thomas Mighill our Deacon, & mathew Boyes ouerseers of the same. In witnesse wherof I doe here sett to my hande & seale."

Thomas Barker.

Witness: Ezekiel Rogers, Thomas Mighell, Mathew Boyes.

Proved 25: 1: 1651 by Thomas Mighill and Mathew Boyce. *Copy of will, Ipswich Deeds, vol. 1, leaf 120.*

Copy of inventory taken 11: 10: 1650, by Humfrey Reyner, Thomas Mighel, Maximilian Jawet and Joseph Jawet: in his purse, 5li. 5s.; his Apparrell, 9li. 15s. 8d.; one Chest of Linin, 9li. 6s. 8d.; in Bookes, 2li. 6s. 8d.; more Linin, 2li. 6s.; one Bed & the furniture about it, 11li.; three Bed Coverings, 3li.; one Bed & the furniture, 13li.; Cushens 13, 3li. 3s. 4d.; A Bed & Cloathes about it, 8li.; A Bed & the ffurniture aboute it, 3li. 5s.; A Table & fforme, 13s. 4d.; one Chest, 5s.; two Boxes, 3s.; fowre Chaires, 6s.; A Table & Table Cloth, 6s. 8d.; some woollen yarne, 2s. 5d.; hemp and fflax, 4li. 10s.; hemp seeds and fflax seed, 15s.; A Chest and A Trunke, 10s.; in pewter, 3li. 11s.; two silver spoones, 8s.; in Brasse, 5li. 4s.; three Iron potts, 1li.; A paire of Andirons, fire shovell, tongs & a *Gable Bauke*, 2li. 5s.; wood vessells, 2li. 10s.; Butter & Porke, 4li. 5s.; in Armes, 5li. 10s.; Baggs & Ropes, 2li.; A Bed stock and measures with such like huselments, 1li. 6s. 8d.; one hive Beese, 15s.; one mare & two Colts, 40li.; six oxen, 43li.; eight Cowes & heifers, 34li.; two Bulls, 6li. 10s.; two steeres & five heifers, 23li.; three Calves, 4li.; 24 sheepe, 24li.; 26 ACres of Corne, 50li.; in hay, 12li.; house & Lande, 150li.; A Cart, 1li. 6s. 8d.; two plows, 1li. 5s.; yoakes & Cheynes, boults & shakels, 1li. 5s.; Iron Tooles, 1li. 5s.; seaven Hoggs, 11li.; in Debts Coming to him, 9li. 6s. *Ipswich Deeds, vol. 1, leaf 121.*

### ESTATE OF BELSHAZZAR WILLIX OF SALISBURY.*

Administration on the estate of Bellshasar Willix, of Salisbury, granted 8: 2: 1651 to his wife Mary Willix. To bring in inventory at next Hampton court. *Salisbury Quarterly Court Records, vol. 1, leaf 25.*

Inventory taken 22: 11: 1650 by Joseph (his X mark) Moyce, Wm. Barnes and Sam Winsley: one feather bedd and bowllster and 2 pillowes and 2 blanketts, 1li. 15s.; 14li. cotten wooll, 8s.; working tooles, one how, owld hatchets, 1li.; 1 throw, 1 plane, 1 briske, 3s.; his wearing apparrell, 2li. 10s.; a grindstoun, 9s. 6d.; lummber, 5s.; 1 pr. stockings, buttons, a band and a bagg, 10s.; total, 7li. 1s. 6d. *Essex Co. Probate Files, Docket 29,974.*

### ESTATE OF RALPH BLASDELL OF SALISBURY.

Administration on the estate of Ralfe Blasdell, intestate, granted 24: 4: 1651 to his widow, Elizabeth Blasdell, and ordered to bring in an inventory at the next court. *Salem Quarterly Court Records, vol. 3, leaf 34.*

### ESTATE OF JOSEPH HOW OF LYNN.

"This is my will & desire —— to take me out of this world—— shall haue all the mouables in & —— as allso the 2 Coues which I —— allso the pide haifer & 3 haifors —— boloks I leue with my wife to *make* —— of to pay all my deats every on that demands anything let them be payd: & what is left my wife to hau it: the house & land I leue to my wiffe vntell the Child Elizebeth how of my on body be 18 yeres of Age & then that shee shall haue if god despose of hur in marag but in case the child should die then my

* See also Records and Files of the Quarterly Courts of Essex Co., Mass., vol. 1 (1911), p. 253.

wife to haue it for euer; if god should so order it that my wife should remaine my widdou & mary no othr man then I leue the land to my wife & hir desposing: the tow cows which we cal mouse & spek to be att my mother hows desposing I mene shee shall haue them to hir self & all so so much of the march as shall find them hay if it be Required vntell my mother be be desesed ||for hir vse|| allso that those which uses the land shall yerly let my mothe[r] haue land bring forth Indian & som english & this during her life or else that she shall haue so much of the land att hir desposing during hir life as may produse it ⸺ in quantaty is six Aker of up⸺ eaite Akers of march liing in ⸺wne march & six Akers of march ⸺ by march now Acording as I haue ⸺ t is my *my* full will & desr & hereto hath set my hand this tenth of febiwary 1650."

Joseph how:

"And for the oursight of what is wrighten I leue to my fathre needom & goodman bread"

"This is my will that my mother If god Take me a way shall haue 2 Acers of Land at the ferder End of y^e Lot next goodman breads: Lot that: he bout of goodman poole: I also Leue to my mother 2 Coues: namly moucy and speck: and them to be her one for Euer and att her desposing: also yt she shall haue as much hay as will sufisantly kepe 2 cous: of y^e hether pece of marsh: Liing next goodman brad one y^e one side and m^r soth one y^e Eather sid: but when god shall Take my mother a way It shall then Retorn to y^e house again I mene y^e marsh olnely: this is my Last will and: desier: toching: my mother: in presents of

Ephraim How."

Proved 24: 4: 1651, by Elizabeth Breade and William Meriam. *Essex Co. Quarterly Court Files, vol. 2, leaf 15.*

Inventory taken 8: 1: 1650-51, by Aline (his + mark) Braide, Edward Burchum and Phillip Kyrtland: too milch kine, 10li.; a too yeare ould heffer, 3li.; thre yearlinge Calves, 5li.; too milch kine, 10li.; too oxen, 18li.; too hogs & too litell pigs, 2li. 4s.; the house, lande and medow, 36li.; a Carte & yocke, 15s.; an Ax & too wedges, 5s. 6d.; a loade of hay, 10s.; a craddell, 5s.; thre pounde of powder, 5s.; twenty pounde of shote, 5s.; a Case & seauen glasses, 5s.; his purse & Aparell, 4li. 10s.; a box, chiste & other lumber, 5s.; in Coren, 1li. 10s.; thre payer of sheets, 1li. 10s.; too pilow Couerings, 5s.; a fether bed & boulster, 2li. 15s.; 4 yards &

a half of cloth, 1li. 13s. 6d.; a ruge & a blanckett, 8s.; six napkines & a table Cloth, 9s.; a bedsteade, 1li.; a Chayer, 5s.; in yaren, 4s.; in puter, 1li. 10s.; a table & too stools, 6s.; a hangine Candellsticke, 2s. 6d.; a gune, 1li.; a Chayer, 2s.; a Copper kettell, 1li.; a tube & soume lumber, 10s.; a spite & fryinge pan & a pece of Iren, 5s.; one Iren kettell, 4s.; a brase potte, 8s.; hooks & hangers, 3s.; a gird Iern, 1s.; trayes & dishes, 2s.; an Iern postnett, 2s. 6d.; a chiste, 3s.; in bookes, 8s.; a diall Case, 8d.; in backer, 5s. Total, 107li. 10s. 8d. *Essex Co. Quarterly Court Files, vol. 2, leaf* 16.

### ADOPTION OF PHILIP FOWLER OF IPSWICH.

Phillip ffowler the elder, of Ipswich, in the presence of Joseph his son and Martha his wife, and with their full consent, adopted as his own son, Phillip, the son of the said Joseph and Martha, 18: 6: 1651. *Ipswich Deeds, vol.* 1, *leaf* 94.

### ESTATE OF WALTER TIBBOTT OF GLOUCESTER.

"1651 the 5 of 4 month. In The nam of god aman I walter Tibbott being in sound and parfete Memberie blessed be god. I Doe make my last will and Tistment I be quieth my bodie To the earthe and my sp[i]rite to god That gaue it In sartaine ||hope|| of The reserecsion of the bodie when The soule and The bodie shall mete Together to reseue Thate Blessed sentanse of Com ye blessed reseue The King prepered for you be for the foundation of the world Itim I make my wif my exseketor and giue To heare my housen together with the land belong belonging to it with t[h]e medowe be long to it the land I boght of sabelond hill and the medowe I boght of Tommas smeth and This I giue to heare during heare lif and after heare Desese I giue This to richard dicke my grandchild who is the right aire I giue to my Dafter mari hasskol The wif of william hasskole fiftene pound in good pay I giue To Josef hasskol sonn to willam my farme at chebake I giue to william hasskoll other Thre sonnes Twenti shelenes a pece to be pote to som good implimont fortheMore I giue my sonn in lawe edward clarke fiue pound mor I giue to John clark and Josefe clark twenti shellenes apece to pot to some good impliments to ras them a stock. Mor I giue elisaberth dick four pound mor I giue to elnor bapsene The wife o[f] James bapsene forti shellens I g[i]ue to sabelone hill Ten shellenes Mor to John hill ten shelnes Mor I giue to william haskoll my clocke The reste of my wearing aparell To my sonn clark I giue Lastly I appoint these Legacies to bee paid that day twelve month after my decease. in witnesse whereof I haue set to my hand & seele. Dated $y^e$ $5^r$ of $y^e$ 4, 1651."

Walter Tibbot [Seal]

Witness: W<sup>m</sup> Perkins, Robert Tucker.

*Essex Co. Quarterly Court Files, vol. 2, leaf 26.*

The will of Walter Tibbot of Gloucester, deceased 14: 6: 1651, was delivered into this court by Robert Tucker, but cannot now be found; a copy whereof is now presented, Mr. Wm. Perkins and Robert Tucker, testifying to the truth of it, upon whose testimony the court, Oct. 19, 1652 doth allow the same. *Mass. Bay Colony Records, vol. 3, page 290.*

Copy of inventory of estate of Walter Tibbot, lately deceased in Gloucester ye 1: 7: 1651, by William Perkins and Robert Tucker: his Dwelling house, Barne & Cowhouse with six Acres of broken up land, twelve Acres unbroken, lying at the lower neck, ten more at the little river & 28 Acres of meadow, 60li.; A ffarme at Chebacco containing fforty Acres of upland & ten of wast medo, 10li.; one yoake of Oxen, 16li.; one yoake of steeres, 9li.; three Cowes, 15li.; one heifer of 3 yeare old, with one yeareling & two Calves, 8li.; nine goates, 4li. 10s.; foure Kidds, 16s.; Ten swine, 9li. 15s.; Corne, 15li.; of howshold goods, pewter, 3li.; one great brasse Kettle, 2li.; 3 Iron potts & one frying pan, 1li. 3s.; one ffether bed, two flock beds with the Coveringe thereunto belonging, 12li.; his wearing Apparell, 7li.; table linen, 1li.; some Tubs, Tramels, tonges, pales, borrds & such small things valued at 1li. 10s.; one Cart, plowe, plowe Chaine, two wedges & one Axe, 1li.; three Cannooes, 2li. 16s.; one bible & some other bookes, 1li. 10s.; total, 181li. *Ipswich Deeds, vol. 1, leaf 115.*

## Estate of Nathaniel Smith.

"I Nathaniel Smith being in sound Mind and perfect Memory, doe dispose of My Monie and goods that is now in New England and elsewhere in wise and Manner following. The sixty three pounds that is in M<sup>r</sup> George Corwins hands due by bond Twenty Pounds of it My will is that it shall bee disposed of to My kinsman Thomas Edwards, Eighteene Povnds to My sister Ruth Halford Tenne Pounds to M$^r$ John Nicolls flaxman and five Pounds to My couzin Nathaniel Edwards. And ten Pounds to My Uncle John Smith. Also My will is that the Monie in James Browns hands and that w$^{ch}$ is in M$^r$ Makepeaces hand Brownes being eight or Ten Povnds and M$^r$ Makepeaces fower Povnds Ten shillings My will is my sister Hannah Mellowes shall have. And I freely give it to her. Moreover the Linnen that I have I doe giue the Napkins and Towels and Table Clothes, and one Halfe of the sheetes to My kinsman Thomas Edwards, and the other halfe of the sheetes to my Sister Hannah Mellowes in New England Moreover that Linnen of mine in My Brother M$^r$ Samvel Wandleys hands, I doe freely bestow it vpon him. Moreover also if their showld be any allowance for the Plundered Estate one halfe whereof is due to mee, I doe giue one halfe of it to My Brother M$^r$ Samuel ffisher, and the other halfe to be distributed betweene My sister Malford and my Sister Wandley, ffor the performance of this according to my true intent and Meaning I doe appoynt and constitute My Kinseman Thomas Edwards and my Couzin Nathaniel Edwards My administrators and Assignes this 19$^{th}$ February 1650. Witnesse My hand and Seale."

Nathaniel Smith

Witness: Samuel Brinsmead, Samuel Oliver.

Certificate of proof printed in Latin. Test. Nathaniel Brent. Michael Oldisworth, Henry Parker, Reg. Jeremia Savage, Jo. Donaldson, Not. Pub. *Copy of Will, Essex Co. Probate Files, Docket 25,701.*

On Sept. 30, 1651, Nath. Edwards and his brother Thomas Edwards, the latter now in England, were appointed administrators of the estate of Nathaniell Smith, deceased, in New England, being nominated in his will, as per certificate of Michaell Oldsworth and Henry Parker, registers. Jeremia Savage and Jo. Donoldson, nota publiqus. Copy of will granted by the prorogative court of London presented to this court to be recorded. *Ipswich Quarterly Court Records, vol. 1, page 25.*

The deputies having considered the case respecting the will of Nathaniel Smyth exhibited in the General Court by Nath. Edwards, declared the said will to be the last will of Nathaniel Smyth and it was allowed 6: 8: 1651 with the consent of the magistrates. *Mass. Archives, vol. 15B, page 73.*

Petition of Nathaniel Edwards that whereas he has lately come over as administrator of the will of Nathaniel Smith, deceased, and proved the will in the last Ipswich Court, and notwithstanding all which, having lately met with some interruption concerning the will by Mr. Joseph Hill of Malden, he now requests that the probation of the will may be confirmed, or if there be just cause of objection by Mr. Joseph Hill against the will, that he may be admitted to plead his cause before the court, having urgent reasons to hasten his return for England. The petitioner's request granted Oct. 15, 1651, the clerk to secure the 10s. due to the country. *Mass. Archives, vol.* 15B, *page* 71.

Whereas Nathaniell Edwards presented to this court a will made by Nathaniell Smyth and several testimonies to prove that the said will was confirmed and allowed by the prorogative court in England, which upon perusal this court doth also declare to be legal and ordered that Nathaniel Edwards should put in a caution to the next County court at Boston, to be responsall for all the estate of the said Smyth being within this jurisdiction in case the will should be reversed, this done with the magistrates consent, 24 : 8 : 1651. *Mass. Archives, vol.* 15B, *page* 74.

A copy of the last will of Nathaniell Smith which Mr. Joseph Hill of Malden presented to the General Court 16 : 8 : 1651 :

"Goods brought with me out of England which amounted to 180li. odd, 38li. 7s. 6d. was Mr. John Wads, of the remainder my brother Halford hath two thirds and myself one, and likewise I was by agreement to have a third part of the gains that was made. Of that part which comes to my share my will is that it be disposed as follows: "two parts of it to my brother mellowes: one parte to william Halford my brother ||Andrew|| Halfords Sonne, in Case of his death to Ruth Halford and the other parte to my Cozen Nathaniell wandley, my will is that the Linnen, Bookes and other things I left in New-England, my Couzen Hanna mellowes should have the Linnen, and Abraham mellowes my bookes for the Linnen I left in England my will is that my Sister mellowes should have one parte, and the other parte to be devided Betweene my Sister ffisher and my Sister walford. for the bookes I left in England my will is that Nathaniell Wandley shall have, and if it please god to restore any thing of the plundered estate my will is that my parte which is halfe, shall be equally devided, betweene all my sisters, and for the Seing of this perfourmed I Constitute and Appointe my brother Edward Mellowes, and my brother Samuell wandley my executors, whereunto I have Sett my hand this first of January 1648."

George Buncker                        Nathaniell Smith

George Buncker deposed that the above was at the date thereof the declared last will and testament of Nathaniell Smith. *Mass. Archives, vol. 15B, page 72.*

### ESTATE OF RICHARD BARRETT OF (LYNN?).

"The last will & Testament of Richard Barrett this 10. 7 m° 1651 ffirst I will that my estate shall remaine with my wife for her maintynance & my Childrens. & then at the yeares end or at the day of her marryage my estate to be deuided, my wife to haue one halfe, & my Children the other halfe, & my sonne out of that halfe shall haue a double portion, And further I giue to my sonne my ffowleing peice It to be kept for him & the ppty of it not Changed, And this is my last will & testament witnes my hand the day & yeare aboue written."

                                     his mark
                             Richard     Barick

Witness: Joseph Armitage, Jane Armytage.
"Nicholas Potter Joseph Armitage to be ouerseers."

Proved 7m: 1651 by Joseph Armitage, sr. and 29: 7: 1651 by Joseph Armitage, jr. *Copy of will, Ipswich Deeds, vol. 1, leaf 119.*

Copy of inventory taken 7m: 1651, by Richard (his mark) Johnson and John Mansfelde: 3 Cowes, 13li. 15s.; one Calfe of a yeare old this winter, 1li.; two piggs, 14s.; Indian Corne & wheate & hay & garden stuffe, 9li. 15s.; househould goods, 9li. 16s.; one fowling peice, 1li. 10s.; two hatts, 10s.; ffenceing stuffe in the woods, 1li.; total, 38li. Debts Dewe to the estate: from Mr. Bennit, 15s.; from Geloo, 12li.; goodman Coock of Salem, 15s. The Debts yt Richard Barret oweth at his Death: To Mr. Kinge, 1li. 10s.; Joseph Armytage, 1li. 18s. 10d.; Robert Borges for eight bushells of corne, 1li. 6s. 8d.; Goodwife Elis, 13s. 6d.; Goodwife Bowtell, 5s.; Mr. Jencks, 2s. 6d.; Mr. Savidg, 1li. 10s.; William Edmonds, 6s.; Goodman Coats, 13s.; Mr. Corbit, 15s.; Mr. South, 10s.; Thomas Beall, 2s. 6d. *Ipswich Deeds, vol. 1, leaf 120.*

Administration on the estate of Rich. Barick granted 30: 7: 1651 to his widow Elizabeth Barick. *Ipswich Quarterly Court Records, vol. 1, page 26.*

### Estate of Honor Rolfe of Newbury.

"Henry Largin of Charlstowne —— house of Thomas Blanchard on n—— where widdow Honour Rolfe lay —— berry lay sick. Shee did declare h—— be; that her sonne Beniam Rolfe should haue the substance of her estate, which was her owne pp estate, & that he should be her sole Executor. Only she gaue these pticulers as followeth, her bedding & Clothes linnen and woollen she gaue to be equally deuided betwixt her two daughters. Also shee gaue twenty shillings a piece to her foure grandchildren to be giuen them five yeares after her death. Also one little Cowe she gaue to her Daughter y$^t$ liues at Newberry. Also of foure peeces of Brasse shee gaue two to her sonne Beniamin, which he should Choose, & to each of her daughters one. The rest shee gaue to her Sonne Beniamine, saueing two pewter platters which she gaue to each of her daughters one. & further shee exprest her mind about a Barne that is built vpon p$^t$ of her sonne Beniamins ground, she gaue to her sonne John Rolfe all her interest in the ground that the Barne stood vpon. this is the substance of her expression as farr as he can remember

"memorandum that p$^t$ of the 22 the whole 23. 24 & p$^t$ of y$^e$ 25 lines were blotted out        Ri. Bellingham.

"Taken vpon oath by the said Henry Largin this 20—12—1650. who further saith that the said Honor Rolfe was of a disposeing memory. before me Ri. Bellingham.

"The Testymoney of George Vaghan Aged abought 23 yeares Concerning the last will of Hono$^r$ Rolfe widdow deceased: 19$^{th}$ of 10$^{th}$ m$^o$ 1650. This Deponent saith that himselfe being in p$^r$fence together with Henry Largin some two daies before the death of the aboue said testator, he heard her make this her last will in maner following. Inprimis She bequeathed all her estate in generall to her yongest Sonne Beniamine Rolfe onely excepted these pticulers which follow: Item to her foure Grand Children she gaue twenty shillings a peec, to be paid them foure or fiue yeare after that time. Item all her Right in halfe an acre of Ground on which the Barne stands and a yonge sowe she gaue to her sonne John Rolfe: Item a little Cowe that she had she gaue to her daughter Hanah Dole. Item all her weareing Cloathes & bedding she gaue to be equally deuided betweene her two Daughters Anna and Hanah: these pticulers abouesaid this deponent tooke spetiall notice of; & further he saith not: only a day after her sonne in lawe Richard Dole comeing to her desired this Deponent to Aske her what she would doe with the three pounds ten shillings in England, & shee Answered that she would that her sonne Beniamine should haue a sute of Cloathes out of it, & the rest he should haue meaning her said sonne in Lawe Richard Dole. The word Beniamine enterlined. Taken upon oath this 20$^{th}$ of the 12$^{th}$ m° 1650 before me William Hibbins"

"The Court vpon the Testimoneys of George Vaughan & Henry Largin of Charlestowne as fare as there Testimonys doe agree is the will & Testa$^{mt}$ of Honour Rofe." *Copy of will, Ipswich Deeds, vol. 1, leaf 123.*

Proved 30: 7: 1651 by Henry Lurgen and George Vaughan. *Ipswich Quarterly Court Records, vol. 1, page 26.*

### ESTATE OF SARAH BAKER OF IPSWICH.

Administration on the estate of Sarah Baker granted 30: 7: 1651, to her kinswoman, Sarah Lumpkin, and inventory received. *Ipswich Quarterly Court Records, vol. 1, page 26.*

Copy of inventory of estate of Sarah Baker, Ipswich, taken the last of the 7m: 1651, by John Whipple and Thomas ffrench: A black stuffe gowne, 1li.; A stuffe pettycoate, 6s.; A Cloth wastcoate, 8s.; A mohaire pettycoate, 1li.; two red pettycoates & two wastcoates, 1li.; one sheete & one bord Cloth, 8s.; small wareing linnen, 1li. 13s. 8d.; total, 5li. 15s. 8d. *Ipswich Deeds, vol. 1, leaf 115.*

### ESTATE OF MRS. ELIZABETH LOWLE OF NEWBURY.*

"The will of Elizabeth Lowle late wife to Jn°: Lowle Deceased made the 17$^{th}$ first m°: 1650. That I Elizabeth Lowle Considering my fraile condition doe Comitt my soule vnto the Lord Jesus my redemer who hath bought me with his blood not Doubting of my resurrection together with all Saints. I doe therefore while I inioy my sences Dispose of that estate God hath Lent me as ffolloweth; I giue to my Sister Tappine one suite of ||my|| weareing lining as one

---

*See also Records and Files of the Quarterly Courts of Essex Co., Mass., vol. IV (1914), pp. 378-381.

forward Cloth one quoife one handkerchife; I giue to my three sonns in Law Jn⁰: Lowle James & Joseph tenn shillings A peece I giue to my sonne Beniamine one siluer Cupp & three siluer Spoones with one third p$^t$ of the howshold stuffe. I giue to my Daughter Elizabeth all the remainder of my Howsehold stuffe Childbed linning & else weareing Apparrell 1 siluer Tunn 1 siluer tipt Jugg 3 siluer spoones one gold ring, 1 siluer bodkine, 2 deskes; & the rest of my Estate Equally deuided betweene my sonne Beniamine & my Daughter Elizabeth after my Debts be sattisfyed with all funerall charges, & else; I will that my brother Thomas Millerd keepe my sonne Beniamine & his estate vntill he goe forth to be an Apprentice & then to be plact forth as my ouerseers thinke fitt; I desire my foure bretherne to be my ouerseers namely bro: tho: millerd Ric⁰: Lowle Abr: Tappine & Will: Gerrish desireing them to see my Daughter Elizabeth be brought vp to her nedle & what else they Judge meete & to disspose of her as I desire to such as are Godly and meete to instruct my Child in the feare of God In witnes hereof I haue put my hand this 10$^{th}$ first m⁰: 1650. I will that if my sonne & daughter die ere they Come to Age that then their portions be deuided between my Husbands Children, Jn⁰: Lowle & James & Ben: mary & Peter Lowle." Elizabeth Lowle.

Witness: George Emery, Peter Tappan, Will: Gerrish.

Proved 30:7:1651, by William Gerish, and 2:8:1651 by Peeter Tappan. *Copy of will, Ipswich Deeds, vol. 1, leaf 118.*

Copy of inventory taken 6m: 1651: in plate 9li. 15s., 4 rings, 24s., 10li. 19s.; a laune Cubbord Cloth & an croscloths, 1li. 2s.; a Table Cloth & 18 handkerchifs, 2li. 5s.; 1 Cubbord Cloth, 4 holland pillowberes, 1li. 17s.; 12 pillowbeers, 1 shift, napkins & table cloth, 3li. 4s.; 7 Aprons, 6 napkins, 1 table cloth, 1li. 8s.; 8 towels, 2 pillowbeers, 3 waskoats, 2 napkins, 1li. 12s. 8d.; 3 pillowbeers, 6 diap. napkins, 1li. 6s.; 2 napkins, 2s. 6d.; 1-2 a table cloth & 1-2 a towell, 1li. 5s.; 1 Cubbord Cloth, 20s.; 1 napkin, 1 p sheetes, 1li. 16s.; 1 Cewshen & 1 Cubbord Cloth, 1li. 12s. 6d.; 2 greene Aprons & 1 muffe, 1li. 10s.; 4 Gownes, 1 p blanckets & 1 pann, 7li. 16s.; small things in Iron, 13s. 8d., 1 beareing cloth, 1li. 3s. 8d.; 1 wt. Cloake, 6s. 8d., 1 red blanckett, 4s., 10s. 8d.; 1 p of wrought Vallents, 2li. 10s.; 1 wrought Cubbord Cloth, 1li. 10s.; 2 greene Curtines, 1 riding Suite, 2li. 15s.; in small things, 2li. 10s.; in Debts, 98li. 7d. *Ipswich Deeds, vol. 1, leaf 119.*

In answer to the petition of Capt. William Gerrish, one of the overseers of the will of Elizabeth Lowle, desiring that there might be an order by this court made for the increase and preservation of the estate for the benefit of the children, it was granted Oct. 19, 1658, that the estate may be let out to the brother of the children of the said Elizabeth Lowle, or to others, as they see best, and to give security. *Mass. Bay Colony Records, vol. 4, page 348.*

The elders and six of the inhabitants of Newbury presented a certificate to the court Sept. 25, 1666, that Benjamin Lowell and Elizabeth Lowell were of age to receive the portions left them by their father and mother, and the court allowed it. *Ipswich Quarterly Court Records, vol. 1, page 155.*

Acquittance of Phillip Nellson of Rowley to Richard Lowle and others, overseers of the will of John Lowle, deceased, and Elizabeth Lowle, of all demands. Dated Feb. 20, 1666.
Witness: Ezekiell Northend, John Pickard.
Sworne to Sept. 30, 1673 by John Pickard and Sept. 29, 1674 by Ezekiell Northend. *Ipswich Deeds, vol. 3, page 326.*

### ESTATE OF THOMAS HAUXWORTH OF SALISBURY.

The court held at Hampton, 8: 8: 1651, appointed Mary Willix administratrix of estate of Tho. Hauxworth, her former husband, who died about nine years ago, intestate.

Inventory of estate of Tho. Hauxworth of Salisbury, taken by Henry Monde and Robart ffitts: one house & house Lott, conteining two acres, more or less, 3li.; one great Lott, 20 acres more or less, 1li.; a planting Lott, conteining fower acres more or lesse, 1li. 10s.; an addicon of lande towards ye ferrie, 3s. 4d.; two meddow Lotts conteining 4 acres more or lesse, 3li.; 4 Goates & two Kids, 2li. 10s.; two shotes, 1li.; 12 bushel of Indian corne & six of wheat, 3li. 3s.; two Iron Potts, 16s.; one frijng pann, 2s.; one Gridiron & one warming pann, 5s.; 3 peuter dishes & 12 trenchers, 6s.; 1 sieve, five spoones & one woodden dish, 1s. 4d.; 2 knives, 3 scythes, 2 howes, 2 Axes, 1 hatchett, 1 steele & steele iron, 10s.; 2 hogsheads, 2 keelars, 1 firkin, 6s.; 1 bedstead, 2 Cheasts, 1 box, 16s.; 1 stoole, 1 Chaier, 2s.; 1 course bed teeke, 1 boulster, 2 pilloes, 10s.; a paier of sheets, 2 shirts, 6s. 8d.; 3

coates, 2 paier of breches, 1 dublett, 1 jackett, 1 hatt, 1 paier of shoes, 1 paier of stockins, 3 bands, 4li. 5s.; total, 23li. 12s. 4d.

*Essex Co. Probate Files, Docket* 12,289.

### Estate of John Osgood of Andover.

"The 12 of Aprill 1650: in the ag of the testator 54 born in 1595 July 23 In the name off God Amen I John ossgood off Andeyer in the County of Essex in new England Being Sick of Body But in Pfect memory do institut and mak my last will and Testament in maner and fforme as ffolloweth Inprins I bequeath ‖and‖ Giue my Soule in to the hand of God my heauenly ffather through the medyation of Jesus Christ my Blessad Saviour and Redeemer my Body to the earth ffrom whenc it was taken my Goods and chatells as ffolloweth Inprinis I do Giue Vnto my Sonn John Ossgood my hous and hous lot with all acomedationes thervnto Belonging Brooken vp and Vnbroken Vp and with all the medow thervnto belonging fforeuer with this proviso y$^t$ my wif Sarah ossgood shall haue the moyety or the on half of the hous and land and medowes during her naturall life. I do Giue and Bequeath to my Sonn Steven Ossgood 25 pound to be payd at 21 yeares of age in Contry pay It I doe Giue to my daughter Mary Ossgood 25 pound to be payd at 18 years off age in Contry pay It I do Giue to my dater Elizabeth Ossgood 25 pound to be payd at 18 yeares off age in Contry pay It I do giue and Bequeath Vnto my daughter hannah Ossgood 25 pound to be payd at 18 years of age in Contry pay It I do Giue to my daughter ssarah Clement 20s It I do Giue to her daughter *Bakah* 20 sshillings to Be payd when she is 7 yeres of age But if she dy before y$^t$ tim it to be null It I do Giue to my Seruant Caleb Johnson one Cow calf to Be payd 3 years Befor his time is out and to be kept at the Cost of my executor till his tim is out It I do Giue to the meeting hous off newbery 18 shillings to Buie A Chushion for the minister to lay his *Book* Vpon: all the Rest of my Goods and Chateal Vnbequeathed I do giue Vnto my sone John Ossgood and to Sarah my wife whom I do mak Joynt executorrs of my last will and testament in wittness thereof [I] set my hand an Seale." John Ossgood.

"I do intreat John Clement of Hauerell and Nichalas hoult of Andever to be ouerseers of this my last will and testament."

John Ossgood.

Witness: Joseph Parker, Richard Barker.
"debt owing to me
m^r Edword Woodman eyght shillings."
Proved 25: 9: 1651, by the witnesses. *Salem Quarterly Court Files, vol. 2, leaf 22.*

Presented by Joseph Parker and Robert Barker, proved by Robert Barker. *Salem Quarterly Court Records, vol. 3, leaf 35.*

Inventory taken by John Clements and Nicholas (his H mark) Hoult, and signed by Sarah (her O mark) Osgood: His purse & apparell, 10li.; fowre oxen, 30li.; two steeres, 10li.; six Cowes, 29li.; seaven young cattle, 14li.; eighteen swine, 25li.; 120 Bushels of wheat, 24li.; 30 Bushels of Ry, 5li.; 120 Bushels of Indian, 15li.; house, lands & meadowes, 80li.; for Rie sowed, 12li.; due upon bond, 20li.; sixty Bushels of Barley, 13li.; fifty Bushels of Pease, 8li. 15s.; a feather bed & furniture, 4li. 10s.; a flockbed being half feathers & furniture, 3li. 16s.; a flock bed & furniture, 2li.; a flock bed & furniture, 2li.; five payre of sheets & an odd one, 2li. 8s.; table linnen, 1li.; fowre payre of pillowbeers, 18s.; nineteene yards of Carsai, 5li.; sixe yards of Sarge, 1li. 4s.; ten yards of Canvace, 15s.; a remnant of Serge, 9s.; penistone ten yards, 1li. 10s.; ten payre of stockins, 18s.; three yards of stuffe, 10s.; twenty two peeces of peauter, 2li.; for ye Copper & brasse, 4li. 14s.; an iron pot, tongs, cottrel & pothookes, 1li.; two muskets & a fowling peece, 2li. 10s.; sword, cutlace & bandaleeres, 1li. 5s.; yarne & cottenwool, 15s.; barrels, tubbs, trayes, cheesemoates & payles, 1li. 10s.; a slead, 5s.; bedsteds, cords & chayers, 14s.; cheasts and wheeles, 16s.; a warming pan, 5s.; fowre Axes, 8s.; three hoes, 8s.; three wedges, 3s.; fowre augers, 5s.; a gouge, two hammers & a broad chisel, 2s. 6d.; for Hay, 8li.; cart & wheeles, 2li.; a dung cart & wheeles, 1li.; a cart roape, 3s.; fiue yoake & the hookes, 15s.; three chaynes, 15s.; ploughs & iron, 1li. 5s.; a Harrow, 1li.; fiue sives, 5s.; a Spade & Crow, 7s.; three Sithes, fiue Sickles, one mathook, pitchforks & a grindstone, 1li.; nayles, 5s.; fower Sacks, 8s.; a hayre cloth, 5s.; bridle & Saddle, 5s.; for Sawes, 10s.; mault, 16s.; a ferkin of Butter, 1li. 8s.; bacon, 2s.; cheese, 2li.; a yard of holland, 4s.; a yard & half of Callico, 2s. 6d.; houshold implements, 1li.; total, 373li. 7s. *Essex Co. Quarterly Court Files, vol. 2, leaf 23.*

### Estate of James Bowtwell of Lynn.

"The will of James Bowtwell Inprimis; I giue to my sonne James Bowtwell one bull Calfe; with the increase, to be payed; when the aforesaid calf is 3 yeare old; And I giue to my daugter sara; one cow calfe at the 29 day of y^e ||sauenth|| month next ensuing the date hereof  And I apointe my wife allice Bowtell sole excecutrix of all my estate; & to bring up my Children; & to dispose of them as she in her wisdome shall haue occassion; And further I giue to my sonne John Bowtell tenne shillings to bee payed at the nine & twenty day of seauen month next ensuing date hereof.

"Lyn the 22$^d$ 6 mo. 1651"

his mark<br>James J. B. Bowtell

Witness: John Deakin, William Longley.

"I apoint these two frends nicolas potter & william Longley to see to the performances herof according to my will, & to assest my wife in what she may haue occassion to mak use of them."

Proved 26: 9: 1651 by the witnesses. *Essex Co. Quarterly Court Files, vol. 2, leaf 24.*

Inventory of the estate of Widow Boutell taken by John Dakin and Richard Blood: One kow and two calves, 8li. 10s.; fore swyne, 12s.; bedding, 7li. 14s.; whearing lining, 3li. 8s.; for her husbands aparall, 5li. 10s. 6d.; brase and puter, 3li. 8s.; bookes, 1li. 2s.; chests, 1li.; in Iren ware and other lumber, 5li. 17s. 6d.; Received of a dett, 2li. 1s.; corne, 1li. Debts, 4li. 19s. Total, 43li. 3s. Endorsed: "Inventory of estate of James Bowtell, deceased." *Essex Co. Quarterly Court Files, vol. 2, leaf 24.*

### Estate of Henry Birdsall of Salem.

Will of Henry Birdsall proved 28: 9: 1651, and inventory brought in. *Salem Quarterly Court Records, vol. 3, leaf 39.*

Inventory taken Nov. 17, 1651 by Tho. Trusler and Edmo. Batter: One dwelling house, outhouses & 1 acre & quar. land, 10li.; 5 acres of upland in the Northfield & half acre of salt marsh in the southfield, 4li. 10s.; two Cowes & hay, 10li. 10s.; 1 feather bed, 1 boulster & 2 pillows, 3li. 5s.; 1 high bedsteed & 1 trundell bedsteed, 1li. 2s.; 1 Covled, 3 blankets & 3 curtayns, 2li.; 1 setle, 5s.; 1 chest, 6s. 8d. & 2 Cubbords, 15s., 1li. 6s. 8d.; 1 small table bord & 2 Joyne stools, 5s.; 2 chaires

& cushines, 3s. and 3 payles, 4s., a meal tubb, 4s., 11s.; 2 Iron pots & 1 kitle, 12s.; 2 brasse kitles, 7s. & 2 brass skillets, 3s., 1 brass morter, 11s.; 3 great pewter platter, 10s. & 3 smale platters, 3s., 13s.; halfe dossen saucers, 1 pewter plate, 1s. 4d., 1 pewter bason, 1s., 2 saucers, 1s., 2 bekers & 1 wine tap, 2s., 4s. 6d.; 1 saltseller, 1s., trencher, 6d., earthen dishes & wooden dishes & bowles, 5s. 6d., 7s.; 1 old sword, musket & halberd, 9s.; books, 5s.; 1 paire Andirons, 3s.; tongs & fore shovels, 2 paire pott hooks, 1s., 2 pair hangers, 5s., 17s.; tubbs & barrells, 3s. & 1 brasse pane, 18d., 4s. 6d.; wearing aparrell, 3 Coats, breeches, dublet, stockings, shooes & 3 shirts, 2li. 17s. 6d.; 4 napkins, 2s., 4 pillow bers, 4s.; 3 pair of sheets, 18s. 4d., 1li. 4s. 4d.; 1 pewter pott, 1s. 6d.; 3 hundred of boards, 18s.; timber, 5s.; tooles for his trade, 2li., 2li. 5s.; 2 swine, 40s. & a remnant of cloath, 12s., 2li. 12s.; 1 bedstead, 15s.; total, 47li. 19s. 10d. *Essex Co. Quarterly Court Files, vol. 2, leaf 25.*

## Estate of Richard Haffield of Ipswich.

Rachell and Ruth Halfield daughters of Richard and Martha Halfield of Ipswich, had by the will of their father, 30li. each, for their portions, to be paid by their mother Martha Halfield, executrix, and have chosen their brother Richard Coy to be their guardian to receive and improve their legacy. The acquittance of Martha Halfield by Richard Coy, he having received the 60li. in house, land, cattle and other goods. Dated Apr. 8, 1652.

Witness: Daniell Hovey. *Ipswich Deeds, vol. 3, page 27.*

"Vpon the 17$^{th}$ daye of y$^e$ 12$^{th}$ month in ye yeare 1638. I Richard Hafeeld of Ipswich in New England, being of body weake & feeble, but of mind & memory pfectly able to make this my last will & testament—as followeth—1. To my two oldest daus. mary & Sara £30 apeece—viz. that £30 w$^h$ I am to rec. of Tho$^s$. fferman for a house sold to Rob$^t$. wallis his man w$^{ch}$ is to be paid at three paiments, £10 at a time, according to y$^e$ tenour of a bill, this £30 as it is rec$^d$ to be devided eqly betxt y$^m$, also 20 acres vpland & meadow at Reedy marsh valued at 20£ to be deuided betxt y$^m$ prsently after my decease: alsoe 10£ in money or my Cow Calfe to be devided betxt y$^m$ & in case either of y$^m$ dye before theye are posest w$^{th}$ y$^s$ my guift then my will is y$^t$ y$^e$ longer liuer to haue y$^e$ whole £60  Alsoe I give to my 3 younger daus. Martha, Rachell & Ruth, to each of y$^m$ 30£ apeece, to be p$^d$ y$^m$ as yᵃ shall com to ye age of 16 yeares old, And my will is alsoe, yᵗ yᶠ any one of yᵐ dy before yᵃ attaine to yᵉ age of 16, yᵗ yⁿ yᵉ whole £90 to fale to yᵉ longer liuers or longer liuer, yˢ sᵈ 90£ to be pᵈ yᵐ as aforesᵈ. I doe enjoyne my wife to yᵉ true & just paiment of it whome I make my executrix of yˢ my last will & testmt." [No signature]

      his mark
Robert ‖= Andrews, George Giddings.

"Wee whose names are vnder written do witness yᵗ yᵉ testator at yᵉ same time did giue vnto his 2 daus. Sara & Mary certaine debts owing to him by these men Goodman Foster 3£ 5s   Richard Waters 2 10   William Avery 1 [£]   Thoˢ. Dorman 1 [£]."

Witness: Geo. Giddings, John Browne.

Geo. Giddings and John Browne came into Ipswich court Sept. 29, 1668 and owned that their names hereunto were their own handwriting.   Robt. Lord. Cleric.

This is a true copie compared with the original on file in Salem Court Recd. Attest.

*New England Historical & Genealogical Register, vol. 3, page* 156.

## Estate of John Bayly of Newbury.

"The 28ᵗʰ of yᵉ 8ᵗʰ mᵒ (1651) This is yᵉ last will: of John Bayly sen: being on his sick bed hee being yett in his right minde & senses. ffirst I giue vnto my Sonne John Bayly my house & land lijng & being in yᵉ Towne of Salisbury during his life; & after my sonnes death his second Sonne Josepth Bayly is to enioy it & if Josephth doth not live to enioy it, then his younger brother is to enioy it, And when Josephth Bayly or his yonger brother cometh to enioy this land he is to pay to his eldest brother John Bayly the some of forty pounds as his Grandfathers guift. And I do likewise make my sonne John Bayly sole Executoʳ of all that ever I have only my Executoʳ is to pay to my wyfe his mother yᵉ some of six pounds a yeare duering hir life pvided she cometh over hither to New-england, likewise my Executoʳ is to pay to my sonne Robert fiueteene pounds pvided also he come over hither to New-england likewise my Executoʳ is to pay to my Daughters his sisters yᵉ some of Tenn pounds a peece pvided they come over hither to new-england butt in case they doe not come over hither butt doe sende by any messenger for their portions, they are to haue fiue shillings a peece for their portions whither sonne or daughte[r]s & all these somes are to bee payed according as it can bee raised out of my land & stocke & likewise it is to bee pay'd to every one of them according as y^e Executo^r & the overseers shall see cause, And farther my Executo^r is to pay for y^e passages of those y^t doe come over hither, of them whither it bee wyfe or children, or any of them  And farther I doe giue to my Sonne John Baylys Childeren either of them a young beast as soone as maybee w^th conveniency, & my Sonne their father is to breed these beasts for eve[r]y of his Childeren till these beasts groeth to cowes or Oxen, & then the childeren are to haue the proffitt of them  And I doe make my brother John Emery sen of Nubery & M^r Thomas Bradbury of Salisbury overseers to see as this to bee performed  In wittness herof I doe sett to my hand y^e day, & yeare aboue written."

his mark<br>Jn° Jb. Bayly Senior.

Witness: william Ilsley, John Emry Jun.

"likewise I doe giue to ||willi|| Huntingtons wyfe & childeren y^t house & land y^t I bought of vallentine Rowell & do desier my overseers to see it made good to hir & hir childeren."

Proved in Salisbury court 13: 2: 1652 by the witnesses. *Copy of will, Norfolk Deeds, vol. 1, leaf 15.*

Inventory taken Nov. 12, 1651, by Mr. Edward Woodman and Thomas Macy: seventy fowre acres of upland fifteene of it broke up, 55li.; Houses, 25li.; 12 Cows, 60li.; Two oxen, 14li.; Two steeres age 3 yeers & vantage, 10li.; ffive Calves, 7li. 10s.; one Bull, 2li. 15s.; one Swine, 18s.; Twenty Acres more or lesse of Meadow, 50li.; household goods & tooles, 13li. 12s. 4d.; Clothes & Bedding, 10li. 12s. 2d.; corne & pvisions, 9li. 13s. 8d.; Two Steeres more, 12li.; total, 271li. 1s. 2d.  *Essex Co. Probate Files, Docket 1,334.*

## ESTATE OF JOHN HARDY OF SALEM.

"30th ith m° 1652 The last will and testament of John Hardie of Salem is as ffolloweth Imprimis I giue vnto Roger Hoscall my son in lawe all my lande lyinge neare bass Riuer (beinge the lande was given me by the towne of Salem) to houlde and inioy all the sd lande to himself and his heires for ever It: I giue vnto my sd son in law Roger Hoscall a steere and a Cowe now in his owne keepinge and one oxx in the hande of William fflint the which oxx my wife shall chuse and apoynt to my son in law out of my three oxen in william fflints hande It: I giue vnto my sd son in lawe all my right and interest in Thomas Varney my apprentice vnless his parents buie his time by payinge the som of seauen pownd that I pd for his time which if they shall doe I give the sd som of seauen pownds to my sd son in law It: I giue vnto my sd son in law his 4 Children: vidz: John William Marke and Elizabeth 4 ewe sheepe of my yongr sheepe to each of them one It I giue vnto Elizabeth the daught$^r$ of my son Joseph Hardy my best ewe sheepe and my best ewe lambe of this yeare. It: I giue vnto my daughter Elizabeth Hoscall one heighfer of two yeare old: It I giue vnto my son Joseph Hardy one quarter pt of the old catch caled the returne: and one quarter pt of the new Catch caled the gift: and one eight pt of the Catch caled the flower It: I giue vnto my sd son Joseph Hardy one ak$^r$ of marsh yt I bought of Jacob Barny and halfe one ak$^r$ that I bought of William Lord lyinge togeath$^r$ neare the cold springe at the head of the south Riuer. also I giue unto my sd son my pt of the house beinge one halfe in which we lay fish beinge on winter Iland

"It: ffor all that remaineth of my estate my debts and legacys being pd. I giue and bequeath vnto by beloued wife Elizabeth Hardy whom I apoynt to be sole executrix of this my last will and testament to order and dispose of all thinges as I haue aboue expressed

"and I doe make Choyce of m$^r$ Charles Gott and Henry Bartholomew whom I doe request to be overseers of this my last will and testament: and in witnis of the truth hereof I have here vnto set my hande and seale the day and yeare first aboue wrighten."  
John Hardy.

Witness: Charles Gott, Henry Bartholomew.

Proved 30: 4: 1652 by the witnesses.

*Essex Co. Quarterly Court Files, vol. 2, leaf 29.*

Inventory taken 8: 4: 1652, by Edmond Batter and Walter Price: One dwelling house & 2 Acres of land, 40li.; 15 acres planting land in southfield, 7li.; 6 acres & 3-4 of salt marsh, 24li.; one farm of 80 acres upland or thereabout & 12 acres medowe, 20li.; halfe a fishe house at winter Iland, 3li.; one fourth part of the Alegatter Catch, 30li.; three fourths of the Catch called Guift, 60li.; one halfe of the Catch called the Returne, 30li.; one boat & Cannow, 1li.; 6 Cowes, 30li. & 4 oxen, 27li., 57li.; 4 yearlings, 8li. & one 2 yeare hiefer, 3li. 10s., 11li. 10s.; 2 weanlinge calves & 1 sucking calf, 2li. 2s.; 1 swine, 30s. & 1 Ramme, 16s., 2li. 6s.; 8 yewes, 12li. & 5 lambes, 3li., 15li.; Mariners Instruments, 2li. & 2 chestes, 16s., 2li. 16s.; 1 bedstead, table & forme, 2li.; waring Aparrell, 13li. 19s.; 25 yds. 1-2 sayle cloath, 28s., 10 yd Stuffe, 35s., 3li. 3s.; five yds. 1-2 broad cloath, 2li. 18s.; 8 yd. Hampton Sarge, 4li. & 4s. & 5 yds. 1-2 cotton, 18s., 5li. 2s.; 1 feather bed & boulster & pillow, 3li. 10s.; 1 Rugge & 1 pr. blankets, 1li. 10s.; 1 paire Cartaynes, carpet & valents, 1li. 5s.; 4 Cushons, 13s.; a Coverled & a Rugge, 20s., 1li. 13s.; 9 Sheetts, 45s. & 5 pillows, 14s., tablecloathes, 2s. 6d., 3li. 1s. 6d.; 1 warming pane, 5s. & 1 brush, 12d., 6s., 3 musketts & 3 swords & bandeler rests, 1 Carbine & a foulinge peece, 4li. 6s.; bulletts & nails, 14s., cases & botles, 4s., 18s.; 150li. shotte, 30s., yarne, 20s., 2li. 10s.; bookes, 20s. & old Irone, 5s. & 1 bell, 12d., 1li. 6s.; 1 lookinge glasse, 2s. & 2 coffers & trunke, 6s., 8s.; 2 feather beds, Rugge, boulster & blankets, 4li. 10s.; 1 bed & beddinge & 2 bedsteeds, 1li. 10s.; netts, linnes & leads, 10s. & 1 woolen loom, 3s., 13s.; Coren upon the ground, 4li., 4li.; corne & malte, 15s.; caske, 5s., 5s.; 2 brass kitles, 15s., Iron potts & brasse, 1li. 15s., pick forks & spads, 5s. & 1 mattocke & tubbs, 3s., 8s.; mortor & pestle, 2s. 6d., scamr, & Andirons, 4s. 6d., 7s.; hakes & pott hookes & tongue, 5s. 6d.; friing pane, gridirone & belowes, 4s.; wooden ware, 5s.; tubbs, form & setle, 11s., 16s.; 3 Chairs, 10s. & 2 hammers & 1 drawing knife, 3s., 13s.; 11 platters & bason & other pewter, 3li. 1s. 6d.; 3 Iron wedges & 2 Iron rings, 6s.; 1 axe & 3 howes, 4s. 6d. & 1 ladder, 18d., 6s.; Cheese presse, 4s., milkpanes, 3s. 6d., 7s. 6d.; 3 runlets & 1 grindston, 7s.; 4 yeares tyme in Elisha Sharpe sold to Mr. Jno. Browne 4li.; Duncan Macall, the scot, has 6 years & 3-4 tyme to serve, 16li.; total, 393li. 4s. 6d. *Essex Co. Quarterly Court Files, vol. 2, leaf 30.*

### ESTATE OF THOMAS WATHEN OF GLOUCESTER.

Administration on the estate of Thomas Wathing granted 28: 7: 1652 to William Sargent. Surety: John Holgrave. *Ipswich Quarterly Court Records, vol. 1, page 31.*

Zeblon Hill, formerly living in Bristall, in Ould England, being here, deposed that Thomas Wathing, son to Edman Wathin, was cousin to William Seargant, said William being his father's sister's son; and that Thomas Wathing went with Robart Gray in Captain Wal's service. Sworn before William Stevens, Robert Tucke and Robert Elwell, commissioners of Gloster, 27: 7: 1652. Debora Joy, aged twenty-seven years, wife of Walter Joy, deposed that Thomas Warren, who died with Prince Rupert, was cousin germane to William Sergent of Glocester and that there was none nearer of kin in this country, and she, being alike related, desired William Sergent to be the administrator of the estate. Sworn to before Increase Nowell, 17 : 7 : 1652. *Essex Co. Quarterly Court Files, vol. 2, leaf 41.*

Inventory taken 4m : 1653, by Zebulen Hill and Steven Glover, both of Gloster : A cote and a pare of briches and a doblet, 1li. 15s. His tools were appraised at 20s. by Goodman Felten of Salem Towne. *Essex Co. Quarterly Court Files, vol. 2, leaf 56.*

### Estate of Ezra Rolfe of Ipswich.

Administration on the estate of Ezra Rofe granted 28 : 7 : 1652, to his widow, Hester Rofe. She presented an inventory, which amounted to 73li. 5s. There were two children, the elder to have 13li. 13s. 4d., and the younger, 6li. 6s. 8d., at the age of twenty-one. The house and land were bound for its payment. *Ipswich Quarterly Court Records, vol. 1, page 31.*

Inventory taken by Edward Browne: one howse, barne & outhowse, ——; 10 acres of land, ——; 2 steares & 2 cowes, 20li. —; 1 payer bellowes, Anvell, vyce & 2 hammors, 5li. —; 1 grinstone & charcoale, 12s. —; 1 ould spade & shovell, 1s. —; 2 ould chests, —; 1 vyce, 10s. —; an ould sawe, 1s.; 3 Iron wedges, 3s.; in steele, 2s.; 20 chapes for swords, 5s.; — duzen kniffe sheaths, 2s.; — fyles, 4s.; 1 sawe, 5s.; 3 smale hammors, 4 payer moulds & other smale tooles wth hanrought Iron, 1li.; 2 boxes 3s. —; 1 fether bed & 1 boulster & 1 pillowe, 2li. 10s.; 1 flock bed & boulster & 2 ould Keverlids, 15s.; 2 payer sheetes & 4 pillowebeeres, 1li. 7s.; in other lyninge, 11s.; 2 suites of Apparrell & a coate, 3li.; 2 hats & other wearinge apparrell, 16s.; 1 smoothinge Iron, 2s. 6d.; 1 musket, bandelleers, belt, sword & other ammunition, 1li. 10s.; pewter, spoones & other smale thinges, 1li. 16s.; 1 brasse kettle & 4 skellits, 1li. 4s.; 2 Iron potts & 1 fryinge pan, 1li. 5s.; tubs, trayes & other lumber, 1li. 5s.; 1 sowe & 2 pigs, 1li. 15s.; A hanger, 3s.; in monie, ——; total, 74li. 16s. —. [de]bpts dewe in the booke, 8li. 14s. 10d., making total, 83li. 10s. 10d.; dabpts dewe to be payd to others, 10li. 5s. —, leaving 73li. 5s. —.

Sworn to in Ipswich court 28: 7: 1652, by the widow of Ezra Rofe. *Essex Co. Probate Files, Docket* 24,109.

### GUARDIANSHIP OF ABIELL CHANDLER OF NEWBURY.

5: 8: 1652, Jno. Cheiney, sr., of Nubery was chosen guardian to his grandchild, Abiell Chandler, aged about two years. *Hampton Quarterly Court Records, vol.* 1, *leaf* 34.

### ESTATE OF JOHN PARTRIDGE OF OLNEY, ENGLAND.

The court 5: 8: 1652, bound Willi. Partridg of Salisbury in 86li. to the Governor and Company of Massachusetts to pay a legacy of 43li., which was given by Jno. Partridg of Olney in Buckinghamshire, to the children of said William Partridg then living, the eldest child to have a double portion. *Hampton Quarterly Court Records, vol.* 1, *leaf* 34.

Will. Partridg of Salisbury informed the court that there yet remained five pounds in the hands of Willi Geynes, Richard Kent and Rodger Tayre of Olney in Buckinghamshire, in old England, being part of the estate of Jno. Partridg of Olney, deceased, and bequeathed to the children of said Willi. Partridg, namely, John, Hannah, Elizabeth, Nehemiah and Sarah. The court 4: 8: 1653, ordered that said Willi. be bound in ten pounds for the distribution of the five pounds. Bond acknowledged in court, 7: 8: 1653, before Tho. Bradbury, Rec. *Hampton Quarterly Court Records, vol.* 1, *leaf* 43.

### ESTATE OF HENRY SOMERBY OF NEWBURY.

Judith, widow and administratrix of the estate of Henry Somersby, deceased, brought in inventory of his estate 30: 9: 1652. She petitioned the court that her son Danyell might have the six acres of land in the little field and half the marsh and meadow, and 5li. at the age of eighteen, and that her two daughters Sarah and Elizabeth might have 13li. and a noble each at the age of sixteen years. If any of the children die, their portion to be equally divided. *Salem Quarterly Court Records, vol.* 3, *leaf* 46.

Inventory of the estate of Henry Somerby of Newbury taken Nov. 6, 1652, by Edmond Grenlefe, Richard Browne and Anthony Somerby: An house and an aker of land that it stands upon, 45li.; 14 Akers of land, 20li.; 11 akers of marsh & meadow, 9li.; 2 steers and a cow & two calues, 18li.; a copper and brewing vessells, 6li. 10s.; 9 swine, 8li. In the parlor: one bedsted and a trundle bedsted with a flockbed and boulster, a rugge and blankett and couerlett and curtaine, 4li. 10s.; one cuberd and cuberd cloth, a table and fourme and chayre and cushion, 1li. 10s. In the kitchen: 4 Iron potts, 2li.; 10 peices of pewter, 3 porringers, one bason & other small peices, one quart pot, 3 drinking cupps, 2li. 10s. In the cellar chamber: one bedsted with featherbed and boulster, blancket, couerlet & curtaines, 5li.; 7 paire of sheets, 4li. 4s.; 3 table cloths, a dozen of Napkins, 5 pillowbears & towells, 2li.; 3 pillowes, one napkin presse, one wooden platter, an earthern platter, 15s.; 2 kettles and a skillet, a frying pan, a spitt, 2 puddin pannes and a warming pan, one pewter chamber pott, a pestle and morter, 2li.; 2 meale seiues, 1 dozen of trenchers, 6 milke vessells, a dozen of pewter spoones, 2 small chayres, 2 cushins, a small table, a case of bottles, a bras small ladle, a trammell & other lumber, 1li. 10s. In the parlor chamber: one bedsted with a feather bed and bolster & rugge, 3li; one chest & foure dry caske, 10s.; one sword & musket & bandeleers, 1li.; one small flockbed in the kitchen chamber and a couerlett & 2 chests and 2 small boxes and two baskets, 1li. 10s.; his weareing apparrell, 2li.; debts due upon booke and bill, 26li. 9s.; total, 164li. 4s.; we finde him to be indebted about 62li. *Essex Co. Quarterly Court Files, vol. 2, leaf 49.*

### Estate of William Averill of Ipswich.

"I William Averill of Ipswich being weake in bodye but of perfect memorye doe make this my last will & testament first I doe bequeath my body to the earth to be deasently buryed in the Burying place of Ipswich, my sperit into the hands of my Saviour the Lord Jesus Christ. And for my outward estate being but small, I doe give unto my children each of them, being seaven in number the some of fiue shillings apeece & the rest of my estate my debts being discharged I give unto Abegal my wife, whom I make sole execotrix of this my last will. In witnes heerof I have heerunto sett my hand & seale the 3$^d$ of the 4$^{th}$ mo. 1652." Will. Averell.

Witness: Andrew Hodges, Renold Foster.

Proved 29: 1: 1653, by the witnesses.

Inventory taken by Reginold Fostr and Andrew Hodgs: One hous Lott & house, 10li.; 10 acres of upland ground &

6 Ac. of meddo, 10li.; 2 kine & 2 two yer old, 16li.; 2 shoats, 1li.; 1 Iron pott, 1 brass pott, 1 frying pan, 4 pewtr plattrs, 1 flagon, 1 Iron ketle, 1 brass ketle, 2 copp., 1 brass pan & some othr smal things, 2li. 17s.; 2 chests, 1 fethr bed, 1 othr bed, 2 payre of sheets, 2 bolstrs, 3 pillows, 2 blanketts, 1 Covrlid, 1 bedstead & othr smal linnen, 5li. 10s.; 2 coats & wearing appel, 3li.; 1 warming pan, 3s.; a tub, 2 pails, a few books, 10s.; a Corslett, 1li.; what shee oweth, 12li.
*Essex Co. Quarterly Court Files, vol. 2, leaf 54.*

### ESTATE OF WILLIAM CRIMP OF (ISLE OF SHOALS?).

Administration on the estate of Willm. Crimp, granted 29: 1: 1653 to Thomas Macye. *Ipswich Quarterly Court Records, vol. 1, page 33.*

### ESTATE OF WILLIAM IVORY OF LYNN.

Inventory of estate of William Ivory of Lin, deceased, filed 29: 1: 1653. Amount, 135li. 9s. 10d. Also a writing filed by Ann Ivory, relict of said William Ivory, as his last will. Declared invalid, for want of an executor. Administration granted to the widow. Deceased's son, Thomas Ivory, was ordered to have twenty pounds of the estate when twenty-one years of age, and Lois and Sarah, two of the daughters, ten pounds apiece when they are eighteen or married. Ruth Baly, a married daughter, to have forty shillings after the death of her mother. Remainder of the estate to go to the widow. *Ipswich Quarterly Court Records, vol. 1, leaf 33.*

Copy of inventory taken 26: 1: 1653, by Edward Burchum (his mark) and Richard Rooton: his purse & aparrell, 11li. 12s.; 3 Kine, 15li.; 3 young Cattell, 9li. 5s.; one Asse, 3li.; 3 Swine, 2li.; Land at Boston, 12li.; Land bought of Mr. Laughton, 12li.; House & Lande, 30li.; Broad Cloth, 5 yards, 4li. 5s.; Cotton Cloth, 12s. 6d.; Linen Cloth, 1li. 12s.; Table linen & Sheets & other things, 6li.; Bedinge in the Chamber, Rug, bed, Boulster & pillows, 1li. 15s.; foure Boxes, 12s.; wheate, 12 bushells, 3li.; A Table & Chest, 15s.; A Musket, Sword & bandeleres & powder, 1li. 17s.; in the Parlor, ffether bed, ruge, pillowes & boulsters, 6li.; in Pewter, 1li. 8s.; A warmeing pan & a Kettle, 14s.; An Iron Pott & a brasse pott, 12s. 6d.; Carpenter Tooles & a grindstone, 2li. 10s.; Bookes, 1li. 6s. 8d.; A Cupbord, Chaire & little Table, 1li. 3s.; two ould Chests & other Lumber, 6s. 8d.; bord Irons &

hookes & some other Small things, 1li.; A Bottle & Lether Jack & some small things, 7s.; Dishes & Milke vessells, 9s. 6d.; water pailes, Beere Barrells & other small things, 10s.; Sives & other Lumber, 5s.; A wheele & Shovell & forke, 6s.; in fflax, 6s.; in flesh, namely Bacon, 2li.; Debts Owing, 2li. *Ipswich Deeds, vol. 1, leaf 126.*

### Estate of William Stevens of Newbury.

"Witnesse by these presents that I william Stevens of Newbury in the County of Essex in Newengland yeoman, being sicke and weake of body but through gods mercy of perfect memory, do make my last will and testament first I bequeath my soule into the hands of my blessed Redeemer with an assured hope of a blessed resurrection, and when it shall please the lord to take me out of this world I bequeath my body to bee buryed in the burying place of Newbury, and for my worldly Goods I bequeath my house and two parts of my land both vpland and meadow to my eldest Son when hee shall be of the age of one and twenty yers and twenty pounds to my son Samuell Steuens when he shalbe at the like age of twenty one yeares, and I appoint Elizabeth my wife my Sole executrix of this my last will and testament and all the rest of my worldly goods vndisposed of I giue to my wife to bring vp my children in the feare of god till they shalbe at the aforesaid age only the third parte of my land after my wiues decease giuen to my Son John Steuens, and in case either of my children shold dye before they shall come to the age of twenty one yeares then the twenty pounds shall returne to my wife In witnesse whereof I the said william Steuens have set my hand and seale may 19$^{th}$ 1653."

William Steuenes

Witness: Anthony Somerby, Rich. Lowle, Robertt Long, Anthony Morse and Benieman Swett.

Robert Long, aged about thirty-two years, made oath before Wm. Gerrish, commissioner, 27 : 4 : 1653, that this will was the last will of William Stevens, as did also Anthony Somerby, in court at Salem, 28 : 4 : 1653, before Henry Bartholmew, clerk. *Essex Co. Quarterly Court Files, vol. 2, leaf 57.*

Inventory of the estate of William Stevens of Newbury, yeoman, who died May 19, 1653, taken June 13, 1653, by Samuell Bidfeild, George (his mark) Little, Anthony Somerby, Francis Plumer and Nicholas Noyes: The house and barne and eleven akers and halfe of land which joynes to the house, eight akers being broken up, 48li.; sixteene akers of exchange and divident land, 6li.; ten akers of meadow and upland neere the mill, 7li. 10s.; ten akers of meadow neere Nich. Noyes neck, 7li. 10s.; two akers of salt marsh, 1li.; two akers of meadow at the little river, 1li.; one oxe, 7li. 10s.; two steers, 3 yere old, 10s.; two cowes, 9 li.; one heifer, 2 yere old, 2li. 15s.; two yeerlings, 4li.; two calves, 2li.; five swine, 3li.; foure akers of Rye and wheat and barly growing, 8li.; an old cart and wheels, a yoake chayne and plough & plough Irons, 1li. 10s.; sithes, axes, spad, shovel & other utinsells belonging to husbandry, 1li. 4s.; a sledd and whelbarrow, 4s.; one bedsted in the parlour with a fetherbed, bolster, 2 blankets and a coverlet and a pillow, 6li.; one chest and a coffer and 2 boxes, 12s.; foure chayres & 2 cushions, 8s.; twenty pound of cotten wooll, 1li. In the little roome: a bedsted and a flock bed and bolster with 2 pillows & blanket and a little flocke bed & other lumber things, 4li.; three paire of sheets, 3li.; his weareing apparell, 10li.; eight yards of cotton cloth, 1li. 4s.; an old coverlet, 7s. 6d.; two table clothes, a dozen of napkins and two pillowbeares, 2li. 10s.; 2 guns and a sword with the rest of his armes, 2li. 10s. In the kitchen: 2 brasse kettles, one brasse pott, 2 brasse skilletts, a brasse candlestick & a skimmer, 2 brass posnets, and a warmeing pan, a brass morter & a pestle, 4li. 10s.; 3 Iron potts, firepan, tongs, pott hooks, andirons, spitt, gridiron, a cleaver and a chafeing dish & other small things, 1li. 10s.; 2 churnes, 3 keelers, 3 small drinke vessells, 4 spining wheels and 5 trayes & other small lumber, 1li. 10s.; eleven peices of pewter, 3 candlesticks, a quart pott, a pinte pott, 2 nips, 3 small salt sellers & 2 porringers, 6 spoones & some small tining things, 2li. 10s.; his books, 1li.; total, 166li. 14s. 6d.

Sworn to by Elizabeth (her mark) Stevens, late wife of the deceased, and Samuell Bidfield, one of the appraisers, 27: 4: 1653, before Wm. Gerrish, commissioner. *Essex Co. Quarterly Court Files, vol. 2, leaf 58.*

### ESTATE OF GEORGE COLE OF LYNN.

Widow Mary Coales of Lin brought into court 28: 4: 1653, an inventory of the estate of her late husband, George Coales, and was appointed administratrix. *Salem Quarterly Court Records, vol. 3, leaf 54.*

Inventory taken 23: 4: 1653, by Edward Burchum and

Nathaniell Handforth: A house & too ackers & a halfe of Land, 12li.; too swien & a pige, 1li.; a kow, 4li. 10s.; fouer pillowes, 18s.; a Chale bed ruge & sheets, 2li. 14s.; a bedsted, 4s.; his aparill, 1li. 19s.; a warminge pan, 10s.; in puter & a Smothinge Iern, 1li. 7s.; too Ieren pots, on brase pot & pot hooks, 1li. 15s.; a grid Iern & a scellitt, 4s. 6d.; a Craddell & too Cussions, 4s.; wooden ware, 10s.; bookes, 8s.; too wheles & a meale tube, 8s.; in Coren, 1li. 3s. 6d.; Cubard & lumbar, 7s. 10d.; a bed & a mantell, 11s. 4d.; flax, woole & Cards, 6s. 6d.; Chiste, barill, table & trunks, 11s. 6d.; thre meale bags & a fryng pan & thre earthen potts, 10s. 6d.; total, 32li. 10s. 8d.; debts Owinge by her, 12s.; debts dew to her, 13s. 6d. *Essex Co. Quarterly Court Files, vol. 2, leaf 56.*

### ESTATE OF WILLIAM TILTON OF LYNN.

The will and inventory of William Tilton of Lynn, deceased, brought in by his widow, 1: 5: 1653. Proved by Edward Burcham and John Hurd. *Salem Quarterly Court Records, vol. 3, leaf 58.*

Inventory taken 16: 2: 1653, by Edward Burchum, Henry Collins and Francis (his mark) Ingols: 2 oxen & five kine, 40li.; six younge Cattell, 14li. 10s.; 3 Calves & five swien, 5li.; in putter, Ieren pots & ould brase, 2li. 7s. 4d.; frynge pan & hooks, 5s.; his purse & aparill & cloth, 7li. 18s.; 2 hogheades, 3 payles & a bottell with other Lumber, 1li. 6s.; too bibles & a hammer, 9s. 6d.; 3 sheepe & 5 lambes, 6li. 13s. 4d.; plow & Ierens & yocks, 15s.; in Lininge, 2li.; in beddinge, bolsters & Coveringe, 6li.; a warminge pan, Chiste & churen, 12s.; in coren, backen & porke, 6li. 10s.; in wheles, sith & yaren grinestone & barley, 2li. 8s. 8d.; house & Lande, 30li.; sword, muskett & bandeleres, 1li. 10s.; total, 128li. 4s. 10d. *Essex Co. Quarterly Court Files, vol. 2, leaf 57.*

### ESTATE OF JOHN PITTICE OF (IPSWICH?).

Inventory of the estate of John Pittice brought in by Margret Pittis, his widow, 27: 7: 1653. Amount, 88li. 17s. 2d. She was appointed administratrix of his estate, and ordered to pay to the five children, being all daughters, five pounds each at the age of eighteen. She was to bring up the children. *Ipswich Quarterly Court Records, vol. 1, page 36.*

Proved by Richard Kemball, sr., and Richard Kemball, jr. *Ipswich Quarterly Court Records, vol. 2, page 31.*

## Estate of John Cogswell, Jr. of Ipswich.*

"——— Cogswell of Ipswitch beinge bound for England ——— considerations movinge me to it have made ——— & my Brother William Cogswell & my Brother ——— Executors in trust & M$^r$ Nathaniell Rojers ——— order & dispose of my children & estate as ———h all see it to be for my good to pay my debts ——— w$^{th}$ my estate for my use & if it should ——— to order it by his pvidence that I Come ——— take y$^e$ Care of my children & breede y$^m$ ——— of God & to learninge, & if any one of y$^m$ be ——— beinge a Good scoler y$^n$ I would have him brought ——— y$^e$ other to be bound prentiss at 10 years ould to a ——— man *where* he may be wel brought vp ——— bandry affairs, & y$^t$ vy y$^t$ should h——— to be ———ut to encrea— daughter *Elisabeth* ——— so ——— is left to b———en y$^e$ *lad* to ——— 2 parts ——— to Samuell & ——— my daughter Eliza*beth* ——— of monye— *di* y$^e$ to her pportion viz in 4 less y$^n$ *to my* sonn samuell ——— if my daughter should be maryed before 21 ——— old y$^t$ she should haue her portion as neer as ——— be Cast vp to be pd to her at her maridge & also my sons to haue theyre portions deliuered at 21 yeres ould whereto I set my hand ——— 3 of december ———3

John Cogswell, Jun$^r$

"——— testifie that ——— ove— John Coggswell Jun —ting into England tould me he had or would make —ill & had made his father his Brother william & Brother Armantage his Executors & further I doe be —*Sen* ——— be *his* owne hand wrighting   Robert Lord

"I *Francis waldo* testifi the *same*." *Essex Co. Probate Files, Docket 5,829.*

Proved 27: 7: 1653. Inventory received. Mr. John Cogswell and William Cogswell, executors. *Ipswich Quarterly Court Records, vol. 1, page 42.*

Inventory of estate of John Cogswell, jr., taken 25: 7: 1653, by John Prockter and Wm. Varnye; one Red Rudge, 1li. 13s. 4d.; 5 Cussings, Culler red, 10s.; Curtens and Vallens, 4li.; one ffeather bed and bolster and two pillowes, 4li.; a litle flock bed, two old blankets, and an old Coueringe, 14s.; two window Curtens, 8s.; one Carpitt, 10s.; two payer of sheets, 1li. 6s. 8d.; one payer of sheets, 15s.; two payer of pillowbers, 13s. 4d.; a dyaper table Cloth, 16s.; 6 napkings,

* See also Essex Co. Quarterly Court Files, vol. 25, leaves 2-25.

1li.; dyaper duble Clutes, 10s.; 7 neck clothes, 16s.; 3 payer of hand cuffes, 6s.; 4 head dressinges, 8s.; 2 lace crossclothes, 5s.; 3 forehead Clothes, 6s.; a shift and a bidgen, and one old bed and stomeger and 2 other Cloutes, 6s.; [A Swathe & a pinquishion, 4s. *copy*] a brush, —; a waskote and nyght houd, 1s.; a payer of white glouffes, 1s.; a payer of stockings, 4s. 4d.; a Childe barringe Cloth, 2li. 4s. 8d.; one stufe gowne, 1li. 10s.; one black gowne, 2li.; a black gowne, 15s.; one petticote, 1li. 10s.; a wascote, 10s.; a petticote, 1li. 6s. 8d.; a white shute, 13s. 4d.; 4 aperens, 1li.; a hatband and Hatte brush, 3s.; a houd, 3s.; a dublet and payer of hose, 1li. 3s. 4d.; a Cloake, 1li.; lethers for stoules, 9s.; Course twolels, 3s.; [6 Course Napkins. *copy*], 4s.; 5 pewter platters [10s. *copy*]; a pewter flaggon [5s. *copy*.]; 3 old pewter pottes, 3 potte gengers [pottingers. *copy*], 3s.; a bassen and spone, 2s.; 2 skingmers, and bastinge laddle, 3s.; one brasse skillet, 3s.; a brase candlestick, 3s.; two tynn Candle sticks, 1s. 6d.; one pestle and Morter, 3s.; one warminge pann, 7s. 6d.; one old dublet, a payer of stockinge, 6s.; a Chamber pott, 2s.; a payer of billowes, 1s.; two payer of Andines, 5s.; a trunke, 10s.; a Chest, 10s.; a litle trunk, 4s.; a pillen, 5s.; 3 scakes 10s.; a tumbrill, 12s.; Blundiviles book, 3s.; more Goods praysed by John Prockter and George Gi—— [Gittans. *copy*], the 26 : 7 : 1653: swayne, 6li.; one bridle, Sadle, stirips and girtes, 10s.; one Rudge, 1li. 10s.; two trayes, 1s. 4d.; one stocke of bees, 12s.; halfe a sworme, 8s.; a payer potthook [2 Chaines. *copy*], 8s. 8d.; [Lamp, 2 stools, one basket. *copy*.], 2 brushes, one bas[ket], Cheese vate, 3s. 6d.; one lether Jack, 2s.; one botle, a salt siller, an houre glase, 5s. 2d.; one spitt, one axe, 5s. 10d.; one brasse kittle, 1li. 13s. 4d.; one brasse kittle, 15s.; one book, Mr. John Collens works, 4s.; one sucken bottle, 6d.; one bedsteed and cord, 15s.; one Roudge, one bed boulster, 2 blankits, 2li. 10s.; one Iron pott and Iron hangers, 8s.; one payer of poot trameles, 2s.; one spad and 7 trayes, 8s. 6d.; one Cheese press, 3 spones and drippen pann, 7s.; one Charne, 2 seves, 4s. 6d.; one beer barrell, one powdering tub, 4s.; one hogshead and virkinge, 2s. 6d.; two barrell, one forke, 3s. 10d.; two betle Rings, a strangen dish, payle, 2s. 10d.; 3 wegges, 4 dishes, 3s. 2d.; Chaynes, one plow sheer, 1li. 6s. 6d.; one table, 6s. 8d.; 5 cowes, 25li.; one bull yeare and Vantag, 2li. 10s.; two hayfers, 10li.; one bull 2 yeare and Vantage, 3li.; one bull, 6li.; one bull stagg, 7li.; one bolster, one dublet, 1li. 4d.; 4 henns, 4s.; one cart and wheels and all the Irons belongen, 2li. 10s.; one Chayne, 3 youckes wth Irons, 15s.; —— [One Cart Rope. *copy*], 5s.; ——, [One pair of Sheetes. *copy*], 8s.; [One pott hanger, 1 Brass skillet, 1li. 4s. 8d. *copy*], 4s. 8d.; [A Cannow, 8s. *copy*]; in Lace, 5li.; 17 yeards of lickren, 1li. 2s.; 2 payer of showes, 8s.; his apperell, 5li.; 2 payer old bootts, 12s.; hay seed, 10s.; a Curriers knyfe, 4s.; 2li. of threed, 6s.; one book, 1s. 6d.; one Chest, 6s.; one skillit, one chamb poot, one porenger, two spones, 5s. 6d.; two payer of crose garner & a payer of esses for doores, 6s. 6d.; a pillen cloth, 6s.; musket and bandelers, 15s.; a saddle, 6s.; 3 hundred of bord, 15s.; a gridian, 1s.; two howses, 14li.; the lease of his farme, 100li.; total, 247li. 5s. 8d.

Received in Ipswich court Sept. 27, 1653. *Essex Co. Probate Files, Docket 5,829.*

On copy of inventory the following: What is owing him: Goodwife winbrough of Boston, 1li.; Mr. Genit, 4li. 1s.; Mark hamms, 36li.; Mr. Webb, 1li.; Hennry Muddle, 38li.; In desperate debts on his book, 28li. 3s. 4d.; total, 94li. 4s. 4d. There is 19li. to be paid out of this Estate to Mr. John Cogswell, Sr. for a child committed to him. *Mass. Archives, vol. 39, leaf 495.*

Mr. John Coggswell and Willm. Coggswell of Ipswich brought in 27: 7: 1664, an account of disbursements for the bringing up of the children of John Coggswell, jr., deceased, unto whom they were executors, and also by the discharge of several debts due from the said John Coggswell to the full value of the estate they received, except the land, which they return to the use of the children, and are discharged of their executorship, they yet to take care of the children until they choose guardians. *Ipswich Quarterly Court Records, vol. 1, page 137.*

### ESTATE OF WILLIAM HOOKE OF SALISBURY.

Administration on the estate of Mr. Willi. Hooke granted 4: 8: 1653, to his widow, Mrs. Ellnor Hooke. Ordered to bring in an inventory to next Salisbury court. *Hampton Quarterly Court Records, vol. 1, page 42.*

Inventory taken by Tho. Bradbury R— (his ↑ mark) Goodale, sr.: 6 Cowes, 30li.; 2 fower yere old steers, 12li.; 3 heiffers & one bull, 14li.; 1 yearlin, 1li. 10s.; 3 sowes, 3li.;

certaine Lumber wch was sould for 5li., 5li.; 2 oxen, 20li.; one farme, 250li.; 3 spotts of meddow, 5li.; total, 340li.

Sworn to in Salisbury court 11: 2: 1654, by Mrs. Hooke, administratrix. The disposing of the estate is referred to the next Hampton court, until when the estate is not to be altered. *Essex Co. Probate Files, Docket* 13,806.

In answer to the petition of Mrs. Elinor Hooke for the disposing of the estate of her late husband, Mr. Wm. Hooke, the court May 23, 1655, gave her power to improve the estate and to have the profits thereof for herself and youngest son, but not to make sale until the court take further order therein. She also was granted liberty to sell certain lands at the eastward, belonging to her first husband, Capt. Norton. *Mass. Bay Colony Records, vol.* 3, *page* 385.

ESTATE OF MICHAEL SPENCER OF LYNN.

Administration on the estate of Mihill Spencer granted 29: 9: 1653 to Garrod Spencer of Linn.

Garrard Spencer brought in an inventory of the estate of his brother, Michaell Spencer, 6: 1: 1653-4. Amount, 22li. 4s. 10d. Garrard Spencer and Capt. Willm. Trask of Salem were ordered to dispose of the estate for the bringing up of Michael's children.

Thomas Robins of Salem had some of the estate of Michaell Spencer, deceased, a bill of 52s. 6d., 2 cowes with rent of same for one year & a rugg of 18s. Court 30: 9: 1654, ordered, with consent of Garrud Spencer, administrator, that Robins was to have it as he had a child of the deceased to bring up. The child's name was Michaell Spencer, and he was six years old.

*Salem Quarterly Court Records, vol.* 3, *leaves* 66, 69, 81.

ESTATE OF JOHN ROBINSON OF SALEM.

Will of John Robinson of Salem proved 29: 9: 1653 by Rich. Prince. *Salem Quarterly Court Records, vol.* 3, *leaf* 67.

Inventory taken 28: 9: 1653, by Elias Stileman and Richard Prince: 1 house & acre of Land, 12li.; 5 acres planting Land, 2li.; 1 3-4 acres of meadowing, 4li.; a peece of meadow at bog pond, 1li.; 5 Cowes, 20li.; 1 heifer, 3li.; 2 Calves, 2li. 10s.; 1 bed & boulster, 1li. 10s.; Couerletts, blanketts & sheets, 1li.; 3 Sutes of Clothes, 2li.; 2 pr. Stockings, 1s. 6d.; bands & Capps, 2s.; 2 pr. shoes, 6s.; 1 warming pan & brass kettle, 1li. 14s.; puter, 6s.; 1 Iron pott & Skillett, 4s.; 2 sheets & a Trunk, 1li.; 1 hhd., 3s.; money, 12s.; severall Lumber goods to the Vallue of 1li.; 40 acres of Land by Geo. Shafling, 3li.; total, 54li. 8s. 6d. *Essex Co. Quarterly Court Files, vol. 2, leaf* 102.

### ESTATE OF THOMAS MILLARD OF NEWBURY.

"M<sup>r</sup> Thomas Millard of Newbury being sick and weake of Body but of sound memory and good vnderstanding did nuncupatively thus declare his last will and testament to be as followeth in the p<sup>r</sup>sence of willm Cotton & Ann his wyfe and John Butler namely That he bestowed his estate vpon his wyfe Ann and his two children Rebecca and Elizabeth to be devided amongst them his wyfe to haue one third part thereof and his two children thother two third pts one third part a peece and to haue it payd them on the day of their marriag and his wyfe not hinder them when they are eighteene yeares of age. And his wyfe Anne to haue the ymprouement of it in the meane tyme. And thus hee exprest himself the Thirtyeth day of August Anno dm one thousand six hundred fifty and three."

Proved 29 : 9 : 1653, by William Cotton and John Butler before Mr. Jon. Glover.

Inventory of estate of Mr. Thomas Millward, who deceased this life Sept. 2, 1653, taken by Percivall Lowle, Richard Lowle and Anthony Somerby: The house, barn and about 20 akers of upland, about five akers of it being broken up, 45li.; twelve akers of salt marsh, 10li.; five akers of salt marsh, 2li.; three akers of meadow, 3li.; five cowes, 21li.; three oxen, 22li.; three calves, 3li. 10s.; halfe of two yearlings, 2li. 10s.; halfe a mare, 6li. 10s.; halfe a horse, 7li. 10s.; the halfe of seaven ewes and a ram, 3li. 10s.; sixe swine, 5li.; 8 pewter dishes, 2 basons, 3 poringers, 1 saltseller, 3 butter dishes, one dozen of spoones, 1 pint pot, 3 tining pudding pans, 2li.; 3 silver spoones, 1 Silver cup, 1 Silver salt seller, 3li. 5s.; his weareing apparrell, 12li. 10s.; one brasse kettle & 2 small brasse kettles, 1li. 12s.; 2 brasse skilletts, a brasse skimmer and ladle, a brasen chafin dish & pewter candlesticke, 1li.; a lattin lanthorne & lamp & a pare of And Irons, 15s.; nine sheets, 9li.; 4 table cloths, a dozen and halfe of napkins, 1li.; 8 pillow beares, 3 towells, 2li.; 2 featherbeds, 2 ruggs, 1 coverlett and 3 blankets, 11li.; a wainscot cubbard and a table, chaires and stooles and some other lumber, 1li.; one truncke and three chests, 3li. 6d.; one bedsted, 12s.; one warmeing pan, 1 small brasen morter and 2 small friing pans, 13s. 4d.; 2 Iron potts and pothookes, 2 prs. of potthangers and a paire of tongs, 1li.; one Iron kettle & spitt, 16s.; one small caske of nailes, 1li.; two small drinke tubs, one churne and two kellers & some other lumber, 8s. 6d.; a cart & 2 plowes and a sled, 2li.; 3 axes or hatchetts, 4 wedgs & hamer and other small Implements, 12s.; a fowleing peice & sword, 1li. 10s.; 2 prs. of bandeleers, 4s.; a gold seale, 1li.; total, 185li. 13s. 10d. Debts due to deceased in England, 85li.; due in this country, 9li. 9s. 6d.; a desperate debt in Virginea, 63li.; total, 157li. 9s. 6d. Whole amount, 343li. 3s. 4d. Ann Millerd made oath to the truth of this statement, 24: 9: 1653, before Wm. Gerrish, commissioner.

*Essex Co. Quarterly Court Files, vol. 2, leaf* 103.

### ESTATE OF WILLIAM BACON OF SALEM.

"The Last will and Testament of m$^r$ William Bacon of Salem, diseased Whereby he gaue to his sonn Isaack his dwelling house and ground and Meddow except some certaine parcells of —— which afterward he shall otherwise see cause; he is to haue it att the age of one and Twentie years. If he dye before one and twentie his wyfe is to haue it. And if his wife keeps hir selfe a widdow his sonn is to liue with hir And shee is to take care of the whole Estate. Item he giues to An Potter one Cowe. Item to his two seruants ffortie shillings apeece Item all his household goods, and all his Chattell and all other moueabls whatsoever to his wyfe m$^{rs}$ Rebeca Bacon And two hundred Acres of Land which is not yet Laid out to his wyfe m$^{rs}$ Rebeca Bacon and Three acers of Land in the tenem$^t$

"As ffor ouerseers Joseph Boyse and Lawrenc Southweeke."
[No signature]
her mark
Witness: George Emery, Elizabeth E. Boy[se].

*Essex Co. Quarterly Court Files, vol. 2, leaf* 105.

Rebecka Bacon brought in an imperfect will of her deceased husband, Will. Bacon, 29: 9: 1653. The estate to be divided equally between her and her son Isaac, who is to have the dwelling house, land and meadow, at the age of twenty-one. If the widow marry again, she is to give security, and bring up her son in a manner suitable to the heir of such an estate. *Salem Quarterly Court Records, vol. 3, leaf* 67.

Inventory taken 26: 7: 1653, by Thoms. Gardner, sr. and Josif (his I mark) Boys, and sworn before Elias Stileman, clerk: House and Land, 50li.; one mare, 10li.; 2 Oxen, 14li.; 5 Cowes, 22li.; 2 Steeres, 9li.; one heifer, 2li.; 3 Calves, 3li.; 9 Sheepe, 15li.; 7 Swine, 5li.; 4 akers of Indian Corne, 4li.; Ten bushels of wheate, 2li.. 10s.; 12 bushels of Rie, 2li. 8s.; 5 bushels of Pease, 1li.; 3 Feather Beads, 6li.; 2 Rugs, 2li.; 3 blanckets, 1li.; Curtaines & Valens for two beads, 2li.; one Flock bead & Covering, 1li. 10s.; 8 payre of Sheetes, 8li.; pillibes, 16s.; Table Lining, 2li.; Carpets & qushens, 1li. 10s.; His wearing aparell, 5li.; Trunks & Chests, 1li.; Beadsteads, 1li.; Chayres & Stooles, 10s.; Brasse & Iiren Vessels, 4li.; Pewter Vessels, 2li.; Plate, 5li.; Books, 2li.; Tooles belonging to his Trade, 2li.; 2 Tables, 16s.; Racks & Tongs, 6s.; Maps & Pictures, 1li.; one Musket & other Armer, 2li.; one Cart & Plow & plowgeere, 2li.; Axes, wedges & other Tooles, 1li. 10s.; total, 184li. 16s. Debts & Legasies, 38li. *Essex Co. Quarterly Court Files, vol. 2, leaf 105.*

### ESTATE OF GEORGE PARK OF (MARBLEHEAD?).

Administration on the estate of George Parke, "feared to be miscaried in a Late Storme" granted Jan. 25, 1653-4 to Mr. Edmond Batter, in behalf of creditors. Signed by Edw. Rawson, secretary. *Salem Quarterly Court Records, vol. 3, leaf 69.*

### ESTATE OF GEORGE CHIN OF MARBLEHEAD.

Administration on the estate of George Chin granted 6: 1: 1653-4, to his widow, Elizabeth Chin of Marblehead. Inventory, 34li. 4s. Debts, 33li. 7d. *Salem Quarterly Court Records, vol. 3, leaf 69.*

Court 28: 4: 1664, ordered that the estate of houses, lands, etc., of George Chin, deceased, in the hands of John Codner, said Chin's successor, be given to said Codner, in consideration of bringing up the children of the deceased, and paying his debts. *Salem Quarterly Court Records, vol. 4, page 133.*

### ESTATE OF JOHN ELIE OF (MARBLEHEAD?).

John Codner was bound 6: 1: 1653-4, to account for what had been received and paid for the use of Jon. Elie, being administrator of his estate. *Salem Quarterly Court Records, vol. 3, leaf 69.*

John Codner had previously brought in an inventory of the estate of John Elie. Amount, 25li. 6s. He stated to the court 27: 4: 1654, that other outstanding bills had been found, so that the amount of the estate was but 20li. 9s., and debts, 19li. 16s. 11 1-2d. *Salem Quarterly Court Records, vol. 3, leaf 73.*

### Estate of John Knowlton of Ipswich.

"This 29$^{th}$: of the 9$^{th}$ m$^{th}$: 1653: I the said John Knowlton being att this p$^r$sent time in perfect memory I make my wife my Executrix & I doe giue vnto margery my wife my house & land & Cattell with other estate for her use & the bringing of my Children up so long as she liues & after her death the remainder to be deuided half of it to my eldest sonne John & the other halfe of it to be deuided betweene my sonne Abraham & my daughter Elisabeth, & if it please God any of my Children do Chang ther Condition it is my desire with the aduice of m$^r$ Symonds & our pastor and the ouerseers and my wife Consenting therto that they should impt something vnto them according as god shall guide you and I giue to Margery my wife all my household goods to be at her owne disposing onely my shop tooles I giue to my eldest sonne John and some of my wearing clothes to my brother william I make m$^r$ Tredwell by brother Wilson & my [brother?] Thomas Knoulton my ouerseers. Theophilus Wilson & Thomas Knoulton sworne testified that John Knoulton was redy to haue subscribed this to be his last will if his wife did accept to be executrix within two dayes which she did & so this is proued to be his will in the Court held at Ipswich the 28$^{th}$ of march 1654." *Copy of will, Ipswich Deeds, vol. 1, leaf 137.*

Proved Mar. 28, 1654. *Ipswich Quarterly Court Records, vol. 1, page 44.*

### Estate of Mrs. Margery Knowlton of Ipswich.

"ffebruary the 20$^{th}$: 1653. This is to Certify that I Margery Knoulton widdow do make my brother Thomas Knoulton Executor to me & Assigne in my stead to fulfill my husbands will in my Roome & also for my selfe to giue to my Children according to our wills, for my household goods which are at my disposeing I doe giue equally to be deuided to my 3 Children John Elisabeth & Abraham, onely I giue my great Byble to John, & all my weareing parrell to Elisabeth & a

Iron pott with a bed tike that is hers & 20ˢ that is John and 2 Candlesticks that are Abraham's. And I make mʳ Tredwell & my brother Wilson my ouerseers. Also Abraham is to haue the yearne & Cloth to make him two shifts & to haue a new hatt. these 3 interlines were made before she set her hand."

her mark<br>Margery Knoulton

[In the margin of the record, midway, is written: "These are beside the Diuision."]

Proved 28: 1: 1654, by Theophilus Wilson, Elisabeth Wilson and Mary Tredwell. *Copy of will, Ipswich Deeds, vol. 1, leaf 138.*

Copy of inventory of estate of John Knoulton and Margery, his wife, of Ipswich, both deceased, taken Mar. 3, 1653, by Robert Payne and Robert Lord: in the Hall: a little table, 4s.; 3 Chaires & 3 old Cushins, 6s. 6d.; one great Byble, 10s.; a broad booke of Mr. Bifields workes, 4s.; 9 other bookes & bibles, 15s.; a Muskett, bandalers, sword, rest, Knapsack with rest moulds & scourer, 1li. 2s.; A Chest with a drawer, 1li.; 6 paire of sheets at 12s. a paire, 3li. 12s.; 3 finer sheets, 1li. 6s.; 3 Course sheets, 14s.; one fine table Cloth, 9s.; 3 other table Cloths, 10s. 6d.; one halfe sheete, 5s. 4d.; 2 paire fine pillow beeres, 18s.; 1 paire of pillow beeres, 5s.; 3 Course old pillow beeres, 2s. 6d.; 10 napkins at 8d., 6s. 8d.; 3 old table clothes & 2 towels, 5s. 6d.; 5 remnants of Canvas & lockrum, 14s.; one shirt, 4s.; Child bed lenen, 26s. 8d., 2 ruffes, 5s., 1li. 11s. 8d.; white thred & a remnant of new cloth, 5s. 4d.; 4 yards & a halfe of pagon at 4s. 6d., 1li. 3d.; almost 4 yards of french serge, 1li. 4s.; one yard of broad Cloth, 12s.; a mantle, 10s.; 4 yards 1-4 of lockrum at 16d., 5s. 8d.; one remnant of red bayes & one of greene, 7s. 4d.; her weareing Clothes, 9li.; her wearing Lennen, 1li. 16s. In the little Parlour: his weareing apparell, 4li.; 2 ould Chests, 10s.; 2 little boxes & a deske with some small things, 5s.; 1yd. blew lennen, 2s. 6d.; a feather bed, a boulster & a straw bed, 3li.; Curtaines & valients, 1li.; one paire of blankets, 1li. 5s.; one rugge, 1li. 6s. 8d.; bedsted & Cord, 8s.; an old trundle bed cord & old strawbed, 5s.; a little flockbed & boulster, 10s.; 5 pillows & 3 blankets, 1li. 10s.; 4 Curtaine rods, 4s. In the shop Kitching & buttery: the shop tooles, 1li. 10s.; leather, 3li. 10s.; in wooden & earthen vessells, 17s. 6d.; a pot of suet, 3s., butter & tub, 9s.; in porke, 1li. 10s.; 2 quarts of oyle & a bottle, 2s.; 43li. of pewter at 16d., 2li. 17s. 4d.; a morter & pestcl & tinne ware, 8s. 10d.; 3 postnets, 6s.; one kettle, 12s., 2 old pots, 12s. 3d., 1li. 4s. 3d.; a scimer & frying pan, 5s.; one kettle, 14s. & a little kettle, 3s., 17s.; 2 tramels, 1 grediron, 2 p potthookes, one paire of tongs, cobirons, spitt, slice & tosting iron, 1li.; an ould warmeing pan, 3s. 6d.; a p of bellows & 2 lamps, 2s. 6d.; 2 vineger bottels & 2 payles, 3s. 4d.; 2 ould wheeles & a paire of scales, 4s. 6d.; in waites, 1 kneading trough, a little table, 2 formes, 2 old Chaires & 2 old Cushens, 8s. 10d.; one flasket & 2 other baskets, 3s. 6d.; 4 wedges & 2 pitchforkes, 10s.; one shovell, one spade, one mattock, one howe & one axe, 9s. In the Chambers: 12li. of Cotten wooll, 12s.; 2 pillow tikes & a boulster tike, 15s.; 3 yards of lensywoollsey, 4s. 6d.; 4 bushells of Indian Corne, 12s.; a flockbed, boulster & straw bed, 1li. 10s.; one rugge & blankett, 2li. 5s.; one bedstead & a Coard, 8s.; one trundlebed, flockbed & boulster, 1li. 15s.; an old blanket & ould Coverlet, 5s.; 2 bushell & halfe of barly, 12s. 6d.; a bill, ads, 2 wry bitts & other lumber, 4s.; a bushell of Indian beanes, 5s.; 4 yards of lennen & Cotton Cloth, 8s.; 13li. of wooll at 14d., 15s. 2d.; 4li. 1-4 of flax & 5li. of towe, 7s. 10d.; 2li. 1-4 of yarne at 2s. 4d., 5s. 3d.; lennen yarne, 1s. 2d.; in rye meale, malt, wheate & hops, 14s.; a Cellar Case, firken, forme & halfe tub, 5s.; 2 sacks & a leather bage, 4s.; a sithe, 2 sickles, hand saw & a half bushell, 10s.; the howse, barne & ground about it, 30li.; 3 acres in the north feild, 5li.; 6 Acres at the pequit feild, 6li.; 3 Acres of meadow at west meadows, 1li. 10s.; 5 acres of marsh, 1li. 5s.; 3 Cowes & one heifer 2 yeare ould, 16li.; one hogg, 14s.; in Debts, 20li. 9s.; A ladder 1s. 4d.; A hyde of leather, 18s. 6d.; more in leather & rosen, 1li. 16s. 6d.; a lookeing glasse, mattock & a wheelebarrow, 5s.; total, 158li. 15s. 3d. Debts owing from the estate, 30li. *Ipswich Deeds, vol. 1, leaf 138.*

ESTATE OF JANE KENNING OF IPSWICH.

"The 14th of 12th mth 1653 This is to Certify that I Jane Kenning being in pfect memory do make my two sisters Elisabeth Wilson and Margery Knowlton to be my Executrixes & they to chuse whom they see fitt to Asist them in the disposing of that which I haue giuen which is as followeth, To John Knowlton I giue Twenty pounde & to the rest of my sisters Children ten pound a peece Elisabeth Knowlton Elisabeth Wilson Seaborne Wilson, & Abraham Knowlton, And to my brother Wilsons sone Thomas three pounds, & the rest for my mothers vse during her life & for that that remaines equally to be deuided in Case there be not enough of that which is left then there is to be a deduction pportionable out of the former gift." [No signature].

Witness: Mary Tredwell, Thomas Knowlton.

Proved Mar. 28, 1654 by Thomas Knowlton and Mary, wife of Thomas Tredwell. *Copy of will, Ipswich Deeds, vol. 1, leaf* 140.

Copy of inventory taken Mar. 3, 1653, by Robert Payne and Robert Lord: one Joyned bedsted, 1li. 6s.; A fetherbed & boulster, curtaines & valents, one pillow & a straw bed, 7li.; one payre of blanketts, 1li. 10s.; a blue Rugge, 1li. 10s.; an ould Rugge, 16s.; a flockbed & boulster, 1li.; A trundle bed, 5s.; 3 payre of sheets, 3li.; 2 payre of sheets, 1li. 10s.; 2 payre sheets, 1li.; one table cloth & one duz: of napkins & one, 18s. 6d.; one pillow beare & 1 paire of old pillowbeers, 6s. 4d.; 3 Towels & a short table cloth, 3s.; A Table, 10s. & a little table, 3s. 6d.; 13s. 6d.; hir weareing lennen, 2li. 1s.; hir red peticoate, 22s., a serge peticoate & wastcoate, 2li. 2s.; hir paragon peticoate, 16s.; a yard & halfe of serge, 9s.; A Cloath wastcoate, 10s.; hir searge Gowne, 2li.; hir Cloth Gowne, 2li. 5s.; hir red peticoate with 2 laces, 1li.; 3 old peticoats, 1li. 2s.; a lensy woollsy Apron, 2s. 6d.; an ould stuffe peticoate & wastcoate of cloth, 10s.; 7 yards of Carsy at 6s. 8d., 2li. 6s. 8d.; 4 yards of blue bayes, 1li.; 2 yards & 1-2 of broad Cloth at 15s. p. yd., 1li. 17s. 6d.; 4 yards of Curtaine stuff, 1li.; a kersy Covering, 1li. 2s.; 2 pillows & a flock boulster, 19s.; 40li. of pewter at 16d., 2li. 13s. 4d.; one postnet, brasse ladle & a spoone, 4s. 6d.; a brasse pott, 12s. 4d.; pins, 3s. 6d., a morter & 2 pestells, 6s. 8d., 10s. 2d.; a paire of Andirons, 6s. 8d.; a great Iron pott & pot hookes, 16s.; an old kettle, 8s. 6d.; a little kettle & 2 pudding pans, 4s. 4d.; a tramell, spitt & firepan, 5s. 9d.; a keeler & 3 trayes, 6s. 8d.; a trundle bed, 4s. 6d.; 6 bushells of wheate, 1li. 10s.; 2 bushell & one peck of Indian, 6s. 9d.; 3 baggs & 3 tubbs & other lumber, 7s. 6d.; 3 Chaires & 3 old Cushins, 4s.; 6 Cushins, 15s.; A Chest & fforme, 11s.; a tub of Porke, 18s.; a paire of bellows & other lumber, 6s. 6d.; one Cowe, 4li. 12s.; the howse & ground aboute it, 35li.; one Sowe, 1li. 1s.; 600 of nayles at 12d., 600 of nailes at 10d., 11s.; 400 of nailes at 7d. & a narrow axe, 2s. 2d., 4s. 6d.; one smoothing Iron, 1s. 6d.; in debts, 71li. 4s. 7d.; total 166li. 7s. 1d. a flock bolster twise prised. *Ipswich Deeds, vol.* 1, *leaf* 141.

### Estate of Mark Quilter of Ipswich.

"february the 7th: 1653: I Marke Quilter of Ipswich in Essex in new England doe make my last will and Testament in manner and forme as followeth. first I doe giue and bequeath unto my wife: during her life my house and the land adioyning thereto And I doe giue to my wife a six acre lott during her life which was giuen mee by the towne Joyning to a lott of goodman warners. which house and lands I doe giue to my son Joseph when my wife shall die, And I doe giue vnto my wife all my meadow ground during her life and after her death to be equally diuided betweene my sonne Marke & my son Joseph. and if it shall please god to take away my son Joseph before my wife then I doe giue his portion to be deuided among the rest of my children my son Marke to haue a double share thereof, I doe alsoe giue my moueable goods vnto my wife to bee at her owne disposing: and I doe giue to my sonne Marke a Six acre lott which I bought of goodman Johnson and ten pounds more when my wife shall die. and if my wife shall die before my son Joseph is of age the vse of my house & the land shall goe to the rest of my Children till Joseph be of age, And I doe giue to my daughter mary & to my Daughter Rebecca & to my daughter Sarah five pounds a peice to be paid when my wife shall thinke meete howeuer to be paid at the death of my wife moreouer I doe giue to my daughter Sarah at present a yeerelinge Cow Calfe which wee call grissles Calfe & the rest of my Cattle to my wife to be at her owne disposing, And I doe make my wife Executor of this my last will and Testament." [No signature.]

Witness: Edward (his mark) Lumis, Danyell warner, Will: Adams, Jun$^r$.

Proved Mar. 28, 1654 by the witnesses.

Copy of inventory taken 23: 12: 1653, by Robert Lord and Daniell Warner; one flockbed, 13s. 4d.; an ould Coverlet & a paire of ould blanketts, 1li. 12s.; one flock Boulster & 3 pillows, 10s.; A little ould flockbed & boulster & strawbed with 2 other straw things, 12s.; one ould Trundle bed, 3s.; 3 paire of sheetes & 3 pillow cases, 1li.; 3 Curtaynes, 1li.; his weareing Cloths, 2li.; 3 ould Chaires & 2 ould Cushings, 4s.; 1 yard & halfe of Cloth, 15s.; A warmeing pan, 10s.; one kettell, one Iron pott, a postnet, tramell & pothookes, 1li. 13s. 4d.; 2 ould lennen wheeles & a Cotton wheele, 5s.; 2 ould axes, 2 wedges, a paire of beetle rings, a bill & som other things, 10s.; 3 sithes, 10s.; 10 bushells of Indian

Corne & 3 bushells of wheate, 2li. 5s.; 2 ould hogsheads & other lumbar, 12s.; 4 bushells of barley & an ould ffunn, 1li. 6s.; an ould table & forme, 5s.; a muskett, bandaleers & sword, 1li.; in pewter, 10s.; A hand saw & other small things, 6s. 8d.; in Cotton & Cotton yarne, 12s.; lennen yarne & hempe, 1li.; A Cart & plough wth what belong to them, 2li. 10s.; 4 steeres & Oxen, 24li.; 5 Cowes, 1  3 yeareling, 3  2 yearelings, 2 yearelings & 2 Calves, 40li.; 2 shoates, 1li.; the house & ground about it, 25li.; 12 Acres of Land & about 12 Acres of meadow fresh & salt, 22li.; in barly at the kill, 13 bushells, 3li. 5s.; total, 137li. 9s. 4d. Debts owing to severall men to the vallew of 14li. 11s. Debts being deducted the estate is 122li. 18s. 4d.

*Copy of will and inventory, Ipswich Deeds, vol. 1, leaf 162.*

### ESTATE OF THOMAS SCOTT OF IPSWICH.*

"This 8$^{th}$ of march 1653-54 I Thomas Scott of Ipswich in Essex in Newengland doe appoint this my last will and Testament as followeth. Inpr I doe giue to my Daughter Elizabeth Twenty & five pounds to her & her heires to be paid the one halfe with in halfe a yeare after by deceace the other halfe with in a yeare after my decease to her & her heires. Item I doe giue to my daughter Abigaille Twenty & fiue pounds to be paid to her & her heires. the one halfe to be paid with in one yeare after my decease the other halfe to be paid with in a yeare & halfe after my decease. Item I doe giue to my daughter Hannah Twenty & fiue pounds to her & her heires to be paid when she is Twenty & one yeares of age, & if shee doe marry before shee be of the age of Twenty & one yeares, The one halfe of it shall be paid at the day of marriage. & the other halfe at the age of twenty and one yeares. Item I doe giue to my daughter Sarah Twenty & fiue pounds. to be paid to her & her heires when she is Twenty & one yeares of age. & if shee doe marry before shee bee of the age of Twenty & one yeares, one halfe shall be paid at the day of her marryage and the other halfe at her age of Twenty and one yeares. Item I doe giue to my daughter Mary Twenty and fiue pounds. To be paid to her & her heires, when shee is of the age of Twenty & one yeares. & if shee doe marry before shee bee Twenty and one yeares of Age. the one halfe shall be payd at the day of her marryage & the other halfe at

* See also Records and Files of the Quarterly Courts of Essex Co., vol. 3 (1913), page 96.

her Age of Twenty & one yeares. And I intend that my daughter mary shall bee maintained out of my estate soe as the executors shall see meete with her labour. Item I doe giue to my son Thomas Scot all my Estate ungiuen: and doe appoint my Brother Richard Kembell and Thomas Rowlinson sen$^r$ and Edmund Bridges executors of this my last will & testament and doe appoint them to be paid whatsoeuer charges they shall be at out of my estate and hereunto I doe set my hand."

Tho. Scott

Witness: Daniel Warner, Will Adams, Jun$^r$.
Proved 28: 1: 1654. *Copy of will, Ipswich Deeds, vol. 1, leaf 163.*

Inventory taken Mar. 17, 1653-4, by John Whipple and Theophilus Wilson: in the parlor, one bedsted wth a feather bed, two feather bolsters, two pillowes with a flock bed, two blankets, a rug, five curtaines and valants, 8li. 15s. 4d.; two chests, one broad box, one Chaire with one old chest with two locks and a warming pan, 15s. 10d.; a Coverled, 12s.; 4 yards quarter and halfe of Canvis at 22d. p yard, 8s.; 2 peeces of Cotten Cloth containing 4 yards and a halfe at 3s. p yard, 13s. 6d.; 4 yards of Cotten Cloth at 2s. 6d. p yard, 10s.; 2 yards of white Cloth, 5s.; 2 yards halfe a quarter of Carsy at 3s. 6d. p yard, 7s.; 2 yards quarter and halfe of red Cotton at 2s. 6d. p yard, 5s. 10d.; a yard and halfe of Carsy, 6s.; a yard and halfe and halfe quarter of serge, 6s. 6d.; a table Cloth, 7s.; 2 small table clothes, 3s. 4d.; a peice of locram, 3 yards, 4s. 6d.; 3 paire of sheetes, 18s.; 5 napkins, 3s. 4d.; 4 pillow beers, 6s.; 2 shirts, 10s.; 2 towells, 1s.; a locke with 2 paire of Joynts, 2s.; 36li. of pewter in the hall at one shilling p li., 1li. 16s.; one kettle weighing 17li., 7s. 8d.; a kettle, 2 posnits & a Scumer weighing 11li. 3q, 10s.; a kettle weighing 16li., 10s.; a brasse morter weighing 4li. 1q., 2s.; a chamber pot, 1s. 6d.; an Iron skillet, 4s.; an Iron kettle, 5s.; 2 Iron potts weighing 53li. and a halfe, 15s.; a trevet 18li., 6s.; a smoothing Iron, 1s.; 21li. of Iron things, 8s. 9d.; a frying pan, 2s. 6d.; a paire of bellowes, a brush with other implements, 6s. 8d.; 6 ocamy spoones, 2s. 4d.; old Iron, 9s.; 2 plowshares, 2s. 6d.; wedges, 2s.; 3 pailes, an old kettle and a spade, 5s.; 3 bookes, 12s. 2d.; a hamer, a paire of pincers and an ax, 4s.; Two muskets, a sword and a paire of bandeleers with a long fowling peece, 1li. 10s.; 500 & a halfe of nailes, 4s.; 3 bells, a hacksaw, a framing saw, a handsaw &

a paire of sheeres, 14s.; 9 old tubs, 10s.; porke, 1li. 11s.; a halfe headed bedsted, a pillow with a paire of blankets and a small bed, 1li. 3s.; 12 Caskes, 6s.; a fan, 3 sickles, 2 sithes with other implements, 7s.; in wearing Clothes, 8li. 3s. 10d.; in money, 2li. 15s. 6d.; 14 yards and a halfe of Cotten Cloth, 2li. 3s. 6d.; girt webb, 1s. 4d.; foure skins with a peece of match, 9s.; lead, 7li., 1s. 2d.; a flitch of bacon weighing 26li. and a halfe, 10s. 10d.; a gowne, 15s.; caps and bands with a paire of stockings, 8s.; wheate, 36 bushels and a pecke, 9li. 1s. 3d.; 55 bushels, 3 peckes of malt, 13li. 18s. 9d.; a brasse frying pan, 3s. 6d.; Indian Corne, 34 bushels, 5li. 2s.; Cattle in the hands of John West with tackling for plow and Cart, 52li.; in the hands of John davis, 5li.; Cattle in the hand of Robert Roberts, 15li.; Cattle at home and swine, 33li. 5s.; a beast in the hand of John Spofford, 6li.; in debts, 4li. 18s.; a house, a barne and land, 129li.; a grinstone, 5s.; total, 318li. 19s. 11d.

Allowed in Ipswich court 28: 1: 1654. *Essex Co. Probate Files, Docket 24,971.*

Richard (his F mark) Kimball and Edman Bridges, on May 10, 1661, acknowledged the receipt from Mr. Ezekell Rogers of 25li. the legacy given to Sarah Scott by her father. Wit: Tho. Lovell and William Goodhue. *Essex Co. Quarterly Court Files, vol. 9, leaf 48.*

Acquittances brought in Sept. 29, 1663, by Richard Kimball and Edmond Bridges, executors of the will of Thomas Scott, under the hands of the legatees, that is, the children of said Scott, of the receipts of their several legacies. Said executors were discharged. *Ipswich Quarterly Court Records, vol. 1, page 123.*

Haniell Bosworth certified, Oct. 1, 1663, that he received 25li. from Richard Kimball and Edmond Bridges, which was a legacy given to his wife Abbigaile by her father, Thomas Scott. Wit: Thomas Lovell, sr., and Thomas Lovell, jr.

Mary (her × mark) Scot certified, Apr. 23, 1663, to the receipt of 25li. from Ezek. Rogers, of Ipswich, which was the legacy left her by her father. Wit: Richard Jacob and Daniel Hovey.

*Essex Co. Quarterly Court Files, vol. 9, leaves 49, 50.*

ESTATE OF SAMUELL SYMONDS, JR. OF IPSWICH.

"I Samuell Symonds Jun$^r$, being very weake in body & of

good memory, doe make this my last will & Testament in mann^r & forme following viz: Imprimis haueing (I blesse God) rest in my heart concerning my euerlasting Condicon, through Jesus Christ my p^rtious Sauio^r, I doe giue vnto my brother Harlakinden Symonds all my lande in wenham, & foure of my best bands. Item I giue to my brother John Symonds three pounds & ten shillings, to be paide next Michaeltide come three yeare, or within one month after his demand of it, in Case he cometh to Newengland in the meane time. Item I giue vnto my brother Samuell Symonds, to my sisters Martha, Ruth, & Priscilla, & to my nephew Samuell Epps, Twenty shillings a peece, to be paide, within one yeare after my deceace. Item I giue to my sister Mary Epps, the little peece of new holland cloth. Item I giue vnto Killigresse Rosse my Chest with the lock & key to it. Item I giue to my brother Samuell all my bookes. Item I giue vnto Rebecca warde fiue shillings. Item I giue vnto my brother william Symonds (whom I appoynt & desire to be my executo^r of this my will) all my lande at Chebacco, in Ipsw^ch: & all the rest of my goods vndisposed of, haueing paid, & discharged all my debts, & duties. In wittness whereof I haue heereunto sett my hand, & seale, Dat 22^th day of the nineth month Anno Dom 1653."

Samuell Symonds.

Witness: James Chewte, Elizabeth Chewte, Samuel Symonds.

Proved 28: 1: 1654 by testimony of James Chute and affirmed by Mr. Samuell Symonds.

Copy of inventory presented 30: 1: 1654: in Lande about sixteene acers lying in Wenham late purchassed of Samuell Kent, 6li.; in lande at Chebacco falls about seaven Acres, 5li.; halfe a Mare & halfe a Colt, 20li.; in bookes & other goods, 10li.; total, 41li.

*Copy of will and inventory, Ipswich Deeds, vol. 1, leaf 161.*

### ESTATE OF RICHARD HOLLINGSWORTH OF SALEM.*

Administration on the estate of Richard Holingworth, granted Mar. 28, 1654, to the widow Holingworth, Capt. William Hathorne, Mr. Henry Bartholomew and Thomas Wilks, all of Salem. *Ipswich Quarterly Court Records, vol. 1, page 45.*

* See also Records and Files of the Quarterly Courts of Essex Co., Mass., vol. 1 (1911), pp. 349, 350, 359.

Mr. Henry Bartholmew brought in an inventory of the estate of Ric. Hollingworth, sr., 27: 4: 1654. *Salem Quarterly Court Records, vol. 3, leaf 72.*

Inventory of Richard Hollingworth of Salem, taken 26: 3: 1654, by Walter Price and Samuell Archard: One dwelling house, an outhouse, and one aker of Lande, 24li.; 4 ten aker lotts on darbie fort side, 12li.; one aker and half of land on the neck neare unto Tho. Picktons, 15s.; 2 akers of lande bought of Mr. Steevens, 2li.; a Cowe, 4li.; 20 akers of lande given by the towne, 1li.; a greate ketch on the stocks, 130li.; a lighter on the stocks, 18li.; a lesser ketch on the stocks, 7li.; 7 loode of timber on the keye at 8s. p loode, 2li. 16s.; 6 loode of sawne timber at 10s. p loode, 3li.; 35 C. of oake plancke at 12s. p C., 21li.; 585 foote of pine plancke at 10s. p C., 2li. 18s. 9d.; trunnells, 1li. 4s.; 400 of inch boords, 1li. 2s.; 966 foote of oake boords at 7s. 6d., 3li. 12s. 4d.; 487 foote of inch and half at 9s., 2li. 3s. 10d.; 3 barrells of Tarr, 3li.; more 536 foote of oake plancke at 12s., 3li. 4s. 4d.; 784 foote of pine at 10s., 3li. 18s. 6d.; a Rudder and keele stem and sterne post for a boate, 1li.; in kettles, potts and a scillett, 2li.; tubbs, 12s.; a frying pan, 2s. 6d.; trenchers, 3s. 3d.; earthen potts, 18d.; a pitch pott, 14s., pails, 12d., 16s. 6d.; pewter, a bras Candlestick, a mortr and spitt, 1li. 16s.; 13 tubbs, a Joyned stool and a forme, 1li. 4s.; 6 Chaires, 12s., andirons, 3s., 15s.; hakes, tongs, grediron and fire shovell, 10s.; 2 Chests and a settle, 1li.; one side Cubberd and box, 18s.; one bed, 2 blanketts and 2 pillowes, 5li.; 3 pr. of Sheets, 40s., a trundle bedsteed, 3s., 2li. 3s.; 3 pr. pillow beares, 12s., a warmeinge pan, 6s., 18s.; one bed steed and Curtaines, 20s., a looking glass and brush, 2s., wearinge apparrell, 4li. 10s., 5li. 12s.; 2 wheeles and a cheese presse, 6s.; 6 napkins, 2 table clothes, 10s., a bed, 2 pr. blankets and bedsted, 2li. 10s.; tooles, Iron Ringe bolts and gin Ropes, 2li. 10s.; a whipsaw, 2 gins and a Rope, 1li.; old Iron, 20s., a drippin pan, 12d., 1li. 1s.; Thomas Warner of Cape Porpus, 1li. 5s.; Jo. Deale of desperatt debt, 5li.; Majr. Sedgwick, 7li.; John Hudson, 20li.; Francis Hudson, 5s.; more 1,000 of oake plancke in the woods, 3li. 15s.; for hewen timbr lyinge on the deputie's farme, 3li. 15s.

*Essex Co. Quarterly Court Files, vol. 2, leaf 131.*

Depositions made in Salem court 30: 4: 1654, concerning the estate of Richard Hollingworth. William Hollingworth deposed that he heard his father, Rich. Hollingworth, often say that the house in which he dwelt was his son Richard's, and that he had given it to him in consideration of work.

Susanna Hollingworth deposed that her husband, Richard Hollingworth said, "I will build another for my wife and myselfe to dwell in."

Nathll. Pickman deposed that Rich. Hollingworth, deceased, said to him that the house on the south end of the lot that was by Mr. Corwethin's house in Salem he had given to his son William Hollingworth, and the house he lived in to his son Rich. Hollingworth, and a parcel of land at Darbie fort side near Mr. Frend's lot, whether 10 or 20 acres, he could not tell. The deceased wished him to build him another house that summer. *Salem Quarterly Court Records, vol. 3, leaf* 76.

### Estate of William Varney of Ipswich.

Administration on the estate of William Varney, intestate, granted Mar. 28, 1654, to his widow, Bridgett Varney. He left three sons and one daughter. Ordered that the eldest son have 8li. within three months, and the other children 4li. each at the age of twenty-one. *Ipswich Quarterly Court Records, vol.* 1, *page* 45.

Inventory of the estate of William Varney of Ipswich, taken 1:1:1653, by George Gidding and John Cogswell: 2 flock beds and flock boulster and 2 pillows, 2li. 10s.; 2 blankets, one sheet & other beding, 1li. 12s.; his weareing aparell, 3li.; bushells of wheat, 15s.; 2 bushells 1-2 of Indian corne, 8s.; in lumborments, 5s.; in axes and tooles, 15s.; a brase pot & frieing pan, 11s.; houses & land, 25li.; in cattell, 22li.; in bookes, 6s. 8d.; total, 57li. 2s. 8d. Debts owing from the estate, 6li. *Essex Co. Quarterly Court Files, vol.* 2, *leaf* 132.

### Estate of John Cooley of Ipswich.

Administration on the estate of John Cooley, intestate, granted Mar. 28, 1654, to the widow, Elizabeth Cooley. The children were three daughters, who were to receive 6li. 13s. 4d. each within three months after demand. *Ipswich Quarterly Court Records, vol.* 1, *page* 45.

Inventory of the estate of John Coolye of Ipswich, deceased, taken Mar. 14, 1653, by Edward Browne and Robert Lord: House & ground about it, 10li.; 6 acres of planting land, 8li.; 2 cowes, 2 heifers, 1 too year ould & one yeare ould, 21li.; 2 shotes, 1li.; one Fetherbed & boulster & floke boulster, 3li.; 2 pillows & one ould flock pillow, 10s.; pr. of ould blanketts & ould rugg & one better Rugg, 1li. 10s.; 1 paire of ould curtayne & valiants, 15s.; one ould bedsted & straw bed, 4s.; a trundle bed, 5s.; 2 pr. of ould sheets, 15s.; pillow beeres, 12s.; 1 table cloth, 4 napkins & a towell, 10s.; 2 ya: hempen cloth, 3s.; all his weareing aparrell, 8li.; 2 ould chests, 6s.; in pewter, 1li.; 2 settells, 2 Skilletts, 1 morter & pestle, 1 brase chafen dish & skimer, 1li. 6s. 8d.; a warmeing pan, 6s. 8d.; one Iron pole & frying pan, dripen pan & a pr. of pot hookes & a tramell, a greediron & spitt, 1li.; a musket, sword & other things belonging to the armes, 1li. 2s.; 5 bushells of corne, 15s.; beetles & wedges, 2 axes, 2 howes, 13s. 4d.; 1 matock spad & shovell & other small toolles, 12s.; a lenen wheele & 2 pr. of cards, 6s.; a poudering tubb, keelor, 2 chaires and other lumbar, 18s.; hempen yarne & hemp & tow, 12s.; one bible & other bookes, 15s.; a payre of bellears, 2s.; 3 skins, 2 bushells of mault, 16s.; total, 66li. 14s. 8d. *Essex Co. Quarterly Court Files, vol. 2, leaf 133.*

### ESTATE OF THOMAS ELITHORP OF ROWLEY.

In answer to the petitions of Widow Ethethrop, Hugh Smith and John Pickerd, the court May 14, 1654, granted the probate of the will of Thomas Ellethrope unto the persons named in the will, they to give security. The eldest son to have 28li., and the three youngest children 20li. each, there being so much clear estate remaining after the widow's 30li. and all debts deducted; but if the estate is more or fall short of 120li. clear, then it to be divided equally among the four children. *Mass. Bay Colony Records, vol. 4, page* 193.

The complaint of Abigaile Elithropp that some estate left her by her husband was unjustly detained from her, and upon her request Oct. 19, 1654, it is referred to the next County court at Ipswich. *Mass. Bay Colony Records, vol. 3, page* 363.

Case of widow Elitrop referred to the General Court; ordered Mar. 27, 1655, with consent of the overseers, Hugh Smith, John Pickard and John Trumble, that they pay her twenty shillings for the year past and 40s. per year in the future, which is for the produce of the two younger children's portions, the stock to be preserved entire. *Ipswich Quarterly Court Records, vol. 1, page* 50.

The two younger children of widow Elitrop to be paid their

portions into the hands of John Wyldes. 24: 2: 1656, John Pickard, executor of Thomas Elitrop, brought the receipt from John Wyldes and the widow, and the two elder children therefor, and the court discharged him. *Ipswich Quarterly Court Records, vol. 1, page* 56.

### ESTATE OF ABRAHAM WAR OF IPSWICH.

"I Abraham war of Ipswich maryed man being weake of body but of parfeckt memorye and vnderstanding doe make this my last will and testament as followeth I comitt my sole to god that gaue it and my body to the earth when I shall departe this life and for my worldly goods I thus dispose of them. my will is that the phissision and other depts that I owe shall bee payde and I giue my daughter to my wife to bring up and I desire her to bring her vp in the feare of god and to haue a care of her as Ife shee war her owne. and I give fiue pounde to my daughter sarah when shee shall come to age. and lastly I make my wife my onely exsecutor and ouerseer of this my laste will and testament. witnes my hand this 22 day of the 3. moneth: 1654."

his mark
Abraham O War
his mark
Witness: Roger Lanckton, William A Simonds, John warner.

Inventory: House & house lott, 25li.; flock bed, 2li. 5s.; 2 pillowes of feathers, 8s.; 2 pillows, 6s.; a hayer bed, 16s.; bedsted and trundle bed, 17s.; boulster and feathers, 1li. 8s.; coverlid and blanket, 15s.; a ruge, 15s.; two payre breches & Jacket, 1li. 5s.; hatt, 14s.; 3 shirts, 18s.; 3 sherts, 18s.; 3 pillow bears, 10s.; a payre shooes, 7s.; 4 bands, 7s. 6d.; chest and boxes, 16s.; 3 Iron potts, 18s.; skellet of bras, 3s.; erthen ware, 6s. 6d.; 3 barels, 8s.; sartaine tubs, 4s.; frying pane, 2s. 6d.; 2 bottles and a cane, 2s.; ―― 5s.; a bras laidele, 2s. 8d.; tine pane, 1s. 5d.; spoones, 2s. 4d.; two blew dishes, 1s. 8d.; the smoothing iron, 6s.; a ―― 2s.; dishes and baskets, 1s. 8d.; hower glase, 1s.; tramell and slice, 4s.; butter, 3s. 6d.; chayers, 4s.; table and two stools, 2s.; two hoes & axe, a wedge, 8s.; 3 sivs, 3 bags, 3s.; a booke, 1s. 6d.; meale, 1s.; trenchers, 9d.; a meale tube, 5s.; ―― 2li. 4s.; two hogsheds, 4s.; a reale, 2s.; a hoge, 15s.; total, 47li. 7s. 4d. *Essex Co. Quarterly Court Files, vol. 2, leaf* 149.

### ESTATE OF JOHN SANDIE OF MARBLEHEAD.

Administration on the estate of John Sandie of Marblehead, intestate, granted 27: 4: 1654, to his widow, Mary Sandy. Inventory, 80li.; the eldest son to have 10li. at twenty-one years of age and the other two children to have 5li. apiece. The widow was enjoined to bring up the children to read and write. *Salem Quarterly Court Records, vol. 3, leaf 71.*

### ESTATE OF DANIEL ROLFE OF IPSWICH.

Administration on the estate of Daniell Roff of Rowley, intestate, granted 27: 4: 1654, to his widow, Hannah Roff. *Salem Quarterly Court Records, vol. 3, leaf 73.*

Inventory of the estate of Daniell Rofe of Ipswich, deceased taken June 24, 1654, by Daniel (his D mark) Thurston, John (his I mark) Gage and Robert Lord: One bedsted & cord, 1li.; a little flock-bed & boulster, an ould Rugge & blanket, 2 paire of sheetes, 16s.; His weareing apparell, 3li. 10s.; a little table and 2 chaires, 2 little stooles, 12s.; one Cradle, 4s.; a warmeing pan, 4s. 6d.; 1 skillet & brase ladle, 3s. 6d., 8s.; one Iren pot, 8s., 1 dozzon of trenchers, 12d., 9s.; one square, 3 agures, a broad axe & a pr. compasses, 12s.; felling axes & one howe, 5s.; other Tooles & an ould sithe & one hinge, 12s., another ould sithe & snath, 2s. 6d.; a hatbrish axe, a pr. of sisers and an ould tubb, 2s.; a fowling peece, 1li. 13s. 4d.; one box, 4s., 1 houre glass, 1s., 5s.; 1 beetle, 20d., one Iron pot, 10s., 11s. 8d.; an ould bible & one other booke, 6s.; one little kettell & a little skillet, 6s.; 2 sives, 2s.; one earthen pot, 4 spoones, 20d., 3s. 8d.; 4 little keelars, 7s., one little poudering tub, 3s., 10s.; 1 ould chirne, one runlet bucking tub & firkin, 9s.; one bottle & other wooden ware, 5s. 6d.; one earthen pot & 20 li. of butter, 10s.; 5 cheeses, 4s.; a pr. of woodin scales & earthen weres, 6s.; an acre of Rye on the ground, 1li.; 4 acres of Indian corne slit corne, 3li.; about 9 acres of wheat & barlye, 16li.; a paire of oxen, 16li. 5s., 1 cart & plough, 32s., 17li. 17s.; a cowe & a calfe, 6li.; one asse, 5li., 11li.; one small sow & 2 piggs, 1li. 10s.; a raper, 22s., belt, 2s., 1li. 4s.; powder & shot, 18d.; a drum & sticks, 2li.; a little fowleing peece, 1li.; a chaire, 18d., 1s. 6d.; owing to the estate, 3li.; the grass that is to be mowne, 1li. 12s.; 3li. of yarne, 5s.; total, 74li. 17s. 8d. Debts due: To Mr. Jewet, 11li., & he requires 9li. more for damages,

20li.; to my father, Humphry Broadstreet, 11li.; to Goodman Weekes of Salem, 6li.; to John Woodam, 6li. 10s.; to Goodman Thurston, 1li. 19s.; to John Gage, 3li.; to Mr. Baker, 10s.; to Nath. Stow, 40s., 2li. 10s.; to Goodwife Elitrip & Marke Quilter, 2li.; to Lieft. Remington, 12s., to Goodman Kemball, 12s., 1li. 4s.; to Mr. Payne, 4s. 6d., to John Tod, 24s., 1li. 8s. 6d.; to Goodwife Lumkin, 3s.; to William Beale, 4li.; to Major Denison, 10s. 6d.; total, 60li. 5s. *Essex Co. Quarterly Court Files, vol. 2, leaf* 134.

### ESTATE OF GEORGE BURRILL, SR. OF LYNN.

"The wille of George Burrill senior ‖ yt after my deathe ‖ my house wherin I dwell I Giue to my sonn francis with all the land and meadow lying near adioyning to it with all farms outhouses &c: and ‖ ye ‖ barn I giu to him yt is neare to ye land of Thomas Chadwell, ‖ Land ‖ formerly william Edward with all the vpland and meadow adioyning vnto it and belonging thervnto This I giue vnto him & his heirs yt is lawfully begotten of his body for ever I giue vnto my sonn John that house wch. formerly was ffrancis his with all the land belonging vnto it and yt pece of land near Rich moors and alsoe I giu him fourteen acrs of salt marsh in Rumley marsh yt is to say six and fiue and three alsoe 8 eight more acres in the last division I giue to my sonn John and his heirs lawfully begotten of his body but in case John should not quietly possess this in regard it was formerly given vnto ffrancis then & my will is that John shall haue my dwelling house and al yt is aboue mentioned to be given to ffrancis alsoe my sonn Georg to haue his now dwelling house w$^{th}$ all the Apurtenances belonging thereto alsoe I giue a cow to my sonn George w$^{th}$ a calf and for the rest of my cattle I giue foure cowes and too oxen ‖ to my sonn John ‖ and all the rest of the cattle to ffrancis also I giue twenty pound a peece to my soon Georg and John and tenn pounds to my sonn francis his child if it liveth if not to the rest of his childeren if he hath any being lawfully begotten of his body alsoe I giue al my movables about the house with linnen and wollin to be equally devided to my three sonns yt is George francis and John and if any moer money shalbe aboue this aboue mentioned ‖yt‖ to be given vnto francis and my Biggest selver cup I giu to Georg with too silver spoons and the lesser silver cup with too silver spoons to John and four silver spoons to francis if ther be eight of them Alsoe that goods which is to com from England my will is if it com safe to be equally devided to my three sonns alsoe my will is that m^r whiting and m^r cobbet and Tho. Laughton with my sonn ffrancis should see this my will fulfiled alsoe my will is that m^r whiting and m^r cobbett shall haue fourty shillings a peece out of my estate and Tho. Laughton twenty shillings all to be paid within one half yeare after my death. Dated 18th october 1653."

George Burill

Witness: Tho. Laughton.

*Essex Co. Quarterly Court Files, vol. 2, leaf 135.*

Will of George Burrill of Lynn was found to be imperfect in respect to executors, and 27: 4: 1654, his three sons were appointed administrators. *Salem Quarterly Court Records, vol. 3, leaf 73.*

Inventory taken 21: 4: 1654, by Francis (his P mark) Ingals and Edward Burchum: One cloath dublett & a paire of Breeches & cotten Drawers, 2li. 10s.; one stuffe dublett & a paire of Breeches, 2li.; one cloath cloake, 3li. 10s.; one cloath dublet & Breeches, 1li.; one stuff dublet & Breeches, wth silver Buttens, 1li. 6s.; one cloath Jurkin & a paire of breeches, 16s.; one fustion dublet, 6s. 8d.; one cloath coat & drawers, 18s.; Tow cloath coats, 1li. 10s.; a short coat & westcoat & breeches, 10s.; one cloath Gowne, 3li. 5s.; one stuffe Gowne, 2li. 10s.; one more stuffe Gowne, 1li. 13s. 4d.; one more stuff Gown, 2li. 5s.; one stuff peticoat, 1li. 6s. 8d.; one more stuff peticoat, 1li.; one kearsy peticoat, 1li. 5s.; one pennystone peticoat, 14s.; one stuff kirtle, 15s.; tow Rideinge hats, 4li. 5s.; one kersy peticoat, 1li. 13s. 4d.; one serge peticoat, 1li.; one kersy weascoat, 10s.; one stuff wescoat, one shagg wescoat & 3 cloath wescoats, 16s.; one cotten wescoat & flannell wescoat & kersy wescoat, 11s. 4d.; one stuff Gowne, 1li.; one cotten wescoat & peticoat, 8s.; one cloath peticoat, 16s.; tow white wescoats, 9s.; one childs peticoat, 3s.; one childs Blankett, 1li. 10s.; two sea Aprons, 11s.; one sea cubberd cloath, 7s.; one stuff wescoat, 6s. 8d.; one sett of curtaines & vallance, 3li. 10s.; one cubberd cloath rought with needleworke, 1li. 4s.; two carpetts, 18s.; one cubberd cloath with fringe, 3s.; three cushens & a peece of stuff, 1li.; 12 yerd & 1-2 kersy, 5li.; 14 yerds of kersy, 5li. 12s.; 8 yerds 1-2 of cotten, 1li. 1s. 3d.; 4 yerd of kersy, 1li. 4s.; 5 yerd 1-2 of stuff, 18s.; one paire of cloath meetings, 2s. 6d.; 13 paire stockings, 1li. 7s. 6d.; a paire of gloves & too maskes, 5s.;

one silke hood scarff and handchetcher, 4s. 6d.; too caps & old stuff, 5s.; peeces of cloath, 3s.; wosted fringe, 2s.; 4 pair stockings, 5s.; cruell & fringe, 3s.; pincushen & a remant stuff, 2s. 6d.; velvett & ribbin, 3s.; a paire bodys, 1s. 6d.; too cloath Hudds, 4s.; a peece stuff and 5 hatts, 1li. 15s. 6d.; 6 cushens, 1li. 1s.; a pcell of shoos, 1li. 14s.; a swath for the backe, 1s.; too paire of course sheets, 16s.; too paire of sheets, 1li. 7s. 7d.; too paire of sheets, 1li. 10s.; too paire of sheets, 1li. 16s.; too pair of sheets, 2li.; three sheets, 2li. 3s. 4d.; one paire sheets, 15s.; one dyapare table cloath, 1li. 4s.; one diaper table cloath, 16s.; too towells, 1s.; one shift, 10s.; 5 old shifts, 4s.; too shift skirts, 6s.; too halfe skirts, 2s.; 14 shirts & shifts, 3li. 18s.; a table towell, 3s. 6d.; a pcell of lace, 2s.; one old sheet, 1s.; one peece of new cloath, 17s. 6d.; one peece of new cloth, 5s. 10d.; one peece new cloath, 1li. 13s. 4d.; one peece new cloath, 5s.; one peece new cloath, 8s. 6d.; six remants of cloath, 7s.; three caps, 7s.; childbed linnen, 2li.; Aprone, 4li.; neck handcatchers & bands, 4li. 7s.; a pockett handcatchers, 1li. 11s.; cubberd cloaths, 2li. 14s.; caps and coyfes, 1li. 2s.; Napkins & towells, 4li. 2s. 6d.; pillow bears, 3li.; double clouts, 9s.; too pcells of old linnen, 1li. 10s.; a paire of bodys & wescoats, 2s. 6d.; a matt for a bed, 3s.; a hatt band & flap, 1li. 5s.; one fetherbed & Bollster, 4li. 15s.; one feather bed & Bolster, 5li. 10s.; one feather bed & Bolster, 4li. 10s.; one Bedstead, curtaines, 2 curtaine rods, matt & coards, 2li. 5s.; one featherbed & too bolsters, 4li.; one fether bed & too old bolsters, 2li. 5s.; five pillows & one bolster ticke, 1li. 10s.; one rugg, 1li. 13s. 4d.; too coverings, 1li. 10s.; 4 blancketts, 3li. 12s.; 4 blancketts, 3li.; 4 blancketts, 1li.; 1 pillian cloath, 3s.; one cloake bagg, 2s. 6d.; curtaine and curtaine rods, 9s.; three spitts, 2s. 6d.; one fowling peece, one curbinne and too musketts, 3li. 1s.; one muskett more, 8s.; too paire of Bandowlerows and a flaske & belt, 8s. 6d.; three swords, 1li. 6s. 8d.; three rest, 3s.; a lead crean for a coop & hallberd, 6s.; 3li. of pewter, 1li. 10s.; 28 1-2li. pewter, 1li. 3s. 3d.; 4 1-2li. pewter & a band pott, 10s. 8d.; a morter & pestle, 5s.; a pcell of cettles, skillets & other brass, 1li. 6s.; a warmingepann, 5s.; a fryinge pann, 3s.; three brass potts, 1li. 16s.; a smoathing Iron with too heaters, 2s. 6d.; for a pcell of Iron warre, 1li. 9s.; one gold ringe, 14s.; six silver spoons, 2li. 3s. 6d.; silver bodkin, thimble, 2 silver buttens, 6s.; too silver bowls, 2li. 10s.; too glasses, 1s.; trenchers, too boxes & too paire of bodys, 3s. 8d.; a pcell of linnen, yearne & winding blads, 4s. 6d.; three chests & foure truncks, 2li.

8s.; a pcell of boxes, 1li. 6s.; foure bibls & a pcell of other bookes, 1li. 13s. 4d.; too linnen wheeles, too chirmes & other lumber, 1li. 4s.; too siffs & a little box with spice, 3s.; too heifers, too years old & a cow, 12li.; one bull stagg, 7li.; three cowes, 13li. 10s.; one steere & one oxe, 12li. 10s.; three coults, 2li. 10s.; foure oxen, 32li.; three cowes, 13li. 3s. 4d.; three ewes, three lambes & one weather, 8li. 8s.; one table, six stools & a cheare, 1li. 12s.; one bedstead, one trundlebed with valance and curtains and too coards, 1li. 12s.; one pcell of nayles small & great, 15s. 4d.; pcell of porke, 2li. 10s.; pcell of wooden ware in the seller, 17s.; pcell of mault, 12li.; pcell of linnes, hookes & other old things, 12s. 6d.; tann leather & whit leather, 11s. 4d.; flax & cloath it is in, 1li. 2s.; pcell of old hoggsheads & other wooden ware in the chamber, 1li. 8s.; pcell of sheeps wool & a Bedstead and coard, 8s. 2d.; pcell of oats & pease, 6s. 4d.; feathers, 4s.; bulletts, shot & powder, 12s. 9d.; too skins and a sife bottom, 2s.; cotton Ribben bindeing, poynts & laces, 4s.; pinns, needles & buttens, 2s. 6d.; black and brown thread, 1s. 6d.; smal bones, gloves & Brimston, 3s.; twine, whipcoard and bowstrings, 1s. 5d.; fishhookes, pinns and old tools, 2s. 6d.; a little box with too sivett boxes, finne thread, smale Inckle and Ribbin in it, 3s.; too snapsackes mach a markinge Iron & a box, 4s. 4d.; spicketts, fossetts, fishhookes, too bookes, little barrell & a pott, 5s.; remnant of cloath, 7s.; hinges for doors and catches for doors, 1s.; Juggs, 4s. 8d.; sisers, spures, knife and Brasse wyer, 3s.; knifes, Bitts for Bridls and too padlocks & small things, 3s.; gally potts, glasses and dager with a knife, 3s.; one cubberd & chest & hower glasse, 18s.; chears, bellows, tables and old tubbs in the house, 7s. 8d.; 7 siths beinge old, 9s.; box of old Iron & steel, 6s.; more old Iron, 14s. 6d.; Iron bills and frows, 12s.; coopers axe, 6s.; coopers crowses, 2s. 6d.; peckaxe, clouts for cart wheels & doore laches of Iron, 4s.; saws, 12s.; axes, 14s. 6d.; adses, 9s.; pirser bits & braces, 5s.; fouer paire of compasses and one file, 3s.; hinges for doors & hammers, 3s.; Augers, 7s.; drawinge knifs, augers, pinncers & truells, 8s.; fouer sickls, 3s.; cleevis fetters & a locke, 4s.; a saddle & brydle, 13s. 4d.; 3 forkes, 3s. 6d.; drawinge knifes & chissels, 3s. 4d.; wedges of Iron, 3s. 10d.; coleters & shares, 15s.; chaines & cleeves, 1li. 1s. 3d.; lead & a little axe, 2s.; salt, naked oats & a trevett, 4s.; cart roops & a siffe, 8s.; dry casks, 8s.; hoops & Barrell heads, 10s.; spads and hooes, 8s. 6d.; Joynters, 9s.; smale caskes, more caskes, 12s.; Barrells, 1li. 2s.; tubbs, 14s.; baggs & sacks, 5s.;

copper furnace & chirme, 1li. 12s.; old chaine & a buckett att well, 2s.; lead wayts, 19s. 2d.; too paire of skailes, 7s.; wood & cooper ware, 8s.; a cheese press, ladder & old wood, 10s.; one plough, cart & wheels, 1li. 10s. 8d.; one dungcart, 10s.; one coller traces & ladder, 3s.; too butts and seaven hoggsheads, 12s.; foure yoakes with Irons, 10s.; a paire of Harrows & old wood, 7s. 6d.; part of a house in Boston, 55li.; upland and meadow and houseinge, 289li. 10s.; debts and Bills, 49li. 18s. 10d.; owing in corne, 3s. 8d.; oweinge in old England, 40li.; in money, 82li. 4s. 10d.; total, 848li. 10s. *Essex Co. Quarterly Court Files, vol. 2, leaf 136.*

### ESTATE OF WILLIAM WAKE OF SALEM.

"The last Will of William Wake: whoe is at this Instant in pffect memory made this 17: 2$^{th}$ 1654. ffirst it is my will and my desire that all due debts and Ingagments wch I doe owe everye man: be discharged owt of my estate: as allsoe all other nessessury Chargis whatsoever in and about my sikness or buryall or about paying and getting vpp my debts as allsoe if there happen any occation about sut or suts of law or any other occations: in and about my prop[er] bisnes and occations: that all chargis about the premisis be Aloude owt of my estate 2$^{ly}$ After all due debts and chargis be sattisfied and payd it is my will that the one halfe of what shall remayne be returned or sent to Ingland to my daughter Katterin Wake if shee be leving: if nott then to be sent to my Bro: John Wake

"3$^{ly}$ it is my will that the other halfe remayning shalbe left in the hands of the overseers: vnto whome I doe giue full power and order to dispose of it according to my priuat directions and Instructions Comitted to them: who will I doupt not faythffully pforme it

"Lastly it is my will: that Hilliard Veren: and Walter Price: shalbe and are Intrusted Joyntly to be my overseers to see the trew pformance of this my last will and testament and In wittnes hearoff I haue sett my hand the daye & yeare aboue written." William Wake.

his mark       his mark
Witness: Tho. I N Smith, Jonathan P Porter.
*Essex Co. Quarterly Court Files, vol. 2, leaf* 137.

Proved 27: 4: 1654. Mr. Walter Price and Hilliard Vearin appointed administrators. *Salem Quarterly Court Records, vol. 3, leaf* 73.

Inventory taken 22: 4: 1654, by Edmond Batter and Elias Stileman: 1 house & orchard & a peece of Lande at ye house, 10li.; 1 halfe headed bedsteed, 8s.; 2 chests, 15s.; 1 Cubberd, 4s. 6d.; 2 Cases & 8 glasses, 4s.; 3 Chaires, 5s.; 1 frying pann, 1s. 6d.; 1 brass Kettle, 1li. 10s.; 1 Iron pott & hookes, 6s.; 1 Gunn, 6s. 8d.; 1 Lampe & 2 old Candle stick, 1s. 6d.; 1 pr. tongs, a spade & handsaw & hatchett, 4s.; 1 Sword & belt, 8s.; 2 Empte Caske, 1s.; English and Cotten wooll, 1s.; 1 square, 1s.; 1 old hatt, 1s.; 2 dos. buttons, 2s.; bookes, 5s.; 3 pewter dishes, 7s. 6d.; a puding pan & erthen things, 1s.; 1 funnell, 3d., a bible, 5s., 5s. 3d.; 2 pr. of blanketts, 1li. 4s.; 1 feather boulster, 1li.; a bedtick of Canvas & a hopp sack boulster, 10s.; 1 greene Rugg, 1li. 5s.; 2 sutes, 1 cloake, 3 pr. of drawers, 2li. 10s.; 3 pr. Stockings, 7s. 6d.; 1 hatt, 6s.; 1 pr. shoes, 2s.; 1 skillitt & small bras kittle, 8s.; 1 qt. pott, 1s.; a 1-2 B: measure & tubb, 2s.; Latten ware, 1s. 6d.; 1 hammer, 12d., earthware & skiming dish, 2s.; 1 chaire, 1s. 6d.; 3 shirts, 12s.; 1 pr. pillowbers, 3s.; 2 napkins, 1s.; 2 sheets, 8s.; 5 towells Course & old, 3s.; 3 Capps & 2 handkercheifes, 3s.; 3 bands, 2s.; 1 Inkhorne and an old silk neckcloth, 1s.; 1 box, 1s. 6d.; 1 pr. billowes, 1s. 6d.; 1 porringer, 4d.; 6 Brlls. salt, 1li.; 1 wooden bottle & an old drawing knife, 1s. 3d.; debts, 33li. 12s.; total, 60li. 8s. 6d. Debtor to severall persons, 60li. 2s. 9d. *Essex Co. Quarterly Court Files, vol. 2, leaf* 138.

### Estate of Thomas Buxton of Salem.

Administration on the estate of Thomas Buxton of Salem granted 27: 4: 1654, to his brother Anthony Buxston. *Salem Quarterly Court Records, vol. 3, leaf* 74.

Inventory taken 5: 4: 1654, by Thomas Gardner sr. and Michaell Shaflen: Aleven akers of Land with A little howse on it liinge in the North Neck, 8li.; six Acares of Corn Indean and English, 4s.; One steare, 6li.; too Cows, 9li.; one heifer, 4li.; too heifers, 6li.; one callfe, 11s.; five swine, 3li. 5s.; one cartt with what belonges to it, 1li.; in mony, 11s.; pewtter and brasse, 1li. 10s.; beding, 1li. 10s.; a musket and furniture to it, 1li. 5s.; his wering Aparell, 4li.; a pres and other lumber, 16s.; total, 52li. 8s. *Essex Co. Quarterly Court Files, vol. 2, leaf* 140.

The court 28: 9: 1654, ordered Anthony Buckston, administrator of the estate of his deceased brother, Tho. Buxston, to pay to the three children of the said Thomas in England, 21li., and Anthony to have the remainder to be divided between himself and his children. *Salem Quarterly Court Records, vol. 3, leaf 79.*

ESTATE OF THOMAS TRUSLER OF SALEM.

The will of Thomas Trusler of Salem proved 27: 4: 1654, by Mr. Thomas Gardner and Robt. Moulton, sr. Inventory brought in. *Salem Quarterly Court Records, vol. 3, leaf 74.*

Inventory taken 5: 1: 1653-4, by Thomas Spooner and Robt. Moulton, sr.: His Mansion or dwelling house Barne or outhousing And Three Acres of land thereto Also one Acre of Land more wth Another house near John Kitchens, 40li.; Three Acres of Land being prt. Marsh & prt. upland wher the Brickill is wth appurtenances, 10li.; Two Tenn Acre Lotts one Near John Smith's Another neare Mrs. Bacon's in Northfield, 10li.; One farme near fathr Moltons Contayning 116 Acres, viz., 100 Upland & 16 of Medow Cost 12li. by purchas, 12li.; 4 bushell of Indean meale, 12s.; 20li. hempe, 10s.; 2li. Cotten wooll, 2s.; Lumber & Tubbs, old Irne & barrell with an ould Cart & 1 bush Corne, 1li. 14s.; 1 grinde stone & 1 Long Ladder, 5s.; Irons belonging to the Cart & plowe as Chaines, 1li. 10s.; 2 Axes, 1 hachet and a woodhook, 6s.; Old Tools, viz. 3 Sawes, hamr., pincrs., siths, augers, 2 wedgs, Iron, bill Ring & elce, 6s.; 2 bushells of seed Barlee, 10s.; 2 bushell of seed Pease, 8s.; one Iron or steele Trapp, 5s.; one Querne or Malt Mill, 1li.; About 24li. of Leaden waights, 6s.; 6 oxen, viz. 4 old ons & 2 yonge ons, 36li.; 5 Cowes at 5li., 25li.; 3 heiffers about 3 yrs. old at 4li., 12li.; 2 yearling Calves at 30s., 3li.; a Sheep or one ewe, 2li.; by 2 swine at 20s., 2li.; one fether Bed, Boulster & pillows at Mr. Edm: Batters, 2 fether beds at home, 6li.; one greene Rugg, 1li. 5s., one Cotten Rugg, 18s., one weaved Covrlet, 5s., 2 Blanketts, 12s., 2 Boulsters, 8s., 3 pillows, 8s., 3li. 16s.; one Carpet, 10s.; Twoe Curtains & Rodds, 10s.; one hower glass, 1s.; one faire gret Looking glass, 6s.; one warming pann, 5s.; one paire of Bellows, 2s. Hous linnen: 3 pr. & one odd Sheete or 7, 2li. 12s.; 2 pr. of pillow beers, 12s.; 2 Table cloths, 9s. and 1 Course one, 2s. 6d.; 6 fine Napkins at 12s., 2 one whes of diap. at 4s. 6d., 4 Couesons, 3s., in all, 4li. 15s. Brass: One broad plat Candlestick of Brass, to hang on a wall, 3s., 2 Brass Candlesticks, 5s., 3 Brass potts, 1li., 2 Bell metle skelets, 5s., 1 smale bras skelet, 1s., 1 bras chafing dish, 1s. 6d., 1 bras Ladle & 1 skimer, 1s., 4 bras ketles old, 12s., 2 bras panns, 1li., in all, 3li. 8s. 6d. Iron: 3 spitts & 2 pr. pothooks, 7s., 2 Iron potts, 18s., 1 greediron & fleshal, 2s. 6d., 2 Racks Coterells or haky, with 1 pr. of Andirons, 9s., 1 fire shovell & firfalk, 1s., 1 wire Candlestick & 2 tin, 6d., in all, 1li. 18s. Woolen wearing apparell: 2 Cloks, 5li., 2 short Coats, 1li., 1 pr. breeches, 15s., 1 dublett, 10s., 1 hatt, 8s., 1 Cloth Capp, 2s., 4 pr. of shoes, 14s., 2 pr. Stockins, 5s., 2 hoods, 5s., in all, 8li. 19s. Linnen wearing apparell: 2 Shirts & 6 faling Bands, 2 wt. Capps, 3 wt. Neckclothes, 2 handkerchers, 12s. Armes: 2 fowling peecs, 1 Muskett & 1 pr. of Bandoleers, Moulds & Rest, 2li.; 1 sword & *Curtle,* 10s.; 2li. powdr & 40 bullets, 5s.; about 24li. of Leaden waights, 2 Bibles & one psalme book, 5s.; one Chest in the parler, 20s.; another chest or Cofer, 4s.; in N. E. silver, 10s.; and Spanish money, 9 pc. of 8, 1li. Pewter: 12 pewter platers, 1li. 8s.; on salt dish, 1s. 6d.; 3 Sawsers, 2 peuter Salts, 1s. 6d.; 3 peuter Basons, 4s. 6d.; 6 peuter porringers, 4s., 1 peutr flagon, 3s.; 1 quart pott, 2s.; 1 pint pott, 1s.; 1 bear boule, 1s.; one wine Cupp, 6d.; one old Chambr. pott & 4 peutr. spoons & 3 *alt*, 1s.; total, 198li. 18s. 6d. Debts due from estate: To the contry, 2li. 15s. 10d.; to Mr. Wm. Browne, 2li. 10s.; to Mr. Phil. Crumwell, 5li. Net estate, 188li. 12s. 8d. *Essex Co. Quarterly Court Files, vol. 2, leaf* 139.

### ESTATE OF WILLIAM AGER OF SALEM.

"The last Will & testament of Will^m: Ager of salem made the 3^d day of y^e first moneth 1653-54 William Ager being Sick & Weake of bodie but in pfict memory did in the presence of us whose Names are vnder written ordaine this as his Last will whereby he did giue & bequeath unto Joseph Ager if he be liueing his now dwelling house & the garden whereon it Stands, but if in case he be not liuing then his sonn Beniamin Ager is to haue it. 2 he gaue unto his sonn Jonathan Ager his tenn acre lott & meadow & Cowe, & if Joseph Ager Came home againe then Beniamin & Jonathan Ager are to deuide the Land & Cow equally betweene them. 3 he gaue unto Abigall Kibben his daughter his feather bed & all that belongs unto the same alsoe he gaue unto her a spitt. 4 he gaue unto Beniamin & Jonathan his sonns & Abigall his daughter all his houshold Stuff to be equally deuided among them. 5 he gaue unto Allice his wife the use of the house

garden tenn acre Lott meadow Cowe & all the household Stuff bed & beding during her life or her widow hood estate & in Case she maried againe then to haue her thirds of the whole Estate, & forthe pformance of this my will I apoynt & ordaine Allice my wife my sole executrix." [No signature]
her mark
Witness: Nathaniell Pickman, Tabitha T P Pickman, Elias Stileman, jr. *Essex Co. Quarterly Court Files, vol. 2, leaf* 141.
Proved 29: 4: 1654, by Elias Stileman and Nath Pickman. *Salem Quarterly Court Records, vol. 3, leaf* 74.

Inventory taken 20: 4: 1654, by Edmond Batter and Elias Stileman: One house and garden plott, 16li.; 8 acres upland, 5li.; 1 acre marsh, 3li.; 1 Cow, 5li.; 1 pigg, 10s.; 1 feather bed, 1li. 10s.; 2 pr. Sheetes, 1li.; 1 Cott Rugg & 3 blanketts, 1li. 10s.; 1 boulster & pillow, 10s.; 1 bedsteed, 12s.; 1 pr. Curtanes and vallance, 10s.; 2 Iron potts & 1 Iron kettle, 1li.; 1 brass kettle & small skillett, 3s.; 1 spade, 3s.; 2 pr. shears & a pressing Iron & reape hooke, 5s.; in pewter, 10s.; 1 warming pan & a Scumer, 7s.; 1 spitt, 2s. 6d.; 1 pistle & morter, 6s. 8d.; 1 pr. tongs & an old fring pann, 2s. 6d.; 1 pr. bellows, 1s. 6d.; 5 chaires, 3s.; 2 axes & 1 hatchett, 2s.; 1 table & 1 chest & Cubburd, 15s.; trayes & dishes & a payle, 2s. 6d.; 1 runlett & sive, 2s.; Lining yearne and waring clothes, 3s.; Lisbourn waire & other erthen vessells, 5s.; a pott hanger, 2s.; bookes, 10s.; 4 B. Indian Corne, 12s.; old beding, 10s.; Lumber waire, 5s.; total, 43li. 14s. 8d. *Essex Co. Quarterly Court Files, vol. 2, leaf* 142.

ESTATE OF THOMAS SCRUGGS OF SALEM.

Administration on the estate of William* Scruggs of Salem, intestate, granted 29: 4: 1654, to his widow. Inventory brought in. An agreement between her and her son-in-law, John Rament, was approved. *Salem Quarterly Court Records, vol. 3, leaf* 74.

Inventory of the estate of Thomas Scruggs, taken 24: 4: 1654, by Roger Conant, Nicholas Patch and William Dodg: Six cows at 5li., 30li.; 2 steers, 10li.; 3 yong heifers & a calf, 10li.; 2 oxen, 18li.; 11 akers of corn on the ground, English & indian, 22li.; the farm & housing, 100li.; 2 potts, one of brasse & on of Iron, 2li.; 2 ketles, 2li. 10s.; a silver boule, 4li.;

* Evidently a mistake for Thomas.

a brass warming pann, 10s.; puter, 10 platters & dishes, 2li. 6s. 8d.; 2 candlesticks, a quart & a pint ——, a salt, all puter, 10s.; 2 brasse acndlesticks, ——king pan and a smale kittell, 7s.; an iron pott, a kettell & a posnet, 15s.; a sheer Cutter, ——, a plow with ould iron, 2li.; a great cleaver, a brasse skimer, 10s.; a ladder, 2s. 6d.; a great chest, 1li.; a cupbord & table ——, 1li. 10s.; a bedsteed, fether ——niture, 10li.; 2 other fetherbeds, 7li. 10s.; a cloth sute with silver ——, 3li.; 2 coats of cloth and ——, 3li.; Tubbs, barrells and ——, 1li.; a wastcoat, 4s.; a dublett and 5 dozen silver buttens, 15s.; 3 bookes, 1li.; total, 244li. 10s. 2d.

Margery (her I mark) Scruggs of Salem, widow, 24: 4: 1654, conveyed to her son-in-law, John Raymont, her land and goods, in consideration of 5li. in hand to be given to her directly and 5li. at the hour of her death to be freely at her disposal; she was to have 20li. a year, paid quarterly as long as she lived and to have the use of necessary household effects.

Witness: Roger Conant, Nicholas Patch, William Dodg. The last two witnesses made oath before Elias Stileman, clerk. *Essex Co. Quarterly Court Files, vol. 2, leaf* 143.

### ESTATE OF RICHARD KENT, SR. OF NEWBURY.

"May the 22th 1654. I Richard Kent senior of Newberry in the County of Essex in New England being verry weake in body but of perfect sence and memory, doe make this my last will and testamt: Imprmis: I giue my soule into ye hands of god my maker, and my body to the earth; In the next place I giue and bequeath vnto my sonne Jon Kent my house and lands to him and his heires for euer, and if my aforesaid sonne John Kent die without any heire, then the afore said house and lands is to be desposed of Jon Bishopp Junior and his heires for euer: ffurther I giue vnto my daughter Sarah or her Children the sume of twenty pounds if they Come ouer to be paid when my Executor comes to be twenty one yeare old, ffurther I giue vnto my louing wife Em Kent tenn pounds per annum to be annually paid her soe Long as she liueth, and the fruit of her apple tree yearly, or thirty pounds to be suddenly paid her wch she pleaseth: Item I giue vnto Mary Kent my Brother Stephens daughter which he had by his first wife, one yearlin heifer calfe, to be paid to her thre yeares after my decease, further I giue vnto my sonne Jon Bishopp 100 trees out of my nurcery to be taken upp when hee pleaseth: likewise I giue vnto my sonne John Bishop, my sonne John Kent in manner as an apprentice till he is compleat nineteen yeares of age, and the said Jo$^n$ Bishopp is to have my sonne John Kent kept at schoole to learne to Reade Write & sipher one whole yeare at my charge, and at the age of nineteene my sonne Jo$^n$ Kent is to enjoy the land, only to be guided by my Ouerseers till he come to the age of one and twenty: and I doe ffurther Order that my sonne John Bishopp William Tittcum and Richard Bartlett be my Ouerseers to pay and receiue all my debts & to lett & sett Order and mannage my buisenes, till my sonne is att nineteene yeares of age: and for euerry day that my Ouerseers meete about this buisenes, I allow they should be paid each man two shillings six pence for their paines; and I doe further order that if either of my Ouerseers afore mentioned, decease before my sonne John Kent Comes to be of age || of ninteene || that then Christopher Bartlett brother to Richard Bartlett shall haue the same power to act with the other Ouerseers in his stead: Alsoe I giue the first Samon that is caught in my wire, yearly to m$^r$ Noice & the second to m$^r$ Roggers of Rowlee till my sonne be of the age of nineteene and then I leaue it to my sonne to doe what hee sees good."

Richard Kent

Witness: William Chandler, John trimman.

"Know all men by these presents that I Richard Kent senior of the towne of Newberry in the County of Essex in New England, being weake in boddy but of perfect sence and memory: wheras I lately Orderred Jo$^n$ Bishopp my sonne in law. William Tittcum & Richard Bartlett; each of them of the said towne and County, to be my Ouerseers to Order and mannage the buisnes they are intrusted with all after my decease: I doe by these p$^r$sents Authorrize allow & giue full power vnto my said Ouerseers aboue mentioned to Receiue demand or gather in any debts as shall be due to the aforesaid Richard Kent, either uppon booke, or by bill or bond, and ffurther I doe allow that if any deny to pay to the aforesaid Ouerseers, that then the ouerseers shall haue power to tach according to law, & to requier damages for want of paymt according to kind In witnesse here of I haue here unto sett my hand this 22$^{th}$ of May in the yeare of our Lord 1654."

Richard Kent

Witness: William Chandler, John trimman.
Proved in Ipswich court 26: 7: 1654 by the witnesses.

Inventory taken June 29, 1654, by John Sanders and John

Bartlett: one dwelling house, 5li.; one barne, 3li.; 4 Acrees of Rie, 5li.; 4 Acrees of Barlee, 4li.; one Acree and 1-2 of Wheate, 1li.; 3-4 of an Acree of pease, 16s.; 4 Acrees of Indean Corne, 4li.; One Orchard about the house to the Vallue of 3 Acrees of Land containing 82 bearing trees and a nurseerey, 40li.; 23 Acrees of Land in tillage about the house, 46li.; 24 Acrees of pasture Land, 12li.; A parcell of Land bought of Mr. Raw— containing about — Acrees, 10li.; 17 Acrees of Meddow ground, 17li.; Two Oxen, 14li.; 4 Cows, 20li.; one two Yearling steare, 3li.; 3 Yearlings, 6li.; 3 Calves, 2li. 10s.; Sixe Swine, 4li.; One Bedd & Boulster & a pare of blanketts & a Rugg, 2li. 10s.; One ffurnice, 7li. 10s.; One drie fatt, 10s.; One muskett, a fowling peice & birding peice, 1li. 5s.; One Sword, 3s. 4d.; 4 Iron potts, 1li.; An ould Copper, 2s. 6d.; ffowre stockes of Bees, 3li.; 3 Iron Wedges, 7s.; three beetle rings, 1s. 6d.; three Axes, 5s.; three hoes, 5s.; one ffro, 2s.; two pair of pott hookes, 2s.; a gridge Iron, 2s.; ould Iron, 2s. 6d.; a crosse bowe, 2s. 6d.; a spaid, 4s.; one plow & Irons, 8s.; one Saw, 2s. 6d.; A Coller and a pair of trases, 6s. 6d.; A frien pann, 2s.; A spitt, 1s. 6d.; A Joynd Cheare, 5s.; two grubbin hoes, 4s.; A pair of scales, 1s.; two Nettes, 10s.; The Lumber about the house, 16s.; debts due to him uppon the Booke, 13li.; poscript more due uppon Booke, 2li. 6s. 6d.; total, 233li. 3s. 4d.

*Essex Co. Probate Files, Docket* 15,378.

### Estate of William Fiske of Wenham.

Administration on the estate of William Fiske of Wennam, intestate, granted 26: 7: 1654, to his widow, Bridgett Fiske. Her house and land are bound to pay the shares of the five children viz: to the eldest son, 10li., to Samuel, the next, 5li., and to the other three, 3li., when they come of age. Inventory brought in. *Ipswich Quarterly Court Records, vol.* 1, *page* 47.

Inventory taken 16: 7: 1654, by Phinehas (his xx mark) Fiske, Austin (his R mark) Killam and Edward Kempe. In the parlor: One bedstead as it stands furnished, viz., with one fetherbed, one fether bolster, 2 fether pillows, one downy pillow, one blanket, one coverlett, vallance, Curtaynes, matt & ——, 10li.; a table, Chaire and a forme, 7s.; two Cushions, 8s. In the Parlor chamber: Table, 4s. 6d.; old chaire, 8d.; Bedstead with certayne Bords, 5s.; a signe with the signe post, 15s.; pcell of hempe, 10s. In the Bed chamber: A bedstead as it stands furnished, 7li.; trundle bedstead furnished, 3li.; Cubbard, 12s.; joyned Chest, 10s.; a *danth* chest, 8s.; two old Trunkes & one Box, 7s.; a warming Pan, 10s. In the kitchen: A smale Table, two smale chaires & a stoole, 5s. 8d.; a brewing stoole, 1s. 6d.; paire of Cob irons, 10s.; two hales, a fire pan & a paire of tonges, 12s.; a spitt & dripping pan, 5s.; a pashell, 1s. In the kitchen Chamber: Certayne old Barrells & other Lumber, 2s.; smale pcel of lethers, 2s.; a hay knife, 4s.; two sives, 2s. 6d.; a pcel of Hopps with a Bag, 6s.; some Indian Corne, 1li. 10s. In the Lentoo: Certayne old killars, Tubbs, a Barrell & Charne, 10s.; Certayne Trayes, Cupps, dishes & other smale wooden things, 10s. 6d.; Certayne Earthen Potts, 1s. 6d.; an iron Pott & Posnet, 17s.; a frying Pan, 2s. 8d.; spade, 1s.; a greate paire of Pincers, 1s.; axe, wedges, Rostiron, Trevett & other old iron, 12s.; lanthorne, lether bottle & 3 Payles, 9s. 6d. In the Cellar: Certayne Casks & the Ale stools, 12s.; a salting Trough & Cover, 10s. Brasse: A Greate kettle & a lesser kettle, 1li. 10s.; a brasse Pott, with two paire pothookes, 14s.; Two skillets in there frames, a basteing Ladle, a Skummer & Lamp, 10s. Peuter & Plate: Sixe Silver spoones, 18s.; seaven Platters, 14s.; one Bason & a Collander, 6s. 6d.; Fower porringers & 8 Peuter spoones, 3s. 8d.; nine Saucers & 4 Salt Sellers, 7s. 6d.; three wine cups, 2 drinking Cupps & a Beker, 5s.; one wine quart, one bere qrt. & a wine halfe Pint, 4s.; two Candlesticks, an old chamber pott & some other broken peuter, 7s.; two lattin panns & a Tunnel, 1s. 6d. Linnen: Seaven paire of sheetes, 7li. 12s.; three paire Pillow beeres, 1li. 4s.; one bord cloth & a dozen Napkins, 1li. 5s.; a suite of Diaper, 5li.; bands & Capps, 10s.; his apparrell, hat & a paire shooes, 2li. 18s. 4d.; his bookes, 1li. 8s.; two swords, a short musket & a Fowling peece, 2li.; his houses & land in Wenham, with their appurtenances, 26li.; Cattaile, 18li.; swine & Pigs, 6li. 13s. 4d.; an old Cart & wheeles, 8s.; all other things not before named, 6s. 8d.; debts due to him by booke, 28li.; total, 141li. 12s. 6d. *Essex Co. Quarterly Court Files, vol. 2, leaf 147.*

### Estate of William Mitchell of Newbury.

Administration on the estate of William Michell of Newbery, intestate, granted 26: 7: 1654 to his widow Mary. Inventory presented. *Ipswich Quarterly Court Records, vol. 1, page 47.*

Inventory taken by Nicholas Noyes and John Allen: 4 acres of Land, 16li.; ——el and an halfe of Indian corne, 4li.; —— Cow, 4li.; —ne Hogge, 1li. 5s.; two pigges, 12s.; Wearing Apparell, 3li.; One flocke bedde, a payre of sheetes and two pillowes and a coverleet, 4li.; two Iron potts, 1li. 2s.; Three skillets and a Kittel, 1li.; Sixe milke pannes, 5s.; fower Earthen pottes, 4s.; In earthen weare, 2s.; One peuter platter, 2s.; Three porringers, 2s. 6d.; A Sawse pan, 1s. 6d.; Another platter, 4d.; Two great tubbes, 5s.; A great boule and a pecke, 2s. 6d.; Two tubbes more, 3s.; firkin and payle, 3s. 6d.; Two beere barrells, 3s. 6d.; Three boxes, 5s. ——; A Craddel, 4s.; A Spade, 5s.; An Axe, 2s. 6d.; A how, 3s.; Bittell Ringes and Saw, 14s.; A rappier, bandeleires & belt, 16s.; A Latin pan, 2s.; total, 35li. 5s. 4d. In debts dewe to be pd. 18li.

Mary Mitchell deposed to the truth of this inventory the 26: 7: 1654, and that it was the whole estate of her deceased husband. *Essex Co. Probate Files, Docket* 18,531.

### Estate of John Perkins, Sr. of Ipswich.

"28th of first m° called March 1654 I John Perkines the Elder of Ipswich being at this tyme sick and weake in body yet through the mercy and goodnes of the Lord retaining my vnderstanding and memory: Do thus Dispose of and bequeath my Temporale estate as ffolloweth first I Doe giue and bequeath vnto my Eldest sonn John Perkines a foale of my young mare being new with foale if it please the Lord shee foale it well also I give and bequeath to my sonn Johns two sonnes John and Abraham to each of them one of my yearleing heyfers: also I give and bequeath to my sonn Thomas Perkines one cow and one heyfer also I giue & bequeath to his sonn John Perkines one ewe to be delivered for his vse at the next shearing tyne also I doe give and bequeath to my Daughter Elizabeth Sarieant one cow and an heyfer to be to her and her children after her Decease as it may please ye Lord they may increase the proffits or increase to be equelly Devided amongst the sayde children also I Doe give to my Daughter mary Bradbery one cow and one heyfer or a young steere to remaine to her & to her children in theyr increase or proffits as it shall please the Lord to bless them and to be equaly Devided to the children: also I Doe give and bequeath to my Daughter Lidia Bennitt one cow and one heyfer or steere to be equaly Devided to her children in theyr increase or proffits after her Decease: I Doe also give vnto my Grand-childe Thomas Bradbery one ewe to be sett apart for his vse at ye next shearing tyne: also I Doe give and bequeath vnto my sonn Jacob Perkines my Dwelling howse together with all the outhowseing, and all my landes of one kinde and other together with all improvements therevpon to be his in full posession & according to a former covenant, after the decease of my wyfe and nott before and so to remaine to him and to his heires forever: all the rest of my estate of one kinde and other I Doe wholy leave to my Deare wife Judeth Perkines apointing and ordaining my sayde wyfe the sole Executrix of this my Last will and Testament Desiring my sayde wife to Dispose of the cattell aboue mentioned according to her discresion as they shall prosper steeres or heyfers as also to Dispose of some of the increase or some of the increase of the sheep to ‖ the ‖ children of my sonn Thomas and of my three Daughters at the Discresion of my sayde wife and this I Doe ordaine as my Last will and Testament subscribed with mine owne hand this twenty eighth Day of y$^e$ first month 1654"

his mark
John Y Perkines

Witness: william Bartholomew, Thomas Harris.
Proved in Ipswich court 26: 7: 1654 by the witnesses.

Inventory taken by William Bartholomew and John Annabl: the dwelling howse and barne wth out howseing, 40li. 60s.; Land about the howse about eight acres, 12li.; more Land unbroake up about fourteen acres, 21li.; a pcell of marsh about six acres at 40s. p acre, 12li.; a pcell of vpland and marsh being much broken about xx acres at 20s. p acre, 20li.; 12 acres of improved Land at 50s. p acre, 24li.; one mare with a mare foale, 25li.; six milch cowes, 30li.; four yearling heyfers & a steere, 11li. 10s.; six ewes at 35s. p, 10li. 10s.; 5 yewe Lambes, 5li.; one yearling weather and two weather Lambs, 2li.; one young calfe, 15s.; one cow at the pasture, a sow & 3 piggs, all, 8li.; one feather bed with bedsteed & furniture, 4li.; one coverlid with other small thinges being Linen most, 2li. 10s.; Left in mony at his decease, 10li.; a cart, plowes, a harow with severall goodes of Lumber as caske, tubbes, cheares, axes, hoes, etc., 5li.; severall ketles, pottes & dishes in the kitchen, 2li.; his wearing aparell, 5li.; total, 250li. 5s.

*Essex Co. Probate Files, Docket* 21,337.

ESTATE OF ROBERT PHILBRICK OF (IPSWICH?).

26 : 7 : 1654 paid out of Robert Filbrike's estate to Robert Dutch, 7li.; Jerimy Belchar, 1li. 10s.; Mr. John Apleton, 9s.; Robert Wallis, 6s. 9d.; John Johnson, 11s. 6d.; and Thomas Miller, 3s. 4d. *Essex Co. Quarterly Court Files, vol. 2, leaf 153.*

ESTATE OF WILLIAM PARTRIDGE OF SALISBURY.

Administration on the estate of Willi. Partridg of Salisbury, granted 3 : 8 : 1654 to his widow Ann Partridg. *Hampton Quarterly Court Records, vol. 1, leaf 50.*

Inventory taken Sept. 5, 1654, by Samuell Hall, Edward ffrench, Robert Pike and John Ensley (Ilsly) : ffower Ackers of Errable land wth an orchard planted upon itt wth the dwellinge howse & other out howses belonginge to itt, 40li.; fforty Ackers of upland, six ackers impved for corne, 20li.; Twenty Ackers of upland vpon meremack river not impved, 1li. 10s.; a plantinge lott in the Neck cont. Eight ackrs, 5 ackers broake upp, 1li. 10s.; ffower Ackers of Medow, 4li.; Seaven Ackrs in ye Barbarie Medows, 3li. 10s.; Eight Ackers of Salt march in ye first devision, 4li.; the last devision of medow pt the sweepage of ye Beach & ptly meremack river about two ackrs, 1li.; Howsehold goods in the howse, one table, 10s.; one bedstead as itt stands Corded, 18s.; one Chist, 8s.; another old bedstead, 2s.; one hide of leather, 1li.; 1 Case of bottles, 8s.; 1 Case of pint bottles, 6s.; one doz. of trenchers, 8d.; a beame & lead weights, 4s.; two Sives, 2s.; an Ioron oven peale, 2s.; a fire shovell, toungs, tramell & girdiron, 7s.; one handsaw, 1s. 6d.; two swords & belts, 18s.; two musketts & one kirbine, 2li. 15s.; one pistoll, 10s.; a Chaire, 5s.; another Chaire & stoole, 3s.; a Crosste cutt saw, 10s.; a tenant saw, 2s.; three broad Howes, 7s.; an old spade, 1s.; a sword & Bandeleres, 5s.; a ffryinge pan, 2s. 6d.; two Sithes, 7s.; 2 Hodgheads & other tubs in ye chambr, 5s.; a spitt, 2s. 6d.; a pcell of Hopps, 10s.; a little table, 4s.; 2 Hatchetts, 2 augurs & other old Iron, 8s.; a Churne, 1 firkin, a cheese presse & 2 old tubbs, 8s.; ffower dozen of Lasts, 6s.; three stone bottles, 2s. 6d.; a powderinge tubb, 1 barrell, one runlett & a pale, 8s.; Aulls, pinsers & other shop tooles, 8s.; An axe, 2s. 6d.; a Grindleston, 13s.; a Cart wheeles & Iron hoopes, 1li. 10s.; two forkes, 2s.; a Saddle & furniture, 10s.; a plowe & Irons, 8s.; 2 yoaks, 2 chaines, 1 paire of hookes & staple, 18s.; a Slead, 6s.; his Wearing Aparrell, 4li.; a brasse Kettle, 6s.; two Iron potts, 13s.; a great brasse Kettle, 2li.; six trayes, dishes & other lumber, 6s. 6d.; 2 pewter dishes, 1 plate, one pint pott, porringer & spoones, 10s.; one ffether bed, bolster, six pillowes & all things belonginge to itt, 2li. 10s.; a fflock bed & appurtenancs, 1li.; Six paire of sheets, 3li.; 4 boxes & a chaire, 8s.; a match lock muskett, 12s.; Cattle: two oxen, 16 li.; ffive milch Cowes, 25li.; ffower steares, 22li.; a mare & Colt, 22li.; a younge horse, 9s.; a Cow & Calfe, 5li. 10s.; 3 weanlinge Calves, 3li.; two Eywes, 2li. 10s.; 5 Ram lambs, 2li. 10s.; two swine, 1li. 10s.; ffive hives of Bees, 5li.; a younge Colt, 7li.; one horse, 10li.; Indian Corne, 6li.; English Corne, 6li.; Haye, 6li.; total, 249li. 5s. 8d.

Ann Partridg testified in the Hampton court 3: 8: 1654, that this is a true inventory.

—————— of the estate that are Certaine: To Richard North, 20li.; to Mr. Wooster, 12li. 13s.; to goodman ffowle, 8li.; to Nathanell Williams, 4li.; to the Currier, 16s.; total, 45li. 9s.; due to be payd out of ye estate to ye Childeren for so much recpt in England, 50li.; payd in debts appeareing since ye Inventory was presented to the Court, over & aboue wch she hath received, 10li.

*Essex Co. Probate Files, Docket* 20,681.

ESTATE OF JOHN PIKE, SR. OF SALISBURY.

"In the name of god Amen The last will & testament of John Pike senior being sick and Weake in body but of pfcct memory. maye 24. 1654. first. I will & bequeath my soule vnto god In the lord Jesus Christ & my body to be buried in Convenient burieinge place & my worldly goods to be bestowed as followeth. first I giue my howse & lande at the old towne at Newbery boath vplande & meddow with my privellidge of Comon || at Newbery || vnto my gran Child John Pike the son of my eldest son John Pike w$^{th}$ that parcell of my lande at the little River. & In Case the saide John Pike doe die without Issue & before he is twenty one yeare old then the saide lande shall pass to his Brother & sisters by equall portions & If they faile then it shall pass to the next of kinn. Allsoe I giue that portion of my lande at the new towne Caled by the name of the pitt boath vplande & meddow vnto my grand Child John Pike the son of my son Robert Pike & In case the saide John Pike die without Issue || or before the age of twenty one ‖ the said lande shall pass to his sisters & if they faile then it shall pass to the next of kinn Allsoe I giue vnto my Daughter Dorothy twenty pounde to be equally devided betwixt her & her Children by equall portions  Allsoe I giue to my daughter ann twenty pounde to be devided betwixt her & her Children by equall portions. Allsoe I giue to my daughter Israell twenty pounde to be devided betwixt her & her Chilldren by equall portions  Allsoe I give to my daughter in law mary the wife of my son John fowrty shillings & I giue to her Children Joseph hanna mary & ruth each of ‖them‖ fowrty shillings  Allsoe I give vnto my daughter in law sara the wife of my son Robert fowrty shillings & I giue to her Chilldren sara Dorathye mary & Elizabeth ‖ each of them ‖ fowrty shillings. allsoe I giue vnto my tenant samuell more the bedsteed that he hath of mine.

"Allsoe I doe. appoynte my two sons John & Robert to bee my executors to see my will pformed & my debts & all Charges paide ‖ soe farr as my estate will reach ‖ & the remainder of my estate within doare & without doare shall be devided betwixt my two said executors my sons John Pike & Robert Pike by equall portions all debts & Charges beinge first discharged & paide  furthermore my will is that in Case my sons John Pike & Robert Pike should Remoue out of the Cuntry with theire famillyes after my decease before my saide grande Chilldren are of the age of twenty one yeare that then it shall be in the power of my saide sons John & Robert to dispose in the waye of sale or otherwise of the saide lande for the benefitt of my saide grand Children respectiuely that is to saye my son w$^{ch}$ is the father shall dispose of that lande w$^{ch}$ is by me given to his owne Child & soe boath respectiuely"

John Pike<br>his mark

Witness: Henry Mondey, John R Raffe.

Proved in Hampton court 3 : 8 : 1654 by Mr. Henry Mondey and Jno. Ral[f]e.

Inventory of estate of John Pike sr., deceased May 26, 1654, taken May 29, 1654, by Mr. Henry Mondy (Mondey), John Roff (Rolf) and George (his o mark) Goldwire (Gouldwire) : His howse & Lande at the old Towne of Newbery, 60li.; his Lande at the new Towne, 60li.; one yonge horse & one mare, a bridle & saddle, 37li.; 7 Cows & 2 yonge Cattell of 2 yeare & vantage, 39li.; one bed & appurtenances, 7li.; on new broad Cloth suite, 3li. 3s. 4d.; one stuff sute & wascot, 2li. 2s.; one Cloth sute, 1li. 4s.; one Cloth Coate, 2li. 10s.; shirts, hankerchers & bands & other linen, 2li. 15s.; 4 paire of stockinges & 2 hats, 1li. 14s.; a paire of boots & 2 paire of shooes, 1li. 2s.; 2 paire of gloves & a paire of mittins, 4s.; one brass pan, one warminge pan, one frieinge pan, 1li. 10s.; one brass pott, one brass possnett, 1li. 1s.; one brand Iron, one and Iron 6s.; a hatchet, a Cuttinge knife to Cut haye & other smale things, 6s. 6d.; a Chest, a box & other lumber, 16s.; In Books, 1li.; in debts, 7li.; a Cheese press & som other lumber, 13s.; total, 230li. 6s. 10d.

Jno. Pike and Robert Pike, executors to John Pike, sr., testified in Hampton court 3:8:1654, that the above is a true inventory.

*Essex Co. Probate Files, Docket 21,893.*

Daniel Henrick of Haverhill with Dorathy his wife, daughter of John Pike, acknowledged the receipt of her legacy of 20li. from her brothers John and Robert Pike, executors of the will of her father, John Pike. Signed June 10, 1654. Witness: Robert Clements, Henry Palmer.

Henry True of Salem with Israell his wife, daughter of John Pike, acknowledged the receipt of her legacy of 20li. from her brothers John and Robert Pike, executors of the will of her father, John Pike. Signed May 1, 1655. Acknowledged May 1, 1655 by Israell True and 15:9:1655 by Henry True before Tho. Bradbury, commissioner of Salisbury.

*Norfolk Deeds, vol. 1, leaf 36.*

Daniell Hendrick of Haverhill granted to his brother John Pike of Newbury and Robert Pike of Salisbury, executors of the will of his father-in-law, John Pike, all his vpland and meadow which belonged to him according to the order of the town of Haverhill in the 4th division to be improved for the use and benefit of his children, Daniell, John, Jotham, Jabez, Israell, Hannah and Dorathie, and that in consideration, the legacy of 20li. to be divided between his wife and children, according to the will of his father-in-law, John Pike. Signed and sealed Mar. 27, 1662. Witness: John Cheney, sr., Nathanell Boulter. *Norfolk Deeds, vol. 1, leaf 139.*

### Estate of George Williams of Salem.

"The last will and testam$^t$ of Georg Williams of salem bearing date the 23$^{th}$ of 7$^{th}$ mo anno 1654 I Georg williams sick in bodie but of sound memorie blessed be the lord doe make this my last will and testam^t and dispose of those goods god hath giuen me in manner & forme following Item I giue and bequeath to marie williams my loving wife my now dwelling house w^th all the land there vnto belonging being about foure Acres and three quarters for and during the naturall life of my said wife and after the decease of my said wife my will is that John williams my eldest sonne shall haue and enioy the said house and land to him and his heires foreuer Item I giue and bequeath to my said wife one third part of my estate viz pt land debts houshould goods and Cattell w^th timber and whatsoeuer I now stand possessed in. Item I giue and bequeath vnto marie Bishop my daughter the sume of five pounds and to her 2 Children five pounds to be divided betwixt them. Item ffor the remain[d]er of my estate vndisposed of I giue and bequeath vnto John Samuell Joseph & Georg williams my sonnes and sara & Bethia williams my daughter[s] to be diuided to them by equall portions saue onlie my daughter sara to haue a double portion in respect of her infirmitie all w^ch portions shall be paid at seuerall tymes as hereafter exprest viz: to my sonne John williams his said portion at the end and expiration of three full yeares from the date of these presents and to samuell williams my sonne his portion at the end of fife yeares and to Joseph williams my sonne his portion to be paid to him at the end of seauen yeares and to Georg williams my sonne the portion to be paid at the end of ten yeares and for a double portion I giue to my daughter Sara my will is shall be paid present and Bethia my daughter her portion it shall be paid when she shall acomplish the age of eighteene Item my will is that marie williams my loving wife and John williams my sonne shall be my executo^rs of this my last will and testam^t and for the better pformance herof my will is that my said sonne John williams & his mother shall endeuor to bring vp and provide for the rest of my Children instructing and teaching them in the trade I now profess vntill they shall come to the age of twentie and one yeare severallie and what advance or loss shall come to the estate before the tymes of paym^t shall expire to belong to all according to their pticular portions and further I doe entreate my loving ffrends Thomas watson & henerie Skerrie the elder and Jefferie massey to be ouer seers of this my said will in witnes of the premises I haue hervnto put to my hand the day and yeare aboue written."

georg williams

Witness: John Horne, Elias Stileman, jr., Thomas Cromwell. *Essex Co. Quarterly Court Files, vol. 2, leaf* 146.

Proved 29: 9: 1654, by the witnesses. *Salem Quarterly Court Records, vol. 3, leaf* 81.

Inventory taken 18: 8: 1654, by Elias Stileman, jr., and Richard Bishop: One house & out buildings wth 4 acres of land at the house, halfe an acre of it in orchard, 40li.; 10 acres of planting Land, 5li.; 3 acres & Quarter of meadow, 12li.; 2 Steeres, 3 yeers & vantage, 11li.; 3 Cowes, 12li.; 3 yeerlings, 5li.; 1 Geilding, 12li.; halfe a Mare & halfe a maire fole, 11li.; 3 Ewe Sheepe, 6li.; 5 Ewe Lambes, 6li. 5s.; 1 wether & 2 Lambes, 1li. 15s.; 2 hoggs, 3li.; 10 Bush. ould Indian Corne, 1li. 10s.; 2 Bush. of Wheate, 9s.; 1 1-2 Bush. Mault, 7s. 6d.; 1 1-2 Bush. pease, 6s.; 40 Bush. New Indian Corne, 5li.; 14li. of white suger, 14s.; 3 yd. 1-4 brodcloth, 2li. 12s. 6d.; 1 yd. 1-2 brodcloth, 1li. 7s.; 2 yds. 3-4 of double shagg, 19s. 3d.; 3 yds. 3-4 of yellow Cotton, 11s. 3d.; 6 yds. of ———, 2li. 2s.; 6 yds. 3-4 of Shagg, 1li. 2s. 9d.; 12 yds. 3-4 of Cotten cloth, 1li. 18s. 3d.; 20 yds. of Sayle Canvas, 2li.; 3 1-2 yds. Linsie Woolsie, 12s. 3d.; 2 3-4 yds. of Wt. Cotten, 5s. 11d.; 1 yd. 1-2 of penneston, 5s.; 4 pr. New shoes, 16s.; 1 sute of clothes Cersey, 2li.; 1 sute & cloke of Searge, 2li. 10s.; 1 Stuff Coate, 15s.; 4 yds. 1-2 pennestone, 18s.; 1 pr. of breeches, 12s.; 4 yds. Lockrum, 8s.; 1 cloth cloake, 1li. 10s.; 1 wastcote, 2s. 6d.; 2 Jacketts & a pr. of drawers, 10s.; 1 hatt, 12s.; 3 pr. Stockings, 8s.; 2 pr. Shoes, 7s.; 2 chests & 1 trunke, 1li. 2s.; 1 chest & box, 8s.; In money, 5li.; 1 feather bed & boulster & 2 pillowes, 14li.; 1 matt, 1s.; 3 blanketts, 1li. 12s.; 1 Greene Rugg, 1li. 10s.; 1 bedsted, 1li.; 3 Curtains, 6s.; 1 feather bed, boulster & 4 pillowes, 3li. 5s.; 2 ould blanketts & rugg, 1li.; 1 trundle bed matt & Cord, 3s.; 1 flockbed, 12s.; 1 feather boulster, 10s.; 1 boulster of wooll, 15s.; 3 blanketts, one Coverlett, 2li. 5s.; 1 Cotten blankett, 12s.; 1 pr. Cotten drawers, 4s.; 1 halfe heded bedsted & matt, 10s.; 1 bedtick & boulster, 12s.; 2 blanketts & 2 ould Coverletts, 1li. 5s.; 1 ould bedsteed, 2s.; 1 yd. 3-4 of Linsiwoolsie, 6s.; 1 yd. 3-4 barbers stuff, 5s.; 1 dieper bourd cloth, 16s.; 1 holland tablecloth, 8s.; 3 dieper napkins, 4s. 6d.; 4 napkins, 3s.; 1 pr. holland sheetes, 2li.; 6 pillowbears, 18s.; 1 pr. sheetes very ould, 4s.; 1 pr. sheetes, 10s.; 1 pr. Cotten sheetes, 1li. 4s.; 3 halfe sheetes ould, 4s.; 2 small bord clothes & 8 towells, 11s.; 2 pr. ould sheetes, 12s.; 1 pr. sheetes, 1li.; 5 shirts, 1li. 10s.; 1 Court Cubberd, 16s.; 1 table & forme,

16s.; 1 chaire table, 8s.; 6 chaires, 8s.; 1li. powder, 2s.; 10 pewter dishes, 2li. 5s.; 2 greater & 2 lesser basons, 10s.; in other pewter potts & old platters, 6s.; Lisbourne waire, 4s.; In hay, 4li.; 2 pailes, 18s.; In Cooper's timber, 6li. 10s.; 1 Copper Kettle, 2li. 10s.; 1 Copper Cettle, 16s.; 1 Brass Cettle, 4s.; 1 Warming pan, 7s. 6d.; 1 Iron pott, 6s.; 1 Iron pott, 3s.; 1 Skillett, 2s. 6d.; 1 frying pann, 1s. 6d.; 1 pr. Andirons, 5s.; 1 Gridiron, 3s.; fire pan & tongs, 3s.; 1 pitt, 2s.; pott hanger & pot hookes, 5s.; a Ladle, 6d.; hourglass, 12d.; 2 sieves, 2s., 3s. 6d.; 1 pr. billowes, 2s. 6d.; 1 bible, 4s.; psalm book, 12d., 5s.; 1 muskett, bandeliers & Sword, 1li.; 1 doz. trenchers, 8d.; 2 yds. of searge, 1li. 10s.; buttons & Silk, 16s.; a Remnant of Stuff, 2s.; 1 pr. Stockings, 2s.; 1 wastcote, 4s. 6d.; 1 doz. bands, 6s.; Silk Cotten ribind, 2s.; thrid, 4s.; Lace & Filletten, 2s.; a peece of Leather, 3s.; 3 axes, 6s., & 3 Cooper's axes, 12s.; 3 frowes, 5s., a hattchett & bill, 2s., 7s.; 2 Spaids, 3s., 4 addses, 15s.; 8 Drawing Knives, 10s.; 2 augers & bung borer, 2s.; 3 pr. Compasses, 3s.; 2 Round shaves & an old adds, 3s.; 1 handsaw, 12d., 2 thwart Sawes, 10s., 11s.; 3 howells, 3s., a sithe, 18d., 4s.; 6 ould howes, 4s.; percer bitts, 1s. 6d.; 2 Joynters, 4s.; Trussing hoopes, 2s.; 2 Cresses, 2s. 6d.; 2 Cressetts, 5s.; a grindstone, 2s.; 100 hewed staves, 5s.; a skiff, 3li. 10s.; severall wood & earth vessells & other Lumber or utensells, 2li. 10s.; In bords & wheate that should have been for the Raite, 1li. 18s.; debts owing to the estate if good & not desperat, 87li. 8s.; total, 326li. 11s. The estate debtor to severall men, 51li. 10s. 7d. *Essex Co. Quarterly Court Files, vol. 2, leaf 146.*

Joseph Williams and Georg Williams, sons of George Williams, late of Salem, deceased, ordered 1: 10: 1654, to dwell with their brother, John Williams, after the manner of apprentices, until they are twenty-one, and be taught the trade of a cooper according to their father's will. Bethiah, the daughter of the deceased, to be given into the hands of some good service or family where she would be well educated. *Salem Quarterly Court Records, vol. 3, leaf 83.*

Isaacke Estye's servant, Joseph Williams, ran away from him, and thereby damaged him. The court 2: 10: 1658, ordered that the portion of said Williams' estate in the hands of Jeffrey Masseye, Tho. Wattson or Henry Skerry, trustees, be kept by them until the court take further order. *Salem Quarterly Court Records, vol. 4, leaf 28.*

## Estate of Mary Williams of Salem.

"The last will and testam$^t$ of Marie williams of Salem widow bearing date the first day of the 8$^{th}$ month Anno 1654 I marie williams sick in bodie but of sound memorie praised be the lord doe make this my last will and testam$^t$ in manner and forme following viz: Impr that wheras my late husband Georg williams deceased by his last will and testam$^t$ did giue and bequeath vnto me besyds his dwelling housse & a Certaine portan of land during my naturall life & one one third pt of all the rest of his estate he died possessed in & out of w$^{ch}$ third part I giue to Sara williams my daughter one halfe of the afforsaid third pt to be improved by the ouersyght of Thomas watson henerie skerrie and Jefferie massey or any two of them for the vse and behove of the said Sara. Itm I giue and bequeath to marie Bishop my daughter the sume of five pounds.

"Itm I giue vnto Samuell williams my sonne five pound Itm. I giue and bequeath to Joseph williams and Georg williams my sonnes and to bethia williams my daughter the remainder of my estate to be improued for the vse and behove of the said Joseph Georg & Bethia by the ffaithfullness and discretion of the aforesaid watson Skerie & masey vntill Joseph & Georg shall acomplish the ag of twentie and one yeares seuerallie and vntill the said Bethia shall acomplish the age of eighteene or be otherwise disposed of in marriag. Itm for my wearing aparell it is my will that for all my woollen Clothes the shalbe equallie diuided betwixt marie Bishop and sara williams my twoo daughters and for my linens they to be diuided betwixt the said marie & sara williams and Bethia williams my daughters by equall portions in witnes of this my present will I haue hervnto put my hand the day and yeare aboue written."

her mark  
marie (|) williams

Witness: Richard Bishop, Thomas Robins.

*Essex Co. Quarterly Court Files, vol. 2, leaf* 148.
Proved 29: 9: 1654 by the witnesses.

The executors were Jeffery Massy, Henry Skerry, sr., and Thomas Watson, though named overseers. *Salem Quarterly Court Records, vol. 3, leaf* 81.

Inventory of the estate of Mary Williams, widow of George Williams, taken 17: 9: 1654, by Elias Stileman, jr., and Richard Bishop: One Cloth goune, 3li. 10s.; 1 Searge Goune, 2li.

10s.; 1 red pettecote & wastcote doub. baise, 2li.; 1 red searge pettecote, 2li. 15s.; 1 doub. Shagg pettecote, 16s.; 1 Linsiewoolsie pettecote, 10s.; 1 Searge pettecote, 7s.; 1 cloake, 1li. 4s.; 1 hood, 2s. 6d.; 1 tafetie Scarfe, 6s.; 1 demycaster, 1li. 2s.; 1 felt hatt, 12s.; 1 pr. stockings, 3s.; 1 pr. Stockings, 12d., 4s.; 1 Searge Apron, 5s.; 1 Say Apron, 10s.; 1 Say Apron, 6s.; 2 blu aprons, 6s., 1 Apron, 12d., 7s.; 1 white demytie wastcote, 9s.; 1 Sleasie Apron, 8s.; 1 dowlass Apron, 5s.; 1 Silk Hood, 5s.; 2 fine holland hancherchers, 10s.; 2 hankerchers, 6s.; 1 Lawne hankercher, 5s.; 2 hankerchers, 3s.; 2 wt. hoods, 7s.; 5 forhead clothes, 7s.; 3 pr. hand cuffs, 1s.; 3 pr. gloves, 7s.; 1 wt. Cotten Wastcote, 4s.; 2 Shifts, 12s., 1 shift, 3s., 15s.; 1 pr. shoes, 3s. 6d.; 6 neckclothes, 6s.; the 1-3 of goods giuen by will of her husband Georg Williams, 79li. 14s. 7 1-4d.; the 1-3 of debts owing to her sd. husband's estate, 29li. 2s. 1-4d.; total, 131li. 3s. 3 1-2d. One third of debts to be payed out of the estate, 17 li. 3s. 6 1-4d. *Essex Co. Quarterly Court Files, vol. 2, leaf 148.*

### ESTATE OF MRS. ELIZABETH HARDY OF SALEM.

Will of widow Elizabeth Hardy proved 1: 10: 1654 by Mr. Edm. Batter and Nathaniell Pickman; but the will was defective for want of executors. Court appointed her son, Joseph Hardy, and Roger Haskall, administrators. Inventory brought in. *Salem Quarterly Court Records, vol. 3, leaf 82.*

Inventory of the estate of widow Elizabeth Hardie of Salem, deceased, taken 11: 9: 1654, by William Dodge and William ———: A certain purchase of house and land late in the possession of Mr. Garvase Gafford, 40li.; a dwelling house in the towne with 2 acres of land thereunto belonging, 40li.; a ten acre lott in the south field, 10li.; a Joynd bedsteed, 1li. 10s.; a wenescot Chest & a sea chest, 1li.; table wth frame & a forme, 1li. 6s.; 4 pewter platters, 1 drinking bole & 1 Candlestick, 12s.; 1 ould warming pan, 5s.; 2 Iron pots & 2 payr of pot hookes, 1li. 5s.; 1 Cheyney bason, 1s. 8d.; 4 pewter dishes, a salt and a bole, 12s.; 1 brass malter, 5s.; 1 musket & 2 swords, all rustie, 12s.; 2 Cuissons, 6s.; 1 Carpett Cloth, 8s.; 3 Cheares, 10s.; 1 pillow beere, 3s.; 1 Cheese press, 3s.; 2 hakes and 2 hookes, 5s.; 2 hand Irons, 1 spitt & 1 ould gridiron, 10s.; 2 litle tables, 1 form and a setle, 10s.; 1 grindlestone, 4s.; 12 bushells of Indian Corne, 1li. 12s.; 2 Iron spads, 3s.;

1 Corne sive, 1s.; 1 ould bed Coverin, 1 blanket and 1 winowing sheete, 12s.; 1 litle brass pot, 2 skellets, 11s.; 2 bushells of wheate, 10s.; 8 Ewe sheepe, 12li.; 1 Ram lamb, 1 weder lambe, 1li.; 1 Calfe, 1li.; 4 Cowes, 1 steere, 21li. 13s. 4d.; 1 Feather bed, 1 pillow, 2 blankets, 1 Rugg, 4li. 10s.; 2 yards 1-2 Coten & wooll mixt Cloth & 2 Cuissons, 16s.; 1 sett of Cortaines & vallance, 1li.; 1 Cloke, 1 peticote, 1 wascote & 1 hood, 3li. 10s.; 3 sheets, 18s.; 2 pillow beeres, 10s.; 1 table Cloth, 1 Napkin, 4 handkerch, 13s. 6d.; 2 Cappes, 1 Croscloth, 1 linen apron, 11s.; total, 151li. 9s. 2d.; debts, 10li. 9s. 2d. *Essex Co. Quarterly Court Files, vol. 2, leaf 149.*

ESTATE OF MRS. ABIGAIL AVERILL OF IPSWICH.

Administration on the estate of Abigaill Averill, intestate, granted Mar. 27, 1655, to her son, William Averill. Eldest son to have a double portion, and the rest of the children a single portion. *Ipswich Quarterly Court Records, vol. 1, page 49.*

Inventory of estate of Abigial Averell, widow and executrix of William Averell, now deceased, taken by Andrew Hodges and Reienold Foster: the house lott and house, 12li.; the six acer lot att muddy River, 4li.; the pequett lott 7 acers, 6li.; six acers of meddow, 5li.; a steer 4 yeer ould, 5li. 10s.; a cow and a haifer, 8li. 10s.; a yeer ould steer an vantage, 2li.; a yeer ould haifer an vantage, 2li.; a calfe, 1li. 4s.; swine, 1li. 15s.; aleven fowles, 8s.; an Iron pott, 1li.; an Iron kettle, 3s. 6d.; frying pan, 2s.; brase skillitt, 2s. 6d.; brase furnes, 1li.; brase kettle, 5s.; warming pan, 2s. 6d.; smoothing Iron, 8d.; brase pan, 7s.; meall trofe, 2s.; two ould paills, 2s.; a ould halfe bushell, 6d.; bar of iron, 2s.; pair of tonges, 1s.; drawing shave, 1s.; fier slice, 4d.; gridiron, 1s. 6d.; pair of pott hooks, 8d.; lampe, 2s. and two tramilles, 2s., 4s.; hour glase, 1s.; cosslett, 14s.; bar of Iron, 1s. 6d.; spitt, 2s.; brasse kettle, 2s.; a pair of nippers and a reaping hook, 1s.; pair of scales and a pound weight, 2s.; hough, 1s. 6d.; four pewter platters, 10s.; two sives, 1s. 6d.; flagon, 2s. 6d.; Sum ould pewter, 1s. 6d.; four earthen vessells, 1s.; bible, 5s.; an ould bible and two other bookes, 5s.; linin wheel, 3s.; mortising axe, 2s, a pair of tow cards, 1s.; hatt bruish, 6d.; a few ould tubbes, 2s.; pine cheast, 6s.; an oke Cheast, 2s. 6d.; a box, 1s. 6d.; bouster filled wth flockes, 3s.; another bouster, 2s.; 3 pillowes, 12s.; fether boulster, 6s.; the fethers of another, 4s.; one pair of sheets, 10s.; one sheet, 5s.; a fether bed, 1li. 10s.; two blankets, 9s.; a cotten blanket, 5s.; a coverlid, 10s.; two ould pillows, 2s.; 3 curtens and valens, 1li.; 2 cuishens, 1s. 6d.; a pair of shooes, 1s. 8d.; a pair of stockings, 1s.; a table cloth, 2s. 6d.; Red cote, 1li.; an ould stufe cote, 4s.; another cloth cote, 10s.; a gound, 1li. 10s.; a wastcote, 10s.; sum other ould cloths, 5s.; a say apron, 2s. 6d.; a cloeke, 8s.; a whood, 5s.; dublet, 9s.; caster hatt, 1li.; an ould hatt, 2s.; white apron, 4s.; two holand handcarchifs, 4s.; an ould holand hancarchife, 1s.; two calico handcarchifs, 1s. 6d.; 5 croscloths and a mufler, 5s.; 4 cowes, 1s. 4d.; a baig, 1s.; cote, 4s. 6d.; hatt, 2s. 6d.; pewtter pott, 1s. 6d.; cheafeing dish, 1s.; an ould tunill with a spindle and a peece of ould linin, 6d.; eighteen bushells and a halfe and halfe a pecke of wheat at 4s. 6d. the bushell, 4li. 3s. 9d.; 80 foote of boerd, 4s. 6d.; a hammer, 6d.; 90 foot of ould plainks, 4s. 6d.; 22 bush. and halfe of indian corn att 2s. 8d. the bushell, 3li.; a hogshead, a wedg an a beetle Ring, 4s.; 9 pound of butter, 4s. 6d.; total, 77li. 4s. 11d. What shee ougheth, 13li. A frame raysed & something done to it to be consd. whether it be the estate of the widdows or otherwise.

William Averill testified in Ipswich court, 27: 1: 1655, that the above is a true inventory. *Essex Co. Probate Files, Docket 1,025.*

### ESTATE OF HENRY SMITH OF ROWLEY.

Administration on the estate of Henry Smith granted Mar. 27, 1655 to Maxemillion Jewett and Frances Parrett, and they to dispose of the children for the present. *Ipswich Quarterly Court Records, vol. 1, page 49.*

The deacons of Rowley, administrators of the estate brought in an inventory of 8li., Mar. 25, 1656. It was apportioned to the two children, who were to be disposed of and cared for by them. *Ipswich Quarterly Court Records, vol. 1, page 54.*

Inventory of the goods of Henry Smith of Rowley, deceased, taken 1: 16: 1654-5, by Richard Swan and John Smith: One sow, 1li.; one muskett wth worme & scourer, 11s.; one sith wth nibs & hoope, 3s. 6d.; one little Chest, 3s. 6d.; one grate, 2d.; one paire of shooes, 4s. 4d.; one Chest, 3s.; one kettle, 9s.; one bagge, 2s. 6d.; ten yards & a quarter of Course Cloath, 15s. 4d.; one reddish Coverlett, 3s. 6d.; one blueish Coverlett, 3s.; in wearing Cloathes, 15s. 6d.; thre Pillowes and a short Cloake, 15s.; one dublett, 7s. 6d.; one pott, 3s.; one feather bed and Pillows, 2li. 5s.; one grid Iron, 2s.; one forme, 8d.; eight pounds & an halfe of bacon, 4s. 3d.; foure pounds and an halfe of puter, 4s. 6d.; one skellet, 6s.; a paire of pepper quarnes, 1s.; one sieve and a bottle, 2s.; one Churne, 2s.; a paire of bandiliers, 1s. 3d.; a sword & belt, 4s.; one spade, 2s.; a salt, 3d.; hempe seed, 8d.; one hatt, 5s.; one paire of forke tines, 4d.; one fire pan, 6d.; one fire pan, 1s.; one dragge, 10d.; one paire of old bootes, 1s. 8d.; one how, 1s. 4d.; one How, 1s.; one wast Coate, 1s. 6d.; one paire of sissars, 2d.; for a tramell & other things, 2s. 8d.; for sith Hoopes, 8d.; for Gunpowder, 1s. 6d.; for a peece of an old Trunke, 6d.; for a heifer, 3li.; for Barly, 1s. 6d.; one knife, 4d.; one Axe, 2s. 6d.; one Lock, 10d.; thre Chickins, 2s.; a paire of bullett moulds, 1s. 6d.; one Harrow tooth, 3d.; total, 14li. 3s. Debts owing: To Joseph Jewet, 2li. 3s. 3d.; Richard Swan, 7s. 6d.; Edward Hassen, 5s.; Thomas Burkby, 3s. 4d.; John Smith, 2s. 6d.; Mr. Ezekiell Rogers, 4s.; John Dresser, 4s. 6d.; John Bointon, 4s. 4d.; Thomas Dickinson, 3s. 8d.; Daniell Roffe, 4s. 3d.; John Pearson, 2s. 6d.; William Acy, 3s.; Maximilian Jewet, 12s. 6d.; Nicholas Jackson, 6s. 8d.; Benjamin Scott, 1li. 4s.; total, 5li. 11s. *Essex Co. Quarterly Court Files, vol. 3, leaf* 48.

### ESTATE OF MRS. ALICE WARD OF IPSWICH.

"Joanah Smith the wife Thomas Smith Elizabeth Perkins wife of Jacob Perkins & Jane Jordon wife to ffrances Jordon Testifie that Alice Ward widdow vpon hir death bed being of pfect memory did commit Sarah Ward hir daughter in Law vnto John Baker & Elizabeth his wife the sayd Sarah ward & hir estate to bring vp the sayd child in the feare of god and gaue vnto the sd Elizabeth Baker hir keyes & desired hir to take of all & to discharge hir debts."

Proved in Ipswich court 27 : 1 : 1655. *Essex Co. Quarterly Court Files, vol. 3, leaf* 9.

Inventory of the estate of widow Alice Ward of Ipswich taken 23 : 11 : 1654, by Robert Lord and John Warner: The house & ground about one acre, 16li.; one flocbed, 1li. 6s.; one fether boulster & 4 pillows, 1li. 12s.; one haire bed, 10s.; an ould rug, an ould coverlet & a blanket, 1li.; a halfe headed bed, trundle bed, mat & cord, 14s.; a peack of hempeseed & the bag, 1s. 8d.; a little bras candellstick & 6 spoones, 2s. 8d.;

ould pewter, 4s.; 2 gally dishes & a lattin puding pan, 2s.; a morter & pestle, 4s. 6d.; a smotheing Iron & 2 heats, 4s.; 1 doozen of trenchers, 8d.; in earthen ware, 4s.; greene ginger, 6d.; 3 Iron pots, 1 frieing pan & a skillet, 1li.; a tramell, pothookes & slice, 4s.; 3 runlets, 5s.; a poudering tub with porke in it, 10s.; a botle & other lumber, 4s. 6d.; a pote with butter in it, 3s. 6d.; a watter paile, 1s.; 3 chaires, a litle table, a forme & 2 stooles, 5s.; two spoones, 4 dishes, a ladell & 3 sives, 2s.; 2 hogsheads, 4s.; 8 bushells of corne, 1li. 1s. 4d.; wheate & a bag, 5s. & 2 baggs, 1s., 6s.; a meale trough & meale in it, 7s. 6d.; an axe & a broad how, 5s. 6d.; a wedge and a psell of hempe & flax, 3s. 3d.; a stufe gowne, red petecote & cloth wastcoat, 2li. 10s.; an ould stufe wastcoat & red petycoat, 16s.; 3 blanketts, 4s. 6d.; 3 old greene aprins, 6s.; 2 hatts, 16s.; a chest & 3 boxes, 10s.; 4 old aprins, 6s.; 2 sheetes, 8s.; 3 shifts, 4s. 6d.; tape binding, 2s.; pins & needles & thred, 2s.; hir weareing lenen, 1li.; childbed lenen, 1li. 2s.; suger 4li., 3s.; sope, 4li., 2s.; 3 glasses, 1s. 6d.; 1 houre glass, 1s.; 2 blankets, 5s. 6d.; suet & talow, 2li., 1s.; pr. stockings, 1s. 6d.; ould lenen, 3s. 4d.; Cokes & henes, 3s. 6d.; wood and a troft and pales, 3s.; a standing stole, 3s. 1d.; total, 37li. 14s. 11d. *Essex Co. Quarterly Court Files, vol. 3, leaf 9.*

### ESTATE OF NATHANIEL MERRILL OF NEWBURY.

"Witnes by these psents that I Nathaniell Merrill of Newbury in the Countie of Essex being sicke of body but through gods mercy of perfect memory I do here make my last will and testament, I first bequeath my soule into the hands of my blessed Redeemer with an assured hope of a joyfull resurection, and my body when it shall please the lord to take me out of this fraile life to bee buryed in the burying place of Newbury, and for my worldly goods I giue and dispose of as followeth Imp$^r$ I giue and bequeath vnto susanna my wife fiue akers of plowable land lying next my brother Johns land and halfe the marsh dureing her naturall life and a cow and three heifers and all my household goods, And out of this estat so giuen to my wife I giue and bequeath vnto my daughter Susanna fiue pounds when she shalbe at the age of twenty yeares then I giue and bequeath vnto my Son Nathaniell (whom I appoint as my true and lawfull heire) all my land and freehold after my wiues decease, and all the working tooles & Implements of husbandry and all the cattell and stocke besids And out of this stocke I appoint that my Son

Nathaniell shall pay theise legacyes as followeth, that is I giue vnto my son John when he shalbee of the age of two and twenty yeers the summe of fiue pounds, And also I giue and bequeath vnto my Son Abraham at the age of two and twenty years fiue pounds, And I giue and bequeath vnto my sonne Daniell also at the age of one and twenty years fiue pound and I giue and bequeath to my Son Abell fiue pounds also at the age of one and twenty years, And I appoint my Son Nathaniell to be my sole executor and all my debts & funerall rites being discharged I appoint him to haue all the rest of my goods & chattels vndisposed and I desire my brother John merill and Anthony somerby to be the ouerseers of this my last will & testament In witnesse whereof I haue set my hand march the eight in the yeare one thousand six hundred fifty foure but if gods puidence should by losses & crosses ||vpon y^e estate|| more than ordinary: then proportionobly to be abated in the legacyes"

his mark<br>Nathaniell n n merrill.

Witness: Richard Knight, Anthony Somerby, John merrell.

Proved Mar. 27, 1655 by John Merrill and Anthony Somerby.

Inventory of the estate of Nathaniell Merrill of Newbury, who deceased Mar. 16, 1654-5, taken Mar. 23, 1654-5, by Daniell (his D mark) Thurston, Richard Knight and Archelaus Woodman: Ten akers of upland and thre akers of marsh with the previledge of a frehold or commonage, 20li.; one cow and a calfe, 4li. 15s.; three heifers of three yeare old & 2 calves, 12li. 10s.; two steers of two yeare old & two heifers, 11li.; three yearelings, 4li.; one old cart & wheeles and sled and an old harow, 1li.; 2 spades, a mattock, a beetle, 4 wedges, a crosscut & a handsaw & 4 axes and 4 hooes, 2li.; 3 old tubs, a fanne, an Iron staple & ring & 2 prongs & shovell, 10s.; his weareing apparell, 2li.; ten bushells of malt & barly, 5 bushells of wheate & nine bushels of rye & about 35 bushells of Indian corne, 10li. 16s.; two muskets and 2 swords with match & powder, 2li.; oats & pease, 10s.; sixe small swyne, 3li.; 2 flock beds & bolsters & 2 paire of sheets old, 4li.; 2 old ketles, 2 skillets & a smal braspot & Iron pot, 1li. 10s.; an old warming pan, fire shovell, grid Iron, tongs, & other small Iron things & a spitt, 12s.; 4 small pewter dishes & a skimmer, dishes & spoones, 12s.; a truckle bedsted, 2 buckets and a pr.

of cottrells, 10s.; a small cart rope & halfe bushell & a pecke, 5s.; a small cubberd & 2 chests, 16s.; one drinke vessel, 2 wheels, one powdring tub, ten milke trayes & 3 cheesfats, 2li.; total, 84li. 6s.; his debts for Rent due to Mr. Cutting, 5li.; in small debts, 2li.

Essex Co. Quarterly Court Files, vol. 3, leaf 10.

### ESTATE OF THOMAS MIGHILL OF ROWLEY.

"The last Will & Testament of Thomas Mighill of Rowley I Thomas Mighill being sicke in body but of pfect memory (blessed be God) doe constitute & appoint this my last Will & testament in maner & forme as ffolloweth. Imp$^r$ I giue & bequeath my soule to God that gaue it in comfortable assurance of a gloryous resurrection at that day, & my body to be interred in the Comon burying place of Rowley aforesaid. Ite my will is that all debts be first discharged & all necessary expences for my decent & Comely buryall. Ite I giue to my loueing wife Ann Mighill one hundred and ten pounds. Ite I giue to my Son Samuell Mighill seauenty pounds to be paid vnto him w$^{th}$in one halfe yeare after the date hereof. Ite I giue to John Mighill eighteene pounds part whereof my Will is shall be paid vnto him out of my inheritance at the place Comonly called the Village, the rest of it w$^{th}$in one yeare, & seauenteene pounds more three yeares after the day of the date hereof: Prouided his Cariage be such dureing that whole time as giue sattisfaction to the Rev$^d$ Elders of this Church of Rowley m$^r$ Ezekiell Rogers m$^r$ Samuell Philips m$^r$ Humfrey Reyner mathew Boyes maxmilian Jewet & ffrancis Parrot or the suruiueing of them. Ite I giue to my Son Thomas mighill thirty pounds & a young black mare that comes three yeares old to be paid into my Son Samuells hand w$^{th}$in two yeares after my death & my will is that it be expended on him towards his bringing up in learning, or otherwise if the abouesaid Elders & brethren Judge meete. And my Will ffurther is concer[n]ing my abousaid Son John mighill that if his Course & caryage be such at the end of the aforesaid three yeares that the aforesaid Elders & Brethren doe not Judge meete that he should haue the said seauenteene pounds abouesaid that then it shall be equally diuided betwixt my two Sons Samuell & Thomas mighill & my will further concerning the Legacy bequeathed to my Son Thomas mighill is that vpon payment of it into my Son Samuells hand as abouesaid his acquittance shall be a full discharge to my Executour & in case my said son Thomas dy before he haue fully compleated the age of twenty one yeares his portio shall fall halfe of it to my Son Samuell & the other halfe of it to my Son Samuell or John as the aforesaid Reuerend Elders & Brethren or the suruiueing of them shall Judge meete. Ite I giue to my Son Ezekiell mighill thirty fiue pounds. Ite I giue & bequeath to my Son Nathaniell mighill thirty fiue pounds. Ite I giue to my Son Stephen mighill thirty fiue pounds w$^{ch}$ three said last Legacyes my will is shall be paid vnto my three said last sons when they shall be twenty one yeares of age. Ite I giue to my daughter mary mighill thirty fiue pounds to be paid to her at the age of twenty one yeares or at the day of her maryage w$^{ch}$ of them shall first be. & in case my wife be w$^{th}$ Child I bequeath thirty fiue pounds to it And in case any of the last mentioned foure or fiue Children dy before the age of twenty one yeares my will is that their portion or portions shall be equally diuided amongst the rest of them; saue only that in Case my said daughter Mary shall mary & after dy before the age of twenty one yeares my will is not that it be repaid againe. And in case my wife desire it my Will is that these last Legacyes bequeathed to my younger Children w$^{ch}$ I had by her be set out for them & shee my said wife to haue the benefitt of them for their education till the age of twenty one yeares. Ite I giue to my sister Ann Tenny one pound. Ite to ffaith Parrot Senior one pound. Ite to the use of the Church of Rowley one pound ten shillings. & in case my estate doe amount to || more || then the discharge of the aforesaid debts expences & Legacyes upon Just apprizall my will is that the ouer plus shall be proportionably diuided amongst my wife and all my Children according to their seuerall disproportions. & lastly I Constitute & appoint my deare & loueing wife Ann mighill as my sole executrix of this my last will & Testament. ||and I|| desire & appoint my trusty & beloued ffriends & Brethren m$^r$ Humfrey Reyner Mathew Boyes maximilian Jewet & ffrancis Parrat as ouerseers their unto. In witnes here of I haue here unto set my hand this 11$^{th}$ of June 1654.

"Before the signing of this my last will & testament I the said Thomas mighill haue and doe by these presents further giue to my wife Ann mighill one ewe to my son Samuell one third pt of my Corne growing at my ffarme at the Pen and one third pt of my Corne at my lott in the northeast ffield containeing about six Acres I also giue to my daughter mary mighill one Ewe."

Thomas Mighill

Witness: Humfrey Reyner, Mathew Boyes, ffrancis Parrat, Maxi: Jewet, John Harris.

Proved in Ipswich court 27 : 1 : 1655 by Maxemillian Jewitt and ffrances Parret.

Inventory taken June 24, 1654, by Maximilian (his I mark) Jewet, Mathew Boyes and Samuell Brockelbanke: his purse and apparell, 7li. 5s. 6d.; foure paire of sheets, 2li.; 5 pillow beares, 13 napkins, one table cloath, 1li. 8s. 6d.; one Carpett, 10s.; two Curtans, 3s.; bookes, 18s.; two Childs mantles, 1li. 5s.; Puter, 1li. 10s.; one bedstead & bedding, 5li. 5s.; bedding in one Chamber, 3li. 13s.; woole and spining, 3li. 10s. 8d.; Corne, meale & mault, 3li. 4s.; baggs, 13s.; haire sieves and other sieves, 5s. 8d.; Corne measures & old tubs, 6s.; Iron tooles in the Chamber, 1li. 12s.; bacon, 5s.; Iron Potts, kettles, a warming pan wth other Vtinsills, 2li. 10s.; Tubbs, trayes & other wooden ware, 1li. 12s.; Sawes, Gallow balke & other Vtinsells, 1li. 2s.; a Table & forme, 1li.; a Boxe, Trunke, Wheele & other things, 18s.; 6 Cushins, 9s.; a Cupboard & a Cushin, 5s.; 5 Chaires, 4s.; one muskett, sword & Bandiliers, 2li. 3s.; one breaking up plow wth her Irons, 1li. 2s.; 3 other Plowes & their Irons, 1li. 1s.; 3 Chaines, 2 bolts & shackells, 16s.; 3 yoakes & tyre for another, 10s. 6d.; axes, spade, dung forkes & other Vtinsills, 17s.; a Cart rope, 2s.; a dung Cart & wheeles & a slead, 1li. 10s.; 6 oxen, 42li.; 5 Cowes, 23li. 5s.; the third pt of a mare, 6li.; one Gray mare, 16li.; Swine, 8li. 10s.; one bedstead & bedding, 1li. 10s.; sheepe, 19li. 10s.; one bull & a steare, 10li.; 4 two yearing Cattle & one 3 yeare old, 14li. 10s.; 2 yearing Calves, 3li. 10s.; the dwelling house, barne & oarchard, 59li.; the kilne wth the Utinsills their to belonging, the kilne yard & Crop their on, 40li.; Arrable Ground at home, 7 Acres and an halfe, 37li. 10s.; 4 Acres & an halfe in the Lott on the right hand Ipswish way, 20li. 5s.; 3 Acres in the Lott on the left hand Ipswish way, 13li. 10s.; 12 Acres in the Northeast ffield, 39li.; 3 Acres of meadow in Satchells, 9li.; 18 Acres of Rough & Salt meadow at the Cowbridge, 38li.; 2 Acres of upland at the ffarme, 1li.; 6 Acres of salt marsh and foure of upland at the ffarme, 19li.; 6 Acres of salt marsh at Mr. Nelsons hand, 7li. 10s.; the ffarme in the Country at the pen, 29li.; 7 Acres & an halfe of wheate & barly at the home Lott, 8li. 5s.; 4 Acres & an halfe of Corne in the ffield on the right hand of the way to Ipswish, 5li. 8s.; 3 Acres of Indian Corne in the other ffield on the left hand the way to Ipswish, 3li. 12s.; in the northeast ffield 4 Acres of wheate and Indian Corne, 4li.; Corne at the pen, 3li.; dung, 2li.; land at the Village, 12li.; 13 gates & an halfe, 10li. 8s.; a buffe Coate, 15s.; an Iron morter, 2s. 6d.; 2 musketts, 2 rapiers & bandiliers, 1li. 16s.; oweing by John Mighill, 1li. 11s. 8d.; total, 571li. 14s. 11d. The debts of the deceased Thomas Mighill, 70li. 10s. 9d.; deducted from the total leaves 501li. 4s. 2d. Out of which said sume all the severall Legacyes mentioned in the Will of the deceased Thomas being discharged their remaines over plus to be divided amongst the partyes specifyed in the Will aforesaid, 81li. 1s. 2d.

Petition of Ezekiell Mighell to the Ipswich court Mar. 25, 1690, as the estate left by our father Thomas Mighill "belonging to yo$^r$ seruant & his Br$^o$ Steuen deceased was not wholy divided betwext us in his life time Brother leaueing three Children, which will haue Right when they Come to Age," that the lands given to us may be devided and the parcells which fall to the children may be improved or kept as their parents think best, and the part belonging to himself may be disposed of according to his discretion; and if the court pleases, to leave the care in the devision to their father, Mr. Robert Greenough, or other guardian.

Mr. Robert Greenough and his wife the mother of said children request that the above petition may be granted.

Petition granted Apr. 22, 1691.

Petition of Samuel Mighell of Rowley, dated Mar. 4, 1694-5, that there may be a settlement of the estate, showing "as his Father Thomas Mighell Formerly of Rowly dec$^d$. made his will & amongst other things therin Contained: had a clause in it That if any of the Children of my first wife died under age they Should inherit one for another; and soe of the Children of his Second wife; but none died under age (except one which the Second wife was then with child with) but all y$^e$ Rest of the Second womans children ariued at full age & are Since all dead, & Ezekiel Mighell the Eldest Son of the Second wife my half Brother dec$^d$. without Issue who died possesed of A Considerable part of my Father Thomas Mighell's Estate & I being the Eldest

Son by y<sup>e</sup> first wife do think I ought of right to Enjoy my S<sup>d</sup> Brother Ezekil's Estate or the greatest part thereof."

*Essex Co. Probate Files, Docket* 18,428.

### Estate of Robert Moulton, Sr. of Salem.

"Salem dated 20<sup>th</sup> febr<sup>y</sup>: 1654-5. By theise p<sup>r</sup>sents be it knowne, that I Robert Moulton Senio<sup>r</sup> being by Gods hand one my sicke bed of pfect memory Doe ordaine & Appoint my sonne Robert Moulton, whole Executor of this my Last will & Testament. I Giue my Daughter Dorothy Edwards twenty marke, Allsoe Two pillow bers marked with R D M. Item My farme I Leaue with my sonne, till my Grandsonne Robert Moulton be twenty one yeares old & then he to Enjoy the one halfe with the Apple trees, & After his father & mothers death to Enjoy the farme wholly, & in Case my Grandsonne Robert dye first that it fall in like manner to his next Elder brother ||& soe|| successively if he That Enjoyes it haue no issue; To Goodwife Buffum I give twenty shillings. To Joshua Buffum ten shillings. The Rest of my Goods & Cattell I leave with my sonne Robert and he to pay my debts."

Robt moulton, Sen.

Witness: George gardner, Henry Phelps, Nich. Phelpes.

Proved 26: 4: 1655 by George Gardner, Henry Phelpes. *Essex Co. Quarterly Court Files, vol. 3, leaf* 14.

Inventory taken by Jo. Alderman and Robert (his R mark) Buffum: One farme with all the housing on it, 35li.; the howses and ground in the towne, 10li.; 8 Cowes, 28li.; 5 yonge Cattell of two yeares old a peec, 11li. 10s.; one steer of foure yeares old, 4li.; two yearlings, 2li. 10s.; seaven wether lambs, 3li. 10s.; one fetherbed and a bolster, a pillow and a coverlid, 14li.; nynne peeces of pewter and a candlestick and a little morter, 1li.; two paire of sheets and two pillowbers and a ruffe and a peace of demetey, 2li. 10s.; one fowling peece and two old muskett bariell and one muskett, 1li. 10s.; one Desk, 3s.; two old Casks, 2s.; for tooles and old Iron, 2li. 12s.; one Iron pott and an old brasse Cettle, 15s.; seven Books, 16s.; other small books, 14s.; halfe a hundred pound of brand, 6s.; halfe an hower Glasse and three old Candlesticks and two lamps, 4s.; two spitts and a old driping pan, 4s.; one chest and an old Trunk and a Case of Bottles wth Glasses, 13s.; an old table and chairs and 2 Jars wth all other things forgotten, 6s.; total, 106li. 5s. Goods at his farmhouse, appraised by Henry Phelps and John Hill, 15: 3: 1655: One irne kittle, 10s.; 2 irne pots & a skillet, 11s.; a brasse kittle & skillet, 5s.; 1 copper kittle, 12s.; 3 pairs of pot hooks, a griddirne, a paire of tongs, a chopping knife & a cleaver, a flesh hooke, a skimmer & a warming pan, 8s.; 3 spitts, 5s.; a whipsaw, 8s.; 4 axes, 12s.; 2 adses, 5s.; halfe a dozen augurs, 6s.; a handsaw & 3 chissels, 4s.; 1 crowe of irne, 4s.; 1 fro, 1s.; 3 hammers, 1s.; woollen cloth & 2 hats, 5li.; linnen cloths, 1li.; a looking glasse & a paire of gloves, 3s.; a chest and a box, 7s.; in bedding, 1li.; pales & tubbs & wooden ware, 10s.; indian corne, 1li. 16s.; a bible, 5s.; total, 15li. 3s. Whole value of the estate, 121li. 8s.; debts, 8li.; total, 113li. 8s. *Essex Co. Quarterly Court Files, vol. 3, leaf 15.*

### ESTATE OF ELINOR TRESLER OF SALEM.

"Salem dated 15$^{th}$ february. 1654. By these p$^r$sents bee it knowne that I Elino$^r$ Tresler, being by gods will vpon my sicke bed, but of perfect memory thankes bee to the Lord, doe Appoint my sonne Henry & Nicholas, to bee Joynt Executo$^{rs}$ of this my Last will & testament. That is to say ‖ I Bequeath ‖ My ffarme To ‖ my sonnes ‖ Henry And Nicholas with the houseing, my ten Acre Lott in the North feild to Henry, My house & ground at the Town to my sonne Edward, My Houshold stuffe I bequeath in this manner one bead to Henry & the other to Nicholas & the sad coloured cloake to Edward & the Other Cloake to Henry, the old Brass Pott & the Least of the Brass Pans, & Two Deepe pewter platte$^{rs}$ & one Broad one & A Couerled & a Blanklett ‖ with ‖ one Paire of sheetes to my sonne Edward, My wascoate Safegard & Goune to goe together, & my Best Petticoate ‖ with the rest of my wearing clothes ‖ to goe together & my Daughte$^{rs}$ to haue them; the Rest of my wearing Linnen to my two Daughte$^{rs}$ & my other Linnen to the Executo$^{rs}$. To John Phelps my Gran-child two oxen & Cheine, with one yew, Item To my Grand Draughte$^r$ Elizabeth one yew. The other two ‖ yewes ‖ to Nicholas his two children. To my Grand-Children Samuell & Edward I giue Either of them a yeareling Calfe. The Rest of my Goods & Cattell to be left with my Executo$^{rs}$ to Pay my Debts & the Legacy bequeathed by my Late husband to his Daughter in England, To witt the summe of Ten Pounds."

her mark<br>
Ellinor E Treslor.

Witness: Robt. Moulton, sr., George Gardner, Robert Moulton, jr..

Proved 26: 4: 1655. *Essex Co. Quarterly Court Files, vol. 3, leaf 16.*

Inventory taken Mar. 13, 1654-5, by Robert Moulton and George Gardner: One farme, with the housing, 20li.: three Cowes, 12li.; three oxen, 18li.; two beasts, two yeare old apeice, 4li.; Foure yearlings, 4li.; foure yewes, 6li.; two hogges, 1li. 5s.; two feather beds, 2 Bolsters, two feather Pillowes, three blankets, two Coverlids, One Rugg, foure paire of sheetes & two paire of pillowbers, 12li. 15s.; three table Clothes, seven napkins, two Course towells, foure handkerchefs, four Coiques, three dressings, two shifts, one white Apron & other small linnen, 1li. 10s.; A Gowne & safegard, a wascoate & a red Peticoate & two old Coates & two wascoates, with a white Cotten wascoate & a short Coate, 3li. 10s.; two Paire of Gloves, 3s.; a Hatt & two Cloath Houdes, 10s.; two Paire of stockings & two pare of shoes, 10s.; two Cloockes & two Carpets, 3 Curtains, 5li.; two Aprons, 8s.; a Greate Chest, a box & two Cofers, 10s.; a Warming pan, a Looking glass & three Candlesticks, one Chafing dish, 16s.; two bras pans & three Brass pots, 2li.; three skillets & two iron pots, 17s.; three Brass kittells, 15s.; ten Pewter platters, 1li.; three pewter pots, 15s.; a Charger with other small Pewter, 10s.; Bookes, 10s.; three spits, two And Irons, two Rackes, a paire of Tongs, a fire shovell & a brass Ladle, 13s.; two fowling peices & A muskett, a sword & a Cutless, 1li. 15s.; three Chaines & a Cart rope, 15s.; a Harrow, 6s.; a Ten Acre lot, 4li.; the house & Barne & foure Acres of ground in the Towne, 20li.; plow yrons with old iron, 10s.; a steele Trapp, 5s.; one Grindstone, 6s.; a paire of Bellowes, 1s. 6d.; weights & scales & measures, 4s.; two Bedsteds, 5s.; 3 spinning wheels, 5s.; an houre Glass, 1s.; two Barrells with Tubs & Pales, 15s.; three Chaires, 3s.; trayes, 2s.; one whipsaw, 5s.; one Crosscut saw, 3s.; three wedges, 2s.; two Beetle Rings, 1s.; small millstones & Irons, 10s.; a Grid Iron toster, 2s.; in Corne, 3li.; total, 131li. 3s. 6d. Debts due: To her brother Edward Phelpes, 10li.; left by her father Tresler's will to his daughter, 10li.; to Mr. Gidney, 5li.; to Mr. Crumwell, 19s.; to Goodman Felton, 1li.; total, 26li. 19s. *Essex Co. Quarterly Court Files, vol. 3, leaf 17.*

## Estate of William Knight of Lynn.

"I william knight in this my last will and testyment do giue my wife Elizebeth the thirds of all my Estate and further that she shall Injoy my dwelling hows So long as she liueth  likwys I giu to my Son John knight forety shillings to be payd tow years after my deceas  Itte I giu to my dafter Ane won shilling and to her children fiu shillings a pease to be payd tow years After my deceas. Itt I giue to ‖ my sone ‖ francis knight fiue shillings when he shall lawfully demand it.  Itt I giue to my dafter hanna forty shillings won year after my deceas  Itt I giue to John ballard forty shillings tow years After deceas or when my wif pleases  Itt I giu to nathanyell ballard forty shillings tow years After my deceas: All and Euery of theas leggacys to be truly payd  The rest of my Estat I will to be Equily diuided amonkst my fowr children wich I had by my last wife Elizabeth

"only I giue to my Eldest Son Jacob a dubbell parcion to be payd in my hows and homelott Adjoyning to my dwelling hows and medow in Rumly march  If this amounts to more then his dubbell portion then it to be payd back to my last childre Equilly diuided likwys If the Sayd hows and land due not amount to a dubbell porttion the[n] it is to be made oup: I further will if any of theas my last children dye before thay come to age: then ther porttions to return to thos that shall suruiue Equaly to be deuided amonkst them  This I will that If my wife maryes then my childrens porttions to be taken from hurs and to be at the ouerseers disposing: I make my wife Elizabeth my lawfull Excekter to Administer on this my last will [and] Testyment I likwys make our brother nicklis potter and Georg keasur and John witt: to be the ouersears of this my last will. To wich I Sett my hand dat the 2 of december 1653."

his mark<br>William C Knight

Witness: John Fuller and Nicholas Potter, both of Lynn.

Potter made oath before Rob. Bridges 27: 4: 1655, and Fuller on 28: 4: 1655, before Elias Stillman, clerk. *Essex Co. Quarterly Court Files, vol. 3, leaf 12.*

Inventory taken 22: 1: 1654-5, by John Fuller and Phillip Kyrtland: Dwelling house, barn and fivten Ackrs of plow land, 46li.; six akers of medow in Rumly march, 10li.; five akers of medow in the town marche, 15li.; two working oxen, 14li.; thre Cows, 13li.; one heaffor in calf, 4li. 1s.; 2

year ould Stear, 3li., one yerling, 1li. 15s., 8li. 15s.; one weaning Calfe, 15s.; 2 Ewes with 2 Ewe Lambs, 4li. 10s.; 2 Ewes with 2 Rame lambs, 4li.; 2 Ewes, 3li. 10s.; 1 wether Shep, 2 years ould, 1li.; three 3 year ould wetthers, 2li. 5s.; one Rame, 15s.; two swyn, 2li.; one fether bede and pillows and bolster and coverlids, 4li.; two flock beds with other furnyture belonging to them, 2li. 10s.; five pare of sheets, 4li.; 8 napkins and a tabell cloth, 13s.; one pillow beare, 2s.; 4 kuchins, 8s.; 2 bede steeds, 18s.; ould chests and a truncke, 10s.; thre brase potts, 1li. 9s.; thre bras kettells, 17s.; one warming pane, 5s.; 4 pewttor dishes, 1li.; 3 wine measurs, 5s. 6d.; 2 wine cups, 2 dram cups, two beare cups, 5s.; severall peases of small pewttor, 5s. 6d.; one Iron pott, one Iron mortter and pestill, 9s.; 2 pare of andyrons, fier shovell and tongs, 8s. 6d.; 2 pare of pott hangers, 3s.; 1 fryinge pane and Iron candellstick, 2s. 6d.; stolls, chears and a tabell, 11s.; beare barrils, tubes, churn, coberd *dewtraft,* 18s.; thre spininge whealls, a pare of woll cards, 8s.; 2 muskitts and kurbyn, 1li. 10s.; two swords, 5s.; two crosscut saws, one narrow axe, a frow and a lathing hamer, a littell hammer, 8s. 6d.; 2 spitts, 2s.; thre sifes, 3s.; the man's wearing apparrell, 3li. 8s. 6d.; carts, plows, yoks and Iron works belonging to them, 2li. 12s.; in mony, 2s. 6d.; a ladder and ould Iron, 5s.; total, 154li. 15s. Due from brother Deken, 6s.; look, 11s.; heed, 9s.; Mikell cambell, 1s.; Joseph Armitag, 5s.; Hugh Aley, 6s.; town, 1s. 6d.; diman, 4s.; Pharrer, 1s.; William Curtis, 6s.; a scote man, 6s.; brother kesar, 2s. 4d.; —— & his Sonn, 12s.; another scotman, 12s. 4d.; total, 9li. 3s. *Essex Co. Quarterly Court Files, vol. 3, leaf 13.*

### Estate of Henry Fay of Newbury.

"Witnese by theise pʳsents that Henry Fay of Newbury in the County of Essex weauer did in his life time, giue and bequeath vnto his brothers children his whole estate his debts being discharged, and that he did desire his friends Robert Long and James Jackman that they would looke to it for said he I will leaue it in your hands vntill they come, this he said often times." Witness: Richard fitts, Robert Long, James Jackman, Joane Jackman. "The Court Inclynes to apʳhend by the testimonyes this to be the will of Henry fay yet suspend the full determination of it till Ipswich court next but leave the estate in there hands & give them power in the mean tyme to pay iust debts & to receiue what is due to the estate p me Robert Lord cleric:

"The deposition of Richard fits of Newbery the said Deponent Testifieth that Henry fay said to him that if hee Died a Singll man then his brothers Children shal haue his estatt this he said often:

his mark<br>Richard U fits

"Taken vpon oth befor me william Titcom commissioner for newbery September 24 1655." *Essex Co. Quarterly Court Files, vol. 3, leaf 36.*

Robert Long testified that Henry Fay said, two days before he died, when he thought he was going to die, that he would leave the estate in his hands and desired him to come & look to it. Sworn in Ipswich court 25: 7: 1655.

Thomas Noyes of Sudbury, yeoman, appointed, under seal, his friends, Mr. Nicolas Noyes of Newbery, gent., and Robert Long of Newberry, weaver, his attorneys to let his house and lands in Newbery, sometime the house and land of Henry Fay, etc. Dated Sept. 20, 1656. Witness: Rich. Lowle, Joseph Mors.

*Essex Co. Quarterly Court Files, vol. 3, leaf 35.*

"The testimonye of James Jackman of Nubery witneseth that Henrye Faye have att several times & plases tould me that he would leave his whole estate when he dyed with Robert Longe and my selfe for his brother's children, if they doe come for itt & that Robert Lounge & myselfe should paye his dettes out of the estate." James Jackman. Sworn in Ipswich court court, 25: 7: 1655.

The deposition of Joane Jackman of Newbury. "This deponent testified that Henry Faye tould her that his brother's children should have what estate he had, but he said he would leave his estate with my husband & Robert Longe untill the said children doe com."

her mark<br>Joan X Jackman.

Taken upon oath before me John Pike, Commissioner for Newbery Sept. 22, 1655.

*Probate papers in the Quarterly Court Records copied by Joshua Coffin and now in the Probate Registry, vol. 1, page 226.*

Robert Long and James Jackman appointed administrators of the estate of Henry Faye Mar. 25, 1656. The estate was to be given to his brothers in England. *Ipswich Quarterly Court Records, vol. 1, page 55.*

Inventory of the estate of Henry Fay of Newbury, weaver, who deceased June 30, 1655, taken by Thomas Hale, Thomas Browne and Abraham Toppan: His house and about seaven akers and an halfe of land lyeing adjoyning, a barne, orchard and garden, and in the little feild foure akers and an halfe, 35li.; about 3 1-2 akers of wheat upon the land, 3li. 15s.; 3-4 aker of Indian corne, 16s.; a loame and warping beame, a spooleing wheele, sleyes and harnesses and other appurtenances, 2li. 10s.; a rugge of cotten, 1li. 8s.; an old pillow, 2s.; his wearing apparell, a cotten paire of breeches and an old coat and Jacket, 16s.; a paire of shooes and stockings & another pair of stockings, 6s.; a musket, 14s.; a brass pott and an Iron kettle and an old frying pan, 1li.; a paire of tongs & an Iron crooke, 2s. 2d.; an old spade and grubaxe & 2 old axes, 4s.; 2 peckaxes and an old hooe, 7s.; 3 wedges of Iron and 2 beetle rings, 3s. 6d.; an handsaw, an ads, 3 gougs, 2 boriers and a gimblet, a draught shave & brest wimble, 8s.; a handhooke, 3 rings & an old trowell, 2 nibs, 3s.; a tennent saw, 2s.; 2 old sithes, 3s.; an old hooe, 1s. 6d.; a hamer & an old skillet, 2s. 6d.; a shirt, 6s. 6d.; a joyned chaire, 3s. 6d.; a peck & halfe peck & a basket, 1s. 10d.; a beare vessell, 1s. 6d.; a poudering tub, 4s. 6d.; a joyned chest, 7s.; a halfe-headed bedsted with a small rod, 9s.; a bible, 4s.; an Inkhorne, 6d.; a wooden bottle, 2s.; 3 bookes, 1 at 1s. 6d., 1 at 1s. and 1 at 6d., 3s.; a wheele and Iron spindle, 3s.; 3 glass vialls, 1s.; a chest and a boxe, 5s.; 3 dozen of buttons of pewter, and a pr. of glasses for the eyes, 1s. 8d.; 2 sieves, 2s.; one small truncke, 2s. 6d.; about six bushells of Indian corne, 15s.; a forme & ladder & wheelbarrow & other lumber, 6s.; 2 hens & 8 chickins, 2s. 6d.; a cow and a calfe, 5li.; a pound weight of lead & halfe pd. & qter, a brass skimer, an Iron foot, a salt box & a small grid Iron, 6s.; twyne & cotten yarne, 1s. 6d.; a new sarge sute, 2li. 12s.; a sith & snede, a tramell, pothooks & wooden platter, 9s. 8d. His debts: To Mr. Woodman, 2li. 9s. 3d.; Steven Greenleafe, 9s.; Robert Coker for plowing, 7s.; Thomas Smith, 1li. 6s. 6d.; Will. Bolton, 3s. 2d.; Will. Richardson for 5 dayes work, 6s.; Goodman Hutchins for the Coffin & a peck of corne, 9s. 8d.; Robert Long, 4s. 6d.; John Bishop, 7s. 6d.; John Bartlet, 1s. 2d.; Anth. Somerby, 2s. 8d.; Steven Swett for the charges at his funeral, 10s.; for rates, 1li. 2s. 11d.; Daniell Peirce,

3li. 8s.; John Bishop, 12s. 6d.; Mr. Dumer, 1li. 10s.; Peter Godfry, 1s. 10d.; Nicholas Noyes, 10s.; Mr. Jewet, 2li. 19s.; Steven Swett, 19s. 5d.; Steven Kent, 1s. 2d.; John Davis, 2s. 2d.; Richard Fits and James Ordway, 6s.; total, 18li. 7s. *Essex Co. Quarterly Court Files, vol. 3, leaf 35.*

ESTATE OF HUMPHREY BRADSTREET OF IPSWICH.

"The last will and testament of Vmphrah Brodstreate of Ipswich, July 21 1655 being weake in boddy doe therfore ordaine this my last will, in manner as followeth: I giue my soule to God that gaue it me, and my boddy to be buried in the buriing place of Rowley, and doe beleue the cumfortable resurrection of the same; as for my outward estate, my will is my farme on which I now dwell, with halfe the commons belonging to me from Ipswich, and all the commons to me from Rowley, shall be my beloued wifes, for the terme of her life, in case she doe not marry, but if she marry, then the one halfe of the farme shall be for the bringing up of my sonn Moses, and in case she dy, before my sonn Moses attain the age of 21, then the one halfe shall be my sonn Mosesis, and the other halfe ||that is the benefit of it|| shall be equally diuided among my fiue daughters, or so many of them as shall be then Liuing, and my will is that when my sonn Moses attains the age of 21: he shall haue and inioy the whole said farm except my wife be then liuing, who shall then enioy halfe the said farme, with all the dwelling house for the terme of her life, and after her death it shall all be my sonn Mosesis. Item I doe giue unto my wife Bridget one brown cow, one ew sheepe, one horse colt. Item I doe giue unto my sonn John all my farme at Mudde riuer, now in the occupation of Richard Camball of Ipswich, with one halfe of my commons from Ipswich soe long as he keeps the farme unsold, but in case he sell it, the commons are to returne ||and belong|| to the farm giuen to my wife. Item I doe giue to my daughter Hannah Rofe 20 ||twenty|| pound. Item I doe giue to my daughter Martha Beale one pound and more. I doe leeue fiftene pounds in the hand of her mother, to be giuen to her or to her child at her discretion. Item I doe ||giue|| to my daughter Mary Brodstreete forty pound. Item I doe giue to my daughter Sarah Brodstreete thirty pound. Item I doe giue to my daughter Rebeccah Brodstreet forty pound: Item I doe giue to my two grand children Danniell, and Hannah Rofe each of them fiue pound to be paid out of the farme by my sonne Moses when they attain the age of 21 years. Item I doe giue to Sammuell Beale ‖fiue pound‖ to be paid as aboue as the said Daniell and Hannah Rofes is. Item I doe giue to the pore of Ipswich one pound. Item I doe giue to the pore of Rowley one pound: and my will is that if my estate doe fall short of the full discharge of all my debts and Legacies then there shall be an equall abatement out of the seuerall Legacies giuen acording to proportion. and I doe intreat my beloued friends M$^r$ Sammuell Phillips, Matthew Boyes, and John Harris, to ioine with my wife, for the disposing of my children in mariage, or otherwise as need may require. and I doe make my wife Bridget Brodstreete Sole exequiteris of this my last will, and I haue hereunto set my hand July 21: 1655:"

Humphri Bradstreet.

Witness: Mathew Boyes, John harris.
Proved 25: 7: 1655 by the witnesses.

Inventory taken Sept. 6, 1655, by Danall thirston and William Lawe: one hat, one cloak and the rest of his cloths, 2li. 10s.; a pair of sheets, two pilowbears, one tabl cloth, 1li.; seven sheets and foure napkins, 1li. 10s.; four cotton blankits, 1li. 4s.; one flock bed, one rugg and one boulster, 1li.; one flock bed, one rug, one boulster, 2li.; one flock bed, one rug, 2 boulsters, one pilow, 2li.; a parsil of sheeps wool, 15s.; a parsil of wheat and a parsil of rie, 2li. 10s.; thre ould chists, one box, 14s.; one bed stead and cortan, 10s.; indian corne, 1li. 10s.; two sieves, 2s.; ould Iyron and two sickls, 5s.; a parsill of barley malt, 10s.; a cros cut saw, 8s.; sertane carpin for tools, 17s.; one kettel, thre iyron pots, one posnit, pot hooks, 2li.; one waring pane, one frying, 4s.; some peuter and a bras candlstick, 1li.; thre bushill of rie malt, 11s.; two bibles and another book, 15s.; two glas bottels, one chear, one smal box, 7s. 6d.; twenty pound of butter, 10s.; tubs and beare vesils, 1li. 1s.; one cubard, two earthin pots, 3s.; four wegs, two beetl rings, 8s.; one spade, one how, 2s.; one grinding stone, 3s.; one cart, one plow with chains and yoaks, 3li.; four oxen, 30li.; nine cowes, 38li. 5s.; one bull, 4li.; two stears, 9li.; two yearlings and one calf, 7li.; two hefers, 6li.; one maire, 16li.; one hors coult, 8li.; thre yewes, thre lambs, 9li.; swine, 10li.; wheat and rie, 6li.; indian corn, 5li.; barley, 1li.; hay, 5li.; a home lot att Ipsig, 8li.; a cannow, 15s.; a muskit, 10s.; hemp, 5s.; in debts that was oweing him, 50li.; in debts he

did owe, 20li.; total, 146li. 10s. The farme where he lived, 160li.; The farme at muddy River, 70li.
*Essex Co. Probate Files, Docket 3,081.*

Bridgett Brodstreet bound 25: 7: 1655, to discharge legacies given in her husband's will. She signed with a mark. *Ipswich Quarterly Court Records, vol. 1, page 52.*

Thomas Rawlison acknowledged the receipt from John Palmer of Rowley in the behalf of Bridget Broadstreete, widow, of 5li. in full satisfaction of all agreements between the husband of the said Bridget, and Thomas Rawlison, sr., concerning themselves and their children according to agreement between Robert Lord and Thomas Rawlison, jr. at Salisbury court. Witness: Joseph Jewett, Edward Browne.

Will. Beale's order to "Mother Bradstrete" "to pay my wife that twenty shillings left mee by my father in his last will." Dated 26: 7: 1655. Receipt of the 20s. by Mr. Jewitt, signed by Martha Beale.

Receipt of Hanah (her mark) Rofe, of Ipswich, of 20li. given by legacy in her father's will, and acquittance of my "Mother Bridget Broadstret." Witness: Mathew Boyes, Sara (her mark) Bradstret.

Receipt of Mary Bradstret of 40li. given her by her father's will and acquittance of her mother Bridget Bradstret. Signed Nov. 7, 1655. Witness: John Grant, Thomas Wood. *Ipswich Deeds, vol. 1, leaf 208.*

Receipt of Joseph Jewett of 10li. from Bridget Bradstret on the account of William Beale "for rent with a great some more for the use of Marble head mill." Witness: Nehemiah Jewett, Abraham Jewett.

Acquittance of "my mother Bradstreet from all debts & demands given or left for us vpon my fathers will," by William Beale and Martha his wife. Signed Aug. 23, 1657. Witness: Rebecka (her mark) Bradstre and Elizabeth Boys.

Acquittance of "my mother Bradstrett," having received "in Cattle the som of Thirty pound which is the full of my wiues portion." Signed 20: 2: 1657 by Nicholas Wallis. Witness: Joseph Jewett, John Harris, Leonard Harriman.
*Ipswich Deeds, vol. 1, leaf 209.*

ESTATE OF WILLIAM KNOWLTON OF (IPSWICH?).

Administration on the estate of William Knowlton, intestate, granted 25: 7: 1655 to his brother, Thomas Knowlton, to whom was committed the care of the widow and children.

Inventory taken July 17, 1655, by Theophilus Willson and Thomas Knowlton: house and ground, medow and Upland, 20li.; 3 pewter disshes and tin candlestick, 10s.; brass kettle, 12s.; little bras pot with holes, 1s. 6d.; little brass kettle old, 2s.; 2 paire of pott hooks, 1s. 8d.; pr. of tongs, 1s. 6d.; broken brass scillet, 1s. 6d.; broken brass ladle, 6d.; 4 Woodden trayes, 2s. 6d.; straning dish, a tunnle, 2 wooden platers and a old traye, 1s. 8d.; lumber, 5s., friing pan, 18d., 6s. 6d.; 2 boxes and a old chest, 5s.; 2 old narrow axes, 1s.; A sive, 12d., tin tunnle, 9 trenchers, 1s. 9d.; A kow, 4li. 5s.; 2 yerlings, vantage, 3li. 11s., 8li.; 3 Calves, 2li. 10s.; 4 shoats, 2li. 10s.; 2 siekles, 1s.; A broad how, 4s.; gun and sword, 14s.; fflock bed and boulster, fflock bed tick and blanket, 1li.; total, 37li. 8s. 1d. Debts that are owing to others for hilling of the ground, 34s., 1li. 14s.; debts besids, 7li.; mor owing, 12s.; mor owing to others, 12s.

Received in Ipswich court, 25: 7: 1655.

A copy of this taken out of the records of the Ipswich court Mar. 11, 1655, received into court Mar. 31, 1691.

Debts oweing from the estate of William Knowlton: To my selfe Tho. Knowlton wch I lent him, 7li.; payd to men for hilling his corne, 1li. 16s.; payd to Jer. Belcher, 3s.; John Browne, 16s. 9d.; Mr. Willm Norton, 5s.; Henry Muddle, 15s.; payd to by cloths for the children, 1li. 16s. 6d.; payd for makeing them & a wastcot for her, 14s. 2d.; to the widdow Varney, 11s.; for a peece of marsh, 12s.; for bringing the goods to the Towne, 10s.; to Willm Coggswell 7s., Goodman ffowler, 6s., 13s.; for 4 hatts, 1li. 1s. 8d.; for shirts for the boyes, 10s.; for Scooling for the boyes, 14s. 6d.; to Goodman Kinsman, 11s. 10d., to Isaack Coussins, 20d., 13s. 6d.; for the Coffin & Grave, 6s. 6d.; to goodman Lomas, 6s. 8d.; to John Emerson, 2s.; 6 paire of shoes for the boyes & a paire for the girle, 14s. 6d.; for a paire of Indenters administration and Inventory & coppes, 3s.; oweing in my booke before his death for corne & shoes, 2li.; The widdow hath of the household stufe, 3li. 9s. 1d.; A petecoat, wastcoat, hatt & a paire of shoes, 2li. 8s. 10d.; a pound of Cotton woole, 1s. 8d.; total, 27li. 14s. 4d.

Thomas Knowlton received of the estate of his brother William Knowlton, deceased, 37li. 8s. 1d. An account of what he has paid out of the said estate: to Robert Kinsman, 11s. 10d.; John Browne, 16s. 9d.; Isaac Cuzens, 2s. 5d.; his Coffin, 5s.; making Cloathes, 14s. 2d.; shoes, 18s. 6d.; Skins for the Boyes, 8s.; to Edward Lumax, 6s. 8d.; Mr. John Emerson, 2s. 8d.; Good. Lord, 2s. 3d.; more paid in June, 7li.; for ye burial of him to mr. Willson, 1s. 6d.; cotten wool and ye Rate then due, 2s. 1d.; for Bringing my Brother to Town when Buried, 12s.; for hilling of his Corne, 1li. 16s.; bringing their Goods to Towne, 10s.; paid to mr. Cogswell, 1s.; Goodwife Fuller, 6s.; Skins for the boyes, 9s. 6d.; four hatts, 1li. 1s. 8d.; one Hatt, 13s. 6d.; A Coat, 1li.; in Shifts, 10s.; to Henry Muddle, 15s.; A coat, 16s.; more in Shoes, 5s. 4d.; to Goodwife Varny, 11s.; Robert Cross, 1s. 8d.; A Coat for William Knowlton, 13s. 6d.; two yards of Cloath, 14s. 11d.; to Richard Jacob, 6s.; my Sister had of me in Houshold Goods and a Cow, 8li. 7s. 11d.; total, 31li. 12s. 10d. And two boyes I kept from their age of five years till they were Eight years old and Cloathed and keept them to Scool, 36li. And I keept a Girle from her age of one year and halfe old till shee Maried.

Received by the court Sept. 24, 1678.

Deacon Thomas Knowlton testified to the truth of a copy of the above account and also that he hath disbursed much more than what is written.

June 19, 1690, before Mr. Sam[ll]. Appleton Assist.

Received in Ipswich Court Mar. 31, 1691.

The request of Thomas Knowlton, sr. of Ipswich, dated Mar. 31, 1691, to the Ipswich court shewing that many years since, he was appointed administrator of the estate of his brother William Knowlton, who died in 1655, leaving a widow and seven children, the youngest about one and one half years old, and he was forced to take care especially of the youngest of them. The estate amounted to about 37li. 8s. 1d. and was insufficient to pay the debts with and bring up the children; he gave in to the court in 1678, two accounts of disbursements, one for 31li. and one for 36li., and as by the accounts it appeared he had paid 50li. more than was inventoried he thought he had been cleared and that his disposal of the estate was for the benefit of the family, especially when they received it and by his sister's importunity consented to the sale of the land, which was valued at about 20li., but now having done that for the widow and children, will this court take such cognizance of the cause as to examine whether the entry of the clearing of said estate be sufficient, if not will they see just cause to do it yet.

Ipswich court, Jan. 2, 1715, granted administration (D. B. N.) on the estate of William Knowlton, Ipswich, to his grandson Capt. Jn°. Knowlton of Ipswich, he giving bond for 200li., Rice Knowlten and Isaac Giddings, sureties. Witness: Samuel Daland, Danl. Rogers.

Mary Mitchell formerly Mary Knowlton, daughter to William Knowlton of Ipswich, deceased, desires that "my Cusen John Knowlton" of Ipswich, late of Manchester, may have administration of any estate that may be thought to be her father's. Dated Winddum, Nov. 10, 1715.

Thomas Knowlton of Norwich, New London Co., desires that "my Cusen John Knowlton" of Ipswich, late of Manchester, may have administration of any estate that may have been his father's, William Knowlton. Dated, Norwich, Nov. 12, 1715.

William Knowlton desires that "my Cusen John Knowlton" of Ipswich may have administration of any estate that may have been his father's William Knowlton. Dated Wenham, Dec. 5, 1715.

*Essex Co. Probate Files, Docket 16,099.*

## Estate of Rev. Nathaniel Rogers of Ipswich.

"The last will and testament of M$^r$ Nathaniel Rogers Pastour of the Church of Christ at Ipswich, as was taken from his owne mouth July 3. Anno Dom: 1655. Concerning my outward estate. To one of the brethren I have left a peculiar charge, which he shall have power in himselfe to doe, and not to suspend. The summe of my estate both in Old England, and New, seemes to amount to about y$^e$ value of twelve hundred pound; of which sume, foure hundred pound is expected from my father M$^r$ Robert Crane in England. To my sonne John, to prevent expectation of a double portion, I have not so bequeathed; he hath never beene by any labour serviceable to to his brethren, but hath beene upheld by their labour, & paine, while he hath beene determining his way. Therefore I giue and bequeath to him an equall portion with his other brethren, viz, y$^e$ sume of one hundred pound of my estate in Old England, and one hundred pound of my estate in New England. To my sonne Nathaniel I give & bequeath y$^e$ sume of one hundred pound out of my estate in Old England; & one hundred pound out of my estate in New England. To my sonne Samuel I giue & bequeath y^e sume of one hundred pound out of my estate in Old England; & one hundred pound out of my estate in New England. To my sonne Timothy I give & bequeath y^e sume of one hundred pound out of my estate in Old England; & one hundred pound out of my estate in New England. To my sonne Ezekiel I give & bequeath the sume of twenty pound, which he shall have liberty to take in my bookes, if he please.

"To my daughter I have already given her at least two hundred pound. The time of y^e childrens receiving their portions either in part, or whole, shall be according to y^e mutuall advice of my Executours, with these godly friends named, viz, my Cousin M^r Ezekiel Rogers, Mathew Boyes, Ezekiel Cheever, who are entreated to advise & counsell in this, & any other case as need shall require. To my three grandchildren, John, Nathaniel, Margaret Hubbard, I give & bequeath to each of them y^e sume of fourtie shillings. To my Cousin John Rogers I give & bequeath the sume of five pound, which is in y^e hands of Ensigne Howlett. To the children of my Cousin John Harris of Rowley, viz, Elizabeth, Nathaniel, John, Mary, I give & bequeath to each y^e sume of twenty shillings.

"To Mary Quilter my maidservant I give y^e sum of three pound. To Sarah ffillybrowne my other maidservant I give y^e sume of ten shillings. To Harbert Colledge in Cambridge I give & bequeath y^e sume of five pounds. To y^e poore I give the sume of three pound. The remaining part of my estate not yet disposed of, I give & bequeath to my deare wife M^rs Margaret Rogers during her life, & after her decease to be equally distributed among my children, by y^e advice of the friends above named. I do ordaine & constitute my deare & beloved wife M^rs Margaret Rogers, and my trusty & welbeloved friends M^r Robert Paine, and John Whipple to be Executours of this my last will, & testament."

Proved in Ipswich court 25: 7: 1655 by M. Ezekell Chever and Dea. John Whipple.

Inventory taken Aug. 16, 1655, by Robert Lord and Moses Pengry: in the Hall: a round table with five joine stooles, 16s.; six chaires & five cushions, 1li.; a trunke, chest & hanging cupboard, 1li. 1s.; 2 spanish platters, 5s.; a small cisterne with other implemts, 17s.; a corslet, musket & fowling peece, 3li.; a p of cobirons & tounges, 7s. In the

Parlour: a short table & a forme, 19s.; 6 cushion stooles & 2 chaires, 2li.; a livery cuphoard, 15s.; a featherbed, boulster, 2 downe pillowes, coverlet, blanket & canopy bedstead, 6li. 18s.; a great chaire, 6s.; 2 pictures, 2li.; a clocke & other implemts, 3li.; a p of Endirons, firepan & toungs, 13s.; 2 window Curtaines & rods, 10s.; a carpet, cuphoard cloth & round table, 1li. 5s.; a treble violl, 10s. In the kitchin: 5 Iron pots & 1 old brasse pot, 2li.; a copper kettell & 2 other old kettells, 4li. 10s.; 3 spitts, p of cobirons, firepan & toungs, forke, tramells & Irons, 1li. 16s. 8d.; a copper & five skillets, 2li. 15s.; 4 brasse candlesticks & a chafing dish, 15s.; a baking pan & a small old kettell, 6s.; 2 pudding-pans, stewing pan & dripping pan, 5s.; a warming pan, mortar & ladle, 10s.; pewter, 153li. 1-2 at 16d. ℔ li., 10li. 4s. 8d.; a Jacke, pothookes & other implemts, 1li.; a kneading trough, tubs & other lumber, 10s.; a trevet [fryeing. *copy*.] pan, 6s.; gally-basine, [glasses. *copy*] & other implemts, 16s.; chafing dish, bedpan & other implemts, 14s. Cellar: [6 beere barrells. *copy*], powdering tubs, 2 leads, [4 trayes a cheese *copy*] presse, beere stalls & some lumber, 4li. 4s. In the Chamber: [a bedsted, curtaines, valencs. *copy*], fetherbed, boulster [mattriss, blanketts, Rugg, flock. *copy*] bolster, 2 downe pillows, 14li. 10s.; [a chest of drawers. *copy*] 2li. 10s.; [a trunke, 3 cushon. *copy*], chaires, 2 stooles, 2li. 14s.; [a sute of greene. *copy*], curtaines & vallence, 1li. 1s.; [3 carpets. *copy*], 3li.; a cuphoard cloth, 1li. 10s.; 2 window cushions, 1li.; a perpetuany coverlet, 1li. 5s.; a carpet, 2 window curtaines & rods, 16s.; a gilt looking-glasse, 6s. 8d.; a chidding wicker basket, 3s.; a table-basket, 2s.; a p of Endirons & toungs, 6s. 8d.; a suit of diaper table linnen, 4li.; another suite of diaper linnen, 2li. 15s.; a diaper cupboard cloth, 1li. 5s.; 2 p of holland sheets, 3li. 10s.; 5 fine pillowbers, 1li. 15s.; p of pillowbers, 12s.; 2 cuphoard cloths & a p of sheets, 1li. 13s.; 23 napkins, 1li. 6s. 10d.; a diaper cuphoard cloth, 10s.; a holland cuphoard cloth, 8s.; 3 holland table cloths, 1li. 5s.; 4 p sheets, 4li. 10s.; 3 towells & a short table cloth, 10s.; a p of pillowbers, 7s.; goods out of England, 21li. 6s. 8d.; 3 p stockins, 1li. 1s. 8d. In ye Hall Chamber: one bedstead & cord, 16s.; curtaines & vallance, 1li. 5s.; a fetherbed & boulster, 4li. 10s.; a flocke bolster & 2 downe pillows, 1li. 2s.; a yellow rugge, 2li.; in English goods, 16li.; 1 p sheets, 15s.; 6 cushions, 1li. 10s.; a couch & an old coverlet, 7s.; in plate, 35li. 18s.; a watch, 4li.; one chest with a drawer, 16s.; 6 cushions, 24s., a curtain & 2 rods, 5s., 1li. 9s.; 6 yds. of Satteniscoe, 1li.; 7 p of old sheets, 3li. 3s.; 2 p course pillowbers, 10s.; 2 small trunkes with old boxes, 10s.; a chaire, trundle bed & litle flockbed, 16s. 6d.; a bedsted, flockbed, coverlet & blanket old, 1li. 17s. In ye Garret over ye Parlour: one bedsted & cord, bed & bolster, 2 old rugs, 4li. 2s.; one chaire, 1s. 2d. In ye Study: his Library, 100li.; a cabinet deske & 2 chaires, 1li. 5s.; a p of creepers & p of toungs, 2s. 6d. In ye chamber over ye Kitchin: 2 flockbeds, blanket, old coverlet, fether boulster & flocke bolster, 3li. [10s. *copy*]; 2 bedsteds & old rug [12s. *copy*], wearing apparrell, [16li. *copy*], wheat & barley in ye barne 20 [200 bushels, 40li. *copy*]; Indian corne 160 bush. at [2s. 6d., 20li. *copy*]; malt 4 bush., 18s.; 2 bush & 1-2 of rye, 10s.; wooll & old caske, [8s. *copy*]; 2 horses, 2 mares, one very old, 2 colts, 6—li. [64li. *copy*]; 7 oxen, 6 cowes, [66li. 13s. 4d. *copy*], 2 yearlings & 2 calves [6li. *copy*]; 3 ewes, 2 lambs, one wether, 9li.; swine, 8li.; 6 acres of Indian corne on ye ground, 9li.; 14 acres of upland & meadow at Mr. Epses, 14li.; ye farme where Good. Cumins is, 130li.; 15 acres on ye Comon, 10li.; ye house & land in Edw. Chapmans hand with ye pasture adjoyning, 120li.; Carts, ploughs & furniture, 4li.; Marsh in ye hundreds, 8li.; ye Dwelling house, Barnes & Orchard & 24 acres of land in comon feild, 200li.; in good debts, 50li.; In old England in Mr. Robert Crane, senior's hand, 400li.; total, 1497li. 12s. 4d.

*Essex Co. Probate Files, Docket 24,042.*

Nathaniell Rogers of Ipswich bequeathed to his son Timothy Rogers of Boston 100li. to be paid out of his estate at Ipswich and he sold his legacy to Mr. William Hubbard of Ipswich and acquits the executors from the payment of the same to any save Mr. Wm. Hubbard. Dated Feb. 5, 1667. Witness: Will. Pateeson, Thomas Dewer. *Ipswich Deeds, vol. 3, page 88.*

### Estate of Joseph Boovey of Lynn.

Administration on the estate of Joseph Boovey granted 27: 9: 1655 to Daniell Salmon. *Salem Quarterly Court Records, vol. 4, leaf 2.*

Ordered 24: 4: 1656 that Mr. Holliock be paid for funeral charges of Joseph Boovey by Danll. Sallmon, administrator, in merchantable wheat. *Salem Quarterly Court Records, vol. 4, leaf 6.*

### Estate of John Bridgman of Salem.

"The will of John bridgman is this that his whole estate shal bee deliuered into m$^r$ curwins hand and when hee hath satisfied him selfe to giu the rest to his daughter."

       his mark   his mark   her mark
Witness: Joseph S boice, Tomes T Averi, Josia X Suthick. *Essex Co. Quarterly Court Files, vol. 3, leaf 31.*

The imperfect will of John Bridgman presented 29: 9: 1655 and Mr. George Corwine appointed administrator. *Salem Quarterly Court Records, vol. 4, leaf 2.*

Mr. George Corwine brought in inventory of estate of John Bridgman 24: 4: 1656. Amount, 44li. 14s. 9 3-4d. The estate to go to said Bridgman's child. *Salem Quarterly Court Records, vol. 4, leaf 7.*

Inventory taken 8: 8: 1655, by Walter Price and Phillip Cromwell: One petticott and wascott, 2li. 5s.; one pr. of brichis and a pr. stokins, 6s.; in woollen and Cotten yaren, 8s.; a Chest, 10s.; 3 blak hatts and a straw hatt, 18s.; a looking glas, a hand baskett and a pot with starch, 3s.; a warming pan, 7s.; one pr. sheets and 3 ould sheets, 1li.; in smale lining, 1li.; a greene ould aprne, a box & a Chest, 10s.; a settle, 5s., an ell canvas, 2s., hops, 8d., 7s. 8d.; a flok bed boulster, 2 pillos, a pr. blankets & 2 Ruggs, 5li.; 5 yds. narrow teek, 12s.; a Curtten and Rod, 5s.; a muskett, sword, bandylers & Rest, 1li. 11s.; in wooden wares in his seller, 12s.; a bible, a psalme booke, 4s.; a pr. dogs, hangers, shovells & tongs & gridiron, 15s.; a friing pann, 16d.; a pr. bellows, 8s. 2d.; a pr. ould boots, 5s.; in severall Iron tooles, 30s.; ould Iron and Iron lumber, 10s.; a smoothing Iron, 20d., 3 pichforks, 3s., 4s. 8d.; 3 bras kittls, 28s., and a spitt, 12d., 1li. 9s.; 2 skilletts, an Iron pott & kittle, 15s.; ould pewter and 2 pewter dishes, 6s. 8d.; 4 ould Chayers, 4s., erthen wares, 7s., 11s.; trayes, seeves, payles & other wodden lumber, 14s.; rayles and ould knives, 2s., an ould Chest, 12d., 3s.; hemp and hurds, 10s., canvas, 3s., 13s.; Cask and a wheele and a Chest, 7s.; corne in the house, 8s.; an ould trundle bedsteed, 5s.; 2 sneads, 2s.; haye and Corne uppon the ground, 4li.; beefe, 45s., garden roots, 5s., 2li. 10s.; a kow and Calfe, 5li.; one house and 15 acres ground and marsh, 25li.; a yeong best, 2li.; Fowles, 5s.; 1li. of powder, 2s.; 2 swine, 2li.; 3 yeong shoats, 1li. 1s.; severall depts dew to him, 2li. 10s. 7d.; total, 69li. 7s. 7d. Debtor to Mr. Curwen for several Accts., 22li. 10s. 5 1-4d.; remayning, 46li. 17s. 1 3-4d. Debts due Mr. Will. Browne, 1s.; Tho. Cuttller, 2s. 4d.; Samuell Cuttller, 7s. 6d.; Mr. Stillman, 1s. 6d.; for Indian corne, 1li. 10s.; total, 2li. 2s. 4d. John Bridgman, creditor by John Neale, 7 dayes work, 14s.; Goodman Lawes for 2 dayes, 4s.; Goodman Browne, 9 dayes worke, 18s.; Mr. Carwythy, 4s.; Ann Potter, 1 bush. 1-2 Indyan, 3s. 9d.; Josyas Sutheke, 6s. 10d.; total, 2li. 10s. 7d.

The debts and what is coming to John Bridgman: "Owing to Goodman Scuder and befe, 2s. 3d., for a pound of salt and he hath paid six pigeons and he hath wrought 7 or 8 days for John Neile and too days work for goodman Laws owing to Elias Stileman, 3s., to frances colins hee hath don nine days work of goodman Browne and is to be payd there, owing to Goodman Rumbal, 3s.; Mr. Carwithe oweth him, 4s., owing to farmer porter, 4s., ana poter oweth a bushel and half of indian corn, Josiah Suthick oweth him 6s. 10d."

*Essex Co. Quarterly Court Files, vol. 3, leaf 31.*

### ESTATE OF REBECCA BACON OF SALEM.

"The last will and Testyment of Rebekah Bacon wido writen the 23 of the i mon 1655 Know all men by thes presants that I make and Constetut my sonn Isaac Bacon my sole Aer and Exsequtor of my whole estat paying all my Detts and leguses that I shall giue Joyning with him Robert Buffam for to be his asistans That hee may haue noo power to lett or sell any thing with out his Consent untell hee Come to age Im: I giue unto my Cossen Anne potter and my Cossen Richard Cherlcraft the 3 Acers of ground at the towne: And the mash ground in the south feeld: And: 2 Cowes: And to Richerd to sheep: And the ||second|| Coltt that the young mare doth bring for his partickqulor benefit And to Cossen anne: and Richerd: the Bead and Bead steed and all the things belongin to it as I Comenly ley upon it exsepting the sheets And I giue unto them: on pare of the best sheets And halfe a dusen of napkins strekt with blue and the table Cloth belongin unto the Round table And to fine touells: on pillobere:

"And: a thurd part of all the bras exsepting the great Coper Cettell: And a thurd part of all the puter and widden houshold stuff: And ech of them a siluer spune And the are to haue halfe the profit that the house and land doth produse toward manetaning of them untell my sonn Come to age: for my desier is that Richerd shall be at my Cossen Anne disposing  And if my sonn shuld dey Befoer hee Come to Age then the whole estat is to Return to my to Cossens exsepting 10$^{11}$: that shall be giuen in sheep for the good of the poer of salem to be disposed by the 7 men a Cording as my desier is that 5$^{11}$ to a man for 7 years And then to pay the 5$^{11}$ Backe to the 7: men to be giuen to: other to poer men for 7 yere moer and so to be giuen from 7 yer to seuen yer to euer

"And if my Cossen Anne dey befoer shee marry then all that I giue hur is to Return to Richard: And if Richard dey that all that I gaue him is to Return to Anne if the both shuld dey with out Ishue then all is to return to my sonn: And if it please the lord to take them all a way before the ar marred and with out Ishue that then the whol estat is to Return to the towne to be dissposed of acording to the former 10$^{11}$ exsepting: 5$^{11}$: a pees that the exsequtor and ouer serers ar to haue out of it  Im: I giue to my man Cornelus all his time freely and ayerling to by him a shutt of Clothes

"I giue to my sister Buffam: my black scarfe And to sister boys my green gown and Red pety cott and to sister sughtwike the black goune and on pety Cote and to sister Auery and hornis each of them a neck hancercho: And all the Rest of my weareing aparell I leue at the dissposing of my Cossen Anne to giue to Abegall what shee see fit: my desier is that my Brother Roberd Buffam shuld Com and dwell in the howse if hee see good and in proue the land and estate left my sonn and a lowe for it what hee shall Judg it worth: And my sonn to liue with him if hee haue a mind to follo husbandry or els to plase him a prentis to some onist seayman I freely dispose of an acker of land w$^{ch}$ Joynes to Captain Trasks meedow, for ye vse of Ann Potter tell such time Isack comes to age  I giue unto Brother Buffam the first Colt that the maer shall bring.  I make and ordane my Brother Jouise Boys and Brother Thomas Auery and Brother nathanell feltonn my ouer seers: And giue unto them: 40$^s$ a pees: The greatest Deat is 3$^{11}$ to be returnd to old England to my sister Judeth that I desier may be donn with speed I giue to my Cossen Jorg Bedell one of the swords ‖which my sonn will‖ and one of Doctor sebes works and on of Docter prestons.  This is my last act and will wittnes my hand and seale."

Rebekah Bacon.

"The mayre being Sould where of goodman buffam should haue y$^e$ 1 Coult y$^t$ came of her I freely dispose of a Steere called lustick at 3 yeares end, In lue of y$^e$ Coult."
  his mark
Witness: Henry H Trask, Geor. Beadle. *Essex Co. Quarterly Court Files, vol. 3, leaf 37.*
Proved 29: 9: 1655 by the witnesses. *Salem Quarterly Court Records, vol. 4, leaf 2.*

Inventory taken July 10, 1655, by Thomas Gardner, sr., and Joseph (his O mark) Boyce, and sworn to by Robt. Buffum: The house, lands, 50li.; 2 oxen, 13li.; 4 Cowes, 17li.; a steere, 5li. 12s.; 2 yearelings, 4li.; 1 Calfe, 1li.; 12 ewe sheepe, 20li.; 2 wetheres, 1 ram, 2li. 5s.; 4 ewe lambes, 1 wether lamb, 4li.; 5 Swine, 3li.; 2 1-2 acres of wheat growinge, 4li.; 5 acres of Indian Corne, 7li. 10s.; Cart & plow & plow geare, 1li. 10s.; 2 sawes, 10s.; 2 Andirons, 4s.; 2 axes, 1 mattocke, 1 crow, 8s.; 2 smothinge Irons, 3s.; 3 payre of pothooks, 1 gridiron & a fryinge pan, 5s.; 4 ould hous, 2 spits, 7s.; 4 plowes, 4 chissels, 1 gouge & 2 hammers, 5s.; 1 hand saw, 2 bitlerings, 1 vice, 1 iron sole, 2 smal wedges, 1 hay knife, 8s.; old Iron, 4s.; an Iron pestle & morter, 7s.; 1 payre of Andirons, 1 payre of tongs & a hake, 5s.; 1 Iron Pot, 5s.; 2 brasse Pots, 12s.; 4 brasse skillets, 7s.; 1 Copper Ketle, 2li. 10s.; 4 brasse candlesticks, a brasse skimmer, a payre of skales & a pot lid, a litle brasse pan & an old warminge Pan, 10s.; 1 Musket wth a fire locke, 2 swords, a payre of bandeliers, 2 bolts, 1 pocket pistol, 2 pike heads & a halfe pike, 2li. 10s.; 3 fether beds, 6li.; 2 Rugs, 2li.; 3 old blankets, 15s.; Curtaynes & vallons for 2 beds, 2li. 10s.; 1 flock bed & coveringe, 1li. 5s.; 9 payre of sheetes, 8li.; 8 Pillow beares, 16s.; 4 table clothes, 23 napkins streked wth blue, 6 fine Napkins, 8 fine towels, 3 Cubbard Cloathes, 6 course towels & 1 shirt, 4li. 8s.; 4 silke Cushions, 2 made, 2 unmade, 3 old cushions, 4 Carpets, 2li.; 1 duble salt silver, 6 silver spones, 1 wine cup & a dram cup of silver, both, 6li.; 3 large peuter platters, 3 a size lesse, 3 more a size lesse, 3 more a size lesse, 1li. 16s.; 1 peuter bason, 5s.; 6 large peuter plates & 6 lesser, 9s.; 19 Peuter saucers & 2 fruite dishes, 11s. 6d.; 1 old Peuter bason & a great plate, 3s.; 2 peuter candlesticks, 4s.; 1 large peuter salt & a smal one, 2 peuter porringers, 3s. 6d.; 1 great peuter flagon, 1 lesser, 1 quart, 2 pints & a halfe pinte, 13s.; 2 old chamber pots & an old porringer, 3s.; 2 great truncks, 1 smal truncke, 1li.; 1 great chest & 4 lesser, 1li. 2s.; A Cabinet, 5s.; 3 Bibles, a Concordance, Calvins Institutions, Luther upon the Galathians, Mr. Shepards Morality of the Sabath, Nicolas Gibbins Disputations, Joshua Symonds bookes, 2 of Dr. Sibs & 1 of Mr. Preston, Markam & 10 smal bookes, 2li.; 4 framed Chaires, 2 wyned Stooles, 14s.; 2 high bedsteds & 2 lower ones, 1li.; 1 longe table, 1 round table & a litle table, 16s.; 1 Cubbord, 2 smal barrels, 2 botles, 2 payles, 10s.; 1 looking glasse, a sun dyal & a case of botles with 5 glasses, a table basket, 5s.; 4 dry caske, 4s.; her wearinge apparrel, 5li.; an old sadle & pillyan cloth, 10s.; 12lb. of wool & 5 lb. of yarne, 1li. 13s.; toal, 195li. 8s. 6d. *Essex Co. Quarterly Court Files, vol. 3, leaf 38.*

### Estate of William Goodridge of Watertown.

Bond of Joseph Jewett of Rowley, merchant, for 200li. to pay to John Hull of Newbury, yeoman, 20li. 12s. 6d. yearly during his life in one beast, three firkins of butter, and the remainder in half wheat and half mault. If John Hull shall depart this life before Margarett his wife then he to pay Margarett or her assigns, 8li. yearly during her life, in one firkin of butter and the rest in half wheat and half mault. If the said Margarett after the decease of her husband shall require the thirds of the farm then the engagement of Joseph Jewett to pay 8li. yearly during her life to be void. If she should die before her husband then the said John to have but 12li. 12s. 6d. yearly during his life. Signed and sealed 6: 1: 1656, by Joseph Jewett. Witness: John Bond, Henry Lunt.

Acknowledged by Joseph Jewett before the Commissioners for Newbury, Mar. 6, 1656. John Pike, Nicholas Noyes. *Ipswich Deeds, vol. 1, leaf 199.*

Bond of Edward Woodman, jr. of Newbury, yeoman, for 200li. to Henry Shortt of Newbury, yeoman, (for the use of John Hull of Newbury), to maintain the "like stock" upon the farm which he bought of John Hull, during the life of the said John Hull, and also to pay all debts and legacies expressed as follows: To Jerimy Goodridge five pounds, which is his portion at twenty one years of age, and five pounds more as a gift from his father-in-law, John Hull one year after his youngest brother's portion is due; and Joseph Goodridge ten pounds at twenty one as above, after the decease of his father and mother fifteen pounds more;

and to Benjamine Goodridge at twenty one, three cows, two steers and after the death of his father and mother five pounds more (provided he acquits Edward Woodman of a cow & her increase which is upon the farm), which if he refuses to do he is to have but ten pounds in all, and to keep the housing & fences belonging to the farme in repair. Signed Apr. 15, 1656 by Edward Woodman. Witness: James Chute, Edward Woodman, sr.

Acknowledged by Edward Woodman Apr. 15, 1656 before Daniel Denison. *Ipswich Deeds, vol. 1, leaf 172.*

Bond of Joseph Jewett of Rowley to John Hull of Newbury, to pay five pounds, which is the portion of Jerimy Goodridge at twenty-one years of age, and five pounds more to said Jerimy as a gift one year after his youngest brother's portion was due; and unto Joseph Goodridge, ten pounds at twenty-one as above, from his father-in-law, John Hull; and to Benjamin Goodridge, at twenty-one, three cows, two steers and five pounds in money. Dated, Apr. 1, 1658. Wit: Robert Lord, Thomas Lord and Thomas Wood. Acknowledged in Ipswich court, Mar. 30, 1658. *Ipswich Quarterly Court Records, vol. 11, page 42.*

Bond of Edmond Moores of Newbury, husbandman, for 200li. to John Hull of Newbury, yeoman, to pay him 20li. 12s. 6d. yearly, during life, in one beast, three firkins of butter and the remainder in half wheat and half mault. If he die before his wife, Margarett, to pay her yearly, 8li. during her life, in one firkin of butter and the rest in half wheat and half mault. But if she should require the thirds of the farm then this to be void. Signed and sealed July 1, 1661. Witness: Robbert (his mark) Adams, James Chute and Richard Dole. Acknowledged July 2, 1661 before Daniel Denison. *Ipswich Deeds, vol. 2, page 31.*

Bond of Edmond Mores of Newbury, husbandman, for 200li. to John Hull of Newbury, to pay to him 5li. in cattle, which is the portion of Jerimy Goodridge at twenty-one years of age, and 5li. more in like pay as a gift from his father-in-law, John Hull one year after his youngest brother's portion is due; and to Joseph Goodridge 10li. in like pay at twenty-one as above, and after the death of his father and mother 15li. more; and to Benjamyn Goodridge at twenty-one, three cows, two steers and after the death of his father and mother 5li. more. Signed and sealed July 1, 1661. Witness: Robert (his mark) Addams, James Chute, Richard Dole.

John (his mark) Hull acknowledged July 2, 1661 the receipt of the first 5li. of the portion of Jerimy Goodridge, and Joseph Goodridge the receipt of 10li., the first pay of his portion. *Ipswich Deeds, vol. 2, page 29.*

Petition to the Ipswich court Apr. 10, 1683, of Jeremiah Goodridge and Joseph Goodridge of Newbury shewing that William Goodridge, their father, deceased, intestate, leaving four children and a competent estate which came into the hands of their mother Margarett Goodridge (though having searched the records we cannot find either will or administration granted) and their mother afterwards married John Hull and the whole estate was conveyed to him: the said John Hull dying left a competent estate to their mother Margarett Hull, who lately dying left (as we understand) all the estate to their brother Benjamin Goodridge: now we ask for your consideration of our just claim to adjust and allot to us what you think may be right of the estate and if there appear any will to the contrary to consider whether it may not be rejected when it seems to carry such injury to your petitioners. Signed Jeramiah Goodridg, Joseph Goodridg. *Essex Co. Quarterly Court Files, vol. 39, leaf 88.*

### Estate of Henry Sewall, Sr. of Rowley.

Mr. Henry Sewall, sr., late of Rowley, died intestate, leaving an estate of about 300li., and his son and heir, Mr. Henry Sewall, was in England, the latter having made Henry Short of Newbury his attorney. Administration granted Mar. 25, 1656, to Mr. Short, who was ordered to lease or use the house and land. *Ipswich Quarterly Court Records, vol. 1, page 54.*

Inventory taken by Joseph Jewett, Mathew Boyes and John Tod: Wearing clothes with sum stufe and cloth, 9li.; Pots and kettles, peutar and bras, 12li. 2s. 6d.; A standig, a case and botles, 6s.; two beds and beding, 12li. 15s.; lining with som cotan blankits and shirts, 15li. 3s. 7d.; a stuing pan, a crow and a saw, 14s.; A Jack and old Iran, 2li. 5s.; thre knives, twine, stele, butons, 5s. 6d.; A sadle and two bridles, storaps and lethers, 1li. 13s. 6d.; four spits, an apron and A drom, 2li. 1s. 6d.; Cortens and vallans and thre quishings, 18s.; a grater and a case with Botles, 7s.; a sword, a belt and bandeleres, 1li.; slings, hookes and eys, 5s. 6d.; a gridg Iron, a clock, bag and old lining, 8s.; a portmantle, two sives, 6s.; poudar and 2 brushes, 6s.; two dozen of fish hookes, 4s.; thre lockes, a box, two cords, 4s.; a Reape Hoke, 1s.; a box, a dosan of spoones, 8s. 6d.; a stomacher, bookes, sceales, a beame and weights, 17s.; a cock, bullits and files, 5s. 8d.; sisers, a bodkin and small things, 2s. 6d.; a salt box, a table, forme and a Cubert, 11s.; a cup, a spoone and a friing pan, 3s.; an axe and trenchers, 3s. 10d.; chairs and a bible, 1li. 3s.; shovells, tonges and poyte, 8s. 6d.; Mace and Ribing, starch and poudarblu, 3s. 8d.; a chist and thre caps, four yards of Cambrick, 1li. 11s.; a lether case, a coyfe and butons, 1s. 10d.; a tronk, a westcote and other things, 4s.; shears, a dagar, an axe, 4s. 6d.; a bag and pepar and a knapsack, 4s.; an iron fork, a rest and five gunes, 2li. 1s. 2d.; bellas, one pair, two tosting Irons, 3s. 6d.; an Iron bar and two tramills, 4s.; a pot of butter, 3s.; a Jug and Shoo Horn and a chist, 1s. 7d.; a tunill and a basket, 1s.; a ladle, a spade, pinsors and a how, 4s.; a sickell, a hamar and a bell, 3s.; a peutar pot, a cloth and a male pillion, a racke, 2s. 4d.; two bands and a cup, a chair, a spit, a trouh, 13s. 6d.; two firkins, a scimar, a pott, a paire of Racks, 13s. 6d.; a booke and a hellar, a map, a spade, a scimar, 12s. 6d.; an axe, two candlesticks, a mattack, an axe, 1li. 8d.; a litle old lining and new, a tinder box, a bell, a clenzer, a scimar, with som old clothes, 1li. 5s. 6d.; four kows, 16li.; twenty thre shepe and a kalfe, 26li.; eight Acors of upland and nine gates, 14li.; the house barn, orchard, and the home lott, 60li.; the farme that Tho. pery dwells on, 70li.; the land at nubery neck, 70li.; total, 330li. 16s. 4d. Debts owing: To Goody Bradstreete for twelve wekes sorgary And taking payns in changing lining, he not being able to heelp himself in his bed, 10li.; to Mr. Carlton, 4li. 12s.; to Joseph Jowett, 7s. 4d.; to Mathew Boyse, 13s. 6d.; to Richard Swan for twelve weekes tendans and wood, washing and provision, 16li. 14s.; for writing, hellping to make up accounts and prizing goods, 9s. 6d.; to Lt. Reminton, 14s.; total, 33li. 10s. 5d.; to John Tod for cost at his buriall and Expences before his death and paying of sum small debts, 11li. 9s. *Essex Co. Quarterly Court Files, vol 3, leaf* 49.

Ordered Mar. 30, 1658, that Henry Short, administrator of Mr. Henry Sewall's estate, pay witnesses in Mr. Sewall's presentment. *Ipswich Quarterly Court Records, vol.* 1, *page* 66.

### Estate of John Ward of Ipswich.

"In y<sup>e</sup> name of god amen: I John Ward: sumtimes resident at Ipswich in new England doe make and ordaine this my Last will and testament for manner and forme as followeth, viz: for that temporall estate of monie goods or chattells: that It hath pleased god to Indow me with I dispose of as ffolloweth: Imprimis: vnto my Cousine m<sup>r</sup> Nathaniell: Ward the sun of my vncle Nathaniell ward I doe giue that house and Land giuen me by my father in his will and that Lies in east mersy in the County of essex in old england: Item to my vncle affores<sup>d</sup> I doe giue the rent and profits that haue Com of that tenement Since: I made Edmund Sharman of Deadham Last my atturney for the receiuing of it: they being in his or the tenants hands still: being next March two yy<sup>s</sup> and a halfe rent: Item I doe giue vnto my Cousine wards of wethersfeild two yongest Suns twentie pounds p peice: to be payd to them when they shall be of age: or one & twentie yeers  Item: I doe giue vnto my Cousine John Barkers eldest daughter: Anne Barker twenty pounds ||It is to be vnderstood John Barker of Boxted in Essex:|| Item I doe giue vnto Samuell Barker: My Cousine John Barkers Son ten pounds: both as sone as it may Conveniently be payd: allsoe I doe Giue ten pounds to my Mothers poore kindred: which I doe desier my Cousin John Barker to distribut as he shall thinke meete Item I doe Giue vnto my Cousine Samuell Sharmans two yongest suns ten pounds p peice: this is to be under stood of my Cousin: Sharman that died sum yeers since in Boston in new england: to be payd to them when they shall be on & twentie yeers by my executor or elce to be payd to them that haue now Care of them (they being Suffitient men) and Giuing bond for the payment of it to the children when they shall be of the age & p phipt

"Item I doe Giue ten pounds to my Cousin philip: Sharman of rood Iland:

"Item My bookes I doe Giue to Thomas Andrews of Ipswich and allsoe my Chirurgern chest and all y<sup>t</sup> is now in it

"Item It is my mind that my Linnen my Cousine Nathaniell ward should haue when he shall Com of age

"It to M<sup>r</sup> Robert Payne I doe Giue twentie pounds desiring him that he would take uppon him my executor shipe to receiue all my depts and Goods what euer and to pay or Cause to be payd the fore recited Leagusies: And there mainner of my Estate he would Lay out in a standing anuity which would haue bestowed uppon Haruard Collidg in Cambridg: and would haue it Improued to the Conuenient bringing up ‖and maintenance‖ of one or more Scollers in the sᵈ Collidg and only such to haue binifet whose estate or frinds cannot other wise maintaine

"It is my desier that the anuity Giuen before to the Collidg should be bought: in such a place and towne where it may be judged most sertaine But If: it: should please God to take me away out of this Naturall ‖life‖ in such a place wher I shall stand need of buriell (as uppon the Land) wher this my Will may be knowen: that then I would haue: fortie pounds bestowed uppon my funerall be fore and then the remainnder to bestowed in an annuety as afforesayd: and In wittnes here of I haue set to my hand and seale this 28ᵗʰ of December 1652."

John Ward.<br>his mark

Witness: Richard Shearman, Thomas + Spule.
Proved Mar. 25, 1656 by Mr. Robert Payne.

Inventory taken by Robert Lord and Mathew Boyes and sworn to in the court at Ipswich by Mr. Robert Payne, 25: 1: 1656: Debt due from Mr. Chute, 2li. 5s.; debt due from Mr. Epps, 6li.; from John Davis, 3li. 14s. 6d.; from Humfry Grifin, 13li. 15s.; by a wharfe morgaged to him by Thomas Lowe of Boston, 19li. 4s.; debt dewe from Thomas Spaule of Boston, 3li. 19s.; from Mr. Phillips of Boston, 36li. 15s. 6d.; from Thomas Haukins of Boston, 22li. 10s.; from Simon Tomson of Ipswich, 25li. 15s.; from John Anniball of Ipswich, 4li. 10s.; from John Johnson of Ipswich, 6li. 12s. 6d.; from Joseph Medcalfe of Ipswich, 12li. 7s. 6d.; from Robert Gutch of Salem, ———; from Samuell Podd of Ipswich, 23li.; from Mr. Powell of Boston, 17li.; small debts, 11li. 10s. 3d.; one old Baye mare with a fole, 17li.; one young mare with a fole, 18li.; two two yeares old mares, 22li.; one yeare old colt, 7li.; the Bald horse, 12li. 10s.; the Baye horse, 14li.; 2 cowes, 9li.; total, 308li. 7s. 3d.

*Essex Co. Quarterly Court Files, vol. 3, leaf 46.*

### ESTATE OF HUGH SMITH OF ROWLEY.

"The nienth moneth the nienteenth day in —1655 Bee it knowne vnto all men by these presents that I Hugh smith being sick in body but yet of perfect memorie doe make this my last will and Testament as in forme followeth Imp my will is that my wellbeloued wyfe Mary shall haue my estate all of it at her dispose for to prouyde for her self withall and to bring vp my Children while that she remayneth vnmaryed and in Case she see Cause to and haue an ofer of mariadge which shee shall accept then my will is that she shall haue her thirds of my estate: allso that she shall haue allowed her fiue pounds out of my estate towards the bringing vp of my youngest sonn: also my will is that my Children shall haue equall portions out of the resedue of my estate saue onely that my will is that my Eldest sonn sammuell smith shall haue half soe much more in portion as any other of my Children: and in witnes hereof I set to my hand the day and yeare aboue written:"

                                          his mark
                                 Hugh $\wedge$ smith
                         his mark

Witness: Thomas Dickanson, William W Jacson, John Trumble and John Pickard.

Proved in Ipswich court 25: 1: 1656.

Inventory taken 14: 10: 1655 by Joseph Jewett and Thomas Dickanson: one mare, 15li.; one ass, 4li. 10s.; foure sheep, 3li. 15s.; two oxen, 14li.; five Cowes, 19li.; one cow and a bull, 7li.; two heifers, 7li.; six calves, 9li.; one steer, 4li.; eight swyne, 6li. 10s.; house and barne and six acres of land and orchards, 40li.; seven acres of land and one half in batcheler plaine, 22li. 10s.; two acre and a quarter of land in the new plaine, 4li. 10s.; eleven acres of meadow, 20li.; foure gates for cattell, 4li.; one gate more, 1li.; wheat and Rye, 8li. 10s.; indian corne, 4li.; eleven score and fourteen pound of wooll, 14li. 12s.; thirtie pound of sheep wooll, 2li. 5s.; one payre of looms with tacklings thereto, 1li. 10s.; one musket and two swords and one pouch, 1li. 10s.; one great Coat, 1li. 10s.; one short coat, 6s. 8d.; one dublet, 12s.; one payre of Cloth brecthes, 8s.; one Jerkin, 12s.; one fustin dublet, 5s.; one short coat and a paire of brecthes of white Cloth, 10s.; one payre of boots, 17s.; one sute of leather, 18s.; one hat, 6s.; one fether bed and bed Clothes and a bed stead, 6li. 10s.; a trundell bed and clothes, 2li.; one rugg in the bay, 1li.; one warming pan, 8s.; a nother bed and clothes, 1li. 10s.; one cart and on plow and chayn, 3li.; hay, 4li.; kettells, pots, tubs, one churne and puter, 5li. 10s.; wheels, chayns and Cushins, 10s.; total, 234li. 11s. 8d.

Debts owing by Hugh Smith: to the children of goodie

Eletrop, 12li. 17s.; Mr. Jewit, 11li.; Elder Raynor, 11li.; John Tod for wooll, 10li.; John Tod for bear and cakes, 1li. 10s.; Thomas Wood for a cofin, 9s.; James Barker his apprentise, 5li.; total, 51li. 16s.

Mary the widow of Hugh Smith deposed 25: 1: 1656 to the truth of this inventory.

*Essex Co. Probate Files, Docket 25,549.*

Jeremiah Elsworth stated that upon his marriage with Mary Smith, he bound himself to Thomas Dickanson, John Pickard and Deacken Jewett, in the sum of two hundred pounds; bond, dated 26: 9: 1657. Wit: Joseph Jewett, Thomas Dickanson and John Tod; conditioned to pay their portions to Hugh Smith's children: viz: Samwell, Mary, Sara, Hannah, Marthay and Edward Smith. *Essex Co. Quarterly Court Files, vol. 3, leaf 127.*

Hugh Smith's estate not being yet divided by any who had power, the court, Mar. 26, 1667, appointed Maxemillian Jewett and Leift. Samuell Brocklebanke to divide the lands into three equal parts, that the said parties concerned in the will might have their proportions, the mother one-third and the children two-thirds. If they could not agree, the court was to determine. *Ipswich Quarterly Court Records, vol. 5, page 39.*

Maximilian Jewett, Leift. Samuell Brocklebanke and Ezekiell Northend, appointed at the first session of this court to make equal division of the lands that were Hugh Smith's, made return Apr. 30, 1667. But the parties concerned came into court and presented an agreement that may be as good for the children of said Smith, and court accepted it and confirmed the rest of the land to Jerimiah Elsworth. *Ipswich Quarterly Court Records, vol. 5, page 11.*

The agreement between Jerimiah Elsworth, Daniell Wickam and Leonard Hariman guardians to some of the children of Hugh Smith: Jerymiah Elsworth is willing that the two sons of Hugh Smith shall have their whole portions out of the lands of Hugh Smith according to the quantity in inventory, and proportions according to their father's will, and also all the houses and lands at home, and four acres of land at the Bachelour field and two cow gates, and all that division of marsh and upland at the end of it in the marsh feild to the path way, and one acre in the new plain at the east end of the land that was Hugh Smith's; also that what lands the said Hugh Smith was possessed of and not inventoried, and what hath been or is to be in any way added to his right, shall be devided among Hugh Smith's children, the mother having her thirds and the two thirds to be devided among the children according to their proportions in the will.

The Court Apr. 30, 1667, accepted of this agreement and the rest of the land confirmed to Jeremiah Elsworth. *Ipswich Deeds, vol. 3, page 36.*

Daniell Wicome of Rowley, carpenter, acknowledges the receipt from Jerimiah Elsworth of Rowley, his father-in-law, of 22li. 2s. 6d., which is the whole portion given to Mary his wife by her own father Hugh Smith. Signed and sealed Feb. 9, 1659, by Daniell Wickam. Witness. Richard Clarke, Nickolas Jackson.

Acknowledged by the witnesses Feb. 14, 1666. *Ipswich Deeds, vol. 3, page 23.*

### Estate of John Friend of Salem.

"The Last will & Testament of John ffreind made y$^e$ 4$^o$: of y$^e$ ii m$^o$: 1655  I John ffriend being weake & Sick of Bodie but of pfict Memory doe ordaine this as my Last will & testament  Imp$^{rs}$ I giue & bequeath unto my Sonn Samuell ffreinds a double portion out of my whole esate personall & Reall: Item I giue unto my daughter Elizabeth pecker: besides that tenn pownds I haue in my hands w$^{ch}$ her granfather gaue her, twente shillings  Item I giue & bequeath unto my other thre children Bethiah Hester & James, Equall portions one as much as y$^e$ other: & for y$^e$ better pformance of this my will I appoynt my Sonn Samuell to be my Executo$^r$, & desire & appoynt my Louing ffriends william Dodg & william King to be my ouerseers in witness whereof I haue hereunto set my hand y$^e$ day & yeer first above written." [No signature]

Witness: George Emery, Edmond grouer, Henry Hericke.

Proved 26: 1: 1656 by the witnesses. Allowed 27: 1: 1656. *Essex Co. Quarterly Court Files, vol. 3, leaf 47.*

Inventory taken 6: 12: 1655, by Roger Conant, John Raiment and Henry Hericke: the mill wth what belongs thereto as also the dwelling house & orchard & ground in all 2 akers, 120li.; 100 akers of ground being most of it rockie, at Manchester, 5li.; at Manchester 30 akers bought of Georg

Williams and 25 akers bought of Samuell Archer and a parsell of land at Kettel Iland cove, 10li.; at Manchester 2 akers salt marsh, 3li.; 20 akers of land bought of Nath. Holton living neere to John Bachelors dwelling, 4li.; 10 akers of land lying on darby fort side neer Forrest river, 2li.; half an aker land neer the buriing place at Salem, 2li.; 3 cows & a heifer, 18li.; a yew, a yew lamb & a wether, 4li. 10s.; 4 swine, 4li. 15s.; a feather bedd & 2 feather bolsters & 2 feather pilloes and a blew & a red rugg, 7li. 10s.; a flockbed & bolster & two blankets the on woollen the other cotten, wth an old rugg & blanket, 1li. 10s.; a bedd of flock & feathers, a fether bolster & 2 blankets, 3li.; 2 paire of sheets the finer at 25s. the courser at 12s., 1li. 17s.; a peece of nu tiking 3 yards & 1-2, 11s. 8d.; 4 pillobies of fine hollan, 1li. 6s.; 2 yards diap. & 3 diap. napkins, 10s.; a cloth sute of kersie, 2li. 10s.; a womans gown of kersie, 2li.; another gown of mild sea, 2li. 10s.; ——— nans hood, 7s.; a doubbell cusshion, 2s. 6d.; 6 great puter platters, 1li. 16s.; 2 old broken puter platters, 3s.; 6 Saucers of wch 2 bigger & 2 middell & 2 least, 5s.; 2 puter cand[l]esticks & a salt, 6s.; a broken quart & pint & littel cup & funnell, a lattin quart & 3 paint dishes, 4s.; a smoothing Iron, 2s.; 3 brasse potts & a brass skillet, 2li.; 3 brasse kittels being old, 1li.; a brasse posnet, 10s.; a chafing dish, a pestell and morter and a littel brasse ladell, 6s.; a warming pan, 3s.; a clock, 2li. 10s.; pothoocks, croocks, hoocks, & hangers, a fier shovel & tongs, a friing pan & spitt, 14s.; a fowling peec and a pistoll, 1li. 10s.; a sword and belt, 10s.; working tooles, 1li. 3s.; chests, bedsteeds, tubs & barrels, tabels and chairs, 1li.; Indian corne 80 busshels, 10li.; 3 saws of wch 2 whipsaws & on crosscut, 1li. 4s.; 2 akers of fresh meado at Topsfeild, 5li.; total, 227li. 10s. 2d. In mony, 2s.

Samuell Frend, executor, testified in Ipswich court 25 : 1 : 1656 that the above was a true inventory. *Essex Co. Probate Files, Docket* 10,208.

### Estate of Thomas Dowe of Haverhill.

"The last will and Testament of Thomas dowe as it was deleuerd or expressed by him on the 29th day of may being in ye yeare 1654 I Thomas dowe although weake in body yet of perfect memory I doe desire to submit my will to gods will and to dispose of my estate to my wife and children as followeth leaueing my wife to be the sole excecutor at present of all my vesable and personall estate first I do giue vnto my louing wiffe Pheby my tow oxen that are now hers and mine and three young beastes beinge now one yeare and vp wards ould and on cow: and tow swine and al my housould goods to be at her disposinge for euer. Also my will is that my eldest son named John dowe at the age ofe twenty and on yeare ould shal in ioy as his inherytanc al the land and housinge that I haue bought in hauerhill ‖and to‖ pay in to his other bro Thomas and Steuen and to his 2 sisters mary and martha as I shall a poynt The house and land being thought to be worth threescore pounds: my second son Thomas shal reseaue at his age of 21 ten pounds or 5 pounds at his age and 5 pounds when he is 22 years and for my son Steeuen he shal haue ten pounds payd him at his age of 21: or 5 pounds at 21 and 5 pound at 22: as lo my will is that John my son shal pay his sister mary and his sister martha at theyre age of 21 ‖ten pound‖ or 5 pounds a peace at 21 and 5 pounds a pece at ther age of 22: as there brothers reseaue theres Also I Pheaby latly wife to thomas dow doe ioyne ‖my‖ consent to this wil of my husband in each pertecular and for my son John dow I doe fully and freely resigne vp all my wright in the house and land when my son shal com to the age of 21 yeares ould wittnes my hand prouided he shal pay to his brothers and sisters as his fathers will is."

her mark<br>
phebya P dowe

Witness: John Eaton, Theo shatswell.
Proved in Salisbury court 8: 2: 1656 by the witnesses.

Inventory taken by John (his F mark) Eaton, James (his V mark) Davis, sr. and Theo. Shatswell: within his house: in brase, 1li. 13s. 4d.; pewter, 3s. 6d.; beddinge, 5li.; linon, 10s.; bedsteeds, 6s. 8d.; in cowpery ware, 16s.; Spining Wheles, 5s.; earthern ware, 1s. 6d.; Iron wares, 2li. 4s.; stooles and things of use, 5s.; his own wearing a parell, 3li.; bookes, 15s.; a gun, 9s. And of his estate abroade: In land the whole fee simple being five acors of acomadashon and 2 such persele of medow, 52li. 10s.; tow oxen, 16li.; on cow, 5li.; 3 eayrling catell, 5li.; 2 Swine, 2li. Total, 95li. 19s.

*Essex Co. Probate Files, Docket* 8,235.

## ESTATE OF JOHN JACKSON, SR. OF SALEM.

"The Last will and Testament of Ino Iackson sen beeinge

in pfect memory make 31 — 11: 1655. Imp$^{rs}$: I bequeath to my wife Mary Iackson fiue pounds sterlinge. Ite I bequeath to margarett Neue thirty shillings. Ite I Constitute & apoynte my Dea[r]ly beloued son ‖In°‖ Iackson my sole Executor  Ite I apoynte M$^r$ Willm Browne and Edmo: Batter: my Ouseers."

his mark<br>Ino. X Iackson.

his mark
Witness: William  I N  Browne, Thomas Smith and Edmond Batter.

Proved —: 4m: 1656. *Essex Co. Quarterly Court Files, vol. 3, leaf 52.*

The executor refused to serve, and administration was granted to said William Browne and Edmond Batter. *Salem Quarterly Court Records, vol. 4, leaf 7.*

Inventory taken 10: 1: 1655-6, by James (his I N mark) Inderwood and Thomas Smith: One small feather bed, 16s.; 1 Coppr. Kitle, 1li. 10s.; 2 Acres of Salt Marsh, 9li.; 1 Cowe, 4li.; 1 yewe sheepe, 3li. 10s.; 1 Greene Rugge, 1li. 10s.; total, 20li. 6s. *Essex Co. Quarterly Court Files, vol. 3, leaf 52.*

## Estate of Thomas Wickes of Salem.

"The Last will & Testament of Thomas Wickes of Salem made y$^e$ 9: 7m°: 1655  I Thomas wickes beinge weake of Bodie but of pfect memory doe ordaine this as my Last will & testament   Imp$^r$ I giue & bequeath vnto Alice my wife y$^e$ one third of all my estate Reall & personall. Ite. I giue & bequeath unto My two daughters Bethiah & Hannah the remainder of my estate to be equally Deuided betweene them the whole estate to remaine in y$^e$ posession of my wife untell my daughters be of y$^e$ age of eighteene yeers ‖either of them‖ or shalbe otherwise disposed ‖of‖ before in mariage, whereby my said wife may y$^e$ better be inabled to bring up my two daughters afores$^d$ & if in Case my wife should mary before my daughters should accomplish y$^e$ age of eighteen yeers either of them or be otherwise disposed of ‖in‖ mariage then the two thirds of my estate giuen & bequeathed to my two daughters Bethiah & hannah to be disposed soe of by my ouerseers that it may be secured for y$^e$ use of my daughters afores$^d$: untell they accomplish y$^e$ age of 18 yeers or shalbe otherwise disposed of before in mariage, & for y$^e$ better pformance of this my will I make Alice my wife my sole executrix, & desire and apoynt my Louing Cousen & ffriends Robert Gray m$^r$ Edmond Batter & Elias Stileman Jun$^r$: to be my ouerseers. in witness where of I haue here unto put my hand the day & yeere first aboue written."

Thomas Wickes.

Witness: Thomas Cromwell, John Bacheler and Anna her mark
A Cromwell. *Essex Co. Quarterly Court Files, vol. 3, leaf 53.*

Proved in Salem court 24: 4: 1656 by Tho. Cromwell and Anna Cromwell. *Salem Quarterly Court Records, vol. 4, leaf 7.*

Inventory taken by Hilliard Veren and Thomas Cromwell: One dwelling house with a shopp & barne & ground, 35li.; 12 acres of upland with 3-4 of an acre of salt & 1-2 of fresh medow, 11li.; 20 acres of land at the head of Bass River, 5li.; 2 acres of land in the towne, 6li.; one mare Colt, 8li.; one Cow & one heifer of a yeare old, 5li. 10s.; one Fatt hogg, 1li. 15s.; in flagges, 2li. 10s.; in working timber, 1li. 10s.; Indian & English Corne, 1li.; in made ware as greene Chayres, wheeles & Reemes, 5li.; 2 cloakes, one great coate, one cloth sute, one stuffe sute, 2 wascoates & 2 pr. of drawers, 10li.; 2 hatts, stockens, showes & boots, 2li.; shirts, capps, hankercheefs & bands, 2li.; 2 Flock beads, 2 bolsters, a pr. of blankets, 2 Coverings & bedsteed, 5li.; 2 musketts, one fowlinge peece, 2 swords, one pr. of bandleers, 3li.; a standing cubbert, one table, 4 Joyne stooles, 4 chayres, 4 chests, 2li. 11s.; 3 chests & 4 boxes, 1li. 10s.; one feather bead, 2 fether bolsters, one under bead with Curtaynes & vallence, 6li.; one Rugg, one Coverlead, one pr. of Carsy blanketts, one pr. Cotten blanketts, 7li.; a bare's skin, 2 bedsteeds with bedcords, 1li. 10s.; 4 fether pillowes, one cubbert Cushing, 1li. 8s.; 2 pr. of fine sheetes, 2li. 10s.; 4 pr. & one sheete, 3li. 5s.; in cash, 2li.; in fine linnen, 1li.; 3 pr. of hollan pillow beers, 1li. 7s.; a larg diaper table cloth & 1 dozen of diaper napkins, 2li.; 20 course napkins, 1li.; in new locrum & holland, 3li. 4s.; 3 doz. pewter, smale & greate, 3li.; one great Copper & Trivett, 3li.; one brass kettle & bras skillett, 10s.; 3 Iron potts, 1 kettle & 1 Skillett, 1li. 15s.; a brasse morter & chafin dish, 2 brass candle stickes, 16s.; one warming pan, 8s.; 2 spitts, 2 pr. of Andirons, 2 haukes, 1li. 12s.; one fire pan, tonges & griderne, 8s.; white earth ware & Voyder, 1li.

10s.; one great chest & one table, 16s.; red earthware & other vtilses, 6s.; 1 looking glass & 1 grater, 6s.; 2 trunkes, 1li.; 2 barrells of beefe, 4li. 14s.; 1-2 C. of Suger, 1li. 5s.; tubbs & barrells & other lumber, 16s.; in plank & boards, 1li.; 2 pigges, 1li.; waites & scales & measures, 10s.; a silver dram cup & silver spoones, 10s.; in tooles, 6li.; a box Smothing Iron, 2s.; in debts upon the book, 20li. 16s.; total, 192li. 10s.; debts, 42li. 10s. *Essex Co. Quarterly Court Files, vol. 3, leaf 53.*

### Estate of John Hart of Marblehead.

Administration on the estate of John Hart granted 24: 4: 1656 to his widow, Florance Hart of Marblehead. Elias Stileman to apportion claims against the estate, etc. *Salem Quarterly Court Records, vol. 4, leaf 8.*

Inventory of the estate of John Hart of Marblehead, taken 14: 1: 1655-6, by Moses Mavericke and Johanne Bartoll: One house wth aboute an acre of ground whereone ye house Standeth & an old Cow house together wth Commonidg for 2 Cowes & 5 acres upland, 36li.; A part in ye farme that was Mr. Humphrey's, 7li. 10s.; 1 acre of meadow at Salem, 3li.; 2 Cowes, 8li.; 1 Calfe ten weekes ould, 15s.; 2 small swine, 1li.; 1 flock beed in ye parlour, 1 Cotten Rugg, 1 boulster & 2 pillowes, feathers, 2 old Curtaines, 2li. 10s.; 1 table, 4 Joynstooles, 15s.; 1 chaire, 2s. 8d.; 2 chests & 1 box, 12s.; 1 pr. of great Andirons, tongs & shovell, 10s.; 2 window Cussions, 5s.; 1 woolin wheele, 3s.; 1 Looking glass, 3s.; 6 pewter dishes, 2 baisons, 1li.; 2 quart potts, 1 candlestick, beaker & wine cup, brass snuffers & small cupp, 7s.; 1 pr. wooll Cards, 2s.; 3 Iron potts, 1li. 5s.; 3 brass Kettles, 1 copper kettle & skillett, 1li.; 1 brass furnace, 1li.; 1 feather bed, boulster & 2 pillowes, 2li. 10s.; 1 pr. Curtaines & Vallance, 1li. 10s.; 1 white Rugg & Coverlett, 1li.; ——elt, 3s. 6d.; [bed]stead & Cord, 5s.; [ta]ble very ould & little, 1s. 6d.; 1 Lanthorne, 1s. 6d.; 3 pr. sheetes, 2 pr. pillowbeers, 1li. 10s.; 1 tablecloth, 1 dos. napkins, 12s.; 1 table in ye Kitchin, 1s. 6d.; 2 tubbs & 2 payles, 5s.; som earthenwaier & other Lumber, 6s.; 1 spitt & hanger for ye chimney, 5s.; total, 74li. 10s. 6d. The estate is debtor to Mr. Corwin, 30li.; Mr. Browne, 8li. 6s.; a bill at Boston, 5li.; Sam. Archard, 2li.; Mr. Elzey, 18li.; total, 63li. 6s. *Essex Co. Quarterly Court Files, vol. 3, leaf 54.*

## Estate of Caleb Johnson of Andover.

Administration on the estate of Caleb Johnson of Andover, intestate, granted Sept. 30, 1656 to Henry Ingalls. Amount of the inventory of the estate, 20li. 8s. *Ipswich Quarterly Court Records, vol. 1, page 58.*

## Estate of Francis Parrot of Rowley.

"I ffrancis Parrat of Rowley intending to take a Journey to England desire as sensible of the frailty of this mortall life to set my house in order & doe therfore constitute and appoin this as my last will and testament in maner & forme as followeth. Impf I giue & bequeath my soule to God that gaue it & my body to be interred as the wise hand of God sees meete whether by sea or land in comfortable hopes of a happy resurrectio at that day. Ite my will is that my debts be first payd Ite I giue to my Loueing wife Elizabeth Parrat one hundred pounds to take it wher shee pleases in land goods & Cattle I also giue to her my house and house lott for her life and after her death my will is that it shall be equally diuided amonge my Children. Ite the rest of my lands goods & Chattles I giue to my Six daughters to be equally diuided amongst them and each of them to haue their equall share paid vnto them at the age of twenty one yeares or the day of their mariage w^ch shall first be And I constitute my wife as my sole executrix of this my last will and Testament And I appoint my Loueing brethren Maxmilian Jewet & Ezekiell Northend as ouerseers of this my last will and testament in witnes hereof I haue herevnto set my hand this 18^th day of Nouember 1655."

ffrancis Parrot

Witness: Ezekiel northend, john palmer.

Proved in Ipswich court Sept. 30, 1656 by the witnesses. *Essex Co. Probate Files, Docket 20,578.*

Inventory taken 15: 7: 1656, by Mr. Joseph Jawet, Max. Jawet, Ezekiel Northene and John Smith: House, orchard and home lott, 70li.; 10 Acres in the northeast feild, 40li.; two Ackers of Bastard marsh, 4li.; two Acres of salt marsh, 5li.; Sawier's Ilande, 35li.; marsh and Broken uplande, 35li.; at the great plaine, 16 Akers of lande, 20li.; ten Akers of medow at the Crayne, 10li.; 13 Gates, 13li.; one Mare, 13li.; two oxen, 11li.; three Cows, 11li.; two steares, 5li.; two yearling Calves, 3li. 6s. 8d.; sheepe, 9li. 10s.; eighteene hogs, 15li.; one Asse, 4li.; due from Andrew Hadon, 6li. 10s.; some Linin, 3li. 13s. 4d.; A bed with Beding, 5li.; another Bed with Beding, 3li.; one Bed, 2li.; malt, 6s.; hemp and flax, 1li.; sheep woll and Cotten woll, 2li.; a sword, 10s.; two tubs and a trough, 2s. 6d.; a payre of scales and weights, 5s.; one Chest, 5s. 6d.; hemp yearne, 1li.; Books, 6s. 8d.; pots, ketles, hooks and a back Iron, 4li.; peuder, 2li.; two Jugs and a frying pan, 1s.; wooden and earthen vessells, 1li.; foure Cushins, 10s.; one Cuberd, 5s.; one Cart, one plow with other Iron Geares, 2li. 10s.; Scives, 3s.; twelve Ackres of Ry, 12li.; thirteene Ackers of Corne, 20li.; Hay, 10li.; fowre hides, 3li.; for hides Taning, 5li. 13s. 1d.; one Musket, 12s.; a brake, 2li. 6s.; total, 357li. 5s. There were a few things of uncertain value, as a hogshead of sugar, his wearing clothes, something in England and 22s. forgotten, for which there was as much debt forgotten. His debts amounted to 63li. 9s. 5d. *Essex Co. Quarterly Court Files, vol. 3, leaf 55.*

### ESTATE OF MACKLIN HUCKSTABLE OF MARBLEHEAD.

Macklin Huckstable of Marblehead, dying intestate about five months since, administration was granted 25 : 9 : 1656, to Mr. Edm. Batter and Mr. Fran. Johnson. Inventory, 29li. 9s. 6d. Insolvent. *Salem Quarterly Court Records, vol. 4, leaf 10.*

### ESTATE OF REV. JAMES NOYES OF NEWBURY.

"The Last will and Teastament of James Noies my will is that my wife shall have the rule and ordering w$^{th}$ the disposing of all my substance I haue; while she keepeth hir selfe in an vnmaryed Condition, And That she will Take counsayle of my Loving ffreinds Cozen Thomas Parker my brother Nicholas Noys & w$^m$ Gerrish; But if she disposeth hir selfe in way of marryage then my will is; That my ffreinds A[b]ove mentioned shall have the disposing of all for the portions of my wife And Children as they shall see meete; in witnes heareof I have put my hand this 17th ocktob : 1656."

James Noies

Witness: W$^m$ Gerrish, Richard Browne, Robert Long.

Proved in Salem court Nov. 21, 1656 by Robert Long and Nov. 26, 1656 by Capt. Wm. Gerrish and Nicholass Noies.

Inventory of the estate of Mr. James Noyes, teacher of Newbury, who deceased Oct. 21, 1656, taken by Richard Knight, Anthony Somerby and Benjeman Swett, and sworn to by Sara Noyes, widow of the deceased, Nov. 21, 1656: The house and seaven akers of land adjoyneing with the orchard, 100li.; foure akers of upland and four akers of meadow, 20li.; twelve akers of marsh or meadow, 30li.; two akers of arable land, 10li.; seauenty-five akers of upland and meadow, 150li.; foure oxen, 22li.; eight Cowes, 27li.; a two yere old steere and two calves, 3li. 10s.; six swyne, 8li.; ten small swyne & 3 shoots, 6li.; two mares and colts, 36li.; his weareing apparrell, 13li. 6s. 4d. In the parlour: one bedsted with two featherbeds, 2 bolsters, 3 pillows, 2 blankets and one rugg, with Curtaines & vallons, 15li.; one presse and a little table and a chest with 3 chayres & 3 Joyned stooles, 2li. 10s.; a little carpet and eight turkey worke cushions, 2li. 15s. In the closset: A case of bottles and some earthern potts and gally potts, 10s. In the hall: One table with a joynd forme and a childs chayre and a livery cubbard and benches, 1li.; a carpet and Cubbard cloth, 10s.; 3 cushions & apaire of And Irons & tongs & fire pan, 1li. In the kitchin: Foure Iron potts with 2 pr. of pott hookes, with 2 pr. of Cottrells & a trevet, 2li.; one Jacke, one spitt, an Iron drippinpan with a fire pan, a pr. of and Irons & other small Iron Implements with 2 frying pans, 2li.; one furnace, a brasse kettle & a small brass pot with two warming pans, a brass morter and pestle and foure brasse skillets and two brass candlesticks with some other old brasen Instruments, 3li.; on one shelfe, one Charger, 5 pewter platters and a bason and a salt seller, 1li. 10s.; on another shelfe, 9 pewter platters, small and great, 13s.; one old flagon and 4 pewter drinking pots, 10s.; one safe, 2 chayrs, one churne and a cheespress with tubs and bucketts and keellers, 2li.; 4 barrells in the seller and 2 powdering tubs & a halfe bushell & other lomber, 1li. In the kitchin Chamber: One bedsted and a featherbed, 2 bolsters, 2 pillowes, one blancket and 2 ruggs, 9li.; a truckle bed and bolster and rug, 1li. 10s.; 2 dozen and halfe of napkins & towels, 1li.; 9 pr. of sheets & 2 table cloths, 5li.; one damask cubbard cloth & towell, 10s.; one fetherbed at the Colledg with a bolster and 2 pr. of Sheets and 2 ruggs, 5li.; 4 holland pillow bears and other pillowbeares, 1li. 5s.; six other table clothes, great and small, & a bolster case, 1li.; one trunck, one chest, 3 boxes & a cabinet and 2 chamber pots, 1li.; one silver bowle & 3 silver spoones & other small peices of silver, 2li. 10s. In the parlor chamber: Two boxes, 4 hogsheds, a musket and a gun and two swords, 2li.; a bolster and a quilt & two blanckets and a parsell of Cotten wooll, 3li. 10s. In the Hall chamber: In Indian corne, a meale trough, a spining wheele & sacks & other lumber, 2li.; 4 trayes, 8 spoones, 2 haire sieves & a tiffiny seive, 12s.; corne in the barne, 10li.; in the study, in books, 30li.; total, 597li. 11s. 4d. Debts due to be paid in England, 16li. 10s.; and to be paid at Boston & in our owne towne about 40li.; total, 56li. 10s. Debts due the deceased, 60li. Sara Noyes, the widow, made oath before Edward Woodman and Nicholas Noyes.

*Essex Co. Quarterly Court Files, vol. 3, leaves 56, 57.*

### ESTATE OF WILLIAM RICHARDSON OF NEWBURY.

Inventory of the estate of William Richardson, deceased Mar. 25, 1657, taken by Gyles (his G mark) Cromlone, Edward (his S mark) Richardson: a house and foure akers of land, 23li.; two cowes, 8li. 5s.; one heifer 2 yere old, 2li. 10s.; one calfe, 7s.; one sow & 3 pigs and a yereling shoot, 2li.; one ewe and foure weather sheepe, 5li.; his weareing apparrell, 1li. 6s.; a bed, one pr of sheets, 2 old rugs & 2 pillows, 4li. 4s.; one Iron kettle & 2 Iron potts, 1li. 12s.; one frying pan and a few earthen potts & dishes, 5s.; one tub & 2 drink vessells, 2 buckets & a hogshead, 11s.; one chest & a box & a spining wheele, 9s.; one sword & bandeleers, 11s.; 2 axes, 1 hatchet, 2 boriers, 1 draughtshave & hand saw and an old hooe, 12s.; a sith & sickle & hooke and 2 prongs & a spade, 10s.; a ladder & other lumber, 5s.; one bible, 8s.; 2 peices of leather to mend shooes, 5s. 2d.; total 52li. ——. Debts due about 1li. 6s. He oweth to Henry Short about 4li. 12s.; to Mr. Jewet, 2li. 15s.; Mr. Macy, 1li. 5s.; Capt. Gerrish, 1li. 4s.; Mr. Woodman, 17s.; other small debts about 1li. 4s.; total, 11li. 17s.

Sworn to by Elizabeth Richardson, wife of William Richardson Mar. 30, 1657, before John Pike commissioner for Newbury. *Essex Co. Probate Files, Docket 23,661.*

### ESTATE OF ANTHONY NEWHALL OF LYNN.

"The Last will and Testyment of Anthony Newhall 1 I will that my grand child Richard hood shall hau on Ewe lamb att the next Encreast 2 I will that my grand chilld

Elizabeth hood shall haue one Ewe lamb at the next Encreas 3 I doe giue my dafftter mary the third part of the Encress of my orchard for Seuen years afftter the datt hearof  4 I doe giue my daffter mary that pcall of ground that lys one the other Syde the brook at the north End of my hows lott uppon Condittyon that her husiband doe bulld a dwelling hows oppon it  5 I will that my dafftter mary shall hau my fether ‖bed‖ afttter my deceas with all things bellonging to it only that my Son John shall hau a boulster fflled with fethers  Theas affowrsayd legasys I giu my daffter mary for her carffull attendanc of me and great payns she hes bin at with me:

"6 of the remayning part of my wholl Esttat I doe giue my Son John newhall tow parts and to my daffter mary I giue one part deuided to Ech of them accourding to my will as followeth  1 I will that my Son John newhall shall haue my hows and land that I now liue in bounded form the brook att the north End vpp to the land of gorg ffrayll at the South End  2 I will that my daffter mary shall hau that lott lying betwixt the land of John hawthorns and John Ramsdell  3 I will that my Son John Shall hau 4 akers of that land that lys by Jonathan hudsons and my dafftter mary tow akers of that land that lys by Jonathan hudsons  4 I will that my Son John shall hau twenty akers of oupland lying oup in the Country

"5 I will that my daffter mary shall hau ten akers of oupland lying in the Country  6 I will that my Son John shall hau 4 akers of that medow that lys oup in the Country and I will that my daffter mary shall hau tow akers of that medow that lys oupp in the Country  7 I will that my Son John shall hau tow akers of Sallt march lying in the town march att the tow tres and 3 akers att m$^r$ neadums and on aker Richard mors and on aker lying in the frech march  8 I will that my daffter mary shall ‖hau‖ 4 akers of Sallt march lying towards goodman Edmonds in Rumlly in the first deuision and tow akers of Sallt march in the last diuydent

"I will that my Son John newhall shall haue Tow Cows and one oxe  I will that my daffter mary shall hau on cow and on stear  I giu my Son John 2 Iron potts and a great bras kettell

"I giu to my daffter mary on bras pan  I giu to John tow pewttur platters and to my dafter mary on platter  I giu to my Son on boulster on ould Couerlid and to my daffter mary on pillow  I giu to my Son John tow par of potthooks and on pott hanger and one frying pan  I giu to my daffter mary on warminge pan  I giu my Son ‖John‖ on new Couerlide and a brase pott  I giue my daffter mary flocks for a littell bed  I giu to my Son John i heckell and to my daffter mary the dubull heckell  I giu to my Son John and my daffter mary the grinston betwixt them  So long as it last  I will that what So Euer of my Estat y$^t$ is not yet giuen or yett deuyded shall be giuen tow parts to my Son John and on part to my daffter mary

"ffurther I will That my Son John newhall and my dafftter mary shall Eche of them hau the produce of Eche others proporttions of my Estat whils I liue and accourding to ther Seuerall proportions to mayntayn me whils I liue  I will that theas Seuerall gifts of my Estat to be ffully Rattyfied and Conffermd affter my dissceas and not beffore to Eche of them

"I will: That if my Son John newhall should dye and hau noe Chilldren That then my hows and lands shall return to my daffter mary and her heirs  I will that nathanell Kertland and mathew ffarrington and John ffuller be ouersears of this my last will & Testyment To wich I wittnes with my hand to be my true and lawffull will.  This 14 day of January 1656"

his mark<br>Anttony  A  Newhall

his mark
Witness: John ffuller, Thomas ———| Couldum, Mathew ffarington, Nathanill kirtland and Jonathan Hudson.

Proved in Ipswich court Mar. 31, 1657 by John Fuller and Mathew Farington.

Proved 30: 1: 1657 by Thomas Couldom and Nathaniell Keartland.

Inventory taken 6: 12: 1656, sworn to by Richard Hood, Mar. 31, 1656: Whearring apparrill, he lying long bedride but small, 2li.; one great brase kettell, 5s.; one brasse pane, 15s.; one littell brass kettell, 5s.; one brase pott, 10s.; one warming pan, 4s.; one skimmor and brass laddell with other ould peasses of brass, 2s.; thre pewttor platters, 10s. 8d.; one pewtter Candellstick, 1s. 6d.; ould peases of pewtor, 3s. 4d.; tow Iron potts, one Iron skillett, Tow par of pott hoks, 18s. 6d.; tow pare of Iron Racks, on Spit with Sertin peases of ould Iron, 9s.; two handsaws, one ould wip saw, one squar, tow ould augurs, one ould handsaw, 11s. 6d.; one Iron punch and one Iron laddell, one Claboad frow, 4s. 6d.; one Carbyn, one ould Sword, 15s.; one singull heckell and one dubell heckell, 8s.; one wyer sife, one ould wyer sife, one hare sife, 6s.; wouden trays and diches, 2s. 6d.; one buttur tub, one bear barrill and a kneading troff with other ould Cask, 8s.; a pare of ould andirons and a frying pane, 6s.; thre ould bybells and thre other ould books, 17s.; seven pans of glas, 10s.; one brase pistell, 8s.; an ould flaskit, one ould box, 1s. 4d.; in lead, 3s.; an ould fether bed and boolster, one pillow and pillow bear, 1li. 18s.; one ould ruge, one ould blankit, 9s.; one ould flock bed, an ould boolster, 10s.; one ould Covelid and tow ould blankit, one fether boolster, one ould fether pellow, one shett, 12s.; one Joyn bedsted and bed cord and matt, 1li. 8s.; one Grenston with an Iron ———, 12s.; one Ewe sheap, 1li. 15s.; one oxe, 5li.; thre Cows, 10li. 10s.; one stear, 2li. 10s.; fowr Iron hops for wheals and one Ex, pins, one Ring, 10s.; one Coverled, 1li. 10s.; one dwelling hows and barne and fiv ackers of land and an orchard att hom, fowr akers of upland by John hawthorns hows, six ackers of upland lying by Jonathan hudssons, eight akers of upland lying by the fresh marsh, therty akers of upland lying oup in the Country, six akers of Salt marsh lying in the town march, six akers in Rumly march, one ackers of fresh march in the town, six akers of fresh march in the Country, due from Edward Richards twenty-five shillings; whe forbare to put any prise oupon the land or howses and cattell becaus the deceased in his will hath divided them to his tow Chilldren ech one ther partt.

*Essex Co. Quarterly Court Files, vol. 3, leaf 105.*

Administration on the estate granted Mar. 31, 1657, to Richard Hud, to settle it according to the will. Administration bond. Overseers appointed by the court: Matthew Farington, John Fullar and Nathaniell Kertland. *Ipswich Quarterly Court Records, vol. 1, page 61.*

GUARDIANSHIP OF THOMAS NELSON OF ROWLEY.

Thomas Nelson chose, in court Mar. 31, 1657, Mr. Joseph Jewett to be his guardian. *Ipswich Quarterly Court Records, vol. 1, page 60.*

ESTATE OF HUGH CHAPLIN OF ROWLEY.

"This 15 day of the firste month 1654 The laste will and Testemente of Hew Chaplin of Rowlay in the Countie of Esexs being sicke in bodie yet perfite in memorie I commite my soule to God thorowgh Jesus Christe And for my out word estaite as followeth Imprimis for my whole estate is at the dessposeng of my beloued wife Elesabeth Chaplin Duringe the time she dus contenew a widdow provided she dowe nothing in dessposing of my estaite with out the Consente ||of|| Thomas Mighell Maxsiemillian Jewite Thomas Diconson Hew Smith John Pickard But if my wife marrie then my estaite to be dessposed of by thes fiue men afore mensoned as after followeth if my esstaite be fourscore ponnds then my wife shall haue Thirtie ponnds And the riste of my estaite to be devided equalie amongst all my Chilldren Onely my Elldeste sonne John Chaplin shall have thre pond more than anie one of my chilldren And my will is that my wife haue thirtie ponndes oute of fourscore ponndes and this preporsion to be cepte whether my estaite be more or lesse." [No signature]

Witness: Joseph Jewett, John Pickard.

Proved in Ipswich court Mar. 31, 1657 by the witnesses. *Essex Co. Quarterly Court Files, vol. 3, leaf* 104.

Inventory of the estate of Hugh Chaplin of Rowley, husbandman, taken Dec. 3, 1656, by Maxemilion Jewit and Thomas Dickanson: house, barn, land and orchard bought of John Dresser, 24li.; one acre of land that is between the house lots of John Burbancke and Peter Cooper on the under side of the way, 4li.; foure acres above street purchased of Thomas Miller, 16li.; foure acres in the field Called batcheler playn together with villadge land, 14li.; five acres of meadow and upland at the farm, 14li.; Comonadge for two Cows, 2li.; two heifers, 5li. 10s.; two Cows, 7li.; one yearing heifer, 2li.; one Spring Calf, 1li.; foure piggs, 2li.; wheat, 5li.; Rye, 3li.; Indian Corn, 2li.; hay, 1li. 10s.; three [pots. duplicate inv.] one kettell and putor, 3li.; beding and linen, 10li. 10s.; one frying pan, one warming pann and tongs and one scellet, 1li.; one wheell, one Smoothing Iron and Sives, 6s. 8d.; milke vessell, bear vessell and tubs, 1li.; fethers, 4s.; hows and Sickels, 4s.; Iron tools, 10s.; wooll, 1li. 10s.; a Sword, 6s. 8d.; hemp and flax, 17s.; one wheell and Cards, 5s.; Chayrs and Cushions and baggs, 18s.; total, 123li. 11s. 4d. Debt owing to Mr. Joseph Jewit, 8li. 10s.

Sworn to Mar. 31, 1657 by the wife of Hugh Chapline and John Pickard.

A duplicate inventory sworn to 29: 7: 1657 by Elizabeth Jackson formerly wife of Hugh Chaplin.

The devision of the estate of Hugh Chaplin according to the true intent of his will, by the overseers, Maxemilion Jewit, Thomas Dickanson and John Pickard Dec. 3, 1656: to his wife, 43li. 18s. 4d.; to the eldest son John Chaplin, 20li.; to each of the other three children [the other three sons. dup. inv.] 17li.

*Essex Co. Probate Files, Docket 4,997.*

The will of Hugh Chapline not being proved within twenty months, ordered Mar. 31, 1657, that the widow forfeit one hundred pounds by the law. *Ipswich Quarterly Court Records, vol. 1, page 60.*

Petition of Elizabeth Jackson to the General Court 6: 2: 1657 for the remitment of a fine of 100li. for neglecting to present her former husband, Hugh Chaplin's will to be probated. It was referred to the next County court at Ipswich. *Mass. Archives, vol. 15B, page 11.*

The General Court 29: 7: 1657, moderated the fine of Nicolas Jackson for not proving the will of his wife's former husband, Hugh Chaplin. *Ipswich Quarterly Court Records, vol. 1, page 64.*

### ESTATE OF JOSEPH BATCHELDER OF WENHAM.

Administration granted Mar. 31, 1657, to Marke Bachelour on the estate of his father. Referred to Salem court for further orders. *Ipswich Quarterly Court Records, vol. 1, page 60.*

Mark Bachelour brought in to the court 1: 5: 1657 an inventory of his father's and mother's estate, amounting to 84li. 10s. 4d. To be paid to his brother John, under twenty one years, and to his sisters, Elizabeth and Hannah, each under eighteen years. *Salem Quarterly Court Records, vol. 4, leaf 15.*

Inventory of estate of Joseph Batchelder, deceased about ten years ago, taken Mar. 30, 1656-7 by James Moulton, Robert Gowing and Tho. Fiske: The Dweling house with 70 Akres of Land Lyeing to it wherof there is 6 Akres of it broken up: with an oarchard: & 7 Akres 1-2 of middow & thirtie Akers of Land more, 70li.; one fether bed & two bolsters & one pillow, 4li.; one bedstead, 8s.; one Rugg, 14s.; one Blanket, 8s.; Curtaines & Curtaine Rods, 10s.; one payre of Sheets, 8s.; one flock Bed, 10s.; one flocke Bed more with a flock Bolster, 8s.; an Iron pott & pott hooks, 9s.; one hake, 3s. 4d.; one Kittell, 16s.; one Brass pann, 5s.; one warmeing Pann, 2s.; one Iron Kittill, 6s.; one Iron Skilit, 5s.; one frieing pann, 2s.; Three Table cloathes & two Nappkines, 1li.; three pillowbeers, 12s.; one pewter platter, 5s.; one pewter Chamber pott, 2s.; other old pewter vessels, 6s.; earthang ware, 1s. 6d.; one Cubboard & Cubboard Cloath, 10s.; one Chist, 8s.; one Cheese press & Cheese fatt, 3s. 6d.; one Sword & belt & Bandilers, 17s.; two Tables, 7s.; one Chayer, 6d.; 4 Trayes, 2s.; one Beetle Ringe & three wedges, 2s. 6d.; Chafeing Dish & Candlestick, 2s.; Books, 15s.; one Cowe & one heifer, 5li. 15s.; total, 90li. 13s. 4d. The Widdow Batchelder is Debt$^r$ to be paid out of the estate 7li. 10s.

Received in Ipswich court 31 : 1 : 1657 and administration granted. *Essex Co. Probate Files, Docket 2,089.*

### Estate of Michael Hopkinson of Rowley.

Petition of John Trumble of Rowley to the General Court 7 : 3 : 1657 for the remitment of his wife's fine for neglecting to administer on the estate of her former husband, Michaell Hopkinson, deceased in 1648, as there was an inventory taken and the estate had in no way been alienated.

The request was granted provided the petitioner give in an inventory to the next County Court and the said Court to dispose of the estate to the woman and her children. *Mass. Archives, vol.* 15B, *page* 204.

Inventory of the estate of Mighill Hobkinson taken 10 : 1 : 1648, by Joseph Jewett and Thomas Dickanson: The house and barne, garden, orchard, yards and swamp below and all of the lower side of the house, 18li.; two acres and a half of broke up land with the seed lying in batcheler plaine, 5li. 10s.; five acres of land broke & unbroke up lying in bradforth lots, 6li. 10s.; eight acres of medow and one of upland at the farme, 21i.; three gates and a quarter, 1li. 10s.; one steer, 2li. 10s.; one steer, 10li.; two heifers of three yeares old, 9li.; three Cowes, 14li.; one yearing, 1li. 6s. 8d.; thre sucking Calves, 1li.; one payre of loomes, 1li.; one shutel 3sh, one tenipel, 1 warping woof, one rings and one payre of heels, 7s., one ridel, 1li. 12s.; three slayes, 9s.; three wheels, 2s. 8d.; twenty bushells of indion Corne, 3li.; Six bushels of wheat, 1li. 7s.; rye two bushels and a halfe, 9s.; baken, 1li. 10s.; one rug, 1li.; Cotton wooll and yarne, 5li. 10s.; five slayds, 12s. 6d.; red Corsay three yards, 15s.;

one hatt, five sh, one payre of shapt brecth, 2d., 17s.; 3 payre of Jerkings, 5s.; one coat, 1li.; one coat, ten sh. one short coat and a jerkin, 1li. 16s. 8d.; one payr of boots, ten sh., one payre breech., 10d., 1li.; one sute, 16s.; breches 6 sh 8 pence and a dublet ten sh., 16s. 8d. one payr of lether breches, 8sh. & lether dublet, 3s. 4d., 11s. 4d.; one bed and bolster, 15s.; shoes 2 payre, 4s.; one cotton blanket, 6s.; one woolen blanket, 4s.; one rugg, 1li.; two blankets and sheets, 1li.; 3s.; three sheets, 6s.; one rugg, 1li.; one sheet, 5s.; one bolster, 2s.; one bed tiking and a blancket, 5s.; two beds, 8s.; Silver, 1li. 14s.; two sives and one payre of cords, 4s. 6d.; one kettell, 1li. 10s.; one kettell 6s., one pot 7s., 13s.; one kettel, two skelets, 2s., 4s.; one warming pan, 8s.; putter 11s., a lanthon 2s., two juggs 1s., 14s.; wood vesell, 10s., pothooks and bellous, 6s. 9d., 16s. 8d.; books, 1li.; armor and powder, 2li.; Sithes 5s., axes, Sawes and Iron tong 20s., 1li. 5s.; one frying pan, 2s.; part of the boat, 10li. 9s.; total 116li. 19s. 8d. Debtor to Joseph Jewit, 6li.; witnes my hand Joseph Jewett 10: 1: 1649. To Mr. Robart Payn 1li.; to William Wild, 1li. 8s.

Testified to be a true inventory in court 29: 7: 1657 by Ann Trumble. *Essex Co. Probate Files, Docket* 13,917.

### Estate of Stephen Waters of (Marblehead?).

Administration on the estate of Stephen Waters granted 30: 4: 1657 to his son, Wm. Waters of Marblehead 30: 4: 1657. *Salem Quarterly Court Records, vol. 4, leaf* 12.

### Estate of John Pickering of Salem.

"In the name of god Amen I Jn° Pickeringe of Salem beeing of pfect mind and memory doe make and Ordayne this last will and Testament in man and forme followinge first I bequeath my soule to my lord god and sauiour: and my body to the earth from whence it came. Impr I Deuid my estate into fiue pts: vidz: lands houses Cattell houshould goods &c.: Ite I bequeath to my son Jn° Pickeringe two parts out of my estate as aboue mencianed: at the age of one and twenty years Ite I bequeath to my son Jn°than one part and halfe out of the estate of mine as aboue said at the age of twenty one years. Ite I bequeath the other pt & halfe to my wife Elizabeth for her mayntenance for her life: puided shee liue vnmaried, & if her part of my estate will not mayntaine her comfortably: that ther shall be an alowance made to her out of my sons pcõns accordinge to the pporcon of their legacies  But if my said wif Elizabeth shall mary againe her next husband to be bound to returne to my two sons their heirs or admnstro$^{rs}$ or assignes ‖to be equaly deuided‖ the same pporcon or value of goods or estate, that he: shall haue: with my said wif when he doth mary her: if she die before ‖him‖.

"Ite I giue to my son Jn$^o$ my musket and Armes compleate and the choise of my foulinge peeces. Ite I giue to my son Jn$^o$athan my other foulinge gune and my Carbine Lastly my will is y$^t$ when my Chilldren comes to age to inioye their pcõns: y$^t$: the increase or losse y$^t$ then shall be found to be in my estate more or less then was at my death shall be borne by them, vidz: my wif & Children  It I make my beloued wif Elizabeth & my sons John and Jonathan my Execũtrix & Executors  It I apoynte & Desire John Horne and Edmond Batter my ouerseers: to see the ffulfilling of this my Last will and I giue to each of them twenty shillings Dated 30$^{th}$ 5$^m$ 1655"

John Pickering

Witness: Edmond Batter, John Horne, ffrancis Lawes and John Kitching.

Proved 1: 5: 1657 by Mr. Batter, John Horne and John Kittchen. *Essex Co. Quarterly Court Files, vol. 3, leaf 128.*

The inventory, amounting to 137li. 3s. 2d. sworn to 1: 5: 1657, by the Widow Pickrin and allowed. *Salem Quarterly Court Records, vol. 4, leaf 14.*

### ESTATE OF HENRY BULLOCK, JR. OF (SALEM?).

Administration on the estate of Hen. Bullock, granted 1: 5: 1657, to his widow, Alice Bullock.  The estate given to the son who was under twenty-one years, to the daughter, under eighteen years, and to the widow for the bringing up of the children.  The feather bed mentioned in the inventtory to be the property of the son after his mother's decease. *Salem Quarterly Court Records, vol. 4, leaf 15.*

Inventory of the estate of Henry Bullocke, jr., taken 10: 10: 1656, by Mr. Thomas Gardiner and Nathaniel Felton: The house and outhouses thereto belonging wth. 20 acres of land thereto belonginge joyninge unto it and 20 acres in the north feild and 6 acres of meadow bought of Mr. Endecodt lyinge in the broad meadow against the farme given to Mr. Bishop and a lease of 8 acres for 6 yeares lyinge in the meadow called willeses meadow, £50; 2 stieres, £8; Cowes, £6; 1 heifer, £2. 10s.; 7 loads of hay, £7; 2 sheepe & 2 ewe lambes, £5; 5 younge swine, £1. 16s.; 15 bushels of Indian corne, £1. 17s. 6d.; 1 feather bed and boulster, £3; 1 Rug and 2 blankets, £2; 2 feather pillows, 10s.; 1 flocke bed and bed and boulster, £1; 1 Coverlet & 2 blankets, £1. 10s.; 2 bedsteads, 15s.; Curtaynes & vallons, £1. 10s.; 2 payre of Sheets, 2 pillowbeares & 2 napkins, £1. 10s.; his wearinge apparel, £6; 2 chests, 15s.; 4 chayres, 8s.; a warminge pan, 5s.; 2 muskets, 1 sword, 2 payre of bandeliers, £1. 15s.; 1 brasse ketle, 10s.; 2 Iron pots, 10s.; 2 frying pans, 5s.; Peuter, 10s.; 1 hake, a payre of tongs & a frye pan, a payre of andirons, a spit & 2 skillets, 13s.; Axes and other workinge tooles, £1; 20 yards of linnen cloth, £1. 10s.; a cradle, 5s.; a pestle and morter, 2s.; planks, 10s.; hemp and flax, £1; flesh, Butter and cheese, £1; old barrels, tubs and payles, 12s.; old lumber, 10s.; a mare colt, £8; total, £119. 18s. 6d. Estate debtor to Mr. Corwine, £2. 8s.; Mr. Willyam Browne, £1. 15s.; Mr. Cromwell, £1. 8s.; Thomas Rootes, 10s.; the Cow keeper, 10s.; Sam Eburne, 8s.; Ralph Tompkins, 7s.; Willyam Robinson, 4s. 2d.; Richd. Leach, 1s. 4d.; Edward Wharton, 12s.; Adam Westgate, 4s.; Widd. Giles, 7s.; Mr. Gardiner, 4s.; total, £8. 18s. 6d. Estate creditor, due from Anthony Nedham, £6; Goodman Herod, 12s.; John Concklinge, £1; John Scot, £2. 10s.; total, £10. 2s.; whole estate, £121. 2s. *Essex Co. Quarterly Court Files, vol. 3, leaf 129.*

### ESTATE OF JOHN ALDERMAN OF SALEM.

"Dated the 3th of 5th mo 1657 The last will & testament of John Alderman he being weake in body but well in mind disposeth of his estate as followeth Impr I giue to mr Norice the best Cowe I haue: Item to mr Eliot one Cow. And one Cowe to the Indians that mr Eliot doth preach unto to be disposed of to them by him: Item I giue one Cowe to mr Thatcher Item I giue one Cowe to mr whiting of Linn Item I giue one Cowe to mr waltom of marbell head. Item I giue one Cowe to mr Cobat Item to John Horne of Salem I giue one heifer Item my house & land which I ualew at 40li my will is that Ezera Clape the sone of Edward Clape: and Nathaniell Clape the sone of Nicholas Clape shall haue it at that price: & pay for it as followeth, viz, to Israell Mason daughter of maior mason tenn pounds, to be paid two years after my decease: the rest to be paid at 3 yeares end by $3^{li}$ a yeare to m$^r$ Norice so long as he liues to Inioy it  Item I giue to John Pickiring, one table 2 stools my Cloke a paire of Cloth briches a paier of worsted stockens & 2 bb barly: Item to Elizabeth Pickirin one greene Cloth suitt  Item to Jonathan Pickirin my Armes & all my Nursery of Apple trees at my ten acre lott  Item I giue to goodwife Bufam 20$^s$ to Josuah Bufam 10$^s$ & to the rest of her Children 5$^s$ a peece. Item I giue to Edward Clape one stufe sute. Item I giue to Prudence Clape her two daughters to Barbara Stoder her two daughters & to Nicholas Clape his two daughters all the houshould stuffe I haue Beding & lining: Item I giue to brother Marshall all my old Aparill  Item I giue to m$^{ris}$ ffellton 10$^s$ to widow Denis 10$^s$ to Goody Curtice 10$^s$ Item I apoynt Edward Clape & John Horne to be ouerseers Edward Clape to be executor. my ouerseers to haue 13$^s$ a peece for ther labor:"

John Alderman

Witness: Edward Clap, John Horne, Henery (his mark) Keny, Jeylls Corye.

Proved Sept. 3, 1657 by Edward Clapp. *Copy of will, Ipswich Deeds, vol. 1, leaf 196.*

Copy of invenrory of estate of Mr. John Alderman, Salem, lately deceased, taken 23: 5: 1657, by Hillyard Veren, Robert (his mark) Buffom: one dwelling house with two acres of ground adioyning & ten Acres of land lying in the north neck & an out lott Containeing about fiuty Acres more or lesse with the meadow belonging to it, 40li.; 7 Cowes, 24li. 10s.; 2 oxen at 11li., 2 heifers & one steere 7li., 18li.; in Corne uppon the ground, 1li. 10s.; 4 bushells of barly & 2 bushells of wheat, 1li. 4s.; in weareing woollen Cloathes, 5li.; in linnen, 2li.; 6 yd. of Searg & som other Cloathing, 3li.; 2 feather beds, 4li.; one pillow & 2 bolsters with 3 old curtins, 1li.; one Coverlett & 2 blanketts, 16s.; one bedsteed, 2 little tables, 2 Joinstools, 1li. 5s.; 2 Chayrs, 2 Chests, one trunk, 1li.; 2 potts, one brasse pan, 2 old Kettles, 1li.; in pewter, 12s., one spitt & 1 warminpan, 1 frying pan with som other utensills, 1li.; plow Irons & Chayne & 2 old howes, 12s.; total, 105li. 17s. The Estate debtr., 4li. 10s.; remainder, 101li. 7s.

Edward Clapp delivered this as a true inventory Sept. 3, 1657 before Samuell Symonds and Daniel Denison. *Ipswich Deeds, vol. 1, leaf 197.*

### Guardianship of Rebecca Bradstreet of Ipswich.

Rebeacha Brodstreet chose Joseph Jewett to be her guardian, and he acknowledged 29: 7: 1657, that he had received her portion of the estate of her father, Humphry Bradstreet, given to her in his will, from her mother Bridgett Broadstreet, executrix of the will. *Ipswich Quarterly Court Records, vol. 1, page 64.*

### Estate of Thomas Rofe of Ipswich.

"I Thomas Rofe being at p<sup>r</sup>sent full of payne and not Knowing what the Lords pleasure is towards me doe make this my last will as followeth I commit my soul into the hands of my saviour the Lord Jesus Christ my body to the earth to be desently buried & for that little outward estate the Lord hath giuen me I leave vnto my deare wife conceiueing it little enough & two little to maynetayne her in the condition she is In & doe apoynt her sole execotrix of this my last will in wittnes whereof I haue heervnto sett my hand this 12<sup>th</sup> of agust 1657"

                Thomas Roof

        her mark
Witness: Robert Lord, Hanah H Day.

Proved in the Ipswich court Sept. 29, 1657 by the witnesses. *Essex Co. Probate Files, Docket 24,128.*

### Estate of Thomas Scott of Ipswich.

Administration on the estate of Thomas Scott granted 29: 7: 1657, to his wife Margret Scott. *Ipswich Quarterly Court Records, vol. 1, page 64.*

Inventory of estate of Thomas Scott, Ipswich, taken Sept. 20, 1657 by John Appleton and William Geed—: his wearing cloths, 2li.; 3 payers of cors sheets, 1li.; in bed and bed cloths & old curta, 3li. 10s.; in peutter, 1li.; 3 old Kettels, 1li. 4s. 6d.; a lettel Kettel, a scummer, a warming pan, litt. scilli, 10s.; too smal Iron potts, 12s. 4d.; Iron things and belows, 12s. 4d.; and old bras frying pan, 2s. 6d.; a payer of larg stilards, 2li.; too old chest and a trunk, 8s. 6d.; a cast with 6 bottel, 5s.; Some books and brasses other implymet, 12s.; 5 old cast, 3s.; hous and barn land, 80li.; in Goodman West hands, 62li.; in wampome, 2s. 6d.; in debts, 27li.; a bed stead, som lumber, 10s.; total, 183li. 12s. 8d. depts yt were owing 184li.

Proved to be a true inventory in Court held at Ipswich, Sept. 29, 1674, by the administratrix.

A letter to Col. Gidnye, Judge of the Probate of wills, dated Jan. 14, 1694, with "the Humble Request of william Rodgers Humbly sheweth that Thomas Scott my Grandfather dyed in Ipswich about thirty and eight yers agoe and made noe will he left my Grandmother with onely two Children viz margerett Scott: my mother and thomas Scott: my sd Grandmother was made an Administratrix to my sd Grandfathers estate but ther was noe settlement made of the sd estat by the Court at all; and my sd uncle thomas Scott went into old England and dyed ther. and when I was about fowr yers old my mother dyed and in a short time after my Grandmother dyed: about sixten yers agoe, my sd Grandfather dyes seazed of agood Considerable estat in land in Ipswich; I am the onely suruiuing person descended from my sd Grandfather and now I am come to the Age of twenty one yers doe humly Craue that your Honnour will Grant Administration to me of the estat of my sd Grandfather that hath not bien leagally disposed of." Signed William Rogers.

A caution, dated Newbury, Feb. 15, 1694-5 to prevent William Rogers being appointed administrator of estate of Thomas Scott, for "I ——— a legal administration (and quiet possession) ——— twelve years sin— from a county court held at Boston." [Signature faded.]
*Essex Co. Probate Files, Docket 24,971.*

### Estate of John Trumble of Rowley.

An Trumble was appointed 29: 7: 1657 administratrix of the estate of her late husband, John Trumble. There were eleven children of three marriages. The estate was ordered to be divided, to four of Mighill Hobkinson's, five of John Trumble's before he married her, and two of his and hers, viz.: To Jonathan Hobkinson, 25li.; Jeremiah Hobkinson, 18li.; John Hobkinson, 18li.; Caleb Hobkinson, 18li.; to John Trumble, 15li.; Hannah Trumble, 8li.; Judah Trumble, 8li.; Ruth Trumble, 8li.; Joseph Trumble, 8li.; and to Abigaill Trumble and Mary Trumble, children of John and An, 20li. each. The rest of the estate, 55li., was allowed to the widow. *Ipswich Quarterly Court Records, vol. 1, page 65.*

Inventory of estate of John Trumble of Rowley, deceased, taken by Joseph Jewit, Maximilall Jewit, Thomas Dickinson and John Pickerd: Hous and barne, gardings, orchards, swamps belowe and all below the house and streett, 26li.; in Bradforth street lots, five acres and a half, 18li.; in Batchelers feild, two acres and a half, 6li.; in the marsh feild comanly called Mr. Dumers farme, meadows & upland, Eight acres, 12li.; Three cowe Gattes and a quarter, 2li. 3s. 4d.; his land in the northeast feild, 4 acre and a half, 5li.; Bought land in batchelders feild, three acre, 9li.; in land at the new plaine, 8li.; in meadowes, 4 acre, 9li.; in 4 gates more upon the Commans, 2li. 13s. 4d.; in corne upon the ground and grass upon the meadows, 14li. 16s.; one mare and one yearing colt, 20li.; Three oxen and one stere, 19li.; Six cowes, 18li.; one hefer of two yere old, 2li. 10s.; Two catle that is one yere old, 3li.; Two calves, 1li.; in swine, 7li.; his apparill, 6li.; in Books, 1li. 6s. 8d.; in a bearing fiuer linen and Three course sheets, 2li. 10s.; one Bed and bed cloathes thereon, 5li.; one Rug and one Covering, 1li. 4s.; in cotten woole, 7li.; Chists & one trunke, Two hogsheads and kushings, 1li. 11s.; one halbird, one sword, one pair of Bandelers, 15s.; more in Beding, one ruge more, 2li.; one sword more, one fouling peice, with kettls, pots & other small matters, 5li. 6s.; In pewter, 1li.; in wooden vessell, 1li.; in Tools belongin to his traid, 1li. 10s.; a saddl, Bridle, apannell, with some other small matters, 14s.; in cart, plow and other Instruments of husbandry, 3li. 10s.; in cowper wood, 10s.; in wheat, malt, Indian, with Bags and other imploments, 2li.; in brick, 4s.; total, 225li. 17s. 10d. Debts owing: To John Tod, 3li. 16s. 3d.; to Mr. Joseph Jewit, 1li.; total, 4li. 16s. 3d.

Sworn to in Ipswich court 29 : 7 : 1657, by his widow Ann Tromble. *Essex Co. Quarterly Court Files, vol. 3, leaf 140.*

### Estate of John Eyers, Sr. of Haverhill.

"The last will and Testament of John Eyers y^e Elder of Haverhill made y^e twelfe of March one thousand six hundred fifty six: fifty seaven: 1^st ffirst I giue vnto my Sonne John Eyers my dwelling house and house Lott, butt my wyfe to haue the ‖my‖ house and Orchyard & the pasture of English grass by the barne, and the leantoo att the South end of y^e barne and to haue libertie in y^e Same Nue barne to lay in such hay or corne as shee shall haue occasion to make vse of duering the tyme of hir Naturall life and att hir death to returne to my Sonne Jn^o Eyers, and duering the tyme of my wiues life my Sonne is to haue the vse of my house Lott and barne, and to pay vnto my wife tenn shillings an acre for every acre of broken vpp land in this my house Lott, and after the end of my wyues life when this falls into my Sonne John Eyers hand then hee shall pay as followes, fiue pound the first yeare after my wyfes death to my Sonne Nathaniell. The second yeare fiue pound to my daughter Hanah the Third yeare fower pound to my daughter Rebecka the fourth yeare fower pound to my daughter Mary: if either my daughters Rebecka or Mary die before this pay bee due vnto them, then it shall remaine vnto their childeren, butt if Nathaniell or Hanah die before it bee due & haue no childe then his or hirs to bee pay'd vnto my Sonne Obediah as is aboue specified to bee pay'd vnto them   2 I giue vnto my Sonne Nathaniell the house & house lott w$^{ch}$ I bought of my Sonn John Eyers and two Cow comons withall the privilidges belonging vnto two cow comons and to haue this when his apprentiship is out with his master ffrench and in the meane tyme my wyfe to haue the disposeing & benefitt of it, and if Nathaniell dies before the expiracon of y$^e$ said time of Nathaniells the said guift to Nathaniell to remaine to my daughter hanah I doe likewise giue to my Sonne Nathaniell my meadow in Haukes meadow, & my north meadow butt nott to haue itt till after the death of my wyfe butt she to haue the vse and benefitt of itt duering hir natural life   I doe likewise enjoyne these my two Sonnes John & Nathaniell not to sell these howses or house Lotts or any part of it to any except they first proffer it to all their other brothers and they to haue the refuseing of it att an other mans price which if either of them shall doe then this my guift shalbe voy'd in Law and his house or land which hee or they shall so sell shall bee forfeited to my other Sonnes:

"I giue my land in y$^e$ vpper and lower playnes to bee equally divided between my Sonnes Robert Thomas & Obediah Eyers and for as much of itt as is broken vpp to pay yearly to my wife for every acre tenn shillings an acre in such corne as shall growe on the say'd land att such price as y$^e$ Contrey rate shalbe pay'd att & if they shall nott impue it for corne then to pay in such pay as shalbee equivalent to corne att contrey price likewise my Sonnes John; Nathaniell; Robert; Thomas; & obediah shall maintaine all ffences aboute this land & to pay all rates which shalbee due vppon y$^e$ same after the yeare one thousand six hundred fifty seven; butt this yeare fifty seaven my wyfe to haue the vse & benefitt of all my land and meadow, and after to bee my Sonnes as is before Specified;

"I farther enjoyne these my Sonnes not to sell any part or parcell of this land without the consent of the other two brothers which if any doe then this my guift to bee voy'd in Law and the land so sould to bee forfeited vnto my other Sonnes provided that my other Sonnes will take it att an other mans price and if either of my Sonnes shall refuse to take my land vppon these termes which are here sett downe then that which any of them shall so refuse provided he haue all or else none of his said land by mee thus giuen shalbee my wifes to dispose of as shee please  I likewise giue to my Sonne Obediah two oxe comons in the comon oxe pasture & two ‖cow‖ cowcomons with all the privilidges belonging to fower commons; and halfe my second division of meadow & vpland and a young calfe of this yeare when it shalbee weanable it shalbe which my wyfe please, and that young Sowe, whose eare hangs downe and all my flaggy meadow I giue to my Sonne Peter the other halfe of my second division of meadow & vpland, & two Oxe comons with all privilidges belonging to two Oxe commons and three acres of land in y$^e$ vpper playne which hee hath allreadie in his possession: I giue my third division of land which is agreed on by the towne to bee lay'd out, I giue vnto my Sonne John Eyers & Peter Eyers to bee equally divided betweene them  I giue to my wife my best Cowe, and to my daughter Hannah my second best cowe, & my other Cowe and three yeare old heifer to my daughters Rebecka & Mary: And all my other goods and Cattell and Swine and house hold stuff vndisposed of I giue vnto my wyfe Hanah Eyers whom I make my Sole Executrix and whom I appoint to discharge all my debts & to take care for my buriall:"

[No signature.]

Proved in Hampton court 6: 8: 1657 by Henry Palmer. *Copy of will. Norfolk Deeds, vol. 1, leaf 58.*

Inventory taken 10: 2: 1657, by Robert Clements, James Davise, Sr. and Henry Palmer: 4 oxen, 25li.; 4 cowes, 2 steeres and a calfe, 20li.; 20 swine and 4 piges, 18li.; one plough, 2 paire of plouing Irons, one harro, one yoke and chaine and a cart rope, 4li.; 2 hoes, 2 axes, 2 shoveles, one spade, 1li.; 2 wedges, 2 bettle ringes, 2 sickels and a reape hook, hangers in the Chimny, tonges and pot hookes, 13s.; 2 potes, 3 kettels, one skillet, a frying pan, a warming pane, 3li. 3s.; in peuter, 1li.; 3 flocke beds and bed Cloathes belonging to them and bedsteeds, 18li.; 12 yards of Cotton

Cloth and Cotton woole and hemp and flax, 4li.; wooden stuf belonging to the house, 1li. 16s. 6d.; 2 wheeles, 3 Chests and a Cubber, 1li. 3s.; 2 muskets and al that belongs to them, 2li. 10s.; bookes, 15s.; in flesh meat, 15s.; about 40 bushell of corne, 7li.; his wearing aparill, 8li.; about 6 or 7 akers of graine in and upon the ground, 9li.; the dweling house and barne and land broken and unbroken with all apurtenances belonging unto it, 120li.; forkes, rakes and other smale imployments about the house and barne, 1li.; In debts oweing to him, 1li. Some things forgoten: betwen 2 or 3 bushels of salt, some nayles, 10s. Total, 248li. 5s. 6d.

This inventory brought into the Hampton court Oct. 6, 1657 by Hanah Eyer executrix to the will of John Eyer, Sr. *Essex Co. Probate Files, Docket* 1,088.

### ESTATE OF THOMAS WATHEN OF GLOUCESTER.

Administration on the estate of Thomas Wathen granted 24: 9: 1657 to Ezekiell Wathen, and he to bring in an inventory. *Salem Quarterly Court Records, vol. 4, leaf 17.*

Inventory, taken 30: 4: 1658: In the hands of Capt. Tho. Clerk, 7li. 14s. 2d. Signed by Ezekiel Wathen who swore in court, June 30, 1658, that this was all the estate of his kinsman, Thomas Wathen. *Essex Co. Quarterly Court Files, vol. 4, leaf 59.*

### ESTATE OF SAMUEL YOE (OF SALEM?).

Administration on the estate of Samuel Yoe granted 24: 9: 1657, to his wife, Rebecca Yoe. Inventory, 12li. 10s. *Salem Quarterly Court Records, vol. 4, leaf 18.*

### ESTATE OF AGNES BALCH OF SALEM.

An illegal will of Agnis Baulch of Salem, deceased, presented 24: 9: 1657. Benjamin Balch appointed administrator. *Salem Quarterly Court Records, vol. 4, leaf 18.*

Widow Anis Woodbery, Nicholas Patch, her brother and his wife, John Hill and his wife, Abigail Hill, Rachill Rayment, Hanah Woodbery and John Grover testified that they knew Anes Ballch more than two years before her death, during her long sickness, and judged that all her estate would not pay Bengeman Ballch and his wife for their trouble, labor and charge. *Essex Co. Quarterly Court Files, vol. 3, leaf 146.*

Inventory of estate of Anes Balsh taken Nov. 25, 1657, by John Rayment and Henery Hericke: One bed and bolster and pilo, £3; two Rugs, £1; one payer of shets, 6s.; one Cot and blancett, £1; 3 Cotes, £1; one waskot and two aprons, 10s.; two shiftes and an aperen and A pocetket hanshercher, 10s.; one pot, a Cettell, one Scelet and payll, 8s.; one hat, 8s.; one bibell, one payer stockings, 10s.; one trunck and Chest, 5s.; one warmen pan, 3s., one Carpet and plater, 8s., 11s.; one Chayer, one Crock, one payer beloes, £9. 11s. Benjamin Balch brought in his bill of charges: Attendance for two years, £15. 12s.; for coming to town to Mr. Curwin, £1; at hir buriall for Cofen and Casks and drink, £2; total, £18. 12s. *Essex Co. Quarterly Court Files, vol. 3, leaf 147.*

Ordered June 29, 1658, that Benjamyn Balch have the estate of Agnis Balch, in order to pay her debts. *Salem Quarterly Court Records, vol. 4, leaf 20.*

### ESTATE OF HUMPHREY GILBERT OF IPSWICH.

"The 14 of the 12 m$^{oth}$ 1657 The last will & Testamente of Humfrey Gilbard haueing his perfect memory dwelling in the boundes of Ipswich after my debts being payde I giue vnto my son John all The middow & Vpland w$^{ch}$ is my farme one hundred Akers more or less & That this farme be let out or Improued acording To my wifes discretian for The bringing of my Child vpp till he com to age or be able to Improve it him selfe and it is my will that twentie pounds be payde oute of The Incom of my farme To my four daughters when They are seaventene yeares of age & in case god Take any of them a way by death be fore the age specied That her proportion shall be equally deuided To the Rest of the sisters or if a second or a Third still it com to she That doe seuiue moreouer it is my will That tow oxen and tow Cows that I haue now In possesion be let oute with the farme I doe also giue vnto my daughter abbigal one heffer of four yeares olde I doe giue vnto my Loueing and deare wiffe Elissabeth Gilbard twelue ackers of vpland with my dwelling Howse I doe likwise giue vnto my wiffe my ffetherbed wth the furniture Therevnto belonging It is my will In Case my son should die in his nonage That what I haue giuen to my son should be equally deuided a mongst my daughters."

his mark<br>Humfre H Gilbard

Witness: Charles Gott, Thomas Hobes, Richard Hutton

Proved in Ipswich court Mar. 30, 1658 and administration granted to Elizabeth Gilbard wife of Humphry Gilbert.

Inventory taken 10: 1: 1658, by Charles Gott, Edward Coborne and Richard Hutton: one payre of Oxen, 12li.; one Red Cow, 4li.; one Cow white faced, 4li. 5s.; one Black Cow, 4li.; one 2 yeare old steare, 2li.; one yearelin Heffer, 1li. 5s.; 3 swine, 2li.; one stuff sute, 13s.; one payre of Hose & one old Cote and wastecote, 14s.; one Hatt, 4s.; 4 payre of shetes, 1li. 10s.; one napkin, 2 old pillebeares, 2s. 6d.; tow bolester Casses, 6s.; one sherte, 4s.; five bandes, 3s. 4d.; one fetherbed & bolster, tow fether pillowes & one bolster case, tow blankits, one Rugg, 7li. 10s.; one bras ketle, 1li. 10s.; one bras skillit, 2s. 6d.; one warmeing pan, 6s.; one pewter dish & fowre spownes, one poringer, tow sawser, one lattin pan, 9s.; tow Iron pots & one Iron skellit, 17s. 6d.; one ax, one hansaw, one shave, 5s.; one payre of Tonges, 3s.; one muskit & sword, 8s.; one plow & Tacklin, 10s.; one smothing Iron, 2s.; earthen ware, 2s. 6d.; Tow Chistes & tow boxes, 16s.; wooddin ware, 12s.; 2 sives, 2s.; Bookes, 8s.; one shepe, 1li. 5s.; one flock bedd, 6s.; one friing pan, 3s.; Tow baskets, 4d.; one payre of shows, 1s. 6d.; one Glass, 6d.; one payre of stockins, 1s.; halfe a ferkin, 8d.; one spade, 1s. 2d.; small Towles, 5s.; one payre of Cardes, 1s. 3d.; one Cros Cut saw, 4s.; Halfe a whip saw, 5s; Howses and Lande, 120li.; total, 169li. 12s. 6d.

Attested to in Ipswich court Mar. 30, 1658 by the widow of Humphry Gilbert.

*Essex Co. Probate Files, Docket* 10,889.

William Rayner, husband of Elizabeth, late wife and administratrix of Humfry Gilbert, deceased, was ordered 26: 4: 1666, to deliver to Hanna Gilbert, daughter of the said Humfry, a great kettle, a box and a pewter platter, which were mentioned in the inventory of the said estate. *Salem Quarterly Court Records, vol.* 4, *page* 162.

The wife of William Geare deposed that she heard Goodman Gilbert say when he made his will that the bed, kettle and some other things were to be Hanna's.

Ellen Haselton, aged about twenty-five years, deposed that

Goodwife Gelbord gave her daughter, upon her death bed, a great brass kettle, a pewter platter and a black box.

Elisabeth Hotten deposed that Gilberd said that there were several things his other wife had given his daughters and he would not alter it. Sworn, 27: 4: 1666, before Wm. Hathorne.

*Essex Co. Quarterly Court Files, vol. 11, leaf 133.*

"The humbell petisyon of the foure dafteres & there husbands of Humphrey Gillburd desesid January the 20: 57," to appoint the four husbands, the petitioners, administrators on said Gilbert's estate that was not given away by will, and six acres of fresh meadow never inventoried by the administrator. Signed by the petitioners, Peter harvi, Richerd Palmer, Richerd Comer, Mosis Ebern. Administration granted to the petitioners. *Essex Co. Quarterly Court Files, vol. 3, leaf 148.*

Inventory of estate of Humphrey Gilbert, that had not been willed away before, taken by Phillip Fowler, and Capt. Gidney, attorney: One paire of oxen, 12li.; cow, 4li.; cow, 4li. 5s.; 2 year old steers and 1 yearlin, 3li. 5s.; 3 swin, 2li.; 2 pair of shetes, 15s.; 2 napkins, 2 ould Pilloberes, 17s.; 2 bolster casis, 6s.; bras skillits and warming pan, 8s. 6d.; spounes, poreng sases, Latin pan, 3s.; 2 iron potes, 1 iron skillit, 17s. 6d.; one paire of tonges, 3s., one musket & sord, prized at 8s., 11s.; Plou & tacklin, 10s.; smuthing iron & erthin ware, 4s. 6d.; 2 chestes & 2 bockes, wooden ware, 1li. 10s.; Boockes, 8s.; sheep, 25s., flockbead, 6s., frying pan, 6s., 2li. 2s.; 2 baskites, 4d., 1 glas, 6d., 10d.; 1-2 ferkin, 8d., 1 spad, 14d., small toules, 5s., 8s. 10d.; one coos cut sau, 4s., half a whipsa, 5s., 9s.; 6 acres of meado yet not inuentarid, 18li.; total, 53li. 11d. *Essex Co. Quarterly Court Files, vol. 4, leaf 19.*

Deposition of Richard Hutten, aged about sixty years, concerning the will of Humphery Gilbert, he being present when it was made, and upon reading the copy finds the folfowing differences between it and his words: 1st, the oxen and cows that were to let out with the farm, in the copy is omitted that when his son came to age or able to improve it he should have them; 2d, the gift to his daughter Abigall was expressed by him towards their bringing up; 3d, the house and twelve acres of land he gave as a jointure. And further testified that notwithstanding the expressions of said Gilbert he saw him sign the will and declare his wife to be his executrix. Thomas Hobbs, aged about sixty four years, testified to the above. Sworn to Mar. 31, 1685 by both parties. *Ipswich Deeds, vol. 5, page 75.*

ESTATE OF JOHN ROBINSON OF IPSWICH.

"This is the last will and testement of me John Robinson of Ipswich whellright being in perfect vnderstanding and memmery doth Bequeth and giue as in maner following I giue to Alles howlett the wife of thomas howlett Ten pounds I doe likewise giue to thomas howlett Junner my Cheast and all my tools and all the Rest of my Estate I doe giue vnto thomas howlett seaner whome I make my sole Exsecketr witnes my hand"

"The 27 of february 1657."

his mark<br>John T Robinson

Witness: James How, John How.
Proved in Ipswich court Mar. 30, 1658 by the witnesses. *Essex Co. Quarterly Court Files, vol. 4, leaf 20.*

Inventory allowed Mar. 30, 1658: Debt of 20li.; debt of 16li.; one oxe, 6li. 10s.; his Tools, 6li. 7s.; his cloathes, 6li. 2s. 6d.; total, 54li. 19s. 4d. Signed by James How. Due to Ensign Howlett for diet, clothes, attendance and physic, 22li. 16s. 3d. *Essex Co. Quarterly Court Files, vol. 4, leaf 21.*

ESTATE OF GEORGE BUNKER OF TOPSFIELD.

Administration on the estate of George Buncker granted June 29, 1658 to the widow, Jane Buncker; and the estate to be divided among said widow, son William Buncker, Elizabeth Buncker, Mary Buncker, Ann Buncker and Martha Buncker, all under twenty-one years of age. *Salem Quarterly Court Records, vol. 4, leaf 21.*

Inventory dated 29: 3: 1658, taken by Thomas Howlett, Frances Pabody, Richod (his R H mark) Huten and Abraham Redington: For working Catil, 36li.; Cowes hefors and Caves, 16li.; One Ewe and two Lambs, 2li.; a Cart and plowes and tackling, 3li.; swine, 2li.; gune and sword, 2li.; bras and pouter, 3li.; tabul and Chares and trayes, tubes and barils, 2li. 3s.; Cowes pelt skines and wheeles, a Rop and bandalers, 2li.; beding and linan and wolan and thirteen pound Coten wol, 8li.; waring Clothing, 3li. 6s.; the Crop of Corne upon the ground, 9li.; dets due to him upon bil, 4li. 11s.; housin and land as namli medo and uplande, the farme Consisting of thre hondered and twelve acres more or les, there be more driblin detes that do not yet apere what tha are; By John Andros, 4li.; by Frances Vsselton, 3li. 14s.; total, 300li. 14s. The estate is debt to severall psons following: To Mr. Tuttle as by bill & otherwise, 9li. 18s. 2d.; Mr. Joseph Juit, 2li. 8d.; Capt. Pendleton, 80li.; Willm. Howard, by bill, 24li.; to the worshipfull Mr. Bradstreet, 22 bushils wheat, 4li. 15s.; Mr. Robert Payne, 2li. 2s. 7d.; Goodman Moulton, 30s. 9d. & Robt. Andrew, 14s. 4d., 2li. 5s. 4d.; Mr. Curwin, 12li. 11s.; Robt. Stiles, 6li., Robt. Pearse, 10s., 6li. 10s.; Mr. Purkings, 50s. and Goodman Gouldsmyth, 18s., 3li. 8s.; Mr. Willm. Payne, 4li.; Thomas Rootes, 2li. 14s. 10d.; Richard Raymend, 20s. & Goody Graften, 24s., 44s.; total, 158li. 13s. 4d.

Elizabeth Bunker was twelve years old; Will., ten years old; Mary, six; An, four; and Martha, one year and a half. *Essex Co. Quarterly Court Files, vol. 4, leaf 60.*

### ESTATE OF WILLIAM WHITE OF SALEM.

Administration on the estate of William White of Salem, deceased sometime since at Vnkaway, granted June 29, 1658, to Mr. William Browne of Salem. *Salem Quarterly Court Records, vol. 4, leaf 21.*

### ESTATE OF THOMAS SCUDDER OF SALEM.

"By the will of God Amen, I Thomas Scudder inhabitant of Salem in Newengland, beinge sick, & weake in bodye, but of perfect strength of memorye, & vnderstandinge, doe appoint, ordeine, & make this my last will & testament. I doe therefore by these presents appoint, & give vnto my welbeloved wiffe Elizabeth Scudder, dureinge her life, all my worldly goodes, & estate whatsoever, of houses, landes, Cattle, & all moveable goodes, & vsentles of what kind soever, & all personall estate whatsoever & I doe allso ordeine, & make, & appoint her my said Wiffe, my full, & sole Execatrixe after my death onely my desire is that after her death, what shee shall leave, of any of my foresaid personall estate, it shalbe devided amongst my Children, John Scudder, & Thomas Scudder, & Hennry Scudder, & Elizabeth Barthelmew, And Thomas Scudder my Grandchilde, the sonne of my sonne William Scudder desesed, & my mynde & will is, that all such estate, as my said wiffe Elizabeth Scudder shall leave after her death, shallbe valewed, & equally devided to my said Children, & Grandchild, & my said Grandchild to have as much as any one of them. Neverthelesse, one Cowe, which I formerlye gave my said wiffe, I doe in noe wise dispose of, butt leaue itt wholly to my said wiffe to dispose of itt, as shee shall thinke good, And that this is my last Will, & testament I have herevnto sett my hand, and seale, this thirtyeth daye of September, one thousand sixe hundred fiftye & seaven:"

his mark<br>Thomas C Scudder<br>his mark

Witness: Richard Waters, Wilom Traske, Joseph F Boyse and Thomas Deutch.

Proved in Salem court June 29, 1658, by Richard Waters and Capt. William Traske. *Essex Co. Quarterly Court Files, vol. 4, leaf 63.*

Inventory of estate of Thomas Scudder, deceased, 1657, taken by Thoms Gardner and Joseph (his X mark) Boys, and sworn to by his widow, Elizabeth (her X mark) Scudder: His house & orchyard, 20li.; three Oxen, 13li.; three Cowes, 9li.; foure sheepe & a lambe, 7li.; two swine, 1li.; Axes & other tooles, 1li.; hempe, 5s. 4d.; two Iron Potts, 10s.; foure brasse kettles, 2li. 10s.; two brasse panns & foure skillets, 1li. 2s.; two spitts, one pott hanger, fire pan, & tonges, one gridiron, one drippinge pan, 14s.; Pewter, 2li. 3s.; one feather bed & bolster & 2 pillowes, 4li.; one bed Coveringe & two blancketts, 1li. 8s.; two paire of sheetes, one pillowe, six napkins, 2li.; one bedd & bolster, 1li.; three sheetes, 10s.; his wearinge apparrell, 3li.; two Cushins & three Curteins, 12s.; two Chests & two boxes, 17s.; one barrell with tallowe, 17s.; Tubbe & pales, 10s.; other Lumber, 10s.; total, 73li. 8s. 4d. *Essex Co. Quarterly Court Files, vol. 4, leaf 64.*

Administration upon the estate of Tho. Scudder, which was left in the hands of his wife who lately deceased, was granted 28: 9: 1665, to Mr. Henry Bartholomew and Hillyard Veren, who were ordered to bring in an inventory. *Salem Quarterly Court Records, vol. 4, page 152.*

## ESTATE OF JAMES PATCH OF SALEM.

Will of James Patch, brought in 8: 7: 1658, and his wife, Hannah, appointed executrix. *Salem Quarterly Court Records, vol. 4, leaf 25.*

"The Last Will and testament of James Patch: Sheweth, that I resigne my soule into the hands of the Lord who hath Given me this spirit, and my body vnto the grave; to be raysed vp by his mighty power at the Resurrect° my Goods I dispose of by this my Last will as followeth. Imp$^r$ I give and bequeath vnto my beloved wife Hannah Patch, my house and lands, orchard, and all the appertaynances of it, belonging to my home groundes, together with that parcell of meadow, Laying near Rich. Dodges, as allso two Cowes, together with ten acres of Rockey land laying on the east side of the home lott, ffor wood: as also all the household stuffe, in the house for the competent bringing up of the children. I give and bequeath unto my Son James Patch, all my part of the ffarme (called Knights farme) both vpland & meadow, all my right there be it more or lesse: together with the two youngest Oxen, and the horse. I doe nextly Give and bequeath vnto my Daughter Mary Patch y$^e$ two oxen that are oldest; togeth$^r$ with one Cow, and allso ten acres of vpland, Laying neare Sawyers Playne.

"Vnto my Daughter Elizabeth Patch I give and bequeath by will, my two midde Oxen, as alsoe one Cow, together with twenty acres of vpland laying by the Land, called Eastyes land, and Joyneing next vnto the sayd land. I doe also by my will appoint my Beloved wife Hanna Patch to be my lawfull exsequitrix, to administer vpon my estate to Receive my dues, to discharge all debts, of mine; with the remainder of my estate, Corne Cattell or other goods, whare belongeing vnto me. ffarther more I doe by will Constitute and ordayne & appoint my two Brothers, viz. Nicholas Woodberry, & John Patch, to be overseers of this my Last will; and to act and Doe in reference vnto my Estate, wife & children, as overseers & ffeofeyes of trust accord. to Law & reason vse to doe: Vnto this my Last will & testament I have Sett my hand vpon the seaventh Day of August. In the year 1658."

James Patch.

Witness: Tho Lowthropp, John hill.

Proved in Salem court 1: 9: 1658. *Essex Co. Quarterly Court Files, vol. 4, leaf 65.*

Proved by Lt. Thos. Lothrop and Jon. Hill. *Salem Quarterly Court Records, vol. 4, leaf 27.*

Inventory taken 27: 6: 1658, by Richard (his X mark) Brackenbury, John Thorndike, Zabulon Hill and John Hill: One dwelling house & barne, one orchyard & 5 akers of land improued, 50li.; 4 akers of Indyan Corne, 8li.; 10 akers of land Rockey, 2li.; 3 akers of meadow, 9li.; 10 akers of land nere Sawyers plain, 10li.; 20 akers of land nere Eastyes lot, 10li.; one third part of knights his farme, 20li.; 6 oxen, one payr, 13li., the next, 12li., the worst, 11li., 36li.; one horse, 12li.; one young Colte, 4li.; 4 Cowes, 12li.; one yearing & 2 Calfes, 3li.; one ewe, one weather, one Rame, one Lambe, 3li.; 2 hogges & 4 smal pigges, 3li.; one third part of a shalop, 10li.; 7 barrills & better of mackeril, 9li.; one waggon, 1 pr. of wheels, 2 plowes & plowtackle, 5li.; axes & workeing tooles, 1li.; 2 musketts & bandeliers, 1 fowleing piece & sword, 3li.; 2 bedds, bedclothes, sheets, Curtain & aperteinanses, 14li.; wearing aparaile, 11li.; 1 yard of broad Cloth & 2 yds of peniston, 1li.; 2 Iron potts, 1 kettle, potthookes, Rackes & 3 Iron wedges, 1li. 12s.; 2 brasse kettles, 3 skellitts, warming pan & Skimer, 2li.; 1 lanthorne besides pewter, lattin ware, smoothing Iron, hourglasse, portingale ware, morter & pestill, 1li.; 2 Chests, 2 boxes, 1 wheele & woodden ware, 2li.; 12 pound of Cotten wooll, 12 pound of flax, 12 pound Linen & 8 pound of Cotten yarne, 4li. 4s.; 1 Doung forke, howes, 1 payr of Cardes & frying pan, 1li.; English corne & flax undrest, 3li.; total, 250li. 16s. *Essex Co. Quarterly Court Files, vol. 4, leaf 66.*

### Estate of Andrew Creeke of Topsfield.

Administration on the estate of Andrew Creeke granted 28: 7: 1658 to Daniell Clarke. The amount of inventory was insufficient to pay bills, by 40s. *Ipswich Quarterly Court Records, vol. 1, page 70.*

Inventory taken Sept. 17, 1658, by Frances Pabody and Robert Andrews of Topsfield: Old clothes, 1li. 3s. 6d.; his sute of better cloths, 2li. 6s.; bannds, bandstrings & hankerchers, 13s. 6d.; a hatt, 13s. 6d.; a bottle, two knives & a spoone, 1s. 10d.; an ax, 2s.; a shirt, 2s.; a pott & pothookes, 10s.; a baskett & a paile, 1s.; a rapier & a belt, 16s.; a cowe in Mathy Stanlyes hands, with a yeares rent almost due, 4li. 8s.; dew to him of his wages, 6li.; a heifers Hyde at the taners, 7s. 6d.; received of Mr. Apleton, 12s.; total, 17li. 17s. 4d. The debts wch. the sayd Andrew owed when he dyed wch. doth allreadye appeare: Oweing to his master Daniell Clarke when they reckoned for his last yeares wages, 11s.; payd to Mr. Wade for a sute of cloths for him, with makeing of them & a paire of stockings, 3li. 10s.; a paire of knit stockings & a shirt, 12s. 6d.; for shoes & leather, 6s. 6d.; payd John Newmarsh his wife for making bands, 2s. 4d.; payd to Goodman Wooddam for him, 2s.; payd to Mr. Willson, 1s. & to Deacon Knowlto, 3s., 4s.; oweing to John Tod, wch. Dan. Clarke is engaged for, 2li. 16s. 9d.; oweing to Mr. William Payne, 4li. 12s.; oweing to Mr. Baker, 1li. 18s.; oweing to Tho. Lovell, 1li. 3s.; oweing to Mr. William Norton, 1li.; oweing to Robert Lord, 1s. 6d.; coffin & wynding sheet & other charges for his buryall, 1li. 8s.; oweing to John Andrews, 12s. 7d.; oweing to Humphry Griffen, 7s.; for tyme Daniell Clarke spent to bring in an Inventory & for entering the order of administration & other fees, 9s.; total, 19li. 16s. 2d. Sworn by Daniell Clarke, 29: 7: 1658, before Robert Lord, cleric. *Essex Co. Quarterly Court Files, vol. 4, leaf 87.*

### ESTATE OF SUSAN FRENCH OF IPSWICH.

Administration on the estate of Susan French, deceased, granted 28: 7: 1658, to her son John French. *Ipswich Quarterly Court Records, vol. 1, page 71.*

Inventory of the estate of Susan French, widow, of Ipswich taken Mar. 10, 1658 by Robert Lord and Phillip (his (|) mark) ffowler: a fetherbed old and small, 2 fether pillows, one old couerlet & blankett, 2li. 10s.; her weareing apparell, 4li.; one old chest & box without a lid, an old Hogshead, 8s.; a linen wheele & 2 chaires, 5s.; an old brase pot & a little ould skillet & little Iron pot, 10s.; 2 pewter dishes poringer & skimer, 8s. 6d.; 2 paire of old shires, ould brase & other small things, 6s. 6d.; a spitt, tongs, grediron & other small things, 12s.; an old warmeing pan & frying, 6s.; 2 small trayes, earthen ware & other lumbar, 5s. 6d.; a cowe old, 3li.; total, 12li. 11s. 6d.

Received in Ipswich court Mar. 29, 1659. *Essex Co. Probate Files, Docket* 10,189.

### ESTATE OF ROBERT CLEMENTS OF HAVERHILL.

"Sept: 6th (58) I Robertt Clements of Haverhill being of perfitt memory blessed be God for itt, doe ordaine & make this my last will, in manner & forme following ffirst I Committ my soule into the hands of God my Creator & maker, beleeving thorough the mirritts Rightousnesse & obedience of Jesus christ my redemer to haue & enjoy life & Salvation

Everlastingly by him. ffor my goods I giue first vnto my wife my house & house lott & all the acomadato⁸ that belonged to itt which shee is to haue during her life, & after her decease to returne to my childorns childorne that are in new england each his pportio to be delivered into ye hands of their parents for their childorns vse. I giue alsoe to my wife my best yoake of oxen I haue, & three of my best cowes, & my mare which brought the *mule* & alsoe my swine & two of my best beds with theire furniture to them & six of my best peauter dishes six spoones, my best brasse pott, & three of my best kittles, & two spining t—rnes, & all hangles on the fire, with fire shoules & tonges & two of ye best coushens, one ——— & a cupp, with all my wooden & Earthen vessells & all manner of clothing that belong to her, as also my byble candlstick & chamber pott. my will is that if there be any goods of mine come out of England this yere or the next my wife shall haue fiue pounds of itt according to ye bill of lading. alsoe I giue my wife all ye Lining in my house ‖excepting two paire of sheetes yt are for my bed‖ & all the Corne in my house barne & growing on the land, & also a debt of seauen pounds & sum odd mony in the hands of John Hutchins for the repaireing the house & fenceing ye home lott. I giue to my wife alsoe what is due to mee ‖or will bee‖ from mr Dumer by bills or Covinants, & alsoe the Cloth that is att the weavers with what woolen yearne & fflaxe is in the house, & alsoe three pounds which is in the hands of mr Cooke of boston I giue her two skillitts, two stockes off the best beese & two chests with locke & caie to them. I giue to my wife the boards I bought at Salisbury to repaire the house. It is my will that one halfe of the goods which I giue my wife that if shee spend not, at her decease it shall returne to my executors to be equally devided among them

"I giue to my sonne Job Clement one fellee which will be two yer old next may. allsoe I give him my best suit of apparell & my best cloake & best hatt, my best paire of shewes & stockens. I giue to my sonne Robertt twenty pound due to mee out of my rentt in England, & which rentt is due to mee more I giue to my three sonnes John, Abraham & Dannell. All the rest of my estate in new england due to mee vpon bonds or bills or any accounts land or goods whatsoever I giue to my sonnes Moses Pengrow, & Abraham Morrill & John Osgood whom I make my executors to see this my will performed & my debts paid & my body laid in ye graue. That which is struck out in the other side at the lower end betweene the 4th & 5th line it was done before it was seald to, & her vnto I sett my hand & seale. I giue to mr ward or minester fiue pounds."

Robert Clements [SEAL]<br>his mark

Witness: Bartell: B H Heath and william white.
Proved in Hampton court 11 : 8 : 1658 by the witnesses.

Inventory of estate of Robert Clemens, deceased Sept. 29, 1658, accepting sum smale debts wch cannott be accounted, taken by Tristram Coffyn, Sr. and William White, one of the executors: his wearing apparell, 16li. 18s.; his purse mony & silver seale, & ring, 1li. 7s.; one bill oweing him, 55li.; one paire of steares, 10li.; twenty bushels of rie, 3li. 6s. 8d.; one cow & thirty bushels of rie, 5li.; in bills, 8li. 15s.; 12li. 15s.; 56li.; 5li.; 6li. 6s.; 14li.; 2li. 3s. 6d.; 4li.; 7li. 12s.; one ingagemt for rent for land, 5li.; foure cows, two steares, one heifer, 22li.; three mares, one fellee, one horse, one colt, 69li.; three cowes, 10li. 10s.; in swine, calves & sheep, 10li. 15s.; beding 25li., 25li. 13s.; a psell of Cotton woole & Cotton yerne Sheeps woole Canmas & fethers, 3li. 1s.; in wheat & Indyan Corne, 2li. 10s.; for chests, turns & cards, potts & kittles, 4li. 17s.; Severall things as viz: fire shovl & tongs, Andiens, spitt, plow chaines & such like Iron things, 5li. 17s. 6d.; in books, fowling pece, tablcloth, napkins, 3li. 18s.; carpett, & warming pan & cotton cloth, 1li. 10s.; his dwelling house & acomadacions, 55li.; Eight loads of hay, 4li. & a psell lining cloth, 5li.; the grist mill, 30li.; one paire of oxen, 12li.; a psell of boards & two stocks of beese, 2li. 13s.; wooden vessels & earthen vessels & one spade, 1li. 16s. 6d.; cotton & lining yearne, 2li. 10s.; a debt of 3li.; a debtt of ten pounds, 10li.; total, 494li. 14s. 2d.

Attested by Moses Pingrie and John Osgood.

Presented the 10 : 8m : 1658 and attested by Moses Pingrin and John Osgood before Robert Pike.

Attested by Abraham Morrill before Tho. Bradbury, recd.

Essex Co. Probate Files, Docket 5,604.

## ESTATE OF MATHEW WHIPPLE OF IPSWICH.

Administration on the estate of Mathew Whiple, intestate, granted Nov. 30, 1658 to his widow Mary Whipple, by Simon Bradstreet and Major-General Denison. *Ipswich Quarterly Court Records, vol. 1, page 71.*

Administration having been granted formerly on the estate to the widow Mary, an inventory was presented Mar. 29, 1659. The land to remain for the children and widow. *Ipswich Quarterly Court Records, vol. 1, page 75.*

Inventory of the estate of Mathew Whipple of Ipswich taken Feb. 4, 1658, by Robert Lord and Edward Browne: a barne nott neere finished with some timbor drawne together & some of it Hewen, 7li.; 30 acres of land upland & meddow 12 of it in tilt & within fence & 56 acres out of fence, 116li.; a horse, 12li.; two oxen, 11li.; one Cow & 2 heifers, 10li.; one sow & 4 small shotes, 2li. 3s. 4d.; In Indian Corne, 3li. 15s.; sadle, bridle, pistolls & furniture, 2li. 10s.; a pillion & pillion cloth, 1li. 15s.; his weareing apparrell & lennen, 10li. 10s.; a bedstead cord & bedding, 6li. 16s.; sheets, pillow beeres & table lennen, 6li.; two sillver spoones, 16s.; In Pewter, 1li. 8s.; a box Iron & heatters, 5s.; one trunke, one chest & boxes, 1li. 4s.; a little table & chaires, 5s. 6d.; on Iron pott, skillett & two sives, 15s.; a mare colt a yeare & vantage, 8li.; a cradle, 10s.; 18 1-2 bushells of wheat, 4li. 3s.; In debts oweing to the estate, 32li.; total, 238li. 16s. 1d. Debts oweing from the estate to be deducted out, 44li. 14s. 4d.; cleare estate, 194li. 1s. 9d.

Received in Ipswich court Mar. 29, 1659. *Essex Co. Probate Files, Docket 29,514.*

### Estate of William Waldridge of (Salem?).

Will. Waldridg had gone out of the country and was probably cast away, and leaving no known attorney, Sam. Archer, marshal, and Tho. Robbins were appointed 30: 10: 1658, to take charge of his estate. *Salem Quarterly Court Records, vol. 4, leaf 28.*

### Estate of John Wright of Newbury.

John Wright, late of Newbury, was possessed of or had a right to goods and chattels in New England, and there being no will, Samuell Symonds and Daniell Denison granted administration of the estate, 30: 10: 1658, to Edward Bragg, and the court ordered it entered. *Ipswich Quarterly Court Records, vol. 1, page 74.*

Inventory taken by Thomas Bishop and Robert Kinsman: "In two ||bills|| both of one date, & ||its|| said (in y$^e$ writing) to be of the same tenor, in y$^e$ one; the party is bound in y$^e$

sume of xl$^{li}$ for y$^e$ payment of 20$^{li}$ In the other the debter is bound in y$^e$ sume of Thirty pounds for y$^e$ payment of 18$^{li}$ and seven shillings. Its also exprest in y$^e$ writings. the one being pformed the other to stand voyde." *Essex Co. Quarterly Court Files, vol. 5, leaf 2.*

ESTATE OF SAMUEL CORWITHY OF (MARBLEHEAD?).

Administration on the estate of Samuell Corwithy, intestate, granted Mar. 29, 1659, to John Gedney. *Ipswich Quarterly Court Records, vol. 1, page 74.*

Inventory taken Mar. 28, 1659, by Hen. Skery and John Marston: a house and foure ackers of ground laying in ye neck, 20li.; a feather beed and on boulster on pillow, 4li. 5s.; two Ruggs & two blankitts, 2li. 15s.; a broad cloch child blankit Couler Reed, 15s.; a holland sheett & a paier of corser sheets besids, 1li. 10s.; beed stead & cord and beed matte, 8s.; three Curttens and Vallance, 12s.; two pilobears, 4s., a diaper tablecloth, 10s.; a chest, 7s., a small trunnk, 4s., 11s.; a bed settle, 4s., two kuisens, 4s. 6d., 8s. 6d.; a small cheest, 3s., a hanging Coberd, 6s., a desk, 2s., 11s.; an Iron, 10s., potthooks, 1s., on hake, 2s. 6d., 12s.; a brase pann, 16s.; a beell mettle morter & pestell, 8s., 1li. 4s.; a warming pann, 4s., a brase kettle, 5s., 9s.; a basson & Ur, 10s., other old pewter, 5s. 6d., 15s. 6d.; two dogg Irons, 4s., a fire Iron, 2s., 6s.; fire pann & toungs & bellows & speett, 4s. 6d.; 4 chaires, 7s., a brush, 1s. 6d., 8s. 6d.; a Rappertt & bandelers & belt, 9s., friing pann & an axe, 4s., 13s.; a looking glase and 1-2 howers glase, 2s. 6d.; a fine baskitt & other lumber, 3s. 6d.; total, 37li. 4s.

Mr. Geedney and Mary Carwethy wife of Samuell Carwethy, deceased, testified the 28: 1: 1659 that this was a true inventory.

Received in the Ipswich court Mar. 29, 1659. *Essex Co. Probate Files, Docket 6,390.*

Mr. John Gedny, administrator of the estate of Samuell Curwithy, was discharged Mar. 26, 1661, having settled the estate according to the inventory. *Ipswich Quarterly Court Records, vol. 1, page 93.*

ESTATE OF TIMOTHY COOPER OF LYNN.

Administration on the estate of Timothy Cooper of Lynn, granted Mar. 29, 1659, to his widow, Elizabeth Cooper. Inventory of his estate amounted to 167li. 11s. Widow to have all the estate, including the house and land, except that she should pay certain portions to the six children, as they came of age, namely, John, the eldest son and Mary, Hannah, Timothy, Dorcas and Rebecah. *Ipswich Quarterly Court Records, vol. 1, page 74.*

Inventory taken Mar. 8, 1659, by Francis Burrill and John (his [] mark) Wit: his weareing cloths, 4li.; the beding I meane all manner of beding and bed steads, 15li. 10s.; yarne, flax and hemp, 2li.; woling yarn and wolle and coten, 10s.; puter and bras and eiorn vessels and pothangers, 4li. 8s.; tabels and chistes and cobbord and chares and whels and cardes, 2li.; saws and axses and hows and other touls and eiorn trad, 3li. 10s.; A musket, sorde and bandeleres and belt, 1li. 10s.; A cart and cart rop and plows and eiorn traid belonging to them, 3li. 3s.; tubes and buckets and such eusfull vessels, 1li.; corn enlish and indein corne, 2li. 10s.; A bibel and other small thinges, 10s.; the dweling hous and housing and upland, 50li.; the meddow, 30li.; oxen and coues and Yonge cattell, 34li.; A mare and swine, 18li.; the shep, 4li.; total, 177li. 1s.; credit 5li. 10s.; Indeted 15li.; leaving total, 167li. 11s.

Mary Cooper aged eighteen, Hanah, sixteen, Timothy, eight, Dorcas, five and Rebeca, three years, to have 15li. each; Jno. Cooper aged twelve years 25li.; the widow the remainder of the estate. *Essex Co. Probate Files, Docket 6,327.*

### Estate of John Tuttle of Ipswich.*

Administration on the estate of John Tuttle granted Mar. 29, 1659, to George Giddinge and Mr. Joseph Jewett, formerly attorneys of the estate. *Ipswich Quarterly Court Records, vol. 1, page 74.*

Whereas Mr. John Tuttle died in Ireland about two or three years ago, and there being no will or administration and the heir appearing and desiring to have the house and land which was his father's, the court ordered Sept. 27, 1659, that if the heir, Symon Tuttle, gave security to repay the rent he shall receive and keep the house in repair, he might take the estate into his possession until the court takes further order, the widow's thirds being reserved during her life.

* See also Records and Files of the Quarterly Courts of Essex Co., Mass., vol. II (1912), pp. 363-366.

Thomas Bishop was the surety. *Ipswich Quarterly Court Records, vol. 1, page* 81.

Mr. Symond Tuttle, bringing in a letter of attorney from Mrs. Joanna, executrix of Mr. John Tuttle, the will of the latter having been approved and allowed in Ireland to the satisfaction of this court, it was ordered 10: 10: 1661, that said Symond Tuttle be allowed as attorney, according to the letter bearing date, Jan. 29, 1660. *Salem Quarterly Court Records, vol. 4, page* 81.

Petition to the court 15: 3: 1661 of Simon Tuttell as attorney to Johanna Tuttell executrix of the will of her husband, John Tuttell shewing that the petitioner's father and her husband was indebted to Mr. Jacob Willet, in London, merchant, about 50li., which not being paid amounted to 111li. here in New England and for satisfaction of the same Mr. Antipas Boyse was made her attorney for the payment of the same out of the stock but instead he had sold of the land in Ipswich; and now we ask for your consideration in the case that we may have release from the same.

The petition having been considered and having seen the discharge given to Mr. Boyse by Mr. Willet it is judged inexpedient to grant any further hearing. Consented to by the magistrates 15: 3: 1662. *Mass. Archives, vol.* 15B, *page* 246.

### ESTATE OF WILLIAM ADAMS, JR. OF IPSWICH.

Administration on the estate of William Addams, jr. of Ipswich, granted Mar. 29, 1659, to William Addams, his father, and John Addams, his brother. The inventory amounted to 218li. The estate was distributed to eldest son William, one half, and one fourth to each of the other two children, when they were of the age of twenty-one years. Elder John Whipple and Thomas Stace, overseers. *Ipswich Quarterly Court Records, vol. 1, page* 74.

Inventory taken 24: 11: 1658, by John Appleton and Robert Lord: the dwelling house, Barne & orchyard together with six or 7 acres of marsh neare to Mr. William Paynes, 70li.; sixty acres or thereabouts of Land on the south syde the River by John Addams, 80li.; one mare, 12li. & a foale, 4li., 16li.; Two oxen, 10li.; three Cowes, 9li.; two ewes & one weather sheepe, 2li. 10s.; Two hoggs & five shotes, 5li. 10s.; one handsaw, 4s.; one broad & narow chessell & goudge,

4s.; two Addes, 4s. 6d.; one croscut saw, 5s.; fowre Augeers, 7s.; five cheesells & goudges for turneing, 5s. 6d.; a percer stock & bitts, 4s.; a hollow shave, 1s.; 4 planes, 5s. 6d.; a sqare, 2s. 6d.; a payre of pinsers, 5d.; one beetle & 2 small wedges, 4s.; 4 axes, broad & narrow, 16s.; a span shakle Ring & staple, 5s.; a chayne & draught yoke, 9s.; an old sled, 1s. 6d.; an old broad How, 2s. 6d.; an old sithe & other old Iron, 3s.; In nayles, dovetailes & other small things, 12s.; a small hande vice, 5s.; a plane, alls & gimlett, 1s. 3d.; two musketts, swords & furniture, 2li. 10s.; one bedsted & cord, 10s.; one fether bed & boulster, one paire of blanketts, a coverlett strawbed & curtaynes, 5li. 10s.; one trundle bed boulster, 2 pillows one blankett and coverlett, 2li. 10s.; one bedsted, bed & boulster, two blanketts, a Rug & a cradle cloth, 3li.; 9 yards of sackcloth, 15s.; 6 yards & a halfe of white cotton, 19s. 6d.; flax, hempe and woole, 16li.; a chest and box without a lid, 5s.; 2 spring locks, 2 cubbard locks, one box lock, one stock lock & 2 paire of dovetailes, 9s.; one box Iron, 4s.; a joyne chest, 6s. 8d.; one pine chest & 3 boxes & leaden diall, 16s.; nyne chaires, 12s.; saddle, pillion & bridle, 1li. 18s.; stufe for 2 joyne tables & 15 foote of board, 1li. 6s.; 6 cushens & 2 old cushens, 13s.; his weareing Apparrell, 10li. 18s.; 8 yards of french searge at 6s. p yard, 2li. 8s.; a yard & halfe of cotten & woole cloth at 3s. 8d., 5s. 6d.; 5 yards 3-4 of canuis, 3 ya: 1-4 lockrom 1 ya: 1-2 of lock: 19s. 6d.; 2 yards cheescloth, 2s. 4d.; gloues, neckcloth & other small things, 5s.; ould stockings, 2s.; his wifes weareing Apparell, 4li. 10s.; in bookes, 1li. 2s.; 11 yards of tikeing at 4s. p ya., 2s. 4d.; in Rebeen & manchestor, 3s.; cotten & lennen yarne, 16s.; 1 paire of fine sheets, 1li. 10s.; 3 pillow beeres, 15s.; one old diaper table cloth & 5 napkings, 1li.; 5 aprins & other lenen of his wifes, 2li. 10s.; childbed lennen, 1li.; bands, caps & pockett handcherchers, 13s.; 7 sheetes & a halfe, 2li.; 3 shifts, 10s.; a long canvas tablecloth, 6s. 8d.; 2 short table cloths, 7 napkings & 2 towells, 12s.; one beareing cloth, 6s., 3 old course pillowbeeres, 4s., 10s.; a paire of gloves, 2s. & money in his purse, 5s. 6d., 7s. 6d.; a grinstone, 8s., 4 silver spoones, 26s. 8d., 1li. 14s. 8d.; in pewter, 30s., 1 pestle & morter, 4s., 1li. 14s.; a skimmer & trenchers, 3s.; a warmeing pan, 7s. & 2 skilletts & a brase pan, 10s., 17s.; two kettells & a brase pot, 2li.; 3 sives, a paile & old tub, 5s.; a fryeing pan, chees pres & two little motes, 8s.; 200 of bricks, 4s.; 2 Iron potts, pothookes & a greediron, 16s.; a kneading trough & other lumber, 5s.; 5

trayes, dishes & earthen ware, 6s. 6d.; Andirons, spitt, fire pan & tonges, 12s.; In beere vessells, poudering tubs, keelers &c., 1li. 5s.; In debts, 25li. 10s.; total 292li. 13s. 7d.; debts to be deducted, 74li.; The cleare estate, 218li. 13s. 7d.

Received in Ipswich court 29: 1: 1659.

At the Ipswich court Mar. 27, 1660 added in debts due to the estate, 48li.; debts due from the estate, 15li.; total clear estate, 251li. 13s. 7d. *Essex Co. Probate Files, Docket 338.*

William Addams one of the administrators of the estate of his son, William Addams, being now deceased, Nathaniell Addams, one of his executors, by his own consent in the place of his father, deceased, acknowledged Mar. 25, 1662, himself bound for the payment of the portions to the children of his brother, William Addams, jr. *Ipswich Quarterly Court Records, vol. 1, page 104.*

Division of the estate of Wm. Addams made by John Addams, administrator, and Elder John Whipple and Thomas Stace, overseers: to the eldest son, 80li. with 45li. in moveable estate; to the other two sons, the other half of the house, barn and six acres of marsh valued at 70li., and 55li. in moveable estate. Allowed in court Nov. 14, 1667. *Ipswich Quarterly Court Records, vol. 5, page 56.*

### ESTATE OF HUGH LASKIN OF SALEM.*

Administration on the estate of Hugh Laskine of Salem, granted Mar. 29, 1659 to Henry Herrick. *Ipswich Quarterly Court Records, vol. 1, page 75.*

Inventory taken Mar. 21, 1658-9, by John Marston and Samuel Pickman: A black dimicaster, 8s.; 3 1-4 yerds of mixt Lincie woolsey, 6s. 8d.; 4 yerds of mixt kersie at 6s. ⅌ yerd, 1li. 4s.; a wainscott chest, 5s.; a red shagg cotton petticoate, 5s.; a mixt Woollen Whittle, 6s. 6d.; 6 ordinarie shifts & 6 ould shifts, 15s.; 2 sives, 1s. 6d.; 9 pecks of Wheat eaten with Weevells, 2s. 3d.; 3 Bushells of Mault, 12s.; 3 Bushells of Indian Corne eaten with Weevells, 5s.; a paire of Boddies & a paire of drawers, 3s.; 3 small wedges & a beetle ring, 2s. 6d.; a brass pann, 10s. 6d.; a pott of suger of about 9 lb., 6s.; 3 brass kettles, 9s.; 3 Iron potts, 15s.; a brass Cullender, a brass Candlestick, & a pewter porringer, 2s.; 3 pewter dishes & 1 small dish & a small bason & a boale, 8s.;

---

\* See also Records and Files of the Quarterly Courts of Essex Co., Mass., vol. II (1912), pp. 157, 160.

a Warming pann & a bell mettle morter, 8s.; a fryeing pann, 11 bands, 2 capps, & 6 handkerchers, 2s. 6d.; a pewter brimm bason, 2s.; 2 pillow beares, 3 crosscloathes & a neck-cloth, 3s.; a small box, 1s.; 2 spades & a dung fork, 2s. 6d.; 3 Bushells & 3 pecks of Mault, 15s.; 4 pc. of porke, 2s. 6d.; 3 pc. of bonie beoffe, 1s. 6d., 4 pc. nought, 4s.; 3 ould wastcoates, 2 ould blanckets & an ould Coate, 4s.; 1 ould petticoate & 2 paire of breeches, 1s.; a small pott of butter & a gallon of oyle, 3s.; a table & forme, a bedstead & 3 ould chaires, 17s. 6d.; 2 mens Coates, 10s. 6d.; & a Cotton cloth apron, 1s. 6d., 12s.; 2 white woollen blanckets, 14s. & a white cotton sheete, 6s., 1li.; fether bed & a flock bed, 3li. 10s.; a fether boalster & a fether pillowe, 15s.; a Canooe, 14s., 2 ould Cushions, 2s., 2 axes & a hatchet, 2s., 18s.; 1 ould crosscutt sawe, 1s. 6d., a black brush & a towell, 1s., 2s. 6d.; 2 Cowles & a peck, 3s., & a loade of wood, 3s., 6s.; a blewe Trucking cloth blanckett, 6s.; 2 pitch forks, 1s., 2 small cobb Irons, 1s. 6d., 2s. 6d.; 2 paire of pott hookes, 1s. 3d. & 2 hake, 2s., 3s. ———; 2 furrs, a tosting fork & a paire of tongs, ———; a smoothing Iron, 4d.; 2 paire of ould shooes & a paire of boots, 3s., 3s.; cloth suite & a wastcoate, 18s.; a mault mill, 2li.; 2 Cowes, 6li. 15s.; a paile & a Mawle, 1s.; a stone Jugg, blewe & white, 2s.; a Tenn Acre Lott, 6li.; 3 quarters of an Acre of Marsh in 2 pl., 1li. 16s.; money in his Pocketts, 9li. 11s.; A debt due from Mr. Edmond Batter, 6li.; a debt due from Mr. Henry Bartholmewe, 9s.; A debt due from Tho. Hayle of Salem, 2s.; total, 52li. 4s. 10d. Debts due from Willm. Hascal, 5li. 8s.; a house plott in Salem, 10s.; debt due from Roger Hascall, 5 Bushels of Indian corne, 15s.; total, 58li. 2s. 10d. *Essex Co. Quarterly Court Files, vol. 5, leaf 15.*

Petition of Damaris (her D S mark) Mansfeild. Her former husband, Tymothie Laskin, died, leaving two small children; and the charges for the burial of her father-in-law amounted to 6li. 10s. The court was asked to settle the matter of the estate. *Essex Co. Quarterly Court Files, vol. 5, leaf 16.*

The court June 28, 1659, ordered two-thirds of the estate to be paid to Damoris Mansfield, who was the wife of Timothy Laskin, son of Hugh Laskin, deceased, and the rest to the wife of Henry Herricke, daughter of Hugh Laskin, deceased; Paule Mansfeild, husband of Damoris, to pay 5li. each to Timothy Laskin's two sons, John and Timothy, who were under the age of twenty-one years. *Salem Quarterly Court Records, vol. 4, leaf 31.*

### ESTATE OF WILLIAM LAMPSON OF IPSWICH.

Administration on the estate of William Lampson of Ipswich, granted Mar. 29, 1659, to widow Sarah. *Ipswich Quarterly Court Records, vol. 1, page 75.*

Inventory taken Feb. 11, 1658, by William Goodhue and Robert Lord: the house & ground aboute it, 40li.; two acres of marsh, 4li.; two steeres, 8li. 10s. 2d.; a cow & heifer of 2y., 6li.; 6 Goates, 3li.; a sow & 5 shotes, 3li.; two kettles, 3li.; 3 Iron pott & 1 Iron skillett, 2li. 5s.; 2 brase skilletts, 9s.; a brase morter, 5s. 6d.; a warmeing pan, 9s.; 7 pewter dishes, 1li. 7s.; a chamber pot, 3 poringers & a pint pot, 5s.; a candlestick, 3s.; 1 dozen ocumy spoones & 1 dozen of pewter, 8s.; a lamp, smootheing Iron & other small things, 12s.; 1 keeler, poudering tub, bucking tub, paile & some other lumber, 14s.; sithes, beatle & wedges & sickles, 1li. 7s.; axes & other tooles, 1li. 12s.; a spad, shovell & howes, 7s.; wheeles & cards, 15s.; 2 old chests & a box, 10s.; wheat threst & unthresht, 32 bushells, 7li. 4s.; Indian Corne, 5li.; tumbrill, wheels, plow & what belongs to them, 3li. 5s.; nayles, 1li.; in bookes, 1li.; one old bedsted & trundlebed, 10s.; 2 old chairs & formes, 4s.; his weareing aparell, 6li.; a sword & belt, 6s. 8d.; sives & earthen ware & other Lumber, 8s.; a fetherbed & 2 bolsters, 3li. 10s.; one bed & other beding, 3li. 10s.; 3 paire of sheets, 3 little pillows & pillowbeares, 2li. 12s.; cotten woole & 1li. of sheeps woole, 8s. 6d.; new cloth, 2li. 10s.; a sack & bag, 5s. 6d.; tobaco, 5s.; bacone, 10s.; hempt and flaxe towe 10s.; total, 117li. 17s. 2d.; debts oweing to him, 7li.; debts that he owed too others, 13li. 7s.; total, 124li. 17s. 2d.; debts to be deducted 13li. 7s.; clear estate, 111li. 10s. 2d.

He left eight children, four sons and four daughters. The eldest son sixteen years last November, the eldest daughter fourteen years, the second son nine and three quarter years, the second daughter seven, third daughter five and one half, fourth daughter four, third son two years last November and youngest son twenty four weeks old.

Administration granted to the widow and ordered that she pay or cause to be paid to the children as they came to age or marriage with her consent, the eldest son 12li. the rest 6li. each and that the house and land stand engaged to make good the legacies. If any of the children die before they come to age then to be divided equally to the survivors. *Essex Co. Probate Files, Docket* 16,264.

Whereas there was security taken of a house and land at Ipswich, for the payment of several portions to the children of Wm. Lampson, deceased, according to Ipswich court record of Mar. 29, 1659, until other security be given, and Thomas Hartshorne of Redding, coming into court and tendering the house in Redding where he now dwells, with fifteen acres of land adjoining, and seven acres of meadow in two several parcels, bounded as is expressed in a writing given in to court, and now on file, in the Salem court records, the court 10: 10: 1661 accepts the latter security and releases the former. *Salem Quarterly Court Records, vol.* 4, *page* 81.

Petition of John Ayres and William Fellows, Nov., 1661: "Wheras o$^r$ Brother william Lampson late of Ipswich dyed intestate and Administration granted by the Honered Court at Ipswich to his widdow our sister Sarah Lampson and devided the estate about halfe to her & halfe to the children being eight in number and whereas shee being about to change her estate to one Thomas Harteshorne of Redding It was agreed that before mariage he should signe and seale a wrighting to give our sayd sister power & liberty to dispose of the one halfe of the estate she brought to him by way of will (of w$^{ch}$ there is sufisient wittness besydes our selues) but by pvidence that wrighting being neglected to be finished before mariage (though then pmised it should be done after) but it is now refused and thereby the children of o$^r$ Brother william Lampson like to suffer And wheras the estate in the Inventory delivered into court was underprised espeshally the Land w$^{ch}$ now appeareth to be worth eightye pound w$^{ch}$ was then prised but forty foure pound

"Our Humble request to this Honered Court is that the children of our brother may Inioy a pt of the advance of there fathers estate and doe humbly intreat (if this Honered Court shall thinke fitt) that the Land may be to pay the childrens portions, it being prised in the Inventory as before exprest & there portions fiftye foure pounds & soe there portions will be advanced twentye six pound & the widdow still haue about halfe the estate and that it would please the court that those children that are put out may haue there portions improved for there use & benifitt ||that|| when they come to age to reciue the same, that being all (as the case now stands) that they are like to haue of there Fathers estate."

Thomas Hartshorne of Redding tendered as security, instead of the land at Ipswich, his house in which he dwells, and fifteen acres of land in Redding, bounded on the north by land of James Pike, on the south by land of Walter Fairefield, on the east and west by the common; also three acres of meadow at Reeva in the same town, bounded on the north by the meadow of Henry Felch and by the common on the other three sides; also four acres of meadow in the great meadow in the bounds of Lynn, bounded on the north by the meadow of Edward Hutcheson, on the south by the meadow of Isaack Harte, on the west by the common, and on the east by Isaack Hart's farm. Accepted 11: 10: 1661.

*Essex Co. Quarterly Court Files, vol. 7, leaves 32, 33.*

### Estate of John Perkins, Jr. of Ipswich.

Administration on the estate of John Perkins, jr., of Ipswich, granted Mar. 29, 1659, to widow Lidia. Amount of the inventory of the estate, 73li. 10s. 1d. He left one young child, new born. The widow to hold the estate until the child was eighteen years old, and then pay the child 14li., or at the day of her marriage, with her mother's consent. *Ipswich Quarterly Court Records, vol. 1, page 75.*

Inventory taken 25: 1: 1659, by William Goodhue and John Dane: Cloth that came from the wevers 56 yard, 8li. 10s.; 14 pound of cotten wooll, 18s. 6d.; on hog, 2li. 4s.; in butter and chese, 1li. 10s.; 3 poringers and 6 pound of suger, 8s. 6d.; in small linin, 2li.; wheatt 22 bushells & a halfe, 3li. 1s. —d.; seventy bushells of barly, 14li.; Inden corne, 1li.; A chest, a tob, a barrell, a halfe barrell, 14s.; the weringe apparell, 4li.; some lumber in severall things, 12s.; A fether bed, a rug, a boulster, 2 blankts, 7li.; A muskett, a sword rest & poutch, 1li. 10s. 5d.; 4 weges, 2 bettell rings, 2 forks, 2 old axes, 2 sithes, 1li.; a plow and Iornes, a yoke & ringe & span shakell, 10s.; in shepe, 2 ewes, 2 yere old wethers, 3li.; a mare colt a yere old, 6li. 10s.; in swine, 10li.; 3 Cowes, 2 steres 5 yere olds, 26li.; a Iorn pott, a skillitt, a fringe pan, 3 dishes peuter, a paell, 2 spoons, 1li. 4s.; a end of ye house at the farme as it cost, 5li. 16s.; total, 103li. 8s. 3d.; debts, 29li. 18s. 2d.; leaving 73li. 10s. 1d.

Received in Ipswich court Mar. 28, 1659. *Essex Co. Probate Files, Docket 21,338.*

## Estate of Mark Symmons of Ipswich.

"The last will & testam$^t$ of Marke Symons who beinge Weake in bodie yet of good & pfect memory doe comit my soule into y$^e$ hand of y$^e$ lord my god as my faithfull creator & my bodie decently to be interred in y$^e$ earth  By this my last will I doe appoynt my beloved wieffe *Ioanah* Symons to be sole executrix of this my last will & testam$^t$ & my estate to be disposed of as followeth viz tt I bequeth to my daughter Susannah Ayres a fetherbed & boulster w$^{ch}$ was her mothers w$^{th}$ y$^e$ worst rugg  tt I bequeathe to Abigaill Pierce a fetherbed & y$^e$ best rugg  tt I bequeathe to John walner iunior one ewe lambe of this yeare

"Allsoe my will is my debyts beinge payde & funerall expences discharged my said wieffe shall inioye all my goods & chattells viz my howse & barne & ground about & belonginge to y$^e$ same w$^{th}$ all y$^e$ pviledges & appurtenances belonginge to y$^e$ same: together w$^{th}$ all my vpland & meadowe w$^{th}$ all my cattell of one kinde & another: I saye to inioy all my reall & psonall estate for y$^e$ full terme of her lieffe: And my will is y$^t$ after y$^e$ decease of my said wieffe my estate to be equally devided amongst our three daughters & y$^e$ children of my daughter ||mary|| Chapman deceased pvided y$^t$ y$^t$ estate w$^{ch}$ anie of them haue receaved alredie shall be vallewed & y$^e$ y$^t$ haue had y$^e$ most y$^e$ y$^t$ haue had least maye all of them after y$^e$ decease of my wieffe haue an equall pportion of all my estate Provided y$^t$ if my said wieffe shall by anie hand of pvidence shall neede more then y$^e$ estate will pduce for her comfortable mayntenance then to haue convaynient supplie out of y$^e$ estate & y$^e$ rest to be devided as aforesaid  Also I apoynt my lo$^g$ bretheren Moses Pengrie & Edward Browne to be oversseers of this my last will & testament dated 25 (2) 1659."

mark symmons

Witness: George Smith, Aaron Pengry.
Proved in Ipswich court Apr. 28, 1659 by the witnesses.

Inventory of estate of Marke Symonds of Ipswich taken May 16, 1659, by Robert Lord and Robert Day: his dwelling house & barne with the ground about it, 80li.; two oxen, 11li.; two steeres & one heifer, 9li.; a mare & foale, 20li.; three cowes, 10li.; 7 ewes & 4 Lambes, 8li.; two shotes, 1li. 16s.; in bookes, 2li. 4s.; his weareing apparell, 5li.; a bedsted & cord, curtaynes & valiants, 1li. 7s.; ye best feather bed & boulster & green Rugg, 6li.; a fetherbed & boulster & red rugg, 4li. 15s.; a bedsted, flockbed & flock boulster & 4 old blanketts, 2li.; a flockbed & 2 blanketts, 1li. 15s.; 3 fether pillows & one old little one, 1li.; 4 paire & an od sheet, 2li. 15s.; 4 pillow beeres, 14s. 6d.; 2 table cloths & one litle one & seaven napkings and old shirt, 1li. 5s.; 2 chests & 3 boxes, 1li. 4s.; a little table, 6s. 8d.; one great chaire & 4 small & too cushons, 8s.; a looking glase, 3s.; 2 glase bottles & 3 earthen poringers, 2s.; 2 brishes, 1s. 8d.; 30li. of pewter at 14d. ℔ li., 1li. 15s.; one chamber pot, 2s.; one great kettell, one midle kettell, 3 small ould ones, 2 old skilletts & a scimer, 4li.; 2 morters & one pestle, 12s.; a warmeing pan, 4s.; a fryeing pan, 4s. 6d.; 2 little Iron potts & paire pothooks, 12s.; a spitt, greed Iron & chafen dish, 5s.; 2 paire *Lamo* Andirons fire pan and a paire of toungs, 10s.; a pewter candlestick, 2s. 6d.; a Tramell, 2s. 6d.; 2 plankes, 2 tressells, forme, cubbord, kneading trough & other lumbar, 16s.; a muskett, coliver & 2 old swords, 1li. 12s.; 2 beere vessells, poudering tub, chirne, cheese press & other lumbar, 1li.; sives, earthen ware, shires, pressing Iron, chees motts & other small things, 8s.; scales & waytes, a halfe bushell, 7s.; 7 bushell Indian corne, 18s. 8d.; wheat about 2 bushell & 1-2, 11s. 3d.; in woole, 5s.; a fann & ould tubs, ould chest & nayles, 18s.; halfe a bush. of rye, 2s.; tooles & old Iron in the bumby, 1li.; a beetell & 4 wedges, a saw & fro, 14s.; 2 old sithes, an old croscutt saw, shovell & some other small things, 11s.; an arrow, axe, hatchet, 3 pitchfork, 6s. 6d.; 2 broad hows, 4s.; a saddell & bridle, 16s.; 18 acres of Land, 36li.; 2 acres of meddow at Mr. Wintrips farme & 1 acre of salt marsh, 5li. 10s.; cart, tumbrill, plow chaynes & yokes, wheeles & Irons & sled, 3li. 5s.; a grindstone, 6s.; In debts oweing to the estate, 36li.; debts oweing from the estate, 13li. 10s.; total clear estate, 257li. 6s. 9d.

Delivered in Ipswich court June 2, 1659 by Joanah Symonds widow of Marke Symonds.

*Essex Co. Probate Files, Docket 27,116.*

Edward Chapman, having received the part of the estate given by Marke Symonds to his children, bound to the county treasurer 24 : 9 : 1659, his house, which was late Mark Symonds, and twelve acres of land in common on north side of the river for payment of the children as they come of age, in all sixty pounds. *Ipswich Quarterly Court Records, vol. 1, page 83.*

### Estate of Benjamin Mountjoy of Salem.

Administration on the estate of Benjamin Monjoye granted June 28, 1659 to his widow. *Salem Quarterly Court Records, vol. 4, leaf 30.*

Inventory of the estate of Mr. Benjamin Mountjoy, taken by William Charles and Joseph Dallever: One Cloake & a suite, 3li. 10s.; one Great copper kettle, 1li. 3s.; one lesser kettle, 7s. 3d.; stewing pan, 6s.; one Skillet, 2s.; one warming pan, 5s.; one scummer, 1s.; Bed & bolster ticking, 1li.; one dozen of pewter dishes, 3li. 10s.; 4 pewter porringers, 6li. 3s.; 4 pewter plates, 2s.; one chamber pot, 4s.; one pewter tankard, 3s.; 6 saucers, 2s.; one little Bason, 1s.; one pewter pint, 1s. 6d.; one little pewter cup, 9d.; one brasse candlesticke & morter, 3s.; two stone jugges, 2s.; one earthen pott, 6d.; two glasse bottles, 8d.; 3 payre of sheetes, 2li. 8s.; 3 payre of pillow bears, 1li.; one table cloth, 9s.; 5 Diaper Napkins, 7s. 6d.; 6 lockram Napkins, 6s.; one hanging candlestick, 2s. 6d.; one lampe, 1s.; one Trunke, 2s.; one chest, 8s.; one fire shovel & tongs, 4s.; one pothanger, 2s.; one old brasse bucket, 2s. 6d.; one smoothing Iron, 2s.; a payre of blankets, 16s.; one Bedsteed, 1li.; one little Table, 8s.; one wooden trey, 8s.; total, 19li. 2s. 5d. *Essex Co. Quarterly Court Files, vol. 5, leaf 10.*

### Estate of William Jigles of Salem.

William Jegles died intestate. Amount of inventory, 148li., ordered June 28, 1659, that the widow shall keep it in her hands for her use. *Salem Quarterly Court Records, vol. 4, leaf 31.*

Inventory of estate of William Jigles taken 26: 3: 1659, by John Browne, John Gardner and Edm. Batter: One dwellinge house & house Lott, 35li.; ten Acres of upland, 3-4 salt marsh & of meadow a small pcell about the upland, 9li. 10s.; 1 Cow, 4li.; 5 yewes, 5li., 1 pige, 4s., 9li. 4s.; 1 Tableboard & 2 formes, 1li.; 1 Chest, 18s.; 1 Cubburd, 12s., 1 bedpane, 12s., 2li. 2s.; p And Irens, 10s.; 1 friing pane, 5s.; 1 earthen basun, 16s.; Basen & Ewer, 2 Candlsticks & Salt, 16s., 7 Cushings, 20s., 1li. 16s.; 1 Remnant of Carsy, 32s.; 1 Carpet & brush, 9s., 2li. 1s.; Aparell, 4li., 1 feather bed, 2 bolsters, 1 Rugg, Curtayns, bedsteed & hangings, 10li.; gune & sword, 5s., brasse, 33s., pewter, 30s., 3li. 8s.; silver beker, 2li., fire shovel, tonges, spit, &c., 4s., 2li. 4s.; 4 Chaires, 1 small Table, 10s., earthen ware, &c., 13s.; bookes, 10s., carpenters tooles, 25s., Iron potts & hangers, 20s., ockum, 3s., 2li. 18s.; sheets & table Linnen, 7li.; new linen, 20s., and an old bed & Rugg, 30s., 2li. 10s.; cash, 3li. 16s., 2 old Chest, table & forme, 15s., 4li. 11s.; flax & yarne, 6s., 1 bushel Indian Corne & bag, 4s., 10s.; 1 Grindston, 2s., 1 kitle, 10s., 12s.; a Katch named William with her apurten., 50li.; total, 145li. 15s.; a small pcell woole, 5s.; a old boate, 2li.; total, 148li.

The children, or three of them, were married in town long since, the other abroad at sea. The eldest son was in England and the master of a ship. On 28: 4: 1659, it was ordered that the estate be left in the hands of the widow Elizabeth, for her necessities while she lived, and be disposed of by the court at her decease. *Essex Co. Quarterly Court Files, vol. 5, leaf* 14.

### ESTATE OF JOHN LEACH, SR. OF SALEM.

"That w^ch John Leach senior spake about the Disposinge of his estate. We whose names ar vnderwritten, beinge both in one roome, about halfe a yeare before the decease of s^d John Leach senior the sayd John Leach comminge in from worke he sayd vnto vs he was so sicke he thought he should haue falln downe dead at his worke: & he did feare that he might at one tyme or other dye suddenly: therefore he did desire of vs both (that if in case it should so fall out) to be witnesses that all that he had he gaue vnto John Leach: and at another tyme hauinge farther conference about the disposinge of his estate vnto the sayd John Leach, we told him there were seueral John Leaches he should doe wel to expresse w^ch of them, he sayd to John Leach the son of Rich^d Leach: sayinge further that he had was but litle. if he should deuide it it would come but to litle."

her mark      her mark<br>
Elisabeth N Buxton, Mary o ffelton.

*Essex Co. Quarterly Court Files, vol. 5, leaf* 12.

Proved June 28, 1659 by Eliza. Buxton and Mary Felton: Richard Leach, executor. Amount of inventory, 33li. 12s. 10d. *Salem Quarterly Court Records, vol. 4, leaf* 30.

Inventory taken 20: 10: 1658, by Daniel (his D R mark) Rea and Henery (his h (( mark) Cooke: House, orchard

& 6 acres of land, 13li.; 20 acres of land & 2 acres of meadow, 3li.; 1 ox, 5li.; 1 Cow, 2li. 10s.; 1 calfe, 18s.; 1 sheep, 16s.; in Corne, 2li. 16s. 6d.; his wearinge apparel, 2li.; his beddinge, 2li.; 1 Cart, 1li.; 1 smal pot & ketle, 10s.; 1 chest, 2 axes & other old Lumber, 1li.; in hay, 1li.; total, 35li. 2s. 6d. In yarne, 1li. 1s.; an old table and a gun and sword, 1li.; total, 37li. 3s. 6d. Debts: To Philip Veren, 6s.; Adam Wesgate, 4s. 6d.; John Ingersol, 3s.; Willyam Curtis, 5s.; Ed. Beecham, 2s. 6d.; Tho. Ricks, 1s. 4d.; the Cow keeper, 4s.; John Burton, 3s.; John Grover, 1s. 4d.; the charges of his burial, 1li. 10s.; rates for 2 yeare, 10s.; total, 3li. 10s. 8d. *Essex Co. Quarterly Court Files, vol. 5, leaf 12.*

### ESTATE OF PETER PITFORD OF MARBLEHEAD.*

Administration on the estate of Peeter Pitford granted June 28, 1659 to Robert Pattashall. *Salem Quarterly Court Records, vol. 4, leaf 31.*

### ESTATE OF RICHARD FRITHY OF (SALEM?).

Richard Stackhouse possessed a ten-acre lot, which was the land of Richard Frithy, deceased, divers years since, and none to claim it. Richard Lambert, deceased, was formerly paid for it June 28, 1659. Mr. Stackhouse ordered to keep it. *Salem Quarterly Court Records, vol. 4, leaf 31.*

### ESTATE OF JOHN WOODIS OF SALEM.

"The last will and testam$^t$ of Jn$^o$ Woodis being weak of body but in pfett memory: 24 (3) 59. Imp$^r$ he gave† vnto Sam$^{ll}$ Very sen 2 oxen and his wearing cloaths  Ite he gaue vnto Alice his Daughter: the wife of Sam$^l$ Very 2 Cowes Ite he gaue vnto Thomas and Jn$^o$ Very the Children of Sam$^l$ very 1: mare  Ite he gaue vnto Sam$^l$ son to Sam$^l$ Very 1: younge horse yeare old and the vantage  It he gaue vnto Elizabeth: the Daughter of Sam$^l$ Very 1: cowe & 1 heifer of 2 years old and 1 Iron pott  It he gaue vnto Sarah the Daughter of Sam$^l$ Verey one Cowe one heifer of three years old and all my beding one Chest and that that is in it and one Iron Kitle my peweter & sixe pounds ten shillings in the hands of Tho:

---

* See also Records and Files of the Quarterly Courts of Essex Co., Mass., vol. 3 (1913), page 283.

† This was written throughout in the first person, and then changed to the third.

fflint Ite he gaue vnto Emme Muse one Cowe  He apoynted & Constituted Sam¹ Verey his son in law his Executor."

[No signature]

Witness: Tho: T Antrum, Thomas T fflint.
                his mark              his mark

Proved in Salem court 29: 4: 1659 by the witnesses.

Inventory of estate of John Wooddes, taken by Thomas James, Thomas (his T mark) Flint and Thomas (his T mark) Antrum: Two oxen, 12li.; 4 cowes, 15li. 10s.; 3 heifers, 9li. 10s.; one maire, 13li.; one horse colt, 6li.; a bed rugge and blanket, 1li. 10s.; a chest and a sheett, 12s.; a 3 pint pot, a pewter bottle and a porringer, 5s.; an Iron pot and pothookes, 10s.; an Iron kettle, 12s.; in Thomas Flints hand, 6li. 10s.; his wearing clothes, 3li.; in mony, 6s.; total, 69li. 5s. *Essex Co. Quarterly Court Files, vol. 5, leaf* 11.

ESTATE OF JOHN CLEMENTS OF HAVERHILL.

Administration on the estate of John Clements, late of Haverhill, "being by God's providence cast awaye," granted July 21, 1659, to Robt. Clements, by Mr. Samuell Symonds and Major Generall Denison. *Ipswich Quarterly Court Records, vol. 1, page* 78.

Court Sept. 27, 1659 confirmed administration granted by Hon. Samuel Symonds and Major-General Denison to Robert Clements upon estate of his brother, John Clements. *Ipswich Quarterly Court Records, vol. 1, page* 80.

Inventory of estate of John Cleman at the time y$^t$ Roberd Cleman takes to that estate taken by James Davis, Bartel Heath and Theo. Shatswell: his accomodations, Three acres & a halfe of houselott more or lesse, bounded on ye east by Isack Cousens & on ye west by a high way; nineteene acres in ye plaine, thirteene acres of it is bounded on ye east by Mr. Robert Clement, Sr., ‖5 of it sould out before I enter opon it‖ & on ye west by Daniell Hendricks, ye other six acres is bounded on ye east by Mr. Ward, & on ye west by Hugh Sherratt: ffowre acres of land lying on ye west side of ye litle river att ye east end of ye towne, as is expressed in ye towne book to lye rate free for ever; one acre & three qters of meadow in ye east meadow by on ye north of Thomas Lilford, on ye south by meadow held by Theophilus Shatswell & widow Dow, five acres of land in ye plaine bought of Tho. Davis bounded on ye east by Mr.

Jewett & on ye west by Mrs. Clement; one acre & halfe of meadow in ye east meadow, wch was formerly Sam. Gilds, bounded on ye east by Richard Littlehale, on ye west by ye upland, 2 acres of meadow layd out at present; The 2 division of upland being thirty two acres more or lesse, lying over agst Andover cornfield from ye greate river by Sowes brooke to a pine marked wth an I & from thence south to a litle white oake marked with an I; & from thence to a blacke oake upon ye greate river banck marked wth an I & from thence upon ye greate river banck to ———.

John clemans acomodashon in ——— tow oxen, the halfe of a white or whitesh mare and the halfe of a gray coult at 2 eayer and vantage, and the halfe of a gray mare coult at one yeare and advantage; on plow, on quarter part of a harrow, linspins, axpins, washers, a ox chayne; and in rent 14 pounds for on peace of lands unlayd out at present, 96 acors which is to be a 3d deveshon of upland, a 3d deveshon of meadow not yet layd out amounting to 4 acors; besides ye right and tytell of all undevided lands yt may be in time layd out and comonage of 8 acors acomodashon throwout. Amount six score and ten pounds.

Received in Ipswich court 27 : 7 : 1659. *Essex Co. Probate Files, Docket 5,587.*

Court May 10, 1660 confirmed administration of the estate of John Clements, upon request of his brother Job and sisters, to his brother Robert Clements. The latter brought in an account of his charges for his voyage to England and Ireland in taking over his brother, John Clements' wife and children. *Ipswich Quarterly Court Records, vol. 1, page 87.*

Petition to the Ipswich court Sept. —, 1659 of Moses Pengry and John Ossgood "that wheras our Nere and deare Brother John Clements By the all disposeing hand of gods providence wth his ffamily was Drowned [as we undoubtedly Beleive] and uppon our cleare Knowlidge by his divers Leters he did very Ernestly sollicit his yonger Brother Robert Clements to Come over with and as a guid to his Wife & children to Irland promising that if he would sell & Bring his family allsoe, Both hee and the rest of his Brethren would doe well for him in Irland, but Beeing soe Dissappoynted on the way and Ther allsoe, we thought it our duty to advise & Incourrage our Brother Robbert, to desire Leters of administration uppon all the Estate of the said John Clements in this Country and are willing it should Be

Confirmed to him if this honoured Court see Cause, judging it short of his dammage & Troubles he mett withall; Ther Beeing in England we Doubt Not in Lands and other Estate suffitient to provide for That one child [if yet alive], in Spaine."

Acknowledged 27 : 7 : 1659 by the petitioners.

An account given in by Robert Clements to the Ipswich court, Mar. 30, 1660 of the charges and losses which "hee sustaned by undertackinge a voige to Ingland and so to Ierland for his brother John Clements beeinge desired by him for the aideing and asistinge his wife and childeren which otherweses Could not have undertacken the voige To goe to him": sum Considerabell loses in puting of my estate to great loss beinge in greate lust upon the undertackinge the voige which I aphernde could not bee less then 10li.; for charges goinge to Pascatawair and for nececaryes for the veoige, 6li.; for The pienge pasage for myselfe wife and 3 Chillderen, 17li.; the losses I sustained the shipe beinge tackine by the spanyard was all I had, 20li.; when I gotte to london in charge there and pasage to Ierland, 19li. 10s.; expences in Ierland whill I staid there, 10li.; for my pasage backe from Irland to London, 8li.; for pasage from london to New Ingland, 15li.; total, 105li. 10s. Allso besides this there is the loss of my time which was a wholle yeare, as allso vearry great hardshipe beeinge I and my Chillderen beeinge Carried capteiv to Spaine and with great hardshipps gotte to Ingland. Signed, Roberd Clements.

*Essex Co. Probate Files, Docket 5,587.*

Job Clements assented to the deduction of the expenses of his brother, Robert Clements' trip to Ireland, from the estate of John Clement, deceased. Dated, 26 : 1 : 1660. *Essex Co. Quarterly Court Files, vol. 5, leaf 84.*

### ESTATE OF HENRY TRAVERS OF NEWBURY.

"This 26th of July 1648 I Henrie Travers of Newbry hauing ocasion to go to sea and know not whether I shall liue to Com againe I do by this present [writing] declar my last will and Testament as followeth first I Giue vnto my sonn James my Housse and halfe acre lot and my 4 acre lot at new towne and my devision Land and my Eight acres of salt marrish and a Copper Kittel and on Iron pott and on Iron skilat and two Goones and two saws and on ox of 4 yer ould and on ‖youn‖ steere of 2 yer ould. 2 Item I Giue vnto my Daughter sara on Cow and a hefer ‖of 3 yer‖ and two brasse potts and ‖my‖ Littel kittel and a fring *pan* and a tabl bord. Itm I giue vnto my wife my bed and Couerlid and a kittel and a scillet and my wheat and barly and my swine and my debts that is owing to me and all my other goods which is not dispose of which ‖in all‖ I ludg will be as good a porcion as on of the Children and mor and my debts being paid. Likewis my will is that my wife shall haue the Increse and Incom of my Estat of both the Childrens vntill they be twelue yers ould tourds ther maintainanc but my will is that my wif should not alter the properti of anie of my goods ‖or lands‖ without thes my ouersears Consent Likwis I do desier my two ffrends Richard Knight and Henri short to se that this my will be performed"

Henrie Travers

Witness: Wileam Ilesly.

Richard Knight testified that this was the act and deed of Henry Travers and William Ilsly testified that he was called to be a witness to such a disposal of his estate and believed it to be his hand.

Inventory taken July 15, 1659, by James (his I M mark) Miricke and Anthony Somerby: a bed bolster & 2 pillowes, 2li.; two paire of sheets, 2 table clothes, 6 napkins, 4 towells, 2li. 10s.; one Rugge and a bed matt, 1li. 14s.; one Iron pott and a small brass pott, 1li. 4s.; A pr of And Irons, a fire shovell & pr of tonges, 9s.; a Tramell, a gridiron, a frying pan & spitt, 11s.; *two* pewter platters, one bason, 2 spoones, two dram cups, one pint pot, one pewter candlesticke and a tin puddin pan, 1li. 3s.; one chaffing dish, a smal brass kettle & the cover of a warmeing pan, 3s.; A brewing tub, 2 keelers & a bucket, 12s.; 2 spining wheels & a Reele & 2 p of cards, 10s.; 2 Rip hookes, a smoothing Iron & a buckets bale, 5s.; 3 Rineing boxes, 8 dishes, 9 trenchers & boules, 10s.; 2 tables, a forme, 2 chayres, 2 boxes and a seive, 17s. 6d.; In fine Earthen ——— porringers, 4s.; one sack and hoo[d], 5s.; A house and foure akers of land with the orchard and eight akers of Marsh land & 8 akers of divident land with priveledg of comonage, 80li. Total, 92li. 17s. 6d. His debts which his wife paid for him after he went away was about 5li.

Received in Ipswich court Sept. 27, 1659.

*Essex Co. Probate Files, Docket 28,078.*

Will of Henry Travers presented, not proved; administration was granted to his widow, Bridgett, now wife of Richard Window. Nicolas Walington, who married his daughter, Sarah Traverse, had already received three pounds, and the court Sept. 27, 1659 ordered the administratrix to pay them twelve pounds more, and to the son, James Traverse, thirty pounds when he comes of age, and the rest of the estate, which amounted to 92li., to the widow, the land to stand bound for the children's portion. *Ipswich Quarterly Court Records, vol. 1, page* 81.

Petition in 1661, of Bridgett Travers of Newbury, wife of Henry Travers, shewing that seven years ago, when her husband went to England, he left two children, a daughter of 10 years, and a son not full three years old. He then made his will and gave "my daughter a cow and an heifer to be paid to her at twelve years of age, and the son at the same age of twelue years to have two steers and foure akers of upland & eight akers of marsh and all the houshold stuffe we had, onely he gaue mee a bed & a couerlet which was very meane, and also I and my children was very mean in apparell: and this was the whole estate of my husband, I had not so much as an house to dwell in and left me also fiue pounds in debt and since he went I have not heard of him but once which is fiue yeares since." Also having paid the fine of 5li. and laid out about 20li. more on the land and building, and her daughter being now married had paid to her two heifers, now desires that she may enjoy the house and land until her son shall be twenty one years, and after to have the thirds during her life. *Essex Co. Probate Files, Docket* 28,078.

James Travers and his mother having petitioned to the General Court to have the action transferred to this court, the court Sept. 25, 1666, saw no cause to alter the order made in Sept., 1659 for disposing of the estate. *Ipswich Quarterly Court Records, vol. 1, page* 156.

### ESTATE OF WILLIAM HOBSON OF ROWLEY.

Administration on the estate of William Hobson of Rowley, intestate, granted Sept. 27, 1659 to his widow, An Hobson. Amount of inventory, 446li., clear estate. Three children. Division: To eldest son Humphry, 150li.; and the two younger sons, 73li. each, when of age; rest of estate to the widow, who was to retain the whole in her hands until the children are of age. Elder Reiner and Maximilion Jewett, overseers. If An should change her estate, she was to give security for payment of the children's portion. *Ipswich Quarterly Court Records, vol. 1, page 82.*

Inventory taken 20: 6: 1659, by Joseph Jawet, Maximilian Jawet and William Boynton: one dwelling house, a Barne and home Lott, 4 Akers more or less, 75li.; 14 Akers of Land lying on the sunn side of the house, 5li. the Aker, 70li.; a swamp Joyning unto the said Lande, 3li.; Gates upon the Comon,; in Batchlers medow thre Akers, 16li.; three Aker of medow at the stratis, 5li.; ten Akers of medow in the east feild with a percel of upland Joyning upon it, 22li.; in farme or marsh feild ten Akers of medow more or lesse and 10 Aker of uplande, 50li.; 200 Akers of Lande lying between Meremak River and Johnsons ponde, 10li.; one meare, 10li.; fowre Cowes, 14li.; two stears, 5li.; one heffer and one Calfe, 14li. 12s.; three yong Calves, 2li.; one horse, 10li.; thirteene Akers of ———, 13li.; 12 Loads of hay, 6li.; his wearing Cloaths, 20li.; shooes and Bootes, 2li. 6s.; hats and a hatt Case, 3li. 6s. 8d.; stockins, shifts, bands, handkerchifs, 2li. 10s.; one paire of stockins and a Raper, 1li.; a paire of pistoles, 2li.; one Coverlet, fowre Blankits, 3li.; one Bed and Beding Cloths, 10li.; one Bed and Beding, 2li.; two Ruggs,; ten yeards of Carsey, 4li.; one peice of Broad Cloth, 9li.; A Chushins and two Carpits, 1li. 13s. 4d.; a Rugg and thre pillows, 2li 10s.; a peece of playne Cotten, 1li.; 7 bushels of wheate, 1li. 11s. 6d.; some Bacan, 12s.; Brass, Iron Potts and pewder, 8li.; wood vessell and Cushins, 3li.; a Chist and a Trunke, 1li.; a bible and other Books, 16s.; trenchers and a brush, 6s.; tooles, 20s., a sadle 25, a Cradle, 6s., 2li. 11s.; swin, 7li.; one ell of Red Cloth, 1li.; certaine Plate, 3li.; two Glasse Cases, 10s.; a Line[n] wheele, 10s. 6d.; some Beare Caske, 10s.; 3 pare of Gloves, 5s.; total, 456li. 1s. 10d. Debts, 10li.

Delivered in Ipswich court 27: 7: 1659 by An Hobson widow of William Hobson.

Bond of John Hobson of Rowley, he having received more of the estate of his mother Ann Hobson than was allowed him by the Ipswich court, to pay his mother yearly 50s. in bread, corn and pork and also to supply her with one half of the firewood she should need, his brother William to supply the other half. Signed and sealed Feb. 28, 1682.

Witness: Nehemiah Jewet and Jane (her I S mark) Simmons.

Acknowledged in court Sept. 28, 1683 by the witnesses.

This was delivered June 10, 1685, by Mrs. Ann Hobson to her daughter as satisfied. Witness: Daniell Wicome, Nehemiah Jewett.

Division of the lands of William and Ann Hobson, deceased intestate, among their children or their heirs, by Daniell Wicom, Nehemiah Jewet, Ezekiel Northend, Samuell Platts and Moses Platts as follows: "William Hobson ye only Surviveing child of sd William & Ann Hobson, deceased & Mr. Thomas Gage who Married ye Relict of Humphry Hobson deceased & Phillip Nelson who married ye Relict of John Hobson deceased: sd Gage his wife being Guardian for her son Humphry Hobson & sd Nelson being Guardian for John Hobson ye Grandchildren of sd William & Ann Hobson."

The Land or dividend in ye west end Oxe pasture is setled & stated as followeth: to Mr. Gage & his wife in behalf of her son Humphry Hobson: Bounded the westerly end upon Land yt belonged to Mr. Ezekiel Mighel ye so-west side by an Elm tree in a swamp: from the sd tree markt on a streight line no-easterly to a Red Oak tree markt (which line parts sd Land from the other division now setled upon William Hobson) & thence bounded by the way yt parts sd Land & sd Williams pt. the other side bounded by a highway yt parts sayd Land & Capt. Wicoms & ye Land Lately Leiut. Lamberts till sd way Comes to ye sd Land of Ezek$^l$ Mighels formerly The next pt of sd Oxe pasture Land setled upon William Hobsen son of sd William & Ann. Bounded by sd Land Layd out to Humphry Hobson son of sd Humphry decd by sd Markt Elm tree in ye swamp, & the Red Oak & ye way on yt side: the west end bounded by sayd Land formerly Ezk$^l$. Mighils extending so-west about thirty & three Rods to a white Oak tree Markt & then easterly to a stump Markt by Samuell Pickards Land: & then bounded Nor by sd Samls Land to a stump & stones in the highway. The next pt of sd Oxe pasture Land setled upon John Hobson Son of John Hobson Late of Rowley deceased sd Nelson who married his mother being his Guardian. Bounded by sd Land layd out to William Hobson by sd white Oak tree Markt In ye swamp, & sd stump Markt neer sayd Pickards Line, he ye sd John being to have all the Remaynder of sd dividend extending to ye place Called ye highway as the Land is bounded.

The far division of upland & Meadow & Marsh ground divided as followes: To Humphry Hobson son of sd Humphry deceased bounded by a stake & stone at ye south end from thence on a streight Line to a stake & heap of stones upon a Little hill, thence on a strait line to a stake & heap of stones by the upland side at ye North End of ye upland & thenc on a straight line to a stake in ye marsh by a Little pond & thenc on a straight Line to a stake at ye Great Creek side which great Creek parts Newberry & Rowly Marshes being ye so-east part of yt division. The other half of sd divission upland & Marsh divided thorow from a Rock & stake in ye Marsh by ye River & to a Rock & stake on ye upland at ye west side of a Cove, & soe to the line Running in ye first division to a stake & heap of stones: William to have the Lower end & John to have the upper end.

The neer divission of upland & Marsh ground divided as followeth: To Humphry ye upper half next ye Roadway downe the Creek to a stake & stone fixed by ye Creek side & thenc on a streight line Cross ye marsh to the upland to a Red Oak tree Markt & thenc on a streight line over ye hill to a black Oak tree markt & thenc on a line to a walnut tree markt & thenc on a streight line to ye outside of ye Land next Ens. Andrew Stickney in his Improvemt. To John Hobson next to sd Humphrys Running downe by the Creek as ye Creek Runs to a stake & stone by the Creek side: & from sd stake cross ye marsh northerly to a poynt of a great Rock: he being to have ye poynt of upland on the southerly side of ye Cove of meadow till it Comes to sd Humphries line allowing a way through it for ye bringing ye Lower part or divission crops of to sayd poynt & along ye way yt leads up ye hill William to have ye Lower part from stake & poynt of Rocks (sd John's bounds) along downe ward to ye Lower end of sayd Marsh Lott: & the upland upon the north side of the Cove yt lies in sd Johns division up to ye former line mentioned yt divideth betwixt Humphrys part & theirs.

The division of ye six Acres of Marsh at ye place called Elders Island as followeth: To John Hobson upon ye so west side bounded by a Creek yt parts widow Johnsons marsh to a stake by ye Edg of ye meadow neer ye great Creek. from thenc on a streight line so-east to a stake by a smale Creek & then as ye Creek Runs till it comes about three Rods of a stake betwext Mr. Philleps marsh & sd marsh haveing a little peice at yt end next Mr. Philleps bounded by a creek till it comes to ye Line. To Humphry Hobson: ye outside divission or no-east side from a stake fixt at ye head of ye creek: yt parts ye twelve Acres & sd Marsh bounded as ye Creek runs to a stake & stone at yt end neer a smale Isleand & from sd stake on a streight line to a stake by the Great Creek yt parts ye other marsh & sd six Acres. To William Hobson ye midle peice divided by ye other forementioned peices on both sides & one end by ye great Creek the other end by Mr. Philleps Marsh.

The outward division of twelve Acres salt marsh divided as followes: To John Hobson ye Lower part next to Joseph Jewets to a white Oak tree upon ye upland & from sd tree cross ye marsh on a streight Line southerly to a stake by a Creek & then as the Creek Runs to the Great Creek. To William Hobson the upper pt of sd divission next Mr. Rogers Marsh to sd white Oak tree & stake before mentioned. And the Lower part of ye midle divission next to James Dickensons & Joseph Jewets: easterly corner by a stake, thenc Running southerly to a stake by a pond end & from yt stake, to a stake at ye head of a little Creek: & thenc as the little Creek Runs until it come to the great Creek & then bounded by the great Creek till it comes to a smale Creek yt parts Ezekiel Mighels Divission of ye six Acres at ye Elders Isleand. To John Hobson: ye upper part of ye midle divission bounded by a creek, next Mr. Rogers his marsh & by a smale creek betwext ye outward divission till it comes to a stake by Joseph Jewets marsh by a pond & then by sd pond to a stake at ye other end & then from sd stake by the pond lineing southerly to a stake by a little Creek: & yn by sd little Creek till it comes into the great Creek againe: yt parts Ezekiel Mighels Divission or third pt at ye Elders Isleand.

The pasture Land divided betwext William Hobson & John Hobson is as followeth: William to have all the pasture Land Lying next to his plowing Land extending against ye Comon to a stake & stone in a hollow: & thenc extending ye length of sd pasture easterly on a streight line to a corner next ye land belonging to Leiut. Lamberts heirs where there is a white oak tree markt with W. H. on one side & I. H. on ye other. John to have all ye rest of sd pasture southerly side of sd two bounds ye stake next ye comon & ye tree at Lamberts corner: Lying betwext sd line & ye feild calld Murley Feild.

The Land Layd out neer Hunsley hill belonging to their Fathers Right divided as follows: To Humphry Hobson Joyneing upon Capt. Wicoms Land at a Red Oak Tree markt that end next Ipswich Line extending from sd tree northerly to an Elm tree markt with H & I & from sd tree cross ye Lott Northerly to a stake & stone & from sd stake & stone extending southerly to an old tree falen with stones at ye Root & from sd stones bounded by Capt. Wicoms Land to ye first bounds. To John Hobson bounded by ye sd Humphrys on ye southerly side at ye Corner next Ipswich line by ye Elm markt with I H. extending northerly to a white oak tree markt with I H. W. from thence extending westerly to a stake & stones. from thence extending southerly to a stake & stones & thenc extending easterly to ye first markt Elm. To William Hobson bounded at ye south Corner next to sd Johns by a white oak tree markt with W. H. I. on ye side next Ipswich extending northerly to a white Oak tree markt with L. H. from thenc extending westerly by Lambert & Boynton to a white oak tree markt with H. thenc extending southerly to a stake & stones a boundary betwext sd Johns Land & it & thenc easterly to ye 1st Oak.

The division of Land cald ye Elders plaine or ye pen Land is as follows: William Hobson to have ye Land & meadow Lying next to Samuell Brocklebanks bounded & set of from ye rest of sayd Land at ye southerly corner by a white oak tree markt & thenc extending norwesterly to a stake & stone fifteene Rods Northeast of the first bounds of ye whole tract & sd William to have ye meadow ground upwards as far as ye foot of the great hill comon Land at a stake & stone neer ye brook.

Humphry Hobson to have ye Land next to Williams bounded by a stake & stone Nineteene Rods Easterly of sd Williams bounds from sd stake ye Line extends southerly to a white oak tree Markt next ye comon. John Hobson to [have the rest of. *copy*.] sd Land cald ye Eldrs division of sd upland upon ye easterly side of sd Humphries & bounded by sd Humphries bounds being a stake & stone at one end & ye white Oak on ye other side or end next ye Comon sd Dividend being bounded by Comon Land in pt & by John Hopkinsons Land in pt. The rest of ye meadow yt belonged to sd Eldrs divission upward of sd William Hobsens bounds is one half to the sd Humphry Hobson & the other half to Jno. Hobson son of sd John Hobson deceased.

The Third of each divisions belonging to Humphry &

John Hobson sons of Humphry & John Hobson deceased which appertaines to the Respective Relicts of Humphry & John Hobson, deceased is not yet set out to sd Relicts: but remaines in their parts yet to be divided to ye sd widows when order for it.

Signed and sealed Sept. 14, 1698.

*Essex Co. Probate Files, Docket* 13,455.

### ESTATE OF JANE LAMBERT OF ROWLEY.

"The last will and Testament of Jaine Lambert widow may the 24: 1659 I Jaine lambert beeing sick in body but of perfect Memory doe make this my last will and Testament in form folowing Imprimous I giue all my land madowes comans and whatsoeuer belongeth to my hous and lott by any right with the said house barnes and what pertaines therto I say all my lands excepting the land in the vilege vnto my eldest son John lambert It I giue vnto him one feather bed with all that belongeth vnto it. It I giue vnto my sonn Jonathan Lambertt forty pounds It I giue vnto my sonn Gershom Lambert forty pounds It I giue vnto him one fether bed with all that belongeth ther vnto It I giue vnto my sonn Thomas Lambert one pewther plater and one linen sheet and one siluer spoone It I giue vnto my Daughter Anne Lambert one great Chist and all that is in it and one trunke and all that is in it one litl box and all that is in it the fether beding which I ly one with all ther belonges vnto it and all my pewther with all my brass and potts and ketls and when thes things is prised, I will that they shall be made vp to the value of sixty pounds provided that if all this estat: the land giuen to John excepted Doe not Amoneitt to thes sumes thus giuen out as aboue-mentioned I will that they shall all abatte proportionably It I make ordaine and Constitute my eldest Sonn John Lambert to be executor of This my will and testament and doe desier and intreat Mr Ezekill Rogers and Mr Joseph Jewit to be ouerseers of this my will and Testament in wittnes that this is my owne free deliberat act and deed I haue setto my hand the day and yere first aboue written."

her mark<br>
Jaine IL Lambert

Witness: Joseph Jewett, Thomas Leauer.

Proved in Ipswich court 27: 7: 1659 by the witnesses.

Inventory taken 22: 6: 1659, by Joseph Jewett and John Tod: one hous, a barn, the orchard and Thre accres of land

Joyning therunto more or les, 80li.; six accres of land in a place Called Sachels ground, 36li.; Two acres of land in the east feild, 10li.; Thre accres more of land in the same feild, 10li.; Eight accres and a half in a place Called the great plaine, 10li.; nine gates and a half, 9li. 10s.; Twenty two Accres of meddows, 80li.; Two accres in the Marsh feild, 2li.; one hundred Acres joyning on Merrimak, 4li.; foure oxen, 22li., and seven Cowes, 28li., 50li.; Eleven young Cattle, 22li.; Swine, 8li. 10s.; Debts owing to the Estat, 78li.; in Corn, 26li.; fiftene load of hay, 8li.; in bras and Puther, 4li.; a warmeing pan, a frieing pan, an Iron Pott, 16s.; in wood vessel and Spouns, 1li.; a raper, 10s., Iron, 2li., yoaks and Chaine, 2li., 4li. 10s.; a bible, 1s., four Chaires, 4s., four quishins, 16s., 1li. 1s.; a Bed, thre boulsters, curtaines and other things, 8li.; in Linen, 2li., a tabl, box, Chist, Trunk, 1li. 5s. 4d., 3li. 5s. 4d.; whelles and Cards, 4s., a bed and beding, 5li., 5li. 4s.; Cotten wool, yearn and hemp, 10s.; a bed and Beding, 7li. 5s.; A hid of lether, 1li.; wearing Cloathes with a peece of cotton and linen Cloath, 9li.; A saddl, bridle and pistil, 1li. 5s.; one mare, 16li., Two horses, 24li., 40li.; total, 539li. 16s. 4d.

Testified to in Ipswich court 27 : 7 : 1659 by John Lambert.
*Essex Co. Probate Files, Docket* 16,181.

### ESTATE OF THOMAS ABBOTT OF ROWLEY.

"I Ezeakell Northen Being desired By Richard Swan father in Law to Thomas Abbott Lately deceased, to goe to the Said Thomas his House to desire him to make his will which is as followeth Inprimis I Giue vnto my Brother Gorge Abbott Ten Pounds, and vnto my Brother Nehemiah Abbott Ten Pounds, and my devission of land at meremacke: also I Giue vnto my Brother Thomas Abbott fiue pounds: The Rest of my Estate I Giue vnto my wife This was the will of the abouesaid Thomas Abbott vpon the last day of the sixt mounth in the yeare 1659"

Witness: Ezeakell Northen, Gemima Burbanke.

"We whose Names ar vnder written Being with Thomas Abbott vpon the fift day of the seuenth mounth in the yeare 1659 Before seuen a clocke in the morneing he being then in his Right vnderstanding and memory he said vnto vs that he had bene perswaded to make his will and he was in such extreme pane when he did it soe as he did not consider the thing as he should haue done. and therfor vpon further consideration ther was something in his former will he desired to alter which was this that haueing giuen his wife his wholle estat, the debts and legacyes being paid, as being his Nearest freind: Now considering that my Bretheren ar next vnto hir: doe therfor Giue my lands vnto my brethren in case that my wife die childless: to those Bretheren that haue childeren or may haue childeren furthermore I Giue vnto widdow Brocklebanke and hir Sons forty shillings."

Witness: maxemillion Jewett, John Tod, James Barker.

Proved in Ipswich court 27: 7: 1659 by the witnesses.

Inventory: One Mare and one Mare fole, 24li.; One Cowe, 3li. 10s.; One oxe, 5li. 15s.; Two Hefers & one steare Calfe, 7li. 5s.; One Sowe & 4 pigs, 1li. 5s.; One Slede and one plow, 10s.; One Sith, 4s.; Two Yookes and one cheane, 10s.; One cart with boult & shakle and cart Roope, 2li. 10s.; One Raper with belt, 15s.; Three Yowes and three wethers, 2li. 10s.; Two litle Tubs and 3 trese, 4s.; Two pales, 2s.; Two bras kettles, 2 litle sclets of bras, one Irne sclett, one Irne poote, one candlstick, 1li. 8s.; earthen poots, 3s.; peuter and Tine things, 1li.; cheares and stooles, 8s.; Bibles, 10s.; Aparel and Cloth for an aparell, 6li. 11s. 6d.; Two Chists and 2 pounds of woole, 16s.; One warming pane and Heales 20s.; Quisings and one Irne huke, 3s. 6d.; One Lamp, 1s.; More wood vesell, 14s.; Bridlebeets and lining Yern with other small things, 10s.; Coton and Sheepp woole, 6s.; One line wheele, 4s.; Two Sickles and one sith, 2s. 6d.; One trea, 1s.; One sheet and one blankit, 7s.; One Tand Calfe skine, 2s. 6d.; Bags and hemp and a head peece, 4s.; Two axes and two beetle hups and Irne weg, 4s.; flax and one sith, 6s. 6d.; Pincers and ould Irne, 2s. 6d.; The Crope of 8 ackers of land, 25li.; Heay, 6li. 10s.; House and hom lot, 30li.; Three Ackers o salt marsh with a poynt of upland and three ackers of fresh medow, 12li.; Thirteen Ackers of upland and medow, 100li.; gats, 2, 2li.; cours yearn for bags 15 pound, 8s.; In bedding & a gun & other things, 7li. 10s.; total, 234li. 15s.

Dorithy Abbott widow of Thomas Abbott testified that this was a true inventory of the estate of her late husband, in the Ipswich court Nov. 24, 1659.

The debts of Thomas Abott: to Elder Wheeples, 2li. 12s.; Mr. Pane, 1li. 4s.; William Law, 2li. 15s. 6d.; Thomas Wood, 8s.; John Grant, 6s.; Henery Ryly, 5s.; James Barker, 9s.; John Jonson, 1s. 6d.; Goodman Porter, 15s.; Samuell Platts, 6s.; John Trumball, 2s. 8d.; John Borbanke, 6s.; Richard

humbs, 1s.; Docter ffuler, 1li.; Goodman Kinsman, 2s. 2d.; Samuell Plumer, 8s.; Ezesekell Northen, 2s.; Wiliam Tene, 1s. 4d.; John Todd, 3li. 8s. 5d.; Mr. Crosby, 1li. 13s.; Joseph Trumball, 1li. 14s.; Samuell Sticknah, 6s.; Mr. Rogers, 5s.; Wiliam Boynton, 2s.; Mr. Jewet, 5li. 14s.; Thomas Abot brother to the deseased, 5li.; total, 29li. 17s. 7d.
*Essex Co. Probate Files, Docket* 137.

Administration on the estate granted 24: 9: 1659, to his widow Dorothy, his will naming no executor. *Ipswich Quarterly Court Records, vol.* 1, *page* 83.

### Estate of Joshua Conant of Salem.

Administration on the estate of Joshua Connant, who died intestate in England, granted 29: 9: 1659 to Mr. Thomas Gardner. Amount of inventory of his estate in New England, 32li. 6s. *Salem Quarter Court Records, vol.* 4, *leaf* 35.

Inventory of Seethe, widow of Joshuah Connant, taken by John Browne and Richard Prince: One bed, one Bolster, a suit of Curtayns and valiants, one Rug and a Blankett and matt, 8li.; five p of shetts and a half shett, 5li.; Eleven napkins, 3 table Cloths, 1li. 7s.; fowr pilow bears, 1li. 4s.; twelve towels, 9s.; for pewter pans and spons, 1li. 6s.; one Cloake, 18s.; one Trunk and on owld Chest, 10s.; one spitt, one payr of Andyrns, 3s.; to Sivs, two Trays, 3s.; one payr of scals and to wayts, 2s. 6d.; one trundl Bedsted and one blankett, 6s.; for wooll, 4s.; 5 stools, 9s.; 9 Chayrs, 13s.; 3 tabls, 1li.; for divers howshowld implements, 8s. 6d.; for bras and Iron, 1li. 10s.; one chest, one box, 1li.; one Carpett, two Coshens, 5s.; one looking glas and two small boxes, 10s.; mony and platt, 1li. 4s.; for 6 shep, 5li.; one kradle, 4s.; one bedsted, 10s.; total, 32li. 6s. *Essex Co. Quarterly Court Files, vol.* 5, *leaf* 62.

Mr. Thomas Gardner, appointed by the last court as administrator of the estate of Joshua Connant, deceased, brought in an acount of the said estate June 26, 1660, and was discharged. *Salem Quarterly Court Records, vol.* 4, *leaf* 39.

Mr. Thomas Gardner's account: a note of what was dewe to mee from Josuah Connant: Wintering of 8 sheepe at 6s. ⅌ sheepe, 2li. 8s.; 32 lode of wood at 4s. ⅌ lode, 6li. 8s.; for a bushell of wheate, 5s.; 3 bushels of Indian Corne, 9s.; payde for him to Jone Cotta, 11s.; dew to Joseph Gardner for 3 yeares rent for his house at 3li. ⅌ yere, 9li.; payd for him to Richard Prince, 13s.; payd to Mr. Browne, 10li.; payd to Mr. Crommell, 5li. 13s. 11d.; total, 35li. 7s. 11d.

Hugh Jones testified that while he lived with his master Gardner, the latter wintered eight sheep for Joshua Connant, and deponent carried in wood to his wife, "I gesse" upward of thirty loads, also corn and wheat, etc.

Jone (her F mark) Cotta, wife of Robert, testified, 20: 4: 1660, that she received of Thomas Gardner of Salem, eleven shillings for the keeping of Josuah Connant's sheep one summer. Phillip Cromwell's receipt dated, June 10, 1659, from "ould m$^r$ Gardner" for a debt of 5li. 13s. 11d.

*Essex Co. Quarterly Court Files, vol. 5, leaves* 116, 117.

### Estate of George Norton of Salem.

Administration on the estate of George Norton granted 29: 9: 1659 to his wife, Mary Norton. *Salem Quarterly Court Records, vol. 4, leaf 35.*

Inventory of the estate of George Norton, taken 22: 7: 1659, by John Porter and Jacob Barney: His wearing apparel, 8li.; a bead with bolsters blankets & rug, 3li.; 3 flock beads with other beading, 1li. 1s.; 6 paire of sheats & 1 tablecloth, 11 napkins, 3 paire of pillibers, 4li. 10s.; Beadstead, 5s.; 1 tronke, 2 Chists, 1li. 10s.; 1 tabell-bord, 1 forme, 3 Chaiers, 6s.; 3 Iron pots, 2 friinge pans, 1 dripinge pan, 1 spitt, 1li. 5s.; 1 Bras kettell, 1 bras pan, skellett & warminge pan, 1li. 5s.; in peutter, 8s.; 4 musskets & a small peace, 2li.; sawes, boarers, axes with other tooles, 2li. 18s. 6d.; flaks, 1li.; 6 akers of Indian Corne, 5li.; in wheate, 5li.; Barley, 16s.; in haye, 6li.; Aples, 1li.; a mare & colt, 15li.; a colt of a year old, 3li.; in hogs & small pegs, 10li. 7s.; 6 oxen, 33li.; 4 Cowes, 14li.; 2 heffers, 5li.; 4 younge Cattell, 7li.; 2 Calfes, 1li. 10s.; total, 134li. 11s. 6d.

Petition of Freegrace Norton and John Norton, children of George, for division of the estate. Mother Mary Norton mentioned. Children: Freegrace, aged twenty-four years; John, aged twenty-two; Nathanyell, aged twenty; George, aged eighteen; Mary, aged sixteen; Mehittabell, aged fourteen; Sarah, aged twelve; Hannah, aged ten; Abigaill, aged eight; Ellizabeth, aged five years.

*Essex Co. Quarterly Court Files, vol. 5, leaf 63.*

## Estate of James Moores of Hammersmith (Lynn).

"The fift day of the fift Moneth one thousand six hundred fifty & nine: was made this last will: of James Moores: at Hammersmith: as followeth I James Moores being now visitted by the hand of god with great sicknes & weaknes: but of perfect memory & hauing my vnderstanding: do Committ my body to y$^e$ Graue & my spirrit to god y$^t$ gaue it: As for my outward Estate that the lord hath bestowed on mee by my labors I dispose of on this wise, One Cow y$^t$ is now feeding I giue to my little daughter: Dorothy: to be sold & Improued to y$^e$ best aduantage as y$^e$ lord shall please to blesse it for y$^e$ good of my said child. as for the rest of my estate: all Just debts being honestly paid: in y$^e$ first place whatsoeuer is Remayning I doe giue & bequeath to my beloued wife Ruth Moores: both of what is myne within doores & also else where in any mans hand or otherwise: to be at her disposall for her good & Comfort & for y$^e$ accomplishment of this my last will I doe appoynt Oliver Purchis & John Clarke: my Louing freinds to be my ouerseers to whose loueing Care & trust I Committ this my last will & the ouersight of my estate to see it pformed & done according to my will heerein & doe heerevnto signe with my hand."

Signum of
James IIII Moores

Witness: Joseph Jenckes, senr, Joseph Jenckes, Juner.

Proved in the Salem court 9m: 1659 by Joseph Jenkes, Sr. *Essex Co. Quarterly Court Files, vol. 5, leaf 66.*

Ruth Moore brought in the will of her husband, James Moore, 29: 9: 1659. No witnesses appeared, and she was appointed administratrix of the estate. *Salem Quarterly Court Records, vol. 4, leaf 35.*

Ruth, widow of deceased, brought in an inventory of the estate. *Salem Quarterly Court Records, vol. 4, leaf 39.*

Inventory taken by Joseph Jenckes and John Hathorne: Swine, pewter, two brass skillets, Iron potts & kettles, a firepan, slice & potthooks, 4 wedges, 2 beetle rings, wearing apparrell, sheets, shirts, a table Cloth, 3 hatts, a flockbed, 3 Fether pillows, a Cubbart & Cubbart Cloth, a Chest, one Chaire, barr of Iron, Linnen wheele, 3 pr. of shooes, ———; a payre of men's stockings, 4s.; other old Lumbar in ye Kitchen, 13s.; butter & Cheese, 1li. 4s.; tools p Colliers use,

3li. 4s. 6d.; total, 56li. 8s. 6d. *Essex Co. Quarterly Court Files, vol. 5, leaf 67.*

### ESTATE OF SAMUEL PORTER OF WENHAM.

John Porter, William Dodge and Mr. Edmond Batter were appointed 29: 9: 1659, administrators of the estate of Samuell Porter, deceased. *Salem Quarterly Court Records, vol. 4, leaf 35.*

"The Last Will and Testament of Sam$^{ll}$ Porter made 10: 12: 1658 being Bound to the Berbadus Itp$^r$ I giue to my dearly beloued wife Hannah Porter the one halfe of my farme during her life Ite I giue to my son Jn$^o$ Porter the other halfe of my farme at wenham: & after the death of my wife the other halfe to Returne vnto him, & one mare to my son: & the Remaynd$^r$ (to my wife) of my estate more or lesse: I desere my ffather Porter & my father in law W$^m$ Dodge & Edmo: Batter to be my Ou$^r$seers."

Samuell Porter

Witness: Edmo: Batter, Sara Batter.

Proved in Salem court 28: 4: 1660. *Essex Co. Quarterly Court Files, vol. 5, leaf 68.*

Inventory taken 22: 4: 1660, by Roger Conant and John Rayment: One house and land at Wenham & other land that was bought of Jno. Denham, 250li.; 2 oxen, 10li., 1 Cowe, 4li., 14li.; 15 yewes & lambs at 6s. 8d., 5li.; mare & Colt, 16li.; a cloath suet, 1li. 15s.; another suet of cloath, 30s., 3li. 5s.; 2 other suet of cloathes, 1li. 14s.; other wearinge aparell, 6li. 17s. 7d.; 2 psalme bookes, 18d., 1 silvr dram Cup, 4s., 5s. 6d.; 2 Chests & 2 boxes, 18s. 6d.; suger & Cotton his pt. at Boston, 30li.; due to him from William Nicoles, 1li.; total, 331li. 19s. *Essex Co. Quarterly Court Files, vol. 5, leaf 69.*

### ESTATE OF EDWARD BROWNE OF IPSWICH.

"I Edward Browne of Ipswich in the county of Essex being att this tyme sick and weake of body but through mercy haueing and Inioying my vnderstanding and memory doe make and ordayne this my last will and testament as followeth Imprimas I committ my Soule into the hands of Jesus christ my Redeemer my Body to be desently buried In the burieing place at Ipswich And for my outward estate that the Lord hath Giuen me I doe dispose as followeth viz.

whereas ‖there was‖ a gift giuen vnto my sonn Thomas by his Aunt wattson in ould England he being dead I accompt my sonn Joseph Browne to be his heire and therfore that gift being thirteene pound to belong vnto him at the age of twenty one yeares and it being in my hands my will is that my sayd sonn Joseph shall haue my eight acres of Land within the common field w^ch I bought of my Brother Bartholmew as alsoe that psell of meddow at the west meddows lyeing beyond the brooke on the west syde of the sayd brooke In leiw of the sayd gift before mentioned And the rest of my estate I leaue vnto my beloued wife ffaith Browne for the tearme of her naturall life and then to be disposed of vnto my children And my will is that after my sayd wiffes decease my sonn Joseph shall haue and Inioy my dwelling house & aptenances & p^rveledges belonging there vnto ‖together with all the rest of my land & meddow‖ pvided he yeald vp the formar Land and meddow which my will is my Sonn John Browne shall haue posses and Inioy And if my Sonn Joseph dye without heires ‖then my Son John Browne to haue & Inioy it and if he the sayd John shall dye without heires ‖then to be vnto my daughters or the surviveing of them And my will is that my sayd wife at her decease shall dispose of my estate among my children And in case my wife shall chang her estat that then she shall giue security that my estat may be desposed off among my children after her decease as aforesayd And doe make my sayd wife sole executrix of this my last will and testament In wittnes of this to be my last will & testament I haue heervnto sett my hand & seale the 9th of february 1659."

           Edward Browne [SEAL]

Witness: Robert Lord, Thomas Lord.

Proved in Ipswich court 27: 1: 1660 by the witnesses. *Essex Co. Quarterly Court Files, vol. 5, leaf 77.*

Inventory taken Feb. 20, 1659, by Moses Pengry and Robert Lord: Dwelling house and aptananses, 50li.; six acres of Land most of it in tilt, 18li.; nyne acres of salt marsh, 16li.; 2 psells of meddow at the west meddows, 14li.; 8 acres of Land, about 6 of it in tilt, 20li.; one fether bed, 2 boulsters, 2 downe pillows, blankett & Rug, 6li.; one bedsted cord, curtaynes, valiants & strabed, 1li. 10s.; eight chaires, 14s.; little boxes, 4s.; a paire of fine sheets, old, 1li.; foure paire of sheets & one od one, 3li.; one paire of pillow beers, 10s.; foure paire of pillow beeres, 2 of ym small, 8s.; 2 table cloths, eleven napkins, 13s.; one course table cloth & 14 course napkins and Towells with some other small lennen, 14s.; His weareing apparell, 7li. 10s.; a muskett, bandeleour, sword & belt & pike, 1li. 10s.; three little tables, 3 chaires & 4 cushens, 15s.; 2 chests and a trunke, 13s. 4d.; 10li. cotten woole, 4li.; sheep woole, 16s.; in cotten yarne, 7li. 14s.; In lennen yarne, 1li.; earthen ware, 7s. 6d.; one warmeing pan, 10s.; one kettell, 3 skilletts, one brase morter, skimer and a little brase ladell and lampe, 1li. 10s.; 2 Iron potts, one iron kettell and morter, 1li.; a frying pan, tramell, potthookes and grediron, 11s.; spitt, firepan, tongs, fireforke, hookes, 8s.; In pewter, latin ware & 2 box Irons, 1li. 10s.; ould pewter, 2s.; a small fether bed, boulster, pillow & other beding, 3li. 10s.; a flock bed, boulster & other beding, 2li. 10s.; ginger & hops, 10s.; 15 bushells & half of wheat, 3li. 18s. 6d.; mault, 6s.; Indian corne, 2li. 8s.; 3 wheeles, finished lennen, 13s. 6d.; wheeles woolen & linnen not finisht, 1li. 16s.; work done toward chaires, 3s. & 15 ———ills, 6s. 9d.; shope tooles, 3li. 6s.; old caske, 13s.; nayles & other small things, 10s.; two cow bells & eares for ———, 3s.; one barrell, firkin & powdering tubs, 12s.; a paire of scales, 3s.; beere vessells, keelers & other lumber, 14s.; 6 trayes, dishes, trenchers, & payles, 13s.; a woolen & linnen wheele & cards, 13s.; kneading trough & fine sives, 8s.; a cartrop & bedline & hand baskett, 12s.; beefe, pourke & suett & tallow, 2li.; halfe a firkin of sope, 10s.; In bookes, 1li.; old baggs, 3s.; one bullock, 6li. 10s.; 2 Cowes, 8li.; 3 cattell about 3 yr. old, 8li., 16li.; 1 bull, 2 yr. old & 1 yr. old, 3li. 10s.; six ewes & a ram, 3li. 15s.; five swine, 2li. 10s.; cart plow & sled, yokes & caynes, 3li.; in hay and peace, 7li.; sythes, 12 axes & hows, beetell & weedges, forks, 1li. 10s.; owing to the estate, 1li. 13s.; total, 225li. 5s. 7d. Debts owing from the estate, 24li. 8s. 1d. Clear estate, 200li. 17s. 6d. *Essex Co. Quarterly Court Files, vol. 5, leaf 78.*

### ESTATE OF JOHN CUTTING OF NEWBURY.

"Bee it knowne vnto all men by theise p<sup>r</sup>sents that I John Cutting of Newbury in the County of Essex in Newengland being through gods mercy in health of body and of perfect memory, Considering seriously mine owne frailty and mortality, endeauoring to leaue mine estate to my relations as may continue loue & peace amongst them, I do hereby make my last will and Testament first I comend my Soule into the hands of my blessed Redeemer Jesus Christ, and my body when I shall decease this life, if I dy in Newbury to be buryed in the burying place in Newbury in hope of a happy resurrection. And for my worldly goods I dispose of as followeth, first I giue and bequeath vnto mary my wife dureing her widdowhood, all my Lands goods and Chattells, And do will and appoint her my sole executrix of this my last will and testament. But if my said wife shall change her Condition and marry againe, then I order and appoint that she my said wife shall pay yearely afterwards dureing her naturall life out of my lands fifteene pounds a yeare. That is to say, To my Daughter Mary the wife of Nicholas Noyes fiue pounds a yeare, And to my Daughter Sara Browne of Charlestowne, the wife of James Browne, fiue pounds a yeare, And to my Grand child Mary the wife of Samuell Moody fiue pounds a yeere, and also out of my stocke to euery one of my Grandchildren and great grandchildren thirty shillings a peice. And at the death of the said Mary my wife, I giue & bequeath vnto my said Daughter Mary Noyes, all that house and land now in the possession of Thomas Bloomfeild that lyeth on the east side of the high way conteineing about fifty or fiue and fifty acres bee it more or lesse both vpland pasture land & meadow and after my said Daughter Mary Noyes her decease to remaine and abide to the proper vse of her Son Cutting Noyes his heires & assignes foreuer 2dly I giue and bequeath vnto my Daughter Sara the wife of James Browne abousaid ||& her heires|| all the house I now dwell in, with the twelue acres of vpland that the house stands vpon, and three quarters of that twenty acres of Salt marsh land lately purchased of m$^r$ Steuen Dummer bee it more or lesse. 3dly I giue and bequeath vnto my Grandchild Mary moody the wife of Samuel Moody abouesaid, all the house and Land that is in the possession of John Dauis with the six akers of meadow in the Birchen meadows, and the quarter part of the twenty acres of the salt marsh Land bee it more or lesse as is abouespecifyed, further I giue vnto her my said Granchild Mary Moody, all that parsell of arable land lately purchased of the said m$^r$ Dumer, lyeing vpon the southwest of the highway betweene the land of Henry shorte on the southeast and John Knights land on the northwest conteineing about twenty or fiue [and?] twenty acres more or lesse. And the first yeare the said Samuell Moody his heirs &c shall possesse the abouesaid parsell of Land, which shalbe after my wiues decease. then the said samuell Moody or his heirs shall pay to my Daughter sara the wife of James Browne aforesaid the summe of forty pounds, But if my Grandchild Mary moody abousaid shall dye without Issue of her owne body, then all the land abouespecifyed that is hereby giuen vnto her, shall after her decease, Remaine equally to bee diuided vnto my abouesaid two daughters Mary Noyes & sara Browne and their Children for euer. And the forty pound that is here mentioned to be paid by Samuell moody vnto my Daughter Sara Browne abouesaid, if paid before, shall be paid backe againe vnto the abouesaid Samuell Moody my Debts and funerall rites being discharged by my said executrix. In witnesse whereof I the aboue mentioned John Cutting haue sett my hand and seale october the two & twentyeth In the yeare of our Lord one thousand sixe hundred fifty nine."

John [SEAL] Cutting
his mark

Witness: Anthony Somerby, John Browne, Nicholas O wallington.

Proved in Ipswich court Mar. 27, 1660 by Anthony Sumerby and John Browne.

Inventory of estate of John Cutting of Newbury deceased Nov. 20, 1659, taken Dec. 16, 1659, by Wm. Gerrish and Edward Woodman: the house which he dwelt in & 12 acres of land with 20 acres of salt marsh, 100li.; the house that John Davis dwells in with 25 acres of pasture & plowland & 6 acres of meadow, 100li.; the farme that Thomas Blomfeild rents of about 70 or 75 acres of upland & meadow & pasture land, 300li.; For plate, a cup & a spoone & his wearing apparell, 16li.; 3 mares and a Colt, 50li.; 4 oxen, 7 cowes & 7 swyne, 59li.; 47 sheep, 23li. In the parlour: one bed & boulster, 2 pillows, a paire of blankets, a rugg and bedstead with Curtaines & vallons, 10li.; one Cubbard & a drawer, 3li.; Eight chayres, 2li.; one draw table, 2li. 5s.; one small table, 5s.; one paire of Andirons, tongs, slice, warming pan, 1li. 5s.; Some small things in yarne & settle &c., 2li. 14s.; spice boxes, &c., 15s.; five cushions, 1li. 6s.; two baskets, 6s.; a glass case beset with earthen ware and a looking glass, 1li. 10s.; a great bible & small & other bookes, 1li. 5s.; three Joyne stooles, 6s. In the kitchin: a great brass kettle, a small copper & smal kettle, a brass skellet & 2 small skellets, a skimmer & 2 brasse candlesticks & morter & pessell, 6li. 10s.; two tramells, a paire of And Irons, spit, tongs, frying pan, 2 small Iron pots & some other small things, 2li.; nine platters, a pottle flagon, a quart pot & pint pot, 2 basons, 2 chamberpotts & other small peices, 5li. 10s.; In earthen ware, 10s.; A brewing tub & 3 drink vessells, a table & forme & 2 buckets & 2 pales, 4 trayes & 2 keelers, a churne, 2 powdring tubs, & a cubberd & other things, wth a wheele, 3li.; a Long saw & hand saw with beetle rings, 6 wedges, a broad axe & small axe, 1li. 10s.; A sadle, bridle & pillion, 1li. 10s.; A Cart & wheels & plow & chaynes & yoaks with some small things, 3li. 10s. In the chambers: 4 chests & a box, 2li. In Linnen: 1 paire of Holland sheets, 2 pr. of flaxen sheets, 4 pr. of other sheets, 6 tablecloths, 1 dosen & 1-2 of napkins, 8 pillow bears, 6 towells, &c. 20li.; A bedsted with a fetherbed, boulster, 2 pillowes, one blanket & a rugg with curtaines and a trundle bed & beding to it, 10li. In the other chamber, a bed with beding or furniture to it, 3li. 10s.; Lumber, 2li.; about 18 bushells of corne & wooll, 3li. 10s.; total, 737li.; debts due: from william Sawyer, 3li.; Peter Godfrey, 26li.; Tho. Blomfeild, 20li.; John Bartlet, 1li.; Mr. Woodman, 3li. 2s.; Sam. Moody, 3li.; total, 56li. 2s.; debts owed to Henry Short, 40li.; Goodman Nicholls, 4li. 10s.; Leift. Sprage, 3li. 10s.; Mr. Broughton, 1li. 12s.; John Lewis, 1li.; Goodman Lynes, 7li.; Joseph Noyes, 6li. 10s.; total, 64li. 2s.

Received in Ipswich court Mar. 27, 1660.

*Essex Co. Probate Files, Docket 6,984.*

James Brown acknowledged 15 : 8 : 1664, the receipt from Samuell Moodey of 20li. being part of the 40li. given him by Mr. Cutting's will; and acknowledged the receipt of the remaining 20li., Nov. 11, 1667. Sworn to June 24, 1675 by Nicolas Noyes. *Ipswich Deeds, vol. 4, page 7.*

### ESTATE OF HENRY TRUE OF SALISBURY.

Inventory of the estate of Henry True of Salisbury taken Mar. 9, 1660, by Robert Pike and Richard (his A mark) Goodall: a debt from one of Salem, 1li. 17s.; a hous and Land att Salem, 50li.; a hous and Land att Salsbury, 45li.; 3 cows, 12li.; a 3 year old stear, 14li.; 2 yearling calves, 2li.; 2 suking calvs, 12s.; 6 sheep, 2li. 10s.; 9 swine, 6li. 10s.; a musket, fowling peec and sword, 2li.; a barell, 2 kelers and other Lumber, 10s.; a spad and ax, 2s.; a bed & bedsteed and appurtainances, 5li. 6s.; a bed & the appurtainances, 9li. 9s.; a cuberd, 1li. 6s.; a chest, 14s.; a box and water cases, 12s.; Table Linen, 1li. 2s.; 3 pillobys, 10s.; a table,

10s.; 2 joynstools, 4s.; 4 chairs, 8s.; a chest, 5s., 2 Irn potts, 16s., 1li. 1s.; a ketle bell metl, 1li.; 2 skelets, 3s., and a warming pan, 10s., 13s.; a skarlett jaket, 1li. 10s.; a hatt band, 7s.; 4 pear of sheetts, 2li. 8s.; 3 bibls, 12s.; an ager, reap hook and other Lumber, 11s.; puter dishes & a bason, 17s.; drinking vesells, 5s.; a smoothing Iron, 5s.; a frying pann and spitt, 6s.; fire tongs & 2 tramell, 5s. 6d.; a debt du from Richard Curier, 16s.; from William ——, 1li.; from Mr. Petter Oliver, 1li. 10s.; total, 174li. 15s. 6d. The house & Land at Salisbury with the accomadasion, aprised at 45li. by Richard (his A mark) Goodall and John Ilsly. Debts which the estate do owe: To Richard North, 40li.; du for the vesell about 9li.; To John Lewes, 1li. 2s. Uncertaine debts: To Frances Skerry, Mr. Woster and Mr. Carr.

Attested to in Salisbury court 10: 2: 1660, by the administratrix. *Essex Co. Probate Files, Docket* 28,178.

### GUARDIANSHIP OF JUDAH TRUMBLE OF ROWLEY.

Judah Trumble and Ruth Trumble chose John Tod as guardian, May 10, 1660. Tod was bound in thirty pounds. *Ipswich Quarterly Court Records, vol. 1, page* 87.

### ESTATE OF EDWARD HOLYOKE OF LYNN.

"The will of mee Edward Holyoke made the xxv. of December 1658. As for the holy faith of the holy one God in Trinitie: & of the holy faith of our glorious Lord the son of God the Lord Jesus Christ the Second Adam I haue composed a booke and do bestowe vpon each of my sonns in Law a booke as their best legacy beeseeching the heauenly father to instruct them & my daughters chiefly in the holy scriptures & vsing that help as a means fro the Lord to vnderstand the scriptures, & the Lord God by his good Spirit blesse the holy scriptures, & this helpe of their ffather & the publique ministery & any sound bookes of instructio ||and I doubt not soe that my booke will giue them an hint of all sound doctrine: and an hint of all false & vnworthy doctrine.|| & it is my hearty desire|| & prayer to God|| that my children & childrens children may delight in the publiq assemblies of the saints & religiously observe the B. Lords day the ch[r]istian Sabbath: & loue priuate and publique prayer yea and secret prayer euery day & loue godly ch[r]istians & delight only in them & that they be not drawen aside by the pleesures or *pfits* & the vaine & fro*ths* company of this evill world w'ch lyes in all wickednesse. And I intreat my children that they bring vp their children wch they haue borne to God in the knowledg of God & of our Lord Jesus Christ The Lord Grant these things to his poore vnworthy servant that I may haue comfort that although I must be taken out of this warld & go to the ganeration of the godly Patriarcks pphetts Apossles & all the godly yet that I haue left among my children & childrens children the holy faith of the son of God for the hope of the life wch is eternall.

"As touching my worldly estate thus I dispose: a yoke of Oxen & my mare I bequeath to my sonn in Law Georg Keysar: my mare foale & a kow to my Son Pickman: 2 a kow to my son Andrewes: a kow to my daughter martyn. These oxen & kine are in the hands of goodman Wilkins of Lynn: the mare & foale is att Romney Marsh: I giue to my son Tuttell that 14$^{ld}$ that yearly he should haue giuen mee since I putt ouer the howse at Boston to him: I never yet had peny of it: 40$^s$ I gaue him of it: so there is 6$^{ld}$ yet behinde: & there is fiue pounds mentioned in goodman wilkins lease that he owes me: 50$^s$ of it I giue to my daughter martyn: & Twenty shillings to my kinswoman Mary Mansfield. & x$^s$ of it to John Dolittle and x$^s$ of it to my kinsman Thomas Morris of new haven. & x$^s$ of it to Hannah Keysar. As touching my Apparell: I giue my best Cloake of that cloth that came fro England to my sonne Holyoke: as also my Coate of the same cloth. I giue my other cloke to my sonn Keysor: my best doublet and breeches to my son Tuttell: my stuff doublet ||and my best Hatt|| to my son Holyoke: & all the rest of my wearing apparell to my son keysar.

"As touching the wholl yeeres rent of this yeere 1658. that is due to me from goodman Wilkins of Lyn. I owe Theodore Atkins 49$^s$ pay him in wheat: I ow John Hull about 22$^s$ pay him in wheate pay m$^r$ Russell treasurer 3 bushell of wheate for John Andreues: viii bushell of wheate to m$^r$ Wilson Pastor at Boston: & 8 bushell of Indian. as for my linnen let all my daughters pt alike: The xx$^s$ goodman Page oweth mee as my son Tuttell can witnesse I giue my Daughter Martyn: There is about xv$^s$ Captaine Sauige oweth mee: intreat him to satisfie my Cousin Davis & the rest giue to my Daughter martyn As for my bookes & writings: I giue my son Holyoke all the bookes that are at Lynn: as also the yron chest. And the bookes I haue in my study that are m$^r$ Broughtons works I giue him: he only can make vse of them: & like wise I giue him all my manuscripts whatsoever: & I ||giue|| him that large new Testam$^t$ in folio w$^{th}$ wast pap betweene euery leafe that I give him. As also mr Ainsworth on the 5. bookes of Moses & the psalms: & my Dictionary & Tremollins Bible in latin: & my Latin coment[ary on] Daniel bound together: these I giue to my son Holyoke. & a pt of the N Testam$^t$: in folio w$^{th}$ wast pap betwene euery leafe: & the great mapps of genealogy & that old manuscript called a *synassight*. the rest for a musket I gaue of old to my son Holyoke. All my land in Lyn & that land & meadow in the contrey neere Reading all was giuen to my son Holyoke when he marryed m$^r$ Pynchons daughter."

Edward Holyoke

Proved June 25, 1660.

M$^r$ Elizur Holioke only son of Edward Holyoke appointed June 25, 1660, administrator to his father's imperfect will.

Inventory of estate of Edward Holyoke of Lynn, who died at Rumney marsh, 4 May, 1660, taken June 19, 1660, by John Tuttell, John Dowlettell: a farme at Lyn, 400li.; 2 oxen, 12li., 4 Cowes, 16li., 3 young cattell, 8li. 10s., 36li. 10s.; 1 Old mare 10li.; 1 two yeere old mare, 8li.; 1 colt, 7li., 25li. Vtensills belonging to ye farme, 10li.; a parcell of land at Nahant about 3 acres, 6li.; A farme at Bever Damme neere Readinge, 150li.; Bookes at lynne & Rumney Marsh, 20li.; Wearinge cloths, 10li., a deske 5s. 10li. 5s.; An iron chest & other chests, 40s., 2 bedsteads, 20s., 3li.; a rest for a muskett, 5s., a little lynnen, 20s., 1li. 5s.; Debts about 19li.; total, 681li. According to our apprehensions of the Estate we judge these to be indiffrent prizes thereof.

Some bookes excepted lent out & not Gott in & the two farmes formerly on marriage Cuven$^t$ to ye sd. Elizur Holyoke.

Elizur Holioke deposed June 25, 1660, this to be a true inventory of his late father's Estate to y$^e$ best of his knowledge & y$^t$ when he knew more he will discover it.

*Suffolk Co. Probate Files, Docket* 242.

## ESTATE OF ERASMUS JAMES OF MARBLEHEAD.

Erasmus James, dying intestate, an inventory of his estate was brought in by his widow, Jane James, June 26, 1660, and she was appointed administratrix. She was to have the estate as long as she remained a widow, and if she died, it was to be equally divided between her son Erasmus and daughter Hester. The debts amounted to 19li. 14s. 10d. *Salem Quarterly Court Records, vol. 4, leaf 38.*

"An inventory of the Estate of Jane James, widdow of Erosmus James deceased," taken by Francis Johnson and Moses Maverick: A Cowe, 4li. 15s., heafer, 3li. 5s., 8li.; a new bedtick & boulster, 2li.; a new green Rugg, 1li. 15s.; a bed & boulster, 2 pillows & 2 pillow beers, a rugg, 2 blankets & sheets, 5li. 15s.; a cheste & a box, 1li.; 6 pewter dishes, 1li.; 9 poringers, 4 Candlsticks, 2 salts, 7 sacers, a pewter beer cupe & small Cupp & 5 earthen cups & Juggs, 1li. 9s. 2d.; A warminge pann, a smothing iron, a spitt, pott hooks, tongs, gridiren and friing pann, 19s.; 3 Iron potts & 2 small Iron kittells, 2li.; Latten ware, pailes, tubs, Chares, boules, trenchers, sives, Cann, table and forme, 1li.; an earthen pott, 5 wedges, an Iron Crow, 2 howes, 15s.; more wooden ware as barrills, hogsheads and other lumber, 11s. 6d.; 10 bushels of Indian corne, 1li. 10s.; other Lumber, 4s.; wareing Cloths of the deceased, 5li.; 5 swine, 3li.; a house and tenn Ackre lott, 50li.; total, 86li. 1s. 8d. "The land in Marblehead w$^{th}$ the house in w$^{ch}$ the deceased liued and died in, beinge in controversie between Erosmus James Junio$^r$ & Richard Reed w$^{ch}$ we knowe not whose it is, but beinge desired by the said Erosmus James Junio$^r$ to be prised we vallew at the some of fortie pounds." Wit: John (his T mark) Legd. Debts of the said Erosmus James at his death: To Arthur Sanden, 13s. 5d.; Mr. John Phillips of Boston, 4li.; Mr. Philipe Crumwell, 4li. 14s. 1d.; Mr. Mauericke, 3li. 7s. 4d.; Fra. Johnson, 3li.; Richard Read, 2li. 10s.; Mr. Corwine, 1li. 10s.; total, 19li. *Essex Co. Quarterly Court Files, vol. 5, leaf 111.*

Court 28: 9: 1665, ordered that all differences between Jane James, widow, and her son Erassmus James, they consenting, be left to the Worshipfull Major Wm. Hathorne and Mr. Moses Maverick to be determined within one month. Also that said Jane should not sell any of the estate except by court order. *Salem Quarterly Court Records, vol. 4, page 154.*

Court 26: 4: 1666, ordered Jane James, widow, liberty to sell the land mentioned in an inventory on file of the estate of her deceased husband, and of the effects to build her a house upon part of the said land or elsewhere in Marblehead. The overplus was to be delivered into the custody of the Worshipful Maj. Wm. Hathorn and Mr. Moses Maverike, to be used for necessities during her life, the two latter having charge of selling the land and building the house, and to order where the house should be built. *Salem Quarterly Court Records, vol. 4, page 166.*

### ESTATE OF WILLIAM GOLT OF SALEM.

Administration on the estate of William Golt, intestate, granted June 26, 1660, to his widow, Mary. *Salem Quarterly Court Records, vol. 4, leaf 39.*

Inventory taken Apr. 21, 1660, by Jefferie Massey and John Kitchin: A dwelling house wth. 16 pole of land aptayning thereunto, 20li.; a feather bed, a feather boulster and an ould pillow, 3li.; one ould Rugg & one ould Covering, 1li.; Curtens and valence, 15s.; 2 beedsteeds wth. 2 bed Cords, 15s.; 1 ould bed, 1 ould boulster, 2 blankets and 1 ould Covering, 1li. 4s.; 3 payre of sheets & 1 odd sheete, 2li.; 3 ould Course napkins, 1s.; 2 Chests, 16s.; 2 Trunkes, 12s.; a Cheare table, 7s.; a Cobbord, 8s.; 2 pewter dishes, 9s.; 3 small ould pewter dishes, 4s. 6d.; 1 pint pot, 1 pewter botle, a pewter candlestick and 2 dram cups, 8s.; a latin puding pan, a latin lamp and a sawce pan, 2s.; 1 brass ketle, 1 ould warming pan and a skellet, 1li. 3d.; 2 Iron ketles, 1 Iron skellet and 1 Frying pan, 16s.; fyre shovell, tongs, hake and hookes, 7s.; 5 Cheares, 5s.; barells, tooles and trayse wth. other wooden Implements, 1li. 1s.; 1 Smoothing Iron wth. heating Irons, 3s.; 9li. of linen yarne, 1li.; Coton wooll and Coton yarne, 8s.; 1 axe, 2 Iron wedges, a shave, a black bill wth. other small Iron tooles, 11s.; shoomakers tooles, 9s.; a bible wth. other small bookes, 11s.; ledder unwrought, 5li.; 1 hamer, 2 ould hatchets wth. ould Iron, 3s.; shoomaker's last wth. stoole trees, 13s.; wearing aparell, 4li. 8s.; a stone Jar wth. other Implemts., 5s. Debts due out of the estate: To Mr. William Browne, 3li. 12s.; Mr. Georg Corwin, 2li. 10s.; Mr. Gedney, 15s.; Mr. Phillip Cromwell, 1li. 16s.; John Porter, jr., 6li. 5s.; Bridgham of Boston, 5li. 2s.; Mr. Batter, 1li. 2s.; the balance of the estat, Rest Cleare, 27li. 2s. 6d. Children of William Goult, deceased: Rebecca, aged nineteen years; Debora, aged about fifteen years; Sara, aged about thirteen years. *Essex Co. Quarterly Court Files, vol. 5, leaf 112.*

Inventory of the estate was brought into court by the widow. Amount, 23li., clear, besides the debts. The court

27: 9: 1660, allowed the children, Rebecka, Deborah and Sara, 4li. each, to be paid in such goods as were inventoried, when they became of age or were married. *Salem Quarterly Court Records, vol. 4, page* 60.

### Estate of John Bradstreet of Marblehead.*

Administration on the estate of John Bradstreet granted June 26, 1660, to his wife, Hana Bradstreet. *Salem Quarterly Court Records, vol. 4, leaf* 39.

Inventory of the estate of John Broadstreet of Marvellhead, lately deceased, taken 14: 4: 1660 by John Bartoll and Joseph Dalliver: One Bible wth. 3 small seabookes, 1li. 6s.; sea instruments, 1li. 5s.; one feather bed, one pillow, one flocke bed, one Cotton Rugg wth. the Bedlinnon, 8li. 17s.; one peece of Hollan, 4li.; eight yds. of Canvas, 24 yds. of Ossembrike, one halfe peece of Blulinnon wth. som Taken, 4li. 5s.; Three Pewter platters, 1 pott, 2 dishes, 2 Iron potts, 3 hangers wth. one Postnett, 2li. 8s.; Beaver, 2li. 5s.; one suit of Waring Apparrell, one Cloke, wth. Sea Cloathes, 33 Chayres, 8li. 3s.; one payre of Curtanes and Vallance, 1li.; Two Cowes, 8li.; one mare, 12li.; howse, 20li.; Fower ten Acre lotts, 30li.; total, 103li. 9s. *Essex Co. Quarterly Court Files, vol. 5, leaf* 114.

Upon petition of Mosses Bradstreet and his sisters about ordering the estate of their brother John Bradstreet, deceased, his widow, now the wife of William Watters, having been appointed administratrix at Salem court, June 26, 1660, the court 27: 7: 1664, ordered the estate as follows: There being an inventory brought into that court, amounting to 103li. 9s., and other estate to the value of 20li. more now being presented, court ordered the four ten acre lots in the inventory appraised at 30li., free from thirds, to be given to Moses and his sisters, in case the said wife of William Watters made claim to her thirds, then ten pounds more out of the other estate, and the rest of the estate to the said Hanah Watters, wife of William. Moses was to have a double portion and the sisters to have the rest, both land and estate, to be equally divided among them. *Ipswich Quarterly Court Records, vol. 1, page* 134.

\* See also Records and Files of the Quarterly Courts of Essex Co., Mass., vol. 3 (1913), p. 183.

A petition having been presented to court by Hana Waters, administratrix of the estate of John Bradstreete, deceased, concerning a portion of the estate disposed of by the last Ipswich court, the court 28 : 9 : 1665, ordered that a summons be sent to all concerned to appear at the next Ipswich court. *Salem Quarterly Court Records, vol. 4, page 152.*

### ESTATE OF LAWRENCE SOUTHWICK OF SALEM.

Will and inventory of the estate of Laurence Sothwick, deceased, brought into court June 26, 1660, by John and Danyell Sothwick, had not been legally proved nor inventory perfected. They were given until the next Salem court to perfect them, and were bound in 400 pounds. *Salem Quarterly Court Records, vol. 4, leaf 39.*

"I Lawrence Sethwick late of Salem in new England now being at the house of Nathaniell Silvester on Shelter Island being weake in body but of sound mind and memory doe make and Ordayne this my last will & Testament The Tenth day of the 5m$^{th}$ 1659 : First I giue and bequeath vnto my Sonne Daniell Sethwick my dwelling house at Salem w$^{th}$ all the houses Orchards gardens & appurtenances. And Gyles Lott, Provided that John Burnell shall haue a house lott on the ground at the further end of the Orchard newly fenc't in. Item my will is That the lott w$^{ch}$ I had of Josiah Sethick shall returne to him againe Item I giue vnto my Daughter Provided fifty pounds sterl to be payd out of y$^e$ stock of Cattle & horses &c Item I giue vnto John Sethick the lott next adioyning to his owne. Item my will is That the great meadow w$^{ch}$ lyes at Ipswich river fenc't in shalbe divided betweene Daniell Setheck and John Burnell equally. Itm I giue vnto Samuell Burton forty shillings Item I giue vnto John Burnell if he stand faythfull in the Truth 2 young steeres & y$^e$ first mare foale Item I giue vnto Henry Traske Marshalls lott ioyning to his Orchard, Provided that Daniell may haue liberty to mow a load of Hay euery yeare therein Item I giue vnto Mary Trask my daughter wife to Henry Traske Tenne pounds sterling I giue vnto Deborah Setchwick and young Josiah each of them fifty shillings sterling Item I giue vnto Ann Potter forty shillings in what shee thinks is beneficiall for her I give vnto Mary Trask daughter to Henry Traske one good serge suyt of clothes and vnto Sarah and Hannah Trask, each of them a suit of clothes I giue and bequeath vnto Samuell and Sarah John Sethicks children to each of them thirty shillings sterling Furthermore my will is That Daniell, my sonne and Provided my daughter shall possesse and enioy all that w^ch remaynes of my estate after debts and legacies payd, and my will above mentioned fulfilled equally to be diuided betweene them, So that Daniell may haue that part w^ch belongs to husbandry. Lastly my will ‖is‖ that in case my wife surviue me she shalbe my executrix, and keep all in possession during her life, and after her decease my will to be performed according as is aboue expressed; And I doe ordayne William Robinson and Tho: Gardiner to be overseers of this my last will and Testament signed & Sealed by me the day and yeare above-written, with my hand and seale following."

his mark
Lawrence L Sethick [SEAL]

Witness: Nathaniell Sylvester, Thomas Harris, Willm Durand.

Proved in Salem court 29: 9: 1660. *Essex Co. Quarterly Court Files, vol. 6, leaf 53.*

Inventory of the estate of Lawrence Southick, taken by William Robbinson and Thomas Gardner: House and land adjoining, 36li.; 25 akers of Land in the north Neck, 20li.; 4 Akers of medoe lying by Ipsige river, 12li.; the Lott lying by John Southick's, 6li.; 4 Oxen, 26li.; 3 Cowes, 14li.; 3 young Cattle, 10li. 10s.; 2 Calves, 1li. 10s.; a mare and horse, 28li.; one horse, 9li.; 19 Swine, 20li.; 8 Sheepe, 3li. 14s.; one Cart and other Plowgeere, 2li. 10s.; 2 beds, 2li.; 3 blankets, 1li. 16s.; 3 sheets, 1li.; 1 ketle, 1li. 8s.; 1 Iron pott, 10s.; Armes, 1li.; a Table & Coberd, 1li.; 1 barel, 2s.; other Lumber, 10s.; total, 196li. *Essex Co. Quarterly Court Files, vol. 6, leaf 54.*

William Robinson and Thomas Gardner testified to the court June 26, 1660 that John Southick and Daniell Southick "haue made a verie fayre agreement about the deviding of their fathers estate." *Essex Co. Quarterly Court Files, vol. 5, leaf 116.*

John and Danyell Sothwick brought in a will and an inventory of the estate of their father, Lawrence Sothwicke, 27: 9: 1660, with a certificate of the children's consent to the division, according to said will, all of which were allowed. *Salem Quarterly Court Records, vol. 4, page 61.*

### ESTATE OF REV. EDWARD NORICE OF SALEM.

"I Edward Norice of Salem In the Countie of Essex in New-England Minister of the Gosple of Jesus christ & Teacher to the Church of christ In Salem aforesaid, for diuers good and Considerable Reasons thereunto me moueing, but more especially hauing Infirmytie upon me W$^{ch}$ may proue uery dangerous, & Mortall, & being In good & perfict memory, doe In the p$^r$sents of these Witnesses ordaine & make this as my Last Will and Testam$^t$: hereby Reuoking all former Will or Wills Legacies & bequeasts by me before this time Named Willed & bequeathed: Imp$^{rs}$ I giue & bequeath my Soule into the hands of Jesus Christ my deare Redeemer, in whose ffaith I haue Liued preached, & now By his Grace hope to dye in, As alsoe my Bodie to the earth from whence it was taken. Item I Giue & bequeath unto my Sonn Edward Norice (my debts being paid) & to his heires foreuer my dwelling house (I now Liue in), W$^{th}$ all the outhouses, gardens, orchards, & arable Land, thereto belonging, & appertaining, together with all my hous holds Stuff, Bookes, goods & chattles moueables and vnmoueables, W$^{th}$ all my debts bills & bonds, & it is my Will that my S$^d$ Sonn Edward Norice be my Sole Executo$^r$ to this my Last Will & Testamen$^t$ desireing & intreating my Louing Friends Jn$^o$ Horne & Richard Prince decons of the church of Salem afores$^d$ to assist my Sonn & be In place & Steed of ouerseers of this my Last Will & Testam$^t$ as Need Requireth, unto W$^{ch}$ in these prsts I haue hereunto sett my hand & Seale the 9$^o$ day of the 10$^o$ m$^o$ Called decemb: one Thousand six hundred fifte seaun 1657"

Edw: Norice [SEAL]

Witness: Walter Price, Elias Stjleman.

Proved in Salem court 27: 4: 1660 by Mr. Price. *Essex Co. Quarterly Court Files, vol. 5, leaf 113.*

Mr. Edward Norice brought in the last will and testament of his father, and it was proved, 27: 4: 1660. *Salem Quarterly Court Records, vol. 4, leaf 39.*

### ESTATE OF HUMPHREY REYNER OF ROWLEY.

"September the 10$^{th}$ Anno Dom 1660. I Vmphrey Reynor, of Rowley, weak in body, yet of perfect memory, doe make and ordaine this my last will and testament. ffirst I

Committt my soule into the hands of God, through Jesus Christ and my body to be interred in Rowley buriall place; according to the discretion of my Exequetors: hopeing ffor a joyfull and blessed Resurrection. And for the outward Estate that God has giuen me I thus dispose of it: ffirst I giue vnto my Son Wigglesworth, for the vse of my grandchild Mercy Wigglesworth one hundred pounds in consideration of a childs portion, and this to be payd, within one half year after my discease, out of certayne goods that are in the hands of m$^r$ John Whipple Senior, & my son John Whipple Junior of Ipswich. Alsoe I giue to m$^r$ Ezekiel Rogers pastor of the church of Rowley ten pounds, to be payd to him within one year after my decease  Alsoe I giue to m$^r$ Samuel Philips ten pounds, to be payd within one year after my discease  ffurther I giue to my grandchildren Vmphrey Hobson, John Hobson, and William Hobson ten pounds apeece, all to be payd or satisfied within one year after my discease  As for all my other estate, both of goods and lands, I leaue it to my beloued wife Mary Reynor, soe long as she continues my wife and at my wifes discease I will that the whole Estate be equally divided between my daughter Whipple, and my daughter Hobson. Item I make my dear wife Mary Reynor Sole exequetrix of this my last will and testament  memorandum  I haue a bill of three hundred pounds ffrom m$^r$ John Whipple Senior & my son John Whipple Junior, which is deu, and to be payd the begining of next october, in this present year 1660  memorandum  that I request my dear brother m$^r$ John Reynor pastor of Dover; and Deacon Jewett of Rowley to be overseers of this my last will and testament: and doe giue to each of them twenty Shillings."

p me Humfrey Reyner [SEAL]

Witness: Ez: Rogers, Samuell Phillips.

Proved in Ipswich court Sept. 27, 1660 by Mr. Ezechiell Rogers.

Inventory taken Sept. 15, 1660, by Maximillian Juett and Joseph Juett: mony and plate, 4li. 12s. 6d.; a cloth cloke, 2li. 10s.; a stuffe cloke, 6s. 8d.; two hoodes, 4s.; a serg cloke, 15s.; a stone grey sute, 1li.; a sadd grey sute with a stufe dublitt, 2li.; a stuffe cloke, 15s.; a dublit, 5s.; a payer of botes & shoes, 10s.; a grene sute wth jacket & drawers, 1li.; two hatts, 13s. 4d.; six payer of stockings, 1li. 5s.; bands, handcercher with shirts, 1li.; a payer of shoes, 2s.; silke, lace, butten, Ribbin & poynts, 1li. 2s.; 3 payer of childrens stocking, 2s.; a pece of grene sey, 10s.; a pece of stuffe, 1li. 10s.; brasse nayles, 4s.; a pece of halfe thick kercy, 3li.; a pece of grene sey, 6s. 6d.; a pece of brode cloth, 9li.; ten payer of stockings, 1li. 17s.; 7 yeards of shag bayes, 1li. 1s.; 6 redd scinns, 1li.; thred tape & sycers, 1li. 5s. 6d.; 5 yeards of red cotton, 10s. curtins and valants, 1li. 10s.; carpetting, 3 yeards, 15s.; 5 blanketts, 2li.; a coverlet, 1li. 8s.; two ruggs, 3li.; a coverlet, 1li. 6s. 8d.; one bedsteade wth ye beding on it, 9li.; a cote, 10s.; another bedstede wth beding, 9li.; one rugg, 1li. 15s.; old carpetts, 12s.; bedding, 3li.; 15 coushens, 2li.; a pece of Cotten & linnen wth 7 pound of flax, 14s.; sheetes & pillowbers, 1li.; table clothes & one dussen napkins, 1li. 5s. 10d.; peuter, 4li.; brasse potts and kettles, 3li.; a crane, tongs, hakes, spitt & andryons, 2li.; a smotheing Iron, morter pestle & Iron plate, 13s. 4d.; payles, treyes, tubbs & barrells, 1li.; truncks, chests, tables, cubbards, 6li.; chayers, 1li.; whele & cards, 5s.; leather and barke, 20li.; pitts & tooles, 2li.; a mare hors & yeareling colt, 30li.; two oxen, 14li.; two young oxen, 12li.; 7 cowes, 28li.; two heffers, 2 calves, 7li.; 16 swine & one ship, 12li.; houseing, barnes wth land about them, 90li.; 7 acres of broken up land, 40li.; 7 acres & a halfe towards Ipswich, 30li.; 8 acres of land in ye comon fence or feilde, 24li.; 6 acres of paster ground, 12li.; 32 acres of meadow, 64li.; 8 acres of upland at ye farme, 8li.; 18 cow commons, 18li.; at merymack 200 acres, 20li.; land at ye pend, 40li.; cart wheles sleedes, plowes, axes, sickles, 4li. 14s.; debts due by bills, 300li.; due for rent, 4li.; bookes, 5li.; 4 acres of indyan corne, 6li.; 3 acres of broken up land toward Ipswich, 10li.; 4 acres of pease, wheat, rye, 6li.; 20 loades of hay and apples, 11li.; a case of knives, 5s.; a saddle, side saddle & bedsteade, 1li. 10s.; bees, 2li.; harrow teth, 12s.; 3 musketts, two swords, 4 rings for wheles, 3li. 10s.; one crosscutt Saw, wimbles, chissells & shreding knife, 12s.; shingleing nayles, 3li.; 4 acres of meadow, 8li.; in ye hand of marmaduk Reyner in old ingland, 40li.; total, 865li. 1s. 2d.

Mrs. Mary Reyner testified in Ipswich court Sept. 27, 1660, this to be a true inventory of her husband's estate and it was allowed.

*Essex Co. Probate Files, Docket 23,289.*

## Estate of Roger Tucker of Salem.

Administration on the estate of Roger Tucker granted 27: 9: 1660 to Mr. George Corwin and he to bring in an inventory to the next Salem court. *Salem Quarterly Court Records, vol. 4, page 58.*

Mr. Georg Corwin, administrator, brought in an inventory, and it was allowed 25: 4: 1661. *Salem Quarterly Court Records, vol. 4, page 70.*

Inventory taken June 25, 16—, by Francis Johnson and Moses Mavericke: ———ards & halfe of Capp Cloth, £1. 6d.; [w]ascoat & drawers, 12s.; —acket & breches grene Cloth, £1; —ew Jackett, 5s.; ——re of but breches, 9s.; 4 yard Canvas, 1s.; ould things, a Jacket, 2s.; a Jackett & breches, 4s.; canvas drawers, 2s. 6d.; a hat, 2s. 6d., a Capp, 6d., a bead Rugg, 2s. 6d., a leather Jacket, 4s., 3 pare ould stockins, 3s., 1li. 2s.; a pare of woosted stockins, 5s.; a pare of greene stockins, 4s.; a swash, 2s. 6d., 3 shirts, 12s., 14s. 6d.; 2 silke neckcloths, 4s.; 1 pare linen drawers, 1s.; 2 pare hullinge hands & a pare gloves, 3s.; 2 pr. gloves more & 2 pare mitiens, 5s.; 9 newfoundland lines, 13s. 6d.; a barrill meckrill, 1li. 5s.; a Coat his man had, 15s.; a hancherker, a capp, 2 ould neckcloths, & a capp, 1s. 6d.; a peare of boots, 6s.; a kittell, 2s. 6d., a bead sacke, 3s., 5s. 6d.; a cheste, 1s. 6d.; total, £9. 14s. This attested by Mr. George Corwin in Salem court 28: 4: 1661. *Essex Co. Quarterly Court Files, vol. 6, leaf 126.*

## Estate of Walter Butcher.

Administration on the estate of Walter Butcher granted 27: 9: 1660 to Mr. George Corwin and to bring in an inventory to the next Salem court. *Salem Quarterly Court Records, vol. 4, page 58.*

## Estate of Thomas Smith.

Administration on the estate of Thomas Smith granted 27: 9: 1660, to Mr. George Corwin and to bring in an inventory to the next Salem court. *Salem Quarterly Court Records, vol. 4, page 58.*

## Guardianship of William Perkins of Topsfield.

William Perkins, aged between nineteen and twenty years, Tobias Perkins, aged about fourteen years, and Elizabeth Perkins, aged about seventeen years, all children of Mr. William Perkins of Topsfeild, chose their father to be their guardian, and it was allowed by the court 27: 9: 1660. *Salem Quarterly Court Records, vol. 4, page 59.*

## Estate of Edmund Nicholson of Marblehead.

Administration on the estate of Edmond Nicholson granted 27: 9: 1660 to his wife, Elizabeth Nicholson. An inventory was brought in, amounting to 150li., and debts, 54li. 4s., which were allowed. Court ordered the estate to be divided as follows: To Christopher, Joseph, Samuell, John, Thomas and Elizabeth, all of the children, ten pounds each, when they reach the age of twenty-one years or are married with their mother's consent; if more debts were brought in, such debts were to be paid before these portions were divided, and if any of the children died, his portion was to be divided among the surviving children. *Salem Quarterly Court Records, vol. 4, page 59.*

Inventory of estate of Edmond Nicolson of Marblehead, taken 22: 9: 1660, by Moses Mavericke, William Nicke and John Legg: Dwelling house, with outhouses and land, 55li.; a Boat fit to goe to Sea with her moreing and Cannoe and other Coardage, 56li. 15s.; One Cow with the Hay, 5li.; one Bed with Bolster, Pillowes, Rug and Blanketts, 3li.; 9 yards of Ticking, 1li. 10s.; sheetts and pillobers, 1li. 3s. 6d.; a peice of white kersie, 1li. 2s.; wearing apparell, 3li. 17s.; 2 Ruggs, 3li. 5s.; 2 pr. of Blanketts, 2li. 10s.; one Bolster and 2 Pillowes, 1li. 18s.; one chest and Box, 10s.; one fowling piece and 3 axes, 1li. 7s.; one sword, 5s.; one Iron pott, 2 Iron kettles, 1li. 5s.; 3 Brasse Kettles and 2 Scilletts, 2li. 18s.; pewter, 1li. 2s.; earthern ware, wooden and Lattin ware, 1li. 9s.; 3 wheeles, 10s.; Lome, sleies, wheele, with Barrle and other Lumber, 3li. 19s.; an old Road with two Bedsteeds, 1li. 15s.; total, 150li. Sworn to by Elizabeth Nicolson, the widow, 28: 9: 1660, before Hilliard Veren, cleric. There were debts to several persons, amounting to 54li. 4s. The children were Christopher, aged twenty-two years, Joseph, aged twenty years, Samuell, aged sixteen years, John, aged fourteen years, Elizabeth, aged eleven years, and Thomas, aged seven years. *Essex Co. Quarterly Court Files, vol. 6, leaf 47.*

### GUARDIANSHIP OF BENJAMIN FAIRFIELD.

Peeter Palfery formerly married Eliza, the wife of John Fayrefeild, deceased, who was then possessed of that estate that her husband Fairefeild left. When she married said Palfery, she did not give bond for security of the children's portions, according to the will of her deceased husband, by which the children were not to have their several portions until Benjamin, the youngest, reached the age of twenty years. Said Palfry desired to be released from the charge of said estate. The court 27: 9: 1660 ordered, Palfrey and the children, Walter, John and Benjamin being present, that, notwithstanding there were some things in the will difficult to be understood, all housing and land of said Fairefeild mentioned in the will should be equally divided among the children, all parties having consented. Palfery was further ordered to pay out of the goods that he had with his wife, Eliza Fairefeild, to the value of 40s. to Walter, the eldest son, which was to be understood to be more than about 3li. which he formerly received of said Palfery. John Fairefeild, the second son, being under age, chose his brother, Walter, to be his guardian, and Benjamin, being about fourteen years of age, chose his father-in-law, said Palfery, as guardian, and agreed to live with him until he reached the age of twenty years, Palfery teaching him to read and write. *Salem Quarterly Court Records, vol. 4, page 62.*

Whereas Benjamin Fairfeild, by consent of Salem county court, 29: 9: 1660, made choice of Peeter Palfery for his guardian, until said Benjamin was twenty years of age, or at said Palfries death, the latter having lately deceased, he chose Mathew Edwards as his guardian, and the court 24: 9: 1663 confirmed it. *Salem Quarterly Court Records, vol. 4, page 123.*

### ESTATE OF CHRISTOPHER CODNER OF (MARBLEHEAD?).

Christopher Codner, dying intestate, an inventory was brought in and sworn to by Mary, the widow, and allowed 27: 9: 1660. Amount, 152li. Mary Codner, the widow, appointed administratrix, and the court ordered to be paid to Christopher, son of said Christopher, deceased, 60li., and to the daughter, 30li., when each reached the age of twenty-one years, or were married; when the said widow married, she was to give security for her said children's portions. *Salem Quarterly Court Records, vol. 4, page 60.*

Inventory taken by John Devorick and William Nicke: House and land, 60li.; a Coubourtt & boxe and beadstead, 3li. 5s.; table & frame & 4 gine stoolls, 1li. 2s. 4d.; arthen ware, as potts & panes & such licke, 15s.; 2 barrells, 4s. 6d., one Cheast, 4s., 8s. 6d.; one skillett, one warmming pane, dusen of treshners, one ladell & one lantorn, 2li. 6d.; wooding ware, as tubbs & trayes, 28s. 3d.; 3 potts & 4 yiorn hookes, 2li.; hoges & axksesse and a sawe, 8s.; 4 Charges and pease of lathour, 12s.; one kittell, one floske bead & boulster, 1li. 14s.; putter, 3li. 20s.; 2 ruggs, 3li. 5s.; one pare of holland sheats, one table Cloth, 2li. 5s.; 7 pillobrs, drayers, 1li. 8s.; 5 sheattes, 2li. 5s.; one bead & boulster, 1li. 16s.; Curttaings & vallings & Cobbartt Cloth and Cushenghs, 2li. 5s.; 3 pare of blancketts, 4li. 5s.; a bead, 2 pillowes and boulster, 3li. 3s. 6d.; one Cheast, a wheall, pare of tongs, 2 basketts, 1li. 2s.; pease of sargh, 4 yd. of holland, 8 yd. moheare, 4li. 6s. 8d.; 8 yards of ttamme, 1li. 8s.; his waring Cloaths, 9li. 17s.; 15 swings, 15li.; 2 Cowes and a heffer, 11li. 10s.; in detts which is due to me, 10li. 17s.; total, 151li. 9d. A daught. 5 yeares old, her name Mary, 30li.; Christ., 3 yeares old, 60li. *Essex Co. Quarterly Court Files, vol. 6, leaf 51.*

Joshua Codner of Marblehead, tailor, having possession of a house and land that was part of the estate of Cristopher Codner, deceased, and whereas Mary, wife of deceased, at the time of her marriage, was to give security for the children's portions, which had not been done, court 28: 9: 1665 ordered, with the free consent of Joshua Codner, that the house be given for security for the payment of 60li. to the children of said Cristopher Codner, to be paid as the children come to age. John Devorix and Cristopher Lattamore, feofees in trust, were discharged, and Richard Downing and Mary, his wife, agreed to bring up the two children free. *Salem Quarterly Court Records, vol. 4, page 155.*

### Estate of William Eliot of (Salem?).

William Ellett, dying intestate, an inventory of his estate was brought in by the widow, and the court 27: 9: 1660, allowed it. Amount, 55li. 8s. 6d., clear estate, besides debts. Court ordered that Sarah, daughter of said Ellett, have one-half the estate, when she became of age or at time of marriage, and the house and land mentioned in the inventory was bound for the child's portion. Sara, the widow of said Ellett, and James Bedde, her now husband, were granted power of administration on the estate. *Salem Quarterly Court Records, vol. 4, page 61.*

### ESTATE OF JOSEPH JEWETT OF ROWLEY.*

"I Joseph Jewett of Rowley, being weake of boddy but per*fect* in understandinge and memory doe make this my last will and test— in manner and forme as followeth, In primis after my debts be payed, I desire the rest of my goods may bee equally diuided am*ong* my seaven children, as well those two that I haue by my last *wife* as the fiue that I had before Allwayes prouided that my eldest sonne Jeremiah Jewett must haue a dubbell portion, of all Estate I haue both in New England, and Olde, whether Personall or Reall, fur—— prouided that one hundred pounds I haue allredy payed to my sonne Phillip Nellson, that shall be counted as part of what I doe now giue him. Item I doe giue unto my sonne Jeremiah Jewett the far*m* I bought of Joseph Muzzy I meane all such Lands bought of h*im* or any other, that are on the Norwest side of the River call*ed* Egipt River, with all the meadow I bought of Nathaniell Stow, *and* Robert Lord Senior, prouided he accept of it at fiue hundred pou*nds* and wheras in the fourth Line it is saide I desire the rest of *my* goods to be equally diuided amongst my seauen children, I m*e*an*e* Lands as well as goods, and if any of these my aboue saide seauen children, should depart this life, before the age of twenty one years, or day of Marriage, then there portions, shall bee equally diuided Amongst the *r*est, allwayes prouided my Eldest son Jerremiah shall haue a doubbell portion, and as for my two yongest Children, and there portion, I leaue to the disposinge of my brothe*r* Maximillian Jewett, and who he shall apoint when he departeth this life, and I make Exequetors of this my last will and Testament, my Brother Maximillian Jewett, and my sonne Phillip Nellson,

* See also Records and Files of the Quarterly Courts of Essex Co., Mass., vol 2 (1912), pp. 298, 317, 318, 325, 434; vol. 3 (1913), p. 241; Essex Quarterly Court Files, vol. 33, leaf 35; vol. 34, leaves 12-18.

my sonne John Car*l*ton, and my sonne Jeremiah Je*wett* allwayes free and willinge, that they shall be satisfied out of— estate, for all such pains a*n*d labour, that they shall be at concerninge the aboue premisses

"Dated the 15: of feburary in the yeare 1660."

Joseph Jewett [SEAL]

Witness: Ezekiel Northend, Mark Prime.

"At the signinge and sealinge hereof I doe giue my Exequitars full power to *make* deeds, and to confirme any Land ⸺ haue sold to any."

Ezekiel Nor*the*nd, Mark Prime.

Proved in Ipswich court Mar. 26, 1661 by the witnesses.

Inventory of estate of Joseph Jewett, deceased Feb. 24, 1660, taken by Ezekiel Northend, Maximillian Jewett and John Pickard: in moneys, 3li.; apparrell, 25li.; house hold stuffe, 12li. 10s.; Beddinge, 38li. 2s.; Linninge, 9li. 8s.; pewter, 8li. 2s.; Brasse, 8li. 10s.; Iron ware, 4li. 18s.; weights and scales, 3li. 4s.; beefe and porke, 20li. 10s.; a cart and furniture for plow, 6li. 3s.; for severall parcells of goods, 188li. 16s.; corne, 61li. 13s.; cattell, 155li. 10s.; horses and mares, 68li.; a Servant, 17li.; wamponpeage, 1li. 5s.; Books, 6li. 17s.; Muzzy farme formerly so called, 500li.; the new house and barne, all the land within Ipswitch fence and without Ipswitch fence and meddows, 604li. 10s.; the house in Rowly with upland and medows, and all out houses and four Commonages, 169li.; The farme at the neck that Corporall Gage doth live upon Contaninge seven hundred and twenty Acres, 332li.; The ffarme that Henry Kingsbury liveth upon contaninge four hundred and twenty Acres, 153li. 10s.; Two hundred and Eighty Acres liinge in Common b*u*ttinge upon Merrimack river, 2li.; A house and orchard and all the upland and meddow liinge in the bounds of Haverhill, 178li.; total, 2607li. ⸺. Due upon Books and Bills, 2491li. 5s.; in Debts and other goods, 55li. 10s.; a pare of stears, 11li. 5s.; total, 2558li. 1s.; Debts due from the Estate, 1876li. 12s. 9d.

This inventory attested by Philip Nellson, John Carleton and Jeremiah Jewett.

Received in Ipswich court Mar. 26, 1661.

*Essex Co. Probate Files, Docket* 14,931.

On Mar. 26, 1661 Maximillian Jewett renounced his executorship to the will of Mr. Joseph Jewett. *Ipswich Quarterly Court Records, vol.* 1, *page* 93.

Upon a motion made by Mr. Carlton, guardian to Patience Jewett, that the court would be pleased to choose some men to make a division of some land between himself and said Patience, which now lay together, Ezekiell Northend and John Tod were named, and the court approved Sept. 29, 1663. *Ipswich Quarterly Court Records, vol. 1, page 121.*

Jerimiah Jewett accepted for his share of land, "the farme that was formarly mussie's farme with all the Land joyneing to it on this syd Egipt River and on the other syde all the meddow land ye upland that lyes betweene this meddow as it is broken up in with the common fence." Acknowledged Apr. 2, 1664.

Maximilyan Jewett, overseer of the two youngest children of Joseph Jewett, deceased, Joseph and Faith, accepted for their portion the house that is upon the field, that was formerly Goodman Gages and Goodman Shatswells, with the barn and the land; the land betwixt the house and Egypt River, with sixteen acres of land within the common fence bought of Goodman Lord and Goodman Kingsbury; the farm that was John Bradstreets containing about four score acres, bounded southeast with Muddye River; six acres bought of Humphry Griffen and three acres bought of John Pinder; four acres of salt meadow bought of Mark Quilter and six acres in the west meadows formerly Goodman Gage's, with as much upland as comes to 64li. 10s. lying between Willson hill and Egypt River. Acknowledged Apr. 2, 1664.

Philip Nelson of Rowley accepted as his share, the farm that was let to Goodman Kingsbury containing four hundred twenty acres, also two hundred eighty acres of upland joining the same farm. Acknowledged Apr. 2, 1664.
*Ipswich Deeds, vol. 2, page 187.*

### GUARDIANSHIP OF NEHEMIAH JEWETT OF ROWLEY.

Nehemyah Jewett, son of Joseph Jewett, chose John Pickard for his guardian, and it was allowed by the court Mar. 26, 1661. Said Pickard was bound in 300li. *Ipswich Quarterly Court Records, vol. 1, page 94.*

John Pickard guardian of Nehemiah Jewett accepted for his portion the dwelling house in Rowley formerly Mr. Bellingham's with all out houses and orchard and yards with five acres of "Ruffe marsh" in the common field; ten acres of salt marsh west of Mr. Nelson's, and five acres of upland joining thereunto; four cow gates with four acres of marsh in Ipswich common field, bought of Marke Quilter, seven acres of meadow in the west meadows formerly Goodman Gages and Goodman Kingsburyes, and the rest of the upland between Willson Hill and Egypt River being the remainder of that land Maximilian Jewett had for the two young children, Joseph and Faith. Acknowledged Apr. 2, 1664. *Ipswich Deeds, vol. 2, page* 187.

Acquittance of John Pickard as guardian of Nehemiah Jewett by Thomas Wood of Rowley. Dated 7: 2: 1664. Witness: Richard Oliver, John Grant. *Ipswich Deeds, vol. 2, page* 190.

### Guardianship of Patience Jewett of Rowley.

Patience Jewett chose Mr. John Carlton as her guardian, it was allowed by the court Mar. 26, 1661. Said Carlton bound himself for a true account of his sister Patience Jewett's portion. *Ipswich Quarterly Court Records, vol. 1, page* 94.

John Carlton guardian of Patience Jewett accepted for her share the farm let to Goodman Gage, also the house in Haverhill with orchard and lands within the bounds of Haverhill. Acknowledged Apr. 2, 1664. *Ipswich Deeds, vol. 2, page* 187.

### Estate of William Odry.

Administration on the estate of William Odry granted Mar. 26, 1661 to Mr. George Corwin and Mr. Edmund Batter, who were ordered to bring in an inventory. *Ipswich Quarterly Court Records, vol. 2, leaf* 62.

Inventory of the estate of Willm. Oaderie, deceased, taken the last of December, 1660, by Walter Price and Elias Mason: A cloake and sute, 4li. 15s.; 1 snugg Coate, 1li. 10s.; 1 sarge sute, 1li. 10s.; 1 gray Coat, 12s. 6d.; 1 Red sute, 11s.; 2 ginting shurtts, at 9s., 18s.; 2 locrum shurts, at 6s. 6d. per, 13s.; 2 ould shurts, 3s. 6d.; 1 canvas Jackett & locrum drawers, 7s. 6d.; 2 pr. ould wosted stokins, 3s. per, 6s.; 1 pr. wedmoll stokins, 16d., 1s. 4d.; 2 pr. of ould wosted stokins, 3s.; 1 pr. yaron stokins, 3s.; 1 cource gray coate and canvas breeches, 14s.; 1 greene cotten sute, 8s.; 1 blak hatt, 10s., 1 coll. hate, 5s., 15s.; 1 mountere Cap, 5s.; 1 neckcloth, 12d., a silk neckcloth, 4s., 5s.; 1 pr. shews, 3s. 4d.; 2 pr. ould shews, 4s. 6d.; 1 psalme book & an Incorne & bible, 7s.; a bedsack & Rugg, 5s. 6d.; 2 pr. mittins, 1s. 6d.; 2 ould lynes wth. Hooks & leads & reels, 5s.; 3 codd lynes, 8s.; 4 Fishing leads, 12d. per, 4s.; 8 Hooks at 12d., 1s.; 1 pr. boots, 14s., 1 od boot, 6s., 1li.; a Chest, 4s., a glas, 12d., 5s.; 1 pr. wosted gloves, 2s. 6d.; his pt. of 15 hundred of fish, about, 30s., 1li. 10s.; a quart pt. of a Cach, 15li.; dew from Robert Starr, 1s. 6d.; dew to him from John Gurvand, 6s. 1d.; dew from Richard Ellyott, 3li. 12s. 2d.; 2 barells makrell, 2li. 10s.; his pt. of three frawghts, his victualls to be deducted, 7s.; total, 41li. 5s. 11d. Sworn in court, 12: 10: 1661, by Mr. George Corwin and Mr. Edmond Batters. *Essex Co. Quarterly Court Files, vol. 7, leaf 46.*

ESTATE OF REV. EZEKIEL ROGERS OF ROWLEY.*

"I Ezekiell Rogers Borne at wethersfield in Esex in old England now of Rowley in Essex in new England being at this time of Good memory and Competent health through Gods mercy, yett not knowing when the lord may be pleased to put an end to this Pillgramage doe Ordaine and make This my last will and Testament And first I will and desire that Everlasting praises be Giuen to the one holy God in Jesus Christ as for all his mercies to me which are innumerable soe for these three Spetiall Blesings: first for my Nurture and Education vnder such a father m^r Richard Rogers, in Catachisme and knowledge of the holy scriptures the want whereof I see to be the maine Cause of the Errors of the times. Secondly that whereas till I was aboue twenty yeares of Age I made but ill vse of my knowlidge but liued in a formall profession of Relligion, the lord pleased by occation of a Sore sicknes which was like to be death to make me to see the worth and Neede of Christ and to take such houlde of him as that I Coulde never let him Goe to this houre whereby I am now encouraged to bequeath and Committe my Soulle into his hands who hath Redeemed it, and my Body to the Earth since he will Giue me with these very eyes to see my Redeemer Thirdly to my Calling even to be a minester of the Gospell the most Glorious Calling in the

* See also Records and Files of the Quarterly Courts of Essex Co., Mass., vol. 3 (1913), pp. 229-235, 263, 275, 313.

worlde which the lord brought into, not without difficulty
for my calling in the time of the hottest Persecution of that
Bloody Hirachy and being inlightened Concerning the euill
and snare of subscription and Cerrimonies I was advised to
giue ouer the thought of the ministry and to betake myselfe
to the study and practise of phisick But the lord mercyfully
prevented it; for though it be a Good and Nessecary Calling; I haue observed that the most through there *owne* cor-
uption haue made it to themselues the very Temptation to
Couetousnes or lust or both, I therfor Chose Rather to lye
hide *about* a dozen yeares in an honerable familly exercising
my selfe in minestiriall dutyes for about a dozen yeares
after my leauing the vnerversity. Then the lord Gaue me a
Call to a Publique Charge att Rowley in yorkeshire whereby
the Gentlenesse of —by mathewe I was fauored both for
subscription and Cerimonies and injoyed my liberty in the
minestry about seaventeene *years* in Comforthable sort Till
for Refusing to Reade that accursed Booke that allowed
sports on Gods holy Sabbath or lords day I was suspended
and by it and other sad signes of the times Driuen with
many of my hearars into New England where I haue liued in
my Pastorall Office about ——— years with much Rest and
comforth Belieueing the way—he Churches here to be according to the present light that God hath Giuen the purest
in the wholle world

"Now Age and Infir*mitie*s Calling vpon me to looke daly
for my Change I professe myselfe to haue liued and to dye an
vnfeigned Hater of all the Bas*e o*pinnions of the Anabap-
tists and Antinomians, and all other phrentiche dotages of
the times that springe from them which God will ere longe
cause to *be* as doung on the earth I doe also protest against
all the evell ffashions and *practi*ses of this Agee Both in
Aparr*ile* and that Generall Disguisement of longe Ruffianlike
haire A Custome most Como*nll*y taken vp at that time when—
Graue and modest weareing of heaire was a part of the Re-
proch of Christ as appeared by the tearme of Round heads
and was carryed on with a high hand not with standing the
knowne Offence of soe m*any* Godly persons, and without
publique expression of there Reasons for any such libertie
taken As for my Est*ate* I will and dispose as followeth ffirst
I doe Bequeath and Giue to my welbeloued wife mary Rogers,
my dwelling house Barne and all the outhouses also my Orchard, Gardens, and the yeards belonging, and pasturage adioyning to the —eed on both sides of the *Brook* also the

hempyearde also the vpper house lott on the other side of the Highway *with* all the land and horse pasture adJoyneing to the same land I Giue hir also sixe Acres of Aurable land By the House of ezekiell Northen and my part of the warehouse pasture also I Giue hir hay Grounde salt and fresh soe much as my Ouerseers shall Judge sufficient to affourd one yeare with another thirty loads of hay and where shee will chuse it and all this only for hir Natureall life also I Giue to my saide wife all my Goods, Household stufe, Cattell, Corne, and all my stocke whatsoeuer, I Giue to my loueing Nephew m$^r$ *S*amuell Stone of conecticot thirty pounds, I Giue to my Cousen his son John ten pounds, to my deere Brother and ffellow officer m$^r$ phillips fiue pounds and aquinas his Iam—in folio, to my Sumtimes servant Elizebeth Tenney ells parratt —en pounds to my loueing Neece m$^{ris}$ *mary* matosins of malldon in esex in ouldengland I Giue ten pounds to my loueing Neece m$^{ris}$ Elizebeth C—ton wife of the preacher of Roterdam in hollande I Giue ten pounds to the wife of my Cousin Rogers of Billrecay I Giue fiue pounds I Giue to my ||two|| present maid servants each of them an ewe lambe all and euery of these seuerall legacyes I will to be paide within one yeare after my death, except Th— into England and Holland which Shalbe redy to be paide as soune as they shall apoint and I *im*poure any from themsellues or any marchant or marchants here that may *r*eceaue it in there behalfe and for There vse and Giue full acquittance as impoured from them that soe my execcutrix or ouerseers may be fully discharged therof I Giue all my latine *b*ookes to harverd Coledge in Cambridge and sume English Bookes as apea*re*s in the Catalogue.

"Item the Rest of my estate in lands that ar not Giuen vnto my wife dureing hir Natureall life that is the land at planting hill the land called Satchwell *g*round and all the rest be it meadow fresh or salt or other vpland what euer and one third part of Gats or Commonage I Giue to the Church and towne of Rowley vpon Condission that they pay or cause to be paid, or legally tender, vnto ezeakiell Rogers the son of m$^r$ Nathaniel Rogers late pastor of the Church of Ipswich, Deceased, the full Some of eightscore poundes in Country pay the one halfe, that is *to* say foure score pounds within one yeare after my Death, the other foure score pounds to be paid the next yeare after that is within two years after my death; and I intreat and appoint m$^r$ John whiple of Ipswich the Rulling Elder to be Gardion for ezekiell Rogers to Receaue or Cause to be Receaued this abousaid eight score pounds, and to Give vnto the Church or towne of Rowley a full discharge and acquittance vpon the Receaueing therof, and in Case the Church or towne of Rowley pay not the abouesaid eight score pounds my will is that thes abouesaid lands that are not Giuen vnto my wife, shalbe assigned and set ouer by my ouerseers vnto Ezeakiell for the abouesaid payment, prouided also that it shall not be in the liberty of the church or towne of Rowley to Giue sell or allien these landes or any part therof or appropriate them or any part of them to any other end or vse then for this, the Better inableing them to carry on the minestry for euer: also all my houses barne and orchard and all my landes pastures and commonages and meadows which I haue Giuen vnto my wife mary Rogers Dureing her Naturall life after hir Decease, I Doe Bequeath and Giue vnto the Church and towne of Rowley to inable them the Better to maintaine two teaching elders in the church, for euer, and vpon that condision I Doe Giue them, the time which I allow them for the setleing of an elder shalbe foure yeares: and soe from time to time as God makes any changes either By Death or Remoueall any other way, and in case that the church or towne of Rowley faille of the condision of providing themsellues of two teaching elders according to the time perfixed that is within foure years after they haue this to inable them the beter and soe from time to time within the said time of foure years after God by his prouidence haue maide any Chainge, my will is that the abouesaid houseing and landes shalbe to the vse of Harvard Colledge at Cambridge in New England I Giue also to the church my Silluer Bowles which they vse for the Communion to be soe vsed still after my wiues Decease and I make and appoint my said welbeloued wife the Solle executrix of this my will and Testament and I appoint maxemillion Jewett and Samuell Brocklebanke to be ouerseers of this my will and Testament, made and signed the 17 of Aprill 1660."

Ezekiel Rogers.

Witness: Samuell Brocklebanke, maxemillion Jewett, John Brocklebanke.

Proved in Ipswich court Mar. 26, 1661 by the witnesses.

Inventory taken Mar. 5, 1660-61 by Deacon Maxemillion Jewett, Ensign Samuel Brocklebanke and John Lambert: a gold ring and a silver Inkhorne and silver, 2li.; all sorts of apparill, 17li. 17s.; silver plate, 20li.; one Dwelling house and barne and out houses with orchard and land lying on the south sid of the street and the Pasturs on both sidds the Brooke, 200li.; Areable land at home fifteene acre, 75li.; more Areabl land in the field, 51li.; in meadowes, 150li.; unbroken upland and pasturing, 70li.; in Commonages, 20li.; three mares, two horses and foure of younger age, 90li.; oxen, 40li.; ten cowes, 40li.; four stears, 18li.; five younge Catle and five calves, 17li.; sheep old and younge, 18li.; swine, 8li.; corne and hay in the barne, 10li.; the best bedd furnished, 20li.; another bedd furnished, 13li. 6s. 8d.; a presse and a litle Table with ther carpits, 1li. 10s.; a trunke and linen in it and one chist, 6li.; another bed and beding, 10li.; another bed and bedding, 5li.; another chist and what is in it, 5li.; another trunke with what was in it, 5li.; cloath of woolen and linen and hempe, 2li.; more Cloath, 2li.; in coten yearne, 1li.; hempe and yearne and flax, 2li.; a litle cobert, one litle table, 10s.; one great presser and round table, 2li.; ten quishings and chares, 3li. 6s. 8d.; more quishings, 1li. 10s.; buffit, stools and formes, 1li.; one clocke, 1li.; mault and barley below & 30 bush. of Indian, 6li. 10s.; in Armore and other Ammunition, 5li.; more wheat & mault, 60 bush. & 20 of Indian, 18li.; flitches of bacon, 3li.; two bedds more with ther bedding, 8li.; sheep woole, 2li.; more hemp, yearne and flax, 4li.; Twentie two peeces of pewther with some smaller, 5li.; brasen vessels, 8li. 10s.; Iron potts, 1li.; spits and frying panes, fire shovls, tongs & other things, 2li.; The Jack, 1li.; Chairs, table, Cobert and stools in the kitching, 1li.; wooden vessels, 2li.; wheels, Linen and woolen, 10s.; axes, hows, sythes, sickls and other edg tools, 2li.; Temses, sives and measurs, 10s.; Carts, plows, chains and yoaks with forks and a cart rop, 5li. 10s.; tumerils, sled, beetle and wedges, 10s.; stocks of bees, 3li.; saddls, Bridle and pilion seat, 1li.; lattin Books in folio, 42li. 10s. 8d.; Lating Books in quarto and other smaller books, 5li.; English Books in folio, 10li. 3s.; English Books in quarto, 13li.; bibls, 1li.; smaller English books, 2li.; debts oweing to the Dead, 53li. 16s. 5d.; in lands that were Thomas Barkers, 400li.; total, 1535li. 19s. 9d.

 Testified to in Ipswich court Mar. 26, 1661 by Mary Rogers wife of Ezekiell Rogers.

*Essex Co. Probate Files, Docket* 23,987.

 Ezekiell Rogers of Ipswich acknowledged the receipt from the Town and church of Rowley of 160li. bequeathed to him by Mr. Ezekiell Rogers of Rowley. Signed and sealed Jan. 6, 1662. Witness: Symon Tuttle, John Whipple.

Sworn in Ipswich court Mar. 31, 1663, by the witnesses. *Ipswich Deeds, vol. 2, page 129.*

Deposition of Samuell Brocklebanke in Ipswich court, Mar. 29, 1670: being with Mr. Ezekiell Rogers pastor of the Church of Rowley when he made his last will, he told him that he would not dispose of any of the land that was his wife's by her former husband, Thomas Barker, only the one half of the warehouse pasture, which he had paid for after their marriage, for all the rest she had it to dispose of, which would be enough to give to her relations. *Ipswich Deeds, vol. 3, page 145.*

### Estate of Joseph Peasley of Salisbury.*

"The ||last|| will and testament of Josef Pesly is that my deats shall bee paid out of my estate and the remainner of my estat wich is left my deats being paid I doe give and dooe beequeaf the on have vnto mery my wiff during her life and I doo giue to my dafter Sera all my hous and lands that I have at Salsbery and I doo give vnto Josef my Sonne all my land that I have upon the plain at Haverell and doo all so giue vnto Josef my Sonn ||all|| medo ling in the East medo at Haverell and doo give vnto Josef my Sonn all my right in the oxespaster at Haverell and doo giue vnto Josef my Sonn five of the common rites that doo be long to the plain I doo give vnto my dafter Elesebeth my forty fouer eakers of vpland lying west word of Haverell and doo giue vnto my dafter Elesebeth fouer Eakers and a have of medo liing in the west medo at Haverell and doo all so give to my dafter Elesebeth fouer of the common rits that doo belong to the plain and doo give vnto my daffter Jean tenn shillen and to my dafter mary tenn Shellens I doo give vnto Sarea Saier my granchild my ||vp||land and medo liing at Speaket reuer and I doo give vnto my Sunn Josef all the re mainer of my land at Haverell wich is not heare disposed of this is my last will and testement being in my righ[t] mind and memere wittnes my hand the 11 of nouember 1660."

Josef pesle

Witness: Phill: Challis, Thomas Barnard, Richard Courrier

* See also Records and Files of the Quarterly Courts of Essex Co., Mass., vol. 3 (1913), p. 146.

"I doo all so make mary my wiffe my Soull exseceter and doo allso leave Josef my Sunn and the esteat that I haue giueen him to my wiffes desposen tell Josef my Sonn be twenty yeares of aige"

Proved in Salisbury court 9 : 2 : 1661 by Phillip Challis and Tho. Barnett.

Inventory taken by Richard Currier, Thomas Barnard and William Barence: 1 grinding stone and crink & bittell rings, 12s.; 1 smothing Iron, 5 wedges and on Iron bar, 1li. 5s.; one pare of and Irons and 2 spits, 4 axes & 2 saws, 2li. 6s.; on crane, 2 tramels, gred Iron & brand Iron and fire slice, on par of cob Irons & tongs, 1li. 14s.; on tow Combe parsel, 10s.; on Iron pot and skelet, pot hokes and flesh hoke and friing pan, 1li. 4s.; 5 howes, 1 Chaine & other Iron work, 1li.; puter and bras, 5li.; 2 guns and on sword, 2li.; all his waring apperell woling and lining, 8li.; Cloth & sarge and tamie, 7li. 13s.; beds and beding, 10li. 18s.; yarn, woll, flax and hempe, 5li. 10s.; Chests, barells, spining wheles and other lumber, 3li.; forty bushels of wheat, 10li.; sixty bushels of Indian Corn, 9li.; three Cows, two heffers & on calfe, 19li.; swine, 3li.; hous and land and meddow, 50li.; 2 bibels and other bukes, 1li. 15s.; total, 143li. 5s.

Inventory taken by James Davice, Sr. and Theophiles Sachell: 12 acors more or les within the playne fenced as it is bounded in the records and so for the rest in record for this 12 acors, 50li.; 18 acors without the fence, 40li.; 44 acors of the 2 deuision over the litel rever westward is bounded, 35li.; 4 scor and 4 of the 3 devision on spicet hill as it is bound, 35li.; a 4th devision of upland yet not perfeted all though granted by the towne, 5li.; 6 acárs of meddow at the east meddow as bound, 20li.; 4 acars & a halfe of meddow at the west meddow bounded, 8li.; 6 acars of 2 devision of meddow at Spicket, 9li.; 4 acors of 3 devision of medow bounded in the new found medow, 5li.; 4 ox commonds & others cow commonds, 16li.; total, 223li.

Testified to by Mary Peasly, executrix.

*Essex Co. Probate Files, Docket* 21,069.

Court 14 : 2 : 1663, ordered that Capt. Rob. Pike, Lt. Phillip Challis and Mr. Tho. Bradbury be impowered to divide the estate of Joseph Peasly, according to his will, all his debts being first paid and to make return thereof to the next Hampton court. *Salisbury Quarterly Court Records, vol.* 1, *leaf* 12.

Court Apr. 12, 1664, ordered that Capt. Pike, Mr. Tho. Bradbury and Leift. Phillip Challis make a division of lands between widow Peasly and Sarah Peasly, now wife of Tho. Barnard, jr., and the housing, according to the will of Joseph Peasly, as soon as they can conveniently. *Salisbury Quarterly Court Records, vol. 1, leaf 20.*

Court Oct. 11, 1664 ordered that the widow Peasly should have libery to make a division of the house and land between her and Tho. Barnett, in behalf of his wife, according to the will of Joseph Peasly, and said Barnett to take his choice, or else the said Barnett to make the division of the land and the widow Peasly to take her choice. If they could not agree, then Willi. Osgood, Richard Currier and Sam. Foot were to make the division. *Hampton Quarterly Court Records, vol. 1, leaf 24.*

### Estate of Mrs. Ann Jewett of Rowley.

"I m$^{rs}$ Ann Jewett of Rowley In the County of esex Being weake of Body But of perfect vnderstanding and memory not knowing how Soone God may be pleased to Call me away by death doe make and ordaine this my last will and Testament It Being that I haue in my owen dispose one hundred pounds I will and dispose of it as followeth Item I will that this one hundred pounds shalbe equally devided a—thes foure of my Children to witt John Allen Ann Allen Isaac Allen and Bossom Allen: only I will and Giue vnto my daughter Ann allen tenn pounds more then the Rest which shalbe that is the ten pounds Giuen Befor the Rest of the hundred be devided: and as for those seuerall pertickulors that ar at my dispose in that Couenant betwene m$^r$ Joseph Jewet and me I *will* that those things that I haue not alredy Giuen to my daughter Prissilla that my sone John allen shall haue a Gould Ring —the sillver wine Cup and the Rest I will and Giue vnto *my* daughter Ann Allen this I acknowledge to be my last *will* made the fist of february one thousand six hundred and *sixty* in wittnes wherof I set to my hand and I appoint m$^r$ Edward Raw*son* and m$^r$ Jeremiah Houchin to see the performeance hereof."

her mark<br>Ann A Jewett

Witness: Samuell Brocklebanke, John harris.

Testified to in Ipswich court Mar. 26, 1661 by Samuell

Brocklebanke and Apr. 29, 1661 by John Harris, and proved May 2, 1661. *Essex Co. Probate Files, Docket 14,874.*

### Estate of Richard Browne of Newbury.

"Bee it knowne vnto all men by theise p<sup>r</sup>sents that I Richard Browne of Newbury in the County of Essex in Newengland being sicke of body but of perfect memory do here make my Last will and testament first I Comend my soule to god in Jesus Christ and my body when it shall decease this life to be buryed in the burying place in Newbury in hope of a ioyfull resurrection, And for my worldly goods I dispose as followeth. first I giue to my Son Joshua Browne when he shallbe of the age of one and twenty yeares, all that parsell of my vpland and meadow that lyeth neere the little Riuer as it is now inclosed, and my fiue acres of vpland adioyneing to Goodm Smiths land, and my share of meadow, which I haue equally with Georg Little, vpon the little Riuer, and a mare colt and two calues and an ewe and my owne freehold for encouragment to liue with his mother vntill he be of the aforesaid age. Secondly I giue to my Son Richard Browne the house and Lott I now dwell vpon with the Lott adioyneing to Robert Longs Land and that parsell of land adioyneing to Richard Pettingalls land ||on bothe sides of the ware|| with my eight acres of salt marsh lying in the great marsh betweene m<sup>rs</sup> Cuttings marsh and Thomas Bloomfeilds marsh, and my parsell of meadow adioyneing to the Land that Beniamin Roafe hath now in possession and the freehold which was Gyles Badgers which belongs to mee, and he my Son Richard shall pay out of his share ten pounds to each of his three sisters within three years after he shall have the said premisses in prossession 3dly I giue vnto my Son Edmund Browne all my share of Land that belongs to mee which was formerly Joseph Carters that is to say halfe the plow land pasture and meadow with the house and barne that hath beene built by mee and halfe the preuiledg of freehold, both Richard and Edmund shall haue their Legacyes at their mothers decease, but if their mother shall chang her Condition and marry againe then they shall haue their portions at the age of one & twenty years. Also to my three daughters Elizabeth Sara and Mary I giue to each of them the summe of ten pounds to be paid out of my stock at the day of their marryage, and if my wife shall marry againe then the stock that I leaue in her hands shall be diuided among my three daughters aforesaid, according to the discretion of my ouerseers, and my wife shall haue the vse of the said stock vntill my daughters shalbe of age for the bringing of them vp, And whereas I am bound to leaue my wife worth threescore pounds, In leiu of it I giue vnto her the thirds of my lands dureing her naturall life, and appoint her to bee the sole executrix of this my last will and testament also I appoint her to pay John Badger his portion out of my estate and that my debts and funerall be discharged, Also the portion abouementioned to my Son Josua I appoint it to be in full of what he shall haue out of my estate so that he shall neuer desire any more in relation of any thing giuen to his brother Joseph deceased by his vnckle Georg Browne deceased If ether of my sons doe die befor he comes to age then his land shal fale vnto the other two and if ether of my dauters shal die before her marrage then her portion shal fale vnto my other two dauters and if my wife chaing her condition by marrag then she shal give security to my ouersers for the paiment of my childrens portions. And I doe appownt my louing frinds Richard Kente and Nicolas Noyes and Robert Long my ouerseers to put in exicution this my wille and testament. Signd and seled with myne owne hands in the presens of vs"

Richard Browne [SEAL]

Witness: Tristram Coffin, Joseph Noyes.

"Farther it is my will & desier that my louing frind Josef Noyce be one of my ouerseers aded to the other three before mentioned.

Wittness & to this will: James Noyes, Moses Noyes."

Proved June 24, 1661 by Moses Noyes before Daniel Denison and Tristram Coffin. *Essex Co. Quarterly Court Files, vol. 6, leaf* 139.

Inventory of the estate of Richard Browne of Newbury, who deceased Apr. 26, 1661, taken, June 5, 1661, by Richard Knight, Anthony Somerby and Steven Grenleff, and proved in Ipswich court, Mar. 25, 1662, by Elizabeth Browne, the widow and executrix: Six and twenty acres of upland & meadow with house & barne and eight and twenty acres of upland and meadow and a house, 1-2 a barne & sixe and twenty acres of upland & meadow, 400li.; a mare and a horse and two yeareling Colts, 46li.; a yoak of oxen and six cowes, 40li.; thre yearling steere & a two yerling heifer, one yerling & 4 calues, 12li.; three ewes, three weathers, 2 lambs, 4li.; A sow, twelue shoots, three pigs, 9li.; Corne upon the grownd, 16li.; his weareing apparrell, 13li. 6s. In the Hall, a bedstead & a trucklbedsted, with a fetherbed, a bolster, 4 feather pillowes, 2 blankets, a coverled & a Ruge with curtaines, a vallons with a flockbed and bolster, a rug and blanket, 15li.; two chests, a trunck, 2 boxes and a case of bottles, 3li.; A Cubbard and Cubbard cloth, a table, a settle, a forme, 2 chayres, one stoole, 4 Cushions and a Cradle, 4li.; two Carpets, 1li. 10s.; A Bason and ewer, 4 silver spoones, a Cupp, a little basen, 6 chiny dishes & a warmeing pan, 3li. 10s.; A paire of Holland sheets & 4 pillow bears, 2li.; Nine sheets & 2 pillow bears, 2li.; one diaper & 2 network cubbard cloths, 1li.; one diaper table cloth & 2 diaper napkins, a Holland tablecloth & 16 napkins, 2li. 5s.; A box, a desck, 2 little pillows & a basket, 10s. In the seller, 4 beare vessells, 6 trayes & a bowle, a keeler, 5 chesefatts, a churne, a poudering tub & butter tub, a koowle & other lumber, 1li. 10s. In the kitchin, two brass potts, a great bras kettle, a little bras kettle, 4 brass pans, 2 brass candlesticks, 2 Skillets, 5li.; A morter and pessill, a chafing dish, a skimmer, a brass Ladle, 1li. 16s.; An Iron pot, 2 tramells, a paire of Andirons, a pr. of tongs & fire shovells, a spitt, 2 pr. of pott hooks, 2 smoothing Irons, a flesh-hooke, a pr. of sheers & a pr. of Snuffers, frying pan & an Iron peele & a pressing Iron & passell, 1li.; two guns and a musket barrell, a sword & amunition & a watchbill & a chopping knife, a Clever & a shreding knife, 2 lamps, 3li. 6s. 8d.; Eleven platters, 2 basins, 5 fruit dishes, 7 porringers, 4 sawcers, 2 salt sellers, a flaggon, 2 quart potts, 2 pint potts, a halfe pint pott, a cup & a beaker, a halfe pint bottle, 2 pewter chamberpots, 6 Alcumy spoones, 6li.; Books & an houre glass, 1li. 10s.; A little table & Cubbard & foormes, a pr. of bellowes & chayres & a cheespresse, a linnen wheele & a woollen wheele & other Lumber, 2 dozen of trenchers, 2 pr. of cards & 2 bucketts, 1li. 15s.; A bedstead In the Chamber over the Hall with a fetherbed, a blanket, a coverled and a Rug & boolster, a matt, 7li.; 2 Chests, 2 boxes, 1li. 10s.; A dozen of Hogsheds & 11 Smal tubs & baggs and sacks and 2 seives & lumber, 2li.; four augers, 2 hedgbills, 2 crosscut saws, a handsaw, 5 hooes, an ads, a hamer, 2 axes, 2 hatchets, a spade and a shovell & other utensells for husbandry & some old Iron, 4li. In the kitchin Chamber, 9 bushels of wheat & about 15 bush. of Indian corne and a halfe bushell, 4li. 10s.; A hors harness, a sadle & a pillion, 1li. 15s.; A cart & dungpot and wheeles, 2 ploughs, 2 yoaks & chayne & 1-2 & other small utensils, 3li.;

two scithes, 2 riphookes, 2 Sickles, 4 prongs, 15s.; 6 stalls of Bees, 6li.; 5 wedges & a pr. of Beetle Rings, 10s.; wooll & yarne, 2li.; ten pounds of Cotten wooll, 10s.; two flitches of Bacon, 1li. 4s.; total, 634li. 3s. Debts due from the deceased: To Nathaniell Badger in England, 25li. 5s.; to Peter Tappan, 1li. 6s.; to Henry Jaques, 3li. 14s.; to John Badger, 1li. 10s.; total, 31li. 15s. *Essex Co. Quarterly Court Files, vol. 7, leaf 95.*

### Estate of Thomas Seers of Newbury.

Administration on the estate of Tho. Seeres granted 25: 4: 1661 to Mary, his widow. Inventory amounting to 79li. 19s. 8d., clear estate, was allowed. *Salem Quarterly Court Records, vol. 4, page 69.*

Inventory of the estate of Thomas Seers of Newbury, who deceased May 16, 1661, taken by William (his W M mark) Moody, Robert Coker and Anthony Somerby: The house & barne & two acres and three quarters of land, 48li.; a cow and a Calfe, 5li. 6s.; three swyne & three pigs, 2li. 8s.; His weareing apparrell, 6li. 14s.; A bedsted, a feather Bed, a Rugg and a blancket, bolster & pillowes, 6li. 10s.; A chest, a forme, table, a cubbard, two spining wheels & two chayres, 1li. 3s.; A tub, a tray, two bowles, two bucketts, & other utensels & lumber, a hayr seive, 15s.; A great brass kettle & little old kittle, 2 little Iron potts & a pr. of pothooks, a bras skillet & a pr. of Cottrills & tongs & warming pan & frying pan & lamp, 2li. 12s.; two pewter platters, a pint pot, a pewter bottle & a porringer, 2 tin sawce pans, 13s.; foer wedges, 2 beetle rings, a spade, a shave, a handsaw, 2 hooes, an axe & a pare of wooll cards, 18s.; a bible, a brush, a smoothing Iron, a flesh hooke, a brass ladle, 10s. In the Chamber: An ould bed & blanket and Rug, 1li. 10s.; A Chest, a box, a meale trough, 1li.; A hogshed, 2 tubs, a bedsted & 2 halfe butts & other Luumber, 17s.; three baggs, 10s.; eight bushells of Indian corne, 1li. 4s.; thre sheets, 1li. 5s.; A coverlet, 1li. 10s. In the seller: A case of bottles, 4s. 6d.; three hogsheads of vineger, 3li.; ten old hogsheads, 1li.; 3 small beare tubs, 2 halfe butts, a Coule & other lumber, 1li.; In corne upon the ground, 3li.; A cannoo, 2 tunnels, a harping Iron, 1li.; total, 93li. Debts: To Henry Jaques, ——; Abrah. Tappan, 3li. 5s.; Mr. Grenleafe, 3li. 3s.; Goodm. Drinker, 1li.; Mr. Woodman, 12s.; Ben. Swett, 10s.; John Bartlet, 6s.; Capt. White,

9s. 4d.; Rich. Fitts, 5s.; John Knight, 3s.; Henry Lunt, 4s.; Peter Morse, 6s.; Robert Coker, 2li. 7s.; total, 13li. 4d. The appraisers made oath, 26: 9: 1661, before Hilliard Veren, cleric. *Essex Co. Quarterly Court Files, vol. 6, leaf 125.*

### ESTATE OF MRS. ISABEL BABSON OF GLOUCESTER.

Administration on the estate of Isabell Babson, widow, granted 25: 4: 1661, to her son, James Babson. Inventory brought in and allowed. *Salem Quarterly Court Records, vol. 4, page 70.*

Inventory of the estate of Isable Babson of Glositer, taken Apr. 9, 1661, by Samuel Delaber and Phillip Stainwood and sworn to in court by James Babson, before Hilliard Veren, cleric: "The vallue of those lands and goods com to twenty seven pounds & six shillings." *Essex Co. Quarterly Court Files, vol. 6, leaf 127.*

### ESTATE OF PHILIP KIRTLAND OF LYNN.

Administration on the estate of Phillip Kertland granted 25: 4: 1661, to his wife Alce, now wife of Eavan Thomas, and Mr. Will. Bartholmew and Mr. Oliver Purchas, the two feofees of trust. Court allowed an indenture or mortgage, together with a schedule annexed, dated 12: 2: 1661, which instrument was made from said Thomas to said Alce, provided the estate be reserved in order that the court may make further proportions to the children out of the said estate. Also, the said widow, not bringing in an inventory of the estate of her husband Kirtland, deceased, according to law, was liable to a fine of 5li. for every month's neglect, which the court respitted till the next General Court. *Salem Quarterly Court Records, vol. 4, page 70.*

William Harker of Lyn, aged about sixty five years, testified that when Phillip Kartland of Lynn was going to sea, he told him that he had left an estate in the hands of his wife, Alice Kartland, etc. Sworn in court.

"Inventory of the moveable estate which Evan Thomas hath and doth enjoy with and by Alice his now wife; Taken before marriage:" Four Cowes, 4li. pr. peece, 16li.; 2 steers of 2 year and vantage at 3li., 6li.; 2 mare colts of a year and vantage, 16li.; 2 smale swine, 16s.; 11 wethers and ewes at 14s., 7li. 14s.; Lambs at 8s. p. pc., 2li.; 57 yds. of

Cloth of Cotton and sheeps wool at 3s. 6d., 9li. 19s. 6d.; 19 yds. 1-2, at 22d. p. yd., 1li. 15s. 10d.; 2 yds. 1-2 of Cotton and lyning cloth at 3s. p. yd., 7s. 6d.; 18 yds. of Searg at 6s. 6d. p. yd., 5li. 17s.; one peece of Penistone, 11s.; 6 yds. of penistone at 4s. 6d. p. yd., 1li. 7s.; 2 yds. of stuff at 4s. p. yd., 12s.; 2 peeces of stuff at 2li. 4s., 2li. 4s.; peece of stuff and a peece of tammie, 14s. 6d.; —— yds. 1-2 of Satinesco at 6s. p. yd., 1li. 13s.; one mantle at 26s., 8 yds. of dimity at 2s. 6d. p. yd., 2li. 6s.; Cards of Lace, 8s. 6d., 13 oz. of silke, 2—0—6 maks, 2li. 9s. Fine sheets, 35s.; one paier of sheets, 20s. maks, 2li. 15s.; table clothes and one hand towel, 19s.; —— yds. of narrow hollond, 9s., one yd. of Lawne, 12s., 1li. 1s.; —— yds. of Carpetting, 11s.; for fine white threed, 12s., 1li. 3s.; —— smale deskes, 6s., 2 paier of scales and wights, 16s., 2 pillow-beers, 30s., one paier of sheets, 30s., 3li.; —— yds. of Cloth, 8s., 8 towels and a boardcloth, 12s., 1li.; napkins, 6s., 2 pillowbeirs, 8s.; one fether bed & pillow, 3li. 6s., 4li.; fether bolster, 10s., a paier of old sheets, 6s., 16s.; a pillow and bolster, 7s. 6d., a green rug, 30s., a blanket, 10s., 2li. 7s. 6d.; one old covled, 20s., Curtaines and vallence, 30s., 2li. 10s.; a blue rug and a blanket, 12s., a paire of Corse sheets, 8s., 1li.; an old flock bed, 12s., a chest, 12s., a press, 25s., 2li. 9s.; a bedstead, 10s., Indean matts, 6s., 16s.; Cotton yarne, 6s., 40li. of wool and lether, 3li. 6s.; an old rug, 5s., ginger, 25s., Coppris, 20s., milsacks, 11s., 3li., 1s.; pewter flagons, platters, & other pewter, 5li. 10s.; a brass kettle and other implments of brass, 4li.; Iron potts and kettls and other things, 5li.; Sword and bandalears, 13s. 6d., a bridle bitt and pannel, 7s., 1li. 6d.; several wodden things, 28s., 2 Chamberpotts & a cass of Bottles, 10s., 1li. 18s.; Chaiers, 8s.; 300 1-2 of board and a spade, 17s. 6d., 1li. 5s. 6d.; ladder & a hoe, 8s. 6d., a wheelbarrow wheele, 2s., and other things, 1li. 8s. 6d.; load of hay, 10li.; one peece of Cotton Cloth, 19s. 3d.; one bill on Samuel Bennet, 2li. 45s.; due in Iron potts from John Diryn, 2li. 5s.; 5 wedges, 2 beetle rings, one spit, a drippin pan, a dung fork, a Iron barr, a blanket and other things, 1li.; in money, 10li.; on bill on Ambrose Cowley, 1li.; total, 160li. 14s. 1d. The following was annexed and entered and recorded, Apr. 29, 1661, by Edw. Rawson, recorder: The house and farm with the apurtnances, 16li.; in wheat, 5li.; four dussen off napkins, 6li. 5s.; to a bill by John Frances, 1li.; to severall debts owinge to ye estat not pd., ——. Sworn in court June 26, 1661 by Alce Thomas,

late wife of Phillip Kertland, deceased, before Hillyard Veren, cleric.
*Essex Co. Quarterly Court Files, vol. 6, leaves 127-128.*

### ESTATE OF JOHN HUMPHRIES, ESQ.*

Administration upon all the estate in New England of John Humphries, Esq., granted 25: 4: 1661, to Mr. Joseph Humphries, his son, and Mr. Edmond Batter, who gave bonds for 100li. *Salem Quarterly Court Records, vol. 4, page 71.*

Inventory of the estate of Jno. Humphreys, Esq., taken 13: 10: 1661, by Edmond Batter and Joseph Humfrey: Jincken Davis of Lyne fined by the General Court to pay Mr. Humphries, 40li.; Jno. Hudson, now of New Haven, fined by the same authority to pay Mr. Humphrey, 20li.; Mr. Jno. Dunster, deceased, sold a windmill from Mr. Humphrey's land, 60li.; the farme at Lyne, now in the Occupation of Edward Ingles, ——; sixe Acres of salt marsh in Rumney Marsh in the Occupation of Richard Jnoson. Court 10: 10: 1661 allowed the inventory and continued Mr. Ed. Batters and Mr. Joseph Humphries as administrators. *Essex Co. Quarterly Court Files, vol. 7, leaf 39.*

Court 10: 10: 1661 gave Mr. Joseph Humphries, administrator, liberty to make use of 30li. of the estate for his necessary expenses. *Salem Quarterly Court Records, vol. 4, page 84.*

Mr. Edmond Batter, who, with Mr. Joseph Humfries, was administrator of the estate, presented an inventory which was allowed. 30: 4: 1663 said Batter was allowed full power of administration in the absence of Joseph Humfries. *Salem Quarterly Court Records, vol. 4, page 119.*

Inventory of the estate of Jno. Humphreys, Esqr., deceased, taken July 3, 1663, by Henry (his mark) Collince and Thomas (his mark) Farrar, and allowed July 3, 1663, in Salem court, as presented by Edmond Batter and Mr. Joseph Humphreys: One farme contayninge one dwellinge house, upland and nine Acres of Salt Marsh in ye hands of Robert Ingles of Lyne, 280li.; six Acres salt Marsh in Rumney Marsh late in the possession of Richard Jnoson of Lyne, 30li.; total, 310li. Re-

*See also Records and Files of the Quarterly Courts of Essex Co., Mass., vol. 2 (1912), pp. 330, 331, 389, 393-395; vol. 3 (1913), pp. 8-11, 106, 107.

ceived of the widow Davis of Lyne for Jenken Davis fine and so a full discharge, 20li.; of Jno. Hudson, for fine to Mr. Humphreys, 20li.; in the hands of Robt. Ingles in consideration of a barn to make good, 277li.; total, 377li. *Essex Co. Quarterly Court Files, vol. 20, leaf 122.*

Court 24: 9: 1663 allowed Mr. Edmond Batter, administrator, to pay himself his just dues from the estate of Mr. Joseph Humfries, for all his charges in the management of the business, taking it from the rent of the farm of Mr. Humfries at Windmill hill in Lynn. Ten pounds was allowed said Batter of an account presented to court, besides another account owned by Mr. Joseph Humphries. *Salem Quarterly Court Records, vol. 4, page 123.*

Mr. Edmond Batter, administrator, having paid Edw. Richards 5li. for his pains about the estate, the court allowed it 27: 9: 1666. *Salem Quarterly Court Records, vol. 4, page 172.*

Court June 25, 1667, advised Mr. Edmond Batter, administrator, to pay a debt due from Joseph Humfryes to John Lake of Boston. *Salem Quarterly Court Records, vol. 5, leaf 4.*

Jno. Davis, aged about thirty years, deposed that whereas there was by agreement of the executors of the estate of John Humphryes, Esq., "that my mother the relict of Jenckin Davis, that as the full of what he was to pay to m$^r$ Humphryes, which was twenty pounds, eighteen pounds of it was paid to m$^r$ Edmond Batter & noe more, & the other forty shillings M$^r$ Joseph Humfryes did dispose thirty shillings to m$^r$ Samuell Whiting seny$^r$ of Lynn & ten shillings to my selfe." Sworn 25: 9: 1668, before William Hathorne, assistant. *Salem Quarterly Court Records, vol. 5, leaf 14.*

Court Nov. 30, 1669, approved a bill of Mr. Tho. Ruckes, charged upon John Humfryes, Esq.'s estate, or so much of it as Mr. Edmond Batter, administrator, should judge justly due. *Salem Quarterly Court Records, vol. 5, leaf 29.*

Whereas the court for several years past impowered Mr. Joseph Humfryes and Mr. Edmond Batter as joint administrators to find what estate Jno. Humfreyes, Esq., deceased, left in the country and to bring in an inventory, Mr. Joseph Humfryes going out of the country, court continued said Batter, making him sole executor. He brought in an inventory in 1663, and now presenting an account of charge and disbursements for said Joseph, also what he had laid out on building and repairing of houses and fences, and the receipts of the profit of the farm, which was allowed 28: 9: 1671. Mr. Batter desired to renounce and be released of his administratorship. *Salem Quarterly Court Records, vol. 5, leaf 54.*

Account of Jno. Humphry's estate, presented to the Salem court, 28: 9: 1671, and allowed upon oath of Edmund Batter: Dr. to what he disbursed to Mr. Joseph Humphreys before he went to England, 35li. 16s. 8d.; to Jno. Floyd for fencing salt marsh, 7s.; to Andrew Mansfield for labor about viewing the fences, 6s. 8d.; to Edward Richards for his paynes & Charges for helping to Inquere out the estate, 5li.; to Mr. Jno. Lake of Boston, 17li. 9d.; to old Mrs. Rucke for old expences, 1li. 14s. 1d.; to Robt. Rane for buildinge of Barne and abatement of Rent, 30li.; to Rich. Hude for Repareing of dwellinge house, 61li. 6s. 10d.; to Mr. Helliard Veren for drawing 2 leases, 5s.; to interest of money to the value near of 60li. for seaven years past, 15li.; to his care and paynes the 7 years past, 10li.; total, 146li. 17s. Cr. ℔ what has been received from Robt. Rane for 4 years Rent, 40li.; what has been received from Richard Hude fo<sup>r</sup> three years Rent, 31li.; total, 71li.

Account of what Mr. Joseph Humphrys received out of the estate while in New England: By Mr. Jno. Hudson of New Haven, 22li.; what he Recd of the Relict of Jenken Davis, 20li.; Francis Ingles pd. to Mr. Jno. Hathorn, 5li.; to Mr. Whitrige of Lyne, 10li.; to Edmund Batter, 10li.; recd of Edmund Batter, 35li. 16s. 8d.; per Jno. Lake of Boston pd. by Ed. Batter, 17li. 9d.; wt. he Received of Mr. Jno. Gedney for a small psell of land sold him in Salem, 2li. 10s.; total, 122li. 7s. 5d. *Essex Co. Quarterly Court Files, vol. 20, leaf 123.*

### Estate of John Sibly of Manchester.

Rachell Sibly, wife of John Sibly, deceased, brought in an inventory of her husband's estate 25: 4: 1661 and was sworn. Said Rachell was appointed administratrix, the widow to have the property for the bringing up of the children. *Salem Quarterly Court Records, vol. 4, page 73.*

Inventory taken June 24, 1661, by Willm. Allen, Pasco

Foot and Rob. Leach: One dwelling house with fifty Acres land, 15li.; 4 Cowes & 1 heifer, 18li.; 2 oxen & 1 Bull, 18li.; 1 heifer & Calfe, 4li.; 5 peggs or swine, 1li. 10s.; pewter, 1li. 15s.; Brass & Iron Potts, 1li. 10s.; Bed & Bedinge, 5li.; Chest, bedsteed & Table, 1li. 10s.; one thousand five hundred boards, 3li. 15s.; total, 69li. 10s. Debts: To Mr. Willm. Brown, about 10li.; Mr. Emory, 25s.; Goodman Joanes, 15s.; Ed. Batter, 4li. 15s.; other small debts, besides what we do not yet understand, 12s.; total, 16li. 17s.; clear estate, 52li. 13s. "he left behind him a Widow & 9 fatherless Children 4 Boyes & 5 girles: the Eldest daughter 19 years old, the next daughter about 17 years: the therd daughter about 15 years: fourth is a son of 12 years." Sworn in court by Rachell Sibly, the widow. *Essex Co. Quarterly Court Files, vol. 6, leaf* 138.

### Estate of James Smith of Marblehead.

"I James Smith of marblehead, being weake in body but (through the mercie of God) of sound mind & memorie, doe make this my last will *will,* in maner & forme following, ffirst I bequeath my soul into the hands of Almighty God, trusting in Jesus Christ alone for Life, & for saluation: Item I giue & bequeth vnto mary Smith my wife, all that my farme called Castle hill, w$^{th}$ ten acres in the South field bought of Joseph Grafton, & now in the hands of Samuell Cutler, during her Life if shee remayne So Long a widdow, & at the day of her death, or marriag w$^{ch}$ shall first happen, then I giue it to my son James Smith: but it is to be vnderstood Richard Rowland my son in Law hath ten pound & in the first purchase of Castlehill; Item I giue vnto my wife my house & land in marblehead bought of Erasmus James & all my share on the farme bought by marblehead of maj$^r$ wm hathorne dureing her life or widdowhood & after her death or marriag w$^{ch}$ shall first happen to my son James Smith, & my will is that after the Death of my son James that this shall Desend to James his Eldest son: Item I giue vnto my wife all my household goods, w$^{th}$in Doors, to her, & her heires for euer, & also 4 of my Cowes. Item I giue vnto Kathren Eburne my Daughter my six Oxen in the hand of Samuell Cutler, Item I giue vnto mary Eburne, my Grandchild Twenty pounds, w$^{ch}$ I order her father to Dispose of & improue for her good, vntill her Day of marriag, or Twenty one yeares: Item I giue to the other fiue Children of my

Daughter Eburne fiue pounds apeece to be improued by the father as abousaid; Item, I giue unto my Daughter mary Rouland the oxe w<sup>ch</sup> I now yoak w<sup>th</sup> one of her husbands; Item I giue vnto my Grandchild Samuell Rowland ten pounds if he be liueing at the Day of my Death, or else the ten pounds to be Devided in equall shares betweene his Brothers, & sisters. Item I giue vnto my Daughter Rowlands other three Children fiue pounds apeece to be improued for their good vntill they come to Twenty one yeares, or marriag, by the ouersight of the ouerseers of this my Last will; Item I apoint mary Smith my wife my sole Executrix & I apoint my trusty ffriend maj<sup>r</sup> wm Hathorne, & my Son Samuell Eburne Ouerseeres of this my last will & doe giue vnto maj<sup>r</sup> wm Hathorne for his paynes ten pounds to be payed him out of a debt in John Deverix hands: And in wittnes that this is my last will I haue here vnto sett my hand, & seale the 9 : 9<sup>ber</sup> : 1660."

          his mark
        James J S Smith [seal]
          his mark
 Witness: Wm Hathorne, Samuell X Eburne.

Proved in Salem court 27 : 4 : 1661 by Maj. Will. Hathorne and Samuell Ebborne. *Essex Co. Quarterly Court Files, vol. 6, leaf 130.*

Will of James Smith was brought into court by his wife, and was allowed 27 : 4 : 1661, as was also an inventory amounting to 592li. 1s. *Salem Quarterly Court Records, vol. 4, page 71.*

Inventory taken June 25, 1661, by Francis Johnson and Moses Mavericke: Nine milch Cowes, 45li.; 1 steer, three years ould, 5li.; 1 bull & 2 heafers, two year ould, 7li.; 5 yearlins, 7li. 10s.; 7 ould sheep & 3 lams, 4li. 5s.; an oxe, 8li.; 6 oxen, 36li.; a mare & Coult, 17li.; 4 swine, 4li.; His house & land at Casteel hill, wth. 10 Akers more purchessed of Mr. Gott ajoyninge, 120li.; 1 Aker of marshe at Foresst river, his pte in the farme purchessed by the men of Marblehead, 36li.; his dwelinge house & land in Marblehead, 110li. In the parlor: A bedd with all its furniture, 10li.; a Cubbard, 2li.; a table & 4 Joynt stules, 1li. 5s.; 3 Chares, 15s.; a cheste, 10s.; a warminge pann, 5s.; one sute as breches & Coat, 2li. 5s.; 4 yds. kersey at 7s. p. yd., 1li. 8s.; 8 yds. sarge at 6s. p. yd., 2li. 8s.; 4 yds. kearsey at 6s. p. yd., 1li. 4s.; 15 yds. water parigan at 3s., 2li. 5s.; a stuff Coat of his, 10s. A brass kittill pott & skillet, 2li. 10s.; an Iron Kittell, 12s., a friing pann, 2s., 14s.;

an Iron pott & skillett, 11s.; pewter, 1li. 4s.; tubs, milke vessell & other Lumber, 2li.; a bedd, bedsted, Rugg, blanketts & pillows, 5li.; Lisburn ware, 10s.; a settell & Chare table, 9s.; a table, a bine, 3 pailes, 8s.; a dripinge pann, smothinge Iron & gridiron, 8s.; tongs, fire shovell & tramells & spitt, 8s. In the Chamber: A. bead, 2 Rugs, 2 blanketts, 3li. 10s.; 2 blanketts, 20s., new cloth, 15s., 1li. 15s.; 8 peare of sheets, 6li.; 1 peare of pillobeers, 2 tablecloths, 14s.; 10 bushells Indian corne, 1li. 10s.; a smith's vise wth. other tules, 1li. 10s.; total, 457li. 1s.; more in debts one ackeer Accompt as the widdow Apprehends, 38li.; total, 492li. 1s. *Essex Co. Quarterly Court Files, vol. 6, leaf* 131.

### Estate of William Witter of Lynn.

"1659 5 6° The last will and testament of william witter being in perfit memory and first I commit my soule to god who gaue it and my body to the earth from whenc it was taken. I giue to my wife Annis halfe my lands, housing and chattels: but in case she chang her name, I bequeath to her but the thirds and to my sonn Josia I giue the other halfe of my lands, housing, and chattels: but in case my wife mary, then I bequeth a duble portion to my sonn Josia and his mother my wife shall haue but the thirds, as aforesaid, prouided that my sonn shall not sell this his inheritanc, but in case hee die w<sup>th</sup> out isseu: then I will that this inheritanc shall bee instated *upon* Robert Burdin and my dafter Hanna, for there posteritis I will my dafter Hanna Burdin shall have a ew, and lamb this time twelfe mounts and I will that my wife Annis bee my sole executor   in witnes here of I haue caused my hand to bee set."

william witter

Witness: Robert Driver, william Harker
Proved in Salem court June —, 1661 by the witnesses. *Essex Co. Quarterly Court Files, vol. 6, leaf* 142.

Inventory taken 15: 9: 1659, by Robert Driver, William Harker and Francis (his ? mark) Ingols: His aparrill, 1li.; in ye hall, one bed and that which belongs to it, 2li.; in ye parler, one bed & that which belongs to it, 5li.; a peec of carsie of foure yards, 1li. 6s.; a chest, 4s.; three pare of shets with other linins, 3li. 10s.; a warming pan, 5s.; in puter, 15s.; in bras, 10s.; an Iron cettle, tow pots and a scellet, 2li.; a friing pan, spit & pothooks, 10s.; tow hoogs, barrils & a salting trough, 6s.; three trays, thre poles and a cimmitt, 6s.;

tow whels & tow pare of cards, 10s.; churn, dishes, spouns & trenchers, 6s.; in wool & flax, 10s.; wheat, inde corne & pese, 3li. 10s.; in hay, 4li.; cart & whels & plough & chains, wth. things belonging, 3li.; a pare of oxen, 13li.; thre cous, 14li.; a mare, 6li. 10s.; swine, 2li. 12s.; housing & land, 66li.; total, 132li. 11s.

Sworn in Salem court 23 : 4: 1661 by Anis Witter. *Essex Co. Quarterly Court Files, vol. 6, leaf* 143.

### Estate of Benjamin Belflower of Salem.

Inventory of the estate of Benjamin Belflower, who deceased Feb. 24, 1660, taken Mar. 16, 1661, by Robt. Moulton and Henry Phelps: Nineteene Acres of Land, 9li. 10s.; houshold stuffe, 4li. 10s.; By Bill, 4li.; serge, 18s.; cotten wooll, 7s. Debts: To my father, 10li.; to Goodman Martin, 3li. Filed with papers of the June term, 1661. *Essex Co. Quarterly Court Files, vol. 6, leaf* 144.

### Estate of John Smith of Rowley.

"This will was made and ssigned the 13 of July 1661 I John smith weake in body but of perfit understanding at this present blessed be god doe make and apoynt this my last will and testament as ‖in‖ forme followeth ‖my debts being paid‖ Item for my outward estate I thus deuide it the one halfe to my wife & the other halfe to my child sarah smith I will alsoe that my wife have my hole estate till she ‖my child‖ come to one and twenty yeres ould or day of her maryage, and my wife shall inioy the other halfe during her naturall life, and ‖at‖ my wife desese I giue my hole estate in land to my daughter smith at my wife desese with my house & barne and out houses & fences to be kept in sufitient repare, excepting tow acres of land I bought of John Tod and 3 acres of medow beyond the ox pastor and 5 acres of medow at the farme liing betwene elder Raners medow & m$^r$ Crosbys and 2 cowes gates of the common, which I giue to my wife to despose of for euer as she says goods and if my wife shod be with child if a daughter all then to be alike during ther naturall [life] and after my wife desese my daughters to diuide w$^t$ estate in land *onely* 3 acres of medow and 2 acres of arable land aboue mentioned & 2 cow gates, prouided it be a son then I giue him my lands after my wife desese and he is to enter of 2 parts of it one & twenty and my wife and daughter is to deuide my estate in goods betwene them and my wife is to haue her thirds during her naturall life and then the hole goes to my son, excepting these perticulers aboue mentioned which I gaue to my wife for euer, I make my wife hole excecutor."

John Smith

Witness: Thomas Tenny, Maxemillyan Jewit, John Johnson.

Proved in Ipswich court Nov. 14, 1661 by Maximilian Jewett and Thomas Tenny before Mr. Samuell Symonds and Maj. Daniell Denison.

Inventory taken July 29, 1661 by Maxemillion Jewett, Ezekiell Northen, John Pallmer and Samuell Brocklebanke: in Apparell and Bookes, 10li. 10s.; In house, Barne, out houses, houselot, orchard and swampe, 60li.; more in Aurable land in the comon feild ten acres, 54li.; in medowes twenty thre acres, 70li.; in commonage, 4li. 10s.; in land at merrimacke, 10li.; foure oxen, 30li.; foure cowes, 20li.; one Bull, 3li. 10s.; thre cattell coming thre yeare ould, 10li.; thre yearlings, 6li.; thre callves, 4li. 10s.; one horse, 13li.; tow mares and one foalle, 32li.; tow yerelinge horses, 15li.; elleven swine, 9li.; wheat on the ground, 7li.; Indian on the Ground, 5li.; Grase on the Ground, 2li.; cart, yokes, chaine, plough, sled, shackells, boults, Axes, sithes, bettell Rings, wedge, cart rope, forkes, whell, Rings, 5li. 15s.; sadell, sword, pistolles, halsters and such furneture for a horse, 3li. 10s.; one Bed with the furneture Belonging unto it, 10li.; one bed more with the furneture belonging to it, 9li.; more bed linen, table linen and other new cloth, 4li. 5s.; putter and tinne and spouns, 1li. 14s.; Brass vessells and Iron, 2li. 15s.; tramell, tongs and such like, 10s.; milke vesell, a beare vesell and earthen ware, 1li.; Corne and mealle, 4li. 5s.; Bacon, 1li.; Bages, ould Ruge, 15s.; horse fetters and other ould Iron things and a peece of leather, 7s. 6d.; whelle, cards, mesures, sives, 12s.; woolle and hempe & yarne, 8s.; Butter and chese, 1li.; table chaires, cushins, 1li. 1s.; one Coubbard and one leather skin and the things in the coubbard, 13s.; in debts due to the deceased, 19li. 17s. 4d.; debts to be paid out of the estate, 19li.; total, 434li. 12s. 10d.

Division of Real Estate in this docket put with estate of John Pickard of Rowley, Mar. 28, 1699, Docket 21,788.

*Essex Co. Probate Files, Docket 25,590.*

### Estate of Humphry Griffen of Ipswich.*

Administration on the estate of Humphry Griffen, granted Nov. 19, 1661, to his widow, Elizabeth, by Mr. Samuell Symonds and Major Genll. Denison. It was ordered that an inventory be brought into the next Ipswich court. *Ipswich Quarterly Court Records, vol. 1, page 97.*

Administration having been formerly granted to Elizabeth Griffen on the estate of her late husband, Humphry Griffen, by the Honered Mr. Samuell Symonds and Major Genrll. Denison, the clerk being present, and now an inventory, amounting to 71li., clear estate, being presented to court Mar. 25, 1662, the estate was ordered to be divided as follows: To John Griffen, the eldest son, 20li.; to the two younger sons, 10li. each; and the rest of the estate to the widow. *Ipswich Quarterly Court Records, vol. 1, page 104.*

Inventory of the estate of Humphry Griffin, late deceased, appraised by James Davis and Theophilus Shatswell, allowed Mar. 25, 1662, in Ipswich court: Wearing apparell, 7li.; beding, boulster, sheets, hanging or curtaines, 9li.; brass, Iron pot, pewter, tinn & leaden waites, 2li. 10s.; gun, pistoll & powder, a rapier & belt, 2li. 10s.; 2 corsletts & another raper and houlsters, 3li. 5s.; a bible, 12s.; axes, beetle rings, wedges & sicles & Irons for fire, 1li. 10s.; chests, payles, bowles, trayes, dishes, beer barrells, chaires, 2li. 15s.; beefe, 3 fatt swine & 3 leane swine, 10li. 10s.; In corne English & Indian in the straw, 40li. 6s.; cart plows, plow Irons, yokes, chaines & timbrell, 4li. 10s.; hows, forks, a spade, shovells, 18s.; a fan, a halfe bushell, 14s.; a yoak of oxen, 15li.; 2 cowes & 2 calves, 11li.; 2 horses, 24li.; in land, upland & meddow, 100li.; debts dew by bill or promise, 52li. 7s.; in cotton woole & a horse coller, 10s.; an ox hyde & a cow hyde, 1li. 3s.; total, 290li. 6d. Debts dew from Griffen to severall men when he dyed was 190li. Copy made, Apr. 1, 1669, by Robert Lord, cleric. *Essex Co. Quarterly Court Files, vol. 14, leaf 149.*

### Estate of Arsbell Anderson of Lynn.

Mr. Oliver Purchase was impowered by the court 26: 9: 1661 to look after and take into his hands the estate of Arsbell Anderson, deceased, and to take an inventory of the

---

\* See also Records and Files of the Quarterly Courts of Essex Co., Mass., vol. 2 (1912), p. 368; vol. 3 (1913), p. 307.

said estate and bring it into the next court. *Salem Quarterly Court Records, vol. 4, page* 79.

John Cleark and Allester Greine were appointed 10: 10: 1661, administrators of the estate of Arzbell Anderson, deceased, and to be accountable to the court held at Salem in November, 1662. An inventory was also brought in and allowed. *Salem Quarterly Court Records, vol. 4, page* 82.

Inventory of the estate of Arzbell Anderson, Scotsman, who deceased at the Iron works at Lyn, 13: 6: 1661, taken 15: 6: 1661, by Edward Baker, Jno. Divan and Oliver Purchis, all of Lyn: Two Bed Blanketts, 14s.; 2 Coarse Shirts, 8s.; his wearing apparrell with 2 hatts, 6li. 5s.; A looking glass, 2s.; 1 yrd. of blew Callico, 1s. 10d.; 1 pr. of Worne Shooes, 3s.; A Rasor, 1s.; 4 Axes, 10s.; A small playne chest, 3s. 6d.; In money, 5s. 10 1-2d.; A small mare & 2 Colts, 18li.; A Small Cow, 4li.; 2 steeres yt. were in my Custody but after his deceased challenged by Corporall Jno. Andrewes to be his upon hire till May next, hee to pay then 20 shillings, wch. I desired to release upon Terms & hee promised mee if he could gett a payre of Oxen I should have them, but afterward he sent & fecht them away early in a morning & as I am Informed by Severall psons, he hath killed one & sold ye other, they were well worth, 12li.; so much as is due to him upon Accots., 12li. 4s. 2 1-4d.; total, 54li. 18s. 5 1-4d. "This is a true Inventory of this estate at ye decease: as is testified by Oliver purchis, a Commissioner in Lyn. Only this to be excepted at prsent one of ye Colts is Strayed & Cannot be found, & Certayne debts are demaunded which I know some to be due." Total inventory, 54li. 15s. 5 1-4d.; debts paid out of the estate, 11li. 3s. 9d.; more for John Clarkes paines, 3li. 14s. 8 1-4d.; 40s. abated upon ye Aprisement of 2 Steers, 2li.; to be paid to Allester Greine by ye Courts order, 38li. "which by ye Courts order is to be pd to Allister Greime upon the old clearks warrant to John Clerke as atteste, 27: 9: 1662, Hillyard Veren, cleric." *Essex Co. Quarterly Court Files, vol.* 7, *leaf* 37.

Allister Mackmallens, aged about thirty years, deposed that for many years, whilst he dwelt in his own native country, in Scotland, he knew Allister Greime and his father and mother, who lived next neighbors to his, the said Mackmallens father's house, and he also knew Arsbell Anderson and his mother, who lived about a mile and a half from them, and the said Arsbell Anderson's mother and Greime's mother were near of kin. This was taken for granted by all the neighbors, and deponent always understood it so and there was never any question about it in Scotland that ever he heard of. Moreover deponent's father and mother had said in his hearing that they were near of kin. Sworn in court, 12:10:1661, before Hilliard Veren, cleric. *Essex Co. Quarterly Court Files, vol. 7, leaf* 38.

Whereas there was administration granted to John Clearke and Allister Greine, upon the estate of Arzbell Anderson, deceased, who gave bond at Salem court, 10: 10: 1662, and returned an inventory, the court 25: 9: 1662 ordered that upon the clerk's warrant to said John Clerk, the latter was to deliver the estate, which was 38li., into the hands of Allister Greime, and his receipt was to be his discharge. *Salem Quarterly Court Records, vol. 4, page* 106.

Account of debts, dated 25: 9: 1662, paid out of Arzbell Anderson's estate, since his decease, by Oliver Purchis: Charges of his Buriall, 2li. 9s. 3d.; keeping his cow In ye Herd yt. summer yt. he dyed, 6s.; debt to Wm. Gibson of Boston, 1li. 9s. 6d.; to Captayne Savage of Boston, 2li. 14s.; to Rowland Mackfashon's order, 5s.; keeping of his cow fro ye end of ye Herd tyme untill ye Court tyme in December past, 7s.; to keeping his mare and colt and keeping them in pasture & Winter meat until ye Court determined in December, 10s.; to Macam Downing, 1li. 17s.; to John Hathorne, 1li. 1d.; to clerk of ye Court for Copies, etc., 5s.; total, 11li. 3s. 9d. *Essex Co. Quarterly Court Files, vol. 7, leaf* 38.

### Estate of Hugh Burt of Lynn.

"The Last will & testimonye of Hugh Burtt being verye weeke of body though of pfect memorye 7 october: 1661. Imp$^r$ I bequeath my bodye to the dust, & my Spiritt to him that gaue: it: It: to my sonn will: Bassitt 2 accors of Salt marsh in the Last devision in Rumny marsh which I bought of Timothye Cooper: which Lyeth next to his (viz) after my wifes desease: then to him & his heires forever: It: to my son Bassett to him, & his heires for ever: fiue acors of vpland Lyeing amongst Henrye Collins Land which I bought of Robt: Mansfeild which is yet vndevided It: I bequeath to my sonn will: Basset all my weareing Apparrell. It: I bequeath to my two granddaughters ‖marye, & Sarah‖ the daughters of my sonn Hugh Birt deseased each of them, a cow when they Come to the age of twentye ||one|| years which are to bee paid by my sonn Edward Burtt because I giue him halfe my Land at my deseas. It: I bequeath to my sonn Edward Burt Halfe my houseing Land & medow vndisposed of in this will: at my desease  It: I bequeath to my Sonn Edward Burtt all my Houseing Land, & medowes vndesposed of (viz) at my wifes desease  It: I bequeath to my wife one Halfe of my Houseing Lands & medowes vndesposed of in this my will (viz) at my desease dureing her Lifetyme  It: I bequeath to my sonn Edward Burt Halfe my chatles sheep & swine at my Desease: & some Corne ||not halfe|| & some haye  It: *It*: I bequeath to my wife all my goods within dores to bee at her dispose:  It: I make my wife my executrix  It: my desyre is that m$^r$ Nathaniell, Handforde & Andrew Mansfeild ||should|| [bee?] overseers of this my will &c: & bequeath Each of them a noble for their paines  Memorandum I acquitt my sonn Edward Burt of all the monyes that ||hee|| receiued of mine in England ||of all debts whateuer|| & alsoe I giue vnto my son Edward Burt all my right & interest in any houseing, or Land in London that came to mee by my brother John Burtt, deseased. In witt$^e$ where of I haue sett my hand the Daye, yeare & aboue ritten this my will being interlyned in the memorandum: & two words in my sonn Edward Legasye."

Hugh Burtt.

Witness: Nathaniell Handforth, Andrew Mansfeild, William bartrum and Richard P Johnson.
his mark

Proved in Salem court 26: 9: 1661 by Andrew Mansfield and Richd. Johnson. *Essex Co. Quarterly Court Files, vol. 7, leaf 24.*

Will of Hugh Burt, deceased, was brought into court by the widow, proved and allowed 26: 9: 1661. *Salem Quarterly Court Records, vol. 4, page 80.*

Inventory of the estate of Hugh Burtt of Lynn, who deceased Nov. 2, 1661, taken Nov. 13, 1661, by Nathanell Handforth, John Deakin and Andrew Mansfeild: Apparrell, 5li.; Beds, boulsters & pillows, 8li. 15s.; Ruggs & Blanckitts, 4li. 4s.; Sheets, pillowbeers, napkins & other Lining, 6li. 19s.; Iron, Brass & puter, 4li. 7s.; Armes & Amunition, 1li. 10s.; Chests & boxes, 1li. 5s.; Tables, forme & Carpett, 1li. 3s.; Lining & woollen yarne, 1li. 5s.; Bybles, 14s.; Apples, 1li.

2s. 6d.; Lumber, 3li. 7s.; wheat & Indion Corne, as haveing Received dalmage, 3li. 13s.; seaven sheepe, 3li.; Three Cowes & one Calfe, 13li. 10s.; Swine, 3li. 17s.; Houseing & Lands, 75li. 10s.; Haye, 2li. 10s.; moneyes, 1li. 10s. All debts that doth apeare being pd., ther remains more dew to the estate, 3s. 3d.; total, 143li. 4s. 9d. Memorandum which was forgotten, Haye, 1li. *Essex Co. Quarterly Court Files, vol. 7, leaf 25.*

### ESTATE OF WILLIAM COCKERELL OF SALEM.

Inventory of the estate allowed 10: 10: 1661. Court ordered that the estate remain in the hands of the widow during her life and that, at her death, it be divided among the children. If she married again, the court was to order the estate as it should see cause. *Salem Quarterly Court Records, vol. 4, page 80.*

Inventory of the estate of Willm. Cockrell, deceased, taken Dec. 6, 1661, by John Browne and Edmond Batter: One dwellinge house, out house and 1-4 Acre land, 30li.; one Acre land neer to Franc. Collince, 8li.; 1 Cowe, 4li. 10s., 1 swine, 10s., 5li.; Rugge, Covrled, 2 pr. blankets, 2 featherbeds & bolsters & 2 Curtaynes, 12li.; pewter, 2li. 10s.; brasse & Iron ware, 40s., 4li. 10s.; 1 Table, Chaires, Chests & other lumber goods, 3li. 8s.; 1 peec & 1 Remnant Ossenbriggs, 3li.; sheets & other linnen, 7li.; 1 suet of Cloaths, 2li.; 3 Remnants Carsy, 2 Remnants Serdge & 1 Remnant broadcloath, 6li.; 1 silver spoone, 5s., & 4 Bushells In Corne, 17s.; total, 81li. 15s. *Essex Co. Quarterly Court Files, vol. 7, leaf 30.*

### ESTATE OF JENKIN DAVIS OF LYNN.

"The tenth of the tenth m° on thousand six hundred sixtie and one In the name of god amen I Jenkin Dauis being weake in body yet of pfit memory doe make this my last will and Testament wherein I doe first commit my soul into the hands of my mercyfull sauiour and redeemer, and my body vnto Cristian buriall. for the portion of goods that god hath bine plesed to giue vnto me I do giue ||them|| vnto Mary my wife, and, to be att her dispose except my Joyners tooles which I do bestow vppon my son John when he has wrought with and for his mother till my debts be paid I doe likwise make my wife my sole executres both to receaue what is due to me from any: and likwise to pay my debts out of that portion of goods I leaue vnto her: and ffarther it is my will that the goods that my wife leaues at her decease shalbe diuided into three parts, two parts to my son John: and the other part to my daughter mary my Joyners tooles my will is that they shall not be in the devidable goods between my son John and my daughter mary but I giue them vnto him, (the form[er] Condison being pformed) ouer and aboue his two parts: the ouer-seeres of this my will is =''

[No signature]

"signed in the psents of vs:" ffrances Ingoles, Nathaniell Hanford, George Dauies, ffrancis Burrill.

Proved in Ipswich court Mar. 25, 1662 by the witnesses.

Inventory of the estate of Jeankine Davis of Lynn taken 27:11:1661 by Nathaniell Handforth: his weareinge cloaths, 4li.; Linnen, 5li. 5s. 6d.; new cloath, 2li. 17s.; more in Linnen, 3li. 7s.; three home made ruggs, 5li.; blankets, 2li. 5s.; Bedinge, 2li. 6s.; Tow bedsteads, 2li. 10s.; Tow cubberds, 2li. 18s.; Tow glass casses, 12s.; Tow tables & a forme, 1li. 15s.; chests & chairs, 2li. 5s.; Three Gunns & a pistle, 2li. 10s.; In Pewter, 1li. 6s.; Iron ware & axes, 2li.; one bible, 8s.; Lumber & Apples, 2li. 5s.; wheate & other Lumber, 2li. 10s.; flax, 15s.; Timber, 6li.; Joyners Tooles, 8li.; one horse, 13li.; one heifer & Tow yearling calves, 6li. 10s.; swinne, 3li. 5s.; houseinge & Land, 101li.; total, 184li. 9s. 6d. To be paid out of this for debts, 70li.

Petition of Thomas Ivorye of Lynn to the Ipswich court Mar. 28, 1682, concerning the condition of Mary Davis, widow of Jenkin Davis of Lynn. She being about ninety years of her age and her reason not being good for about four years she is not able to make any bargain with her son John Davis for her care; and she being my mother-in-law has been with me for four years and we now ask for 4s. a week for the care of her.

The court impowers Thomas Laughton, Sr. and Francis Burrill, Sr., to sell so much of the widow's estate as to enable them to pay the 4s. per week for the past and for the future as long as she may live.

*Essex Co. Probate Files, Docket 7,274.*

ESTATE OF JOHN GOYTE OF MARBLEHEAD.

Administration on the estate of John Goyte, intestate, granted Mar. 25, 1662 to Mary Goyt, his widow, and Mr.

William Steevens, her father. *Ipswich Quarterly Court Records, vol. 1, page* 103.

An inventory was presented Mar. 25, 1662, of the estate, amounting to 34li. 6s. Court Mar. 31, 1663 found that there were six pounds put into the inventory in land that was not his estate, so the inventory should be 28li. 6s. *Ipswich Quarterly Court Records, vol. 1, page* 116.

Inventory of John Coite: Three cowes, 12li.; 6 swine, 3li.; one Cowe, 5li.; to bedsteds, 10s.; one stere, 5li.; one Chest, 5s.; one sute of Carsie, 1li. 15s.; one chest, 8s.; upland and marsh, 6li.; to hundred of bords, 8s.; total, 34li. 6s. *Essex Co. Quarterly Court Files, vol. 9, leaf* 9.

### ESTATE OF ISAAC WAKLYE OF GLOUCESTER.

Isaack Waklye with Henry Muddle and John Pomary having been cast away at sea, and none appearing to desire administration of his estate, and William Browne, constable of Gloster, presenting papers of the estate amounting to 6li. 1s., he was given charge Mar. 25, 1662 until further order. *Ipswich Quarterly Court Records, vol. 1, page* 103.

Administration on the estate granted June 24, 1662 to Thomas Very, the inventory having been brought into the last Ipswich court, and he was to dispose of the estate for the discharging of all just debts. *Salem Quarterly Court Records, vol. 4, page* 93.

### ESTATE OF HENRY MUDDLE OF (GLOUCESTER?).

Henry Muddle with Isaack Waklye and John Pomary having been cast away at sea, and none appearing to desire administration of his estate, and William Browne, constable of Gloster, presenting papers of the estate amounting to 14li. 16s. 10d., he was given charge Mar. 25, 1662 until further order. *Ipswich Quarterly Court Records, vol. 1, page* 103.

Administration on the estate of Henry Muddle, intestate, granted Apr. 17, 1662 to Mr. Peeter Duncan, he was ordered to bring in an inventory to Salem court. *Ipswich Quarterly Court Records, vol. 1, page* 106.

Inventory presented to the court 30: 4: 1663 by Mr. Peeter Duncan. *Salem Quarterly Court Records, vol. 4, page* 119.

"Whereas there was a writtinge delivered unto Ipswich

Courte in March anno 1662 By the Selectmen of Gloucester w^ch they Called an Inventary, in these words:" Two Barrells mackrell, Richard Beefard indebted unto the sd Muddle, 8s.; one old Coate, 5s.; one new wascoate, 15s.; one suite of Kersey, 2li.; one Coate, 14s. 6d.; one pare of French heele shooes, 5s.; two pare stockings, 10s.; one sharte, 7s.; one hatt, 14s.; one Lockram Sharte, 9s.; one sharte, 10s.; one lockram sharte, 10s.; one halfe silcke neekcloath, 6s.; one Linen necke Cloath, 1s. 6d.; 1 handcharchife, 6d.; 1 pr. yarn Gloves, 1s. 6d.; 1 pr. Leather Gloves, 1s. 6d.; 1 Codline, 3s.; 1 dozen & 1-2 hookes, 4s. 6d.; 1 pue, 6d.; a Chest, 2s. 6d.; Cape, 5s.; 4 3-4 yds Cape Cloath, 16s. 7d.; one heyfor wee find in Henry Walker's hands, 2li. 10s.; wee find in Osman Duch's hands, 3li.; total, 14li. 16s. 10d.; since which time received in June, 1663, of Robert Ellwell, 2 quintalls merchantable fish, 1li. 12s.; making total 16li. 8s. 10d. Charges for wintering a hyfer wch. I payd Hen. Walker for, 12s.; in Osman Duches Debt paid Before his Death, 2li.; To the Clarke of Ipswich for writtinges, 2s.; for my Journey to Salem aboute this Buisnesse, 5s.; total, 2li. 19s. Sworn in court by Peter Duncan.

Another account, dated Gloucester, Aug. 6, 1661, was also presented by Peter Duncan: Henry Mudle, Debitor, Aug. 6, to balance of former acctt., 10s. 1d., to sugar, 7d.; Aug. 9, to John French, the Tayler, 5s. 6d., wine and Rume at severall tymes, 1li. 16s. 5d.; Oct. 28, to Caske for 2 tun barrells, 28s. p. tun, 2li. 16s., to marchandise for 7 1-2 yds. Canvas, 14s., for threed, 3d.; Aug. 29, to sugar, 6d.; Aug. 30, to marchandise for thread, 6d., to rum, 1 gallon, 6s., wine 4 gallons, 3 qtrs. delivered to Jno. Gent p. his order & 22 1-2 li. sugar, 1li. 5s. 1d.; Nov. 20, brandy 1 quart, 2s., wine & rum, 1li. 9s., poorke 386li. at 4d. p. li., 6li. 8s. 8d., bisquits for 2-1-0 at 21s. p., 2li. 7s. 3d., marchandise for 2 holland neck-cloathes, 8s.; Nov. 28, to Thomas Millett, sr., for 2 bushells Indian Corne, 6s.; total, 18li. 15s. 10d. Henry Muddle, Creditor, Oct. 12, 1661: Oct. 20, By fish 4 quentalls refuse att 11s. p. qntl., 2li. 4s.; Mar. 1, By 159li. porke wch. the selectmen of Gloucster Delivered as they said to mee Beinge a parte of ye 386li. of porke wch. I Charge one the other side wch. the selectmen delivered mee at 5d. p., 3li. 6s. 8d.; Oct. 20, 1662, by the acctt. of his Estate wch. is Due to mee upon Ballance of this acctt. 13li. 5s. 7d.; total, 18li. 15s. 10d. *Essex Co. Quarterly Court Files, vol.* **9**, *leaf* 20.

### Estate of John Pomary of (Gloucester?).

John Pomary with Isaack Waklye and Henry Muddle having been cast away at sea, and none appearing to desire administration of his estate, and William Browne, constable of Gloster, presenting papers of the estate amounting to 4li. 11s. 11d., he was given charge Mar. 25, 1662 until further order. *Ipswich Quarterly Court Records, vol. 1, page 103.*

There being some estate of John Pomery, late deceased, in the hands of the widow Browne of Gloster, the marshal of this court June 24, 1662, was ordered to dispose of it according to the court's order. *Salem Quarterly Court Records, vol. 4, page 96.*

### Estate of James Mudge.

James Mudg, with Aniball Lane and William Homan, having been by God's providence cast away, and no will appearing, the court Mar. 25, 1662, granted administration upon his estate to Walter Sussex, a partner with them, and ordered him to bring in an inventory to the next Salem court. *Ipswich Quarterly Court Records, vol. 1, page 103.*

### Estate of Aniball Lane.

Aniball Lane, with James Mudg and William Homan, having been by God's providence cast away, and no will appearing, the court Mar. 25, 1662, granted administration upon his estate to Walter Sussex, a partner with them, and ordered him to bring in an inventory to the next Salem court. *Ipswich Quarterly Court Records, vol. 1, page 103.*

### Estate of William Homan.

William Homan, with James Mudg and Aniball Lane, having been by God's providence cast away, and no will appearing, the court Mar. 25, 1662, granted administration upon his estate to Walter Sussex, a partner with them, and ordered him to bring in an inventory to the next Salem court. *Ipswich Quarterly Court Records, vol. 1, page 103.*

### Estate of John Lookeman.

John Lookeman, with Nicolas Lookman, John Hart and Richard Holeman, having been cast away, and no will appearing, the court Mar. 25, 1662, granted administration upon his estate to Mr. George Corwin and Mr. Moses Maverick, and ordered them to bring in an inventory to the next Salem court. *Ipswich Quarterly Court Records, vol. 1, page* 103.

### ESTATE OF NICHOLAS LOOKMAN.

Nicholas Lookman, with John Lookeman, John Hart and Richard Holeman, having been cast away, and no will appearing, the court Mar. 25, 1662, granted administration upon his estate to Mr. George Corwin and Mr. Moses Maverick, and ordered them to bring in an inventory to the next Salem court. *Ipswich Quarterly Court Records, vol. 1, page* 103.

### ESTATE OF JOHN HART.

John Hart, with John and Nicolas Lookman and Richard Holeman, having been cast away, and no will appearing, the court Mar. 25, 1662, granted administration upon his estate to Mr. George Corwin and Mr. Moses Maverick, and ordered them to bring in an inventory to the next Salem court. *Ipswich Quarterly Court Records, vol. 1, page* 103.

### ESTATE OF RICHARD HOLMAN.

Richard Holeman, with John and Nicolas Lookman and John Hart, having been cast away, and no will appearing, the court Mar. 25, 1662, granted administration upon his estate to Mr. George Corwin and Mr. Moses Maverick, and ordered them to bring in an inventory to the next Salem court. *Ipswich Quarterly Court Records, vol. 1, page* 103.

### ESTATE OF SIFFORYE COCK.

Sifforye Cock, with John Anard and Tobiah Beckes, having been cast away, and no will appearing, the court Mar. 25, 1662, granted administration upon his estate to Mr. Edward Ting and Mr. James Brading, and ordered them to bring in an inventory to the next Salem court. *Ipswich Quarterly Court Records, vol. 1, page* 103.

### ESTATE OF JOHN ANARD.

John Anard, with Sifforye Cock and Tobiah Beckes, having been cast away, and no will appearing, the court Mar. 25,

1662, granted administration upon his estate to Mr. Edward Ting and Mr. James Brading, and ordered them to bring in an inventory to the next Salem court. *Ipswich Quarterly Court Records, vol. 1, page 103.*

### ESTATE OF TOBIAH BECKES.

Tobiah Beckes, with Sifforye Cock and John Anard, having been cast away, and no will appearing, the court Mar. 25, 1662, granted administration upon his estate to Mr. Edward Ting and Mr. James Brading, and ordered them to bring in an inventory to the next Salem court. *Ipswich Quarterly Court Records, vol. 1, page 103.*

### ESTATE OF THOMAS SMITH OF SALEM.

Administration on the estate of Thomas Smith, intestate, granted Mar. 25, 1662, to Mary Smith, relict of Thomas Smith and ordered her to bring in an inventory to the next Salem court. *Ipswich Quarterly Court Records, vol. 1, page 104.*

Inventory of the estate of Thomas Smith, late of Salem, taken 17: 4: 1662, by Jefferie Massey and Tho. Rootes: A dwelling house and quarter of an acre of land, 18li.; one Cowe, 4li.; 3 sheepe & 3 lambes, 2li. 10s.; 1 sowe, swyne & 2 shuits, 2li. 8s.; 1 feather bed, 3 feather boulsters & 4 feather pillows, 8li.; 2 beds fild wth. Flockes & otherwise, 2li.; 1 halfe head bedstead & 2 other bedsteeds, 1li. 4s.; 1 Greene Pott Rug, 1li. 8s.; 2 white blankets, 1li. 5s.; 2 bed Coverings, 1li. 10s.; 5 payre of Canvas sheets, 2li. 10s.; 5 payre of pillow beeres, 18s.; 5 table napkins, 12s.; 2 pewter dishes, 5s.; 1 pewter quart & 1 pewter pint, 7s.; 5 sawsers of pewter, 2s.; 1 beaker, 1 Cupp, 3 potenshees, 1 Candlesticke & 1 salt, 12s.; 2 basons, 1 Chamber pott, 1 brass candlestick & 2 bras cups, 15s.; 2 brass ketles, 2li. 15s.; a little brass ketle & a brass skellit, 6s.; 2 Iron pots & one Iron possnett, 18s.; 1 truncke, 1 Chest, 12s.; 2 Frying pans and a warming pan, 12s.; 2 spits, 2 hakes, a gridiron and five shovells & tongs, 16s.; over sea dishes of severall sorts, 1li.; 6 Cheares & 2 litle tables, 12s. 5d.; 2 hogshed barrells and other treene ware, 1li.; sword, musket & bandalires, 1li. 6s.; 3li. wool, 4s.; a shuete of apell, viz., Coate & breeches, 2li. 10s.; Coate, briches & wascote, 1li. 15s.; 1 hatt, 8s.; 1 payre of shag, 1 pare of stockens, 10s.; 2 shirts, 12s.; 2 shirts, 10s.; total,

63li. 15s. Debts out of the estate, 34li. 9s. 5d. The widow was not able to come to court, but the inventory was allowed at Salem court, 26: 9: 1662, and the estate given into the hands of the widow for the bringing up of the children. *Essex Co. Quarterly Court Files, vol. 8, leaf 95.*

### ESTATE OF GEORGE SMITH OF SALEM.

Administration on the estate of George Smith, intestate, granted Mar. 25, 1662 to his mother, Mary Smith, and ordered her to bring in an inventory to the next Salem court. *Ipswich Quarterly Court Records, vol. 1, page 104.*

Administration on the estate of George Smith, granted 25: 9: 1662, to Jeffery Marsy and Thomas Rootes, who were ordered to bring in an inventory. *Salem Quarterly Court Records, vol. 4, page 104.*

Inventory of the estate of George Smith, deceased, was allowed 30: 4: 1663, and his mother, the widow Smith, was appointed administratrix. *Salem Quarterly Court Records, vol. 4, page 119.*

Inventory of the estate of Georg Smith, late of Salem, taken Mar. 9, 1662-3, by Jefferie Massey and Tho. Rootes: One Cloth Cloke, 2li. 5s.; a short Coate, a wastcote, a payre of stuff breeches and an ould Coate, 3li. 8s.; 2 ould shirts, 7s.; 1 hatt, 7s.; 1 hatt, 3s.; 4 bands, 4s.; 8 handkerchifs, 8s.; 2 payre of stockings, 6s.; debts due, 1li. 6s.; total, 9li.; debts owing the estate, 2li. 11s. 3d. *Essex Co. Quarterly Court Files, vol. 9, leaf 20.*

### ESTATE OF RICHARD ELIOTT.

Richard Eliott with John Garven, having been cast away, and no will appearing, the court Mar. 25, 1662, granted administration upon his estate to Mr. George Corwin, and ordered him to bring in an inventory to the next Salem court. *Ipswich Quarterly Court Records, vol. 1, page 104.*

### ESTATE OF JOHN GARVEN.

John Garven with Richard Eliott, having been cast away, and no will appearing, the court Mar. 25, 1662, granted administration on his estate to Mr. George Corwin, and ordered him to bring in an inventory to the next Salem court. *Ipswich Quarterly Court Records, vol. 1, page 104.*

## Estate of John Balch of Salem.

Administration on the estate of John Balch, intestate, granted Mar. 25, 1662, to Mary Balch, the widow, and ordered her to bring in an inventory to the next Salem court. *Ipswich Quarterly Court Records, vol. 1, page 104.*

Inventory of the estate of John Balch of Salem, taken 19: 1: 1662, by Roger Conant and Samuell Corning: His house with 5 akers of land adjoyning, 35li.; the quarter part of his father's farm, about 50 akers, 50li.; two akers & half of meadoe in the old planters' salt marsh, 12li.; a mare and colt, 15li.; a Cow, 4li. 10s.; a fetherbed & bolster, a rugg, blankets & purtinances & bedsted, 10li. 10s.; another bed & bedsteed wth the purtinances, 6li. 10s.; some other smale bedding, 2li.; peuter platters & porringers, 5li.; a kettel, 2 skellets, a warming pan & skimer, 1li. 12s.; a smale iron pott & smale kettel & od iron, 8s.; 2 chests, a cubbord, and boxes, 2li.; a littel table and 4 chairs, 16s.; his waring apparrell, 10li.; 2 cusshions & some sea garments, 1li. 3s.; pillobiers, sheets and napkins, 6li. 10s.; a fring pan, a bellose & smoothing iron, 8s.; 2 hatts, 1li.; an eighth part of a ketch prised at 26li., but this is still owing for, and more also; total, 189li. 17s. There is owing to Lott Conant of Marblehead, 26li.; more in other debts 4li.; total, 30li. Debts to be added to John Balch's debts: Due to Captin Price, 9li. 16s. 3d.; his funeral expences, 2li. 1s. 6d.; for keeping a sick and weakly child, viz., Mary Balch, six months, 10s.; to the doctor, 10s. *Essex Co. Quarterly Court Files, vol. 8, leaf 23.*

Inventory amounting to 159li. 17s., was allowed June 24, 1662. The whole estate was to be divided between the widow Mary and the child Mary, and was to remain in the hands of the widow until the child became of age or married. *Salem Quarterly Court Records, vol. 1, page 97.*

Whereas administration was granted to Mary Balch on the estate of her late husband Jo. Balch, and the Salem court in the fourth month, 1662, divided the estate between said Mary Balch and Mary, the daughter of John Balch, deceased, and now said daughter being deceased, it was ordered Mar. 31, 1663, that Benjamine Balch, after the end of seven years, should enjoy all the lands that belonged to said John Balch, 50 acres more or less, the said Mary to enjoy all the improved land, upland and meadow, during the term of seven years. *Ipswich Quarterly Court Records, vol. 1, page* 115.

William Dodge acknowledged judgment Sept. 26, 1665, to Capt. Walter Price for a debt of John Balch, deceased, said Dodge's wife being executrix of the estate of said Balch. *Ipswich Quarterly Court Records, vol. 1, page 146.*

The agreement of Benjamin Balch and William Dodge that the first settlement at Salem court should stand, the land and moveables to be divided equally, and the debts due when John Balch died to be paid by them equally, provided that all later settlements be made void and that each shall hold that part which is now in his possession. The three acres of meadow expressed by deed of gift to William Dodge, also the 2 1-2 acres of marsh at Salem shall be accounted as part of Benjamin Balch's estate and there shall be 16li. allowed for the debts. Signed 1: 2: 1682.

Sworn to in Ipswich court Mar. 28, 1682 by Benjamin Balch and William Dodge, and allowed. *Ipswich Deeds, vol. 4, page 438.*

### Estate of William Adams of Ipswich.

The will of William Addams proved Mar. 25, 1662, and inventory received. *Ipswich Quarterly Court Records, vol. 1, page 104.*

An agreement made Apr. 24, 1668, between Nathaniell Addams of Ipswich and Samuell Addams his brother; that all the lands and goods which William Addams their father had bequeathed to them should be equally divided between them according to the true meaning of the will, allowing convenient maintenance unto his wife during her life, and paying such portions as their father had bequeathed unto his daughters. The house and barn and all the land about the house wherein the said Nathaniell now dwelleth containing about 16 acres, also another division of land lying between the land of Samuell Addams, brother to Nathaniell and the land of Thomas Stace, bounded by a long hill running down from the thick woods to a piece of meadow appertaining to John Addams, our brother, that he bought of Anthony Potter, also another piece of meadow being upon the Black brooke, bounded northwest by a point of upland running down to the brook & southeast by the land of Symon Stacy, shall belong unto Nathaniell and his heirs forever. All the land that is now in the occupation of Samuell Adams, being an entire parcell of land joining to Mr. Saltonstall's farm shall belong to him and his heirs forever. And all the goods and chattells that are at present in the possession of either of them shall so continue to them and their heirs. Signed and sealed Apr. 24, 1668 by Samuell Addams. Witness: William White, Thomas Waite.

Acknowledged June 30, 1668 by Samuell Addams. *Ipswich Deeds, vol. 3, page 79.*

### Estate of John Dorman of Topsfield.

Administration on the estate of John Dorman, intestate, granted Mar. 25, 1662 to Mary Dorman, the widow, and the inventory was allowed. *Ipswich Quarterly Court Records, vol. 1, page 104.*

Inventory taken Feb. 12, 1661, by Francis Pebody and Samuell Brocklebanke: One booke and Aperell, one cloke, 2li. 5s. 6d.; one jackit and briches, 2li.; one wascoate, 7s.; one dublit and a paire of briches, 1li. 1s.; three paire of stockins, 8s.; Gloves, 6s.; one Inkhorne, 4d.; one neckcloath, 8d.; one hate, 10s.; another wascoate jackit and two paire of briches, 1li. 15s.; one paire of boots, spurs and 2 paire of shooes, 1li. 1s.; in sheets, shirt and other linen, 2li. 15s.; 4 cushins, 12s.; 4 bands and 3 handkercheifers, 9s. 6d.; one bedstead and beding on it, 7li. 8s.; musket, sword and amunition, 1li. 15s.; puter and spounes, 12s. 6d.; one drinkeing ———and brase skellitt, 4s.; in earthen and wooden dishes and trayes, 6s. 4d.; in chest and boxe, 9s.; in one Iron pot and pothookes, 12s.; wheat, 3li.; one meall trough and one sith, 3s.; in flaxe and hempe, 16s.; in two swine, 2li. 13s.; in two cows, one stere calfe, 10li. 6s. 8d.; in Indian corne unthrashed, by estimation about therty bushell, 3li.; more in wheat unwinowed, about 4 bushell, 1li.; total, 46li. 1s.; in debts dew to the deceased from Thomas Baker, 4 bushels of wheat, 1li.; debt due from Peter Cowper as part of portion, 21li.; debt due by bond from Thomas Dorman, 50li.; debts to be paid out of the estate, 8li. 6s. 6d. "Be this knowne unto all men that Thomas Dorman of the towne of Topsfeild Hath and doth freely expresse himselfe that for a quiete and loueing Agreement betwene peter couper and him in differance about that estate that the said peter couper did expect that his daughter should haue bene estated in, he would Giue unto the said Mary dorman." *Essex Co. Quarterly Court Files, vol. 7, leaf 94.*

### ESTATE OF WILLIAM HARKER OF LYNN.

Inventory of the estate of Willylam Harker taken Dec. 26, 1661, by Thomas Marshall, Franceis (his P mark) Ingolles and Henry Collins: Howsing, upland and meadow, 60li.; one yoke of oxen and thre cows and fowr load of hay, 27li.; tow mars and on Coult, 36li.; thre yearling calfs, 3li. 16s.; six sheap, 3li. 2s.; thirten Swyn, 5li.; forty tow buchils of English and Indyan Corn, 7li. 3s. 6d.; The man and woman wearing Aparell, 7li. 10s.; one fether bed, tow Rugs, tow pare of Blankits, 7li. 13s.; seven pillows, 1 pillow bear, one bolster, 2li. 15s.; fowr pare of sheets, 2li. 2s.; seven yards of ——— Cloth, thre yards Cotton Cloth, 2li.; nyn yards ———, six yards of serge, 4li. 12s.; Eight yards ——— alf of red Shag, 1li. 9s.; ten pound ———en wooll, 10 pound of hony, 17s. 4d.; one ould ———, 3li. 5s.; 2 brace ——— iron pott, and on ———, 2li. 14s.; two Sp———, tongs and ——— 13s. 6d.; Twenty ———, 17s.; one axe, ——— knife, 3s.; presing ——— Iron 6s.; warming ———, 3s.; one Croscut ——— ells, 1li. 3s.; thre Ches——— and other ———, 1li.; one Churn, one Erthen pot and other things, 5s. 6d.; six pound of wool, one Stak of bees, 1li. 6s.; one pannell, Cask and other lumber, 17s.; one brydell, one spad, one plow, 3s. Proved in Ipswich court, Mar. 25, 1662 before Robert Lord, cleric. *Essex Co. Quarterly Court Files, vol. 7, leaf 98.*

### ESTATE OF DANIEL RINGE OF IPSWICH.

"The last will and Testament of Daniell Ringe of Ipsw[ch] this 3[d] day of ffebruary 1661. In the name of God Amen I Daniell Ringe being of pfect memory and understanding do dispose of that outward estate that God hath giuen mee in manner as followeth In the first place I comit my soule to Allmighty God and my body to decent buryall I giue unto Mary my beloued wife one third part of my ffarme now in the hands of Daniell Davison during the terme of her naturall life, and after her decease to be deuided amongst my three Sonnes the Eldest to haue a double share thereof I giue and bequeath unto my three Sonnes Daniell Roger and Isaack my farme aboues[d] to bee deuided amongst them the Eldest to haue a double part therof the two youngest to be equall, and they to take possession therof at the age of one and twenty my wiues third part being reserued for her during her life and then her thirds part to bee deuided according to y$^r$ proportion abouesayd. I giue and bequeath unto my three daughters Mary Susanna and Sarah Thirty pounds to each of them and they to haue possessio therof at ye age of sixteen or at the time of their marriage I leaue my house and lands now in y$^e$ possessio of Thomas wayt unto my Wife to emproue till my youngest two Daughters shall bee of age that if they desire it they may haue the same for their portions allowing the ouerplus of their portions to my other Daughter as part of her portion or if they Desire it not, to bee left to y$^e$ Executo$^{rs}$ to dispose of for y$^e$ discharge of my Daughters portions.

"My mind and will is that if my Eldest Son shall dye without children that his portion shall be left to the two yonger Brothers the Elder of them two to haue a double share therof, puided that he allow to each of his Sisters fiue pounds, and if both the Eldest dy childlesse the youngest to inherit their portions allowing to each of my Daughters ten pounds, or if the youngest leaue no children the two Eldest to inherit his portion the Eldest hauing a double share and if the two youngest leaue no children the Eldest to inherit their portions paying to Each of my Daughters ten pounds. If my wife marryeth my mind is her husband shall giue sufficient security for what estate he is possessed of by my wife, for the discharge of my childrens portions The remainder of my Estate I leaue to my wife to Dispose of at her decease Equally amongst all my children My mind is that if my wife marryeth my children shall haue liberty if they desire it to bee disposed of to good seruices as they shall think meet to whom they are betrusted Which to Confirme I haue herunto set my hand this third of february one thousand, six hundred sixty and one I Constitute and appoint my louing friends Deacon William Goodhue and Daniell Houey sen$^r$ of Ips$^{wh}$ And my wife Executo$^{rs}$ and Executrix of this my Last will and Testam$^t$ and Rich$^d$ Hubberd and John Dane sen$^r$ ouerseers."

his mark<br>Daniel C Ringe

Witness: Robort Kinsman, Junier, Richard Jacob.

Proved in Ipswich court Mar. 25, 1662 by Robert Kinsman and John Dane.

Inventory taken by John Whipple, 3d and John Whipple,

Jr.: The Goods in the house and first in ye Parlor: One chest with Apparell, 7li. 10s.; Two chests, 10s.; A Bedstead and bedding, 6li. 10s.; Three chayres and Cushions, 5s. 6d.; One warming Pan, A brush & looking glasse, 11s.; a Piece of Taffaty, 1li. 10s.; A case with 7 Glasses, 3s. 6d.; A chest and 3 Boxes, 12s.; A carpet, 15s.; One dozen of Napkins, 1li. 10s.; A dozen of Napkins, 12s.; A Table cloath & Two Pillowbeers, 10s.; Sheets & other linnen, 4li. 4s.; A Table, 1li. 10s.; Saddles, bridles & furniture for traiping, 3li. In the Hall: In Peuter, 3li.; skillets and dishes, 1li.; An iron kettle and pot, 10s.; firepan, tongs & spitt, 14s.; A musquet, 1li.; A pot & kettle, 1-s.; A morter, 5s.; chesmotes, trayes & other lumber, 1li. 2s.; Carpenters tooles, 7s.; Other tooles & two bottles, 2s.; Two Axes, 5s.; An iron Pot, a Kneading trough, —s.; cheespresse, barrells & firkins, 1li. 3s.; a Piece of beeswax, 4s. In the chamber: In bedding, 3li.; ——— for an ordinary, 1li.; Indian corne, seaventy bushells, 10li. 10s.; Wheat twenty five bushells, 6li. 5s.; Oates, Rye and peas, 2li.; Bed and bedstead, 2li.; More wheat & barly, 2li. 10s.; In flesh meat, 2li.; In mony, 2li. 12s. Without the house: A cart & wheels, yokes, chaynes, 3li. 10s.; hay, 2li. In Cattle: one horse, 10li.; Two oxen, 12li.; Nine Cowes, 40li. 10s.; foure Yearlings, 5li.; A Bull, 3li.; A three yeer old steer, 4li.; Three heyfers, 7li. 10s.; foure Calves, 1li.; Twenty-five swine, 14li.; five acres of Rye upon ye ground, 5li. In Land: A farme in the hands of Daniel Davison Conteyning by estimation an hundred and ten acres, 182li.; A house and land in ye towne in ye hands of Thomas Wayt, twelve acres, 70li. Debts: By Daniell Davison, 19li.; William Rayner, 5li.; Richard Walker, 3li.; John Adams, 4li. Sum total, 463li. 11s. Debts out of ye estate: To Mr. William Hubbard, 70li.; John Whipple, Jr., 8li.; Mr. John Payne, 6li.; In other debts about 20li.

Proved in Ipswich court Mar. 25, 1662.

*Essex Co. Probate Files, Docket 23,714.*

### GUARDIANSHIP OF DANIEL TILTON OF LYNN.

Daniell Tilton chose Samuell Tilton as his guardian, and the court allowed it Apr. 8, 1662.

Court Apr. 8, 1662 ordered that Joseph Shaw pay to Daniel Tilton 40s. in consideration of what service he had done for him since he was fourteen years old.

Court Apr. 8, 1662 ordered Sam. Tilton to put in security to Daniel's portion in binding over land.
*Salisbury Quarterly Court Records, vol. 1, leaf 3.*

ESTATE OF ANN LUME OF ROWLEY.

Administration on the estate of Ann Lume, intestate, granted Apr. 17, 1662, to Judith Lume and Susanah Lume, her daughters. *Ipswich Quarterly Court Records, vol. 1, page 106.*

Inventory taken Apr. 16, 1662, by Maxemillion Jewett and Samuell Brocklebanke: Aparell, 4li.; one bed, with furniture on it, 4li. 10s.; puter and Tin, 1li.; brase and Iron vessels, 1li. 2s. 6d.; wooden vessell, 10s.; table, chaires and cushings, 16s.; whelle and cards, 4s.; house and land, 20li.; three cowes, one calfe and one 2 yeareing, 17li.; total, 49li. 2s. 6d. Allowed Apr. 17, 1662. *Essex Co. Quarterly Court Files, vol. 7, leaf 98.*

The Ipswich court Mar. 18, 1664 ordered an equal division of the estate of Ann Lumbe between her two daughters, Judith and Susannah Lumbe, the house and lot to Susanna and the moveables to Judith Lumbe.

Acknowledged by Joshua Bradley to be the agreement between his wife Judith and his sister Susanna, which he approveth before me Daniell Denison. *Ipswich Deeds, vol. 2, page 225.*

Deposition of Samuell Brocklebanke, aged about 36 years, being in court when an inventory of the estate of Ann Lum was presented, and before administration was granted to the two daughters of the said Ann, that he heard John Pickard son of the aforesaid Ann say he did not desire to have the administration but desired that it might be granted to his sisters, and also that he did not expect any of the estate. When administration was granted to the two sisters equally, he was desired to be helpful to them in the division. Sworne in Ipswich court Mar. 29, 1664.

William Stickney deposed that John Pickard did own to him in way of discourse what is expressed by Lt. Brocklebanke in the testimony above written. Sworn in Ipswich court Mar. 29, 1664.

*Ipswich Deeds, vol. 2, page 197.*

## Estate of Thomas Dickinson of Rowley.

"I Thomas Dickinson of The Towne of Rowley in The County of esex being weake of Body but of perfect vnderstanding And memmory doe make And ordaine This my last will and Testament  In primis my will is That my welbeloued wife Jennett Dickinson shalbe my Solle excequtrise for To pay all my debts and to pay my childeren Those portions That I by will doe Giue vnto Them; And also To demand and Recouer all debts that are or may be due vnto me by bills bonds or otherwise and To doe any Thinge belonging To such an excequtorise.  Item I will and Giue vnto This my welbeloued wife halfe of ‖my‖ Dwelling house halfe of my barne halfe of my orchard and halfe of my swampe below my orchard and all my land aboue The barne about Twellue Acres be it more or lese And Three Acres of meadow one acre of it in batchelor meadow and Two Acres in the northeast feild as also one acre more of salt marsh in the marsh feild bounded by deacon Jewets marsh on the west and by marsh of John pickards on the north and also i doe Giue vnto hir Two Gates on the Towne common al this I doe Giue hir dureing hir naturall life  Item  I will And Giue vnto my son James dickinson The other halfe of my houseing barne orchard and swampe below the orchard and all other my lands meadowes and Commons that belonge vnto me with The Towne of Rowley (excepting my village land and Two Acres of meadow in The great meadow be it more or lese.)  Item I doe Giue vnto my son James dickinson foure score Acres of land more or lese being my deuission of land in that land Commonly called merrimack land buting against merrimacke Riuer with the priueledges belonging vnto the said fourscore acres of land and likewise I doe Giue vnto my son James my houseing barne orchard and swampe and lands aboue the barne and meadow and commons That I haue giuen vnto my welbeloued wife for her naturall life to be his vnto his proper use and behoufe after his mothers decease.  Item I doe further Giue vnto my son James my cart and plough and furneture belonging There To also I giue vnto him my loumes and furneture belonging There To

"Item out of The Rest of my estate That is in my village land and Two Acres of meadow in the Great meadow that was before excepted and in my stocke moueables bills bonds or any other estat that is or may be due vnto me out of This Remaneing part of my estat I will and Giue vnto my foure daughters each of Them one hundred pounds and my will is that that fifty pounds That I haue giuen vnto my daughter Sarah alredy shalbe acounted as part of that which I doe now giue And if any of my childeren die before they attaine to the age of Twenty one yeares or day of marriage Then There portions to be devided equally among the rest and if my Son James depart This life haueing noe child Then the one halfe of those lands I giue him to Returne to be equally devided among The Rest of my daughters or Theire heires The other halfe I giue vnto his wife if then liueing to be for hir use dureing hir nattural life and then to returne after hir decease to be equally devided among my other daughters or there children if ther be any then liueing Item I will and Giue (the Three hundred and fifty pounds being paid out of this estat that I here apoint for the payment of my daughters portions) all the Remaineing part of that estat vnto my welbeloued wife To be vnto hir owne proper use and To despose of as she shall Thinke meete; And my will is that my wife shall haue hir liberty to chuse which halfe of my dwelling house she will for to liue in dureing hir life; And I appoint John pickard and Samuell Brocklebanke To be ouersseers of This my last will and Testament which I Confirme with my owne hand this eighth of march one Thoussand Six hundred and sixty one or sixty two"

Thomas Dickanson

Witness: Samuell Brocklebanke, John trumble.

Proved in Ipswich court Apr. 17, 1662 by the witnesses. *Essex Co. Probate Files, Docket 7,678.*

An inventory of the estate received in court Apr. 17, 1662. *Ipswich Quarterly Court Records, vol. 1, page 106.*

### Estate of Thomas Lee of Ipswich.

"The last Will and Testament of Thomas Lee of Ipsw^ch In the name of God amen I Thomas Lee of Ipswich being at this present time of perfect memory and understanding doe dispose of that outward estate that God hath giuen mee in manner as followeth: In the first place I comit my soule to God and my body to decent buryall. My mind and will is that Alice my beloued wife shall haue the sole disposing of my farme and the rest of my estate upon these Considerations that is to say. That my Grandson Richard Lee shall liue and abide with her untill he shall bee two and twenty yeares of age then my whole estate to be Deuided and Richard shall haue an equall share with my wife only my wife shall haue the use of my now Dwelling house during the terme of her life unlesse she shall bee willing that they both may liue together but if my wife should marry my mind is that shee shall haue fiue pounds euery yeare out of my estate during the terme of her life, and the abouenamed Richard to haue my estate at y$^e$ age of two and twenty. My mind allso is that if my wife shall continue a Widow and enjoy such a share of my estate as is aforesaid that after her decease my foresayd Granchild shall inherit all that estate shee shall leaue, Twenty pounds being excepted which I giue and bequeath to my Daughter Susanna now in England or her children if any of them shall bee here to demand the same within y$^e$ space of seauen yeares from this present time My will is that Richard my Grandchild shall not haue liberty to Alien sell or bargaine my farme or any part therof but that it bee reserued entire to him and his heires. If my wife shall not think meet that Rich$^d$ my Grandchild should abide with her for the p$^r$sent shee shall haue liberty to dispose of him to some Good seruice till he shall come to bee at the age of two and twenty In witnesse of this my Will and testament I haue hereunto set my hand and seal this nineteenth of March one thousand six hundred sixty one I constitute and appoint Allice my wife onely Executrix of this my last will and Testament."

            his mark
          Thomas T Lee (seal)

 Witness: Richad Brabrook, James gregory.

 Proved in Ipswich court Apr. 17, 1662 by Richard Hubbard and Richard Brabrooke.

 Inventory of estate of Thomas Lee, deceased Mar. 23 last past, taken Apr. 10, 1662 by George Giddinge and Daniel Hovey: the wearing Close, 2li. 5s.; a payer of bulloks, 12li.; seven Cows & their Cafs, 31li.; 2 buls, 5li.; one heifor, 2li.; 4 yockes, 4li.; a sow & 7 shoats, 3li. 3s.; beding, 4li. 10s.; 2 chests, on box, a tabl, old tubs wth other lumber, 2li.; an old bibl wth other trad, 6s. 8d.; bras & pewter, 2li. 8s.; an old musket, 10s.; 2 axses, betl & wedges & hows, a Clever, a bill, a smal saw & such like, 1li.; siths & sikles, 10s.; 3 saks, 6s.; a tumbril, on plow, 15s.; 2 Chayns, a shar & colter wth expins, 1li.; sadl, pillion & bridl, 1li. 10s.; seed Corn, 2li. 5s.; iron hoops for vesels, 8s.; a shovel, 1 spad & hamer, 2s. 6d.; a fan, 10s.; a payr of feters & *brpe &c*, 4s.; house & barn wth the homsted wth ye upland withing ye fence & 2 parsels of salt marsh, ye one in ye great marsh next hog iland ye other next chebaco river, 120li.; total, 198li. 3s. 2d. Debts amounting to about 40li.

Testified to in Ipswich court Apr. 17, 1662 by Alice wife of Thomas Leigh.

*Essex Co. Probate Files, Docket 16,659.*

### ESTATE OF SAMUEL SHERMAN OF IPSWICH.

In answer to the petition of Samuell and Nathaniell Sherman and Mary Clarke children of Samuell Shearman, long since deceased, the committee of the court having considered the petition and answer of Mr. Colebron, one of the administrators to that estate, returned that the petitioners had no such cause of complaint therein, which the court May 7, 1662 allowed and confirmed. *Mass. Bay Colony Records, vol. 4, page 47.*

### ESTATE OF DANIEL REA OF SALEM.

"Whereas there hath been a Will begun to be made by Daniell Rea of Salem, lately deceased, but he not being able to finish it, whereby great inconvenience is like to arise to his Children, if it be left as it is, Wee therefore whose names are vnderwritten, takeing it into our Consideration, haue made this our Joynt Conclusion & Agreement, (if the Honored Court ‖now Assembled‖ please to Accept of, & Confirme the same) in Manner as followeth. ffirst, that his sonne Joshua Rea shall haue y$^e$ Improuement of the whole farme, where he lives, & when his sonne Daniel is growne vp to y$^e$ Age of Twenty one yeares, he shall have halfe y$^e$ farme, & his father to have y$^e$ other halfe, dureing y$^e$ terme of his owne life, & also of his wives widdowhood, in Case she should outlive him, & then that halfe also to be his sonne Daniels, & so y$^e$ said Daniel then to haue y$^e$ whole farme, which is y$^e$ proper Will of y$^e$ Testator. Secondly, that y$^e$ said Joshua Rea shall haue the vse & improvement of the seventeene Acres of land, lying on Salem North River, vntill his two daughters, Rebecca & Sarah, exprest in y$^e$ will, shall attaine to y$^e$ age of sixteene yeares, & then they to haue y$^e$ land with y$^e$ improvement of y$^e$ same equally divided betwixt them. Thirdly that y$^e$ said Joshua Rea, shall have also the one Acre & halfe on the South Rivers side in Salem, as his proper right, to dispose of as he shall see cause. ffourthly, that his sonne

Thomas Lothrop, & his wife, shall haue the ffarme, Comonly Called Captaine Damports farme, as their proper right, to dispose of, as they please, provided that the five pound, paid already by me to Capt. Damport, in a Cowe, be allowed me out of y$^e$ other estate. fifthly that our Mother shall have y$^e$ Thirds, of all of this Estate, dureing her life. Lastly, for the rest of y$^e$ Estate, we leave it to the wisedome of the Honoured Court, to dispose of the same, as they shall thinke best, according to lawe."

"This aboue writing or agreement is by the Court alowed of & is to be as the Courts determination & ordering of the estate of Danyell Ray deceased being consented ‖there‖ to by y$^e$ children of y$^e$ deceased in Court at Salem: 4 $^{mo}$ 1662 atteste, Hillyard Verin Cleric:"

Proved in Salem court 24: 4: 1662. *Essex Co. Quarterly Court Files, vol. 8, leaf 16.*

Inventory of the estate of Daniell Ray, taken by John Porter and Jacob Barney: His apparell, 7li. 11s. 10d.; a feather bed, 2 bolsters and 3 pillowes, 4li.; 2 Coverletts, 1li.; 2 blanketts, 1li. 10s.; 2 pillow beares, five sheets, 1li. 10s.; a kettle with other small things, 2li.; 2 dishes and a pinte pot, 8s.; 2 Iron skilletts and a frying pan, 12s.; a paire of pot hangings & a paire of Tongs, 10s.; a paire of fetters, an axe, & a hatchet, with other things, 12s. 6d.; a pecke, 3 traies & a platter, 4s.; a paire of traisses & a halter, 2s.; a winowing sheet & 4 sackes, 10s.; 6li. of wooll, 6s.; a saddle & pillion, 1li.; a chest & a bedsted, 18s.; a Chaire & 2 Joynt stooles, 4s.; a paile with 2 stooles, with other things, 2s.; 3 yards & a halfe of Cloth, 1li. 15s.; a mare & a Colt, 14li.; a Cow & a Calfe, 5li. 16s.; 6 sheepe, 2li. 8s.; 17 acres of land in the north field, 25li.; an acre & a halfe of salt marsh upon the South river, 5li.; a farme of 160 acres of upland & 10 acres of meadow, 150li.; debts due to the deceased, 14li.; total, 239li. 19s. 4d. Proved 26: 4: 1662. *Essex Co. Quarterly Court Files, vol. 8, leaf 17.*

Joshua Ray was appointed June 24, 1662, administrator of the estate of Danyell Ray, deceased, who died intestate, but his mind being understood and his children agreeing thereto, they drew up a writing about the division of part of the estate, as land, etc., leaving the other part to the court's ordering. The court approved the writing, and concerning the other part of the estate, Joshua Ray, son of the deceased, was to have 25li. and Capt. Tho. Lothrop, said Daniel's son-in-law, was to have all the rest of the estate, provided he keep and maintain his mother, the widow, during her life. *Salem Quarterly Court Records, vol. 4, page 94.*

### ESTATE OF JOHN STEVENS OF ANDOVER.

Administration on the estate of John Steevens, intestate, granted June 24, 1662 to his widow, Eliza Steevens. An inventory amounting to 463li. 4s., was also allowed. Court ordered that John Steevens, son of the deceased, should have 74li. paid at demand, and Timothy, Nathan, Ephraim, Joseph, Benjamin and Mary, the other children, should have 37li. each, paid at age or time of marriage, and the remainder of the estate to be at the disposal of the widow. *Salem Quarterly Court Records, vol. 4, page 94.*

Inventory of the estate of John Steevens of Andover, taken Apr. 28, 1662, by Nicholas Noyes, George Abboott, sr., Richard Barker and Nathan Parker: His wearing Aparrell, 10li.; In the hall, two beds with there furniture, 15li.; One Chest & foure boxes, 1li.; Eight payre of sheets, foure Bolster cases and three payre of Pillow beeres, 7li. 10s.; Three table cloaths, one dozen of Napkins, with other sleight things, 2li. 5s.; in ye kitchin, one Brasse Pott, foure small Kettles, one Skillett, a Scummer & Warming pan, 2li.; one Iron Pott, an iron posnett, two payre of potthookes, two trammells, a spitt, a payre of tonges & firepan, a payre of cob irons with a smoothing iron & a trivett, 1li. 10s.; six peuter platters, two basens, two porrengers, foure drinken cupps, a salt sellar, a chamber pott, a dozen & halfe of spoones and a latten pan, 2li. 5s.; A tableboard & forme, foure chayres, two cushens, two dozen of trenchers and halfe a dozen of dishes, 14s.; a muskett, corslett & headpeece, a sword & cutlass & holbert, 2li. 5s.; bible, with other books, 1li.; In the Leanetoo, Barrells, wheeles, treyes, with other lumber, 2li.; In the chamber, Bedding, 5li.; wheate, twenty Bushells, Indian corne, ten Bushells, 6li. 10s.; A bridle & sadle & pannell, 1li.; two flitches of Bacon, 2li.; Baggs, 1li.; Flax & yarne, 5li.; Old tubbs & other lumber, 10s.; Sawes, axes, pronges, with other working tooles, 3li.; Eight oxen, 51li.; Six cowes, 24li.; a heifer & two yearlings, 6li.; three calves, 1li.; swine, 12li.; A colt and an Asse, 4li.; horse, 10li.; three sheep, 1li.; one stocke of bees, 10s.; Carts, sleads, yoakes, chaines, plowes &

plow irons, ropes and tackling to it, 6li. 2s.; house, barnes, upland & meadow and corne upon ye ground, 200li.; debts, 2li. The sequell of this inventory was given by the deceased to his eldest sonn John Steevens: A house, orchard and land, 50li.; one cow, two steers of two yeare old & a yearling, two swine and two sheepe, 15li.; All ye rights & privilidges that is to be granted by ye towne by virtue of twenty-five Acres of ground granted to mee, John Steevens; three acres of home meadow, 9li. "These testyfye yt I John Steevens doe accept of the above specifyed estate appointed mee of my father before his death in full satisfaction for my portion amounts to seaventy foure pound prouided the honoured Court at Psalem shall see good to confirme it Wittnesse my hand John Steevens." Total, 463li. 4s. Elizabeth Steevens, widow, made oath in court before Hillyard Veren, cleric. *Essex Co. Quarterly Court Files, vol. 8, leaf 18.*

ESTATE OF CORP. JOHN ANDREWS OF IPSWICH.*

Administration on the estate of John Andrews granted June 24, 1662 to Mr. Tho. Andrewes. An inventory was also allowed, excepting the farm and the crop upon the ground, which latter were referred to the next Ipswich court, partly because the farm was mortgaged and partly because of the failure of the crop by reason of the drought, and he was to provide for the widow and children until the court take further order. *Salem Quarterly Court Records, vol. 4, page 95.*

Inventory of the estate of Corpll. John Andrews, taken May 23, 1662, by John Dowlettell, John Hathorne and Andrew Mansfeild: One dwelling house, 150li.; tow barnes, 90li.; a bake house, 2li. 10s.; an orchard, 100li.; an hundred acres of upland and medow belonging to the farme, 590li.; one horse, 12li.; tow Cowes & tow caulfes, 12li.; one three yeare ould steere, 5li.; six sheepe & three lambs, 5li. 5s.; to forty acres of corne upon the ground, 40li.; one grinstone, 16s.; a tumbrill & a paire of Iron bound wheeles, 4li.; a ladder, 10s.; five swine, 6li. 5s.; tow stocks of bees & tow swarmes, 2li. 10s.; an Iron furnis, 3li.; an Iron trumill, 7s.; tow horse collers & trases, &c., 12s.; five axes & a mathooke, 1li. 1s.; tow howes & a spad, an ads & a frow, 13s.; tow

* See also Records and Files of the Quarterly Courts of Essex Co., Mass., vol. 3 (1913), pp. 46, 47, 162-166.

plowes with irons & a colter & sheare, 1li. 14s.; three chaines, yoaks, chaine & bolts, 1li. 11s. 6d.; a stone cart & sleid & a ould cart body & a dubble brake, 1li. 15s.; three forks & a paire of fetters, 9s. In the kichin: Tenn ould pueter platters, quart potts & other ould pewter, 3li. 4s.; half a dussen of ould spoones, tow old brass kittles & ould pott and a warmeing pan & a candle stick, 2li. 7s. 6d.; Iron potts, one Iron kitle, one Iron skillett & other ould things, 1li. 15s.; severall ould wooden things, 8s.; severall augers, chissells & other ould Iron things, 2li. 5s.; tow cross cut sawes, a paire of andirones & paire of tongs & slice, 1li. 9s. 6d.; tow tramills, a gridiron, a spitt, a smoothing iron & a paire of sheirs, 15s.; tow muscutts, a fouling peece & 2 paire of skeals & waites, 3li. 14s. 6d.; a pike, tow chairs, & tow ould tubbs & 3 dussen of trenchers, 15s.; a woolen wheele, 2 cans, glases & gally potts, 8s.; a sadle, bridle, pistolls, holsters, belt & Cutlis & pillion, 5li. 5s. In the Parlor: Tow bedsteds, one fether bed, bolster, 2 pillows, a rug & curtaines, 6li. 10s.; a trunke, 2 boxes, 2 chairs, one cubburd & cloath, 2li. 2s.; table, 5 cushins & 5 chanye dishes, 1li.; his wearing apparill, 5li. 10s. In the chamber over the chichin: 5 paire of sheets, 2 table cloaths, 12 napkins, 4 pillow beers & a chest, 6li. 7s.; a bedsted, 2 flock beds, three pillos, one rug, one blankett, 3li. 10s.; one table, tow wheels & other ould lumber, 1li. In the garret: Tow Cosletts & other ould lumber, 2li.; on flock bed, bolster & 2 coverlids, 16s.; a gun, 5s.; in the seller, 2 barrills, 10s.; beetle & wedges, 5s.; total, 1083li. 19s. 6d. To halfe a barn at Ipswich, 6li.; bed, 4li. 15s.; 6 pewter dishes, 1li. 5s. 6d.; flax, 4li.; debts recoverable, 16li. 18s. 10d. Estate is debtor: To funeral charges, 2li.; houshold expenses, 2li. 11s.; to ye honoured Mr. Simon Bradstreet, about 400li.; other debt demanders, 314li.; to an assurance, 40li. Sworn by Mr. Thomas Andrewes in Salem court.

The Cattle and moveables conteined in ye Inventory of ye Estate of Corporal John Andreus, which was presented to ye County Court held at Salem 26: 4: 1662, 127li. 9s. 6d.; debts due to deceased, 40li. 11s.; the Corne upon ye farme and other pduce, 30li. 19s.; total, 198li. 19s. 6d. Out of which is to be deducted: Funeral Charges and expences before Salem court, 4li. 17s. 6d.; family expences since, 15li. 16s. 11d.; Charges about ye Corne, 6li.; ye administrators own labor, time, charges, &c., 10li. Debts demanded and presented to Salem court and since examined, as opportunity would serve, 312li. 14s. 9d. The foregoing account was presented to court at Ipswich in Sept. last, and then omitted to be left on file. The court sitting in Salem, 2: 5: 1663, ordered it to be safely kept in the court records. *Essex Co. Quarterly Court Files, vol. 8, leaf 20.*

Court Mar. 31, 1663 appointed Capt. Thomas Marshall, Mr. Oliver Purchase and Sergt. John Porter a committee to set off to Sarah, relict of Corpll. John Andrews, deceased, her third part of her late husband's farm, not meddling with the forty acres purchased of Mr. Price. *Ipswich Quarterly Court Records, vol. 1, page 117.*

### ESTATE OF JOHN ROW OF GLOUCESTER.

"In the name of god Amen: I John Row in my will and Testament; being in my perfect sences doe giue and Resine my soule to god that gaue it: and my Body to the earth to be Buried; and my goods: I despose of; As followeth: I giue all my wholle estat which god hath bestowed upon me; to my wife and my to sonns; That is to say to my wife; and my sonne John; and my Sonn huah; to be equally deuided Betweene them and to euery one a like: and as for my wife: if her third part of goods will not maintaine her; it is my will y$^t$ my too sonns shall maintaine her all her dais; if in case shee liue unmaried; And if she doe mary, what goods she haue at her decease shall be equaly deuided to my to sonns: That is to say what estate she haue; at her day of mariage; and if either of these to sonns dye unmaried his estat shalbe his Brothers that doe Remaine a liue: and in wittnes hereof I set my hand; Dated y$^e$: 15$^{th}$: of y$^e$ 8: m$^o$: 1661:"

his mark<br>John  O  Row senier:

his mark
Witness: John I I Collens senier, Steuen Glouer, John Collens Junier.

Proved in Salem court 24: 4: 1662 and the widow and her sons John and Hugh appointed administrators to divide the estate according to the mind of the testator.

Inventory taken Apr. 2, 1662, by Samuel Delaber, John (his I mark) Collings and William Browne: Two Cowes, 10li.; 1 Cowe, 4li.; 2 dry Cowes, 9li.; 1 old Cowe, 4li. 10s.; 1 yocke of oxen, 16li.; 1 yocke of oxen, 15li. 10s.; 3 Cattle of 2 years, 6li.; Cart & wheles, 2li.; plow shears, chaines &

harnes, 1li. 12s.; 2 hamers, 4 weges, 9s.; 2 sawes, 3s.; old axces, 10s.; 2 pecaxces, 5s.; 1 hoe, 2s.; spad & shuvels, 7s.; pickes forke, 6d.; shot mowels, 1s.; pot huckes, 5s.; tongs & crucks, Iron pots, 18s.; 2 Cittles, 12s.; peuter, 5s.; sheves, 5s.; 1 ass, 2li.; seves, 3s.; 3 Rakes & old sithe, 2s.; a wheelbara, 2s.; Swine, 2li.; 4 bushells of wheat, 1li.; peaes, 14 bushels, 2li. 9s.; tember vessels, 10s.; one gun, 12s.; bed & bed Clothes, 8li.; Clothing, 4li.; Chest & nails, trunk & books, 14s.; Friing pan, warming pan, 5s.; 1 grining stoo., 1s. 6d.; a bars skin, 5s.; Twenty busshelle of indian, 53li.; Baken, 2li.; Ropes & bags, 10s.; rep hoackes, 4s.; augers, chest and ades, 8s. 9d.; Lanhorne & skales, 5s.; Cotten stockens, 8s. 4d.; rye, 3 bushels, 10s. 6d.; salt & salt meat, 7s. 6d.; Thre pounds, ten shillings Due det to John Roe; Lands, 100li.; total, 205li. 16s. 10d. John Roe indetted Fourty shillings. Sworn by Brigitt Row, the widow, and John Row, her son, June 9, 1662, before Samuel Symonds.

*Essex Co. Quarterly Court Files, vol. 8, leaf 26.*

### ESTATE OF DAVID LEWIS OF SALEM.

An inventory of the estate of David Lewis was allowed June 24, 1662 and Samll. Archerd was appointed to administer in behalf of the country, and to be accountable to this court. *Salem Quarterly Court Records, vol. 4, page 98.*

Inventory taken June 22, 1662: In Mr. Corwin's hand, in fish, 17li. 16s.; a sea bead and covering & old cloathes, 2li.; wearing cloathes & Linnen, 2li. 10s.; total, 22li. 6s. The estate is Dr. to Mr. Corwin, 5li. 6s.; for ye Coffine & other things at his buriall, 12s.; for exspences & time of one about his busines, 10s.; total, 16li. 8s. The rest of the estate the debts being discounted, 5li. 18s. *Essex Co. Quarterly Court Files, vol. 8, leaf 27.*

### ESTATE OF THOMAS WILKES OF SALEM.

Administration on the estate of Tho. Wilkes, that he had in this country, granted June 24, 1662 to Mr. Edmond Batter. An inventory, amounting to 100li. 6s. 11 1-2d., was presented to this court. *Salem Quarterly Court Records, vol. 4, page 98.*

Inventory of the estate of Thomas Wilks, deceased, that was found in Boston in November, 1661, by John Wiswall and John Lake: Aparell and small things, 7li.; 1 small pcell of goods as p. Invoys, 2li.; 10 p. small stockings, 6s. 8d.; 6 1-4 linnen & woolen, 12s.; 5 yds. 1-2 Red cloath, 1li. 2s.; 9 yd. 1-2 gray Carsy, 2li. 7s. 6d.; gloves, laces & silke, 7s. 6d.; 3 grosse & 9 doz. buttons, Coat, 12s. 9d.; 2 grosse, 8 doz. brest buttons, 9s.; 2 yds. Coifing stuffe, 3s. 4d.; 13 yds. 1-4 shage at 3s. 4d. p., 2li. 4s. 2d.; 14 yds. Course woolen cloath at 3s. p., 2li. 2s.; 28 p. gloves, 1li.; 1 great Bible, 6s.; 3 peeces Sardge at 4li. 5s. p., 12li. 15s.; 16 yds. 1-2 duble Beys, 4li. 2s. 6d.; 24 yds. Browne Lynen, 5li. 4s.; 1 Coverled, 18s. & old Carpet, 3s. 6d., 1li. 1s.; 1 old Satinnisco gowne, 1li. 6s.; Incle mancster & some ode things, 2s. 6d.; packing cloath & Cord, 2s.; 19 yds. Carsy at 5s. 4d. p., 5li. 1s. 4d.; 14 yd. flaninge, 1li. 16s.; hatte and Case, 8s.; 1 Child Blanket, silv. lace, 1li. 10s.; Chest, boxe, &c., 2 stone Juggs, 11s.; 3 hhds. Suger, Neate, 15 C. 3qt. 1li., 15li. 15s. 3d.; 14 Gallon Rum at 3s. p., 2li. 2s.; total, 70li. Inventory of goods in Salem, taken in December, 1661, by Walter Price and Hillyard Veren: One pcell goods of small wares, 3li. 1s. 3d.; 1 pcell Ironmonger's wares, &c., 2li. 10s. 11d.; 1 pcell small wares, 1li. 4s. 1d.; 1 pcell small wares, 2li. 10d.; 1 friing pane, 2s.; 25 yds. Course Carsy at 4s. p., 5li.; 14 yds. tickinge at 3s. p., 2li. 9s.; 7li. old Iron & kitle, 1li. 7s. 11d.; 14li. peper, 28s., 2 grosse, 5 doz. hooks & eyes, 5d., 1li. 13s.; thimbles & nails, 3s. 7 1-2d.; 150li. Cotton, 3li. 15s.; 270li. suckets, 3li. 7s. 6d.; 1 pcell small wares, 3li. 11s. 10d.; total, 30li. 6s. 11 1-2d. *Essex Co. Quarterly Court Files, vol. 8, leaf 28.*

Court 25: 9: 1662 ordered Mr. Edmond Batter, administrator to send only 40li. of the estate to England to the widow, and to keep the remainder until the court takes further order. *Salem Quarterly Court Records, vol. 4, page 106.*

The request of Robert, son of Tho. Wilkes, deceased, made 26: 4: 1666, that he might have the estate of said Wilkes, which amounted to about 30li., in the hands of Mr. Edmund Batter, administrator, who held it for said Robert until he became of age, delivered to him for his own use. Court understanding that he was now of age and able to improve it, ordered that it be delivered to him. *Salem Quarterly Court Records, vol. 4, page 165.*

Robert Wilkes' receipt to Mr. Edmond Batter, dated 18: 10: 1666, for 36li., in full of what was due him from his father's estate. Witness: Hillyard Veren, jr., and Hillyard Veren, sr. Entered in the court records by Hillyard Veren, cleric. *Salem Quarterly Court Records, vol. 4, page* 178.

ESTATE OF HENRY COOKE OF SALEM.

Administration on the estate of Henry Cooke, intestate, granted June 24, 1662 to Judeth, his wife, and Isaack, his eldest son, and an inventory was allowed. It was ordered that the whole estate remain in the hands of the widow until the children become of age, except that Isaack was to have 5li. in hand, and, after his mother's decease, to have the house and land adjoining valued in the inventory at 60li. The other children were to have 10li. each at age or time of marriage. "Ye ordering of this estate is null and refers to what y$^e$ court have further ordered as apeers in y$^e$ records of y$^e$ second session of this court." *Salem Quarterly Court Records, vol. 4, page* 98.

Inventory of the estate of Henery Cooke, late deceased, 14: 11, 1661, taken by Nathaniel Felton and Henry Bartholmew: His dwelling house and the land adjoining, 60li.; the Cowpen lot, beinge 5 acres, 20li.; 9 acres of land at the great coave, commonly called Towne's lot, 10li.; the house, orchard and land, about 21 acres that was formerly bought of Willm. Nichols, 40li.; a farme lot of 40 acres, neare Mr. Downing's farme, 6li.; 6 acres of meadow lyinge by Bishop's farme, 5li.; 8 acres of meadow lyinge neare the land of Hen. Phelps, 8li.; an acre of land in the towne next to Mr. Norrice & the housinge upon it, 30li.; 2 oxen, 12li.; 1 Cow, 5li.; 4 two yeare old heifers, 12li.; 2 yearlings, 3li.; a horse, 12li.; In beddinge wth. 2 payre of sheets, blankets and a rug, 5li.; hempe & flax, 2li.; a bed teecke & boulster, 2li. 10s.; a brass ketle, an iron pot & ketle, a skillet, 2 platters, a table & a Cupboord, 3li.; a sadle & bridle, a payre of skales, a payre of stilyards & a steele, 2li.; Barly and pease, 4li.; In beddinge, 1li. 10s.; a polaxe, 2 cleivers, 3 axes, 3 wedges, a hammer, beetle rings, a thwart saw, 2 muskets, a rapier, a sword & bandeliers, a fryinge pan, an old warminge pan & a morter, 2li. 10s.; some old bookes, a fire shovel & tongs & other smal utensils, 1li.; a Cart and plow wth. tacklinge thereunto belonginge, a slyd, 2 sytes, 3li. 10s.; his wearing apparrel, 5li.; total, 255li. Sworn in court June 24, 1662 by the widow, before Hilliard Veren, cleric.

Henery Cooke debter: To Mr. Corwinne, 16li. 17s. 4 3-4d.; Mr. John Browne, 8li. 2s. 11d.; Mr. Bartholomew, 8li. 13s. 10d.; Mr. Gidney, 4li. 15s.; Henery Bullocke, 4li. 7s.; Willm. Flint, 25li. 10s.; John Pickeringe, 15s.; Nathaniel Norton, 14li.; Francis Lawes, 1li.; Mr. Cromwel, 2li. 2s. 9d.; Mr. Gardiner, 2li. 1s. 10d.; Richard Bishop, 1li. 10s.; Ezekeil Wathen, 2li. 10s.; total, 92li. 5s. 8 3-4d. Inventory, 255li.; debts, 92li. 5s. 8 3-4d.; rest, 162li. 14s. 4 3-4d. Henery Cooke's children were Isacke, aged twenty-two years, Samuel, twenty, John, fourteen, Henery, eight, Judith, eighteen, Rachel, sixteen, Mary and Martha, twelve, and Hanna, four years. *Essex Co. Quarterly Court Files, vol. 8, leaf 24.*

John Burton and Samuel (his O mark) Eburne certified, Jan. 10, 1661, that "beinge w$^{th}$ Henery Cooke about 3 or 4 houers before his decease perceiuinge he was in perfect memory spake to him about the settinge of his house in order, for the peace of his famely after his dicease: and that if he had done it when he had had more strenght, It would haue ben more comfortable for himselfe, his answer was, that he had some reason for it and that he would leaue al to his wiues disposinge, then after some tyme of respite he sayd that his wil was that his son Isacke should haue his Dwellinge house with the land thereunto belonginge, then beinge demanded when, he sayd after the decease of his wife, & then he sayd that his daughter Judith should haue the Cowpen land and more he would haue spoken concerninge the rest of his children but was not able." *Essex Co. Quarterly Court Files, vol. 8, leaf 25.*

Upon further consideration about ordering the estate of Henry Cooke, deceased, it was ordered July 7, 1662, that Isaack, the eldest son, have 24li., and the other children, John, Henry, Judith, Rachell, Mary and Hanna, 12li. each, payable at age or time of marriage, and the widow was appointed administratrix. *Salem Quarterly Court Records, vol. 4, page* 100.

### Estate of Robert Gray of Salem.

"The last will and testament of Rob: Gray of Salem being sicke in bodie but of pfect vnderstandinge is as followeth Impmis I giue vnto my daught$^r$ Elizabeth Gray that peece of grounde runninge alonge by the side of m$^r$ Endicotts and buttinge against Thomas oliuers It: I giue vnto my son

Joseph my barne and one quarter of an aker of grounde to it to be laid out for him at the discretion of my ouerseer It: to my son Robert I giue my kitchin with som grounde vnto it reserving a convenyent passage for my wife into the orchard and to the well which I also reserv to be laid out at the discretion of my ouerseers It: I giue vnto my other three children Bethiah Hannah and Mary my third pt of the Ketch to be soulde and equallie diuided amonge them It: I giue vnto my seruant Elizabeth Wicks: three pownds provided shee dwell with my wife to the end of the next somer It: I: giue to George Hodgis a quadrant a fore staffe a gunters scale and a p of Compassis And for the rest of my estate what soeuer I giue and bequeathe it vnto my beloued wife Elizabeth Gray whom I make executrix of this my last will and testament and doe apoynt my beloued friends m<sup>r</sup> John Brown and Henry Bartholmew the overseers of this my last will and testament

"in witnes herevnto I haue set my hand the first of the iith m° 1661."

Robert Gray

Witness: John Browne, Henry Bartholmew.

Proved in Salem court 25: 4: 1662 by the witnesses. *Essex Co. Quarterly Court Files, vol. 8, leaf 29.*

Inventory taken 5: 12: 1661, by John Browne, Richard Prince and Henry Bartholmew: One dwellinge house with a kitchin and barne and the land belonging to it, 300li.; one third pt. of a Ketch, 140li.; one Cowe, 5li.; two yonge horses, 15li.; one swine, 14s. In the parlor: One fetherbed, two bolsters, a pillow, a Rugge and blankett, curtaines and vallence with the bedsteed, 14li.; one trundle bedsteed, one fether bed, a pillow, Coverlid and matt, 4li.; one table, a case of drawers, two chaires, 6 stooles, a setle, 3 less chaires, two trunkes and 2 casis of botles, 7li.; one large lookinge glass with som earthen dishis and pictures, 2li.; a tin lanthorne, 4 basketts and som glassis, 10s.; 2 silver booles with som other plate, 4li.; 7 p. of sheetes, 7li.; Table linen and pillow beares, 9li. 10s.; Childbed linen, hollon and other linin, 6li. 10s.; woolin yearne, Cupboard clothes with othr small things, 2li. 5s. In the litle Chamber: One feather bed and bolster, Rugge, blankett and bedsteed, 9li.; a chest with linin, woolin and other goods, 10li.; 4 old blanketts and 2 pillowes, 1li. 18s.; a table, 3 casis, a forme, a setle and chaire, 3li. 5s.; a lookinge glass and 3 pictures, 1li. In the Kitchin: One fether bed, a bolster, 2 pillowes, a Rugge and blankett, 6li.; a trundle bed, with the furniture, 2li. 5s.; brass, pewter and earthware in 2 butteries, 6li.; brass and pewter in the kitchin and 2 p. of stilliards, 7li. 10s.; 2 potts, 2 chests, a table, with other lumber, 6li.; in the chamber, a bed and beddinge with the bedsteed, 3li.; a cradle, 3 chests and other lumber, 1li. 10s.; old Iron, Ropes, blockes, 5 guns and a sword, 6li.; 6 sackes and a pcell of Rossen and brimston, 1li. 10s.; in the Cellar, a firkin of sope, a Jarr of oyle and a grindstone, 1li. 14s.; his wearing apparrell, 24li.; total, 588li. 1s. *Essex Co. Quarterly Court Files, vol. 8, leaf 30.*

## Estate of William Browne of Gloucester.

"I William Browne of Glocester in the County of Essex in New-England being by Gods providence Cast upon my Bed of Sicknesse and not knowing how neare my departure out of this world may be at hand doe therefore declare and make knowne this my last will and Testament in manner following and first I Committ and Commend my Soule unto God the Father of Spirits and my body to the Grave to be decently buried by my good freinds Surviving And in the next Place I give and bequeath unto my Sonne in Law Abraham Robinson Two Acres of Meadow being Situate & lying on the North Side of little good Harbour as also two Acres of vpland being Situate and lying next the burying place on the South West Side thereof in Glocester aforesayd as also three Acres ‖of meadow‖ be it more or lesse Situate and lying at Annasequam So Comonly Called next to the Meadow of John Collins Sen on the North-East & butting upon the mayne Creeke or River as also halfe that my Parcill of vpland being Situate & lying in the Fishermans Feild between the Land of Jeffrey Parsons also halfe that my Parcell of vpland Lying at the Eastern Poynt and adioyning to the Land of Robert Elwell also I giue and bequeath unto my Sayd Sonne in Law one Cow and two Ewes also a Bed and a Bolster together with a Rugge & one Blanckett these Lands Goods & Chattells aforesayd to be Delivered to the Sayd Abraham my Sonne in Law together with one Iron Pot when hee Shall attayne the Age of twenty one years to have and to hold the Sayd Goods Lands & Chattells to him & his Heires for evar that is in Case hee Shall accept of what I have here given & bequeathed unto him in this my last will & Testament But if hee Shall not accept of what is here bequeathed & given unto him then it is my will that all the aforesayd

Lands Goods Chattells Shall fall to my Executresse anything herein contayned to the Contrary in any wise notwithstanding. Furthermore it is my will and I doe by these Psnts assigne & appoynt my Daughter Mary Browne to be my Heire & Executresse of all the rest of my estate onely it is my will that my wife Mary Browne Shall injoy the benefit vse & profit of all this my estate now last expressed unto which my Daughter Mary is Heire I Say it is my will & I doe hereby appoynt & determine that my Sayd wife Shall injoy all the benefitt vse & profit of this my estate now last expressed untill my Daughter Mary doth marry or attayne the age of Eighteene yeares and then when Shee Shall attayne the age of eighteene yeares or otherwise if Shee doth marry before Shee doth attayne the Sayd terne of yeares then It is my will and I doe hereby appoynt and determine that my Daughter Mary Shall presently injoy halfe the benefitt & Profitt of this my estate last expressed to her owne proper vse & behoofe any thing herein Contayned to the Contrary in any wise notwithstanding and after the death of her Mother Shee Shall injoy the other halfe which her Mother was to injoy while Shee lived that is to say Shee my Sayd Daughter after the Decease of her Sayd Mother Shall have an injoy all that my estate last expressed to which I have appoynted her Executresse to Her & her Heires for Ever But if my Sayd Daughter Should dye before Shee doth marry or before Shee doth attayne the age of Eighteene yeares then it ‖is‖ my will & I doe hereby appoynt and determine that her Mother Surviving Shall have full power to injoy & dispose of all this my estate last expressed But if my Sayd Daughter doe Survive or out-live her Mother and dye before Shee attayne the age of Eighteene yeares or before shee doth marry then it is my will & I doe hereby appoynt & determine that my Sonne in law Abraham Robinson above expressed Shall have & injoy that estate abovesayd unto which I have Constituted & appoynted her to be Heire to him & his Heires for ever Any thing herein Contayned to the Contrary in any wise notwithstanding In witnesse whereof I the Sayd William have hereunto Set my hand the twenty & ninth day of Aprill Anno Dom one thousand Six hundred and Sixty two."

            William Browne
           his mark

Witness: John Emerson, John I Collins Sen, Philip Haywood.

Proved in Salem court 25: 4; 1662 by the witnesses. *Essex Co. Quarterly Court Files, vol. 8, leaf 31.*

Inventory taken at Glositer, May 13, 1662, by John Emerson, Samuel Delaber, John Collings and Philip Staynwood: Two oxen, 17li.; 3 Cowes & calves, 16li.; 7 ewes and 4 lambs, 4li. 2s.; 1 rame, 6s.; 2 oxen, 12li. 10s.; 3 yere old bull, 4li.; 2 to yers old, 5li.; 6 swine, 3li. 10s.; one yerling, 1li. 10s.; Cart and whele, 1li. 15s.; plowe harnis, 1li.; one pair of new wheles, 2li.; One Cannow, 10s.; Axcel, 7s.; houes, 4s.; to shivels, 1s. 6d.; pich forkes, 2s.; Augers, 3s.; Draing knife, 3s.; Truell & huck, 2s.; one hamer, 1s.; fire pan & toungs, 3s.; A gredion & friing pan, 6s.; pothucks and crucks, 13s.; smuthing eirns, 2s.; Billowes, 1s.; 4 seves, 5s.; 4 Bages, 4s.; spitt, 4s.; Stillerds, 14s.; fouling peace, 1li.; 5 pots and a Iron Skillet, 3li. 10s.; 4 peuter Dishes & one Bason, 2li. 1s. 6d.; 1 quart, 2 pints, half pint, 13s.; 2 wine bolles & dram Cup, 2s. 6d.; 1 Candellstick, 3s.; one puter Cuck, a salter and a saser, 4s. 6d.; Spoones, 2s.; A warming pan, 11s.; A dripping pan, 2s. 2d.; Snuffers, 2s; Paynted Dishes, 2s.; Timber Vessells, 3li. 2s.; Chests, 1li. 6s.; wheeles for spinning, 8s.; Scales & weights, 4s.; Two Tables & a Stoole, 1li. 14s.; Trenchers & a Grater, 1s.; Bands, handkerchiefs, Neck-cloths, 10s.; A knife & a sheath, 1s.; Shirts, 1li. 10s.; Three payre of Sheets, also one old sheete, 3li.; Table Napkins, 15s.; Board cloths, 1li. 5s.; Table cloaths, 14s.; old Linnen, 6s.; wearing Apparell, 9li. 10s.; Shooes, 10s.; Red karsey, 18 yards, 6li. 7s.; Trucking cloth, 10s.; Red Cotton, 8s.; Narrow karsey, 1li. 3d.; Cotton cloth, 6s.; Leads & Lines, 12s.; An Houre Glasse, 1s.; wool, 12s.; woollen yarne, 1li. 8s.; An Iron Lampe, 1s.; Cotton wool, 6s.; cotton yarne, 4s. 8d.; salt, 6s.; Bedding, 15li.; wheat, 1li. 12s. 6d.; Indian Corne, 9s.; malt, 6s. 6d.; one Hide, 8s. 6d.; a Bible, 10s.; House & Lands, 90li.; total, 223li. 7s. Sworn by Mary Browne, the widow, June 9, 1662, before Samuel Symonds. *Essex Co. Quarterly Court Files, vol. 8, leaf 32.*

### ESTATE OF LAWRENCE LEACH OF SALEM.

"Larance Leach Aged 85 years or thereabouts beinge parfitt in memory neer a yeare before his death expressed himselfe vnto vs whose names are heervnder written in the disposing of that w^ch hee had, we beinge vrgente w^th him to make his will his expressions to vs was this first he said that he did owe thirtie ||pounds|| for the mill & his will was that his wife should pay his debts and when his debts ware paid that shee should take all hee had." John Porter, John Bacheller.

Proved in Salem court 25: 4: 1662 by the witnesses and Elizabeth wife of the deceased appointed administratrix. *Essex Co. Quarterly Court Files, vol. 8, leaf 33.*

Inventory of the estate of Lawrence Leach of Salem, deceased, taken by John Porter and Jacob Barney: His wearing apparell, 3li.; 2 feather bolsters, 1li.; 3 feather pillowes, 12s.; 1 Coverlet & 2 Ruggs, 1li. 10s.; 2 blanketts, 1li. 5s.; a Fether bed & 2 flocke beds, 3li.; 2 paire of sheetes, 1li. 10s.; 3 pillow beares, 6s.; 3 small table clothes, 10s.; 1 single sheet, 4s.; a bedsted and a Chest, 1li. 10s.; 5 Chaires, 15s.; 3 barills, a tub & 8 trays, 1li. 5s.; a table, a forme & 3 dishes, 6s.; 3 old brasse kettles & a skillet, a Chafindish & 1 Candlestick, 2 Iron pots & a skillet, 1li. 6s. 8d.; 1 Iron kitle & a morter, 2li. 10s.; a spit & a dripping pan & a frying pan, 10s.; 6 pewter dishes, 1li. 5s.; a Baskett with other Lumber, 5s.; 2 Cowes, a heyfer & a Calfe, 12li.; 5 small swine, 4li.; the howse, with 2 acres of land with the orchard, being parte of the said 2 acres, 30li.; a mill, 40li.; 20 acres of land not improved on Ryall side neare John Bacheler, 10li.; 15 acres of meadow neare John Porters farme bought of Mr. Downing, 20li.; a Bible with another Booke, 5s.; total, 138li. 14s. 8d. *Essex Co. Quarterly Court Files, vol. 8, leaf 34.*

ESTATE OF ANNE FULLER OF (SALEM?).

"Anne ffuller widdow aged 79 yeares being *very* sicke and weake, beinge in perfect memory *and* 2 or 3 dayes before her decease desired vs [whose] names ar vnderwritten to be witnesses to this her disposinge of what she had, & first she sd her wil was that her son Richard Leach should have her 5 acre lot for the charge of her burial, & her red wastcote she *gave* vnto Bethiah Farrow, and her ———— that John Leach & Sara Leach haue on of her Cowes betweene them & what she had more she gaue unto her son Richard Leach."

his mark
Jonathan Willcott, John  E  Rowdon.

Proved in Salem court 25: 4: 1662.

Richard Leach was appointed administrator of the estate

of Ann Fuller, having brought into court a will and inventory of the said Ann Fuller, which were allowed 25 : 4 : 1662.

Inventory taken by Nathaniel Felton and Anthony Buxton: Five acres of Land, 7li.; two Cowes, 8li.; a Coverlet, 1li.; 2 blankets, 1li.; a bed teeke & a bolster, pillowes & 3 sheetes, 1li. —; her wearing apparell, ————; ————st, 5s.; a bible, 2s.; total, 23li. 17s. 6d.

*Essex Co. Quarterly Court Files, vol. 8, leaf 35.*

### Guardianship of Jonathan Hopkinson of Rowley.

Jonathan Hopkinson made choice of his father, Richard Swan, as his guardian, Sept. 30, 1662. *Ipswich Quarterly Court Records, vol. 1, page 109.*

### Estate of Elias Stileman of Salem.*

Administration on the estate of Elias Stileman of Salem, intestate, granted Sept. 30, 1662, to Elias Stileman of Portsmouth, son of the deceased, who was ordered to bring in an inventory. *Ipswich Quarterly Court Records, vol. 1, page 109.*

Elyas Stileman, administrator of the estate of Elyas Stileman, sr., deceased, was given liberty 25 : 9 : 1662, to perfect the inventory and bring it in to the next Ipswich court. *Salem Quarterly Court Records, vol. 4, page 108.*

Mr. Elias Stileman presented an inventory of his deceased father's estate, which was allowed 24 : 9 : 1663. *Salem Quarterly Court Records, vol. 4, page 125.*

Inventory taken 7 : 9 : 1662, by Edmond Batter and Hillyard Veren: A dwelling house, 50li.; one Acre of salt marsh, 5li.; 3 1-2 acres of pasture land, 14li.; about 2 acres & half of ground in ye south feild, 3li.; 6 swine, 3li. Goods in the parler: a bed with the bedsted & all ye furniture belonging, 10li.; a table & forme & two Carpitts, 1li. 5s.; 8 chayers, 1li. 10s.; a Cubbord cloath & 3 Cushens, 2li.; 8 cushens, 8s.; one old Bible, 2s. 6d.; 4 pr. hollan sheets, 8li.; 5 Cource hollan sheets, 3li.; 1 pr. Calico sheets, 1li.; 2 pr. Cource sheets, 2li.; table cloathe, 2li.; 5 pr. pillow beers, 1li. 10s.; 15 towells, fine & cource, 14s.; 1-2 doz. fine napkins, 15s.; 2 doz. 1-2 napkins, 1li. 16s.; 12 Cource napkins & a cource table cloath,

---

* See also Records and Files of the Quarterly Courts of Essex Co., Mass., vol. 3 (1913), p. 108.

9s.; a warming pan, 10s.; 1 pr. And Irons & tongue, 1li. In the hall: a table, 2 formes, 1li. 5s.; a Cubbard cushing, 2s. In pewter: new wine qrt., pt. & 1-2 pt. potts, 1li. 12s.; a flaggon, 3 qrt. potts & pt. potts & cupps, 2li.; worne pewter, 2li.; pewter platters, sasers & bassons, 1li.; new pewter: 9 platters, 2li. 10s.; latten ware, 10s. In ye Hall chamber: a bead, 2 coverings, bolster, pillow & a blankett, 3li. 10s.; chares, table & form, old ones, 6s. In ye parler chamber: one bead, one bolster, to pillowes, a rugg, 2 blanketts, curtins, vallenc & bedsteed, 7li.; an old table & forme, 2s. In the kitching: one muscott, 10s.; 2 spitts, 1 pr. rackes, gridiron, 2 pr. hauckes, tongues, fire pan, beefe pricker, 1li. 12s.; 3 Iron potts & on kettle, 2li.; on Iron thripin pan, frying pan & one pestle & morter, an old Jack, 1li.; bras scales & waites, 5s.; 2 brass Kittles, 1li.; a brass scumer & ladle, 5s.; old Iron, 2s. 6d. & a spade, 30d., 5s.; trenchers, & wooden platters & bottle, 10s.; earthen ware, 3s.; 4 baggs, 12s.; 2 seeves, 2s.; a copper, 3li.; a bellowes, funnell & other lumber tubbs, canns & shovell, 13s. In the Kitchin chamber: one bead & 2 bolsters, 2 white blanketts & 2 red blanketts, 5li.; 2 Coverleads, 1li. 8s.; 2 chests, 1li.; wearing apparrell, 10li.; 3 hatts, 15s. In the seller: wine viniger, 1li.; ould caske, 10s.; 1 pr. malt Milstones, 5s.; a hamaker, 10s.; aprentice boye, 9li.; total, 176li. 12s. 6d. The estate owes to severall men that is known, 279li. 12s. 4d. *Essex Co. Quarterly Court Files, vol. 9, leaf 74.*

### Estate of John Brabrooke of Newbury.

"This 27th of June 1662 I John brabrooke of newberie being sicke in body butt of good memorie do here make my last will and testament as foloweth  first I Comit my soule to god to Inioy him and secondly for my outward Estat I giue vnto my mother on Cow and all my wering Clothes that Cow I mene which is in my vnkl shorts hands  3[dly] I giue vnto my mother and my brother samuell and my brother Josep and my sister Elizabeth and my sister sarah and my sister Rebeca and my sister Rachell all that Estate which is mine in England to be Equally devided between them  4[thly] I giue vnto my brother Thomas and my brother Josep my mare and Coult to be devided between them. Likwis I giue vnto my brother Josep on yew and lamb  Likwis I giue vnto my frend Cormack fiue shillings  Likwis I giue vnto my mother mor fifteen shillings  Lastly I giue vnto my brother Thomas all my Interest in the house and Land at watter toune after my mother desese allso I giue vnto my sister Elizabeth on Cow which is at samuell Moodys Likwis I desier my vnkell short as my frend to se this my will to be performed."

[No signature]

Witness: Richard Knight, James Jackman.

Proved in Ipswich court Sept. 30, 1662 by Henry Short and Richard Knight.

Inventory of the estate of John Bradbrook of Newbury, deceased June 28, 1662, taken by Nicholas Noyes and Samuel Moody: his weareing apparrell, 4li.; A bible, 3s.; in mony, 4s. 3d.; a paire of Gloves, 2s.; a box with small things in it, 6s.; House & Land after his mothers deceas, 60li.; In England, 30li.; A mare and colt, 12li.; Two cowes, 9li. 10s.; In Samuell moodyes hands, 18s.; total, 117li. 3s. 3d. His debts due to the phisician & the charge of his funerall, 1li. 10s.

Attested to in Ipswich court Sept. 30, 1662 by Henry Short.

*Essex Co. Probate Files, Docket 2,980.*

John Brabrooke of Newbury made a nuncupative will, which was proved in court, but named no executor. Court Nov. 13, 1662, appointed Henry Short, yeoman, of Newbury, administrator of the estate. *Ipswich Quarterly Court Records, vol. 1, page 110.*

### Estate of Philip Call of Ipswich.

"I Philip Call of Ipswich in New England in the county of Essex being sicke of body but Inioying my memorye and vnderstanding doe make this my last will and testament, for my outward estate w$^{\text{ch}}$ God hath Given me I thus dispose after my debts are discharged I giue unto my wife mary Call all my land in old England dureing her naturall Life and after her decease my will is that my sonn Phillip Call shall haue and inioy the same to him and to his heires for euer and Alsoe I doe giue vnto my sayd wife mary Call my House and Land about it in Ipswich in New england aforesayd for the terme of her naturall Life and after her death my will is my daughter mary call shall have and Inioye the same and my will is that if any of my children departe this life before they come to age or the sayd lands come into there possesion then the surviveing shall haue and Inioy the whole and my will is that my sonn Philip call shall haue a cow and my daughter mary a calfe to be impued for there vse & benifitt and for the rest of my estate I giue vnto my wife for to helpe bring vp my children and after her death what is left my will is shall be devyded amongst my children acording to her discression  Item I make my ‖wife‖ sole executrix of this my last will and testament  In wittnes that this is my last will & *and* testament I haue heervnto sett my hand the sixth day of may 1662 In wittnes that this is my will."

*Php* Call

Witness: John Caldwell, Richard smith, Robert Lord.
Proved in Ipswich court Sept. 30, 1662 by the witnesses.

Inventory taken June 14, 1662, by Robert Lord and John Caldwell: The house & aboute an acre of Land, 40li.; 2 cowes and year old heifer, 11li.; 4 swine, 2li.; his weareing apparell, 3li. 10s.; a bed & bedsted & furniture, 8li.; linery cubbert, 15s.; 2 chests, 10s.; 3 paire of sheets & one od sheete, 3li. 10s.; 4 pillowbeeres & a cubber cloth, 1li. 5s.; 2 short table cloths, 6 napkins & 3 towells, 15s.; a trunke, hatt case & table baskett, 10s.; a little table and 3 chaires & one cushen, 12s.; a glass case, tipt jugg, gally dishes & a broken silver spoone, 12s.; a cubbard, old little table & 4 chaires, 8s.; 2 keelers, a chirine & other wooden ware, 1li. 10s.; bras kettles & skilletts, 1li. 10s.; an Iron pott & pott-hookes, 12s.; a warmeing pan & fryeing pan, 8s.; a paire of Andiorns, fire pan & lampe, 14s.; an axe and smotheing Iron, 6s.; in pewter dishes, potts, candlestick & poringers, 2li. 10s.; tinn ware & gally dishes & other small things, 5s.; in girtweb & other things about his trade, 3li. 10s.; a paire of bellows, old bible & other small things, 5s.; 8 bushells of Indian Corne, 1li. 4s.; bacon, 1li.; in Land England, 250li.; debts oweing to the estates, about 26li. 10s.; Turkye Hill lott & Scotts Hill lott, 4li.; a muskett, 12s.; total, 367li. 13s. Debts oweing from the estate about 26li.

Allowed in Ipswich court Sept. 30, 1662.

*Essex Co. Probate Files, Docket* 4,528.

### Estate of Henry Lunt of Newbury.

"Witness by theese p^rsents, that I Henry lunt of Newbery in the County of Essex in New england, being but weake in body, but of sound & pfect memory, for diuerse Causes & considerations me therevnto moueing, doe make my last will & testament, & doe dispose of my landes goods & Chattels as followeth; first I bequeath my soule whensoeue$^r$ it shall depart out of my body into the handes of my redeemer Jesus Christ, with an assured hope of a blessed resurrection, & my body to be buried, wheare it shall please the lord at death to cast me. Then next to Ann my wife I giue & bequeath dureing her natureall life my dwelling house barne Archard w$^{th}$ the pasture ground the houses stands in, with my ground ioyneing to the pasture as allso Eight Ackers be it more or less in the litle feild, as allso my meddow in the mashes on this side plum Iland riu$^r$, Allso I giue vnto my sonn Daniell all the Corne ground & pasture ground, w$^{ch}$ was formerly Thomas Dowes as allso all my mash ground at plum Iland, And my will is that my son Daniell shall giue to my Daughter Presilla Twenty poundes to be paide her at the age of Twenty one years, and if she marry before, then to pay her within halfe a yeare after her marriag, Allso I giue vnto my Daughters Sarah Mary & Ellezabeth to ech of them Twenty pounds, to be paide out of my goods & Chattells, when they attaine to the age of Twenty one yeares, Allso I giue vnto my son John Twenty pounds & to my son Henry ffiue pounds, to be payde out of my goods & Chattells at the age of Twenty one years, & till then my will is that my son John & my son Henry shall be at my wifes disposeing, Allso my will is that after my wifes decease I giue vnto my son John & to my son Henry my dwelling house barne Archard ——— the land it stands in wth my ground ioyneing to the pasture, as allso Eight Ackers be it moore or lesse in the litle feild as allso my meddow in the mashes on this side plum Iland riu$^r$; ||exept that at Jerreco as they call it|| to ech of them an equall portion And my will is that my son John & my son Henry after my wifes decease shall pay vnto my daughters Sarah presilla Mary & Ellezabeth to ech of them Ten pounds to be payde by them equally that is to say by my two sones John & Henry within one whole yeare after my wifes decease Allso I giue unto my sonn Daniell after my wifes decease the meddow or mash ground at Jerreco as they Call it w$^{ch}$ is exepted aboue from John & Henry & interlined And I appoynt Ann my wife the sole executrix of this my last will and Testament And I Apoynt Anthony Mo——— senior & Abraham Toppan senior to be the ou$^r$seers of this my last will and Testament  In witness whereof I the saide Henry Lunt haue set my hand *and* seale this eight of July one Thousand Six hundred Sixty & Two

"my will is that my debts & funarall rites be discharged & if my daghter p'silla dy before the age of Twenty one years or of marriage that then the Twenty pounds be deuided amongst her brothers & sisters equally, And my will is allso that my wife Ann shall haue liberty of Three Cowes pastureing in my son Daniells pasture as long as she liueth."

"Signed sealed & deli*vered* as my act & deede after the words interlineed exept that at Jerroco as they Call it."

"The *mk* of"
Henry lunt [SEAL]

Witness: Willam Mooudy & Abraham Toppan.
Proved in Ipswich court Sept. 30, 1662 by the witnesses.

Inventory taken Aug. 5, 1662 by Wm. Gerrish, Hen. Short and Robert Long: weareing apparell, 16li.; Books, 12s. Armes, 50s., 3li. 2s.; Land & Howsing, 354li.; 4 oxen & 4 steers, 52li. 10s.; 4 Cowes & other Catle, 32li.; Corne, 41li. 17s.; Cart, yokes, chaines sithes, axes, plowes, dragg prongs, sawes, wedges, 10li. 5s.; Lumber, 3li.; Bedding in the Lower roome, 8li. 10s.; Boxes, chest & bedsteed, 1li. 10s.; Lining, 15li. 15s.; woodden wares, 2li. 14s.; table bord, stooles, 1li. 14s.; pewter, 4li. 18s.; Brass, 3li.; Iron potts, spitts & other Iron, 2li. 5s.; Earthen wares, 1li.; Chest & spining wheeles, bacan, 1li. 18s.; Lining yarne, 1li. 10s.; wooll & Corne, 3li. 4s.; Bedding in the Chambers, 9li. 2s.; blankets & Curtins, 1li.; Cloth, 5li. 12s.; debts, 3li. —s.; debts, 34li.; debts owing to be payd 38li. 17s.; total, 575li.

Allowed in Ipswich court Sept. 30, 1662.

*Essex Co. Probate Files, Docket* 17,382.

## ESTATE OF THOMAS ROWELL OF ANDOVER.

Administration on the estate of Thomas Rowell, intestate, granted Sept. 30, 1662, to Marjery Rowell, his widow, and an inventory amounting to 123li. 3s. was brought in. According to a contract before marriage, the widow was to have half the estate, and the court ordered 29li. 10s. to be paid to Jacob Rowell, his son; to his grandchildren, the children of his son Valentine Rowell, 7li., that is, 40s. to the eldest son and 20s. each to the other five children. Jacob Rowell was to receive his portion at the age of twenty-one years and the widow was to have liberty to pay the 7li. to the grandchildren. *Ipswich Quarterly Court Records, vol.* 1, *page* 109.

Inventory taken June 16, 1662 by John Ossgood, Richard Barker and John (his I mark) louioy: the house and baren and shoope, 24li.; a parsell of land by the house fence and sowed, 40li.; 3 Akers of land neare the hous unfenced, 3li.; [a parsell of land forther in the woods unfenced and all sould butt five akers to cristever ossgood but not yet asuered unto him all which valed at, 12li. 10s. This crossed out.]; medow ground, 12li.; 2 Oxen, 14li., 2 Cowes, 10li., 24li.; a marre, 8li., 2 Calves, 1li., 4 sheepe, 3 lambs, 2li. 1s., 11li. 16s.; 7 swine, 5li. 10s., 3 stookes of bees, 1li. 10s., 7li.; 6 bush. wheat, 4 bush. Indean coren, 2li. 2s.; 1 fether beed and boulster and 2 pillowes and Rooge, 6li.; 1 flookbeed and boulster and Rooge, 2 blancetes, 3li.; 3 payer of sheets, 1li. 10s.; 3 payer of pillowbears, 10s., 2li.; waring Aparell, 2li. 10s.; 1 Cubbord, 10s., 3 Cheests 1li.; 1 box, 5s., 1li. 15s.; 3 Iron pottes, 1 posnat, 1 skellet, 1li. 4s.; 1 brass keetell, 1 skemer, 1 bras morter, 1li.; pewter, 2 platers, 1 bason, 1 Chamber pott, 6s.; 2 beer boulls, 2 saceers, 1 poringer, 1 Candellstik, 3s.; 1 smoothing Irone, 1 lampe, 5s.; 1 warmeing panne, 1 fryeng pan, 1 speet, 5s.; fier panne, tonges, tramell and Chafin dish, 6s.; Carpenders tolles, 1li. 6s.; 3 goonnes, 1li. 10s., 1 sworde and beelt, 7s., 1li. 17s.; 1 matte hook, 1 pek, 2 exess, 3 wegges, 4 beetl Rings, 14s.; 1 Chaine, 1 Coulter, 1 yooke, 1 plow, 1 sleed, 15s.; 2 speening wheeles, 4 Chayers, 4 Cquishinges, 10s.; wooden vesells, 2 barells, 1 keller, 2 poudering tubs, 8s.; 1 tubb with trayes, pailes, seefes and other ould vesells, 10s.; earthen vesells, 2 payer Cards, 2 sikells, 6s.; debts dew to him, Mr. dane, 3li. 17s. 6d.; John lovioy owes, 3li. 2d.; Steeven Ossgood, 7s. 6d.; George Abbet, Senior, 2s. 6d.; Robert Collince of Ipswich, 5s.; Willeam Avery, Ipswich, 11s.; Robert Kensman, Ipswich, 2s. 6d.; total, 156li. 10s. 2d.; debtes hee owes: Mr. Horen, 19li. 12s. 3d.; Mr. John Geedney, 11s.; Phillep Whorten, Boston, 3li.; Sameuell Willeams, Salem, 1li.; Mr. Robert Payne, 1li. 10s.; Mr. John Appleton, 1li.; John Whipell, 1li.; Will bukly, 14s.; total, 28li. 7s. 3d.

Allowed in Ipswich court Sept. 30, 1662.

Since this inventory was made there is lost thre swine and a shepe; in dets aperes aboute twenty shillings.

On reverse of paper: Income, 156li. 10s. 2d.; debts, 28li. 7s. 3d.; cattle dead, 5li.; take out her estate, 50li.; remaine, 73li.; her halfe, 36li. 10s.; remaine, 36li. 10s.; to her child, 25li. 10s.; to his 6 grandchild, the eldest 2li. ye rest 1li. 7s.

Anti nuptial agreement of Thomas Rowell of Salisbury with Margere Ossgood widow of Christopher Ossgood of Ipswich: to take her children, two sons and two daughters as his own and to give her one half of his estate at his decease besides the portion which he shall have with her, paying to the children their several portions mentioned in their father's will. Signed Feb. 24, 1650.

his mark<br>Thomas F Rowell.

     his mark
Witness: Phillip P ffowler, Edman bridges, William Chandler.
Allowed in Ipswich court Sept. 30, 1662.
*Essex Co. Probate Files, Docket 24,324.*

Additional inventory of the estate of Tho. Rowell brought in June 28, 1681 by his son Jacob Rowell and to whom administration is granted for that, taken by Dudley Bradstreet and Tho. Chandler: one hundred acres of upland being the great devission in Andever, 100li.; 25 acres of upland on the Indian plaine being the third devission, 30li.; meddow on the west side of Shawsheen River in 4 pcells, 30li.; 5 acres of meddow which was ye last devission of meddow, 15li.; 7 acres & 1-2 of upland, which was the swamp devission, 7li.; total, 182li.

As there is 12li. mentioned in the former inventory for meddow, I have left out 5-1-2 acres of meddow as it was laid out by the lot layers which is worth more than 12li. Jacob Rowell.

The above omitted by his mother, Margery when she gave in the former inventory. Sworn to in Salem court by Jacob Rowell.

*Essex Co. Probate Records, vol. 302, page 5.*

### ESTATE OF WILLIAM WILD OF IPSWICH.

"I william wild of Ipswich in the county of Essex in New England being at present Sicke and weake of body but through Gods mercye Inioyeing my vnderstanding and memory doe make & ordaine this my last will and Testament first I giue my soule into the hands of Jesus christ my Redeemer my Body to be desently buried And for my outward estate which the Lord hath beene pleased to giue I dispose of as followeth After my debts & funerall expences are discharged I doe giue and bequeath vnto ||my|| beloued wife Elizabeth wild my dwelling house and all my land for the toorme of her naturall Life, and after her decease I giue all my sayd house and Land I doe giue vnto John wild the sonn of John wild of Topsfield my Kinsman Item I doe giue and bequeath vnto my Kinsman John wild Senior of Topsfield tenn pounds w$^c$h he the sayd John wild hath in his hands of myne & doe order the bond I haue of him for it to be rendered vp vnto him after my decease Item I doe giue vnto Robert Amis the sum of five pounds to be payd by my executrix within one yeare after my death Alsoe I giue vnto marke warner the Summ of five pound Alsoe I giue vnto Hanah Lampson the summ of *ten* pounds to be payd by my executrix as my Overseers shall apoy$^t$ and the rest of my estate I leave vnto my beloued wife Elizabeth wild whom I make sole executrix of this my last will and testament And I doe desire my loueing freinds Theophilus willson william white & Robert Lord senior to be my overseers to see that this my last will be pformed acording to the true intent & meaneing therof And it is my will and mynd that If my Kinsman John wild Junior depart this life before he come ||to|| age or before the sayd house & Land comes into his possesion that then it be devided among the children of John wild senior vnless the Sayd John leaue heires then to be vnto them In wittnes that this is my last will & testament I haue heervnto sett my hand the Sixt day of may in the yeare one thousand Six hundred sixty two 1662"

William Wild

Witness: Theophilus wilson, William White, Robert Lord.

Proved in Ipswich court Sept. 30, 1662 by Theophilus Willson and Robert Lord.

Inventory taken June 26, 1662 by Theophilus Wilson and Robert Lord, jr.: the dwelling house, orchyard, & ground about it & 6 acre planting lott, 46li.; a mare and three colts, 31li.; two cowes & 2 yearlings, 11li. three oxen, 18li.; 6 hoggs & 3 piggs, 4li. 10s.; in the hall, 2 little tables, 6s.; 3 chaires, 2 formes & a stoole, 7s. 6d.; a cubberd, 2 chests & a box, 1li. 4s.; a kneading trough, one tub, two Keelers, 5 trayes, 2 beere vessells & paile, 12s.; one poudering tub & od wooden things, 6s.; earthen ware, 5s.; one chamber pott & other pewter, 13s.; a bras kettell, skillet & warming pan, 1li. 4s.; 2 Iron potts & other Iron things, 1li. 4s.; 6 old axes, 3 old sickles, 3 wedges, one broad how, 2 beetell rings & a hammer, 1li. 2s.; In weareing apparrell, one cloake, jackett,

Breeches & hatt, 6li. 14s.; a searge sute, 1li. 10s.; a cloth coat & sute & other old apparrell, 1li. 10s.; 2 paire of shoes & 4 paire of stockens, 1li.; one yard & halfe of woollen cloath, 4s. 6d.; 7 yards of co—— wooleing cloath, 1li. 1s.; ——— paire of sheets, ——— table cloaths, ———, 5li.; ——— a dozen ——— napkins, 9s.; 7 shirts, 1li. 15s.; three cushons, 5s.; one bedsted, 1li.; curtaines & valence, 1li. 15s.; a fether bed, boulster & 3 pillows, 4li. 10s.; a blankett, coverlet & Rugg, 3li.; one bedsted, strawbed, flock boulster, blankett & coverlett, 1li. 15s.; drest hempe, 10s.; barke tubs, 5s.; sheepe woole, 5s.; coslett, pike and sword, 1li. 4s.; a tub with 4 bushells of wheate, 1li. 1s.; one ewe & lamb, 4s.; a fowling peece, 18s.; a crosecut saw, 5s.; debts owing to the estate, 71li. 10s. 6d.; total, 225li. 14s. 6d. debts owing from the estate, 5li.

Received and allowed Sept. 30, 1662.

*Essex Co. Probate Files, Docket* 29,827.

### Estate of Abraham Morrill of Salisbury.

"I being weake in body, yet hauing the perfect use of my memory doe make this as my last will & testament; Im: my will is that what euer debts I owe to any man be first payd out of my estate, And the ressidue of my estate I doe dispose of as followeth, I giue unto my Deare & louing wife the one halfe of my whole estate whether in Housing lands cattle debts due to me from any or moueables or what euer els is mine; & this to be hers to dispose of as she shall see cause either in her life *time or** at her death, 2$^{ly}$ I giue to my eldest sonne Isaack Morrill a double portion *of** the othur halfe of my estate to be payd to him at the *age* of one & twenty yeares or day of marriage; 3$^{ly}$ The rest of the sayd halfe of my estate I giue unto my *other** five children Abraham Jacob sarah Moses & Lidda Morrill to be equally deuided betweene them, & to be enioyed by them as they come to the age of one & twenty yeares; or at the day of marriage; 4$^{ly}$ My will is if any of my foresayd six children die before the come of age to inioy there portion that then there portion be deuided betweene the seruiuing children equally. 5$^{ly}$ My will is my whole estate be kept, & improued together & noe deuission made untill my eldest sonne Isaack come to age to receiue his

* Worn off; words supplied from the record.

portion; & afterwards as much as may be with any conueniency; 6ˡʸ My will is that my deare & louing wife & my eldest sonne Isaack Morrill shall be the executors of this my will 7ˡʸ My request is that my louing friend Mʳ Thomas Bradburry & my louing brother Job Clement be the ouerseers of this my last will & testament.  June the 18th 62."

             his mark
         Abraham Œ & Morrill

Witness: John stebines, Tobias Daves, Rhoda Remington, Mary wise.

Proved in Hampton court Oct. 14, 1662 by Tobias Daves and Ms. Rohda Remington and the widow Morrill accepted the executorship.

Inventory taken by Tho. Barnard, John Weed and William (his V mark) Barns: 3 horse kind, a mare & a fole, 46li.; 5 Oxen, 35li.; 4 cowes & one heiffer, 20li.; 2 two years old, 2 yearlins & 3 calves, 11li.; 8 sheep, 4li.; 11 Swine kinde, 12li.; the now dwelling house, 56 acres of land, oarchyard & out howsen, 90li.; 19 acres of land uppon ye neck att ye old towne, 22li.; a grant of tenn acres of land, 5li.; a right in Mr. Halls farme, 3li.; 10 acres of meadow in ye new meadows, 15li.; 9 acres of meadow in the great meadows, 20li.; two higle pigledee Lotts, 18li.; 10 acres of meadow in ye bareberri meadows, 20li.; 2 Sweepages & 2 acres in Mr. Halls farme, 10li.; the house at ye towne & ye house Lott, 40li.; a 3d pt of ye corne mill at Haverhill, 20li.; part of a vessell, 26li.; due from Henry Sawer, 5li.; from Richard Currier, 3li.; in corne, 12li.; a plough sled, yoaks & chaynes, 1li. 10s.; ye shop tooles & Iron tooles & steel, 14li.; 4 gunns, 3 potts, houshold goods & other Iron, 6li.; brass & peuter, 3li. 10s.; beds & bedsteds & beding belonging to them, 22li.; his weareing cloathes & a peece of cloath, 12li.; for chests, barrell tools & other wooden vessels, 4li.; hay, 7li. Total, 507li. Wt may bee either debtor or creditor ℈ book, by reason of ye obscuritie wee cannot yett finde out. Attested Oct. 14, 1662 by the widow Sarah Morrill, executrix.

Petition of Sarah Mudget alias Morell concerning the division of the estate of her former husband, Abraham Morell for consideration to be made of the charge she had been at about the estate and the bringing up of their children. The youngest, a daughter named Ipsabe born about six months after her husband's death, and the other young children were Lide not two years old, Moses about five, Abraham between seven and eight, Sarah about ten; and she lived a widow about three years.

Dated Salisbury, Apr. 5, 1694.

Whereas Abraham Morrell late of Salisbury bequeathed to his widow Sarah one half of his whole estate and unto his children viz., Isaack, Jacob, Abraham, Moses, Sarah Rowell alias Morell and ——— Severance alias Morrell the other half, and no division being yet made they have chosen Col. Daniel Pierce, Dea. Tristram Coffin, Capt. Peter Coffin, Capt. Stephen Greenleafe and Mr. Thomas Currier of Amesbury to make a division according to the will, and have entered into a bond of 200li. to abide by their decision. Dated May 16, 1694.

Jacob Morrill, Moses Morill, Onesephrus Page, and Sarah (her V mark) Page acknowledged the receipt from their brother Isaac Morrel, executor with their mother Sarah, widow of Abraham Morrel, of their legacies given us in the will of their father, Abraham Morrel. Signed and Sealed Apr. 12, 1697. Witness: Thomas Wells, John Hartshorn.

Sarah Morrell as administratrix signed this instrument in the presence of Henry True, William Carr.

Isaac Morrell accepted the executorship of his father, Abraham Morrell's will and it was allowed Jan. 31, 1703-4.

An additional inventory taken by Tho. Currier and John Kimball: a Lot of Land in a devition above the mill of ninty acres, 22li.; a lot of twenty five acres in a devition next Hampton line, 10li.; a lot in a devition in the great neck of two acres and half, 3li.; a lot in the Cow Common of ten acres, 10li.; about 3 quarters of an acre of medow and the Commonage, 12li.

Sworn to by the executor Jan. 31, 1703-4.

*Essex Co. Probate Files, Docket* 18,787.

ESTATE OF VALENTINE ROWELL OF SALISBURY.

Administration on the estate of Vallentine Rowell, late of Salisbury, deceased, granted Oct. 14, 1662 to his relict, Joane. *Hampton Quarterly Court Records, vol. 1, leaf 4.*

Ordered Oct. 14, 1662 that L. Challis and Rich. Currier were to make distribution of Vall. Rowell's estate to the widow and children, she to have one half. *Hampton Quarterly Court Records, vol. 1, leaf 6.*

GUARDIANSHIP OF ISRAEL WEBSTER OF IPSWICH.

Israell and Nathan Webster, sons of Jon. Webster, deceased, presenting their desires in writing, together with their mother's consent, with Jon. Cheny, sr., Robt. Long and Wm. Elsly as witnesses, and said Israell Webster being present in court and manifesting his desire also, that his father-in-law Jon. Emory and brother-in-law Jon. Emory, jr., might be appointed guardians, the court 25: 9: 1662 appointed them guardians, and also ordered that the bond given into Ipswich court for security for the children's portions remain in full force. *Salem Quarterly Court Records, vol. 4, page 105.*

Petition of Israel Webster, aged eighteen years, and Nathan Webster, aged sixteen years, for appointment of John Emery, sr., and John Emery, jr., as their guardians, signed also by Mary (her mark) Emery. Witness: John Cheney, sr., Robert Long and William Elsly. *Essex Co. Quarterly Court Files, vol. 8, leaf 88.*

ESTATE OF GEORGE FARR OF LYNN.

"The will of goodman far my will is that my sonne John should haue the lot of ground that lieth betwen the ground of Captan martialls and the ground of goodman winters allso I giue tow acers of salt march which is in Roumly march to my sonne John to him and his ares for euer Also it is my will that my sons lazerous and Bengamin should haue my hous and all the land About it and the lot that lyeth near the land of Captan ||martiall|| and iohn lueces to them and to thare ares for euer and if onny of them die before he be at age then thare porshon shall goe to my sones that doth life ether iohn lazerous or Bengamin Also it is my will that my wife shall haue hare thirds of all my estat so long as she doth reman a widdow but in Cas shee should marry then hare thirdes should sease and shee shall haue that which shee and hare sones shall Agree for and after har desease hare thirdes shall goe to my three sones namely iohn lazerous and Bengemin Also it is my will that my sone ioseph shall haue fifty shillings when he Comes to age Also it is my will that my four douter[s] namly mary marthr: Elizebeth and sarah shall haue fifti shilins apese and mary and martha should haue it paed to them tow yeare after my desease and that Elisabeth and sarah shall haue thares paed to them fouer yeare after my deseas  Also it ‖is‖ my will that ‖my‖ mare and Cattel and my houshould goods shall be for the euse of my famely  It is my will m<sup>r</sup> laton and ffrancis Burrill and allin Brad iuner shall be the ouerseers of my wif and Children."

his mark<br>George  G  far

Witness: Henery Sillsbey, ffrancis Burrill.
"dated the first of July 1662."
Proved in Salem court 26: 9: 1662 by Henry Silsby. *Essex Co. Quarterly Court Files,*'vol. 8, leaf 92.

Inventory taken 24: 9: 1662, by Henry Collins, sr., and Henery Sillsbey: Beding, 1li. 10s.; baggs, sifes and roopes, 1li. 2s.; a table and forme, 12s.; pcell of barrells, wheels, chairs and forme, 13s. 6d.; pcell of milking vessells and barrells, a churne, 17s.; one pottage pot, one kettle, a smothing Iron, one fryinge pann & a paire of tongs, 17s.; five old Axes & one spade, 11s. 6d.; one cart roope, 8s.; tow siths, tow forkes and a handsaw, 7s.; one muskett and a sword, 15s.; one pcell of old bookes and tow pots & old pecke and a paire of spininge cards, 6s.; one bettle & wedges, 4s.; thirty Bush. of Indian corne, 4li. 10s.; one weavers lume wth the tacklings, 2li.; one cart and whels and one plough with the tacklings, 1li. 10s.; one paire of oxen, 12li.; tow cows, 8li.; one heifer, 1li. 15s.; one calfe, 1li.; three hoggs, 4li. 10s.; tow piggs, 10s.; one mare, 8li. 10s.; one dwellinge house and some outhousinge wth. the lote it stands upon, 20li.; eight acres of upland, 16li.; eight acres more of upland, 16li.; tow acres of salt marsh in Rumley march, 5li.; total, 109li. 8s.

Attested 26: 9: 1662 by the widow. *Essex Co. Quarterly Court Files, vol. 8, leaf 93.*

ESTATE OF REV. WILLIAM WORCESTER OF SALISBURY.

"I willi: Worcester being ‖Sick &‖ weake of body but of sound & pfect memorie doe make & ordeine this my last will & Testam<sup>t</sup> as followeth: Imp my will is that my beloued wyfe: shall haue that bonde of fiftie pound w<sup>ch</sup> is due vnto me from Thomas clark of Boston Iron munger: she secuering my daughter in Law Rebecka Bilie of w<sup>t</sup> remaynes due to hir out of y<sup>t</sup> bonde  Also my will is that my wyfe shall haue the vse & benefit of my dwelling house oarchyard & house lott duering the time of hir widohood; & three cowes comonage: duering y<sup>e</sup> sd term  Also that my wyfe shall haue w^t moneys soever ar due in England: for rent: for w^t lands & houseing belongs vnto her: or may otherwayes be given vnto her, or any other wayes due  Itt: I doe giue & bequeath vnto my Sonn Samuell worcester my last higledee pigledee lott of Salt marsh lyng towards Merimack Rivers mouth: & also a silver wine bole that hath y^e letters of his name ingraven vppon it & a thousand of pine board towards the finishing of his house: as also all my wareing Apparrell; my minde is y^t my grandchilde willia: worcester ——— Samuels childe shall haue y^e Sylver wine boule ——— named Itt: I doe giue & bequeath to my daughter Susana ——— my pide mare Colt:: It: I doe giue vnto my grand childe Rebecka stacy five pound in houshould stuff: such as her grandmother shal thinke meet It: I doe giue & bequeathe to my Sonne william worcester all my vpland w^thin y^e bounds of the new towne of Salisbury: w^th all rights & privilidges thervnto belonging as also my first Higgle pigledee lott of Salt Marsh: & all my lott of Sweepage at the beache: by my land at y^e newtown: my meaning is: my twenty acre lott butting vpon merimack River & the sevnty acres granted vnto mee by the towne of Salisbury lying next: to the land of Cap^t Pike: n esterly: Itt: I doe give & bequeath vnto my Sone Timothie worcester & to my Sonn Moses woster all the remaynder of my lands both vpland Marsh & meadow, lyng & being w^thin the bounds of the old towne of Salisbury w^th all rights, Comonages & privilidges thervnto belonging (Except before Exepted) to bee equally divided between them: p^rsently after my decease  Also I doe give vnto my said Sonns Timothe & Moses: my dwelling house, orchyard & house Lott: after their mothers death or day of mariage w^ch first happens: to bee equally divided between them & to haue the barne p^rsently after my decease w^th free egress & regress vnto y^e sd barne: to cary hay or corne or y^e like: Always pvided that the marsh Lott: w^ch was formerly my wyfes by hir former husband m^r John Hall: remayne to the vse of my Said wyfe hir heires & assignes for ever. It: I doe giue & bequeath vnto my Sonne william: my pide mare: & a cowe that is cald short & fiue povnd in houshold goods:: all other guifts by any to my said sonne being Comp^rhended in y^e abouesd estate giuen ||by me|| vnto him  It: I doe giue & bequeath vnto my Sonne Timothy my old horse: & a cowe cald: Cherry & fiue pound in houshold goods. It: I doe giue & bequeath vnto my Sonne Moses my young mare between two & three yeare old & also the young heifer & fiue pound in household goods: It: I doe giue vnto my grandchild willia worcester: my Cow cald the Barbar. It: I do giue vnto my Daughter stacy: y$^t$ cowe which is cald the young cowe: & also my two yearling steers It: I doe giue vnto my grand Childe Rebecka stacy: my two yeare old steere It: my will is that all the Cattle: before named in this my will: be wintered w$^{th}$ the hay pvided for them if y$^e$ owners please I doe giue vnto my Daughter Rebecka: Bylie: my brass Chafendish; & also I giue vnto her a booke of m$^r$ Anthony Burgases concerning the tryalls of grace, as a small token of my Specyall loue vnto hir It: I doe giue vnto my servant mayde Hannah Hendrick: tenn shillings. It: I doe appoint my loueing freinds Cap$^t$ Robert Pike my brother Edward ffrench: Richard wells & m$^r$ Tho: Bradbury to bee overseers of this my will & testam$^t$ & for the care & paynes theirin I doe bequeath vnto each of them twenty shillings to bee payd vnto them: out of my library in some good ||English|| autho$^{rs}$, as they shall like off Lastly my will is that my dearly & welbeeloved wyfe: Rebecka worcester to bee my sole Executrix vnto this my last will & testament It: my will is that after my wyfe hath taken hir owne books out of my library & w$^t$ others she think meet for hir vse; & y$^e$ ——— *ond x ryd* ——— books to my overseers as afore ————— books shalbe sold———— s willia: Timothie ————— portion: It: my will is that all ————discharged & pay'd the ————— remayne & bee to y$^e$ —————utrix afore named."

Witness: Tho: Bradbury, Robert Pyke, Edward ffrench, Richard Wells.

"wheras it is be ————— remainder of ————— giuen to my Sonns ————— to each an equall p ——— that my books shalbe ————— yte: to dispose of a ————— I haue given to my ————— this 18$^{th}$ day of Octobr"

Witness: Tho: Bradbury, John Severance.

Proved Dec. 2, 1662 by Capt. Robert Pike and Capt. Thomas Bradbury, and the addition by Capt. Thomas Bradbury and John Severance before Samuell Symonds and Daniel Denison and the will delivered to the clerk of the county court of Norfolk to be by him communicated to said Court according to law.

Inventory of estate of Rev. Mr. William Worcester of Salisbury taken 6: 9: 1662 by Edward French, Richard Wells, Nicholas Noyes: money & plate, 20li.; wareing Apparrell, 25li.; the bedding & furniture in ye parlor, 15li. 7s.; the beding, table & Chayer in ye studdie, 3li.; the bedsted & bedding in ye parlor Chamber, 4li.; a small Chest wth household linnen, 4li.; a little box wth linnen, 1li. 11s.; a Trunke, 10s.; bedding, bedsted & furniture in ye kitching Chamber, 12li.; a trundle bed wth ye furniture, 5li.; a great Cheast wth pilloes, Rugg, blankets & Cushins, 7li.; a great trunk wth furniture in it, 15li.; a small trunke of linen, 9li. 10s.; a cheast of linen in ye passage, 9li.; goods in ye Clossett, 7li.; Yarn & other linen, 3li.; in peuter, 10li.; in Brass, 8li.; Iron & tinn, 7li. In ye Hall: Chayers, forme, table, Cubard, etc. 2li.; severall small things in ye lower Clossett, 10s.; Tubbs & milk vessell & other lumber in ye seller, 3li. 10s.; working tooles, 3li.; in ye garrett in Indian Corne & other lumber, 8li.; The dwelling house, barne & hen house, house Lott & planting Lott, 100li.; tenn acres of fresh meadow, 40li.; ye comonage, 12li.; the last division of upland, 5li.; about 9 acres of upland att ye newtown, 45li.; the Sweepage at ye beach & the first Higledee pigledee lott of Salt marsh, 20li.; the last Higledee pigledee lott of Salt marsh, 3li.; the 6 acre lott of Salt marsh yt was Mr. Jno. Halls, 10li. In Cattle: the lame mare, 5li.; ye pide Mare Colt, 8li.; ye old pide mare, 14li.; the bald facet Horse, 10li.; the young Mare given to Moses, 9li.; two Oxen, 14li.; a Cow cald Cherrie, 5li.; Cow cald barbar, 4li. 5s.; Cow cald Golding, 4li. 10s.; cow cald short, 4li. 15s.; cow cald Madkitt, 4li. 5s.; cow cald brown, 4li. 5s.; a heiffer at Kimbals, 4li.; a brown heiffer, 3li. 10s.; a ffinch steere, 3li. 10s.; 2 yearling steers, 4li. 10s.; 8 Ewes & 4 lambs, 5li. 10s.; 2 Swine & 4 piggs, 5li.; 70 acres att ye Newtown wch was Mr Biles, 20li.; in goods, 5li. 9s.; a bill of fifty pound due from Mr. Clarke of Boston Iron munger, 50li.; a bill from Ben Kimball, 1li. 10s.; in bookes, 30li.

Presented to the Salisbury court 14: 2: 166[2-3].

*Essex Co. Probate Files, Docket* 30,679.

Court 14: 2: 1663 ordered that the Worshipfull Major Eliezar Lusher take Mrs. Worcester's oath to the inventory of Mr. Worcester's estate presented by her as executrix. *Salisbury Quarterly Court Records, vol.* 1, *leaf* 11.

## Guardianship of Sarah Partridge.

Sarah Partridg chose Capt. Robert Pike as her guardian and the court confirmed it 14: 2: 1663.

Ordered that Capt. Robert Pike demand of Anthony Stanian and his wife, administratrix to Will. Peaslee, the amount which Will. Partridg received in old England as the legacies given to the children of said Partridg. This was to be delivered at the next county court at Hampton, according to said Partridg's bond.

*Salisbury Quarterly Court Records, vol. 1, leaf 12.*

Court 13: 8: 1663 ordered that Mr. Stanian deliver to Joseph Shaw his wife's portion, 13li., before the next Salisbury court, and to have the remainder of the children's portions ready, also to give said Shaw's interest for five pounds of said portion for what time he keeps it after it is due.

*Hampton Quarterly Court Records, vol. 1, leaf 17.*

## Estate of Anthony Colby of Salisbury.

Inventory of the estate of Anthony Collby, late of Salisbury, deceased, taken Mar. 9, 1660, by Sam. Hall, Tho. Bradbury and Tho. Barnett: His waring Apparrell, 2li. 10s.; 1 feather bed & bolster & old Cotten Rugg, a payer of course sheets & a course bed case, 4li. 15s.; one old warming pan, 3s. 4d.; an other feather bed, feather pillow, feather bolster & a payer of sheets & Cotten Rugg, 4li. 10s.; about 8li. of sheeps wooll, 10s. 8d.; five pound of cotton wooll, 5s.; 10li. of Hopps, 6s. 8d.; a bed case, feather pillow & bolster case, a payer of sheets & old cotten Rugg, 1li.; an Iron pott, pott hooks & Iron skillett, 6s. 8d.; a copp. kettle & a payer of tramells, 1li.; a little old brass skillett & old morter & pestle, 3s. 4d.; trayes & other dary ware, 15s.; a landiron, gridiron, frying pan, old cob iron, 5s.; in old peuter, 3s. 4d.; 4 scythes, 8s.; 2 pillow beers, 3s.; table, two joynstooles, 2 chayres, 1li.; old swords & 2 old muskets, 1li.; one chest & one box, 10s.; an old saddle & a pillion, 10s.; old lumber, 10s.; a grindle stone with an Iron handle, 3s. 4d.; a new millsaw & 1-2 an old one, 1li.; a croscutt saw & half a one, 1li.; a broad how, 3 forkes, a rake, 2 axes & an Iron Spade, 12s.; 5 yoakes, 10s.; 2 Iron cheynes, 10s.; halfe a tymber cheine & a new draft cheyne, 1li. 15s.; an old tumbrill with an old payer of wheeles, 1li.; 2 sleades, 1li.; a long cart & wheels & Spanshakle & pin & 4th pt. of an other cart, 2li.; a plough

& plough Irons, 10s.; 2 Canoas & 1-2 a canoa, 3li. 15s.; 6 oxen, 42li.; 6 Cowes, 27li.; 2 3 yeare old steers, 7li.; 2 Yearlins, 3li.; 2 calves, 1li.; 7 swine, 5li. 5s.; 8 sheep, 4li.; 1 mare & colt, 20li.; 1 horse, 10s.; a dwelling house & barne & 14 acres of upland in tillage, 70li.; a pasture of about 30 acres, 20li.; 2 lotts att yt wch is cald Mr. Hall's Farme, 5li. 10s.; about eighteen acres of fresh meadow, 40li.; ye accoodacon bought of Mr. Groome, 6li.; 2 lots of sweepage & one higgledee piggildee lott, 4li.; 60 acres of upland towards pentucett bounds with meadow to be laid out, 10li.; ye 8th pt. of ye old saw mill, 30li.; 40 bushells of wheat, 9li.; 10 bushels of barley & 6 of rie, 3li. 4s.; about 60 bushels of Indian corne, 9li.; total, 359li. 19s. 4d. Copied from the files of the Norfolk county court records, and sworn to by the widow Colby, Tho. Bradbury, rec.

Anthony Colby, debtor: To Sam. Worcester, 1li. 7s.; Willi. Osgood, 2li. 9d.; Goodman Tappin, 1li. 2s. 6d.; Abram Morrill, 2li. 10s. 10d.; John Tod, 10s.; Tho. Clarke, 9s.; Mr. Russell of Charlstown, 10li.; Mr. Gerish, 5li. 8s. 6d.; Mr. Woodman, 2li. 14s.; Jno. Bartlett, 2li. 2s. 1d.; Steven Sweat, 2li. 5s. 5d.; John Webster, 13s.; Steven Greenleif, 13s.; Goodman Peirce, 10s.; Goodman Cillick, 3li.; Jno. Lewis, 1li. 10s.; Orlando Bagly, 5li. 19s.; Jno. Blower, 6s.; Mr. Worcester, 1li. 13s. 6d.; Mr. Bradbury, 16s. 9d.; to the widdow Colby, 10li.; Henry Jaques, 2li. 10s.; Willi. Huntington, 11s.; John Severans, 1li. 13s. 8d.; Jno. Clough for grass, 6s.; for 9 weeks worke, 8li. 2s.; total, 68li. 14s. 7d. Debtor p Contra: Rodger Eastman, 10s.; Robert Clements, 1li. 5s.; from ye town, 9s.; Jno. Maxfield, 2li.; Leonard Hatherlee, 1li.; Sam. Worcester, 14s. 6d.; Goodman Morrill, 1li. 10s.; Steven Flanders, 6s.; Goodman Randall, 6s.; boards at ye saw mill, 3li. 7s. 6d.; loggs to make 2000 of bord, 2li. 5s.; for work done to ye estate, 1li. 2s. 6d.; total, 14li. 15s. 6d. *Norfolk Co. Quarterly Court Files, vol. 1, leaf 33.*

The division of the estate of Anthony Colby of Salisbury, late deceased, made by Tho. Bradbury and Robert Pike, Apr. 9, 1661, by order of the county court held at Salisbury. To ye widdow for hir part & the two youngest children: ye dwelling house, barne and 14 acres of upland in tillage, 70li.; ye ferrie meadow, 30li.; ye household goods, 19li. 19s. 4d.; a yoake of Oxen, 14li.; 3 Cowes, 13li. 10s.; 7 Swine, 5li. 5s.; in sheep, 2li. 10s.; in Corne, 21li. 4s.; the boggie meadow, 10li. To John Colby: an acre of land aded to his halfe acre at his house, 2li. 16s.; two cheyns, 10s.; a yoake of oxen, 15li. 10s.; Mr. Groom's accomodacons, 6li.; in sheep, 1li. 10s.; a cart & wheels, span, shackle & pin & ye 4th pt. of another cart, 2li. To Sarah, ye wife of Orlando Bagly: one Cowe & one 3 yeere old steere, 8li.; a young horse, 10li.; another Cowe, 4li. 10s.; p. Isaac Colby, 5li. 16s. More payd by Isaac Colby to Orlando Bagly for ye which the estate was debtor, 5li. 19s. 8d. To Samuell Colby: one yoake of oxen, 13li.; the pasture, 20li. To Isaac Colby: the eleven lotts of marshe at Mr. Hal's farme, 2 lotts of sweepage & one higledee pigeledee lot, 9li. 10s.; 2 yearlins, 3li.; ye part of ye saw mill, 30li. To Rebecka Colby: a Cowe, one 3 year old steere & ye mare colt, 14li.; two Calves, 1li.; a bed & bolster, 4li. 10s.; p. Isaac Colby, 2li. 11s.; p. Sam. Colby, 5li. 4s.; in corne, 11s. This division was consented to by the widow Colby and all the children who were of capacity. Confirmed by the Norfolk county court at Salisbury, 14: 2: 1663, and recorded by Tho. Bradbury, rec. *Norfolk Co. Quarterly Court Files, vol. 1, leaf 34.*

Upon the petition of Susanna Whittredge formerly Colbie the Ipswich court Mar. 28, 1682 granted her power with the advice of Samuell Colbie and Thomas Colbie to sell enough of the estate left in her hands by her former husband for her necessary support in her old age, not exceeding the value of two of the parts or shares which the court Apr. 9, 1661 allotted to her for her part of the estate.

Petition of Thomas Challis, Orlando Bagly, Ephraim Weed and Ebenezer Blasdell for some part of the estate of their grandfather Anthony Collby formerly of Salisbury left in the hands of their grandmother Susanna widow of Anthony, administratrix to his estate, afterward Susanna Whithredg, deceased: the Court Ordered the division of the estate Apr. 9, 1661, and it was allowed 14: 2m: 1663. Also such of us as have married the daughters of John Collby, deceased, eldest son of said Anthony and Susanna by virtue of the last will of John Collby, as we are informed that Samuell Collby of Amesbury the only son surviving (although not the eldest) of said Anthony and Susanna, hath letters of administration granted him unto the estate of Susanna Whithredg, deceased, and hath exhibited a large account of debt from the estate and also he designeth a further application for liberty for alienation of more of said estate.

We address ourselves to the court "where we think we

ought for y‍ᵉ interposing & improvement of yᵗ authority for yᵉ prevention of yᵉ evacuation of yᵗ estate whereunto we have right (as we think) out of half gills or gills, and yᵉ exhausting & wasting thereof by such embezelling trifles," also crave your advice whereby we may be orderly possessed of our rights. Dated Sept. 28, 1698.

Citation to Samuell Coleby to appear before Jonathan Corwin, Esq., at the house of Mr. Frances Elles to take administration on the remaining estate of Anthoney Coleby of Amesbury, deceased. Dated Salem, Nov. 16, 1699.

Said citation read to Samuell Coleby Nov. 18, 1699 by Ebenezer Blasdell, Constable of Amesbury.

*Essex Co. Probate Files, Docket 5,896.*

### Guardianship of Moses Worcester of Salisbury.

Moses Worcester chose Richard Wells as his guardian and the court 14: 2: 1663 approved. The court also desired said Goodman Wells to take care of Timothie Woster's estate, his land, meadow and housing. *Salisbury Quarterly Court Records, vol. 1, leaf 10.*

Division of the house and land given to Timothie Worcester and Moses Worcester, both of Salisbury, by their father Mr. William Worcester: Timothy to have the now dwelling house, orchards, barn, houselot and half of a great meadow lot, and one half of all ye common rights belonging to said house and land, except ye meadow, &c. Moses is to have a planting lot, one half of ye great meadow, and share in the 500 acres, meadow in Mr. Hall's farm, and all ye division of land above ye mill, &c. It is also agreed that Richard Wells, Isaac Buswell, Edward French and Samuell Felloes, all of Salisbury, to determine any allowance that may be made to either in the penalty of 20li. Dated Mar. 12, 1666-67.

Susanna (her S mark) Worcester, wife of Timothie Worcester, releases dower. Acknowledged Sept. 17, 1667, before Robert Pike, commissioner. *Norfolk Deeds, vol. 2, leaf 104.*

### Estate of Mrs. Mary Smith of Marblehead.

"Marbellhed the 28ᵗʰ daye of march 1663: The last will and Testament of Mary Smith wife vnto the late, Jeames

Smith of mabelhed aforsed That is to saye, I bequeth my Soule to God, & my body, to [be] buried at marbellhed at the vsuell place of buring Nextly I giue my great Brasse kittel vnto my daughter Cathoron Eborrun. And for all my peuter, I giue, to boath my Dafters Catharon, And Marye, to be equally shared between them. Allso I giue all my linning vnto my too daugters aforesaied, to be equally shared between them. And my too great Chares I giue the one to my dafter Catheron and the other, to my Dafter Mary Roulland abousd And my tabell, & stooles, I giue to my dafter mary Rouland, and allso the great Chest, Allso my spitt, dripping pan, the smothen Iron, and gridiron. And for my grand childeren, I giue & Conferm vnto Samuell Rouland, and Joseph Rouland all the legases that my husband Jeames Smith, left for them, And three pounds which is yet behind *vnpaid** vnto my grand *child mary Eborne; And these three Legasies** I doo heerby order and apoynt my tennant *Samuell Cutler to** paye, *That is to say tenn** pounds to Samuell aforesaied and five pounds to Joseph & three pounds to mary Eborne, as aboue. Morouer I giue to my dafter Mary Roulands flue children, fiue Cows to each of them one, And for my dafter Catherons Children, I giue to Mary and Rebeca Eboron, each of them a Cow, And the Rest of my Cattell, being three steers, a heffer & a Calfe of a yeer ould I giue vnto my dafter Cathorons fouer younger Children namly moses Hanna & Jeames & Sara; to be equally deuided amongst them, only my will is that Jeames shall haue the thre yeer ould steere. My ffether bed too bolsters I giue vnto my grandchild Samuell Eborne, and allso my Iron pott. And to marye Eboron, I giue my littell Joynt Chare, and my Box to Rebeca Eboron, And as for all debts that is dew to me, my on debts, that shall appeere dew to my Creditors being payed, the Rest I giue & bequeth to my too dafters Catheron Ebron, and Mary Rouland abouesaied.

"Allso, I giue vnto my son Jeames Smith my ffether bed in the Parler, with all things that doo belong vnto itt, with the bedsteede, My mare, and my Hors I giue vnto my Sonn Jeames to be Improued for his Children, the mare being now in fould, the Coalt when it falls I giue to my to grandchildren Samuell & Josep Rouland My great Cobber I giue

---

* These italicized words torn from the original will are supplied from a copy in Essex Co. Quarterly Court Files, vol. IX, leaf 11.

to my dafter Eboren, as allso my Round tabell, & an Iron skillet, My Pott I giue to my grandchild Mary Rouland my great Iron kittell I giue to my grandchild Mary Eboron, my brasse skillett to my dafter Rouland my green Rugg I giue to Samuell Eborn w^{th} the bed aforesaied. my Red Rugg I giue to my dafter Eborne. And my to pare of blankets I giue to my to dafters, to each one pare. And the Rest of the my stuffe I giue betwen my to dafters aforesaied, to be equally deuided among them."

"At the sinning heerof, the word Rouland strooke out, & the word Eborne put in the margent in the 29 line in the other side is — of march aforesayd."

her mark<br/>Mary   3   Smith

Witness: Will^m Pitt, Joseph Rowland, mary aborn.

Proved before Wm. Hathorne 25: 2: 1663 by Willim Pitte and Mary Aborne and received in Ipswich court May 5, 1663.

Inventory taken Apr. 13, 1663 by Francis Johnson and Moses Mavericke: 2 steers & a heafer of 2 years ould & one steer of 3 years ould & one yearlin, 13li. 10s.; 7 Cowes, 35li.; 3 swine, 2li.; a mare wth foale & a horse 2 years, 23li.; the bead, boulster, beadsteed, Cortains, Rugg, blanket & the other things belonginge to the bead in the parler, 8li.; a Cubbard, 1li. 10s.; a table, 4 Joynt stooles & 2 Cheares, 1li. 15s.; 2 Cushings, 3s.; a great Cheste, 16s.; in the Cheaste: a hatt, 10s.; Apron, 5s.; hood, 8s.; 6 yds. & a halfe Carsey, 1li. 19s.; 18 yds. stuffe, 3s. ℔ yd., 2li. 14s.; a man sutte of Cloth, 2li.; a peare stockins, 5s.; black gowne, 1li. 10s.; kersey peticoote, 1li. 10s.; read peticoote, 1li. 10s.; read sarge peticoote, 1li. 10s.; black Cloth gowne, 1li. 10s.; a wastcoote, 15s.; monny, 10li. 2s.; read kersey peticoote, 1li. 10s.; total, 27li. 18s. 6d. In the midle Roome: a feather bead & 2 boulsters, 3li. 10s.; Rugg, 1li. 10s.; 2 blanketts, 1li. 5s.; a sheet, 10s.; a round table, 10s.; settle, 5s.; Chare, 4s.; dripine pann, gridiron & Smothinge iron, 10s.; a great Iron kittell & an Iron pott & skilett, 18s.; 7 pewter dishes, 10s. 6d.; a bason & 2 plats, 4s.; 2 Chamber potts, 5s.; a pint pott, 3s. 6d.; 2 cupps & a salte, 1s. 6d.; a chafing dish & Candlestick of brasse, 6s.; a tine pann, 12d.; Lesburne ware, 10s.; a deske, 2s. 6d.; a great brasse kettell, 2li. 2s.; a brasse pott, 8s.; brasse skillet, 2s.; friing pann, 12d.; pouderinge tubb, chese presse & other wooden Lumber, 1li. 10s.; warminge pann, 5s.; trundle beadsteed & flocke bead, 10s.; read Rugg,

Coton blankett & boulster, 2li.; 3 yds. of Cotton, 7s.; 2 cotton blanketts, 15s.; 2 wheles, 7s.; 3 bushells of corne, 9s.; 8 peare sheets, 8li.; 2 table cloths, 10s.; 4 napkins, 4s.; 2 holon pilowbeers, 5s.; 4 pillows & pillow beers, 15s.; a pichfork, 2 howes, spade, an Iron & mall, ould axes, tongs, fire shovell & hangers, 15s.; total, 144li. 3s. 6d.

Received in Ipswich court May 5, 1663.

*Essex Co. Probate Files, Docket 25,670.*

"the bead and furnytver belonging to itt: in the whish the sd mary Smith dyed in: she gave itt to her sonn James Smith then leven in ould ingland: the bead and furnyture was this—one beadsted: one bead; tto boulsters: and two pellowes: and one pare of blanketts: one rouge: and the Curtains and vallings: and one bead matte: and Cord: then belonging to itt. this is a truth: I then being present when this was so given Jane James—this she said is my deare sonn James Smiths, 18<sup>th</sup>-10-63. A Sute of Clothes of Casa Catrin oborne and a pare of woosted stockings. mary aborne." *Essex Co. Quarterly Court Files, vol. 9, leaf 10.*

There being a paper called the last will and testament of Mary Smith presented and no executor named, court May 5, 1663, granted administration to Samuell Eborne, Richard Rowland and Major William Hathorne, or any two of them. They were ordered to dispose of the estate according to the mind of the deceased expressed in the aforesaid paper. *Ipswich Quarterly Court Records, vol. 1, page 119.*

### ESTATE OF THOMAS ANTRUM OF SALEM.

"The Last Will and Testament of Thomas Antrum beinge of pfect Memory Inprimis I giue to: Isaack Burnape the son of my daughter Burnape ten pounds at the age of twenty one years to be paid: if he dye before to be giuen to my son Obadiah Antrum Item I giue to Thomas Spooner my horse Colt Item I giue to Helyard Verin five pounds Item I giue to Obadiah Antrum my son all the Remaind<sup>r</sup> of my estate but in Case it should please god to take away by death my son before the will be proued: that then the Childe or Children of my daughter Hannah Burnape: (who hath hade her full porcon Already) shall haue the estate devided amongst them at the age of eighteene years. Morour I apoynte Edmond Batter my Executor for this my will and

Thomas Spooner and Helyard Veren my Ouerseer as witnes my hand: this 24 of 11 ᵐᵒ 1662"

his mark
Thomas + Antrum

Witness: Thomas Spooner, William Woodcocke.
Proved in Salem court 3: 5: 1663 by the witnesses.

Inventory of the estate of Thomas Antrum of Salem, taken Feb. 17, 1662, by Elias Stileman and John Ruck: Cattell lett to hire, 70li.; by soe much due for hire of ye said cattell, 10li.; by soe much due for a farme he sold in his life time, 80li.; 2 peeces of march containing 1 1-4 acres, 6li.; 2 steers, 3 yeare old a peece, 9li.; 1 mare at Lyn, 10li. & 1 mare in ye woods if not lost, 8li., 18li.; a stone colt, 8li., 2 brass Kettells, 2li., 3 Iron potts, 2li. 2s., 12li. 2s.; 1 brass pot & 2 bell mettle skilletts, 15s.; 2 brasse skilletts & pott hoockes, 8s.; 1 skumer & brass ladle & pestle & morter, 6s.; 1 brass candlestick & chamber pot, 3s., 6 pewter platters, 18s., 1li. 1s.; 3 plates & 3 pewter dishes, 6s.; 30 old basons & 5 saucers & old pewter, 8s., 1 sword, 30d., 10s. 6d.; bookes, 4s., a stone bottle, 6d.; a bucking tubb, 2s., 6s. 6d.; At Goodman Spooners, 1 loome, 25s., 6 pr. sleas & harnesse & shuttle, 25s., 2li. 10s.; 2 1-4 yrd. wt. cotten cloath, 5s., 2 cource sheets & 4 old bagges, 5s., 10s.; an Iron kettle, 7s., 2 old brass kettles, 2s., 9s.; a beame & scales & shott waite, 5s.; 2 old basketts & a littel woole, 1s.; 2 pr. stockens, 5s.; 12 yrds. Kersy, 6s. p. yrd., 3li. 12s., 3li. 17s.; 3 yellow Curtaines & vallens, 20s., a green Curtaine & carpett, 1li. 7s.; 1 whittle, 10s., & 1 shagg mantle, 4s., a broad cloath stamell mantle, 1li. 14s.; 1 Jump cloake & hood for a woeman, 1li. 10s.; 2 cloakes & 1 long coate, 5li.; 1 Hatt & Portugall capp, 8s., 5li. 8s.; 1 muffe, 1s., 17 1-4 yds Linnen cloath, 24s., 1li. 5s.; 3 long coates, 2li., 3 pr. breeches, 2 dublets, 3 short coats & wascoats, 3li., 5li.; 1 feather bead & bolster, 4li., 1 old feather bead & bolster, 2li., 6li.; 1 flock bead & bolster, 20s., 3 feather pillowes, 10s., 1li. 10s.; 1 pr. course sheets, 8s., 1 blew Rugg, 35s., 1 green old Rugg, 5s., 2li. 8s.; a wt. blanket, 1 blew & 1 Cotten blankett, 1 new wt. blankett, 1li., 25 yds. Cotton cloath, 3li., 2s. 6d., 8 bands, 2 capps, 3s., 3li. 5s. 6d.; 12 yds. tiking, 36s., 4 Cource & 5 worne shifts, 14s., 2li. 10s.; 1 Lind. wascoat, 2s., & skirt, 2s., 1 pr. sheets, 12s., 5 cource sheets, 10s., 1li. 4s.; 1 pr. pillow beers, 4s., a wenscot chest & 1 plaine chest, 14s., 18s.; 1 old settle chest, 12d., 3 chaires, 2s., 1 box, 1s., 2 pr. shooes, 6s., 10s.; frying pan,

18d., a hauck, chamber pot, suckling bottle & porenger, 3s., 4s. 6d.; a brass candlestik & lamp, 18d., 2 Jugg bottles, 18d., 2 1-2 yrd. penestone, 10s., 13s.; a bible, 10s.; in money, 6li. 15s. 6d.; 5 pillow beers in a box, 10s., 7li. 15s. 6d.; 5 napkens, 3 towells, 8s., 3 table cloathes, 10s., a remnt. of holland, 3s., 1li. 1s.; 1 holland sheete, 13s., 5 cource sheets, 16s., 2 boxes, 4s., 1li. 13s.; 5 spoones, & 1 Iron candle stick, 2s. 6d.; total, 263li. 6s.

*Essex Co. Quarterly Court Files, vol. 9, leaf 24.*

The will of Thomas Antrim, presented by Edmond Batter, was allowed and proved May 5, 1663, and said Batter was ordered to give in the original to the clerk of the Salem court, both of the will and inventory. *Ipswich Quarterly Court Records, vol. 1, page 117.*

### ESTATE OF JOHN BENNET OF MARBLEHEAD.

Administration on the estate of John Bennet granted 30: 4: 1663 to Margaret, his widow. Inventory, 76li. 2s. The estate was to remain in the widow's hands, save the house and land appraised at 50li., which after the widow's decease, was to go to her daughter Mary, wife of Elias White, and to her daughter's maid's child Joane had by her first husband, Christopher Codner. *Salem Quarterly Court Records, vol. 4, page 115.*

An invoice, dated June 29, 1663, of the estate of widow Benett of Marvelhead: For a house Lot and fence, 50li.; four Swine, 6li.; four heifers, 7li.; a fether bed and furniture, 5li.; one Rug, 2li.; a Coate, 1li. 5s.; Iron, Brasse and puter, 2li. 5s.; a table, box and Chist, 12s.; total, 76li. 2s. *Essex Co. Quarterly Court Files, vol. 9, leaf 15.*

### ESTATE OF COL. THOMAS READ OF (SALEM?).

Whereas there was an attorneyship given to Mr. Danyell Epps from Colonel Thomas Read, who had an estate in land and other ways in this country, the said Colonel Reade having deceased, said Epps was appointed 30: 4: 1663 administrator of the estate to bring in an inventory to the next Ipswich court. *Salem Quarterly Court Records, vol. 4, page 116.*

Widow Read complained that Robert Pease withheld her thirds of about six acres of land which her husband Thomas

Reade was possessed of in his life time while she was his wife. Court 28: 4: 1670 ordered Hilliard Veren, Henry Skerry, sr., and John Tompkins to lay out her thirds according to law. *Salem Quarterly Court Records, vol. 5, leaf 33.*

### Estate of Thomas Flint of Salem.

"Dated Aprill the first 1663. This present writing doth declare that I Thomas fflint being one my sicke bed, doe leaue this as my Last will & testament. To my wife I giue fiftie Acres of emprowed Land & my meadow & housing. To my sonne Thomas I Giue thirtie acres of vpland one my ffarme next to M^r Gardners as hee sees fit not entrenching one his mothers meadow or broken land as also ten pounds in Corne or Cattell all which he is to enjoy at age: As *also after* my wives decease to enjoy two thirds of my farme I bought of which was M^r Higginsons & Goodman Goodall, & in case his mother doth marrie then that he shall enjoy the one halfe of the emprowed Lands & meadow & housing To my sonnes George & John, I give all my Land I bought beyond the River, to enjoy equally devided to them when they are at age or at theire mothers decease yf shee die before, it is my will that yf George die without seed, then my sonne John to enjoy his part, & yf John die without seed then my sonne George to enjoy his parte To my sonne Joseph I give the other third part of my Land which was M^r Higginsons & Goodman Goodalls, It is provided that my sonne Joseph enjoy it at his mothers decease, & yf my sonne Thomas die without seed vnmarried then his part to fall to my sonne Joseph & Contrariwise yf my sonne Joseph die without seed then his part to fall to Thomas & soe to pass from one to another yf hee that enjoyes it die without issue. To my daughter Elizabeth I Giue thirtie pounds at marriage in Corne & Cattell, & I doe appoint my sonne Thomas when he enjoyes his two thirds as abouesaid then to pay to my Daughter Elizabeth & in case the farme fall into Josephs hands before he is of age or after he to pay her the said ten pounds I doe appoint my wife whole executor, I entreate my Two freinds M^r William Browne Senio^r & Goodman Moulton to bee my overseers, to see this my will & testament pformed, & this I Leaue at my Last will and Testament. In witness wheareof I set to my hand."

T. F.

Witness: Robert Moulton, Joseph Pores marke, Job Swinerton Juner.

"my will is that my wife at her death giue the estate shee leaues to my children whome shee will  my desire is that my freind Job Swinerton Junior be joined with m<sup>r</sup> Browne & Goodman moulton." *Essex Co. Quarterly Court Files, vol. 9, leaf 16.*

Proved in Salem court 30: 4: 1663 by Robert Moulton and Job Swinerton. *Salem Quarterly Court Records, vol. 4, page 116.*

Inventory taken Apr. 14, 1663, by Robert Moulton, Samuel Verry and Henry Phelps: The Farme, 120li.; land Bought of Goodman Goodall, 20li.; land bought beyond Ipswitch River, 41li.; neate Cattell, foure oxen, 20li.; two yongue steeres, 5li.; sixe two yearlings, 12li.; a bull, 3li.; a Mare & Foale, 15li.; two horses, 20li.; a Yongue horse, 5li.; a Cart & plow, chaine, axes, howes, 3li.; Indian Corne, ten Bushels, 1li. 10s.; a Bushell Rie, 4s.; two Kittles & a pot, 1li.; pewter, 12s.; bed & bedding, 10li.; wearing clothes, 10li.; chest & lumber, 1li.; swine, 10li.; a flitch of bacon, 1li.; William Curtess is debtr., 6li.; land bought, 1li. 10s.; total, 330li. 16s.  Thomas Flint, debtr.: To Mr. Browne, 15li.; Goodman Goodall, 20li.; Goodman Cowdrie, 3li. 15s.; Goodman Clarke & Lieutenant Smith, 16li. 5s.; Goodman Canterbury, 3li.; other small debts, 7li. 13s. 4d.; total, 65li. 13s. 4d. *Essex Co. Quarterly Court Files, vol. 9, leaf 17.*

### ESTATE OF MATHEW WHIPPLE OF IPSWICH.

Whereas there was an estate of Mathew Whiple of Ipswich, deceased, which was ordered at a court held at Ipswich, Mar. 29, 1659, to be given to Mary, wife of said Mathew and their child, that is, the land to the said child and the rest of the estate to the widow, the child having since deceased, the court 30: 4: 1663 appointed John Whiple, son of Mathew Whiple, father of said Mathew, deceased, administrator of the estate of the child, and to bring in an inventory to the next Ipswich court. *Salem Quarterly Court Records, vol. 4, page 117.*

John Whiple, having brought in an inventory of the estate of Mathew Whipple, amounting to 175li., court Sept. 29, 1663 ordered two parts to said John Whipple and one part to Joseph Whipple, his brother. *Ipswich Quarterly Court Records, vol. 1, page* 122.

"John Whipple, sonn of Mathew whipple: ffather of the saide Mathew deceased hath with the consent of Alexander Tompson taken possession according to law of the house & Land or estate which was ordered to the child being made Administrator by the court held at Salem" 2:5:1663. Witness: Richard Walker and Daniell (his mark) Davison of Ipswich. *Ipswich Deeds, vol. 2, page* 169.

### Estate of Robert Sallows of Salem.

Robt. Sollas, dying intestate, the widow, Freeborn Sollas brought in an inventory of his estate and 30:4:1663, was appointed administratrix. She was ordered to pay the children had by her late husband, Hanna, Mary, Sara and Robert Sollas, 10li. each at age, and to give bond for the payment of the children's portions at such time as she change her condition by marriage. *Salem Quarterly Court Records, vol. 4, page* 117.

Inventory of the estate of Robert Sallos, taken by Tho. Lowthropp, John Thorndike, Richard (his y mark) Brackenbury and John Pache: Wearing Cloathes, 8li. 15s.; woster & yearne, woolen & lininge, 1li. 10s.; boots & showes, 12s.; fishing lines & leads, 13s.; bands, table-cloathes & napkins, 5li. 11s.; five paire of sheets, 5li. 2s.; shirts & one ould waskcott, 10s.; one musket, sword & bandlears, 1li. 10s.; bedding, 3li. 11s.; barrels, 11s.; flax & leade, 18s.; in beding, 10li. 9s.; towe chests, one truncke, towe boxes, 1li. 14s.; two bedsteeds, 12s.; bookes, 1li.; Iron ware, 2li. 13s.; one smothin Iron & looking glas, 8s.; puter, 2li. 3s.; earthen ware, 16s.; wood ware, baskets, spinning wheeles, 1li.; lumber, 1li.; one Cowe, 5li.; two pigs, 1li. 10s.; house & ground, 75li.; one prentice box which cost 10li.; one Cannow, 1li. 1s.; total, 143li. 9s. 6d. In fish, 8li. 10s.; in salt, 1li. 4s. *Essex Co. Quarterly Court Files, vol. 9, leaf* 18.

### Estate of Thomas Sallows of Salem.

Grace, wife of Thomas Sollas, deceased, presented an inventory of his estate amounting to 70li. 15s. 5d., and 30:4:1663 was appointed administratrix. Court ordered to the children as follows: to Thomas, 4li., and to Mary, Robert and Abigail, 40s., each at age. *Salem Quarterly Court Records, vol. 4, page* 118.

THE PROBATE RECORDS OF ESSEX COUNTY. 419

Inventory of the estate of Thomas Sallowes, taken June 4, 1663, by Elias Stileman and Tho. Rootes: One house & one acre & halfe of Land, 60li.; one Cowe, 4li. In ye parlour: one feather bed & 2 boulsters, 2 pillowes, 1 pr. of white blanketts, 1 blue Rugg, a straw bed, curtaines & vallance & bedsted, 8li.; 1 Court Cubbard, 12s.; a wainscort chest, 10s.; 1 table & 2 joyne stooles, 10s.; 1 carpit, 9s.; 3 boxes & 3 chaires, 8s.; 1 warming pan & pr. tongs & fire shovell, 8s.; 1 Cushion for a Cubbard's head, 1s. In ye Hall: 1 ould feather bed & 1 pr. blanketts, 1 feather boulster, a canvas bed & a boulster case, 1 greene rugg, 1 bedsted, curtaines & vallance, 5li.; 1 pr. blanketts, a feather pillow & 2 canvass bed case, 1li.; 1 settle, 5s. & 9 chaires, 13s.; 6 cushions, 6s., 3 feather pillows, 4s., 10s.; 2 hakes, 1 pr. tongs, a spit & gredeiren, 6s.; 1 frying pann, old, 12d., & smothing Iron, 2s. 6d.; 2 Iron potts, 1 Iron kettle & skillett, 14s.; 2 brass kettles & 2 skillett, 1li. 6s.; 1 Looking glass & a Jugg bottle, 1li. 6s.; 2 bookes of Mr. Burroughs & 2 ps. bookes, 10s.; 1 brush, 9d., 2 pr. pott hookes, 2s., 2s. 9d.; in wearing clothes, 3li.; 9 pewter dishes, 1 bason, 2 small basins, 2 quart potts, 8 porrengers, 4 spoones, 1 beaker & a boule & 1-2 pint pott, 7 saucers, 2 salts, 1li. 15s.; 1 brass candlestick & 2 brass Ladles, 5s.; in Latten waire, 3s.; Lisburne ware & glasses, 10s.; 2 doz. of trenchers & 6 spoones, 1s. 6d.; 15 woodn. dishes & 3 trayes, 5s.; 3 sives, 3s., 2 chests, 6s.; small table, 4s., 13s.; 1 musquet, 10s.; 2 baggs, 5s., & old sea beds & beding, 15s., 1li.; 13 sheetes, 3li. 10s.; 3 calleco table clothes & 1 ossingbriggs, 15s.; 2 old cobberd clothes, 2s., 6 Lockm. napkins, 8s.; 12 pillow-beers, 20s.; 6 small ones, 3s., 1li. 3s.; 14 towells & 1 table cloth, 14s.; 5 shirts & 1 white demyty wastcote, 1li. 10s.; 2 old axes, wedges & erthen potts, 8s.; in Lumber, old barrells & tables & pals, 10s.; 1 Lining bask good & 2 old, 3s.; in a part of a stage & house at ye Messery, 1li. 10s.; 4 codlines, 2 pr. of shoes & portugall capp, 10s.; 1 doz. handkerchiefs & 6 bands, 10s.; 6 pr. Stockings & a spinning wheele, 12s.; a pestle & morter of brass, 2s. 1d.; total, 105li. 11s. 3d. Debtor: to Mr. Wm. Browne, 18li. 15s. 10d.; to Wm. Allen, 16li.; total, 34li. 15s. 10d. *Essex Co. Quarterly Court Files, vol. 9, leaf 19.*

ESTATE OF JOHN CUMMINGS OF SALEM.

Whereas John Comins, mariner, late of Salem, had been lately out upon a voyage and it being feared that he was lost, all his estate in the hands of John Orme of Salem and all else to be found in this country, said Orme was ordered 30: 4: 1663 to inventory and return the same to the next Salem or Ipswich court. *Salem Quarterly Court Records, vol. 4, page* 118.

Mr. John Gardner and John Ormes were appointed 24: 9: 1663 administrators of the estate of John Commins, deceased, that is in this country, and were ordered to bring in an inventory to the next court. *Salem Quarterly Court Records, vol. 4, page* 124.

Inventory of the estate taken in the custody of John Ormes of Salem, Nov. 26, 1663, by Edmond Batter and Walter Price: 111 yds. of Canves at 18d. pr. yrd., 8li. 6s. 6d.; 20 yds. of brod Lining at 2s. p. yd., 2li.; 63 yds. of Ossinbredge at 15d. yd., 3li. 18s. 9d.; 56 1-2 yds. of Canves at 18d. yd., 4li. 4s. 9d.; 42 yds. of Canves at 18d. pr. yrd., 3li. 3s.; 3 peces of tufted holond at 2s. 2d., containing in all 45 yrds., 4li. 17s. 6d.; 34 yds. of blew Lining at 3s. pr. yd., 5li. 2s.; In money, 4li.; A sute of Cloathes And Wastcoate, 2li. 5s.; A Cloake, 30s., and hat, 15s., 2li. 5s.; A feather bed, bolster, on pillow and 2 blankites, 7li. 12s.; total, 47li. 14s. 6d. *Essex Co. Quarterly Court Files, vol. 9, leaf* 64.

Mr. John Gardner, administrator of the estate of John Comings, presented an inventory and the court Mar. 29, 1664, ordered him to pay the debts and to keep the rest of the estate until the court take further order. *Ipswich Quarterly Court Records, vol. 1, page* 126.

Samll. Cummins, son of John Cummins, was appointed June 29, 1669, administrator of the latter's estate, in the hands of Mr. John Gardner, the former administrator, who was discharged. Said Cummins gave bond to pay the children's portions. *Salem Quarterly Court Records, vol. 5, leaf* 24.

### Estate of William Cantlebury of Salem.

"whereas the lord our god hath appoynted his servants to set there houses in order, to the prayse of his name, the comfort of their owne soules and the peace of their famelyes. Therefore I Willyam Cantlebery of Salem though weake in body yet in perfect memory in obedience vnto christ my sauiour do commit my body to earth in its season: hopinge when christ who is my life shal appeare: to be brought agayne w$^{th}$ him in glory.

"And for my outward estate I doe thus dispose thereof makinge this my last will & testament  Inprimis, I giue vnto Beatrice my wife, my house and orchard, & the land lyinge betweene the land of Richard Leach & John Rowden: the which house and land I giue to her & to be at her dispose. Item: I giue vnto Beatrice my wife: all my moueable goods, all my Catle: both younge and old, & horse and mares  All the which foresayed house and land: mouable goods and Catle I giue vnto her frely, & to be at her dispose: Prouided, that in case my wife should marry to another husband: my children be not depriued, of what my wife shal leaue at her decease. Item: I giue vnto my son John: the 3 quarters of the farme.  I bought of mr George Corwine (the 20 acres excepted, that I disposed of to Job Swinnerton) only Inioyninge him, to pay as legacyes out of the same, twenty pounds to my Daughter Ruth, & twenty pounds to my Daughter Rebbecca & her children. Item: my will is in case my son John shal depart this life, or shal not come to take possession of the sayd farme, I giue vnto him, for that is my will that he shal come in person to take possession: or else: If he depart this life, or doe not come to take possession thereof I giue then the sayd farme bought of mr George Corwinne as aforesayd, vnto my daughter Ruth: Inioyninge her to pay as a legacy vnto my ‖daughter‖ Rebbeca, thirty pounds, & in case my daughter Ruth: shal by gods providence, be disposed of in marriage, the profit of the sayd farme shal be hers, vntil, my son John shal take possesson as aforesayd: the legacyes beinge payd, both the w$^{ch}$ foresayd legacyes ar to be payd vpon the entry vpon the farme. Item I constitute & apoynt Beatrice my wife to be sole executrix of this my last wil and testament Item: I Constitute, and appoynt my lovinge ffreinde mr John Croade ouerseer of this my last wil and testament

"That this is my last wil & testament witnes my hand & seale Dated the 2$^{th}$ of April 1661."

signum<br>Willyam O Cantlebery

Witness: John Porter, sen., Nathaniel ffelton.

Proved in Salem court 3: 5: 1663 by the witnesses. *Essex Co. Quarterly Court Files, vol. 9, leaf 22.*

Inventory taken June 25, 1663 by Thomas Gardner, sr.,

and Nathaniel Felton: A farme wth. appurtenances, 220li.; his dwellinge house with land adjoyninge, 60li.; a house & orchard, 20li.; 7 oxen, 49li.; 6 Cowes, 27li.; 2 heifers, 7li. 10s.; 3 yearlings & 3 calves, 9li.; 8 bigger swine, 10li.; 3 lesser swine, 1li. 4s.; 1 horse, 10li.; 1 mare & yearlinge Colt, 15li.; 9 smal piggs, 1li. 7s.; 1 feather bed, 3li.; 1 Rug, 1li. 10s.; 1 boulster, 3 blankets, 2 pillows, 2li. 10s.; a payre of sheets & 2 table cloths, 1li. 6s.; 3 payre of sheets, 1li. 10s.; 5 Course pillow beares, 6s.; 1 old flock bed, 10s.; 1 old Rug & 3 blankets, 2li. 10s.; 1 brass ketle & a brasse skillet, 1li. 5s.; 2 Iron potts & 1 iron ketle, 2li. 5s.; 1 hake, 2 payre of pot hooks & a gridiron, 10s.; a bedstead wth. old curtaynes & vallons, 1li. In Peauter & lattin ware, 8s.; 1 chest, 2 old coffers, 10s.; 1 table & 2 chayres, 12s.; 1 musket, 2 swords & bandeleirs, 1li.; 1 sadle & pillyon & a pannel, 1li. 10s.; 3 payles & 6 trayes, 10s.; Indian Corne, 1li. 10s.; In Bacon, 3li. 5s.; Iron chaynes & plow tacklings, 2li.; his waringe Apparel, 5li.; In mony, 1li.; In old lumber, 1li.; Corne growinge, 4li.; total, 470li. 8s. Creditor: By Tho. Robins, 17li. 10s.; Richard Hutton, 2li. 5s.; widd. Flint, 2li. 16s.; total, 22li. 11s. Debtor: To Mr. George Corwinne, 11li. 11s. 8d.; Mr. Price, 1li. 9s. 2d.; Mr. Browne, 30li.; Mr. Gardiner, 1li. 2s.; John Marsh, 1li. 9s. 10d.; Francis Lawes, 3s.; rent of the farme, 20li. *Essex Co. Quarterly Court Files, vol. 9, leaf 23.*

The court 28: 4: 1664 appointed Leift. Tho. Putnam and John Porter, sr., to lay out and bound, in convenient time, the thirds of a farm of William Cantlebury, deceased, according to the will and inventory, for the use of Bettrice, the widow. *Salem Quarterly Court Records, vol. 4, page 131.*

### ESTATE OF JOHN CALIE OF NEWBURY.

Administration on the estate of John Calie of Newbury, intestate, granted Sept. 29, 1663 to John Calie, his son. *Ipswich Quarterly Court Records, vol. 1, page 121.*

### ESTATE OF ROBERT ROBERTS OF IPSWICH.

Administration on the estate of Robert Roberds intestate, granted Sept. 29, 1663 to Susan Roberts, the widow. Inventory amounting to 160li. was brought in and there were eight children left. Court ordered that John Roberds, the eldest son, should have 12li., and the other children 6li. each, at age or marriage. If the widow should marry again, court ordered that the other children should have 10li. each instead of 6li., and her husband was to give security. *Ipswich Quarterly Court Records, vol. 1, page 122.*

Inventory of the estate of Robert Roberts of Ipswich lately deceased, taken July 20, 1663 by Regnald Foster, sr., Tho. Clarke and Thomas Knoulton: Dwelling house and barn, 20li.; cart & wheeles & plough with the furniture to them, 5li. 5s.; 2 oxen, 13li. 10s., 4 Cowes, 16li., 2 steers, 8li., 3 Calves, 1li. 16s., 39li. 6s.; 10 acres of land at Chebacco, upland & meddow, 20li.; 11 swine and tenn piggs, 16li. 6s. 8d.; halfe a mare & half a horse, 9li.; a sheep fold, 2li.; 4 Ews, 4 lambs, a Ram and a wether, 4li. 6s.; ground improved, 5li.; 3 Canows, 5li.; a bed and Covelett, 5li. 10s.; a bed and Coverlets & pillows, and bolster, 6li. 12s.; 2 blanketts, 3 pillows, 1li. 12s. 6d.; a bed & Bolster, 2li. 10s.; Indean Corne, 6li.; Bacon & Porke, 1li. 10s.; his aperrall, 5li.; fethers, 18s.; wooll, 1li. 2s.; Bedsteds, 2li. 16s.; a Cubberd, 10s.; Chest, 3 boxes, a Case of Bottells, 1li. 6s.; Sheetes & pillow beers, 5li. 2s.; pewter & warminge pan, 2li.; pots, kettell, skillets, fier souell & tongus, 2li. 8s.; a table, 5s., Chaiers, 5s., wheels, 5s., a Cradle, 5s., 1li.; a Iron pott, 6s.; milke vessells, tubbs & other nessessarys, 2li.; Bettle, wedges, axes & hows, 1li. 8s.; Instruments for his trade, 1li.; 3 bushels of malt, 18s.; post & Rayles, 7s.; pouder & shott, 12s. 6d.; 2 pare of sheres, 2s.; due to me from divers debters, 4li.; total, 181li. 11s. 8d. *Essex Co. Quarterly Court Files, vol. 9, leaf 47.*

Whereas there was an order made at the court Sept. 29, 1663 for the husband of Susanna Roberds to give security for the payment of the portions of Robert Roberds' child set by the court, it was ordered Sept. 28, 1669, that Thomas Perrin give such security to Robert Lord, clerk. *Ipswich Quarterly Court Records, vol. 5, page 99.*

### Estate of William Gardner.

William Gardner, fisherman, dying intestate, his brother ———— Gardner and Mr. Edmond Batter were appointed Sept. 29, 1663, administrators of his estate, and ordered to bring in an inventory to the next Salem court. *Ipswich Quarterly Court Records, vol. 1, page 122.*

## Estate of Samuel Winsley of Salisbury.

Administration on the estate of Mr. Sam. Winsley, late of Salisbury, deceased, granted 13: 8: 1663 to Sam. Winsley and he was ordered to satisfy Mrs. Ann Winsley, widow, for her jointer so far as the estate will go, and to give in his account to the next Salisbury court. *Hampton Quarterly Court Records, vol. 1, leaf 17.*

Whereas the court Apr. 12, 1664 was informed by Sam. Winsley that he had delivered to his mother, Mrs. Anne Winsley, 20li., also to deliver what estate was in the inventory to her when she required it, court accepted this as an answer to said Mrs. Winsley, there being no estate to make good the bond given by Mr. Winsley to make good her jointure or annuity. *Salisbury Quarterly Court Records, vol. 1, leaf 22.*

Inventory taken June 27, 1663, by Tho. Bradbury and Andru Grele: purse & aparrell, 4li. 2s. 6d.; his wearing linnen, 1li. 10s.; Iron tooles, 7s.; a Spining wheele, 4s.; a wheelbarrow, 2s. 6d.; in Ocumy, 8s.; a payer of Scysers, 3d.; 2 barrells, 4s.; nayles, 2s. 6d.; total, 6li. 4s.; 3 pillobeers, 9s.; 3 napkins, 9s.; 1 payer of sheets, 13s. 4d.; a woollen wheele, 4s.; 2 stooles, 1s. 6d.; 19 pound of yarne, 19s.; total, 2li. 15s. 10d.

Sworn to in Hampton court 13: 8: 1663.

On reverse of paper: 300 foot of board, 13s. 6d.; Humphry Willson debtor, 1li.; Samuell Tillton of Hampton, 5s. 6d.; Mr. Taylor, 18s.; for a cloakbag he lost, 7s.; Edward Gove, 18s. 2d.; Steven Greneleife to pay for Peter Coffin, 10s.; Sam. Robins, 2s.; due from Henry Roby for paying for 2 atachmts serving for his brother Sam and for a wittness at Hampton Court, 5s.; total, 4li. 19s. 2d. *Essex Co. Probate Files, Docket 30,176.*

## Estate of Theophilus Shatswell of Haverhill.

"The Last will of Theophelus Satswell: Datted y<sup>e</sup> twenteth day of y<sup>e</sup> fourth: m<sup>o</sup> in y<sup>e</sup> yeare of o<sup>r</sup> lord one thousand six: hundred Sixty & thre  Memorandum: In y<sup>e</sup> name of y<sup>e</sup> Lord Amen. I Theophelus Satswell being but weake in bodey, but of perfitt memory doe Bequeath my soull to god that Gaue it & in his time my bodey to y<sup>e</sup> graue in a christian & deasent maner of buriall & my goods to be: Dispozed of as followith viz: I giue to my eldist Daughter Mary dureing her life one hundred & tenn: Acres of Adishon to y^e 3^d deuishon of upland with all privledges to it belonging, & one & thirty Acers of 2^nd deuishon Adjoyneing to wilya: Deales Land & six: aceres of planting Land adjoyneing to his Land by y^e great riuer And one partiell of y^e East meadow with a 3^d partt of my Salt marsh at Salsbury & hogghill meadow Also half of my 4^th deuishon of vpland for quantity and quallity it being in y^e whole thre hundred & 15 acers w^th all Preuiledges therevnto belonging & a young gray hors & y^e vse of a payer of bullocks two years ‖allready receiued‖ w^th other things Allso I giue unto my daughter Lidea: dureing her lif ‖y^t farme‖ beyond Spickitt riuer as it is bounded bettwen Steuen Kentt And Wilyam Simons & y^e meadow y^t lyeth out of y^e farme vpon y^e brook at y^e head of thomas Dauises 3d Deuishon half y^e meadow being gourg corlis & half mine not yett parted & a white mare & y^e coult y^t cam of The mare calle[d] her mothers mare with other things alreadey receiued Also I giue Hanill Clark my whole pportion of hauks meadow & y^e 3d deuishon of vpland belonging To Sauages Land Layed out beyond haukes meadow vpon a chaing betweene Robertt Swan & I & tenn pounds al If he stay w^th me or mine untill he be one & twenty years of age: ‖or else null all‖ And I make my wif Susanah & my Daughter Hannah Executors & Administrato^s all my other Lands houseing catle & all other herrediments And at y^e Death of my wif then my will is y^t my Daughter Hannah shall be sole Administratour & if hannah dye then y^e other sisters Adminestring, Also my will is in all aboue written y^t my lands after the desease of my daughters Shall goe to there children by y^e heade to part alike & if any of my daughters dye leaueing no child nor children Then her partt so dyeing shall be to all y^e liueing children alike pportion pseeding from her other Sister Further I Desire my Brother Wilyam Sargent: & my Kinsman Lefttenent Philip challis To be my ouer Seers To Se this my will fulfillid accord: to y^e tennor of it."

Theophelus Shatswell.

Witness: Jonathan Singltary, Edward clarke.

Proved in Hampton court 13: 8: 1663 by Edward Clark.

Jonathan Singltary, aged forty nine or thereabouts made oath July 1, 1680 that he wrote the above at the desire of Theophilus Satchwell and saw him sign it.

Inventory taken Sept. 8, 1663 by John Eaton, sr. and John Emmerry, sr.: one bed & bedsteed in ye chamber & ffurniture belonging to it, 5li.; another bed in ye same chamber & ffurniture to it, 4li. 10s.; sheetes & pillowbeeres & table linnen, 4li.; in English goods brought in for a debt, 9li. 6s.; 2 chests, a little trunck, a hogshead & other lumber, 2li.; her wearing apparrell, 5li.; in ye kitchin: pots, kettells, pewter & other nessessary houshold stuff, 5li.; a parcell of old indian Corne in ye chamber, 1li.; a corslett & pike & sword, 1li. 10s.; sheeps wooll & cotton wooll, 1li.; a bed & bedding in ye upper chamber & other nessessary things, 2li. 10s.; his wearing apparrell, 5li.; a parcell of carpenters tooles & tooles for husbandry, 2li. 10s.; a cart & plow & cart rope, 2 yoakes & 2 chaines, a horse harnesse, a bridle, saddle & pillion, 5li.; a parcell of wheate in ye barne, 5li.; hay, 7li.; 4 tun of pork cask, 1li. 4s.; a pcell of flax undrest, 10s.; ———, 8li.; indian Corne upon ye ground, 12li.; house & barne, orchard, homelott & timber to repaire the house, 40li.; 2 acres & a halfe of land by Ed. Clarkes house lott, 12li. 10s.; a pcell of planting Land in ye plaine, 45li.; land att ye Iland, 10li.; 2 parcells of meadow att ye east meadow, 10li.; his North meadow, 12li.; 3 higly pigly salt marsh lotts att Salisbury, 12li.; 36 acres of upland in 2 parcells, adjoyning to Will. Deales lott below ye little river, 30li.; his 3 division of upland, 90li.; his 4th division of upland, 40li.; a pcell of meadow att hoghill meadow, 1li.; his pt in beare meadow, 12li.; a pcell of meadow in hawkes meadow, 12li.; 88 acres of upland of ye 3 division, 45li.; 3 cowes & a heifer, 18li.; 2 oxen & 2 steeres, 27li.; 2 mares, 3 colts, one riding horse, 2 yearling colts & one yearling colt, 65li.; his pt in ye oxe comon, 20li.; in swine, 9li.; 3 sheepe, 1li. 10s.; 30 acres of upland or thereabouts joyning to his 3 division in lieu of yt he wanted elsewhere, 20li.; 110 acres of his addition to his 3 division of upland, 30li.; his pt of yt meadow wch is to be devided betwixt him & George Corlis, 8li.; in debts about 2li.; in debts yt he doth owe about 14li.; for anything unseen or forgotten, 10s.; total, 759li. 10s. More for five Comonages, ——. Attested in Hampton court 13: 8: 1663 by Susanah Satchwell relict and executrix of Theophilus Satchwell.

*Essex Co. Probate Files, Docket 25,121.*

Petition of Edward Clarke of Haverhill to the court at Boston, May 29, 1671 shewing that Theophilus Satchwell in his will gave to his youngest child nothing in particular but left her to be joint executrix with his wife. The said daughter being afterward married, died in childbed, and her husband also died a few months afterward leaving a young child; the estate all being the mothers during life it was thought that by the daughter being executrix, after the mother's death that she would have all the lands and the mother gave the son-in-law a deed of land but the relations opposed it asserting that it was entailed land to the other children. Now the son in law has left no estate only this land and many debts and as executor Edward Clark appeals to this court for advise and direction in the matter as there is nothing to care for the child with.

Referred to the County Court of Norfolk to find the true state of the case and return to this court that they may be better enabled to order the settleing of the estate. *Mass. Archives, vol.* 15B, *page* 241.

Petition of Haniell Bosworth of Ipswich to the Ipswich court Apr. 10, 1683, he being guardian of Abiall Messer of Haverhill and administrator of the estate requesting that the estate may be settled on the said Abiall according to the will of Theophilus Shatswell of Haverhill, his grandfather, and also that Isarell Ela may be appointed guardian and administrator in his place, he being very weak of body, till he come of age to choose for himself. He also states that he has received but one small warming pan and three smale puter platers, the rest of the moveables John Grifin had and hath not yet given account of.

Bond of Abiall Mercier of Haverhill of 1500li. administrator, with James Sanders and Elisha Davis, both of Haverhill as sureties, Signed and sealed June 19, 1704. Witness: John How, Daniel Rogers.

Inventory of the estate of Theophilus Satswell, Abial Mercer administered on which was not otherwise disposed of by the will, taken June 29, 1705 by Jonathan Handick (Hindrick. *copy*) and Samuel Dalton: his homelot six acres, 40li.; Land in The great plaine, 40li.; Three accres of Est medow, 15li.; five acre of north medow, 10li.; medow at bare medow, 13li.; Twenty two acres of ox comon, 30li.; Land on the Ileland, 15li.; nine rights in the comon, 20li.; a percel of Land, 12li.

Sworn to by Abiall Mercier, admr., July 9, 1705.

*Essex Co. Probate Files, Docket* 25,121.

Theophilus Satchwell in his will appointed his wife and Hannah his daughter to be executors and they both dieing before they had completed their trust and the two surviveing daughters having renounced their right of administration the Court appointed Abiall Mercier of Haverhill only child of said Hannah and grandson to said Theophilus Satchwell administrator of the estate. Signed and sealed at Ipswich June 19, 1704 by John Appleton. *Essex Co. Probate Records, vol. 308, page 230.*

### Estate of John Pickworth of Manchester.

"The last will and testement of John Peckworth made the 27 of the 4: month 1663  I John Peckworth being weake & seke of bodey but of Peffet memorey haue ordayned this as my last will & Testyment  Imprymes I giuefe and bequeth vnto my wellbeloued ||wife|| An Peckworth my wholle estate as hows land and Catell and howshowlld goods and she to injoye the same as long as she leueth if liueing and dying in a widows estate but if she other wyis changh her condition and marey then she only to haue her thirds of w$^t$ then: the estate is: and after her changh eyther by deth or marege  Then my Elldest sonne John Peckworth is to haue the hows medow And 25 aekers of land w$^{th}$ the p$^t$ of the nek that lyeth betwene Aberham W$^t$yare and my sellfe: for the rest of my land which is 30 akers bowght of Robert morgon with the medow that belongeth to yet my 3 sonns Samuell Joseph and Beneiemen is to haue the same as fore mentioned by my son John as he is to haue his after my wife soe they to inJoye the sam allsoe: and my sonn Samuell is to haue the 6 aekers that lyeth upon the nek nex to Robert Leachs lot that was giuen me by the Plantation ||manchester|| and the land that lyeth by the saw mill: and for my Part of the samill I thus disspose of yet I leauef yet w$^{th}$ my wife as the rest of my estate only my sonn Samuell to act in her behalfe with the rest of my fortuen and he to be Payed for his labower and to haue half the Profect that yet brings in if the estate howld out then my to elldest dawghters Ruth marsterson and Haner Coollens is to haue 40 shillens a peace when the rest fore mentioned haue theyers: and to my yongest son Beniemen and my yongest Dawghter Abegall I giue a cow callfe the same to be thyer after my decese and the Profet that comes in by the increase furthermore yet is my will that if the hows medow & ground that my son John is to haue cometh to more than a dobell Portion when the estate is pryesed then he is to elld up out of his only he is left to his leberty for the redemeing of his land and to pay w$^t$ yet comes to for to make up the sengell Portions: and for the beter Performance of this my will: I apoynt my wife An Peckworth w$^{th}$ my to Sons John and Samuell to be Administraters and desyers and apoynts my well beloued friends Thomas Jones and William Benet to be ouer seares where unto I here set my hand."

John Pickworth

his mark

Witness: John L Hutson, Samuell friend.

Proved in Salem court 25: 9$^{\text{b}}$: 1663 by the witnesses. *Essex Co. Quarterly Court Files, vol. 9, leaf 71.*

Inventory taken Aug. 25, 1663, by William Allen and Robert Leach: The hows wth the meadow and lans, 25 ackers, 35li.; more land and medow, 16li.; a peace of medow at Kettell Illand, 4li.; a sheare of the saw mill, 30li.; 3 cowes and a calfe, 16li.; a horse wth a sadell, 11li. 10s.; a pcell of swyn, 6li.; a cover and a prcell of bowlts, 1li. 10s.; a prcell of carpenters toolls, 2li.; a fethers bed wth the coweferins, 8li.; pots & ketells & skellets, a fryine pan and hooks, 4li. 5s.; a spet, 3s.; more howshowld stof, erthen and wooden ware, 10s.; more beding wth. the coweferin, 2li.; a pare of cart whealls and Plow, 2li. 10s.; a fowllin Peace, 1li. 5s.; a prcell of Pewter and warmin pan, 3li.; wheat in the barein, 1li. 10s.; enden Corne, 10s.; a Cubowrd, Tabell, stoolls, chayers, chests, 2li. 10s.; his warein Clothers, 8li. 10s.; 7 yds. of coten, 1li. 1s.; more 9 yds. of flaning, 1li. 7s.; kersey, 1li. 7s.; Lining, 7li.; Boots, 16s.; total, 168li. 4s. Sworn by Ann Pickworth, the widow, in Salem court. *Essex Co. Quarterly Court Files, vol. 9, leaf 70.*

## ESTATE OF RICHARD ROOTEN OF LYNN.

"This is the Last will and Testement of Richard *Rooton* First I commit my soulle and body to God that *gave it* First I will and bequeve all that I haue to my ——— whille shee Liues saue Sagemore hill. and ——— close and, to steares, to cowes which I beequeue *to* my kinsman Edmond Rooton, and After my wifes Desease I will that all I haue to bee my kinsman, Edmond Rooton, allsoe I will that hee shall haue a bed with al y$^t$ doeth belonge to it of such as I haue of mine one Allsoe I will that Edmond Rooton haue for his Conuenesy halfe an Acor of ground vpon the hill yt was owld Tilltons to builld him a howse vpon: with tene Poundes

towards his builldings I will; that hee haue it, where hee may have —— most Conuenient, to builld him a howse vp*on*.
—— Allsoe I will: that if Johnathan Hartshorne — continew with my wife and Edmond Rooton —— tearm of yeares I doe grant vnto him fiue — Allsoe I will that our Pastor, m$^r$ whiting haue forty shilling giuen vnto him Allsoe I will that Henery Rhods haue twenty shillings to bee giuen him, I will to giue vnto Gorge Tayler twenty shilling. Singhued Sealled and Deliuered in the Presents of vs whose names are vnder written. this: 12$^{th}$ of June 1663."

his mark<br>Richard h Rooton<br>[SEAL]

"This his will and Testament was written when hee was in his Perfect, memory this Adicion was written beefore the signeing and sealling heare of,"

Witness: Henery Rhodes, Robert Driuer, ffrancis Burrill.

"It is my will that —— my wife my chefe E*xecutrix* and Henery Rhods my ouersers, and Gorge Tayler with him."

Proved in Salem court 25: 9: 1663 by Henry Roads and Robert Driver. *Essex Co. Quarterly Court Files, vol. 9, leaf 72.*

Inventory taken Sept. 20, 1663 by Nathaniell Handforth and Francis Burrill: Coates and breaches, 4li. 18s.; a new shute, 1li. 10s.; in stockins, 7s.; hates, 1li. 6s.; shurtes, 1li.; shooes, 7s. 6d.; beding, 3li.; pillowes, 1li.; tikes, 16s.; a Pillow, 6s.; fether Pillows, 2li.; fether bed, 2li.; a bed, 16s.; 3 blankets, 1li. 7s.; in Coverletes, 3li.; a coverlet, 1li.; a grene Ruge, 1li. 2s.; a cotten Ruge, 1li. 10s.; blankets, 3li. 4s.; grene Cotten, 7s. 6d.; Coate, 5s.; in broad Cloth, 2li. 6s.; cersy, 4li. 3s. 6d.; Red Penestone, 4s.; serge, 2li. 6s.; blew Cotten, 3s.; in Cotten and Linen Cloath, 1li.; sheetes and Pillow tikes, 10li. 16s.; Napkins, 10s.; blew Calleco, 4s.; Linen and bandes, 10s.; Potes and kettells, 2li. 10s.; a brase kettell, 1li. 12s.; a warming Pane, 6s.; a Morter and Pestell, 6s.; tonges and shouffell, 12s. 6d.; Pewter, 2li. 7s. 6d.; gunes and sordes, 2li. 10s.; chestes, 1li. 10s.; a tike, 8s.; cheres and stolles, 12s.; a Tabell and forme, 1li.; a bedsted and Cubard, 1li. 10s.; two Restes, 1s.; Earthen Potes, 1s.; bookes, 12s.; tubes and other Lumber, 1li. 3s. 6d.; wolle, 10s.; hopes, 2s.; tubes, 8s.; Flaxe, 1li. 5s.; a Rope, 2s.; Corne, 2li. 2s.; trenchers, 2s.; sives, 2s.; Oyle Jares, 2s. 6d.; wheeles, 4s.; barly, 2li. 10s.; wheate, 2li. 10s.; Ingen Corne, 2li. 10s.; Eyren, 2li. 18s.; Inglish haye, 3li.; sallt mash, 6li.; a Pare of Oxen, 14li.; cowes, 18li.; steres, 8li.; heffers, 9li. 10s.; caves, 2li. 10s.; shepe, 4li.; a mare and coult, 15li.; swine, 4li.; land, 131li.; howses, 15li.; cart and whells and other things belonging, 2li. 10s.; fries, 5s.; mony, 20li.; a brase Potte, 3s.; Plow Eyrens, 8s.; Dettes owing to her, 11li. 15s.; other debts, 1li. 15s.; more, 2li.; in yarden, 6s.; more, 1li. 17s. 2d.; total, 281li. 6s. 8d.

Paid out of the estate since her husband's death: To Mr. King, 7s.; the Cowkeper, 8s.; for sumering of cattell, 14s.; more laid out, 1li.; more, 7li.; total, 9li. 9s. *Essex Co. Quarterly Court Files, vol. 9, leaf 73.*

### ESTATE OF RICHARD LITTLEHALE OF HAVERHILL.

Inventory of the estate of Rychard Littlehale of Haverhill, deceased Feb 18, 1663, taken Mar. 18, 1663-4 by Bartholomew Heath and Henry Palmer: a house and 4 akers of house lot, 35li.; 4 akers of planting land in the plane, 20li.; 4 akers of meadow, 12li.; four score and 8 akers of 3 devition land wth the adition, 22li.; 4 previledges of common, 12li.; 20 akers of out land more, 5li.; 120 akers of 4th devision of land which is granted but yet not layd out, 18li.; one cow and a 3 yeare old heifer, 9li.; one swine, 1li. Goods in the house: two table bords, a bedsteed, 1li. 10s.; 6 chaires, one chest, a cradle and two boxes, 1li. 8s.; some other woodden lumber as Payles, traies, Platters, dishes and the like, 2li. 13s.; Peuter and earthen vessels, 2li.; two Iron Pots and an Iron kettle, 1li. 4s.; a brase kettle, 5s.; Iron things, two tramels, 5 wedges, 4 axes, sickle, shave, spade, hamer, two sawes, 3 hoes, presing Iron and two paire of sheares with some other smale Iron things, 3li.; 3 hogsheads and a linen wheele, 1li.; a bed and bolster and bed cloathes and pellows, 3li. 10s.; 3 paire of shetes and Pellobes and other linen in a chest, 5li.; another bed and bed cloathes, 1li.; two boxes of linen and other things in them, 5li.; bookes, 1li.; 120 Pound of tobacco, 6li.; 20 Pound of cotten woole, 1li.; 40 Pound of sope, 1li.; his weareing cloathes, 5li. 13s.; new cloth which was to make him cloaths with thred, silk and buttens, 2li. 13s.; his armour, 1li.; In debts oweing to him, 15li. 18s. 6d.; some of his wives cloathes, 10li.; total, 205li. 14s. 6d. Debts which he owed about 7li. *Essex Co. Probate Files, Docket 16,891.*

### Guardianship of Joseph Trumble of Rowley.

Joseph Trumble came into court Mar. 29, 1664 and chose his brother, John Trumble, as his guardian. The latter was bound to pay said Joseph his portion when it was due. *Ipswich Quarterly Court Records, vol. 1, page 127.*

### Estate of Thomas Barnes of Salem.

Administration on the estate of Thomas Barnes of Salem, intestate, granted Mar. 29, 1664 to Mary Barnes, his widow, and to bring in an inventory to the next Salem court. *Ipswich Quarterly Court Records, vol. 1, page 126.*

Mary Barnes, relict of Thomas Barnes, deceased, presented an inventory of her husband's estate, amounting to 217li. 5s. 9d., which was allowed 28: 4: 1664. The estate to remain in her hands, and she to pay to Benjamin, son of the deceased, 60li., at the age of twenty-one, and 30li. to Mary, the daughter, at the age of eighteen or time of marriage. The dwelling house and ground adjoining were to remain for security. *Salem Quarterly Court Records, vol. 4, page 131.*

Inventory taken 12: 11: 1663, by Walter Price and Elias Stileman, and proved by oath of the widow: A dwelling house & orchard, shop & outhouses, 100li.; 5 acres of upland in south feild, 8li.; 1 horse, 8li.; 1 Cow, 4li.; 1 swine, 15s. In ye shopp, 9 chaldr. of Coles, 20li.; 18 C. of Iron in ye shopp, 22li.; 2 Ankers, 2li.; in smithes tooles, 18li. 1s. 6d.; a malt mill, 15s. In ye hall, 1 feather bed, boulster & pillow, 4li.; 1 green rugg, 10s.; 1 pr. blanketts, 1li.; Curtaines & vallance, 1li. 10s.; 1 bedsteed, 1li. 15s.; 1 feather bed & boulster more, 2li. 10s.; 1 rugg green, 1li.; 1 pr. of wt. blanketts, 1li. 10s.; 1 trundle bed steed, 5s.; 1 settle & wainscot Chest, 1li. 10s.; 1 Court Cubbard, 12s.; 1 deske & box, 1li.; 2 tables, 10s.; 3 Joyn stooles & 1 forme, 8s.; 7 chaires, 7s., 1 Jack, 15s., 1li. 2s.; 1 pr. of doggs & pr. andirons, old, 6s.; 2 hakes, tongs, fire shovell & spit, gridiron & Lanthorne, 12s.; 1 Cubard cloth & cushion; 2 Windo Curtains, 12s.; pewter, 1li. 10s.; erthern waire & glass bottles, 10s.; 1 warming pan & smothing Iron, 10s.; 1 brass Kettle & chaffing dish, 2li. 15s.; 1 silver dram Cupp, 5s.; 2 Iron Kettles & a brass skillet, 12s.; 1 case of Knives, 4s.; 1 Looking glass, 12d. & 2 dos. trenchers, 2s., 3s.; 3 bookes, 8s.; 1 baskett, 18d., case & bottles, 14s. 6d.; 1 Cutless, 1 sword, 1 pr. pistolls, 2 belts & 1 old saddle & bridle, 2li.; 9 spoones, 3s.; 2 brushes, 4s.; waring apparrell 11li. 4s.; 17 napkins, 25s., 2 tableclothes, 5s., 1li. 10s.; 8 pillow beares, 15s.; 1 fine table cloth, 1li. In ye parlour, 1 feather bed & bolster rugg & 2 blanketts & bedsteed, curtaines, vallance, 5li. 10s.; 1 settle, 3 chaires, 1 chest, 16s.; 10 pr. sheetes, 5li.; 6 boulster cases, 12s.; Course towells & old Napkins, 10s.; earthen waire in a case, 5s.; a Window Curtaine, 1s. In ye Kitchen, 2 old brass Kettles, 6s.; 2 Iron potts & chaffing dish, 12s. 6d.; 1 brass & 2 Iron skilletts, 10s.; a frying pan, Ladles & scumer, 4s. 6d.; a pestle & morter & 2 seives, 4s. 6d.; 1 Cullendr. & 2 pud panns, 4s.; earthen waire, 10s.; wood. boules, pailes & Keilers, 10s.; a sifting trow, 4s. & a Lampe, 5s. In ye Hall Chamber, 1 chest, 4s. & a Cradle, 5s., 9s.; 2 Spining wheeles, 6s.; a pillion & Cloth, 15s.; a halfe headed bedsteed & an old flock bed, two blanketts & Coverlett & matt, 1li. 10s.; a bed case & matt & pillow, 6s.; 3 pillows & 1 pillow beare, 1li.; 2 musquets, 15s.; 1 pr. of shirt buttons, 3s.; 1 yere & 5 mo. in a servant, 5li.; Lumber, 5s.; debts owing & Iron bak and an ould Kitle, 94li. 14s. 3d.; total, 337li. 18s. 9d. By Severall men unto whome the Estate is Indebted, 120li. 13s. *Essex Co. Quarterly Court Files, vol. 10, leaf 4.*

### Estate of Robert Rogers of Newbury.*

Administration on the estate of Robert Rogers, intestate, granted Mar. 29, 1664 to Susanah Rogers, his widow, and ordered to bring in an inventory to the next Salem court. *Ipswich Quarterly Court Records, vol. 1, page 126.*

Inventory taken by John Emmerry, Sr. and Abraham Toppan, Sr.: house & land at plum ileland, 65li.; 3 swine, 3li.; a bill due from Will. Troter, 8li.; in Joseph Plummers handes, 1li. 10s.; in Nicholas Noyce his handes, 18s.; a gun, 2li.; Cotton wooll, 1li. 10s.; yarne, 1li. 10s.; my husbands aperrell, 2li. 10s.; the bedding, 6li. 10s.; bookes, 15s.; sheetes & lining, 2li. 10s.; a whipp saw, 12s.; in brass, 1li.; in pewter, 1li.; an iron pott, hanger, frying pan & other smale iron things, 1li.; in lumber, 2li. 10s.; total, 101li. 15s. The widdow is indebted to Richard Dowell, 4li. 7s.

* See also Records and Files of the Quarterly Courts of Essex Co., Mass., vol. 3 (1913), pp. 186-189.

Susanah Rogers testified in Ipswich court 27: 7: 1664 that this is a true inventory of her husband's estate.

He left four children: Robert Rogers, aged Apr., 64, fourteen years, Thomas, last July 12, twelve years, John, last March, ten years and Elizabeth, last Feb., six years. *Essex Co. Probate Files, Docket* 24,055.

### ESTATE OF GEORGE FRAILE OF LYNN.

Administration on the estate of George Fraile of Lynn, intestate, granted Mar. 29, 1664 to Elizabeth Fraile, his widow. An inventory amounting to 184li. 14s. was brought into court. Said Fraile left one son and four daughters. Court ordered that the son have 40li. and the daughters 20li. each at age or marriage. *Ipswich Quarterly Court Records, vol.* 1, *page* 126.

The relict of George Fraile presented an inventory of her husband's estate, which was allowed 28: 4: 1664. *Salem Quarterly Court Records, vol.* 4, *page* 134.

Inventory of the estate of George Frayle of Lynn, deceased 9: 10: 1663, taken by Thomas Laughton, Thomas Putnam, John Putnam and John (his — mark) Tarbey: houseinge and upland, 50li.; salt & fresh meadow, 40li.; tow cows, 8li.; one cow & three steers, 14li.; foure younge cattell, 7li.; eight sheep, 4li.; hay, 5li.; foure shoots, 1li. 10s.; one bed with all bedinge, 6li.; one bed more wth bedinge, 3li.; one table cloath & six napkins, 5s.; foure pillowbears, 10s.; foure paire sheets, 4li.; foure sheets more, 2li. 10s.; his wearinge apparrell, 7li.; one bed more & bedinge, 4li.; chests & a box, 1li. 5s.; Iron potts & brasse with pot hooks, 3li.; in pewter, 1li.; one warming pan, 8s.; in wooden lumber, 2li. 5s.; in armes, 2li.; tooles, 5li. 14s.; five bookes, 10s.; pcell of small Iron things, 1li.; table, chears & stools, 10s.; siths & hoos, 8s.; mault & corne, 2li. 3s.; yearne, 4s.; one peece of new cloath, 1li. 10s.; timber, 2li.; ladders, breaks & wheelbarrow, 12s.; in provision, 3li. 10s.; total, 184li. 14s.

Received in Ipswich court Mar. 29, 1664. *Essex Co. Probate Files, Docket* 10,120.

Elizabeth (her 8 mark) Frayle brought into court, 28: 4: 1664, a further account of the estate, dated 19: 4: 1664, that there were owing to George Frayle of Lynn, 6li. 12s. 8d., and that he owed 7li. 14s. 9d. *Essex Co. Quarterly Court Files, vol. 10, leaf 13.*

### ESTATE OF WILLIAM BEARD.

Administration on the estate of William Beard, intestate, granted Mar. 29, 1664 to John Devrix and he ordered to bring in an inventory to the next Salem court. *Ipswich Quarterly Court Records, vol. 1, page 126.*

### GUARDIANSHIP OF SARAH SMITH OF (ROWLEY?).

Sarah Smith came into court Mar. 29, 1664 and chose Daniell Wickam, her brother-in-law, as her guardian. The latter was bound to pay said Sarah her portion when it was due. *Ipswich Quarterly Court Records, vol. 1, page 127.*

Daniell Wycom, guardian to Sarah Smith acknowledges the receipt from Jerimiah Elsworth of 22li. 2s. 6d., her portion, and acquits the said Jerimiah Elsworth and Mary his wife executrix to Hugh Smith her former husband, of all the said portion or legacy. Signed Dec. 7, 1664 by Daniell Wickam. Witness: Ezekiell Jewitt and Abraham Jewitt.

Acknowledged Dec. 28, 1665 by the witnesses. *Ipswich Deeds, vol. 2, page 253.*

### ESTATE OF WILLIAM GOOSE OF SALEM.

Court having been informed that Mr. Goose died many years ago and that there was no will found or proved, nor administration granted, and that Mrs. Goose was distracted and not able to provide for herself, the town of Salem having been at great expense to support her for several years, administration upon the estate was granted Mar. 29, 1664 to the selectmen of Salem. They were ordered to bring in an inventory of the estate of William Goose, deceased, to the next Salem court, with a bill of the charges for Mrs. Goose. *Ipswich Quarterly Court Records, vol. 1, page 127.*

Widow Jackson, formerly the wife of Mr. William Goose, was not capable, owing to her present distemper of head, to look after herself. Her estate was inventoried 28: 4: 1664 and amounted to 14li. 12s., which was to remain in the Salem selectmen's hands, and to be used for her necessary expenses. *Salem Quarterly Court Records, vol. 4, page 132.*

The inventory of Wm. Goose's estate found in the hands of Mary Jackson, widow, taken June 28, 1664, by Jefferie Massey, Thomas Jeggells and John Pickering: A dwelling house, with an acre of upland belonging, 50li.; an ould feather bed, 1 boulster & 2 small pillowes, an ould Rug & an ould blankett, 4li.; a little table & 3 ould Cheares wth. a deske, 10s.; total, 54li. 10s.

Paid by the town of Salem for the relief of the relict of Willm. Goose, deceased, from 1656 to 1663, 39li. 18s.; rest to the estate of Will. Goose, 14li. 12s. Taken out of Salem town records by Edmond Batter, for the selectmen. *Essex Co. Quarterly Court Files, vol. 10, leaf 8.*

### ESTATE OF GERSHOM LAMBERT OF ROWLEY.

"I Gershom lambert in the county of Essex of Rowley in new England being sicke of body but of perfect understanding and memory. I do make this my last will and testament in manner and forme as followeth. I commend my soule to god. and my body to the graiue and I do dispose of that Estate that god hath given me as followes. Inprimis after my debts be paide I giue my Ant Rogers my horse, and I giue my brother John lambert my cloath coate, and my Bootes and I giue my best suite to my brother Thomas Nelson and I giue to John Spaffard, senior a gray jacket and breches, and I giue to Charles broune two paier of shooes, and two paire of stockings and I giue the rest of my cloaths to Richard lighten, and I giue to my cousen elizabeth platts fiuety shillings, and I giue to my brother thomas lambert my pistells, and my sward and my sadle a ——— my breast girt and I giue the halfe thousand Acres of upland — the meddow proportianable to the halfe thousand Acres of upland which my Ant Rogers gaue me which lieth in the bounds of Rowley, which lieth in the diuisian of land commonly called Rowley uillage. I giue this land to my brother Thomas Nelsons children, equally to be diuided amongst them that is the children I meane which my sister An hath by my brother Thomas Nelson, and all the rest of my estate I giue to my brother Thomas Nelson, and I make my brother Thomas Nelson executor of this my last will and Testament and hereunto I set my hand and seale the sixtenth of Ma[r] one thousand six hundred and sixty fouer."

his mark<br>
Gershom  L  Lambert.

"This will of Gershom Lamberts was Read unto him and he owned it in euery of the p^rtickulers of it and set these leters of his name and his seal to it," in presence of the witnesses.
Witness: Samuell Brocklebanke, Ezekiel Northend, John Brocklebanke.
Proved in Ipswich court Mar. 29, 1664 by Samuell Brocklebanke and Ezekiell Northend. *Essex Co. Quarterly Court Files, vol. 9, leaf* 109.

### Estate of Mrs. Mary Miller of Newbury.

"Know all men by theise psents that I Mary Miller widdow of ———— of body but of perfect memory Do here make my last will and testament disposeing of my worldly goods as followeth ^r I giue and bequeath eleuen pounds due to me in Rent from *Benja*min Roafe vnto my Daughter Sara the wife of James Browne as also foure Cowes that is in the possession of the said *Benj*amin Roafe vnto my said daughter Sara Browne and the ——— that is in Henry Tewksburyes hands I giue vnto Mary Moody the wife of Samuell Moody, the said Samuell paying *to my* aforesaid Daughter Sara Browne twenty shillings ———— two oxen that is in my son Nicholas Noyes his hands *I g*iue to my said son Nicholas, prouided that he pay also to my said Daughter Sara Browne eight pounds out of the said oxen as also I giue my said Daughter Sara Browne thirty fiue shillings *w*hat Henry Tewksbury oweth vnto me and thirty shillings tha*t S*amuell moody oweth vnto me, and ten shillings that is behind of rent in the hands of John Dauis and fifty shillings in the hands of Nicholas Noyes of my Rent since last year I also giue vnto my said Daughter Sara Browne and a feather bed I giue also vnto her my said daughter *also* a siluer spoone and the little ———— my daughter Mary the wife of Nicholas Noyes, and the ———— Dram cup I giue vnto my Grandchild Mary Moody; and my linnen and cloathes & other goods left I *dis*pose of to be deuided equally among them my two daughters ———— grandchild abouesaid as also I appoint my son James *Bro*wne to be the executor of this my last will and testament ——— my debts & funeral being discharged nouemb: 26^th 1663 In witness wherof I haue set my hand."

her mark<br>Mary MA Miller

Witness: Anthony Somerby, Henry Short.
Proved in Ipswich court Mar. 29, 1664 by the witnesses.

Inventory of the estate of Mrs. Mary Miller, widow, deceased Mar. 6, 1663, taken by Henry Short and Anthony Somerby: foure cowes, 18li.; three oxen, 21li.; her weareing apparrell, 20li.; four pr. of sheets, 5 pillowbeares, two table clothes, 6 napkins, 3li. 10s.; one feather bed, one boulster, 3 pillowes, one Rug, 2 blanckets with curtaines and [va]llons, 12li.; six platters, 1li. 10s.; five cushions, 1li.; a chest, a box with drawers, a looking glasse, 1li.; one silver spoone, one silver wine Cupp and a silver dram cup, 1li.; total, 79li.

Attested in Ipswich court Mar. 29, 1664 by James Browne.

*Essex Co. Probate Files, Docket 18,445.*

### ESTATE OF JOHN ROLFE OF NEWBURY.

"This 4$^{th}$ (3$^{d}$\*) of februrie 1663 I John Roffe of Newbry being often sickly am willing while my memorie is good to dispose of my outward Estat not knowing how soon I may be desolued and leue this world Therefore I do ordain and make my last will and Testament as followeth first I Comitt my soule to god and my body to the Erth to be buried 2$^{dly}$ I give and bequeth my house and all my land I have in salsbery with all the priviliges and apurtenances be longing ther vnto in *said* salsbery vnto my daughterr Hestur sanders the wife of John Sanders during hir life and thirtie pounds more: and after hir decease to Remain vnto hir Children of hir body by Equall portions Itm I give and bequeth vnto sarah Cottell the wife of willm Cottl besid twenti pounds I formerly gave hir I give hir twenti pounds more and vnto hir two Children sarah Cottl and Ann Cotle tenn pounds a peece to be Improved by willm Cottl for ther benifit Itm I giue vnto my Grand Children Isac Ring and Josep Ring tenn pounds a peece and vnto Elizabeth shropshere and hester Ring twentie pounds a peece Itm I giue vnto Thomas whittyre ||for his|| Children ten pounds Item I giue vnto the Church of newbre twenti shilings Itm I giue vnto Richard whittyr my sisters sonn tenn pounds and vnto his sonn John whityr five pounds Itm I giue vnto John Rofe my brothrs sonn tenn pounds and vnto his two daughtrs marie and Rebeca Rofe fiue pounds to be Improved equaly for ther benifit

"Itm I give vnto beniamn Rofs son John Roffe tenn pounds and his sonn benimin Roffe five pounds to be Im-

\* The day of the month was changed in the original instrument.

proved for ther benifit Itm I give vnto Ann Gardner the wife of Richard gardner five pounds Item I give vnto honore dole the wife of Richard dole my — Item I giue vnto Richard dols six Children fortie shillings and ——— Item I giue vnto heneri lesenby Richord dols servant ten shillings Itm I giue vnto mari Kinrick tenn shillings and a plater of pewter Likwis I do ordain and apoint my louing Kindsman Richard dole to be my Executur to discharg and pay all the former ligacies and debts and Charg that may a Rise for my funerall.or otherwise and I desir my three frends Henri short willm moody and Richard Knight to be my ouer seers to see this my will to be performed and my will is that all the legacies should be paid within a yere and half after my decease"

his mark<br>John R Roffe (SEAL)

Witness: Richard Knight, Cornelius Connor, Hen: Short,
   his mark
william w-m moodye.

Proved in Ipswich court Mar. 29, 1664 by Richard Knight and William Moody. *Essex Co. Probate Files, Docket 24,116.*

### ESTATE OF ALEXANDER KNIGHT OF IPSWICH.

"In The Name of God Amen. The tenth day of ffebruary in the yeere of o$^r$ Lord one thousand six hundred sixty & three. I Allexander Knight the vnproffitable seruant of God weake in body, but strong in mind doe willingly & with a free hart render & give againe into the hands of my Lord God & Creator my spirit, which hee of his fatherly goodnesse gaue vnto mee, when hee first fashioned mee in my mothers wombe makeing mee a liueing & a resonable creature nothing doubting but that for his infinite mercies sake set forth in the p$^r$tious blood of his dearely beloued sonne Jesus Christ o$^r$ onely sauiour & redeemer, hee will receiue my soule into his Glory, & place it in the Company of the heauenly Angells & blessed Saints: And for my body I Comitt it to the earth wherof it Came; nothing doubting but according to the Article of my faith at the great day of the Generall Resurrection when wee shall appeare before the Judgment seate of Christ I shall receiue againe the same by the mighty power of God who is able to subdue all things to himselfe, not a Corruptible weake & vile body as it is now, but an incorruptible imortall strong & pfect body in all poynts like vnto the Glorious body of my lord & Sauiour Jesus Christ. And for the portion of these earthly things which God hath lent mee I dispose as followeth, first I giue vnto my Loueing wife my howse & howse lott & all my other goods & debts during her naturall life, (my debts being discharged) Item I giue vnto my eldest Daughter Hannah Knight at the age of one & twenty yeares six Acres of marsh & Six Acres of planting land, Item I giue vnto my loueing wife all the rest of my planting land & marsh during her naturall life, my will is also after my wiues deceace, that my planting land & marsh before named be equally diuided betwene my other daugters, Sarah & Mary & my sonne Nathaniell, And also that my sone Nathaniell haue my howse & howse lott, besides his part in my planting land & marsh aforesaid. And further my will is that all my howsehold goods be equally diuided betwene my three daughters & my sonne Nathaniel after my wiues deceace. And I doe ordaine & appoynt my wife Hanna Knight And William Inglish ||of Boston|| to be my executors of this my last will & Testament, And if it shall happen any of my Children before named to depart this life before their portions be due, my will is that those that be liueing shall share their portion or portions equally betweene them. Also my will is that if any Ambiguity doubt or question doe arise by reson of the impfection or defect of, or in any Clauses words or sentences in this my last will & Testament, or my true intent & meaning therin, I will that the further & better explanation interp$^r$tation & Construction of the said doubt & ambiguity be by my said executors expounded explained & interp$^r$ted according to their wisdome & discretion. In witnes wherof I haue hereunto sett my hand & Seale in the p$^r$sents of"

        his mark
      Alexander O Knight [SEAL]

Witness: John Whipple, James Chute, Robert Lord, Jn'r.

Proved in Ipswich court Mar. 29, 1664 by James Chute and Robert Lord, Jr.

Inventory taken by Jno. Denison, Walter Roper and Francis Wainewright: 32 Acers of land & a house, 120li.; Brass & pewter, 3li. 7s.; Bedding & furniture, 4li. 13s.; a Trunk & Chest & box & chairs and table & paile and keeler and trayes & other ould things, 1li. 14s.; Cloaths of his, 8s.; one small Cow, 4li.; swine, 1li. 10s.; 2 wheels, 5s.; Books, 5s.; ould Iorn things & 2 sives, 8s.; 1 pr tongues & tramell

& pothookes, 8s.; 1 doz. spoons, 6s.; in Goodman Bishops hand, 14s.; a silver spoone, 5s.; in Mr. Jewits hands, 26li.; total, 164li. 3s. 11d. The debts of Allexander Knight: to Jno Denison, 10s. 3d.; Mr. Baker, 8s.; Jno. Whipple, 3s. 6d.; Jno. Wiet, 3s.; ffr. Wainewright, 2li. 12s. 1d.; total, 3li. 16s. 10d. To Aaron Pengre, 7s.

Received in Ipswich court Mar. 29, 1664.
*Essex Co. Probate Files, Docket* 15,941.

### Estate of Richard Wickam of Rowley.

Inventory of the estate of Richard Wickam taken Feb. 26, 1663, by Maxemillian Jewett and Samuell Brocklebanke: in aparrell, 4li.; the beding for one bed, 4li.; beding and bedstead for another bed, 2li.; two paire of sheets, 1li. 8d.; pots Iron and brase and Cettles and skellits and other things belonging them for the house, 2li.; the houses and land at home lot, 22li.; land in bredforth street lots, 9li.; land in pollipod lots, 5li.; land in the new plaine, 4li.; [on]e acre of medow called the Spring acre, 5li.; 3 acres of upland and meadow at farme, 15li.; 3 acres of salt marsh, 12li.; more upland in the farme 107 Rod, 15s.; 4 acres of upland in the common, 3li.; in land called the village land, 15li.; one pare of oxen, 11li.; 3 Cowes, 2 steares and 3 other smaller catell and 2 calves, 23li.; in young swine, 21li.; cart, plow cheines and yoakes and other such things, 2li. 10s.; axe, beetell, wedges, howes and such other small things, 10s.; chaires and wooden vessels, 1li.; total, 144li. 1s. 8d.

Attested to be a true inventory by An Wickam in the Ipswich court, ———, 1664. *Essex Co. Probate Files, Docket* 29,792.

Daniell Wickam of Rowley, carpenter, upon receipt of one paire of oxen and some other small things, and also to have one acre of meadow in Batchelor's meadow after his father, Richard Wickam's decease, acknowledged himself satisfied of any further expectation of portion from his father or his estate. Signed and sealed Aug. 9, 1662. Witness: Maxemilian Jewett and Samuell Brocklebanke.

Maxemilian Jewett and Samuell Brocklebanke testified to this being the act and deed of Daniell Wickam in Ipswich Court Mar. 29, 1664. *Ipswich Deeds, vol. 2, page 201.*

### Estate of William Deale of Haverhill.

"I William Deale of Haverhill in y^e County of Norfolke in New England; being weake in body; but of perfect Memmory; and Nott knowing how ye Lord May be pleased to deale with me; I doe Make this my Last will; Imp^r I doe bequeath my soule into y^e hands of him y^t gave it me; tt After all my debts be payd I doe give unto my deare and Loueing wife Mary Deale all my Lands and goods to be att hir dissposall; tt I doe will y^t my two Children shall have twenty pounds A pece when they Come at age or day of Marridge; I doe Meane att twenty one yeares: and Sixteene yeares y^t y^e twenty pounds shalbe payd tt I doe make my deare and Loveing wife Mary deale Administratrix of my whole Estate ffebruary ye: 14^th 1664."

his mark<br>
William O Deal (SEAL)

Witness: John Carleton, Phill: Challis.

The will presented to court Apr. 12, 1664 but not proved, the administratrix, as she was called, refusing to have anything to do with the will. *Norfolk Co. Quarterly Court Files, vol. 1, leaf 38.*

Administration on the estate granted Oct. 10, 1665 to Edward Clarke of Haverhill and ordered to bring in an inventory. *Hampton Quarterly Court Records, vol. 1, leaf 32.*

Inventory of the estate of William Delle taken 3: 3: 1665, by William Sargent, Sr. and Lt. Phillep Challis both of Salisbury: house, 1li. 10s.; Land brocke up and unbrocke up ajoyning to ye house, 80li.; in staveses by the water side, 4li.; 2 coues and a calfe, 9li. 10s.; wering aparill, 7li.; linin, 2li.; wodin ware, 12s.; a cheste, 4s.; yarne, 6s.; iern were for husbindre, 1li. 15s.; a friing pan, 3s.; a bellte, 10s.; chilldrenes blanckites, 10s.; an ell of brode cloath, 1li.; a paire of pistels, 10s.; his thurd divishan Land, 5li. 15s.; whete and inian corn, 3li.; a sack, 3s.; total, 118li. 8s.

Presented to Hampton court 10: 8: 1665 and attested to by Mary Deale. *Essex Co. Probate Files, Docket 7,463.*

### Guardianship of Widow Mary Willix of Salisbury.

The widow Willix of the town of Salisbury being in no capacity to order and improve her estate by reason of a strange kind of distracted and distempered condition that she had been in for a long time, it was ordered Apr. 12, 1664, that Capt. Tho. Bradbury, Richard Wells and Edward French take care of her estate for her comfortable subsistence, to see her house finished, according to agreement with Wm. Osgood, and in case of need to sell part of her estate for the finishing of the house and procuring stock. *Salisbury Quarterly Court Records, vol. 1, leaf 21.*

Ordered 9 : 2 : 1667 that the estate of Thomas Hauxworth, deceased, some-time of this town, be committed to the improvement of Onezeverous Page, who married said Hauxworth's daughter, who was to provide for the maintenance of the relict of Hauxworth, his wife's mother. Page had power also to exchange or sell part of the estate, with the approbation of Tho. Bradbury and Ric. Wells. If his mother-in-law proved more than ordinarily burdensome to him by reason of her age and other infirmities, the town of Salisbury should afford timely help. *Salisbury Quarterly Court Records, vol. 1, leaf 46.*

### GUARDIANSHIP OF MARTHA SMITH OF (ROWLEY?).

Martha Smith chose Nathaniell Elitrop to be her guardian May 5, 1664, and he was bound in 40li. to pay her her portion when due. *Ipswich Quarterly Court Records, vol. 1, page 130.*

Nathaniell Elithorp, guardian of Martha Smith acknowledges the receipt from Jerimiah Elsworth of 22li. 13s. 6d. her portion, and acquits the said Jerimiah Elsworth and Mary his wife (late wife and executrix to Hugh Smith her former husband) of all the said portion or legacy. Dated Nov. 8, 1664. Witness: Maximilian (his mark) Jewett, John Boynton.

Acknowledged by Nathaniell Elithorp Apr. 6, 1665 before Samuell Symonds. *Ipswich Deeds, vol. 2, page 233.*

### ESTATE OF JONATHAN LAMBERT OF (ROWLEY?).

Administration on the estate of Jonathan Lambert, intestate, granted May 5, 1664 to his brother John Lambert and he was ordered to bring in an inventory to the next Ipswich court. John Lambert was bound in forty pounds. *Ipswich Quarterly Court Records, vol. 1, page 130.*

Inventory of the estate of Jonathan Lambert taken 24: 7: 1664, by William Acie and Richard Swan: a maire and a colt and a young horse, 20li.; more receved of Mr. Richard Parker merchant of Boston, 10li. 9s. Estate debtor: for wintering a mare and colt, 1li. 5s.; for administration granting, 2s. 6d.; one journey to Boston, two men 3 dayes horse and man, one journey more to Boston, one man 3 dayes, 12li.; money due, 10s.; paid to the man that attended on Jonathan, 2li.; to the ship doctor, 15s.

Attested in Ipswich court 27: 7: 1664 by John Lambert. *Essex Co. Probate Files, Docket* 16,188.

### ESTATE OF ELIZABETH COCKERILL OF SALEM.

Edward Clapp and Frances Collens presented an inventory of the estate of Elizabeth Cockerill, deceased, amounting to 102li. 2s. Administration was granted 28: 4: 1664 to Edward Clapp, Frances Collens and Andrew Woodbery, who married the three daughters of said widow, who, after all just debts were paid, were to divide the estate among them. *Salem Quarterly Court Records, vol. 4, page* 129.

Inventory taken June 27, 1664, by Jefferie Massey and Hennery Skerry: One dwelling house & out house with a quarter of an acre of ground adjoining, 32li.; two Cowes & one swine, 7li.; two feather beads with theire furniture, 14li.; pewter, 2li. 15s.; iron potts & hangers, fire shovell & tongues, 20s., 3li. 15s.; brass kettles, skellets, a candlestick & brass morter, 1li. 15s.; 12 yrds. osenbrige & about 20 yrds. cource holland, 3li. 15s.; 6 pr. of sheets, 1 doz. napkins & other linen, 12li. 17s.; 4 yrds. broad cloath, 40s.; 2 yrds. 1-4 Carsy, 14s., 2li. 14s.; a black cloak, 25s., her wearing aparell, 6li. 13s., 7li. 18s.; tables, stooles, chaires & chests & other lumber, with 2 seives, a sword & old muscutt, 3li.; two bibles, 11s., cash, 12li., a silver spoone, 5s., a ring, 12s., 13li. 8s.; total, 102li. 2s. *Essex Co. Quarterly Court Files, vol.* 9, *leaf* 136.

### ESTATE OF MRS. GRACE SALLOWS OF (SALEM?).

Robert Lemon, presenting an inventory of the estate of Grace Sollas, widow, late deceased, amounting to 113li. 13s. 3d., which was allowed, was appointed 28: 4: 1664 administrator of the estate. He was ordered to pay to her son Thomas Sollas, 30li. at the age of twenty-one years, to son Robert, 15li., to daughter Mary, 15li. at age or marriage, and the survivors to have the deceased childrens' portions, if any die before they come of age. *Salem Quarterly Court Records, vol. 4, page 132.*

Inventory of the estate of Grace Sallowes, deceased, taken June 29, 1664, by Thos. Pickton and Thom. Rootes: One house & an akre & halfe of land, 60li.; one cowe, 4li. In the parlor, one feather bed, 2 bolsters, 2 pillowes, one pare of white blankets, a blew Rugg, a straw bed, Curtaines & valence & bedsted, 8li.; a Court Cubberd, 12s.; a wainscot Chest, 10s.; a table & Joynt stooles, 9s.; a Carpet, 9s.; 3 boxes & 3 Chaires, 8s.; a warming pan, a paire of tonges & fire shovell, 8s.; a cushion for a Cubberd's head, 1s. In the hall, 1 old feather bed, a paire of blankets, a feather bolster, a canvas bed & bolster case, a greene Rugg, a bedsted, curtaines & valance, 5li.; a paire of blankets, a feather pillow & a canvis bedcase, 1li.; a settle & 9 Chaires, 13s.; 6 Cushions & 2 feather pillowes, 10s.; 2 hakes, a paire of tongs, a spit & grediron, 6s.; a frying pan & smoothing Iron, 2s. 6d.; 2 Iron pots, an Iron kettle & skillett, 14s.; 2 brasse kettles & 2 skillets, 1li. 6s.; a looking glasse & a Jugg bottle, 1s. 6d.; 2 bookes of mr. burroughes & 2 psal. bookes, 10s.; a brush & 2 paire of pott hookes, 2s. 9d.; wareing Clothes, 3li.; 9 pewter dishes, 1 bason, 2 small Basons, 2 quart pots, 8 porringers & 4 spoones, one beaker & a boule, 1-2 pint pot, 7 sawsers, 2 salts, 1li. 15s.; a brasse candle stick & 2 brass ladles, 5s.; Latten ware, 3s.; lisbone ware & glasses, 10s.; 2 dozen trenchers & 6 spoones, 1s.; 15 wooden dishes & 3 trayes, 5s.; 3 sieves, 2 Chests, a small table, 13s.; a musket, 10s.; 2 baggs & old seabeds & bedding, 1li.; 13 sheets, 3li. 10s.; 3 kalico table cloathes & one ozingbrig, 15s.; 2 old Cubberd cloathes, 6 lockrom napkins, 8s.; 12 pillowbeires, 1li. 3s.; 15 towells & a table cloath, 14s.; 5 shurts & a dimity waiscoate, 1li. 10s.; 2 old axes & wedges & earthen pots, 8s.; in lumber as old barrells & tubs & pailes, 10s.; a basket & 2 old ones for linnen, 3s.; in a pt of stage & house at the misery, 1li. 10s.; 4 Codlines, 2 pare of snuds & a portagall cap, 10s.; a dozen of handkercheifes & 6 bands, 10s.; 6 pare of stockins & a spinning wheele, 12s. & a pestill & morter of Brasse, 2s. The womans childs cloathes, Childrens small linnen, 1li. 10s.; a silke skarfe & hood, 12s.; 3 white aprons & weareing linnen, 2li. 5s.; 3 sutes of womens apparell, 3li.; a bareing blanket & Childes weareing Cloathes, 15s.; total 113li. 13s. 3d. Estate was debtor to Mr. Browne, 18li. 15s. 10d.; to Will. Allen, 16li.; total, 34li. 15s. 10d. *Essex Co. Quarterly Court Files, vol. 10, leaf 5.*

### ESTATE OF HENRY HARWOOD OF SALEM.

"29th 4th mo 1664 Wee whose names are here vnderwritten, do witnesse yt being desired by bro: Harwood (ye afternoon before his death) to be with him to help to make his will, he did then expresse himselfe for ye substance thus that it was his will, yt his wife should haue the vse of his wholl estate while she liued, & after her deceas it should be diuided between his wiues daughter Elizabeth Nixon, & his Kinswoman  onely one legacy he expressed his will to giue to ye church viz foure pound to ye Church to help ye poor in bearing the charge of the Lords Supper. this had then been written but for some interruption; he saying he would take another time for it, neither he nor we thinking he had been so near to his end." John Higginson, Henry Bartholomew.

"I Henry ||Bartholmew|| haue subscribed to what is aboue written onely that pticuler of devidinge the estate betweene his kinswoman and his wiues daughter but in discource it did apeare to me it was his minde to giue her a pt of his estate after his wiues decease" Henry Bartholmew

Proved in Salem court 28: 4: 1664. *Essex Co. Quarterly Court Files, vol. 10, leaf 9.*

Administration on the estate was granted 28: 4: 1664, to the widow, and it was ordered that the estate remain in the widow's hands for her use for life. At her death, the housing and land was to go to Jane Flinder, wife of Richard Flinder, the kinswoman of said Henry Harwood, and the rest of the estate to Elizabeth, wife of Mathew Nixon, her daughter. If the widow should be in want, she had liberty to sell any part of the estate. "The will & Inventory filed up in the court records 9mo 71 with other papers concerned." Copy made by Steph. Sewall, cler. *Salem Quarterly Court Records, vol. 4, page 133.*

Inventory of the estate of Henry Harwood, late of Salem, taken 10: 1: 1663-4, by Joseph Grafton, George Gardner, John Gardner and Henry Bartholmew: A dwellinge house with outhousinge and three akers of lande belonging, 50li.; ten akers of lande in the south field, 20li.; five akers of lande on Darbie forte side, 5li.; two Cowes, 9li.; nine ewe sheepe, one wether, and 10 lambes, 7li. 10s.; one swine, 15s. In the inner Rome, 5 pewter plattrs, 17s. 6d.; one pewter bowle, one beaker, 2 bras candlesticks and 3 poringrs, 15s.;

17 peecis of blew and wt. earthware, 8s. 6d.; 3 p. of sheetes, 1 duzzen of napkins, 3li.; 2 smale table clothes and 2 half sheetes, 10s.; 4 pillowbeares, a towell and a napkin, 16s.; bands and shifts and other small linen, 2li. 10s.; one feather bed, 2 bolsters, 2 pillowes, a Rugge and blankett, 7li.; wearing apparrell, 4li.; 2 blanketts, 14s.; a table and frame, 6 stooles, 1 chest and trunke, 3 boxes and a cup boord, 3li.; 4 chaires, 3 cussions, and a basket, 12s. In the midle rome, one feather bed, 2 bolsters, 2 pillowes, a Rugge and curtaines, 7li.; 6 p. of sheetes, 1 p. cotton sheetes, 5li. 10s.; 2 table clothes, 18 towells, 1li. 4s.; a table and frame, 3 chaires and three chests, 1li. 5s.; 3 brass ketles, 3 brass skilletts and a warminge pan, 3li.; 4 pewter plattrs., 2 basons, 2 qua. potts and chambr. pott, 1li. 5s.; a brass chafinge dish and morter, 10s.; for bookes, 1li.; two musketts and a Javelin, 1li. 5s.; fire shovell and tongs, a pr. Andiron, a gridiron, a spitt, 2 p. pot hangrs., 1li. 10s. In the Kitchin, three Iron potts, a ketle and scillet, 1li. 10s.; earthen panes and tubbs and trayes and other lumbr, 1li. 10s.; debts, 8li. 17s. 6d. In the Chamber, 2 flock beds with the Coveringe and aptenancis, 2li. 10s.; Indian and English graine, 2li.; ould Iron and other lumber, 1li. 10s.; leather shooes and bootes, 5li.; shoemakers tooles and a graplin, 1li.; total, 163li. 14s. 6d. Debts, a legise to Mathe Nixons wife, 5li.; other small debts, 5li. Allowed 27 : 4 : 1664. *Essex Co. Quarterly Court Files, vol. 10, leaf 10.*

The court 29 : 9 : 1664, gave Widow Harwood liberty to sell ten acres or five acres of land, as per inventory on file, also some part of her other goods which she could best spare, for her present support, provided it be by advice of the selectmen of Salem or Worshipfull Major Wm. Hathorne. *Salem Quarterly Court Records, vol. 4, page 139.*

Whereas there was an action commenced by Richard Flinder against Jeremiah Buttman concerning part of the estate of Henry Harwood, deceased, and there being further contention likly to arise, Mr. Edmond Batter, Mr. Hen. Bartholmew and Leift George Gardner were chosen by the court 28 : 4 : 1670 auditors of the estate. What they could not settle was to be settled by the court. *Salem Quarterly Court Records, vol. 5, leaf 34.*

Mr. Edmand Batter, Mr. Hen. Bartholmew and Leift. Georg Gardner, appointed by a former court at Salem to settle the estate of Hen. Harwood, made return 28: 9: 1671, that they do not find that Mathew Nixon had a legal right to what was given his wife, she dying before she was possessed of it. Richard Flinder was appointed administrator of the estate. *Salem Quarterly Court Records, vol. 5, leaf 52.*

Inventory of the estate of widow Harwood, deceased, now in possession of Richard Flinder, appraised, 24: 11: 1669, by Walter Price and Samuell Gardner: One fether bed, one boulster, two pillows, one ould Rugg, one paire of ould blanketts & curtens with vallence, 9li.; one ould fether bed, one boulster, two ould blanketts, one very ould Rugg, fower litle pillows, 5li. 2s. 6d.; two ould boulsters and two ould blanketts, 1li. 5s.; 7 paire of ould sheets, 4li.; 2 table cloths, 5 pr. of smale ould pillobers, 3 napkins, wth. 3 or 4 ould towells, 1li. 1s.; two Chests, two ould Trunks & two ould boxes, 1li. 6d.; 2 coats wth. two ould Wascotts & a cloake, 2li. 10s.; one ould safgard & 4 paire of stokins & ould hat & 2 Cushings, 15s.; one brass kittle at 22s. 6d.; curten rods, 3s.; two stools, one ould Chayer & one Indian Baskett, 4s. 6d.; two payells, 4 woodin dishes, one killer & on paire woodin skales, 4s. 6d.; two bras skilletts, one brase paire of skales & an Iron skillett, 8s.; to 15 peecis of ould pewter & a small pestell, 1li. 6d.; an ould spitt fyer pan tongs & grediron & leaden wayt, 10s.; in erthen ware, 15d., two ould bedsteeds, an ould table, 2 straw beds, 1li. 1s. 3d.; a Cheese press and a ould matt, 5s.; total, 29li. 13s. 3d. *Essex Co. Quarterly Court Files, vol. 18, leaf 20.*

Return of Edmund Batter, Henry Bartholmew and George Gardner, with the consent of Rich. Flinder and Jeremiah Butnam, dated 28: 9: 1671, in the settlement of the estate: that the debts should first be paid; that the moveable goods be given to Mathew Nickson, which formerly were credited to his wife; that Jeremiah Butnam should enjoy the house and land now possessed by him, except a small strip of land from Rich. Flinders' house to the sea, for which the latter was to allow Butman some of his land most convenient for said Butman; of if Flinder desired the house and land, he was to pay Butman 60li., which had been laid out about the house, and care and pains about the widow Harwood, and that it be paid within the term of twelve months from date in fish at current price; said Butman was to have liberty to dwell in the house one whole year from date. They also found a debt of 25li. due to Mathew Nicksen. *Essex Co. Quarterly Court Files, vol. 18, leaf 21.*

### ESTATE OF WILLIAM STUART OF LYNN.

William Stuart, dying intestate, an inventory was presented 28: 4: 1664, by Sara, his wife, amounting to 39li. 3s. 11d., which was allowed. Said Sara was appointed administratrix. *Salem Quarterly Court Records, vol. 4, page 134.*

Inventory of the estate of Willyam Stuward taken by Thomas Bancroft and Robert Gowing: Two cows, 9li.; 1 mare, 2 yeare, 7li.; fife young shots, 2li.; his wearing close, 3li. 12s. 6d.; two hats, 16s.; the flocke beed & beed close, 5li. 6s.; a payer of shets, two towilles & a pellowber, 1li. 6s.; two eyern pots & two payer of pot hokes, 1li. 6s.; 2 fryin pan, 2s.; a smothing eyrin 2s. 6d.; fouer puter platers, 14s.; a puter pote & 6 sponns, 3s. 6d.; a brase scillet, 5s.; a dossen of trenchers, 1s. 3d.; woding vissels, 3s.; a churne, 6s.; a pail & two mylke pans & pot, 3s.; one sefe, two betelrings & an wedg, 3s. 8d.; one hansawe, ould how, two ould axes, 6s. 6d.; one raper & a barell of a goun & a locke, 1li. 16s.; two saxe & on sithe, 7s.; a cuberd & chist, 13s.; a sadell & a bridell, 1li.; a payer of cards, 3s.; a Carte boody, boxes and hoopes, 1li. 8s.; in lumber, 12s. Sworn to by Sara Stuart, the widow, before Hillyard Veren, cleric. *Essex Co. Quarterly Court Files, vol. 10, leaf 10.*

### ESTATE OF RICHARD ELLITT.[*]

Richard White dying intestate, and being indebted to the widow Smith for diet, court 28: 4: 1664, ordered that the amount of the inventory, 2li. 14s., be given to widow Smith toward her bill, she to administer upon the estate. *Salem Quarterly Court Records, vol. 1, page 134.*

Inventory of the estate of Richard Ellitt, taken Mar. —, 1662-3, by Jefferie Massey and Tho. Rootes: A short Coate & a p. breeches, 2li.; an over worne Caster, 10s.; an ould shirt, 2s.; a payre of ould stockings, 2s.; total, 2li. 14s.

Copy of Salem court record of 30: 4: 1663, the widow Smith was appointed administratrix of the foregoing estate and ordered to keep it in her hands & not make payment to

---

[*] The name on the original appears to be **Richard Ellitt** though endorsed as **Rich. White** and so entered on the Court record.

any out of it for a twelfth month to come without the court's order. Copy made by Hillyard Veren, cleric. *Essex Co. Quarterly Court Files, vol. 10, leaf 12.*

### ESTATE OF HENRY BULLOCK OF SALEM.

"December 21 1663 whereas the lord our god hath appoynted his servants to set their houses in order to the glory of his name the comfort of their owne herts and the peace of their famelyes Therefore I Henery Bullocke inhabitant in Salem in assurance of his rich mercy and grace in Jesus Christ my sauiour & in obedience to his commandment, doe commit my soule vnto him commendinge my spirit into his hands who hath redemed me & yeelding my body to the earth in its season, hoping when christ who is my life shal appeare to be brought agayne by the power and goodnes of my god and to appeare with him in glory And for my outward estate I doe thus dispose of it In primis I giue vnto Elisabeth my wife, my dwelling house and out houses therevnto belonginge with all the land adioyninge vnto it, which is about eight acres more or lesse Item I giue vnto Elisabeth my wife 4 acres of meadow, lyinge in the broad meadow that bordereth on the farme that was giuen to mr Bishop all the which houses and lands she is quietly to enioy the tearme of her life Item my wil is that after the decease of my wife the lands and houses aforesayd be giuen vnto my grand child John Bullocke the son of my son Henery Bullocke deceased If he so long shal liue & if the lord shal take him away before he come to the age of 21 yeares then I giue the sayed houses and lands to his sister Elisabeth Bullocke & if she dy childlesse I giue the sayd houses and lands to my son Thomas Bullocke & his heyres Prouided Notwithstandinge that in case my wife continue in her widdows estate & shal want for her necessary mayntenance then it shal be lawful for her to make sale of the houses and lands aforesayed giuen vnto her & then only what doth remayne of my estate at her decease shal be giuen vnto my two grand children aforesayd to be equally deuided Item I giue vnto John Bullocke aforesaid after the decease of my wife the bed where on I doe commonly ly & the funiture there unto belonging which my wife is to keepe in reperatione duringe the tearme of her life Item I giue vnto my son Thomas Bullocke ten pounds to be payd vnto him on yeare after my decease If he come to demand it

"Item: In case my wife shal haue no cause to sel the sayd house & land for her necessary mayntenance but do leaue them to my grand childe John Bullocke as aforesayde then my will is that he shal pay vnto his sister Elisabeth Bullocke halfe the worth of the sayd house and lands as they shall be indifferently valewed by two indifferent men. Item my wil is that If eyther of my grandchildren should depart this life vnmaryed & before they come to age that which I haue giuen to that ‖departed‖ shal be giuen to that w$^{ch}$ doth surviue & in case they both depart this life before they come to age then that w$^{ch}$ I haue giuen them shal be giuen to my son Thomas Item my wil is that in case my wife shal sue for her therds in the land I gaue vnto my son Henery & w$^{ch}$ is sould vnto Henery Cooke that then it shal be lawful for the heyres of my son Henery to take possession of the hovse & land aforesayd giuen to her Item I constitute Elisabeth my wife Executrix of this my last wil & testament & Willyam flint & Nathaniel ffelton ouerseers of my wil & giue to each of them 20$^s$."

signum
Henery H Bullocke
his mark

Witness: John Pudne, Thomas O Smal, Nathaniel ffelton.

Proved in the Salem court 29 : 4: 1664 by the witnesses. *Essex Co. Quarterly Court Files, vol. 10, leaf 6.*

Inventory taken Jan. 4, 1663, by Thomas Gardiner, sr. and Nathaniell Felton: His dwellinge house & outhouses with the land thereunto belonging, 40li.; 4 acres of meadow, 5li.; 2 Cowes, 5li.; 3 smal swine, 1li. 8s.; 8 feather bed & bolster, 1 greene Rug, 2 blankets, 3 pillows, 1 Coverlet, 8li.; 1 flock bed & bolster, 3 Cotten blankets, 1 pillow, 2li. 10s.; 5 Sheets, 2li. 10s.; 2 old chests & 2 boxes, 12s.; a bedstead, 6 chayers, 12s.; 6li. yarne, 5li. cotton, 13s.; scales & weights, 5s.; 3 brasse ketles, 1li. 10s.; 2 Iron pots, 15s.; Peuter, 12s.; a warming pan, 4s.; a morter & pestle, a fyre shovel & tongs & a halve, 5s.; a fryinge pan, a chafendish and old candlesticke, 5s.; a bedstead & old tubs, 10s.; a bucken tub & 2 payles, 5s.; a spade, 4 wedges & ax, 7s.; old Lumber, 10s.; his weareing apparel, 5li.; total, 76li. 13s. Crediter per John Sutchicke, 4li.; John Upton, 4li.; Willyam Flint, 9li. 12s.; Nath. Felton, 4li. 10s.; Isacke Cooke, 4li.; total, 26li. 2s. Sum total, 99li. 15s. Debter to Captayne Corwinne,

1li.; the charges of his burial, 1li.; in other smal debts, 1li.; total, 3li. *Essex Co. Quarterly Court Files, vol. 10, leaf 7.*

### ESTATE OF SAMUEL BEADLE OF SALEM.

"I Samell Beadle being by Gods pvidents sick & weake of body: yett through the Lords mercy of pfect memorye, doe make this my last will & testament: as followeth: Imp$^r$ I giue vnto my son nathanyell Beadle ten shillings: it being as much as I conciud convenyent vpon divers good considerations also with respect to what I haue alredy don for him It I giue to my daughter Dorithy forty shillings ffor the rest of my estate, moueables and vnmoueables, what euer God haue giuen me in this world, (when all my Just debts are paid) I giue to my three smalest children now at home with me, namly Samuell, Thomas, and Elizabeth, equally to be devided betweene them, & to be paid at the age, of 21 years my sons & my daughters at ye age of 18 yeares or maryed & of y$^e$ three viz: Samuell Thomas & Elizabeth y$^e$ survivers at the time of payment to haue y$^e$ deceased pt devided And lastly I doe apoynt my Loveing freind m walter price to be my executor of this my will & m$^r$ John Croad & Hillyard veren ouerseers witnes my hand this 12$^{th}$ of march 1663-64."

Samuell Bedle.

Witness: Hillyard veren, Thomas Watson.

Proved in Salem court 30: 4: 1664 by the witnesses. *Essex Co. Quarterly Court Files, vol. 10, leaf 11.*

Will of Samuell Beadle was proved 30: 4: 1664, by Mr. Walter Price and Hilliard Veren and an imperfect inventory was presented. Administration was granted to Samuell and Nathanyell, sons of Samuell Beadle, deceased, who were to perfect the inventory and bring it into Salem court. Mr. Walter Price, the executor named in the will, refused to serve. *Salem Quarterly Court Records, vol. 4, page 133.*

### ESTATE OF JAMES PRIEST OF SALEM.

"Whereas by an awefull dispensation of god, James Priest the son of James Priest late of Salem unnaturally made away himselfe & left some small estate behind him, an Inventory of which goods was taken by Mr. Edmund Batter & Leiut John Holbrooke & a full agreement made with all psons concerned the approbation & confirmation whereof was to be Issued at Ipswich Court," the said James Priest, surviveing, appointed his son-in-law, "Shadrach Tore of Brauntry" to be his lawful attorney and asked the favor of the Court in reference to the settling of his estate on him, his aged father. Signed Sept. 19, 1664.

his mark<br>James I P Priest.

Witness: Wm. Torrey, Josiah Torrey.

Inventory taken 12 : 5 : 1664, by Edmond Batter and Theodore Price: 1 Cotten Rugge & a Canvas bedcase, 1li. 5s.; 3 pr stockings, 7s., 1 hatte, 5s., 12s.; 2 suets of Aparrell, 7li. 10s.; in money, 2li. 10s.; Linnen cloaths, 1li.; 2 wastcoats & old Coate, 15s.; 1 Chest, books, lead & bullets, 12s.; 1 gun, Rapier & bandlier, 14s.; total, 14li. 18s.
Received in Ipswich court Sept. 27, 1664.

*Essex Co. Probate Files, Docket 22,746.*

Administration on the estate of James Preist of Salem, intestate, granted 27 : 7 : 1664, to his father, James Preist of Weymouth. An inventory, amounting to 14li. 18s., was presented, which was ordered to remain in his hands until the court took further order. *Ipswich Quarterly Court Records, vol. 1, page 134.*

### GUARDIANSHIP OF HANNAH SMITH OF ROWLEY.

Hanah Smith of Rowley chose Leonard Harriman as her guardian, 27 : 7 : 1664, and he was bound to pay her her portion when it became due. *Ipswich Quarterly Court Records, vol. 1, page 133.*

Lenord Heryman of Rowley, guardian of Hanah Smith, acknowledges the receipt from Jerimiah Elsworth of 22li. 2s. the portion left her by her father, Hugh Smith, and fully acquits the said Jerimiah Elsworth and Mary his wife forever. Signed Mar. 26, 1666. Witness: Abraham Jewitt, Jonathan Platts.

Acknowledged Feb. 28, 1666 by the witnesses. *Ipswich Deeds, vol. 3, page 26.*

Joseph Trumble of Rowley acknowledges the receipt from Leonord Hariman, guardian of Hanah Smith his wife, of 22li. 2s. 6d. her portion. Signed May 10, 1669. Witness: Samuell Brocklebanke, Daniell Wickam.

Acknowledged in Ipswich court Sept. 27, 1670 by Joseph Trumble. *Ipswich Deeds, vol. 3, page* 161.

### ESTATE OF NICHOLAS TUCKER OF MARBLEHEAD.

Administration on the estate of Nicolas Tucker of Marblehead, intestate, granted 27: 7: 1664, to his brother Andrew Tucker of Marblehead, fisherman, and he was ordered to bring in an inventory to the next Salem court, that the estate might be disposed of to the right heirs. Andrew Tucker and Mathew Price, sureties. *Ipswich Quarterly Court Records, vol. 1, page* 133.

An inventory of the estate of Nicholas Tucker having been presented to the court 29: 9: 1664, by Andrew Tucker, administrator, and Mathew Price, though somewhat imperfect, yet it was accepted, and the administrator was discharged of his bond, and held in another bond of 20li. for the perfecting of the inventory for the next Salem court. *Salem Quarterly Court Records, vol. 4, page* 141.

Inventory taken by Andrew Tucker: One Rugge, Cost at Mr. Willm. Brown's, 2li.; 1 suet of Cloaths, 2li. 15s.; 1 bagge of Linnen, 1 feather pillow, 2 silke Neckcloath, ———; 1 Barrell Green ginger, cost 5li.; 1 Cabin Rugge, 1 Canvas bed sake, ———; 1 pr. boots & barrell, 1li.; hier of Boat, sumr. voiage, 4li.; 1 short Cape, ———; what is due from Samll. Condey, heir of third of boate, winter vioage, 4li. 13s.; 1 fowlinge peece to Jno. Pedericke, 2li.; 16 pr. stockings, 3 suets sea cloaths, 4 pr. shoos, 5 pr. drawers, Hooks, lines & leads, ———; Rich. Norman is Indebted, 3s.; Willm. Watters, 3s.; Elias Henly, 3s.; Nich. Foxe, 3s.; Jno. Pedericke, 3s.; Thomas Ellis, 3s.; Jno. Harris, 3s.; Jno. Pederick, the losse, 3s.; Jno. Stacy, 3s.; Elias Henly, 6s.; due to Elias Stileman, deceased, 1li. 18s. 8d. *Essex Co. Quarterly Court Files, vol. 10, leaf* 76.

Andrew Tucker, administrator of the estate of Nicholas Tucker, was bound 27: 4: 1665, to bring in a perfected inventory to court to be held in June, 1666, in Salem. *Salem Quarterly Court Records, vol. 4, page* 145.

### ESTATE OF JOHN ANNABLE OF IPSWICH.

Administration on the estate of John Anaball, intestate, granted Nov. 10, 1664, by the honored magistrates, Mr. Samuell Symonds and Maj. Genll. Denison, to Anna, the widow, and she was ordered to bring in an inventory to the next Ipswich court. *Ipswich Quarterly Court Records, vol. 1, page 137.*

Anna Aniball, administratrix, brought in an inventory amounting to about 180li., clear estate. Court Mar. 28, 1665, ordered that the estate remain in her hands for the bringing up of the children, and she was to pay to the eldest son, John Anaball, 20li., and 10li. each to the rest of the children, three sons and three daughters, at age, the land to be security. *Ipswich Quarterly Court Records, vol. 1, page 141.*

Inventory of the estate of John Anaball of Ipswich, lately deceased, taken Nov. 7, 1664, by Robert Lord: the dwelling house & barne & land about it, 80li.; 6 acres of marsh and foure of upland, 40li.; a small fether bed, boulster, 2 pillows, old rugg, ould curtaines, valants & 2 blanketts & bedsted, 5li. 10s.; a trundle bed & beding belonging to it, 2li.; a chest & 2 boxes, 16s.; a mantell & another old one, 1li.; a paire of Andiorns, 10s.; one old warmeing pan & other small things, 8s.; one flockbed, 2 bousters, old coverlett & bedsted, 2li. 10s.; five paire of sheets, 4li. 10s.; 4 pr. of pillowbeers, 1li.; 3 table cloths, 1 dozen of napkins & a towell, 1li. 15s.; one old chest, kneading trough & other lumber, 10s.; his weareing apparrell, 5li.; an old bedstead, chest & some other things, 1li.; in pewter, 2li. 5s.; tinn ware, 15s.; brasse, 1li. 2s.; 2 Iron potts, tramells, potthookes & other things, 2li. 5s.; 2 presing Irons & sheeres, 10s.; wooden ware, 2li. 10s.; 2 wheeles & cardes, 9s.; 2 little tables & chaires, 16s.; a cradle & what belongs to it, 10s.; 2 axes, hows and other tooles, 1li.; an ould cubberd, 2 sives & small things, 10s.; bookes, 1li.; Indian corne, 60 bushells, 8li.; 3 cowes & 3 young cattle & hay to winter them, 19li.; hoggs and shotes, 7li.; a young horse, 5li.; English corne, 5li.; apples & garden stuffe, 16s.; butter & biefe, 10s.; debts oweing to the estate, 22li. 17s.; debts oweing from the estate, 47li. 2s. 5d.; total clear estate, 181li. 2s. 7d.

Received in Ipswich court Mar. 28, 1665. *Essex Co. Probate Files, Docket 743.*

### ESTATE OF THOMAS SPOONER OF SALEM.

Administration on the estate of Tho. Spooner, granted

29: 9: 1664, to Elizabeth Spooner, relict of Tho. Spooner, and an inventory, amounting to 333li. 3s. 8d., was allowed. Whereas there were several grand-children, namely, John, Elizabeth, Hana, Sara and Thomas, children of John Ruck by his wife, the daughter of Thomas Spooner, court ordered, it being consented to by said John Ruck, that the children have 120li. out of the said estate, payable at age, to John, 40li., and to the others 20li. each. The remainder of the estate was to be left in the hands of the widow for her own use. Mr. Edmond Batter and John Ruck were appointed overseers. *Salem Quarterly Court Records, vol. 4, page* 140.

Inventory taken 15: 9: 1664, by Edmund Batter and Hillyard Veren: A dwelling house, with out houses & 13 acres of land adjoining, 150li.; 1 3-4 acres of marsh & about 6 acres of upland lying in the south field, 16li.; 3-4 of an acre of marsh in ye north feild, 6li.; about 37 acres of upland in the north feild, 40li.; 2 oxen, 2 steers & 5 Cowes, 40li; 1 horse, 1 steere, 1 heifer, 2 calves, 13li.; 1 swine and 4 sheep, 3li.; a Cart & dung pott, with chaines, yoakes, Harrow & plow, 4li.; 2 loomes & sleas, 5li. In the parlor, a beadsteed, beading & furniture, 7li.; 2 tables, 6 Joyn stooles & a Carpitt, 2li.; 7 chaires & cushions & 2 smales stooles, 2li.; 2 swords, 2 belts & a staff, 1li.; a looking glass & som earthware, 6s. 8d.; bookes, 2li.; wearing apparrell, 12li.; 7 pr. sheets, 5 pr. pillow beers, 1 doz. napkins, 3 table cloathes, & some other linnen, 5li. In the hall, 2 chests, a settle & 3 boxes, 1li. 10s.; a high bead, truckle bead & ye beading, 8li.; 2 hatts, 20s., 1 saddle & pillion, 20s., 2li.; a linnen wheele & 2li. of yarne, 10s.; 2 old cushions & some other lumber, 5s. In the kitchen, an old table, forme, stooles & chaires, 12s.; axes, augers, hoes & some other tooles, 1li.; pewter, 20s., Iron potts, bras, & haukes, 4li.; some pailes & wooden lumber, 10s. In the chamber, a beadsteed, 10s.; a feather bead, flock bead & beading & chest, 5li.; old cask & some other lumber, 10s.; a cheese press & dary vessells, 10s.; total, 333li. 3s. 8d. *Essex Co. Quarterly Court Files, vol.* 10, *leaf* 75.

## Estate of John Bartoll of Marblehead.

John Bartoll, dying intestate, an inventory of the estate was brought into court 29: 9: 1664, by Parnell, his wife, amounting to 71li. 10s., and debts owing to several men of 64li. 18s. 5d., which, upon oath of said Parnell, were allowed, and she was appointed administratrix. The clear estate was 6li. 11s. 7d. *Salem Quarterly Court Records, vol. 4, page 142.*

Inventory taken Nov. 16, 1664, by Moses Maverick and William (his W mark) Charles: Two cows, 8li.; bull, 2li.; yearling, 1li.; three swine, 3li.; 4 acres of land and fences, 12li.; 6 in the farme bought of Major Hathorn, 6li.; 2 acres of medow liing at Capan, 4li.; 1 Cows Common, 2li.; one fourth part of a stage and land liing to it, 5li.; 2 beds mad of silkgras with bolster and blankits, 3li. 10s.; a great Copper, 3li. 10s.; one Iron pott, an Iron Ketle, 2 bras skilletts, one Iron scillott and towoe brass scillots, 3li.; 5 pewter platters and a bason, 1li.; peuter, 16s.; a morter and a bras skillet, 8s.; 2 dripin pans, 6s.; a handsaw, 1s. 6d.; a bible, 10s.; wearing aparell, 8li. 15s.; Earthen and wooden ware, 1li.; 2 Chests, 12s.; mony, 1li. 4s.; 1 paire of boots, 1li.; bands and hankershirs, 7s.; land bought of Robert barcus near Goit's house, 2li. 10s.; total, 71li. 10s.; estate is debter to severall men, 64li. 18s. 5d. Daniel Bartoll took oath in court before Hillyard Veren, cleric. Debtor, as appeared by Mr. Curill's booke, 30li. 18s. 9d.; Mr. Mossis Maverick's booke, 9li. 4s. 8d.; Mr. William Brown's book, 5li. 4s. 6d.; John Codner, 7li. 3s.; severall smale Dts. demaunded by severall men, 12li. 7s. 5d.; total, 64li. 18s. 5d. Demanded by Mr. B , 1li. 6s.; John Clemants, 12s.; Goodman Samson, 9s.; William Raimant, 3li.; Thomas Pittman, 10s.; Goodman Dixe, 10s.; Goodman Palmiter, 18s. 1d.; Mark Pitman, 1li. 5s.; Richard Croker, 1li.; William Littfoot, 2li. 15s.; Mr. Gidnie, 2s. 4d.; total, 12li. 7s. 5d. *Essex Co. Quarterly Court Files, vol. 10, leaf 77.*

## ADDENDA

### Estate of Richard Ingersoll of Salem.*

Inventory of the estate of Richard Ingerson of Salem, dated Oct. 4, 1644, taken by Townsend Bishop and Jeffery Massy: Seven Cowes, 34li.; 2 young steers, 4li.; 2 young heifers, 4li. 13s. 4d.; a bull and bull segg, 7li. 10s.; a paire of Oxen, 14li.; paire of steeres, 11li.; bull and bull segg, 8li. 10s.; 3 calves, 3li.; 3 swine, 4li. 10s.; halfe a pig, 4s.; 2 horses, a mare, colt and foal, 28li.; Indian corne, 4li.; pease in the barne, 2li.; Ry & wheate, 5li. 12s.; Ry, 1li. 15s.; Hay, 3li. 15s.; the 3d pt of a cart, 8s. 4d.; the third pt. of a Tumbrill, 5s.; the third pt of a Harrow, 1s. 8d.; the 3d pt of 3 yoakes & chains, 4s. 8d.; the 3d pt of 2 plowes, 6s. 8d.; hemp & flax, 5s. 6d.; a farme, 80 acres, meddow, 20 acres, 14li. 13s. 4d.; another farme 75 acres, 7li.; 26 acres, 2 houses, 2 acres a quartr of salt marsh, 26li. 7s. 6d.; Debts due to the estate, 6li. 19s.; bedsteed & beding, 4li. 14s.; another bedsteed & bed, 1li. 15s.; press cubbord, 14s.; a peece of locrum, 3s. 4d.; a warming pan, 4s.; 2 cushins & a chaire, 10s.; pewter, 10s.; 2 dripping pans, 10s.; a great Iron Kettle, 1li.; 2 Iron potts, 1li. 10s.; brasse Kettle, 4s.; a settle, 6s. 8d.; cheese fatts, 3s.; churne, 4s.; Kneading trough, 4s.; seive, 1s. 4d.; 7 traies, one milke pan, 5s. 4d.; milk paile, 4s.; cheese, 6s. 8d.; oates, 8d.; malt & wheate, 8s.; spinning wheele, 2s. 6d.; woollen wheele & cards, 5s. 4d.; moose skin sute, 2li.; cloath sute & coate, 1li.; total, 213li. 19s. Proved in court, 1: 11: 1644, by Ralph Fogg, p. curia. Copy made and brought in court Mar. 30, 1669 by Hilliard Veren, cleric. *Essex Co. Quarterly Court Files, vol. 14, leaf 34.*

### Estate of John Cogswell, Jr. of Ipswich.

A copy of this will, *see ante* page 156, proved 27: 7: 1653, may be found in Essex County Quarterly Court Files, vol. 23, leaf 137.

---

* See *ante* page 43.

# INDEX.

Abbott, Abbet, Abboot, Abbot, Abot, Abott, Dorothy, 302, 303.
  George, 84, 86, 301, 377, 396.
  Nehemiah, 86, 301.
  Thomas, 86, 301-303.
Aborn, Aborne, Eaborne, Ebborne, Ebern, Eborn, Eborne, Eboron, Eborrun, Ebron, Eburne, Oborne, ——, 349, 412.
  Catherine, 348, 411-413.
  Hannah, 411.
  James, 411.
  Mary, 348, 411-413.
  Moses, 266, 411.
  Samuel, 256, 349, 411-413.
  Sarah, 411.
  Thomas, 24.
Abre, Abree, Thomas, 39.
Acie, Acy, Axe, Axey, James, 55, 124.
  William, 203, 443.
Adams, Addams, John, 278, 280, 366, 370.
  Nathaniel, 280, 366.
  Robert, 231.
  Samuel, 366, 367.
  William, 64, 167, 169, 278, 280, 366.
Addis, Addiss, Adies, ——, 101.
  William, 102.
Adze, *see* Tools.
Ager, ——, 49.
  Alice, 184, 185.
  Benjamin, 184.
  Jonathan, 184.
  Joseph, 184.
  William, 58, 184.
Alderman, John, 40, 42, 210, 256, 257.
Alford, William, 38.
Allen, Allin, Andrew, 99.
  Ann, 338.
  Bossom, 338.
  Faith, 99.
  Isaac, 338.
  John, 190, 338.
  William, 18, 347, 419, 429, 445.

Alley, Aley, Hugh, 56, 214.
Ambross, Henry, 102, 103.
Amesbury, 401, 409, 410.
Amis, Robert, 398.
Ammunition, *see* Weapons.
Anard, John, 362, 363.
Anderson, Arsbell, 353-355.
Andirons, *see* Utensils.
Andover, 141, 244, 291, 377, 395, 397.
Andrews, Andreues, Andreus, Andrew, Andrewes, Androes, Andros, Androws, ——, 33, 52, 313.
  Elizabeth, 27.
  John, 5-8, 27, 28, 268, 272, 313, 354, 378-380.
  Robert, 3, 27, 28, 145, 268, 271.
  Sarah, 380.
  Thomas, 27, 28, 234, 378, 379.
Animals (domestic).
  Ass, 152, 176, 236, 245, 377, 381.
  Beasts, 19, 22, 107, 146, 170, 212, 226, 230, 231, 240.
  Bullocks, 90, 130, 308, 374, 425.
  Bulls, 4, 6, 22, 29, 31, 32, 71, 83, 106, 108, 125, 130, 143, 146, 157, 158, 208, 218, 236, 308, 348, 349, 352, 370, 374, 388, 417, 457, 458.
  Calves, 4, 6, 8, 10, 14, 20, 22, 26, 27, 29, 32, 48, 56, 61, 64, 71, 74, 75, 80, 83, 85, 91, 97, 99, 100, 108, 121, 124, 125, 130, 131, 133, 136, 143, 146, 147, 151, 154, 155, 159, 160, 162, 167, 168, 176, 177, 182, 183, 185, 188, 191, 193, 201, 205, 208, 211, 214, 216, 218, 220, 225, 226, 229, 233, 236, 243, 244, 246, 247, 251, 253, 260, 262, 267, 271, 274, 289, 295, 302, 304, 311, 319, 322, 335, 337, 339, 340, 342, 348, 352, 353, 357, 358, 367, 368, 370, 371, 374, 376-378, 388, 389, 393, 396, 400, 403, 408, 409, 411, 422, 423, 428, 429, 431, 441, 442, 456, 458.

INDEX

Animals (domestic).
  Cattle, 6-8, 10, 11, 13, 15, 16, 18, 19, 47, 67, 73, 84, 93, 96-99, 112, 116, 120, 125, 127, 129, 142, 144, 152, 155, 163, 167, 170, 173, 177, 189, 191, 194, 196, 204, 208, 210, 211, 231, 236, 240, 244, 250, 254, 260, 262, 267, 268, 270, 277, 285, 301, 304, 308, 314, 318, 319, 328, 333, 335, 352, 379, 380, 395, 396, 399, 403, 405, 406, 411, 414, 416, 417, 421, 425, 428, 431, 434, 441, 455.
  Colts, 20, 96, 108, 112, 116, 120, 125, 128, 130, 171, 180, 190, 191, 193, 197, 217, 225, 227-229, 235, 242, 246, 256, 260, 271, 274, 275, 284, 290, 291, 304, 306, 310, 314, 322, 339, 340, 343, 349, 354, 355, 365, 368, 376, 377, 391, 392, 398, 404, 406, 408, 409, 411, 414, 422, 425, 426, 431, 444, 458.
  Cows, 4, 6-9, 14, 16. 20, 22, 23, 26, 29, 31, 32, 34, 35, 43, 44, 48, 50, 54-58, 61, 64, 65, 71, 73-75, 77, 80, 82, 83, 85, 87, 90, 91, 95-101, 106-110, 112, 116, 117, 120, 121, 123-125, 128, 130, 131, 133, 136, 137, 141-144, 146, 147, 149, 151, 154, 155, 157-162, 165-168, 172, 173, 176, 177, 180, 182-185, 188, 190, 191, 193, 194, 197, 201, 202, 204, 205, 208, 210, 212, 213, 216-218, 220, 221, 225-227, 229, 231, 233, 235, 236, 239-244, 246-248, 250, 251, 253, 256, 257, 260-262, 264-267, 269-275, 277, 278, 281, 282, 284, 285, 287, 289, 290, 293-295, 301, 302, 304-306, 308, 310, 311, 313-315, 317, 319, 322, 324, 326, 335, 337, 340, 342, 343, 348, 349, 351-357, 359, 363, 365, 367, 368, 370, 371, 374, 376-378, 380, 383, 385, 386, 388-393, 395, 396, 398, 400, 403-406, 408, 409, 411, 412, 418, 419, 422, 423, 426, 428, 429, 431, 432, 434, 437, 438, 440-442, 444-446, 449, 451, 455-458.

Animals (domestic).
  Ewes, 26, 99, 147. 160, 180, 183, 190, 191, 193, 207, 208, 211, 212, 214, 218, 225, 239, 247, 267, 271, 278, 284, 285, 287, 302, 306, 308, 339, 340, 343, 350, 386, 388, 391, 399, 406, 423.
  Filly, 273, 274.
  Foal, 278, 285, 302, 313, 352, 400, 417, 458.
  Gelding, 197.
  Goats, 18, 23, 27, 29, 30-32, 34, 35, 40-42, 48, 91, 102, 135, 140, 282.
  Heifers, 4, 6-9, 20, 23, 31, 32, 34, 36, 39-41, 44, 47, 48, 54, 55, 61, 75, 80, 82, 83, 87, 90, 91, 96-101, 106-108, 112, 116, 120, 123-125, 128, 130, 131, 133, 147, 154, 157-159, 162, 165, 173, 180, 182, 183, 185, 186, 190, 191, 201, 203-205, 213, 218, 236, 239, 242, 247, 251, 253, 256, 257, 260, 262, 264, 265, 267, 274, 275, 282, 285, 289, 290, 293-295, 302, 304, 315, 322, 326, 337, 340, 348, 349, 358, 360, 370, 374, 377, 383, 389, 393, 400, 403, 404, 406, 411, 412, 415, 422, 426, 431, 456, 458.
  Hogs, 6, 22, 48, 50, 56, 74, 75, 83, 91, 95, 97-100, 106, 123, 128, 130, 131, 165, 175, 190, 197, 212, 242, 245, 271, 278, 284, 304, 398, 403, 455.
  Horse, riding, 426.
  Horses, 19, 125, 128, 160, 193, 194, 218, 225, 235, 270, 271, 274, 275, 289, 295, 301, 318, 319, 322, 328, 335, 340, 352, 353, 358, 370, 377, 378, 383, 385, 400, 404, 406, 408, 409, 411-413, 417, 421-423, 425, 426, 429, 432, 436, 444, 455, 456, 458.
  Kids, 18, 27, 30, 32, 40, 41, 133, 140.
  Kine, 124, 131, 152, 155, 313.
  Lambs, 42, 55, 91, 124, 147, 148, 155, 180, 191, 197, 201, 210, 214, 218, 225, 229, 239, 247, 248, 256, 267, 269, 271, 285, 306, 333, 340, 343, 349, 350, 363, 378, 388, 391, 396, 399, 406, 423, 446.

INDEX 461

Animals (domestic).
  Mares, 4, 6, 9, 20, 29, 30, 32, 80,
    96, 97, 100, 106, 108, 110, 112,
    116, 120, 125, 128, 130, 160,
    162, 171, 190, 191, 193, 194,
    197, 206, 208, 218, 225, 227-
    229, 235, 236, 244, 246, 260,
    273, 274, 277, 278, 285, 289-
    291, 295, 301, 302, 304, 306,
    310, 313, 314, 317-319, 328,
    335, 340, 349, 351, 352, 354,
    355, 365, 368, 376, 391, 392,
    396, 398, 400, 403, 404, 406,
    408, 409, 411, 412, 414, 417,
    421-423, 425, 426, 431, 443,
    444, 449, 458.
  Mule, 273.
  Oxen, 6, 9, 16, 20, 22, 29, 31,
    32, 61, 71, 80, 83, 96, 97, 99,
    100, 106, 108, 109, 112, 113,
    116, 118, 124, 130, 131, 133,
    142, 146, 147, 154, 155, 159,
    160, 162, 168, 176, 177, 180,
    183, 185, 188, 193, 208, 211-
    213, 218, 225, 229, 236, 240,
    244, 246, 248, 250, 257, 260,
    262, 264-267, 269, 270, 271,
    273-275, 277, 278, 285, 289,
    290-292, 301, 302, 304, 306,
    310, 313, 314, 319, 322, 335,
    340, 348, 349, 351-354, 368,
    370, 377, 380, 383, 388, 395,
    396, 398, 400, 403, 406, 408,
    409, 417, 422, 423, 426, 431,
    437, 438, 441, 456, 458.
  Pigs, 3, 4, 7, 14, 27, 32, 34, 41,
    45, 48, 55, 64, 74, 75, 80, 83,
    85, 100, 102, 107, 123, 131,
    136, 149, 155, 176, 185, 189-
    191, 243, 247, 251, 262, 271,
    287, 302, 304, 340, 342, 348,
    398, 403, 406, 418, 422, 423,
    458.
  Rams, 31, 147, 160, 193, 214,
    229, 271, 308, 388, 423.
  Sheep, 26, 55, 56, 100, 124, 128,
    130, 147, 155, 162, 183, 191,
    197, 201, 208, 214, 217, 227-
    229, 233, 236, 241, 244, 247,
    250, 256, 265, 266, 269, 274,
    277, 278, 284, 289, 303, 304,
    310, 311, 319, 322, 335, 349,
    356, 357, 363, 368, 376-378,
    396, 400, 408, 409, 426, 431,
    434, 446, 456.

Animals (domestic).
  Shoats, 27, 74, 83, 91, 109, 124,
    140, 152, 168, 174, 220, 226,
    246, 247, 275, 278, 282, 285,
    340, 363, 374, 434, 449, 455.
  Sows, 3, 27, 32, 34, 35, 41, 42,
    55, 74, 75, 85, 121, 137, 149,
    158, 166, 176, 191, 202, 247,
    262, 275, 282, 302, 340, 363,
    374.
  Steers, 4, 6, 7, 14, 20, 22, 29, 30,
    32, 44, 47, 48, 56, 64, 71, 75,
    82, 83, 85, 97, 99, 100, 108,
    112, 116, 124, 125, 128, 130,
    133, 142, 146, 149, 151, 154,
    158, 162, 168, 180, 182, 185,
    188, 190, 191, 193, 197, 201,
    205, 208, 210, 214, 218, 229,
    231, 236, 244, 246, 248, 250,
    253, 256, 257, 260, 262, 265,
    266, 274, 282, 284, 285, 293-
    295, 311, 318, 328, 335, 340,
    343, 349, 354, 359, 367, 370,
    378, 395, 405, 406, 408, 409,
    411, 412, 414, 417, 423, 426,
    429, 431, 434, 441, 456, 458.
  Swine, 18-20, 23, 36, 42, 57, 61,
    65, 71, 73, 77, 82, 98, 108, 133,
    142-144, 146, 147, 151, 152,
    154, 155, 160, 162, 170, 182,
    183, 188, 189, 193, 201, 205,
    208, 214, 218, 225, 226, 229,
    236, 240, 243, 246, 256, 260,
    262, 265-267, 269, 273, 274,
    277, 284, 293, 295, 301, 305,
    308, 310, 311, 315, 319, 322,
    335, 337, 342, 343, 348, 349,
    351-353, 356-359, 363, 367, 368,
    370, 377, 378, 381, 385, 388-
    390, 393, 396, 400, 406, 408,
    412, 415, 417, 422, 423, 426,
    429, 431-433, 440, 441, 444,
    446, 451, 456-458.
  Wethers, 26, 180, 191, 197, 214,
    225, 229, 239, 271, 284, 302,
    340, 343, 423, 446.
  Yearlings, 8, 32, 44, 61, 80, 83,
    100, 121, 123, 124, 133, 147,
    154, 158, 160, 168, 188, 197,
    205, 210, 212, 214, 218, 220,
    225, 229, 253, 266, 271, 340,
    349, 352, 370, 371, 377, 383,
    388, 398, 408, 409, 412, 417,
    422, 457.
Animals (wild).

Animals (wild).
  Beaver, 317.
  Stag, 157, 180.
  Wolf, 7.
Ann, Cape, see Cape Ann.
Annable, Anaball, Aniball, Anniball, Anna, 455.
  John, 191, 235, 454, 455.
Annisquam, 386.
Antrum, Antrim, Obadiah, 413.
  Thomas, 290, 413-415.
Anvils, see Tools.
Apples, see Food.
Appleton, Apleton, ——, 6-10, 271.
  John, 192, 258, 278, 396, 428.
  Samuel, 4, 221.
Appleyard, Sarah, 111.
Apprentices, 11, 21, 39, 44, 62, 82, 118, 139, 147, 148, 156, 187, 198, 228, 237, 261, 283, 391.
Aprons, see Clothing.
Archer, Archard, Archerd, Samuel, 172, 239, 243, 275, 381.
Armitage, Armantage, Armatage, Armitag, Armytage, ——, 156.
  Jane, 136.
  Joseph, 27, 100, 136, 214.
Armor, see Weapons.
Arms, see Weapons.
Asington, Eng., 82.
Aslet, John, 120.
Asses, see Animals (domestic).
Atkins, Theodore, 313.
Attorney, power of, 15, 16, 114, 215, 277, 278, 415, 453.
Audeley, Edmond, 11.
Augers, see Tools.
Austines, Thomas, 124.
Averill, Averell, Abigail, 151, 201.
  William, 151, 201, 202.
Avery, Averi, Averye, ——, 3, 228.
  Christopher, 102.
  Joseph, 3.
  Thomas, 226, 228.
  William, 145, 396.
Awls, see Tools.
Axes, see Tools.
Ayres, Eyer, Eyers, Hannah, 261-263.
  John, 261-263, 283.

Ayres, Mary, 261, 262.
  Nathaniel, 261.
  Obadiah, 261, 262.
  Peter, 262.
  Rebecca, 261, 262.
  Robert, 261.
  Susanna, 285.
  Thomas, 261.

Babson, Bapsene, Eleanor, 132.
  Isabel, 343.
  James, 133, 343.
Bacon, ——, 41, 183.
  Isaac, 161, 227, 228.
  Rebecca, 161, 227, 228.
  William, 161.
Bacon, see Food.
Badger, Bagir, Giles, 78, 79, 339.
  John, 80, 340, 342.
  Nathaniel, 342.
Badgeth, Eng., 113.
Bagly, Baggerly, ——, 10.
  Orlando, 408, 409.
  Sarah, 409.
Bags, see Utensils.
Bags, cloak, see Clothing.
Bailey, Baly, Bayley, Bayly, Edna, 92, 93.
  James, 92.
  John, 92, 101, 145, 146.
  Joseph, 92-94, 145.
  Richard, 92-94.
  Robert, 145.
  Ruth, 152.
  William, 40.
Baize, see Cloth.
Baker, ——, 13, 177, 272, 441.
  Edward, 354.
  Elizabeth, 203.
  John, 203.
  Robert, 13.
  Sarah, 138.
  Thomas, 367.
Balch, Ballch, Baulch, Agnes, 263, 264.
  Annis, 96, 263, 264.
  Benjamin, 96, 97, 263, 264, 365, 366.
  Freeborn, 96.
  John, 96, 365, 366.
  Mary, 365.
Ballard, John, 213.
  Nathaniel, 213.
  William, 24.
Bancroft, Thomas, 449.

Bandeliers, see Weapons.
Bands, see Clothing.
Barbadoes, 306.
Barber, Barbor, Barbour, ——, 41.
  Faith, 40.
  John, 40, 41.
Barber's stuff, see Cloth.
Bark, 322.
Bark, see Vessels.
Barker, Barcus, Anne, 234.
  James, 85, 237, 302.
  John, 234.
  Mary, 129.
  Richard, 142, 377, 396.
  Robert, 142, 457.
  Samuel, 234.
  Thomas, 85, 94, 111, 117, 128, 129, 335, 336.
Barley, see Food.
Barnard, Barnett, Sarah, 338.
  Thomas, 336-338, 400, 407.
Barnes, Barence, Barns, Benjamin, 432.
  Mary, 432.
  Thomas, 432.
  William, 130, 337, 400.
Barney, Barny, Jacob, 52, 147, 304, 376, 389.
Barns, see Buildings.
Barrels, see Utensils.
Barrett, Barick, Barret, Elizabeth, 137.
  Richard, 136, 137.
Bartholomew, Barthelmew, Bartholmew, Bartholmewe, Bartlemew, ——, 47, 101, 384.
  Abraham, 52.
  Elizabeth, 268.
  Henry, 51, 74, 77, 91, 117, 147, 153, 171, 172, 269, 281, 383, 385, 446-448.
  Richard, 51, 52.
  Thomas, 52.
  William, 51, 120, 191, 343.
Bartlett, Bartlet, Barttlet, Batlet, Batlett, Christopher, 86, 187.
  John, 86, 87, 187, 216, 311, 342, 408.
  Richard, 86, 87, 187.
  Sarah, 46.
Bartoll, Bartol, Daniel, 457.
  Joanna, 243.
  John, 60, 317, 456.
  Parnell, 456.

Bartrum, William, 356.
Basins, see Utensils.
Baskets, see Utensils.
Bass River, 146, 242.
Bassett, Basset, Bassitt, William, 355.
Bast, ——, 4.
  John, 4.
Batchelder, Bachelder, Bacheler, Bacheller, Bachelor, Bachelour, Bachiler, Batcheler, Batchelor, ——, 6, 253, 260, 441.
  Elizabeth, 252.
  Hannah, 252.
  John, 239, 242, 252, 389.
  Joseph, 78, 252.
  Mark, 252.
Batherne, George, 16.
Batt, Batty, ——, 103.
  Christopher, 103.
  Nicholas, 24.
Batter, Battar, Batters, ——, 39, 118, 120, 316.
  Edmond, 118, 143, 147, 162, 182, 183, 185, 241, 242, 245, 255, 281, 287, 306, 330, 331, 345-348, 357, 381, 382, 390, 413, 415, 420, 423, 436, 447, 448, 452, 453, 456.
  Sarah, 306.
Batty, see Batt.
Beach, sweepage of, 192.
Beacham, Beachum, ——, 35.
  Ed., 289.
  Mary, 35, 37.
Beadle, Bedell, Bedle, Dorothy, 452.
  Elizabeth, 452.
  George, 228, 229.
  Nathaniel, 452.
  Samuel, 452.
  Thomas, 452.
Beakers, see Utensils.
Beale, Beall, Martha, 217, 219.
  Samuel, 218.
  Thomas, 136.
  William, 177, 219.
Beans, see Food.
Beard, William, 435.
Beaver, 56, 119.
Beaver Dam, 314.
Beckes, Tobiah, 362, 363.
Becket, ——, 119.
Beckwell, George, 104.
Bedde, James, 327.

Bedding, see Furnishings.
Beds, see Furnishings.
Bedsteads, see Furniture.
Beef, see Food.
Beefard, Richard, 360.
Beer, see Drinks.
Bees, 21, 22, 61, 106, 130, 157, 188, 193, 273, 274, 322, 335, 342, 368, 377, 378, 396.
Beeswax, 22, 370.
Beetle rings, see Tools.
Beetles, see Tools.
Belcher, Belchar, Jeremy, 192, 220.
Belflower, Benjamin, 351.
Belknap, Belknapp, Abraham, 26.
Mary, 27.
Bell, John, 9.
Bellingham, ——, 329.
Richard, 110, 114, 137.
Samuel, 121.
William, 120, 121.
Bellows, see Tools and Utensils.
Bells, 148, 233, 308.
Belts, see Clothing.
Bennett, Benet, Bennet, Bennit, Bennitt, ——, 136, 415.
John, 415.
Lydia, 190.
Margaret, 415.
Samuel, 46, 56, 344.
William, 429.
Bertram, see Bartrum.
Betts, Richard, 103.
Beverly, see Bass River.
Bexby, Bigsby, Joseph, 82.
Bible, see Books.
Bidfield, Samuel, 153, 154.
Biggins, see Clothing.
Bile, ——, 406.
Billerica, 333.
Bills, see Tools.
Birding piece, see Weapons.
Birdsall, Henry, 26, 143.
Birkin, James, 16.
Biscuit, see Food.
Bishop, Bishopp, Byshop, ——, 256, 383, 441, 450.
John, 23, 84, 119, 186, 187, 216, 217.
Marie, 196, 199.
Rebecca, 84.
Richard, 3, 197, 199, 384.
Thomas, 52, 95, 275, 278.
Townsend, 43, 458.

Bitnar, Sarah, 99.
William, 99.
Bits, see Horse Equipment.
Bixby, see Bexby.
Blacksmith, see Trades.
Blanchard, Blanchar, Thomas, 23, 137.
Blankets, see Furnishings.
Blasdell, Ebenezer, 409, 410.
Elizabeth, 130.
Ralph, 130.
Blood, Richard, 143.
Bloomfield, Bloomfeild, Blumfeild, Blumfield, Henry, 37.
John, 12.
Thomas, 12, 309-311, 339.
Blower, John, 408.
Board cloths, see Furnishings.
Boards, see Manufactures.
Boat, see Vessels.
Bodices, see Clothing.
Bodkins, see Tools.
Bog pond, 159.
Bolsters, see Furnishings.
Bolton, William, 216.
Bolts, see Tools.
Bond, John, 34, 36, 230.
Books, 9, 16, 21, 22, 31, 33, 39, 43, 45, 47, 48, 55, 57, 58, 61, 64, 67, 69, 78, 80-82, 85, 87, 89, 92, 93, 95, 97, 105, 112, 117, 119, 123, 129, 132, 133, 135, 141, 143, 144, 148, 149, 151, 152, 154, 155, 158, 162, 164, 169, 171, 173-176, 180, 182, 185, 186, 188, 189, 195, 201, 208, 210, 212, 216, 218, 223, 225, 230, 233, 234, 240, 243, 245, 247, 250, 253, 254, 258, 260, 263, 265, 266, 274, 279, 282, 285, 288, 295, 308, 310, 312, 313, 314, 316, 320, 322, 328, 332, 335, 337, 341, 352, 367, 377, 381, 383, 389, 395, 403, 405, 406, 414, 418, 419, 430-434, 440, 447, 453, 455-457.
Ainsworth, Mr., on the five books of Moses and the Psalms, 314.
Aquinas (folio), 333.
Bibles, 7, 12, 23, 25, 29, 31, 33, 34, 39, 45, 46, 48, 49, 51, 54, 55, 57, 58, 61, 64, 67, 75, 77, 78, 87, 92, 100, 119, 120, 121, 123, 125, 133, 155, 163, 164, 174, 176, 180, 182, 184, 198,

INDEX 465

Books.
  Bibles, 201, 211, 216, 218, 226, 229, 233, 247, 250, 264, 273, 277, 295, 301, 302, 310, 312, 316, 317, 331, 335, 337, 342, 353, 356, 358, 374, 377, 382, 388-390, 392, 393, 415, 444, 457.
  Bifield's Works, 164.
  Blundeville's book, 157.
  Broughton's Works, 313.
  Bruised Reed, 9.
  Burrough's books, 419, 445.
  Calvin's Institutions, 230.
  Collins, John, works of, 157.
  Concordance, 230.
  Deceitfulness of Man's Heart, 77.
  Dictionary, 314.
  Dod's Works, 31.
  Dunham's Works, 31.
  Dyke's Works, 54.
  English authors, books of, 405.
  English books, 333, 335.
  Genealogy, maps of, 314.
  Gibben, Nicholas, Disputations of, 230.
  Horse book, 30.
  Latin books, 333, 335.
  Latin commentary, 314.
  Luther upon the Galatians, 230.
  Manuscripts, 314.
  Maps, 162, 233.
  Markam, 230.
  Of God's All Sufficiency, 77.
  Parchment, 48.
  Perkins' Works, 7, 9.
  Physic book, 30.
  Practical Catechism, 92.
  Practice of Piety, 30.
  Preston, Dr., works of, 30, 54, 228, 230.
  Psalm books, 49, 58, 64, 184, 198, 226, 306, 331, 445.
  Purchase Pilgrimage, 67.
  Sea books, 317.
  Sermon book, 58.
  Seven Treatises, 9.
  Shepard's Morality of the Sabbath, 230.
  Sibbs, Dr., books of, 228, 230.
  Spouse Royal, 9.
  Symonds, Joshua, books of, 230.
  Testaments, 9, 39, 314.

Books.
  Tremollin's Latin Bible, 314.
  Trials of Grace by Anthony Burgess, 405.
Boothaunches, see Clothing.
Boots, see Clothing.
Boovey, Joseph, 225.
Borges, Robert, 136.
Borman, ——, 9.
Boston, 44, 51, 55, 104, 119, 120, 152, 158, 181, 225, 234, 235, 243, 247, 273, 306, 313, 315, 316, 346, 347, 355, 381, 396, 403, 406, 440, 444.
Bosworth, Abigail, 170.
  Haniel, 105, 170, 427.
Bottles, see Utensils.
Boulter, Nathaniel, 195.
Bourne, Borne, ——, 35.
  Joanna, 34.
  John, 58.
  Mary, 34.
Bow, see Bowstrings.
Bowls, see Utensils.
Bowstrings, 180.
Bowtell, Boutell, Bowtwell, ——, 136.
  Alice, 143.
  James, 143.
  John, 143.
  Sarah, 143.
Boxes, see Furniture.
Boxted, Eng., 234.
Boyce, Boice, Boyes, Boys, Boyse, ——, 35, 228.
  Antipas, 278.
  Elizabeth, 161, 219.
  Joseph, 161, 162, 226, 229, 269.
  Matthew, 85, 93, 129, 206-208, 218, 219, 223, 232, 233, 235.
Boynton, Bointon, ——, 299.
  John, 203, 443.
  William, 295, 303.
Brabrooke, Brabrook, Bradbrook, Elizabeth, 391, 392.
  John, 391, 392.
  Joseph, 391.
  Rachel, 391.
  Rebecca, 391.
  Richard, 374.
  Samuel, 391.
  Sarah, 391.
  Thomas, 391, 392.
Brackenbury, Richard, 270, 418.
Bracy, ——, 6.

Bradbury, Bradbery, Bradburry,
——, 103, 408.
  Mary, 190.
  Thomas, 146, 150, 158, 191, 195, 274, 337, 338, 399, 405, 407-409, 424, 443.
Brading, James, 362, 363.
Bradley, John, 18.
  Joshua, 371.
  Judith, 371.
Bradstreet, Bradstreete, Bradstret, Bradstrett, Broadstreet, Broadstret, Brodstreate, Brodstreet, Brodstreete, ——, 6, 25, 30, 233, 268.
  Bridget, 217-219, 258.
  Dudley, 397.
  Hannah, 317.
  Humphry, 30, 177, 217, 218, 258.
  John, 217, 317, 318, 329.
  Mary, 217, 219.
  Moses, 217, 218, 317.
  Rebecca, 217, 219, 258.
  Sarah, 217, 219.
  Simon, 274, 379.
Bragg, Edward, 275.
Braintree, 453.
Brakes, see Tools.
Bran, see Food.
Brandy, see Drinks.
Brass, see Utensils.
Brazier, see Trades.
Brazor, ——, 6.
Bread, Brad, Braide, Breade, ——, 131.
  Allen, 56, 131, 403.
Bread, see Food.
Breeches, see Clothing.
Breed, see Bread.
Brent, Nathaniel, 134.
Brewster, Francis, 15.
Bricks, see Manufactures.
Bridges, Edmund, 169, 170, 397.
  Robert, 114, 213.
Bridgman, John, 226, 227.
Bridles, see Horse equipment.
Brigden, Mildred, 64.
  Thomas, 64.
Brigham, Bridgham, ——, 316.
  Sebastian, 85, 111, 117.
Brimstone, 70, 180, 386.
Brinsmead, Samuel, 134.
Bristol, Eng., 15, 16, 148.

Broadcloth, see Cloth.
Brocke, John, 117.
Brocklebank, Brockelbanke, Brocklebanke, ——, 302.
  Lt., 371.
  John, 334, 437.
  Samuel, 208, 237, 299, 334, 336, 338, 339, 352, 367, 371, 373, 437, 441, 453.
Broughton, ——, 120, 311.
Brown, Broune, Browne, ——, 65, 119, 227, 243, 304, 361, 417, 422, 445.
  Bartholomew, 307.
  Charles, 436.
  Edmund, 339.
  Edward, 62, 63, 95, 149, 173, 219, 275, 285, 306, 307.
  Elizabeth, 339, 340.
  Faith, 307.
  George, 22, 23, 340.
  James, 119, 134, 309-311, 437, 438.
  John, 35, 118, 119, 145, 148, 220, 221, 287, 303, 307, 310, 357, 384, 385.
  Joseph, 22, 307, 340.
  Joshua, 23, 339, 340.
  Margery, 23.
  Mary, 339, 387, 388.
  Michael, 22, 23.
  Nicholas, 44.
  Richard, 22, 23, 80, 150, 245, 339, 340.
  Sarah, 309, 310, 339, 437.
  Thomas, 14, 216, 307.
  William, 19, 20, 77, 102, 184, 227, 241, 256, 268, 316, 348, 359, 361, 380, 386, 387, 416, 419, 454, 457.
Browning, ——, 24.
Brushes, see Utensils.
Buckets, see Utensils.
Buckles, see Horse equipment.
Buckley, see Bukly.
Bud, John, 36.
Buffet, see Furniture.
Buffum, Bufam, Buffam, Buffom, ——, 210, 228, 229, 257.
  Joshua, 210, 257.
  Robert, 210, 227-229, 257.
Buildings.
  Bake house, 378.
  Barns, 16, 17, 20, 42, 47, 54, 55, 60-62, 64, 71, 80, 84, 90, 91,

## INDEX

Buildings.
Barns, *continued*, 93, 96-98, 106, 109, 112, 129, 133, 137, 149, 153, 160, 165, 170, 177, 183, 188, 191, 208, 212, 213, 216, 225, 233, 236, 242, 247, 250, 251, 253, 258, 260, 261, 263, 270, 273, 275, 278, 280, 285, 295, 300, 322, 328, 329, 332, 334, 335, 339, 340, 342, 346, 347, 351, 352, 366, 372, 374, 378, 379, 385, 394, 396, 404, 406, 408, 410, 423, 426, 429, 455, 458.
Cow houses, 17, 60, 61, 74, 106, 133, 243.
Fish house, 147.
Frame, 91, 202.
Hen house, 406.
Houses, 4, 7, 11-17, 19-23, 26-29, 32-37, 39-44, 47, 50, 52-58, 60-62, 64, 65, 67, 71, 73, 74, 77, 80, 81, 83-85, 90-95, 97-100, 102, 104, 106, 109, 110, 112, 115, 122, 123, 129-133, 140-147, 149-155, 158-163, 165-168, 170, 172, 173, 175, 177, 181-186, 188, 189, 191-194, 196, 197, 199-201, 203, 208, 210-213, 215-217, 220, 225-229, 231-234, 236-238, 240, 242-244, 246-258, 260, 261, 263-266, 268-270, 273, 274, 276-278, 280, 282-288, 292-295, 300-302, 304, 306, 307, 309-313, 315-320, 322, 324, 326-330, 332-334, 336-340, 342, 344, 345, 347-352, 356-358, 363, 365, 366, 368-374, 378, 383-385, 388-390, 392-396, 398, 400, 402-404, 406, 408-410, 415, 416, 418, 419, 421-423, 425, 426, 428-434, 436, 438, 440-446, 448, 450, 451, 455-458.
Mansion, 183.
Mill house, 109.
Mills, 22, 23, 37, 109, 112, 113, 115, 116, 154, 219, 238, 274, 389, 401, 410.
Mills, corn, 400.
Mills, malt, 281, 432.
Mills, saw, 408, 409, 428, 429.
Sheepfold, 423.
Shop, 164, 242, 396, 432.
Warehouse, 113.
Windmill, 345.
Workhouse, 91.

Bukly, William, 396.
Bulfinch, John, 40.
Bull, ——, 4.
　John, 4.
Bullets, *see* Weapons.
Bullock, Bullocke, ——, 41.
　Alice, 255.
　Elizabeth, 450, 451.
　Henry, 40, 255, 384, 450, 451.
　John, 450, 451.
　Susan, 40.
　Thomas, 450, 451.
Bulls, *see* Animals (domestic).
Bunker, Buncker, Ann, 267, 268.
　Elizabeth, 267, 268.
　George, 136, 267.
　Jane, 267.
　Martha, 267, 268.
　Mary, 267, 268.
　William, 267, 268.
Burbanke, Borbanke, Burbancke, Burbant, Jemima, 301.
　John, 80, 251, 302.
Burcham, Burchum, ——, 41.
　Edward, 56, 100, 124, 131, 152, 154, 155, 178.
Burdin, Hannah, 350.
　Robert, 350.
Burgess, *see* Borges.
Burial, cost of, 58, 123, 235, 264, 272, 281, 289, 355, 365, 379, 381, 392, 452.
Burkby, Birkby, Thomas, 80, 203.
Burnape, ——, 413.
　Hannah, 413.
　Isaac, 413.
Burnell, John, 318.
Burnum, Robert, 28.
Burrill, Borrell, Burrell, Francis, 56, 177, 178, 277, 358, 403, 430.
　George, 56, 177, 178.
　John, 177.
Burt, Birt, Bort, Burtt, ——, 119, 123.
　Edward, 33, 123, 356.
　Hugh, 33, 122, 123, 355, 356.
　John, 356.
　Mary, 355.
　Sarah, 355.
Burton, John, 289, 384.
　Samuel, 318.
Buswell, Isaac, 410.

468 INDEX

Butcher, Walter, 323.
Butler, John, 9, 160.
Butman, Buttman, Jeremiah, 447, 448.
Buttall, ——, 119.
Butten, ——, 119.
Butter, see Food.
Buttery, 164.
Buttons, see Clothing.
Buxton, Buckston, Buxston, Anthony, 182, 183, 390.
    Elizabeth, 288.
    Thomas, 182, 183.
Bylie, Bilie, Byley, Bylye, Henry, 102, 103.
    Rebecca, 102, 103, 403, 405.

Cabbages, see Food.
Cabinet, see Furniture.
Cake, see Food.
Caldwell, John, 393.
Calico, see Cloth.
Calie, Caly, Abraham, 4.
    Emme, 4.
    Jacob, 4.
    John, 422.
    Rebecca, 4.
    Thomasine, 4.
Call, Mary, 392, 393.
    Philip, 392, 393.
Calves, see Animals (domestic).
Cambell, Camball, Michael, 214.
    Richard, 217.
Cambric, see Cloth.
Cambridge, 80, 223, 235, 333, 384.
Campbell, see Cambell.
Candall, Edward, 58.
Candlesticks, see Utensils.
Canes, see Clothing.
Canoe, see Vessels.
Cantlebury, Canterbury, Cantlebery, ——, 417.
    Beatrice, 421, 422.
    John, 421.
    Rebecca, 421.
    Ruth, 421.
    William, 420-422.
Canvas, see Cloth.
Cape Ann, 457.
Cape Ann Side, 18, 92.
Cape Porpoise, 172.
Capon, Elizabeth, 12.
Caps, see Clothing.
Carbine, see Weapons.

Cards, see Tools.
Carlton, Carleton, ——, 111, 233, 329.
    Edward, 94, 99, 111.
    John, 328, 330, 442.
Carner, ——, 25.
Carpenter, see Trades.
Carpets, see Furnishings.
Carr, ——, 312.
    William, 401.
Carrots, see Food.
Carter, Joseph, 339.
Carthrick, Carthricke, ——, 64.
    Michael, 62-64.
    Mildred, 62, 63.
    John, 62, 64.
    Sarah, 63.
Carts, see Tools.
Carwithin, Carwethy, Carwithe, Carwythy, Corwethin, Corwithy, Curwithy, ——, 173, 227.
    David, 60.
    Mary, 276.
    Samuel, 276.
Cartwright, Cartwrit, Cortwrite, ——, 7.
    Bethia, 12.
    Elizabeth, 12.
    William, 7.
Cary, James, 13.
Case, leather, 233.
Casements, 112.
Casks, see Utensils.
Castle hill, 348, 349.
Catcham, Jo., 64.
Catches, see Tools.
Cattle, see Animals (domestic).
Cavis, William, 93.
Chadwell, Thomas, 177.
Chafing dish, see Utensils.
Chains, see Tools.
Chairs, see Furniture.
Challis, L., 401.
    Philip, 386-338, 425, 442.
    Thomas, 409.
Challis, see Cloth.
Chamberlin, Chamberline, ——, 62.
    Joanna, 103.
    Samuel, 103.
Chandler, Abiel, 150.
    Thomas, 397.
    William, 84, 187, 397.
Chape, 149.

INDEX 469

Chaplin, Chapline, Elizabeth, 251.
Hugh, 250-252.
John, 251, 252.
Chapman, Edw., 225.
Edward, 286.
Mary, 285.
Charcoal, 149.
Chargers, see Utensils.
Charles, William, 60, 287, 457.
Charlestown, 137, 138, 309, 408.
Charlton, 119.
Chebacco, 98, 132, 133, 171, 423.
Chebacco river, 106, 375.
Cheese, see Food.
Cheesecloth, see Cloth.
Cheese press, see Utensils.
Cheever, Chever, Ezekiel, 223.
Cheney, Cheiney, Cheny, John, 13, 121, 150, 195, 402.
Cheny, see Cloth.
Cherlcraft, Richard, 227, 228.
Chests, see Furniture.
Chichester, William, 60.
Chickens, see Fowls.
Chin, Elizabeth, 162.
George, 60, 162.
Chisels, see Tools.
Church, 4, 10, 34, 47, 80, 81, 126, 206, 207, 320, 321, 333-336, 438, 446.
Churchman, Hugh, 32, 33.
Churns, see Utensils.
Chute, Chewte, ——, 235.
Elizabeth, 171.
James, 47, 54, 171, 231, 440.
Lionell, 46, 47.
Nathaniel, 47.
Rose, 47.
Cillick, ——, 408.
Cistern, 223.
Clapp, Clap, Clape, Edward, 256, 257, 444.
Ezra, 256.
Nathaniel, 256.
Nicholas, 256, 257.
Prudence, 257.
Clark, Clarke, Cleark, Clearke, Clerk, Clerke, ——, 119, 133, 406, 417.
Daniel, 271, 272.
Edward, 132, 425-427, 442.
Haniel, 425.
John, 132, 305, 354, 355.
Joseph, 132.

Clark, Katherine, 65, 67.
Mary, 375.
Nathaniel, 84.
Richard, 80, 238.
Thomas, 263, 403, 408, 423.
William, 65.
Cleavers, see Tools.
Clement, Cleman, Clemans, Clemants, Clemens, Clements, ——, 291.
Abraham, 273.
Daniel, 273.
Job, 273, 291, 292, 399.
John, 141, 142, 273, 290-292, 457.
Robert, 195, 262, 272-274, 290-292, 408.
Sarah, 141.
Cloaks, see Clothing.
Clocks, see Furnishings.
Cloth, 5, 14, 34, 36, 38, 41, 49, 51, 61, 68, 69, 76, 78, 79, 92, 93, 120, 132, 138, 144, 154, 164, 166, 167, 169, 178-180, 186, 195, 197, 199, 202, 204, 232, 257, 281, 282, 284, 295, 302, 306, 313, 321, 335, 337, 344, 350, 352, 358, 364, 376, 382, 395, 400, 412, 431, 434, 458.
Baize, 90, 164, 166, 200, 322, 382.
Barber's stuff, 197.
Broadcloth, 54, 55, 97, 148, 152, 164, 166, 195, 197, 271, 276, 295, 322, 357, 414, 430, 442, 444.
Calico, 36, 38, 69, 142, 202, 354, 430.
Cambric, 233.
Canvas, 5, 36, 69, 87, 106, 142, 164, 169, 182, 226, 274, 279, 317, 323, 330, 331, 360, 368, 420.
Canvas, sail, 197.
Cap cloth, 323.
Cape cloth, 360.
Challis, 155.
Cheesecloth, 69, 279.
Cheny, 46.
Coifing stuff, 382.
Cotton, 34, 36, 97, 127, 148, 152, 154, 165, 169, 170, 178, 197, 198, 200, 212, 262, 274, 279-281, 295, 301, 322, 331, 344, 368, 388, 413, 414, 429, 430, 451.

470  INDEX

Cloth.
  Cotton and wool, 279.
  Damask, 66, 69, 106, 246.
  Darnacle, 48, 95.
  Darnex, 35, 75, 98.
  Diaper, 29, 32, 36, 38, 45, 64, 66, 69, 75, 78, 79, 90, 106, 112, 128, 139, 156, 157, 179, 183, 189, 197, 224, 239, 242, 276, 279, 287, 341.
  Dimity, 200, 210, 344, 419, 445.
  Dowlas, 69, 200.
  English goods, 426.
  Felt, 200.
  Filleting, 198.
  Flannel, 39, 178, 382, 429.
  Frieze, 68.
  Fustian, 38, 93, 178, 236.
  Genting, 330.
  Grosgrane, 36, 68, 69.
  Hair cloth, 142.
  Hempen cloth, 174, 335.
  Holland, 5, 29, 38, 48, 66, 69, 78, 90, 106, 128, 139, 142, 171, 200, 202, 224, 239, 242, 246, 317, 326, 341, 344, 360, 385, 413, 415, 444.
  Holland, tufted, 420.
  Inkle, 180.
  Inkle mancster, 382.
  Kersey, 34, 35, 57, 78, 142, 166, 169, 178, 197, 239, 242, 253, 280, 287, 295, 322, 324, 349, 350, 357, 359, 360, 382, 388, 412-414, 429, 430, 444.
  Lawn, 46, 139, 344.
  Linen, 5, 38, 45, 50, 52, 69, 76, 78, 81, 93, 97, 121, 127, 129, 152, 164, 165, 179, 184, 200-202, 211, 233, 245, 256, 274, 288, 300, 301, 317, 322, 323, 335, 344, 360, 382, 406, 414, 418-420, 429, 430, 454.
  Linen, broad, 420.
  Linsey woolsey, 5, 38, 48, 56, 57, 75, 165, 166, 197, 200, 280.
  Lockrum, 34, 66, 158, 164, 169, 197, 242, 279, 287, 330, 360, 419, 445, 458.
  Manchester, 279.
  Mohair, 138, 326.
  Ossembrike, 317, 357, 419, 420, 444.
  Packing cloth, 382.
  Paragon, 164, 166.

Cloth.
  Penistone, 142, 178, 197, 271, 344, 415, 430.
  Perpetuana, 224.
  Plush, 66.
  Ribbon, 179, 180, 198, 233, 279, 322.
  Ribbon binding, 180.
  Sackcloth, 90, 279.
  Sail cloth, 148.
  Satin, 85.
  Satinesco, 225, 344, 382.
  Say, 38, 66, 200, 239, 322.
  Sempiternum, 66.
  Serge, 5, 12, 69, 78, 97, 106, 142, 148, 164, 166, 169, 178, 197-200, 216, 257, 318, 321, 326, 330, 337, 344, 349, 357, 368, 382, 399, 412, 430.
  Serge, French, 279.
  Shag, 35, 178, 197, 200, 280, 363, 368, 382, 414.
  Silk, 38, 75, 78, 90, 182, 198, 229, 322, 323, 331, 382, 454.
  Stammell, 414.
  Stuff, 7, 34, 35, 38, 41, 45, 51, 52, 57, 61, 75, 78, 79, 92, 93, 95, 112, 117, 138, 142, 148, 157, 166, 178, 179, 195, 197, 198, 202, 204, 242, 257, 265, 313, 321, 322, 344, 349, 364, 412.
  Taffety, 200, 370.
  Tamme, 326, 337, 344.
  Tape, 78, 322.
  Tape binding, 204.
  Tapestry, 66.
  Ticking, 48, 93, 226, 239, 279, 324, 382, 414.
  Tow, 36, 121.
  Trucking cloth, 36, 281, 388.
  Velvet, 35, 179.
  Water paragon, 349.
  Woolen, 5, 50, 52, 184, 211, 280, 281, 335, 382, 399, 418.
  Worsted, 39, 323, 330, 331, 413, 418.
Clothing, Wearing Apparel, etc., 5, 13, 18, 22, 23, 31, 32, 34, 44, 47, 48, 50, 55, 56, 58, 64, 67, 68, 71, 72, 80, 81, 85, 87, 92, 93, 99, 100, 102, 106, 108, 109, 111, 117, 121, 123, 124, 127, 129, 131, 133, 138, 139, 142, 143, 146, 148, 149, 151, 152, 154, 155, 158, 160, 162-164,

INDEX 471

Clothing, Wearing Apparel, etc., *continued*, 167, 170, 172-174, 176, 182, 185, 190, 191, 193, 199, 202, 205, 208, 211, 214, 216, 128, 220, 221, 225, 228, 230, 232, 233, 240, 245-247, 249, 256-258, 260, 263, 267, 269, 271-275, 277, 279, 282, 284, 285, 287, 289, 290, 295, 301, 302, 304-306, 308, 310, 313-317, 324, 326, 328, 334, 341, 342, 350, 352-356, 358, 365, 367, 368, 370, 371, 374, 376, 377, 379, 381-383, 386, 388-393, 395, 396, 399, 400, 404, 406, 407, 417-419, 422-424, 426, 429, 431, 433, 434, 436-438, 440-442, 444, 445, 447, 449, 451, 455-457.
Aprons, 36, 38, 39, 41, 45, 46, 57, 78, 85, 139, 157, 166, 179, 200-202, 204, 212, 226, 232, 264, 279, 281, 412, 445.
Aprons, sea, 36, 178, 202.
Bag, cloak, 179, 424.
Bands, 13, 23, 34, 36, 42, 45, 51, 68, 69, 91, 117, 130, 141, 159, 170, 171, 175, 179, 182, 184, 189, 195, 198, 233, 242, 265, 271, 272, 279, 281, 295, 321, 364, 367, 388, 414, 418, 419, 430, 445, 447, 457.
Bandstrings, 271.
Basque, 419.
Bearing cloths, 78, 90, 139, 157, 279.
Belt, leather, 66.
Belts, 149, 179, 379, 433, 442.
Biggins, 69, 157.
Bodices, 5, 7, 8, 39, 45, 52, 57, 78, 179, 280.
Bones, 180.
Boot tops, 68.
Boothaunches, 128.
Boots, 23, 31, 36, 48, 52, 68, 75, 79, 92, 117, 128, 158, 195, 203, 226, 236, 242, 254, 281, 295, 321, 323, 331, 367, 418, 429, 436, 447, 454, 457.
Breeches, 14, 34, 45, 75, 78, 92, 141, 144, 149, 175, 178, 184, 197, 216, 226, 236, 254, 257, 281, 313, 323, 331, 349, 363, 364, 367, 399, 414, 430, 436, 449.

Clothing, Wearing Apparel, etc.
Breeches, leather, 92, 254.
Buttons, 39, 70, 78, 130, 180, 182, 198, 233, 322, 382, 431.
Buttons, pewter, 216.
Buttons, shirt, 433.
Buttons, silver, 5, 127, 178, 179, 186.
Buttons, steel, 232.
Cane, 175.
Cape, 360, 454.
Caps, 14, 38, 49, 51, 66, 68, 78, 79, 85, 91, 117, 159, 170, 179, 182, 184, 189, 201, 233, 242, 279, 281, 323, 414.
Caps, mountero, 331.
Caps, Portugal, 414, 419, 445.
Cloak, jump, 414.
Cloaks, 5, 35, 38, 41, 45, 54, 66, 68, 69, 90, 133, 139, 157, 178, 182, 184, 197, 200-203, 211, 212, 218, 242, 257, 273, 287, 303, 313, 317, 321, 330, 364, 367, 398, 414, 420, 444, 448.
Clouts, 157, 179.
Coats, 5, 12-14, 36, 42, 45, 51, 57, 61, 68, 70, 75, 78, 79, 90, 92, 93, 106, 120, 141, 144, 149, 152, 178, 184, 186, 195, 197, 202, 209, 212, 216, 221, 236, 242, 254, 264, 265, 281, 313, 323, 330, 349, 360, 363, 364, 382, 399, 414, 415, 430, 436, 448, 449, 453, 458.
Coifes, 35, 36, 38, 45, 46, 69, 78, 139, 179, 212, 233.
Combs, 117.
Crosscloths, 36, 38, 45, 46, 78, 139, 157, 201, 202, 281.
Cuffs, hand, 38, 157, 200.
Demicastor, 200, 280.
Doublets, 34, 38, 45, 57, 68, 78, 90, 92, 141, 144, 149, 157, 178, 184, 186, 202, 203, 236, 313, 321, 367, 414.
Doublets, leather, 14, 90, 254.
Drawers, 5, 13, 14, 79, 178, 182, 197, 242, 280, 321, 323, 330, 454.
Dressings, 212.
Dressings, head, 157.
Fan, wicker, 75.
Forehead cloths, 69, 139, 157, 200.
Girdles, 38, 39, 90, 93.

472  INDEX

Clothing, Wearing Apparel, etc.
  Gloves, 13, 38, 39, 45, 70, 78, 80, 90, 102, 117, 157, 178, 180, 195, 200, 211, 212, 279, 295, 323, 331, 360, 367, 382, 392.
  Gloves, leather, 360.
  Gowns, 7, 24, 31, 35, 36, 38, 40, 41, 45, 46, 69, 78, 85, 112, 138, 139, 157, 166, 170, 178, 199, 202, 204, 211, 212, 228, 239, 382, 412.
  Haling-hands, 323.
  Handkerchiefs, 36, 45, 46, 48, 51, 68, 78, 85, 117, 139, 179, 182, 184, 195, 200-202, 212, 242, 271, 281, 295, 321, 323, 360, 364, 367, 388, 419, 445, 457.
  Handkerchiefs, lace, 35.
  Handkerchiefs, neck, 38, 39, 179, 228.
  Handkerchiefs, pocket, 38, 264, 279.
  Hat bands, 157, 179, 312.
  Hat case, 295, 382, 393.
  Hats, 5, 9, 13, 14, 23, 34-36, 39, 41, 42, 45, 50-52, 57, 61, 64, 68, 75, 78, 79, 90, 92, 93, 117, 136, 141, 149, 164, 175, 179, 182, 184, 189, 195, 197, 200, 202-204, 211, 212, 218, 220, 221, 226, 236, 242, 254, 264, 265, 271, 273, 295, 305, 313, 321, 323, 331, 354, 360, 363-365, 367, 382, 391, 399, 412, 414, 420, 430, 448, 449, 453, 456.
  Hats, castor, 202.
  Hats, riding, 178.
  Hats, straw, 45, 226.
  Headcloth, 45.
  Head piece, 302.
  Hoods, 35, 38, 41, 45, 57, 70, 75, 157, 179, 184, 200-202, 212, 239, 293, 321, 412, 414.
  Hoods, silk, 179, 200, 445.
  Hose, 14, 68, 79, 157, 265.
  Hose, leather, 5.
  Jackets, 5, 68, 90, 92, 141, 175, 197, 216, 312, 321, 323, 330, 367, 398, 436.
  Jackets, leather, 68, 79, 323.
  Jerkins, 42, 75, 178, 236, 254.
  Kirtle, 69, 178.
  Lace, 5, 35, 46, 78, 95, 157, 158, 166, 179, 180, 198, 322, 344, 382.

Clothing, Wearing Apparel, etc.
  Lace, bone, 45.
  Lace, seaming, 38, 66.
  Lace, silver, 382.
  Linen, 5, 7, 24, 29, 31, 35, 36, 44-46, 57, 69, 78, 85, 123, 137, 138, 143, 164, 166, 195, 199, 204, 211, 212, 226, 232, 257, 275, 279, 337, 358, 381, 424, 430, 442, 445, 447, 453.
  Mantles, 69, 70, 93, 164, 208, 344, 414.
  Masks, 178.
  Mittens, 49, 178, 195, 323, 331.
  Muffler, 202.
  Muffs, 34, 36, 139, 414.
  Neckcloths, 38, 39, 45, 157, 182, 184, 200, 279, 281, 323, 331, 360, 367, 388, 454.
  Pattens, 46.
  Petticoats, 7, 31, 34-36, 38, 40, 41, 45, 46, 57, 70, 78, 112, 138, 157, 166, 178, 200, 201, 204, 211, 212, 220, 226, 228, 280, 281, 412.
  Pockets, 281.
  Points, 5, 180, 322.
  Portmantle, 233.
  Purse, 5, 50, 56, 100, 124, 129, 131, 142, 152, 155, 208, 274, 279, 424.
  Rings, 139, 274, 444.
  Rings, gold, 46, 85, 120, 139, 179, 334, 338.
  Ruffs, 69, 78, 164, 210.
  Sack, 293.
  Safeguards, 35, 211, 212, 448.
  Satchel, leather, 93.
  Scarfs, 57, 200, 228.
  Scarfs, silk, 179, 445.
  Sea clothes, 317, 365, 454.
  Seal, silver, 117, 274.
  Shifts, 7, 36, 39, 45, 57, 69, 139, 157, 164, 179, 200, 204, 212, 221, 264, 279, 280, 295, 414, 447.
  Shirts, 13, 23, 34, 36, 42, 48, 51, 64, 68, 78, 87, 90, 117, 140, 144, 164, 169, 175, 179, 182, 184, 195, 197, 216, 220, 229, 232, 242, 265, 271, 272, 286, 305, 321, 323, 330, 354, 360, 363, 364, 367, 388, 399, 418, 419, 430, 445, 449.
  Shoe-strings, 5.

INDEX 473

Clothing, Wearing Apparel, etc.
  Shoes, 7, 13, 14, 22, 23, 31, 34, 36, 39, 42, 45, 48, 49, 51, 52, 57, 64, 68, 79, 86, 117, 119, 128, 141, 144, 158, 159, 175, 179, 182, 184, 189, 195, 197, 200, 202, 212, 216, 220, 221, 242, 247, 254, 265, 272, 273, 281, 295, 305, 321, 322, 331, 354, 367, 388, 399, 414, 418, 419, 430, 436, 447, 454.
  Shoes, French heel, 360.
  Skirts, 45, 179, 414.
  Stockings, 5, 13, 14, 22, 31, 34, 36, 39, 42, 45, 49, 51, 52, 56, 57, 64, 68, 78, 79, 90, 117, 130, 141, 142, 144, 157, 159, 170, 178, 179, 182, 184, 195, 197, 198, 200, 202, 204, 212, 216, 224, 226, 242, 257, 264, 265, 272, 273, 279, 295, 305, 321-323, 330, 360, 363, 364, 367, 381, 382, 399, 412-414, 419, 430, 436, 445, 448, 449, 453, 454.
  Stockings, leather, 14.
  Stockings, wednoll, 330.
  Stomacher, 38, 157, 233.
  Straddle band, 39.
  Suits, 5, 9, 13, 14, 36, 42, 51, 57, 61, 68, 75, 76, 79, 90, 92, 93, 106, 120, 138, 149, 157, 159, 182, 186, 189, 195, 197, 216, 228, 239, 242, 254, 257, 265, 271, 273, 281, 287, 306, 318, 321, 330, 331, 357, 360, 363, 399, 412, 413, 420, 430, 436, 445, 453, 454, 458.
  Suits, leather, 68, 79, 90, 236.
  Suits, riding, 139.
  Swash, 323.
  Swathe, 70, 157, 179.
  Waistcoats, 5, 7, 12, 31, 34-36, 38, 39, 41, 45, 46, 51, 56, 57, 68, 69, 78, 79, 138, 139, 157, 166, 178, 179, 186, 195, 197, 198, 200-204, 211, 212, 220, 226, 233, 242, 264, 265, 281, 323, 360, 363, 364, 367, 389, 412, 414, 418-420, 445, 448, 453.
  Wallet, 5.
  Watch, 224.
  Woolen, 14, 24, 137, 199, 257, 337.
  Whittle, 69, 280, 414.

Clough, John, 408.
Clouts, see Clothing.
Coal, 49, 432.
Coales, Mary, 154.
Coats, ——, 136.
Coats, see Clothing.
Cobbet, Cobat, Cobet, Cobit, ——, 83, 178, 256.
  Samuel, 55.
Cobirons, see Utensils.
Coborne, Edward, 265.
Cocall, ——, 35.
Cock, Sifforye, 362, 363.
Cockerell, Cockerill, Cockrell, Elizabeth, 444.
  William, 357.
Cocket, Samuel, 55.
Codner, Christopher, 325, 326, 415.
  Joane, 415.
  John, 162, 163, 457.
  Joshua, 326.
  Mary, 325, 326.
Coffers, see Furniture.
Coffin, Coffen, Coffyn, ——, 125.
  Peter, 401, 424.
  Tristram, 274, 340, 401.
Coffins, 41, 49, 58, 216, 220, 221, 237, 264, 272, 381.
Coffins, see also Burials.
Cogswell, Coggswell, ——, 221.
  Elizabeth, 156.
  John, 156, 158, 173, 458.
  Samuel, 156.
  William, 156, 158, 220.
Coifes, see Clothing.
Coit, Coite, Goit, Goyt, Goyte, ——, 457.
  John, 60, 358, 359.
  Mary, 358.
Coker, Robert, 216, 342, 343.
Colby, Colbie, Coleby, Collby, ——, 408, 409.
  Anthony, 407-410.
  Isaac, 409.
  John, 408, 409.
  Rebecca, 409.
  Samuel, 409, 410.
  Susanna, 409.
  Thomas, 409.
Cole, George, 154.
Colebron, ——, 375.
Collars, see Horse Equipment.
College, The, 115, 246.
Collier, see Trades.

Collins, Colins, Collens, Collince, Collings, Coollens, Francis, 227, 357, 444.
  Hannah, 428.
  Henry, 100, 155, 345, 355, 368, 403.
  John, 380, 386-388.
  Robert, 396.
Colman, see Cowllman.
Combs, see Clothing.
Comer, Richard, 266.
Compass, see Tools and Vessels.
Conant, Connant, Joshua, 303, 304.
  Lot, 365.
  Roger, 185, 186, 238, 306, 365.
  Seeth, 303.
Concklinge, John, 256.
Concord, 44.
Condey, Samuel, 454.
Connecticut, 333.
Connor, Cornelius, 439.
Cook, 57.
Cooke, Coock, ——, 136, 273.
  Hannah, 384.
  Henry, 288, 383, 384, 451.
  Isaac, 383, 384, 451.
  John, 384.
  Judith, 383, 384.
  Martha, 384.
  Mary, 384.
  Rachel, 119, 384.
  Richard, 60.
  Samuel, 384.
  Thomas, 119.
Cooley, Coolye, Elizabeth, 173.
  John, 173.
Cooper, Couper, Cowper, Dorcas, 277.
  Elizabeth, 276.
  Hannah, 277.
  John, 277.
  Mary, 277.
  Peter, 251, 367.
  Rebecca, 277.
  Timothy, 276, 277, 355.
Cooper, see Trades.
Copperas, 344.
Coral, 32.
Corbit, ——, 136.
Cord, 382.
Cordage, see Vessels.
Corlis, George, 425, 426.
Cormack, ——, 391.
Corn, see Food.

Cornelius, 228.
Corning, ——, 35.
  Elizabeth, 35.
  Samuel, 365.
Cornish, ——, 34.
Corselet, see Weapons.
Corye, Giles, 257.
Cotta, ——, 34.
  Jone, 303, 304.
  Robert, 41, 304.
Cottell, Cotle, Cottl, Ann, 438.
  Sarah, 438.
  William, 438.
Cotton, ——, 107.
  Ann, 160.
  Elizabeth, 333.
  William, 160.
Cotton, see Cloth and Manufactures.
Cottrels, see Utensils.
Couldum, Thomas, 249.
Cousens, Coussins, Cuzens, Isaac, 220, 221, 290.
Coverings, see Furnishings.
Coverlets, see Furnishings.
Cowdrie, ——, 417.
Cowley, Ambrose, 344.
Cowllman, Thomas, 21.
Cowpen lot, 383.
Cows, see Animals (domestic).
Coy, Richard, 144.
Cradles, see Furniture.
Crane, Robert, 6, 222, 225.
Crane meadow, 244.
Cranes, see Utensils.
Creeke, Andrew, 271.
Crimp, William, 152.
Croad, Croade, John, 421, 452.
Croker, Richard, 457.
Cromwell, Cromlon, Cromlone, Crommell, Cromwel, Croomwell, Crumwell, ——, 212, 256, 304, 384.
  Anna, 242.
  Giles, 53, 247.
  Philip, 58, 184, 226, 304, 315, 316.
  Thomas, 53, 197, 242.
Crooks, see Tools.
Crosby, ——, 303, 351.
Cross, Crose, Crosse, Anne, 125.
  Hannah, 125, 126.
  John, 4, 125-128.
  Margaret, 80, 120.
  Robert, 221.

## INDEX  475

Cross garner, 158.
Crosscloths, see Clothing.
Crows, see Tools.
Croxen, John, 34.
Cuffs, see Clothing.
Cullenders, see Utensils.
Cummings, Comings, Comins, Commins, Cumins, Cummins, ——, 225.
  Joanna, 34, 35.
  John, 34, 419, 420.
  Samuel, 420.
Cupboard cloths, see Furnishings.
Cupboards, see Furniture.
Cups, see Utensils.
Curill, ——, 457.
Currier, Courrier, Curier, Richard, 312, 336-338, 400, 401.
  Thomas, 401.
Currier, see Trades.
Curtains, see Furnishings.
Curtiss, Curtess, Curtice, ——, 257.
  Richard, 60.
  William, 214, 289, 417.
Curwin, Corwin, Corwine, Corwinne, ——, 59, 61, 101, 119, 226, 227, 243, 256, 264, 268, 315, 381, 384.
  Capt., 451.
  George, 57, 65, 138, 226, 316, 323, 330, 331, 362, 364, 421, 422.
  Jonathan, 410.
Cushions, see Furnishings.
Cutlass see Weapons.
Cutler, Cuttller, Samuel, 227, 348, 411.
  Thomas, 227.
Cutting, ——, 206, 339.
  John, 308, 310, 311.
  Mary, 309.

Dagger, see Weapons.
Dairy ware, see Utensils.
Dakin, Deacon, Deakin, Deken, ——, 214.
  John, 123, 124, 143, 350.
Daland, Samuel, 222.
Dalliver, Dallever, Delabar, Delaber, Joseph, 287, 417.
  Samuel, 60, 343, 380, 388.
Dalton, Samuel, 427.
Damask, see Cloth.
Damport, Capt., 376.

Dane, Daine, ——, 396.
  Francis, 80, 100.
  John, 28-31, 284, 369.
Daniel, Roger, 16.
Darnex, see Cloth.
Davenport, ——, 101.
Davis, Daves, Davice, Davies, Davise, ——, 313, 346.
  Sergeant, 11.
  Elisha, 427.
  George, 358.
  James, 240, 2, 290, 337, 353.
  Jenkin, 345 347, 357, 358.
  John, 170, 217, 235, 309, 310, 346, 357, 358, 437.
  Mary, 357, 358.
  Thomas, 290, 425.
  Tobias, 400.
Davison, Daniel, 368, 370, 418.
Day, Hannah, 258.
  Robert 285.
Deacons, 35, 38, 39, 128, 129, 202, 320.
Deale, Delle, Jo., 172.
  Mary, 442.
  William, 425, 426, 442.
Dedham, Eng., 284.
Demicastor, see Clothing.
Denham, John, 306.
Denison, Maj., 177.
  Maj. Gen., 274, 290, 353, 455.
  Daniel, 122, 281, 257, 275, 340, 352, 371, 405.
  John, 440, 441.
Dennis, Denis, Denise, ——, 24, 257.
  Samuel, 84.
  Sarah, 84.
Dent, Francis, 11.
Derby fort, 42, 172, 173, 239, 446.
Desks, see Furniture.
Devereux, Deverix, Devorick, Devorix, Devrix, John, 60, 326, 349, 435.
Dewer, Thomas, 225.
Diaper, see Cloth.
Dick, Dicke, Elizabeth, 132.
  Richard, 132.
Dickinson Dickanson, Dickenson, Diconson, James, 298, 372, 373.
  Jennett, 372.
  Sarah, 373.
  Thomas, 203, 236, 237, 251-253, 259, 372, 373.

Dillingham, Dillingam, ——,6-8.
  Edward, 6-10.
  John, 6-10.
  Sarah, 3, 4, 7-10.
Diman, ——, 214.
Dimity, see Cloth.
Diryn, John, 344.
Dishes, see Utensils.
Divan, John, 354.
Dixe, ——, 457.
Dodge, Dodg, Richard, 270.
  William, 185, 186, 200, 238, 306, 366.
Dole, Dol, Hannah, 138.
  Honore, 439.
  Richard, 84, 138, 231, 439.
Dolittle, Dowlettell, John, 313, 314, 378.
Doliver, see Dalliver.
Donaldson, John, 134.
Door latches, see Tools.
Dorlow, Kathrin, 46.
Dorman, John, 367.
  Mary, 367, 368.
  Thomas, 25, 54, 145, 367.
Doublets, see Clothing.
Dover, 321.
Dow, Dowe, ——, 290.
  John, 240.
  Martha, 240.
  Mary, 240.
  Phebe, 240.
  Stephen, 240.
  Thomas, 239, 240, 394.
Dowell, Richard, 433.
Dowlas, see Cloth.
Downes, Thomas, 6, 9.
Downing, ——, 8, 9, 65, 383, 389.
  Macam, 355.
  Mary, 326.
  Richard, 326.
Dowse, Francis, 44.
Drawers, see Clothing.
Dresser, John, 80, 203, 251.
Dressers, see Furniture.
Dressings, see Clothing.
Drinker, ——, 342.
Drinks, 264.
  Beer, 41, 49, 237.
  Brandy, 360.
  Rum, 360, 382.
  Wine, 41, 360.
Dripping pans, see Utensils.
Driver, Robert, 33, 100, 350, 430.
Drums, see Weapons.

Dudley, ——, 6.
  Samuel, 103.
  Thomas, 4, 8.
Dummer, Dumer, ——, 30, 112, 115, 217, 260, 273.
  Joanna, 113.
  Richard, 107, 108, 110, 111, 113-116.
  Stephen, 309.
  Thomas, 113.
Duncan, Peter, 359, 360.
Dunster, John, 345.
Durand, William, 319.
Dutch, Deutch, Duch, Osman, 360.
  Robert, 192.
  Thomas, 269.

Earthen ware, see Utensils.
East Mersey, Eng., 234.
Eastern Point, 386.
Eastman, Roger, 408.
Easton, see Eston.
Eaton, John, 240, 425.
Edmonds, ——, 248.
  William, 136.
Edwards, Edward, ——, 34, 36.
  Dorothy, 210.
  Matthew, 46, 74, 325.
  Nathaniel, 134, 135.
  Richard, 40.
  Robert, 46.
  Thomas, 134.
  William, 177.
Eggs, see Food.
Egypt river, 28, 29, 54, 98, 327, 329, 330.
Ela, Israel, 427.
Elders, 68, 88, 91, 104, 111, 128, 140, 206, 207, 333, 334.
Elder's Island, 297, 298.
Elder's plain, 299.
Elie, Elly, Daniel, 111.
  John, 162, 163.
Eliot, Eliott, Ellett, Ellitt, Ellyott, ——, 256.
  Richard, 331, 364, 449.
  Sarah, 327.
  William, 326, 327.
Elithorp, Elethorp, Eletrop, Elithropp, Elitrip, Elitrop, Ellethrop, Ellethrope, ——, 174, 177, 237.
  Abigail, 174.
  Nathaniel, 443.
  Thomas, 80, 125, 126, 174, 175.

Ellis, Elis, Elles, ——, 136.
  Francis, 410.
  Thomas, 454.
Elsworth, Jeremiah, 237, 238, 435, 443, 453.
  Mary, 435, 443, 453.
Elvin, ——, 76.
Elwell, Ellwell, Robert, 148, 360, 386.
Elzey, ——, 243.
Emerson, John, 220, 221, 387, 388.
  Thomas, 11.
Emery, Emerey, Emerie, Emmerry, Emory, Emry, ——, 58, 100, 348.
  George, 20, 35, 36, 51, 59, 139, 161, 238.
  John, 3, 53, 83, 146, 402, 425, 433.
  Mary, 402.
Endicott, Endecodt, Endecot, Endecott, Endicot, ——, 6, 24, 255, 384.
  John, 16, 39, 43, 51.
England, 4, 8, 24, 46, 51, 61, 72, 76, 78, 81, 99, 104, 106, 109, 114-116, 123, 134, 135, 138, 148, 156, 161, 178, 181, 183, 193, 211, 216, 222-225, 228, 232, 234, 244, 245, 247, 259, 273, 288, 291, 292, 294, 303, 307, 313, 322, 342, 347, 356, 374, 382, 391-393, 404, 407, 418.
English, see Inglish.
Enon, 18, 19.
Epps, Epse, ——, 225, 235.
  Daniel, 415.
  Mary, 171.
  Samuel, 171.
Erington, Thomas, 24.
Esticke, Elizabeth, 51.
Eston, Nicholas, 107.
Estye, Eastyes, ——, 270, 271.
  Isaac, 198.

Fairfield, Fairefeild, Fairefield, Fairefild, Fairfeild, Fayrefeild, ——, 325.
  Benjamin, 73, 325.
  Eliza, 325.
  Elizabeth, 73, 74.
  John, 57, 73, 325.
  Walter, 73, 284, 325.

Fans, see Clothing and Tools.
Farr, Far, Benjamin, 402.
  Elizabeth, 402.
  George, 33, 402, 403.
  John, 402.
  Joseph, 402.
  Lazerous, 402.
  Martha, 402.
  Mary, 402.
  Sarah, 402.
Farrar, Pharrer, ——, 214.
  Thomas, 345.
Farrington, Farington, Ed., 27.
  Matthew, 249, 250.
Farrow, Bethiah, 389.
Fay, Faye, Henry, 23, 214-216.
Feathers, see Furnishings.
Felch, Henry, 284.
Fellows, Felloes, Fellowes, Samuel, 410.
  William, 11, 283.
Felt, see Cloth.
Felton, Fellton, Felten, Feltonn, ——, 149, 212, 257.
  Mary, 288.
  Nathaniel, 228, 255, 383, 390, 421, 422, 451.
Fences, 4, 16, 58, 62, 71, 74, 84, 120, 231, 261, 273, 275, 318, 328, 329, 337, 347, 351, 375, 396, 415, 457.
Fencing, ——, 58, 136.
Fenn, ——, 119.
Ferry, the, 140.
Fetters, see Horse equipment, and Tools.
Field, Feald, Feld, ——, 35, 58.
Files, see Tools.
Filleting, see Cloth.
Fillybrowne, Sarah, 228.
Fire dogs, see Utensils.
Firelock, see Weapons.
Fire pans, see Utensils.
Fire shovels, see Utensils.
Firewood, 295.
Firkins, see Utensils.
Firman, Ferman, ——, 7.
  Sarah, 95.
  Thomas, 95, 144.
Fish and fishing, 147, 331, 360, 381, 418, 448.
  Casting net, 47, 48.
  Fish house, 147.
  Hooks, 180, 233, 331, 360, 454.
  Leads, 148, 224, 331, 388, 418, 454.

## 478 INDEX

Fish and fishing.
  Lines, 148, 180, 331, 388, 418, 454
  Lines, cod, 331, 360, 419, 445.
  Lines, hair, 48, 70, 90.
  Lines, Newfoundland,
  Mackerel, 271, 323, 331, 360.
  Nets, 148, 188.
  Reels, 331.
  Salmon, 187.
  Snood, 445.
  Stage, 419, 445, 457.
  Weir, 187.
Fish house, see Buildings.
Fisher, ——, 135.
  Samuel, 134.
Fisherman, see Trades.
Fisherman's field, 386.
Fiske, Fisk, ——, 20.
  Bridget, 188.
  John, 20, 37, 74, 77.
  Phineas, 77, 188.
  Samuel, 188.
  Thomas, 252.
  William, 57, 74, 77, 188.
Fitts, Fits, Jeremy, 99.
  Richard, 214, 215, 217, 343.
  Robert, 140.
Flagons, see Utensils.
Flags, 242.
Flanders, Stephen, 408.
Flannel, see Cloth.
Flasks, see Utensils.
Flax, 45, 50, 56, 61, 66, 70, 71, 75, 78, 79, 85, 97, 100, 106, 124, 129, 153, 155, 165, 180, 204, 245, 251, 256, 263, 271, 273, 277, 279, 282, 288, 302, 304, 322, 335, 337, 351, 358, 367, 377, 379, 383, 418, 426, 430, 458.
Flax seed, 56, 61, 64, 129.
Flesh, see Food.
Flinder, Jane, 446.
  Richard, 446-448.
Flint, ——, 422.
  Elizabeth, 416.
  George, 416.
  John, 416.
  Joseph, 416.
  Thomas, 290, 416, 417.
  William, 146, 384, 451.
Floyd, John, 347.
Fogg, Ralph, 26, 39, 458.
Food.
  Apples, 304, 322, 356, 358, 455.

Food.
  Bacon, 33, 42, 45, 83, 142, 153, 155, 170, 203, 208, 253, 282, 295, 335, 342, 352, 377, 381, 393, 395, 417, 422, 423.
  Barley, 25, 33, 42, 92, 97, 142, 154, 155, 165, 168, 176, 183, 188, 203, 205, 209, 218, 225, 257, 284, 293, 304, 335, 370, 383, 408, 430.
  Beans, 45.
  Beans, Indian, 165.
  Beef, 6, 226, 227, 243, 281, 308, 328, 353, 455.
  Biscuit, 6, 360.
  Bran, 210.
  Bread, 41, 49, 295.
  Butter, 5, 14, 22, 44, 55-57, 128, 129, 142, 164, 175, 176, 202, 204, 218, 230, 231, 233, 256, 281, 284, 305, 352, 455.
  Cabbages, 14.
  Cake, 287.
  Carrots, 14.
  Cheese, 5, 22, 44, 55, 57, 97, 128, 142, 176, 256, 284, 305, 352, 458.
  Cinnamon, 5.
  Corn, 4, 6, 18-20, 23, 32, 33, 35, 36, 39, 41, 44, 49, 57, 61, 65, 71, 73, 74, 77, 78, 80, 82, 83, 85, 90, 93, 96, 97, 99, 100, 106, 108, 109, 120, 123, 130, 131, 133, 136, 143, 146, 148, 155, 174, 176, 181, 183, 192, 204, 207-209, 212, 216, 220, 221, 226, 245, 247, 257, 260, 261, 263, 267, 270, 273, 289, 295, 301, 304, 311, 328, 333, 335, 340, 342, 352, 356, 357, 378, 379, 394, 395, 400, 404, 408, 409, 413, 416, 422, 430, 434.
  Corn, English, 20, 56, 131, 182, 185, 193, 242, 277, 353, 368, 455.
  Corn, Indian, 3, 14, 18, 20, 22, 33, 39-42, 44, 48, 50, 55-58, 64, 66, 74, 75, 82, 92, 97, 106, 123, 124, 131, 136, 140, 142, 162, 165, 166, 168, 170, 173, 176, 182, 185, 188-190, 193, 197, 200, 202, 205, 209, 211, 216, 218, 225, 227, 229, 236, 239, 242, 247, 251, 253, 256, 260, 271, 274, 275, 277, 280-282,

# INDEX 479

Food.
  Corn, Indian, *continued*, 284.
    286, 288, 303, 304, 308, 313,
    315, 322, 335, 337, 341, 342,
    350-353, 357, 360, 367, 368,
    370, 377, 381, 388, 393, 396,
    403, 406, 408, 417, 422, 423,
    426, 429, 430, 442, 455, 458.
  Eggs, 49, 56.
  Flesh, 256, 263.
  Fowls, 49.
  Fruit, 4, 19, 57.
  Garden roots, 226.
  Garden stuff, 136, 455.
  Ginger, 65, 204, 308, 344, 454.
  Grain, 263, 447.
  Grain, English, 123, 447.
  Honey, 368.
  Hops, 64, 85, 165, 189, 192, 226, 308, 407, 430.
  Mace, 233.
  Malt, 5, 14, 48, 52, 55, 64, 66, 70, 79, 97, 142, 148, 165, 170, 174, 180, 197, 205, 208, 218, 225, 230, 231, 245, 260, 280, 281, 308, 335, 388, 423, 434, 458.
  Meal, 14, 109, 125, 175, 204, 208, 352.
  Meal, Indian, 183.
  Meal, rye, 165.
  Meat, 355, 370, 381.
  Milk, 7.
  Oatmeal, 85.
  Oats, 39, 45, 124, 180, 205, 370, 458.
  Pease, 22, 42, 45, 92, 142, 162, 180, 183, 188, 197, 205, 308, 322, 351, 370, 381, 383, 458.
  Pepper, 233, 382.
  Pork, 14, 22, 119, 128, 129, 155, 164, 166, 170, 180, 204, 281, 295, 308, 328, 360, 423, 426.
  Provisions, 146, 434.
  Raisins, 5.
  Rye, 5, 6, 9, 41, 48, 74, 142, 154, 162, 176, 188, 205, 218, 225, 236, 245, 251, 253, 274, 286, 322, 370, 381, 408, 417, 458.
  Salt, 77, 109, 180, 182, 203, 227, 263, 381, 388, 418.
  Spices, 5, 49, 180.
  Suet, 57, 164, 204, 308.
  Sugar, 35, 49, 58, 65, 197, 204, 243, 245, 280, 284, 306, 360, 382.

Food.
  Veal, 49.
  Vinegar, 342.
  Vinegar, wine, 391.
  Wheat, 22, 25, 33, 42, 48, 50, 55, 57, 66, 74, 76, 82, 86, 92, 97, 123, 124, 136, 140, 142, 152, 154, 162, 165, 166, 168, 170, 173, 176, 188, 197, 198, 201, 202, 204, 205, 209, 216, 218, 225, 229-231, 236, 251, 253, 257, 260, 268, 274, 275, 280, 282, 284, 286, 293, 295, 303, 304, 308, 313, 322, 335, 337, 341, 344, 351, 352, 357, 358, 367, 370, 377, 381, 388, 396, 399, 408, 426, 429, 430, 442, 458.
  Wheat, English, 14, 47.
Foot, Pasco, 348.
  Samuel, 388.
Forehead cloths, *see* Clothing.
Forest river, 239, 349.
Forks, *see* Tools.
Forms, *see* Furniture.
Foster, ——, 107, 145.
  Reginald, 151, 423.
  Reynold, 201.
Fowle, ——, 34, 36, 193.
  Ann, 6, 9, 10.
Fowler, ——, 220.
  Joseph, 132.
  Martha, 132.
  Philip, 4, 25, 122, 132, 266, 272, 397.
Fowling piece, *see* Weapons.
Fowls (domestic), 85, 201, 226.
  Chickens, 203, 216.
  Cock, 204.
  Hens, 157, 204, 216.
  Poultry, 78, 80, 108.
Fowls, *see also* Food.
Fox Hill, 27.
Foxe, Nicholas, 454.
Fraile, Frayle, Frayll, Elizabeth, 434.
  George, 248, 434.
Frames, *see* Furniture.
Frances, John, 344.
Francklin, Franckling, ——, 28.
  Elizabeth, 28.
  William, 108.
French, ——, 261.
  Edward, 121, 192, 405, 406, 410, 443.

French, John, 272, 360.
  Susan, 272.
  Thomas, 138.
Friend, Freind, Frend, ——, 173.
  Bethiah, 238.
  Hester, 238.
  James, 238.
  John, 238.
  Samuel, 238, 239, 429.
Fries, 431.
Fringe, see Furnishings.
Frithy, Richard, 289.
Frows, see Tools.
Fruit, see Food.
Frying pans, see Utensils.
Fuller, Fuler, Fullar, ——, 221.
  Dr., 303.
  Anne, 389, 390.
  John, 213, 249.
Funnels, see Utensils.
Furnaces, see Tools.
Furnishings, Household, 22, 108, 129, 136, 139, 146, 161, 163, 184, 185, 220, 227, 240, 254, 257, 262, 270, 294, 333, 348, 351, 400, 403, 404, 405, 408, 428, 429, 440.
  Bed case, 407, 433.
  Bed case, canvas, 419, 445, 453, 454.
  Bed clothes, 258, 260, 262, 271, 295, 381, 431, 449.
  Bed cords, 39, 45, 48, 57, 61, 75, 77, 93, 95, 98, 142, 157, 164, 165, 176, 179, 180, 192, 197, 208, 224, 225, 242, 243, 250, 275, 276, 279, 285, 307, 316, 413.
  Bed linen, 317, 352.
  Bed lines, 90, 128, 308.
  Bed mats, 14, 48, 57, 61, 64, 66, 250, 276, 293, 413, 433.
  Bed sacks, 57, 323, 331.
  Bed stock, 129.
  Bed teaster, 111.
  Bed ticks, 20, 42, 44, 93, 99, 127, 140, 164, 182, 197, 220, 254, 287, 315, 383, 390, 430.
  Bedding, 23, 34, 37, 39, 50, 54, 73, 93, 96, 109, 112, 113, 120, 123, 137, 138, 143, 146, 148, 152, 155, 173, 182, 185, 208, 211, 232, 236, 240, 245, 251, 257, 258, 260, 267, 274, 275, 277, 282, 289, 295, 301, 302,

Furnishings, Household.
  Bedding, continued, 304, 308, 311, 322, 328, 335, 337, 348, 353, 358, 365, 367, 370, 374, 377, 383, 386, 388, 395, 400, 403, 406, 417-419, 426, 429, 430, 433, 434, 440, 441, 445, 455, 456, 458.
  Beds, 12, 14, 18, 20, 23, 28, 29, 34, 35, 38, 40, 45, 54, 56, 73, 74, 79, 91, 96, 97, 99, 100, 111-113, 124, 125, 129, 148, 152, 155, 157, 159, 170, 172, 179, 185, 188, 194, 211, 225, 227, 229, 232, 236, 242, 245, 247, 249, 254, 256, 258, 260, 264, 265, 269, 271, 273, 279, 282, 288, 290, 293-295, 301, 303, 304, 310, 311, 315, 316, 319, 324, 326, 335, 337, 342, 348-350, 352, 356, 365, 370, 371, 377, 381, 386, 390, 391, 393, 400, 409, 412, 413, 416, 417, 423, 425, 426, 429-431, 434, 441, 450, 458.
  Beds, canvas, 419, 445.
  Beds, feather, 4, 7, 22, 27, 31, 32, 35-37, 40, 42-44, 48, 49, 55, 57, 61, 64, 66, 69, 74, 77, 81, 83, 85, 90-93, 95, 97, 99, 102, 105, 106, 127, 130, 131, 133, 142, 143, 148, 149, 151, 152, 154, 156, 160, 162, 164, 166, 169, 174, 179, 183-186, 188, 191, 193, 197, 201-203, 210, 212, 214, 224, 229, 236, 239, 241-243, 246, 248, 250, 252, 255-257, 264, 265, 269, 272, 276, 279, 281, 282, 284, 285, 287, 300, 307, 308, 311, 316, 317, 341, 342, 344, 357, 363, 365, 368, 376, 379, 385, 386, 389, 396, 399, 407, 411, 412, 414, 415, 419, 420, 422, 429, 430, 432, 433, 436-438, 444, 445, 447, 448, 451, 455, 456.
  Beds, flock, 22, 27, 29, 32, 38, 42, 44, 47, 48, 52, 55, 64, 66, 69, 85, 87, 90, 95, 98, 102, 105, 106, 127, 133, 142, 149, 151, 154, 156, 162, 164-167, 169, 173, 175, 176, 190, 193, 197, 203, 205, 214, 218, 220, 225, 226, 229, 239, 242, 243, 250, 252, 256, 262, 265, 266, 281,

INDEX 481

Furnishings, Household.
  Beds, flock, *continued*, 286, 304, 305, 308, 317, 326, 341, 344, 363, 379, 389, 396, 412, 414, 422, 433, 447, 449, 451, 455, 456.
  Beds, hair, 175, 203.
  Beds, sea, 51, 381, 419, 445.
  Beds, silk grass, 457.
  Beds, straw, 33, 66, 78, 164-167, 174, 279, 307, 399, 419, 445, 448.
  Blanket, child's, 276, 382, 442.
  Blankets, 4, 12, 14, 20, 22, 27-29, 31-33, 35-38, 40, 42-45, 47, 48, 52, 55, 57, 61, 64, 66, 69, 74, 75, 79, 85, 87, 90, 91, 93, 95, 97-99, 105, 106, 117, 121, 123, 127, 130, 132, 139, 143, 148, 151, 152, 154, 156, 157, 159, 160, 162, 164-167, 169, 170, 172-176, 178, 179, 182, 183, 185, 188, 197, 201-204, 211, 212, 218, 220, 224-226, 229, 232, 239, 242, 246, 247, 250, 252, 254, 256, 257, 264, 265, 269, 272, 276, 279, 281, 284, 286, 287, 290, 295, 302-304, 307, 310, 311, 315, 316, 319, 322, 324, 326, 341, 342, 344, 350, 354, 356-358, 363, 365, 368, 376, 379, 383, 385, 386, 389-391, 395, 396, 399, 406, 412-414, 419, 420, 422, 423, 430, 432, 433, 436, 438, 445, 447, 448, 451, 455, 457.
  Boardcloths, 12, 45, 75, 78, 79, 127, 128, 138, 189, 197, 344, 388.
  Board linen, 21.
  Bolster cases, 22, 38, 69, 246, 265, 266, 377, 407, 419, 433, 445.
  Bolster ticks, 38, 45, 165, 179, 287.
  Bolsters, 4, 7, 12, 14, 18, 20, 27, 28, 36, 37, 40, 42, 43, 48, 57, 61, 64, 66, 69, 74, 77, 79, 81, 83, 85, 87, 90, 91, 93, 95, 97-99, 105, 106, 112, 121, 127, 130, 131, 140, 143, 148, 149, 151, 152, 154-157, 159, 164-167, 174-176, 179, 183, 185, 188, 193, 197, 201, 205, 210, 212, 214, 218, 220, 224-226, 239, 242, 243, 246-248, 250,

Furnishings, Household.
  Bolsters, *continued*, 252, 254, 256, 257, 264, 265, 269, 276, 279, 282, 284, 285, 287, 293, 301, 303, 304, 307, 308, 310, 311, 315, 316, 324, 326, 341, 342, 344, 353, 356, 357, 365, 368, 376, 379, 383, 385, 386, 390, 391, 396, 399, 407, 409, 411-414, 419, 420, 422, 423, 431-433, 436, 438, 445, 447, 448, 451, 455, 457.
  Bolsters, feather, 31, 43, 44, 49, 66, 69, 74, 106, 127, 169, 182, 188, 197, 201, 203, 225, 239, 242, 248, 250, 281, 316, 344, 363, 389, 407, 414, 419, 445.
  Bolsters, flock, 35, 38, 43, 45, 47, 48, 66, 74, 85, 90, 166, 167, 173, 174, 201, 224, 225, 253, 286, 399, 414.
  Bolsters, hop sack, 182.
  Bolsters, wool, 197.
  Carpets, 20, 36, 38, 61, 66, 69, 100, 105, 106, 111, 148, 156, 162, 178, 183, 200, 208, 212, 224, 229, 246, 264, 274, 287, 295, 303, 322, 335, 341, 344, 356, 370, 382, 390, 414, 419, 445, 456.
  Chair case, 68.
  Clocks, 90, 112, 224, 232, 239, 335.
  Cloth, 14.
  Coombsacks, 47.
  Coverings, 36, 45, 66, 85, 97, 99, 117, 124, 129, 133, 155, 156, 162, 166, 179, 201, 229, 242, 260, 269, 316, 363, 381, 391, 429, 447.
  Coverlets, 4, 7, 12, 14, 20, 22, 27, 29, 32, 37, 38, 40, 43, 44, 47, 48, 55, 57, 61, 64, 69, 75, 79, 81, 85, 87, 90, 93, 95, 98, 105, 106, 121, 127, 143, 148, 149, 151, 152, 154, 159, 160, 165, 167, 169, 175, 183, 188, 190, 191, 197, 202, 203, 210-212, 214, 224, 225, 242, 243, 248-250, 256, 257, 272, 279, 293-295, 316, 322, 341, 342, 344, 357, 376, 379, 382, 385, 389-391, 399, 423, 430, 433, 451, 455.
  Cradle cloth, 279.

482　INDEX

Furnishings, Household.
　Crewel, 70, 179.
　Cupboard cloths, 20, 38, 64-66, 68, 69, 90, 105, 106, 139, 151, 178, 179, 224, 229, 246, 253, 305, 326, 341, 379, 385, 390, 393, 419, 432, 445.
　Cupboard cloths, network, 341.
　Cupboard cloths, sea, 178.
　Curtain rods, 48, 105, 164, 179, 183, 224-226, 252, 448.
　Curtains, 14, 35, 38, 41, 43, 45, 48, 57, 61, 64, 66, 68, 69, 75, 77, 79, 81, 85, 90, 95, 98, 99, 105, 106, 127, 139, 143, 148, 151, 156, 162, 164, 166, 167, 169, 172, 174, 178-180, 183, 185, 188, 197, 201, 202, 208, 212, 218, 224, 226, 229, 232, 242, 243, 246, 252, 256-258, 269, 271, 276, 279, 285, 287, 301, 303, 307, 310, 311, 316, 317, 322, 326, 341, 344, 353, 357, 379, 385, 391, 395, 399, 412-414, 419, 422, 432, 433, 438, 445, 447, 448, 455.
　Curtains, window, 90, 105, 156, 224, 432, 433.
　Cushions, 5, 7, 20, 23, 33, 42, 43, 45, 55, 58, 61, 66, 68, 69, 85, 90, 93, 95, 105, 111, 128, 129, 139, 141, 144, 148, 151, 154-156, 162, 164-167, 178, 179, 183, 188, 200-202, 208, 214, 223, 224, 229, 232, 236, 239, 245, 251, 260, 269, 273, 276, 279, 281, 286, 287, 295, 301-303, 308, 310, 322, 326, 335, 341, 352, 365, 367, 370, 371, 377, 379, 390, 393, 396, 399, 406, 412, 419, 438, 445, 447, 448, 456, 458.
　Cushions, cupboard, 66, 127, 242, 391, 419, 432, 445.
　Cushions, Turkey work, 246.
　Cushions, window, 224, 243.
　Feathers, 64, 107, 142, 175, 180, 201, 243, 251, 274, 423.
　Flocks, 249.
　Fringe, 178, 179.
　Fringe, silk, 66.
　Fringe, worsted, 179.
　Hamaker, 391.
　Hangings, 64, 83, 106, 287, 353.

Furnishings, Household.
　Keys, 36, 47, 66, 70, 203.
　Linen, 12, 57, 61, 73, 78, 85, 91, 106, 134, 135, 139, 149, 152, 155, 164, 177, 179, 191, 204, 211, 232, 234, 240, 242, 251, 257, 267, 273, 284, 301, 308, 313, 314, 328, 335, 350, 356-358, 367, 370, 385, 388, 395, 406, 411, 431, 433, 437, 444, 456.
　Linen, childbed, 106, 164, 279, 385.
　Looking glass, gilt, 224.
　Looking glasses, 36, 39, 64, 70, 77, 148, 165, 172, 183, 211, 212, 226, 230, 243, 276, 286, 303, 310, 331, 354, 370, 385, 418, 419, 432, 438, 445, 456.
　Mantle, 155, 455.
　Mats, 95, 179, 188, 197, 203, 303, 341, 385, 433, 448.
　Mats, Indian, 344.
　Mattress, 112, 224.
　Napkins, 5, 7, 12, 21, 22, 27, 29, 32, 36, 38, 45-48, 55, 64, 66, 69, 75, 78, 79, 85, 87, 90, 95, 97-100, 102, 106, 124, 128, 132, 134, 139, 144, 151, 154, 156, 157, 160, 164, 166, 169, 172, 174, 179, 182, 183, 189, 197, 201, 208, 212, 214, 218, 224, 227, 229, 239, 242, 243, 246, 253, 256, 265, 266, 269, 274, 279, 286, 287, 293, 303, 304, 308, 311, 316, 322, 341, 344, 356, 363, 365, 370, 377, 379, 388, 390, 393, 399, 413, 415, 418, 419, 424, 430, 433, 434, 438, 444, 445, 447, 448, 455, 456.
　Padlocks, 180.
　Pictures, 162, 224, 385.
　Pillow beers, 12, 18, 21, 27-29, 31, 32, 36, 38, 42, 45-48, 54, 55, 59, 61, 64, 69, 75, 79, 83, 85, 90, 95, 97-99, 102, 106, 112, 128, 139, 142, 144, 149, 151, 154, 156, 160, 162, 164, 166, 169, 172, 174, 175, 179, 182, 183, 189, 197, 201, 208, 210, 212, 214, 218, 224, 225, 227, 229, 239, 242, 243, 246, 250, 253, 256, 265, 266, 275, 276, 279, 281, 282, 286, 287,

# INDEX 483

Furnishings, Household.
  Pillow beers, *continued*, 303, 304, 307, 311, 315, 322, 324, 326, 341, 344, 350, 356, 363, 365, 368, 370, 376, 377, 379, 385, 389, 390, 393, 396, 407, 413-415, 419, 422-424, 426, 431, 433, 434, 438, 445, 447-449, 455, 456.
  Pillow cases, 167.
  Pillow coverings, 41, 131.
  Pillow ticks, 165, 430.
  Pillows, 4, 7, 14, 22, 27, 28, 31, 33-37, 40, 43, 44, 57, 61, 69, 75, 79, 85, 90, 91, 93, 95, 97, 99, 102, 105, 106, 112, 121, 124, 130, 140, 143, 148, 149, 151, 152, 154-156, 164, 166, 167, 169, 170, 172-175, 179, 183, 185, 190, 193, 197, 201-203, 210, 214, 216, 218, 226, 243, 246-248, 250, 252, 257, 264, 269, 276, 279, 282, 293, 295, 308, 310, 311, 315-317, 324, 326, 341, 342, 344, 350, 356, 368, 376, 379, 385, 386, 390, 391, 396, 399, 406, 413, 419, 420, 422, 423, 430-433, 436, 438, 445, 447, 448, 451, 455.
  Pillows, down, 188, 224, 307.
  Pillows, feather, 22, 35, 38, 45, 47, 48, 52, 74, 77, 98, 127, 175, 188, 212, 239, 242, 250, 256, 265, 272, 281, 286, 305, 341, 363, 389, 407, 414, 419, 430, 445, 454.
  Pillows, flock, 45, 48, 174.
  Pillows, sea, 51.
  Pin cushions, 45, 69, 157, 179.
  Quilts, 66, 105, 247.
  Rods, 14, 41, 216, 324.
  Rug, cabin, 454.
  Rugs, 4, 14, 28, 31, 35, 36, 38, 42, 43, 47, 48, 55, 57, 66, 69, 74, 77, 78, 81, 83, 90, 91, 93, 95, 97-99, 105, 106, 121, 132, 148, 151, 152, 155-157, 159, 160, 162, 164-166, 169, 174-176, 179, 182, 183, 185, 188, 197, 201, 203, 212, 216, 218, 224-226, 229, 236, 239, 241-243, 246, 247, 250, 252-254, 256, 260, 264, 265, 276, 279, 284-288, 290, 293, 295, 303, 304, 307, 310, 311, 315-317,

Furnishings, Household.
  Rugs, *continued*, 322-324, 326, 331, 341, 342, 344, 350, 352, 356-358, 363, 365, 368, 379, 383, 385, 386, 389, 391, 396, 399, 406, 407, 412-415, 419, 422, 430, 432, 433, 436, 438, 445, 447, 448, 451, 453-455.
  Rugs, cradle, 78, 95.
  Screen, 106.
  Sheets, 5, 7, 8, 12, 21, 22, 27-29, 32-34, 36, 38, 41, 42, 45-48, 52, 54, 55, 57, 61, 64, 66, 69, 75, 78, 79, 83, 85, 87, 90, 91, 95, 97-100, 102, 105, 106, 112, 121, 128, 131, 134, 138-140, 142, 144, 148, 149, 151, 152, 154-156, 158-160, 162, 164, 166, 167, 169, 172-174, 176, 179, 182, 183, 185, 189, 190, 193, 197, 201, 202, 204, 205, 208, 210-212, 214, 218, 224-227, 229, 239, 242, 243, 246, 247, 250, 252, 254, 256, 258, 260, 264-266, 269, 271, 273, 275, 276, 279, 281, 282, 286-288, 290, 293, 300, 302-305, 307, 311, 312, 315, 316, 319, 322, 324, 326, 341, 342, 344, 350, 353, 356, 357, 363, 365, 367, 368, 370, 376, 377, 379, 383, 385, 388-390, 393, 396, 399, 407, 412-415, 418, 419, 422-424, 426, 430, 431, 433, 434, 438, 441, 444, 445, 447-449, 451, 455, 456.
  Sheets, calico, 390.
  Sheets, flaxen, 5, 7, 38, 95, 311.
  Sheets, Holland, 38, 66, 69, 197, 224, 276, 311, 326, 341, 390, 415.
  Sheets, winding, 272.
  Starch, 226, 233.
  Stockbed, 38.
  Table-cloths, 5, 7, 27, 32, 38, 42, 47, 48, 55, 64, 66, 69, 85, 90, 95, 98-100, 102, 106, 112, 124, 129, 132, 134, 139, 148, 151, 154, 156, 160, 164, 166, 169, 172, 174, 179, 183, 201, 202, 208, 212, 214, 218, 224, 227, 229, 242, 243, 246, 253, 274, 276, 279, 286, 287, 293, 303-305, 307, 308, 311, 322, 326,

## INDEX

Furnishings, Household.
  Table-cloths, *continued*, 341, 344, 350, 370, 377, 379, 388-390, 393, 399, 413, 415, 418, 419, 422, 433, 434, 438, 445, 447, 448, 455, 456.
  Table-cloths, calico, 419, 445.
  Table-cloths, Holland, 66, 197, 224, 341.
  Table-cloths, ossenbridge, 445.
  Table linen, 133, 142, 152, 162, 224, 275, 288, 311, 352, 385, 426.
  Tassels, 38.
  Towels, 5, 32, 36, 38, 47, 48, 64, 66, 69, 75, 90, 99, 102, 107, 112, 134, 139, 151, 157, 160, 164, 166, 169, 174, 179, 182, 197, 212, 224, 227, 229, 246, 279, 281, 293, 303, 308, 311, 344, 390, 393, 415, 419, 433, 445, 447-449, 455.
  Valances, 38, 45, 61, 64, 66, 68, 69, 75, 77, 90, 95, 98, 105, 106, 111, 112, 139, 148, 156, 162, 164, 166, 169, 174, 178, 180, 185, 188, 201, 202, 224, 229, 232, 242, 243, 246, 256, 276, 285, 303, 307, 310, 316, 317, 322, 326, 341, 344, 385, 391, 399, 413, 414, 419, 422, 432, 433, 438, 445, 448, 455.
  Woolen, 73, 177, 267, 385.
Furniture, 440.
  Band box, 4.
  Bed, high, 456.
  Bed, side, 98.
  Bedsteads, 4, 14, 20, 23, 36, 37, 42, 43, 48, 55, 57, 61, 64, 66, 70, 71, 75, 77, 90, 92, 95, 97, 98, 102, 105-107, 112, 121, 124, 128, 132, 140, 142-144, 148, 151, 152, 154, 155, 157, 161, 162, 164, 165, 169, 172, 174-176, 179, 180, 185, 186, 188, 189, 191, 192, 194, 197, 208, 212, 214, 218, 224, 225, 227, 230, 236, 239, 240, 242, 243, 246, 252, 256-258, 262, 276, 277, 279, 281, 282, 285-287, 303, 304, 310, 311, 314, 316, 322, 324, 326, 341, 342, 344, 348, 350, 358, 359, 363, 365, 367, 370, 376, 379, 385, 386, 389-391, 393, 395, 399, 400,

Furniture.
  Bedsteads, *continued*, 406, 411-413, 418, 419, 422, 423, 425, 430-433, 441, 445, 448, 451, 455, 456, 458.
  Bedsteads, canopy, 224.
  Bedsteads, half-headed, 18, 66, 95, 170, 182, 197, 203, 216, 363, 433.
  Bedsteads, joined, 66, 166, 200, 250.
  Bedsteads, truckle, 205, 246, 341, 456.
  Bedsteads, trundle, 37, 43, 45, 56, 75, 92, 95, 100, 105, 106, 128, 143, 151, 164-167, 172, 174, 175, 180, 189, 197, 203, 225, 226, 236, 279, 282, 303, 311, 385, 386, 406, 412, 432, 455.
  Benches, 65, 107, 246.
  Box, apprentice, 418.
  Box, spice, 310.
  Box with drawers, 438.
  Boxes, 4, 5, 12, 14, 23, 27, 29, 32, 36, 39, 44, 45, 47, 48, 56, 57, 64, 70, 75, 77-79, 81, 85, 90, 92, 93, 95, 98, 105, 107, 111, 129, 131, 140, 149, 151, 152, 154, 164, 169, 172, 175, 176, 179, 180, 182, 189, 190, 193, 195, 197, 201, 204, 208, 211, 212, 216, 218, 220, 225, 226, 233, 242, 243, 246, 247, 250, 265, 266, 269, 271, 272, 275, 279, 281, 282, 286, 293, 300, 301, 303, 306, 307, 311, 315, 324, 326, 341, 342, 356, 365, 367, 370, 374, 377, 379, 382, 392, 395, 396, 398, 406, 407, 411, 414, 415, 418, 419, 423, 431, 432, 434, 440, 445, 447-449, 451, 455, 456.
  Boxes, case of, 70.
  Boxes, chest of, 95.
  Boxes, iron, 56.
  Buffet, 112, 335.
  Cabinet, 225, 229, 246.
  Case of drawers, 385.
  Cases, 385.
  Chair table, 198, 316, 350.
  Chairs, 18, 22, 27, 36, 39, 41-43, 45, 47-50, 55, 56, 61, 63-65, 68, 71, 75, 77, 79, 81, 85, 89, 92, 95, 97-100, 105, 107,

Furniture.
  Chairs, *continued*, 109, 123, 124, 129, 132, 140, 142, 143, 148, 151, 152, 154, 160, 162, 164-167, 169, 172, 174-176, 180, 182, 185, 188, 189, 191-193, 198, 200, 204, 208, 210, 212, 214, 218, 223-226, 233, 239, 242, 243, 246, 251, 253, 256, 257, 264, 267, 272, 275-277, 279, 281, 282, 286, 288, 293, 301-305, 307, 308, 310, 312, 315-317, 322, 335, 341, 342, 344, 349, 352, 353, 357, 358, 363, 365, 370, 371, 376, 377, 379, 385, 389, 390, 391, 393, 396, 398, 403, 406, 407, 411, 412, 414, 419, 422, 423, 429, 430-434, 436, 440, 441, 444, 445, 447, 448, 451, 455, 456, 458.
  Chairs, framed, 230.
  Chairs, joined, 4, 127, 188, 216, 411.
  Chest, Chirurgeon, 234.
  Chest, iron, 313, 314.
  Chest of drawers, 224.
  Chest with drawer, 164, 224.
  Chest with lock and key, 273.
  Chest, settle, 414.
  Chests, 5, 13, 14, 20, 22, 23, 25, 27, 29, 32-34, 36, 39-45, 47-50, 52, 55-57, 61, 64, 66, 70, 75, 77, 79, 81, 85, 87, 89-93, 95, 97-100, 102, 105-107, 111, 112, 117, 121, 123, 124, 127, 129, 131, 132, 140, 142, 143, 148, 149, 151, 152, 154, 155, 157, 158, 161, 162, 164, 166, 169, 171, 172, 174, 175, 179, 180, 182, 184-186, 189, 192, 195, 197, 201, 202, 204, 206, 210-212, 214, 216, 218, 220, 223, 226, 229, 233, 239, 242, 243, 245-247, 253, 256-258, 260, 263-267, 269, 271, 272, 274-277, 279, 282, 284, 286-290, 295, 300-306, 308, 311, 312, 314-316, 322-324, 326, 331, 335, 337, 341, 342, 344, 348-350, 353, 354, 356-360, 363, 365, 367, 370, 374, 376, 377, 379, 381, 382, 385, 386, 388, 389, 391, 393, 395, 396, 398, 400, 406, 407, 411, 412, 414, 415, 417-419, 422, 423, 426,

Furniture.
  Chests, *continued*, 429-431, 433, 434, 438, 440, 442, 444, 445, 447-449, 451, 453, 455-457.
  Chests, joined, 31, 56, 189, 216, 279.
  Chests, sea, 4, 42, 200.
  Chests, wainscot, 200, 280, 414, 419, 432, 445.
  Coffers, 37, 148, 154, 184, 212, 422.
  Cots, 264, 322.
  Couch, 224.
  Cradles, 6, 71, 131, 155, 176, 190, 256, 275, 295, 303, 341, 386, 423, 431, 433, 455.
  Cradles, bed, 33.
  Cupboards, 4, 63, 75, 79, 98, 105, 112, 143, 151, 152, 155, 180, 182, 185, 186, 189, 206, 208, 214, 218, 230, 233, 245, 253, 263, 277, 286, 287, 305, 310, 311, 316, 319, 322, 326, 335, 341, 342, 349, 352, 358, 365, 379, 383, 393, 396, 398, 406, 411, 412, 423, 429, 430, 445, 447, 449, 455.
  Cupboards, court, 65, 197, 419, 432, 445.
  Cupboards, hanging, 223, 276.
  Cupboards, livery, 224, 246.
  Cupboards, press, 458.
  Cupboards, side, 172.
  Cupboards, standing, 242.
  Cupboards, wainscot, 160.
  Desks, 4, 66, 70, 139, 164, 210, 225, 276, 314, 341, 344, 412, 432, 436.
  Drawer, 310.
  Dresser, 89, 105, 128.
  Foot, 34, 36.
  Foot path, 56.
  Foot stool, 90.
  Form, joined, 246.
  Forms, 23, 36, 43, 55, 57, 65, 66, 89, 105, 107, 112, 129, 148, 151, 165, 166, 168, 172, 188, 197, 200, 203, 204, 208, 216, 224, 233, 281, 282, 286-288, 293, 304, 311, 315, 335, 341, 342, 356, 358, 377, 385, 389-391, 398, 403, 406, 430, 432, 456.
  Frames, 23, 65, 200, 326, 447.
  Napkin press, 151.

Furniture.
  Press, 112, 182, 246, 335, 344.
  Presser, 335.
  Settle, bed, 276.
  Settles, 39, 57, 77, 143, 148, 172, 174, 200, 226, 310, 341, 350, 385, 412, 419, 432, 433, 445, 456, 458.
  Standard, 21, 232.
  Stools, 21, 43, 49, 50, 61, 65, 79, 90, 92, 93, 97, 98, 100, 105, 118, 123, 132, 140, 157, 160, 162, 175, 176, 180, 189, 192, 204, 214, 224, 240, 257, 302, 303, 335, 341, 376, 385, 388, 395, 398, 411, 424, 429, 430, 434, 444, 447, 448, 456.
  Stools, ale, 189.
  Stools, brewing, 189.
  Stools, close, 66.
  Stools, cushion, 79, 224.
  Stools, joined, 43, 64-66, 70, 95, 143, 172, 223, 230, 242, 243, 246, 257, 310, 312, 326, 349, 376, 407, 412, 419, 432, 445, 456.
  Stools, leather, 66.
  Stools, standing, 204.
  Table, draw, 310.
  Table boards, 42, 57, 92, 143, 287, 293, 304, 377, 395, 431.
  Table chair, 71.
  Tables, 4, 21, 23, 27, 29, 36, 43, 44, 46, 54, 55, 61, 63, 65, 66, 71, 77, 79, 95, 97-100, 105, 107, 112, 121, 123, 129, 132, 148, 151, 152, 155, 157, 160, 162, 164-166, 168, 175, 176, 180, 185, 186, 188, 189, 192, 197, 200, 204, 208, 210, 214, 223, 224, 227, 230, 233, 239, 242, 243, 246, 253, 257, 267, 275, 277, 281, 286-289, 293, 301, 303, 308, 310, 311, 315, 319, 322, 326, 335, 341, 342, 348-350, 352, 356-358, 363, 365, 370, 371, 374, 379, 383, 385, 386, 388-391, 393, 398, 403, 406, 407, 411, 412, 415, 419, 422, 423, 429, 430, 432, 434, 436, 440, 444, 445, 447, 448, 455, 456.
  Tables, joined, 31, 89, 105, 279.
  Trunks, 14, 32, 34, 36, 45, 50, 52, 55-57, 66, 70, 85, 90, 95,

Furniture.
  Trunks, *continued*, 97, 99, 105, 112, 127, 129, 148, 155, 157, 160, 162, 179, 189, 197, 203, 208, 210, 214, 216, 223-225, 229, 233, 243, 246, 257, 258, 260, 264, 275, 276, 287, 295, 300, 301, 303, 304, 308, 316, 322, 335, 341, 363, 379, 381, 385, 393, 406, 418, 426, 440, 447, 448.
Fustian, *see* Cloth.

Gage, ——, 329, 330.
  Corp., 328.
  John, 32, 176, 177.
  Thomas, 296.
Gaines, Geynes, Daniel, 44.
  Jane, 44.
  John, 44.
  Samuel, 44.
  William, 150.
Gardens, 4, 37, 47, 64, 184, 185, 216, 253, 260, 318, 320, 332.
Gardner, Gardiner, Gardnar, ——, 6, 108, 256, 304, 384, 416, 422, 423.
  Ann, 439.
  George, 210, 212, 446-448.
  John, 287, 420, 446.
  Joseph, 303.
  Richard, 439.
  Samuel, 448.
  Thomas, 162, 182, 183, 229, 255, 269, 303, 304, 319, 421, 451.
  William, 423.
Garford, Gafford, Gervase, 35, 200.
Garven, Gurvand, John, 331, 364.
Gatchel, John, 60.
  Samuel, 60.
Gates, 75, 94, 209, 233, 236, 237, 244, 253, 260, 295, 301, 302, 330, 333, 351, 372.
Geare, William, 265.
Gearringe, ——, 51.
Gedney, Gedny, Geedney, Gidney, Gidnie, Gidnye, ——, 212, 276, 316, 384, 457.
  Capt., 266.
  Col., 259.
  John, 276, 347, 396.
Genit, ——, 158.
Gent, John, 360.
Gerrish, Gerish, ——, 16, 17, 408.

Gerrish, Capt., 247.
  Johan, 68.
  William, 16-18, 67, 68, 71, 139, 140, 153, 154, 161, 245, 310, 395.
Getchel, see Gatchel.
Gibson, William, 355.
Giddings, Gidding, Giddinge, Gittans, Gittings, George, 11, 145, 157, 173, 277, 374.
  Isaac, 222.
Gilbert, Gelbord, Gilbard, Gillburd, ——, 265, 266.
  Abigail, 264, 266.
  Elizabeth, 264, 265.
  Hannah, 265.
  Humphry, 264-266.
  John, 264.
Giles, Gilds, Gyles, ——, 256, 318.
  Samuel, 291.
  William, 6.
Gillow, Gillo, Gillowe, John, 91.
Gimlet, see Tools.
Ginger, see Food.
Girdles, see Clothing.
Glass, 90, 250.
Glasses for the eyes, 216.
Glasses, see Utensils.
Gloucester, 101, 102, 132, 133, 148, 149, 263, 343, 359-361, 380, 386, 388.
Glover, Jonathan, 160.
  Stephen, 149, 380.
Gloves, see Clothing.
Goats, see Animals (domestic).
Godfrey, Godfry, Peter, 217, 311.
Goffe, Amy, 13.
  Hannah, 13.
  John, 13, 14.
  Susan, 13.
Goldsmith, see Gouldsmyth.
Goldwire, Gouldwire, George, 194.
Golt, Goult, Deborah, 316, 317.
  Mary, 316.
  Rebecca, 316, 317.
  Sarah, 316, 317.
  William, 316.
Goodall, Goodale, ——, 23, 416, 417.
  Elizabeth, 65, 71, 72.
  John, 65.
  R., 158.
  Richard, 311, 312.

Gooderson, William, 25.
Goodhue, William, 170, 282, 284, 369.
Goodridge, Goodridg, Benjamin, 231, 232.
  Jeremiah, 230-232.
  Joseph, 230-232.
  Margaret, 232.
  William, 230, 232.
Goog, Gouge, Ann, 50.
  William, 50.
Goose, ——, 35, 65, 435.
  William, 46, 435, 436.
Gorames, John, 120.
Gott, Got, ——, 35, 349.
  Charles, 38, 39, 147, 265.
Gould, Zaccheus, 33.
Gouldsmyth, ——, 268.
Gove, Edward, 424.
Gowing, Robert, 252, 449.
Gowns, see Clothing.
Grafton, Graften, ——, 268.
  Joseph, 24, 26, 118, 348, 446.
Grain, see Food.
Grant, Hannah, 120.
  Jane, 80.
  John, 219, 302, 330.
Grass, 54, 176, 260, 352, 408.
Grass, English, 260.
Graves End, 6.
Graves, Mark, 100.
Gray, Bethiah, 385.
  Elizabeth, 384, 385.
  Hannah, 385.
  Joseph, 385.
  Mary, 385.
  Robert, 148, 242, 384, 385.
Great Yarmouth, Eng., 76.
Greely, Grele, Andrew, 102, 424.
Greenfeild, Samuel, 11.
  Susan, 11.
Greenleafe, Greenleff, Greenleif, Greenleife, Greneleife, Grenleafe, Grenlefe, Grenleff, Grenleife, ——, 17, 79, 342.
  Edmund, 16, 68, 79, 150.
  Stephen, 216, 340, 401, 408, 424.
Greenough, Robert, 209.
Greenoway, Ursly, 18.
Gregory, James, 374.
Greime, Greine, Allister, 354, 355.
Gridirons, see Utensils.

Griffin, Griffen, Grifin, Gryffin,
    Elizabeth, 353.
  Humphry, 27, 28, 235, 272, 329,
    353.
  John, 27, 353, 427.
Grindstones, see Tools.
Groome, Groom, ——, 408, 409.
Grover, Edmund, 238.
  John, 263, 289.
Guardians, 24, 28, 32, 72, 85, 86,
    144, 150, 158, 237, 250, 258,
    296, 312, 324, 325, 329, 330,
    333, 370, 390, 402, 407, 410,
    427, 432, 435, 443, 453.
Gudderson, William, 54.
Guns, see Weapons.
Gurvand, see Garven.
Gutch, Robert, 235.
Gutterson, see Gudderson.

Hadon, Andrew, 245.
Haffield, Hafeeld, Halfield, Martha, 144.
  Mary, 144, 145.
  Rachel, 144.
  Richard, 144.
  Ruth, 144.
  Sarah, 144, 145.
Haines, William, 43.
Hair bottoms, 52.
Hakes, see Utensils.
Hale, Hayle, Thomas, 21, 23, 216,
    281.
Halford, ——, 135.
  Andrew, 135.
  Ruth, 134, 135.
  William, 135.
Hall, Hal, ——, 103, 400, 408-
    410.
  John, 102, 404, 406.
  Rebecca, 102.
  Samuel, 192, 407.
Halsted, Halsteed, William, 93,
    94.
Hamm, Mark, 158.
Hammers, see Tools.
Hammersmith, 305.
Hamond, ——, 118, 119.
Hampton, 11, 401, 424.
Handkerchiefs, see Clothing.
Hanforth, Handforde, Handforth,
    Hanford, Hanfort, Nathaniel, 44, 50, 56, 123, 155, 356,
    358, 430.
Hangers, see Utensils.

Harbert, John, 51.
Hardy, Hardie, ——, 26.
  Elizabeth, 147, 200.
  John, 146, 147.
  Joseph, 147, 200.
Harker, William, 343, 350, 368.
Harnesses, see Horse Equipment
    and Tools.
Harriman, Hariman, Heryman,
    Leonard, 219, 237, 453.
Harris, Elizabeth, 223.
  John, 208, 218, 219, 223, 338,
    339, 454.
  Mary, 223.
  Nathaniel, 223.
  Thomas, 191, 319.
Harrows, see Tools.
Hart, Harte, Florence, 243.
  Isaac, 284.
  John, 59, 60, 243, 361, 362.
Hartshorn, Harteshorne, Hartshorne, John, 401.
  Jonathan, 480.
  Thomas, 283, 284.
Harvard College, 223, 235, 333,
    334.
Harvi, Peter, 266.
Harwood, Harwod, ——, 447,
    448.
  Elizabeth, 51.
  Henry, 446-448.
Haselton, Ellen, 265.
Haskell, Hascal, Hascall, Haskall, Haskoll, Hasskol, Hasskole, Hasskoll, Hascoll,
    Elizabeth, 147.
  John, 147.
  Joseph, 132.
  Mark, 147.
  Mary, 132.
  Roger, 146, 200, 281.
  William, 132, 133, 147, 281.
Hassen, Edward, 203.
Hatchets, see Tools.
Hatherlee, Leonard, 408.
Hathorne, Hathorn, Hawthorn,
    ——, 101.
  Capt., 59.
  Maj., 457.
  Anna, 101.
  John, 248, 250, 305, 347, 355,
    378.
  William, 18, 52, 65, 101, 171,
    266, 315, 346, 348, 349, 412,
    413, 447.

Hats, *see* Clothing.
Haugh, Martha, 104.
  Samuel, 104.
Haukes, ——, 261.
Haukins, Thomas, 235.
Hauxworth, Thomas, 140, 443.
Haverhill, 141, 195, 239, 240, 260, 272, 290, 328, 330, 336, 400, 424, 426-428, 431, 442.
Hawes, Haws, Alis, 46.
  Frances, 46.
  Matthew, 46.
  Robert, 46, 74.
  Thomas, 46.
Hawkes, *see* Haukes.
Hawkins, *see* Haukins.
Hay, 20, 22, 45, 50, 55, 56, 74, 80, 85, 93, 100, 112, 123, 124, 130, 131, 136, 142, 143, 193, 195, 198, 218, 226, 245, 251, 256, 260, 274, 289, 295, 301, 302, 304, 308, 318, 322, 324, 333, 335, 344, 351, 356, 357, 368, 370, 400, 404, 405, 426, 431, 434, 455, 458.
Hay seed, 158.
Haywood, Philip, 387.
Heartbreak hill, 106.
Heath, Bartholomew, 274, 290, 431.
Heed, ——, 214.
Heifers, *see* Animals (domestic).
Hemp, 13, 19, 45, 48, 55, 64, 70, 75, 78, 79, 97, 100, 107, 128, 129, 168, 174, 183, 188, 204, 218, 226, 245, 251, 256, 263, 269, 277, 279, 282, 301, 302, 335, 337, 352, 367, 383, 399, 458.
Hemp seed, 20, 55, 64, 129, 203.
Hempyard, 333.
Hendrick, Handick, Hendricks, Henrick, Hindrick, Daniel, 195, 290.
  Dorothy, 195.
  Hannah, 195, 405.
  Israel, 195.
  Jabez, 195.
  John, 195.
  Jonathan, 427.
  Jotham, 195.
Henly, Elias, 454.
Hens, *see* Fowls.
Herbert, *see* Harbert.
Herrick, Hericke, Herricke, Henry, 238, 264, 280, 281.

Hersome, Mary, 57.
Herod, ——, 256.
Hibbins, ——, 8, 10.
  William, 10, 138.
Hides, 97, 245, 388.
  Cow, 21, 32, 42, 353.
  Heifer, 271.
  Ox, 353.
Higginson, ——, 416.
  John, 446.
Higledee Pigledee, 400, 404, 406, 408, 409, 426.
Hill, Hilles, Hills, Abigail, 263.
  Elin, 46.
  John, 133, 211, 263, 270.
  Joseph, 116, 135.
  Mary, 60.
  Zebulon, 132, 133, 148, 149, 270.
Hilton, William, 3.
Hinds, Hindes, James, 24.
Hine, 57.
Hingham, 107.
Hives, 130, 193.
Hobbs, Hobes, Thomas, 265, 267.
Hobson, Hobsen, ——, 321.
  Ann, 294-296.
  Humphry, 294, 296-300, 321.
  John, 295-300, 321.
  William, 120, 294-299, 321.
Hodges, Hodgis, Hodgs, Andrew, 151, 201.
  George, 385.
Hoes, *see* Tools.
Hog hill, 425.
Hog Island, 375.
Hogs, *see* Animals (domestic).
Hogsheads, *see* Utensils.
Holbrooke, John, 452.
Holgrave, ——, 91.
  John, 148.
Hollingsworth, Holingworth, Hollingworth, Richard, 13, 34, 171-173.
  Susanna, 173.
  William, 172, 173.
Holman, Holeman, Richard, 361, 362.
Holmes, Holme, Huellme, Humbs, Obadiah, 40, 41.
  Richard, 120, 303.
Holsters, *see* Weapons.
Holte, Hoult, Nicholas, 3, 141, 142.
Holton, Nathaniel, 239.

490                               INDEX

Holyoke, Holioke, Holliock,
——, 225, 313, 314.
  Edward, 312, 314.
  Elizur, 314.
Homan, William, 361.
Honey, see Food.
Hood, Hud, Hude, Elizabeth,
    248.
  John, 100.
  Mary, 248.
  Richard, 247, 249, 250, 347.
Hoods, see Clothing.
Hooke, ——, 102.
  Elinor, 158, 159.
  William, 158, 159.
Hooks, see Fish, Tools, and
    Utensils.
Hooks and eyes, 95, 232, 382.
Hopkinson, Hobkinson, Caleb,
    259.
  Jeremiah, 259.
  John, 259, 299.
  Jonathan, 259, 390.
  Michael, 92, 120, 253.
  Mighill, 259.
Hops, see Food.
Horne, Horen, ——, 35, 396.
  John, 38, 39, 197, 255-257,
    320.
Hornis, ——, 228.
Horse equipment, etc.
  Bits, 85, 302, 344.
  Breast girt, 436.
  Bridle, 127, 142, 157, 180, 194,
    232, 260, 275, 279, 286, 301,
    302, 311, 335, 344, 368, 370,
    374, 377, 379, 383, 426, 433,
    449.
  Buckles, 85.
  Collars, 353, 378.
  Ferrule, 85.
  Fetters, 352.
  Girt, 157.
  Girt web, 170, 393.
  Halter, 376.
  Harnesses, 341, 381, 426.
  Leathers, 232.
  Pannel, 127, 260, 344, 368, 377,
    422.
  Pillion cloth, 90, 158, 179, 230,
    233, 275, 433.
  Pillion seat, 335.
  Pillions, 128, 157, 233, 275, 279,
    311, 341, 374, 376, 379, 407,
    422, 426, 433, 456.

Horse equipment, etc.
  Saddles, 106, 112, 128, 142, 157,
    158, 180, 192, 194, 230, 232,
    260, 275, 279, 286, 295, 301,
    311, 322, 335, 341, 352, 370,
    374, 376, 377, 379, 393, 407,
    422, 426, 429, 433, 436, 449,
    456.
  Side-saddle, 322.
  Spurs, 180, 367.
  Stirrups, 5, 157, 232.
  Traces, 181, 188, 376, 378.
Horses, see Animals (domestic).
Horton, ——, 25.
Hose, see Clothing.
Hotten, Elizabeth, 266.
Hour glass, see Utensils.
Houses, see Buildings.
Hovey, Hovie, Daniel, 28, 144,
    170, 369, 374.
Howard, William, 20, 126, 268.
Howe, How, ——, 131.
  Edward, 12.
  Elizabeth, 12, 126, 127, 130.
  Ephraim, 131.
  James, 61, 81, 105, 267.
  John, 267, 427.
  Joseph, 130, 131.
Howlet, Howlett, Ensign, 82,
    223, 267.
  Alice, 267.
  Thomas, 4, 28, 32, 61, 81, 267.
Hubbard, Hubard, Hubberd,
    ——, 105.
  John, 223.
  Margaret, 223.
  Nathaniel, 223.
  Richard, 369, 374.
  William, 104, 105, 225, 370.
Huckstable, Macklin, 245.
Hudson, Hudsson, Hutson, Francis, 172.
  John, 172, 345-347, 429.
  Jonathan, 248-250.
Hull, John, 230-232, 313.
  Margaret, 230-232.
Humphrey, Humfrey, Humfreyes, Humfries, Humfry,
    Humfryes, Humphreys,
    Humphries, Humphryes,
    Humphrys, ——, 65, 248,
    345, 346.
  John, 345-347.
  Joseph, 345-347.
Hunsley hill, 299.

# INDEX 491

Hunter, Mary, 80, 81.
  Robert, 80, 81.
Huntington, William. 146, 408.
Hurd, Heard, Herd, Herde, Edmund, 81.
  John, 81, 155.
  Luke, 81, 82.
  Sarah, 81, 82.
Hurds, 226.
Husbandman, *see* Trades.
Hutcheson, 284.
Hutchins, Houchin, Howchin,
  ——, 216.
  Jeremy, 111, 338.
  John, 273.
Hutton, Huten, Hutten, Richard, 265-267, 422.

Ilsley, Elsly, Ensley, Ilesly, Ilsly, John, 192, 312.
  William, 79, 140, 293, 402.
Inderwood, James, 241.
Indian plain, 397.
Indians, 256.
Indigo, 51, 66.
Ingalls, Ingalles, Ingals, Ingils, Ingles, Ingoles, Ingolles, Ingols, Ann, 99.
  Edmund, 99, 100.
  Edward, 345.
  Elizabeth, 99, 101.
  Faith, 101.
  Francis, 27, 50, 56, 100, 155, 178, 347, 350, 358, 368.
  Henry, 99-101, 244.
  John, 99, 101.
  Mary, 100, 101.
  Robert, 99, 101, 345, 346.
  Samuel, 99-101.
  Sarah, 101.
Ingersoll, Ingersol, Ingerson, Inkersell, Ann, 43.
  Bathsheba, 43.
  George, 43.
  John, 43, 289.
  Nathaniel, 43.
  Richard, 25, 43, 458.
Inglish, William, 126, 440.
Ink, 93.
Inkhorns, *see* Utensils.
Ipswich, 3, 4, 10, 11, 25, 27, 28, 32, 43, 46, 47, 52, 53, 60, 62, 81, 82, 85, 87, 88, 93, 95, 97, 100, 103, 104, 106, 108-110, 117, 119, 121, 122, 125-127,

Ipswich, *continued*, 132, 138, 144, 149, 151, 155, 156, 158, 163-165, 167, 168, 170, 171, 173, 175, 176, 190, 192, 201, 203, 208, 209, 217-219, 221-223, 225, 234, 235, 258, 259, 264, 267, 272, 274, 275, 277, 278, 282-285, 299, 306, 321, 322, 328, 330, 333, 335, 353, 360, 366, 368, 369, 373, 375, 378, 379, 392, 396, 397, 402, 417, 418, 422, 423, 427, 439, 454, 455.
Ipswich river, 318, 319, 417.
Ireland, 277, 278, 291, 292.
Iresonn, Edward, 56.
Iron, *see* Metals, Tools and Utensils.
Iron monger, *see* Trades.
Iron works, 120, 354.
Isbell, Ann, 40, 41.
  Robert, 40, 41.
Ivory, Ivorye, Ann, 152.
  Lois, 152.
  Sarah, 152.
  Thomas, 152, 358.
  William, 152.

Jacie, Jesse, Henry, 111.
Jackets, *see* Clothing.
Jackman, James, 214, 215, 392.
  Joanna, 214, 215.
Jackson, Jacksonne, Jacson, ——, 34, 435.
  Elizabeth, 120, 251, 252.
  John, 12, 34, 50, 59, 97, 240, 241.
  Kathren, 97.
  Margaret, 12, 51.
  Mary, 241, 436.
  Nicholas, 203, 238, 252.
  William, 80, 236.
Jacob, Richard, 170, 221, 369.
James, Erasmus, 314, 315, 348.
  Hester, 315.
  Jane, 314, 315, 413.
  Thomas, 290.
Jaques, Henry, 342, 408.
Jarrat, Elizabeth, 98.
  John, 98.
  Susanna, 98.
Jars, *see* Utensils.
Jeffrey's Creek, 18.
Jenkes, Jenckes, Jencks, ——, 136.
  Joseph, 305.
Jeoffreys, Robert, 108.

Jericho, 394.
Jerkins, *see* Clothing.
Jewett, Jawet, Jewet, Jewit, Jewitt, Jowett, Juett, Juit, Juitt, ——, 176, 217, 219, 237, 247, 291, 303, 321, 372, 441.
  Abraham, 219, 435, 453.
  Ann, 338.
  Ezekiel, 435.
  Faith, 329, 330.
  Jeremiah, 327-329.
  Joseph, 32, 93, 94, 111, 129, 203, 219, 230-233, 236, 237, 244, 250, 251, 253, 254, 258-260, 268, 277, 295, 298, 300, 321, 327-330, 338.
  Maximilian, 81, 93, 129, 202, 203, 206-208, 237, 244, 251, 252, 259, 295, 302, 321, 327-330, 334, 352, 371, 441, 443.
  Nehemiah, 219, 296, 329, 330.
  Patience, 329, 330.
Jigles, Jeggells, Jegles, Elizabeth, 288.
  Thomas, 436.
  William 287.
Jobitt, ——, 100.
Johnson, Jonson, ——, 65, 93, 167, 297.
  Caleb, 141, 244.
  Elizabeth, 128.
  Francis, 245, 315, 323, 349, 412.
  John, 128, 192, 235, 302, 352.
  Richard, 136, 345, 356.
  Robert, 116, 117.
Johnson's pond, 295.
Jones, Joanes, ——, 348.
  Hugh, 304.
  Thomas, 429.
Jordan, Jordon, Francis, 54, 203.
  Jane, 203.
Joy, Deborah, 148.
  Walter, 149.
Jugs, *see* Utensils.

Keagle, John, 65.
Keelers, *see* Utensils.
Keene, Ephraim, 60.
Kegs, *see* Utensils.
Kellem, *see* Killam.
Kelly, Abel, 13, 15.
Kemball, *see* Kimball.
Kempe, Edward, 188.
Keniston, Allen, 101.
  Dorothy, 101.

Kenning, Jane, 165.
Kent, Kente, Kentt, ——, 6.
  Em, 186.
  John, 186, 187.
  Mary, 186.
  Richard, 3, 13, 65, 83, 84, 116, 150, 186, 187, 340.
  Samuel, 171.
  Stephen, 83, 85, 186, 425.
Keny, Henry, 257.
Kersey, *see* Cloth.
Ketch, *see* Vessels.
Kettle Island, 429.
Kettle Island cove, 239.
Kettles, *see* Utensils.
Kesar, Keasur, Keysar, Keysor, ——, 214, 313.
  George, 213, 313.
  Hannah, 313.
Key (wharf), 172.
Keys, *see* Furnishings.
Kibben, Abigail, 184.
Kidwel, Nicholas, 108.
  Rachel, 108.
Killam, Kellem, Austin, 188.
  Elizabeth, 12.
Kiln, 168, 208.
Kiln, brick, 183.
Kiln, hair, 85.
Kiln utensils, 208.
Kimball, Kemball, Kembell, Kimbal, ——, 177, 406.
  Benjamin, 406.
  John, 401.
  Richard, 127, 155, 169, 170.
King, Kinge, ——, 27, 100, 136, 431.
  Deliverance, 118.
  Dorothy, 117, 118.
  Hannah, 118.
  John, 118.
  Mehitable, 118.
  Richard, 3.
  Samuel, 118.
  William, 117, 118, 238.
Kingsbury, ——, 329, 330.
  Henry, 328.
Kinrick, Mary, 439.
Kinsman, Kensman, ——, 220, 303.
  Robert, 221, 275, 369, 396.
Kirtland, Kartland, Keartland, Kertland, Kirtland, Kyrtland, Alice, 343.
  Nathaniel, 249, 250.
  Philip, 131, 213, 343, 345.

INDEX    493

Kirtle, *see* Clothing.
Kitchen, Kitchin, Kitching, Kittchen, John, 183, 255, 316.
Knapsacks, *see* Weapons.
Knight, Knights, ——, 35, 270, 271.
  Alexander, 439, 440, 441.
  Ann, 107.
  Elizabeth, 213.
  Francis, 213.
  Hannah, 213, 440.
  Jacob, 213.
  John, 3, 213, 309, 343.
  Mary, 440.
  Nathaniel, 440.
  Richard, 3, 16, 17, 22, 23, 67, 68, 71, 79, 83, 84, 205, 246, 293, 340, 392, 439.
  Sarah, 440.
  William, 28, 213.
Knives, *see* Tools, Utensils, and Weapons.
Knowlton, Knoulton, Knowlten, ——, 272.
  Abraham, 163-165.
  Elizabeth, 163, 165.
  John, 98, 163-165, 222.
  Margery, 163-165.
  Mary, 222.
  Rice, 222.
  Thomas, 89, 163, 166, 219-222, 423.
  William, 163, 219-222.

Lace, *see* Clothing.
Ladders, *see* Tools.
Ladles, *see* Utensils.
Lake, John, 346, 347, 382.
Lambert, Lambertt, Lt., 296, 298, 299.
  Ann, 94, 300.
  Francis, 94.
  Gershom, 94, 300, 436, 437.
  Jane, 94, 128, 300.
  John, 94, 300, 301, 334, 436, 443, 444.
  Jonathan, 94, 129, 300, 443, 444.
  Richard, 289.
  Thomas, 94, 128, 129, 300, 436.
Lambs, *see* Animals (domestic).
Lamps, *see* Utensils.
Lampson, Hannah, 398.
  Sarah, 282, 283.

Lampson, William, 282, 283.
Lanckton, Roger, 54, 175.
Lane, Aniball, 361.
Langley, Abel, 81.
Langton, ——, 25.
  Joseph, 25.
  Mary, 25.
  Roger, 25.
  Sarah, 25.
Lanterns, *see* Utensils.
Largin, Lurgen, Henry, 137, 138.
Laskin, Laskine, Hugh, 280, 281.
  John, 281.
  Timothy, 281.
Lasts, *see* Tools.
Lattamore, Christopher, 326.
Latten ware, *see* Utensils.
Laughton, ——, 152.
  Thomas, 24, 178, 358, 434.
Law, Lawe, Lawes, Laws, ——, 227.
  Francis, 255, 384, 422.
  William, 218, 302.
Leach, Lech, ——, 35.
  Elizabeth, 389.
  John, 288, 389.
  Lawrence, 20, 388, 389.
  Richard, 256, 288, 389, 421.
  Robert, 348, 428, 429.
  Sarah, 389.
Lead, *see* Metals.
Lead crean for a coop, 179.
Leader, ——, 100.
Leanto, 377.
Leather, 13, 14, 64, 70, 79, 83, 87, 93, 125, 157, 164, 180, 189, 198, 247, 272, 326, 344, 352.
Leather, *see also* Manufactures.
Leather, hide of, 165, 192, 301, 352.
Leather jack, 153, 157.
Leaver, Thomas, 128, 300.
Lee, Leigh, Alice, 373-375.
  Richard, 373, 374.
  Susanna, 374.
  Thomas, 373-375.
Legg, Legd, John, 60, 315, 324.
Leighton, Laighton, Laton, Layghton, Lighten, ——, 403.
  Richard, 436.
  Thomas, 27, 44.
Lemon, Lemmon, Robert, 65, 444.
Lesenby, Henry, 439.

Lewis, Lewes, David, 381.
  Edmund, 123, 124.
  John, 124, 311, 312, 408.
  Robert, 34.
  Thomas, 124.
Lightfoot, Lightfoote, Littfoot, Anne, 56.
  Frances, 50, 55, 56.
  Isabel, 55.
  John, 55.
  William, 457.
Lilford, Thomas, 290.
Lincolnshire, Eng., 55.
Linen, see Cloth, Clothing, and Furnishings.
Linsey woolsey, see Cloth.
Lisbon ware, see Utensils.
Lisson, Nicholas, 60.
Little, George, 153, 389.
Littlehale, Littleale, Richard, 22, 23, 291, 431.
Lock and key, 171.
Lockrum, see Cloth.
Locks, 36, 45, 47, 66, 70, 119, 169, 180, 203, 233.
  Box, 90, 279.
  Chest, 90.
  Cupboard, 279.
  Hanging, 75.
  Spring, 279.
  Stock, 279.
Logs, 408.
London, 51, 55, 134, 278, 292, 356.
Long, Longe, Lounge, Robert, 153, 214-216, 245, 339, 340, 395, 402.
Longley, William, 143.
Look, ——, 214.
Looking glass, see Furnishings.
Lookman, Lookeman, John, 361, 362.
  Nicholas, 361, 362.
Looms, see Tools.
Loomwork, 5.
Lord, ——, 221, 329.
  Robert, 4, 48, 54, 63, 95, 106, 117, 127, 145, 156, 164, 166, 167, 173, 176, 203, 215, 219, 223, 231, 235, 258, 272, 275, 278, 282, 285, 307, 327, 353, 368, 393, 398, 423, 440, 455.
  Thomas, 231, 307.
  William, 39, 147.
Lothrop, Lowthropp, Thomas, 270, 376, 377, 418.

Lovejoy, John, 396.
Lovell, Thomas, 117, 170, 272.
Lowe, Thomas, 235.
Lowell, Loule, Lowle, ——, 17.
  Benjamin, 68, 139, 140.
  Elizabeth, 65, 67, 68, 71, 72, 138-140.
  James, 67, 72, 139.
  John, 15, 16, 23, 53, 65, 67, 68, 71, 72, 138-140.
  Joseph, 67, 72, 139.
  Mary, 67, 68, 72, 139.
  Percival, 160.
  Peter, 67, 139.
  Richard, 65, 67, 68, 71, 72, 139, 140, 153, 160, 215.
Luece, John, 402.
Lumber, 66, 130, 220, 224, 256, 258, 311, 357, 358, 395, 407, 418, 433, 449.
Lume, Lum, Lumbe, Ann, 371.
  Judith, 371.
  Susanna, 371.
Lumis, Lomas, Lumax, ——, 220.
  Edward, 167, 221.
Lumkin, Lumpkin, Lumpkyn, ——, 177,
  Richard, 11, 43.
  Sarah, 138.
Lunt, Ann, 394, 395.
  Daniel, 116, 394, 395.
  Elizabeth, 394.
  Henry, 230, 343, 393-395.
  John, 394.
  Mary, 394.
  Priscilla, 394, 395.
  Sarah, 394.
Lusher, Eleazer, 406.
Lynes, ——, 311.
Lynn, 11, 12, 24, 26, 32, 44, 50, 55, 59, 91, 99, 122, 123, 130, 136, 143, 152, 154, 155, 159, 177, 178, 213, 225, 247, 256, 276, 284, 305, 312-314, 343, 345-347, 350, 353-358, 368, 370, 402, 414, 429, 434, 449.
Lynn, see also Hammersmith.
Lyon, John, 60.

McCall, Duncan, 148.
Mace, see Food.
Mackerel, see Fish.
Mackfashon, Rowland, 355.
Mackmallens, Allister, 354.

Macy, Macie, Macye, ——, 247.
  Thomas, 23, 146, 152.
Mahew, Mahur, ——, 8.
Makepeace, ——, 134.
Malden, 135.
Malden, Eng., 333.
Malford, ——, 134.
Malt, see Food.
Manchester, 222, 238, 239, 347, 428.
Maning, ——, 113.
Mansfield, Mansfeild, Mansfeilde, Mansfelde, ——, 56.
  Andrew, 56, 347, 356, 378.
  Damoris, 281.
  John, 136.
  Mary, 313.
  Paul, 281.
  Robert, 355.
Mantle, see Furnishings.
Mantles, see Clothing.
Manufactures.
  Boards, 49, 107, 133, 144, 158, 172, 198, 202, 243, 273, 274, 279, 344, 348, 359, 404, 408, 424.
  Boards, oak, 172.
  Bricks, 260, 279.
  Clapboards, 64.
  Cloth, 273.
  Cotton, 65, 168, 277, 306, 382.
  Iron, hand-wrought, 149.
  Leather, 316, 322.
  Linen, 308.
  Nails, 5, 13, 39, 64, 70, 84, 142, 148, 161, 166, 169, 180, 263, 279, 282, 286, 308, 322, 381, 382, 424.
  Nails, brass, 322.
  Pipe staves, 34, 35.
  Planks, 113, 202, 243, 256, 286.
  Planks, oak, 172.
  Planks, pine, 172.
  Posts, 423.
  Rails, 226, 423.
  Resin, 165, 386.
  Soap, 52, 119, 204, 308, 386, 431.
  Staves, 198, 442.
  Tallow, 204, 269, 308.
  Timber, 39, 74, 112, 144, 172, 196, 198, 242, 275, 358, 426, 434.
  Wool, 124, 128, 208, 337, 342, 351, 352, 388, 395.
  Worsted, 69, 257.

Manufactures.
  Yarn, 5, 39, 51, 52, 56, 58, 69, 78, 97, 106, 124, 132, 142, 148, 155, 164, 165, 176, 179, 230, 253, 277, 288, 289, 301, 302, 310, 330, 335, 337, 342, 352, 360, 377, 406, 418, 424, 431, 433, 434, 442, 451, 456.
  Yarn, cotton, 56, 93, 107, 168, 216, 226, 271, 274, 279, 308, 316, 335, 344, 388.
  Yarn, flaxen, 107.
  Yarn, hempen, 174, 245.
  Yarn, linen, 57, 64, 79, 165, 168, 185, 271, 274, 279, 302, 308, 316, 356, 395.
  Yarn, linsey, 56.
  Yarn, woolen, 129, 226, 273, 277, 356, 385, 388.
Maps, see Books.
Marblehead, 59, 65, 117, 162, 176, 243, 245, 254, 256, 276, 289, 314, 315, 317, 324-326, 348, 349, 358, 365, 410, 411, 415, 454, 456.
Mariner, see Trades.
Marking iron, see Tools.
Marsh, John, 422.
Marshall, Martiall, ——, 257, 318.
  Capt., 402.
  Thomas, 368, 380.
Marsterson, Ruth, 428.
Marston, John, 276, 280.
Martin, Martyn, ——, 313, 351.
Mason, Mazon, Maj., 257.
  Elias, 330.
  Emme, 57.
  Israel, 256.
Massey, Marsy, Masey, Masse, Massey, Masseye, Massy, ——, 35.
  Jeffrey, 20, 35, 51, 52, 59, 96, 97, 118, 196, 198, 199, 316, 363, 364, 436, 444, 449, 458.
Match, 170.
Mather, Nathaniel, 122.
Matosin, Mary, 333.
Mats, see Furnishings.
Mattocks, see Tools.
Mattox, Mattackes, John, 36.
Mattstone, John, 35.
Maverick, Mavericke, Maverik, Maverike, ——, 60, 315.
  Moses, 60, 243, 315, 323, 324, 349, 362, 412, 457.

Maxfield, John, 408.
Meal, see Food.
Measures, 129, 182, 208, 212, 243, 335, 352.
  Half bushel, 75, 79, 82, 89, 165, 201, 206, 246, 286, 353.
  Half peck, 33, 58, 71, 75, 89, 216.
  Peck, 33, 42, 71, 79, 82, 89, 190, 206, 216, 281, 376, 403.
  Pint, 66.
  Pottle, 66.
  Quart, 66.
  Yard, 33.
Meat, see Food.
Medicine, 267.
Meeting house, 32, 99, 141.
Mellowes, ——, 135.
  Abraham, 135.
  Edward, 136.
  Hannah, 134, 135.
Merchant, see Trades.
Meriam, William, 131.
Merit, Nicholas, 60.
Merrill, Merill, Merrell, Abel, 205.
  Abraham, 205.
  Daniel, 205.
  John, 83, 204, 205.
  Nathaniel, 204, 205.
  Susanna, 204.
Merrimac, 120, 301, 322, 352.
Merrimack ridge, 108.
Merrimack river, 108, 192, 295, 328, 372, 404.
Messer, Mercier, Mercer, Abial, 427, 428.
  Hannah, 428.
Metals.
  Iron, 49, 71, 431, 432.
  Iron, bar, 85, 89, 201, 233, 305, 337, 344.
  Iron, old, 50, 89, 97, 100, 112, 123, 148, 172, 180, 183, 188, 210, 214, 218, 226, 229, 232, 286, 302, 316, 341, 382, 386, 391, 447.
  Kettle brass, 39.
  Lead, 49, 52, 71, 92, 170, 180, 250, 418.
  Steel, 49, 50, 140, 149, 180.
Metcalfe, Medcalfe, Joseph, 28, 62, 235.
Mighill, Mighel, Mighell, Ann, 206, 207.

Mighill, Ezekiel, 207, 209, 210, 296, 298.
  John, 206, 207, 209.
  Mary, 207, 208.
  Nathaniel, 207.
  Samuel, 206, 207, 209.
  Stephen, 207, 209.
  Thomas, 86, 98, 117, 129, 206-209, 251.
Mill house, see Buildings.
Millard, Millerd, Millward, Milward, Ann, 160, 161.
  Elizabeth, 160.
  Rebecca, 160.
  Thomas, 65, 68, 139, 160, 192, 251.
Miller, Mary, 437, 438.
Millett, Thomas, 360.
Mills, see Buildings.
Millstones, see Tools.
Ministers, 141, 274, 320, 331.
Miricke, James, 293.
Misery, the, 419, 445.
Mitchell, Michell, Mary, 189, 190, 222.
  William, 189.
Mittens, see Clothing.
Mohair, see Cloth.
Mondey, Monde, Mondy, Moneday, Henry, 140, 194.
  William, 21, 83.
Money.
  Noble, 356.
  Silver, 66, 87, 184.
  Spanish, 184.
  Wampum, 66, 258.
  Wampumpeag, 5, 328.
Moody, Moodey, Moodye, Mooudy, Mary, 309, 310, 437.
  Samuel, 309-311, 392, 437.
  William, 342, 395, 439.
Moore, Moor, Moores, More, Mores, Dorothy, 305.
  Edmund, 72, 231.
  James, 305.
  Richard, 91, 119, 177.
  Ruth, 305.
  Samuel, 194.
  Thomas, 77.
Morgon, Robert, 428.
Morrill, Morell, Morill, Morrel, Morrell, ——, 408.
  Abraham, 273, 274, 399-401, 408.
  Ipsabe, 400.

Morrill, Isaac, 399-401.
　Jacob, 399, 401.
　Lydia, 399-401.
　Moses, 399-401.
　Sarah, 399-401.
Morris, Thomas, 313.
Morse, Mors, Mose, Mosse, Anthony, 153.
　Dorothy, 54.
　Hannah, 54.
　John, 54.
　Joseph, 25, 47, 53, 54, 215.
　Peter, 343.
　Richard, 248.
　William, 21.
Mortar and pestle, see Utensils.
Morton, William, 100.
Motte, ——, 107.
Mottley, Robert, 4.
Moulton, Molton, ——, 183, 268, 416, 417.
　James, 24, 252.
　Robert, 183, 210, 212, 351, 417.
Mountjoy, Monjoye, Benjamin, 287.
Moyce, Joseph, 130.
Mo——, Anthony, 394.
Muddle, Mudle, Henry, 158, 220, 221, 359-361.
Muddy river, 60, 201, 217, 219, 329.
Mudge, Mudg, James, 361.
Mudget, Sarah, 400.
Mufflers, see Clothing.
Muffs, see Clothing.
Murley Feild, 298.
Muse, Emme, 290.
Muskets, see Weapons.
Mussey, Mussy, Mussye, Muzye, Muzzall, Muzzey, Muzzie, Muzzy, ——, 328, 329.
　Benjamin, 29-31, 126, 127.
　Bridget, 28, 30, 31.
　Ellen, 29, 31.
　Joseph, 29-32, 327.
　Mary, 29-32.
　Robert, 28, 30-32.

Nahant, 314.
Nails, see Manufactures.
Nantucket, 84.
Napkins, see Furnishings.
Neale, Neile, John, 227.
Neckcloths, see Clothing.
Needham, Neadum, Nedham, ——, 248.

Needham, Anthony, 256.
　Edmund, 44.
Needles, see Tools.
Needlework, 66, 178.
Nelson, Nellson, Nulson, ——, 114-116, 208, 330.
　Ann, 436.
　Elizabeth, 94.
　Joane, 109, 110.
　Mercy, 110, 116.
　Philip, 72, 94, 110, 115, 140, 296, 327-329.
　Samuel, 111.
　Thomas, 109-111, 113-116, 120, 121, 250, 436.
Neve, Margaret, 241.
Nevill, Nevell, William, 25.
Newbury, 3, 6, 12, 13, 15-18, 21, 22, 34, 53, 65, 67, 72, 78, 82, 85-87, 107, 108, 113, 116, 137, 138, 140, 141, 145, 146, 150, 153, 160, 186, 187, 189, 193-195, 204, 205, 214-216, 230-232, 245-247, 259, 275, 292, 294, 297, 308-310, 339, 340, 342, 391-393, 422, 433, 437, 438.
Newbury neck, 233.
Newfoundland, 323.
Newhall, Anthony, 247, 249.
　John, 248, 249.
New Haven, Conn., 117, 119, 313, 345, 347.
Newman, John, 28, 29.
　Richard, 16.
Newmarsh, John, 272.
Nichols, Nicholls, Nicoles, Nicolls, ——, 311.
　John, 134.
　William, 306, 383.
Nicholson, Nicolson, Christopher, 59, 324.
　Edmund, 59, 60, 324.
　Elizabeth, 324.
　John, 324.
　Samuel, 324.
　Thomas, 324.
Nicke, William, 324, 326.
Nixon, Nickson, Nicksone, Elizabeth, 12, 446.
　Mathew, 446-449.
Norington, Robert, 117.
Norman, Richard, 60, 454.
Norris, Norice, Noris, Norrice, ——, 34, 101, 256, 257, 383.
　Edward, 320.

North, Richard, 193, 312.
North river, 375.
Northend, Northen, Northende, Northene, Northin, Ezekiel, 72, 93, 94, 111, 140, 237, 244, 296, 301, 303, 328, 329, 333, 352, 437.
　Jeremy, 120.
Northy, John, 60.
Norton, ———, 30, 122.
　Capt., 159.
　Abigail, 304.
　Elizabeth, 304.
　Freegrace, 304.
　George, 12, 57, 304.
　Hannah, 304.
　John, 32, 63, 88, 104, 105, 110, 122, 126, 127, 304.
　Mary, 12, 304.
　Mehitable, 304.
　Nathaniel, 304, 384.
　Sarah, 304.
　William, 30, 220, 272.
Norwell, ———, 6, 8, 10.
　Increase, 10, 149.
Norwich, Conn., 222.
Noyes, Noice, Noies, Noyce, Noys, Noyse, ———, 187.
　Cutting, 309.
　James, 245, 246.
　Joseph, 311, 340.
　Mary, 309, 310, 437.
　Moses, 340.
　Nicholas, 67, 68, 71, 153, 154, 190, 215, 217, 230, 245, 247, 309, 311, 340, 377, 392, 406, 433, 437.
　Sarah, 246, 247.
　Thomas, 215.
Nursery, 186, 188, 257.

Oakum, see Vessels.
Oatmeal, see Food.
Oats, see Food.
Odry, Oaderie, William, 330.
Oil, 107, 164, 281, 386.
Oldisworth, Michael, 134.
Oliver, Olliver, ———, 23.
　Christopher, 15, 16.
　Joane, 15, 16.
　John, 15-18.
　Mary, 18.
　Peter, 312.
　Richard, 330.
　Samuel, 134.
　Thomas, 384.

Olney, Eng., 150.
Orchard, 16, 60, 61, 84, 97, 112, 182, 188, 192, 197, 208, 216, 225, 233, 236, 238, 244, 246, 248, 250-253, 260, 269, 270, 278, 288, 293, 300, 318, 320, 328-330, 332, 334, 335, 352, 372, 378, 383, 385, 389, 394, 398, 400, 403, 404, 410, 421, 422, 426, 432.
Ordinary, 370.
Ordway, James, 217.
Orme, Ormes, John, 420.
Osgood, Ossgood, Abigail, 121.
　Christopher, 121, 122, 396, 397.
　Deborah, 121.
　Elizabeth, 121, 141.
　Hannah, 141.
　John, 141, 273, 274, 291, 396.
　Margery, 122, 397.
　Mary, 121, 141.
　Sarah, 141, 142.
　Stephen, 141, 396.
　William, 338, 408, 443.
Oxen, see Animals (domestic).

Padlocks, see Furnishings.
Page, ———, 313.
　Onesiphorus, 401, 443.
　Sarah, 401.
Pails, see Utensils.
Paine, Pane, Payne, ———, 9, 177, 302.
　John, 370.
　Mary, 37.
　Robert, 31, 43, 63, 88, 89, 105, 164, 166, 223, 234, 235, 254, 268, 396.
　Thomas, 37.
　William, 105, 107, 126, 268, 272, 278.
Palfrey, Palfery, Palfray, Palfree, Palfrey, Palfrie, Palfry, Sergeant, 118.
　Eliza, 325.
　Peter, 38, 39, 58, 96, 97, 325.
Pallgrave, Paulgrave, Ann, 50, 51.
Palmer, Pallmer, Henry, 195, 262, 431.
　John, 219, 244, 352.
　Richard, 266.
　Thomas, 92.
Palmiter, ———, 457.
Pans, see Utensils.

# INDEX 499

Park, Parke, George, 162.
Parker, ——, 7, 8, 108.
  Henry, 134.
  Joseph, 142.
  Nathan, 377.
  Ralph, 60.
  Richard, 444.
  Thomas, 245.
Parrett, Parrat, Parratt, Parrot, Elizabeth, 244, 333.
  Faith, 207.
  Frances, 202, 206-208, 244.
Parsons, Jeffrey, 386.
Partridge, Partridg, Patridge, Ann, 192, 193.
  Elizabeth, 150.
  Hannah, 150.
  John, 150.
  Nehemiah, 150.
  Sarah, 150, 407.
  William, 46, 103, 150, 192, 407.
Patch, Pache, Elizabeth, 270.
  Hannah, 269, 270.
  James, 269, 270.
  John, 270, 418.
  Mary, 270.
  Nicholas, 96, 97, 185, 186, 263.
Pateeson, William, 225.
Pattashall, Robert, 289.
Patterson, *see* Pateeson.
Peabody, *see* Pebody.
Peach, John, 60.
Pearson, Person, John, 27, 203.
Pease, Peas, Peasse, ——, 40, 41.
  John, 40-43.
  Margaret, 40, 41.
  Marie, 41, 42.
  Robert, 40-43, 415.
Pease, *see* Food.
Peasley, Peaslee, Peasly, Pesle, Pesly, ——, 338.
  Elizabeth, 336.
  Jean, 336.
  Joseph, 336-338.
  Mary, 336, 337.
  Sarah, 336, 338.
  William, 407.
Pebody, Pabody, Francis, 267, 271, 367.
Pecker, Elizabeth, 238.
Pederick, Pedericke, John, 454.
Peeters, ——, 65.
Pell, ——, 55, 56.
  Hannah, 55.
Pendleton, ——, 104, 106.

Pendleton, Capt., 268.
Pepper, Robert, 128.
Pepper, *see* Food.
Pequot field, 165.
Perkins, Perkines, Perkings, Purkings, ——, 5, 54, 55, 268.
  Abraham, 11, 190.
  Elizabeth, 203, 324.
  Jacob, 191, 203.
  John, 4, 190, 191, 284.
  Judith, 191.
  Lydia, 284.
  Thomas, 190, 191.
  Tobias, 324.
  William, 133, 324.
Perrin, Thomas, 423.
Pery, Thomas, 233.
Peters, *see* Peeters.
Petticoats, *see* Clothing.
Pettingell, Pettingall, Richard, 20, 43, 339.
Pewter, *see* Utensils.
Phelps, Phelpes, Edward, 212.
  Henry, 210, 211, 351, 383, 417.
  John, 211.
  Nicholas, 210.
Philbrick, Filbrike, Robert, 192.
Phillips, Philips, Phillepes, Philleps, ——, 27, 235, 298, 333.
  John, 76, 315.
  Samuel, 206, 218, 321.
Physician, *see* Trades.
Pickard, Pickerd, John, 72, 140, 174, 175, 236, 237, 251, 252, 260, 328-330, 352, 371, 372.
  Samuel, 296.
Pickering, Pickeringe, Pickirin, Pickiring, Pickrin, Elizabeth, 254, 255, 257.
  John, 254, 255, 257, 384, 436.
  Jonathan, 254, 255, 257.
Pickman, ——, 313.
  Nathaniel, 173, 185, 200.
  Samuel, 280.
  Tabitha, 185.
Pickton, Thomas, 36, 172, 445.
Pickworth, Peckworth, Abigail, 428.
  Ann, 428, 429.
  Benjamin, 428.
  John, 428, 429.
  Joseph, 428.
  Samuel, 428, 429.
Pictures, *see* Furnishings.

500 INDEX

Pierce, Pearce, Pearse, Peirce, Perce, ——, 408.
  Abigail, 285.
  Daniel, 79, 216, 401.
  Robert, 268.
Pigeons, 227.
Pigs, see Animals (domestic).
Pike, Pyke, Capt., 338, 404.
  Ann, 194.
  Dorothy, 194.
  Elizabeth, 194.
  Hannah, 194.
  Israel, 194.
  James, 284.
  John, 193-195, 215, 230, 247.
  Joseph, 194.
  Mary, 194.
  Robert, 103, 192-195, 274, 311, 337, 405, 407, 408, 410.
  Ruth, 194.
  Sarah, 194.
Pikes, see Weapons.
Pillion, see Horse Equipment.
Pillows, see Furnishings.
Pin cushions, see Furnishings.
Pinder, ——, 6, 9, 10.
  John, 329.
Pine Island, 108.
Pingrie, Pengre, Pengrie, Pengrow, Pengry, Pingrin, Aaron, 285, 441.
  Moses, 223, 273, 274, 285, 291, 307.
Pins, 166, 180, 204.
Pins, see also Tools.
Piscataqua, 292.
Pistols, see Weapons.
Pit, brass, 27.
Pitchforks, see Tools.
Pitford, Peter, 289.
Pitman, Pittman, Mark, 457.
  Nathaniel, 13.
  Thomas, 60, 457.
Pits, 198, 322.
Pitt, Pitte, William, 412.
Pittice, Pittis, John, 155.
  Margaret, 155.
Planes, see Tools.
Planks, see Manufactures.
Planter, see Trades.
Planters, old, 365.
Plasse, William, 49.
Plates, see Utensils.
Platters, see Utensils.
Platts, Elizabeth, 436.

Platts, Jonathan, 453.
  Moses, 296.
  Samuel, 296, 302.
Ploughs, see Tools.
Plum Island, 7, 394, 433.
Plummer, Plumer, Francis, 153.
  Joseph, 433.
  Samuel, 303.
Plush, see Cloth.
Podd, Samuel, 235.
Pole, iron, 174.
Pollard, George, 59, 60.
Pomery, Pomary, John, 359, 361.
Poole, ——, 131.
Pore, Joseph, 417.
Pork, see Food.
Porringers, see Utensils.
Porter, Portor, ——, 227, 302, 306.
  Hannah, 306.
  John, 96, 97, 304, 306, 316, 376, 380, 389, 421, 422.
  Jonathan, 181.
  Nathaniel, 26, 38.
  Samuel, 306.
Portsmouth, 390.
Posnet, see Utensils.
Pot hooks, see Utensils.
Pots, see Utensils.
Potter, Poter, Ann, 161, 227, 228, 318.
  Anthony, 366.
  Luke, 44.
  Nicholas, 91, 136, 143, 213.
Poultry, see Fowls.
Powder, see Weapons.
Powell, ——, 235.
Pressing irons, see Utensils.
Price, ——, 58, 101, 119, 380, 422.
  Capt., 365.
  Matthew, 454.
  Theodore, 453.
  Walter, 13, 57, 147, 172, 181, 226, 320, 330, 366, 382, 420, 432, 448, 452.
Pride, John, 91.
Priest, James, 452, 453.
Prime, Mark, 328.
Prince, ——, 34, 36.
  Richard, 159, 303, 304, 320, 385.
Procter, Prockter, Proctor, ——, 6, 95.
  John, 156, 157.
Pudne, John, 451.

Punches, *see* Tools.
Purchase, Purchas, Purchis, Oliver, 305, 343, 353-355, 380.
Purse, *see* Clothing.
Putnam, Putman, Putnum, John, 434.
  Thomas, 18, 24, 422, 434.
Pynchon, ——, 314.

**Quadrant**, *see* Vessels.
Quern, *see* Tools.
Quilter, ——, 25.
  Joseph, 167.
  Mark, 167, 177, 329, 330.
  Mary, 167, 223.
  Rebecca, 167.
  Sarah, 167.
Quilts, *see* Furnishings.

**Raisins**, *see* Food.
Rakes, *see* Tools.
Ramsdell, John, 248.
Randall, ——, 408.
  John, 104.
Rane, Robert, 347.
Rapier, *see* Weapons.
Rawlison, Thomas, 219.
Rawson, Edward, 8, 14, 65, 68, 87, 162, 338, 344.
Rayment, Raimant, Raiment, Rament, Raymend, Raymont, John, 185, 238, 264, 306.
  Rachel, 263.
  Richard, 268.
  William, 457.
Reyner, Raner, Rayner, Raynor, Reiner, Reynor, ——, 351.
  Elder, 237, 295.
  Elizabeth, 265.
  Humphry, 81, 86, 93, 98, 99, 117, 129, 206-208, 320, 321.
  John, 321.
  Marmaduke, 322.
  Mary, 321, 322.
  William, 265, 370.
Razor, 354.
Rea, Ray, Daniel, 288, 375-377.
  Joshua, 375, 376.
  Rebecca, 375.
  Sarah, 375.
Read, Reade, Reed, ——, 415.
  Col., 415.
  Esdras, 57, 77.
  Richard, 315.
  Thomas, 415, 416.

Reading, 283, 284, 314.
Reap hooks, *see* Tools.
Redington, Abraham, 267.
Redknap, Joseph, 91.
Redverne, Isabel, 117.
Reedy marsh, 144.
Remington, Reminton, Lt., 177, 233.
  Rhoda, 400.
Rhode Island, 234.
Rhodes, Rhods, Roads, Henry, 430.
Rial Side, 389.
Ribbon, *see* Cloth.
Richards, Edward, 250, 346, 347.
Richardson, Edward, 247.
  Elizabeth, 247.
  William, 216, 247.
Ring, Ringe, Daniel, 368, 369.
  Hester, 438.
  Isaac, 368, 438.
  Joseph, 438.
  Mary, 368, 369.
  Roger, 368.
  Sarah, 369.
  Susanna, 369.
Rings, *see* Clothing, and Tools.
Rix, Ricks, Margaret, 118.
  Thomas, 289.
Robbins, Robins, Samuel, 424.
  Thomas, 159, 199, 275, 422.
Roberts, Roberds, John, 422.
  Robert, 170, 422, 423.
  Susanna, 422, 423.
Robinson, Robbinson, Abraham, 102, 386, 387.
  John, 78, 159, 267.
  William, 25, 256, 319.
Roby, Henry, 424.
  Samuel, 424.
Rogers, Rodgers, Roggers, Rojers, ——, 30, 52, 93, 110, 111, 120, 187, 298, 303, 333, 436.
  Daniel, 222, 427.
  Elizabeth, 434.
  Ezekiel, 110, 114, 115, 121, 128, 129, 170, 203, 206, 228, 300, 321, 331, 333-336.
  John, 82, 222, 223, 434.
  Margaret, 82, 223.
  Mary, 332, 334, 335.
  Nathaniel, 9, 82, 88, 104, 156, 222, 225, 333.
  Richard, 331.

Rogers, Robert, 433, 434.
  Samuel, 223.
  Susanna, 433, 434.
  Thomas, 434.
  Timothy, 223, 225.
  William, 259.
Rolfe, Raffe, Ralfe, Roafe, Rof, Rofe, Roff, Roffe, Rolf, Roof,
  Anna, 138.
  Benjamin, 137, 138, 339, 437, 438.
  Daniel, 122, 176, 203, 217, 218.
  Ezra, 149, 150.
  Hannah, 176, 217-219.
  Henry, 21.
  Hester, 149.
  Honor, 137, 138.
  John, 21, 84, 137, 194, 438, 439.
  Marie, 438.
  Mary, 84.
  Rebecca, 438.
  Thomas, 258.
Ropes, *see* Tools.
Rootes, Thomas, 256, 268, 363, 364, 419, 445, 449.
Rooton, Rooten, Rowton, Edmond, 429, 430.
  Richard, 27, 152, 429, 430.
Roper, Walter, 440.
Ropes, George, 41.
Ross, Killicrest, 171.
Rotterdam, Holland, 333.
Row, Roe, Bridget, 381.
  Hugh, 380.
  John, 380, 381.
Rowden, Rowdon, John, 389, 421.
Rowell, Jacob, 395, 397.
  Joanna, 401.
  Marjory, 395, 397.
  Sarah, 401.
  Thomas, 395, 397.
  Valentine, 146, 395, 401.
Rowland, Rouland, Roulland, ——, 412.
  Joseph, 411, 412.
  Mary, 349, 411, 412.
  Richard, 348, 413.
  Samuel, 349, 411.
Rowley, 60, 72, 80, 81, 84, 86, 92-94, 98, 109-111, 113-117, 120, 128, 129, 140, 174, 187, 202, 206, 207, 209, 217-219, 223, 230-232, 235, 238, 244, 250, 251, 253, 259, 294-297, 300,

Rowley, *continued*, 301, 312, 320, 321, 327-331, 333-336, 338, 351, 352, 371, 372, 390, 432, 435, 436, 441, 443, 453.
Rowley, Eng., 332.
Rowlinson, Rowlandson, Rowlison, Bridget, 32.
  Joseph, 122.
  Thomas, 32, 169.
Roxbury, 7, 8.
Ruck, Rucke, Ruckes, ——, 41, 347.
  Elizabeth, 456.
  Hannah, 456.
  John, 414, 456.
  Sarah, 456.
  Thomas, 346, 456.
Ruffs, *see* Clothing.
Rugs, *see* Furnishings.
Rum, *see* Drinks.
Rumball, Rumbal, ——, 49, 227.
Rumney Marsh, 44, 100, 177, 213, 248, 250, 313, 314, 345, 355, 402, 403.
Rupert, Prince, 149.
Russell, ——, 313, 407.
Rye, *see* Food.
Ryly, Henry, 302.

Sacks, *see* Utensils.
Saddles, *see* Horse Equipment.
Sadler, Anthony, 121.
  Martha, 121.
Safeguards, *see* Clothing.
Sagamore hill, 429.
Saier, Sarah, 336.
Salem, 3, 6, 10-13, 18, 21, 24-26, 34, 36, 37-43, 46, 49-51, 57, 58, 65, 67, 73, 74, 77, 91, 96, 101, 117-119, 123, 136, 143, 146, 149, 159, 161, 171-173, 177, 181-186, 195, 198-200, 210, 211, 226-228, 235, 238, 240, 241, 243, 254-257, 263-268, 269, 275, 280, 281, 287-289, 303, 304, 311, 316, 318, 320, 323, 326, 347, 351, 357, 360, 363-366, 375, 381-384, 388-390, 396, 410, 413-416, 418-420, 432, 435, 436, 444, 446, 450, 452-455, 458.
Salisbury, 21, 23, 40, 102, 121, 130, 140, 145, 150, 158, 192, 193, 195, 273, 311, 312, 336, 397, 399, 401, 403, 404, 406-410, 424-426, 438, 442, 443.

INDEX 503

Sallows, Salace, Sallos, Sallowes, Sollas, ——, 35.
　Abigail, 418.
　Freeborn, 418.
　Grace, 418, 444, 445.
　Hannah, 418.
　John, 59.
　Martha, 59.
　Mary, 418, 444.
　Michael, 58, 59.
　Robert, 59, 418, 444.
　Samuel, 59.
　Sarah, 418.
　Thomas, 59, 418, 419, 444.
Salmon, Daniel, 225.
Salmon, see Fish.
Salt, see Food.
Salt cellars, see Utensils.
Salt marsh, 16, 27, 36, 44, 83, 84, 102, 108, 112, 113, 143, 147, 154, 160, 177, 192, 208, 239, 241, 242, 244, 248, 250, 286, 287, 292, 298, 302, 307, 309, 310, 330, 339, 345, 347, 355, 365, 372, 375, 376, 390, 402-404, 406, 425, 426, 431, 441, 458.
Saltonstall, Saltenstall, ——, 4, 7, 9, 367.
　Richard, 4, 6, 8-10, 16, 114.
Sams, Thomas, 60.
Samson, ——, 457.
Sanden, Sandie, Sandin, Sandy, Arthur, 60, 315.
　John, 176.
　Mary, 176.
Sanders, Saunders, Hester, 438.
　James, 427.
　John, 16, 17, 21, 26, 67, 68, 71, 102, 187, 438.
Sandwich, 6, 9.
Sandy bridge, 112.
Sargent, Sarieant, Seargant, Sergeant, Sergent, Elizabeth, 190.
　William, 108, 148, 149, 425, 442.
Satin, see Cloth.
Saucers, see Utensils.
Saws, see Tools.
Savage, Savidg, Savige, ——, 100, 136, 425.
　Capt., 313, 355.
　Jeremiah, 134.
Sawyer, Sawer, Sawier, Edward, 80.

Sawyer, Henry, 400.
　William, 20, 311.
Sawyer's Island, 244.
Sawyer's plain, 270, 271.
Scales and weights, see Tools.
Scarfs, see Clothing.
Scarlet, Anne, 24.
　Joseph, 24.
　Margaret, 24.
　Mary, 24.
Schooling, 220.
Schools, 62, 94, 125, 126.
Scissors, see Tools.
Scotland, 354, 355.
Scott, Scot, Abigail, 168.
　Benjamin, 203.
　Elizabeth, 168.
　Hannah, 168.
　John, 256.
　Margaret, 258, 259.
　Mary, 168-170.
　Sarah, 168-170.
　Thomas, 28, 32, 109, 168-170, 258, 259.
Scott's Hill, 393.
Scruggs, Margery, 186.
　Thomas, 185.
　William, 185.
Scudder, Scuddr, Scuder, ——, 227.
　Elizabeth, 268, 269.
　Henry, 268.
　John, 118, 268.
　Mary, 118.
　Thomas, 268, 269.
　William, 268.
Scullard, Scullar, Sculler, Mary, 83, 84.
　Samuel, 53, 82, 84.
　Sarah, 83, 84.
Scythes, see Tools.
Seal, gold, 161.
Seaman, see Trades.
Sedgwick, Maj., 172.
Seed corn, 374.
Seers, Seeres, Mary, 342.
　Thomas, 342.
Serge, see Cloth.
Servants, 6, 9, 10, 13, 15, 25, 107, 120, 141, 161, 198, 223, 228, 328, 333, 385, 405, 433, 439.
Settles, see Furniture.
Severance, Severans, John, 405, 408.
　Lydia, 401.

Sewall, Henry, 232, 233.
  Stephen, 446.
Shackles, see Tools.
Shaflen, Shafling, Shaflinge, George, 160.
  Michael, 182.
  Myhill, 42.
Shag, see Cloth.
Shallop, see Vessels.
Sharpe, ——, 101.
  Elisha, 148.
Shatswell, Sachell, Satchell, Satchwell, Satswell, Seatchwell, ——, 6-9, 111, 112, 329.
  Hannah, 425, 427.
  Johan, 60, 61.
  John, 60, 61.
  Lydia, 425.
  Mary, 424.
  Richard, 60, 61.
  Susanna, 425, 426.
  Theophilus, 61, 240, 290, 337, 353, 424-428.
  William, 7.
Shaw, Joseph, 370, 407.
Shawsheen river, 397.
Sheaffe, ——, 119.
Shearing, 190, 191.
Shears, see Tools.
Sheep, see Animals (domestic).
Sheets, see Furnishings.
Shelter Island, 318.
Sherman, Sharman, Shearman, ——, 85.
  Edmund, 234.
  Nathaniel, 375.
  Philip, 234.
  Richard, 235.
  Samuel, 234, 375.
  Thomas, 6.
Sherratt, Hugh, 290.
Shifts, see Clothing.
Ship, see Vessels.
Shipley, Ann, 35.
Shirts, see Clothing.
Shoemaker, see Trades.
Shoes, see Clothing.
Shops, see Buildings.
Short, Shorte, Shortt, ——, 391, 392.
  Henry, 13, 22, 65, 79, 83, 84, 116, 230, 232, 233, 247, 293, 309, 311, 392, 395, 437-439.
Shot, see Weapons.
Shove, ——, 80.

Shovels, see Tools.
Shrimpton, ——, 119.
  Edward, 51.
Shropshere, Elizabeth, 438.
Shuttles, see Tools.
Sibly, John, 347.
  Rachel, 347, 348.
Sickles, see Tools.
Sieves, see Utensils.
Sign post, 188.
Sign (tavern?), 188.
Silk, 70, 344, 431.
Silsby, Sillsbey, Henry, 403.
Singeltarie, Singltary, Jonathan, 425.
  Richard, 40.
Skelton, ——, 10.
  Samuel, 10.
Skerry, Skerie, Skerrie, Frances, 312.
  Henry, 36, 41, 196, 198, 199, 276, 416, 444.
Skiff, see Vessels.
Skimmers, see Utensils.
Skins, 33, 170, 174, 180, 221, 322.
  Bear, 242, 381.
  Calves, 32, 70.
  Calves, tanned, 302.
  Cows, 267.
  Goat, 32.
  Moose, 458.
Skipper, Skeper, Kathrine, 99, 100.
Skirts, see Clothing.
Sleds, see Tools.
Sleighs, see Tools.
Smal, Thomas, 451.
Smith, Smeth, Smyth, ——, 105, 339, 449.
  Lt., 417.
  Edith, 78.
  Edward, 237.
  George, 285, 364.
  Hannah, 237, 453.
  Henry, 202.
  Hugh, 120, 174, 235-238, 251, 435, 448, 453.
  James, 42, 348, 349, 410, 411, 413.
  Joanna, 203.
  John, 120, 134, 183, 202, 203, 244, 351, 352.
  Martha, 237, 443.
  Mary, 19, 20, 236-238, 348, 349, 363, 364, 410, 412, 413.

Smith, Nathaniel, 133-136.
  Richard, 393.
  Samuel, 18, 20, 236, 237.
  Sarah, 19, 237, 351, 435.
  Thomas, 19, 20, 42, 132, 181, 203, 216, 241, 323, 363.
Smoothing irons, see Utensils.
Snuffers, see Utensils.
Soap, see Manufactures.
Somerby, Somerbe, Somersby, Sumerby, Anthony, 86, 87, 150, 153, 160, 205, 216, 246, 293, 310, 340, 342, 437, 438.
  Daniel, 150.
  Elizabeth, 150.
  Henry, 79, 150.
  Judith, 150.
  Sarah, 150.
South, Soth, ——, 131, 136.
Southmate, Southmead, Millissent, 101.
  William, 101.
Southton, Eng., 104.
Southwick, Setchwick, Setheck, Sethick, Sethwick, Sothwick, Sothwicke, Southick, Southweeke, Southwicke, Sughtwike, Sutchicke, Sutheke, Suthick, Suthicke, Suthweek, ——, 39, 41, 228.
  Daniel, 318, 319.
  Deborah, 318.
  John, 318, 319, 451.
  Josiah, 226, 227, 318.
  Lawrence, 161, 318, 319.
  Provided, 318, 319.
  Samuel, 319.
  Sarah, 319.
South river, 375, 376.
Sowe's Brook, 291.
Spades, see Tools.
Spain, 292.
Spaulding, see Spolding.
Spaule, Spule, Thomas, 235.
Spencer, Spenser, Garrett, 159.
  Jerard, 27.
  John, 107, 108.
  Michael, 159.
  Thomas, 107, 108.
Spices, see Food.
Spicket hill, 337.
Spicket river, 336, 425.
Spinning wheels, see Tools.
Spits, see Utensils.

Spofford, Spaffard, Spawforth, John, 170, 436.
  William, 9.
Spolding, Spouldyng, Edward, 77.
Spooner, ——, 414.
  Elizabeth, 456.
  Thomas, 183, 413, 414, 455, 456.
Spoons, see Utensils.
Sports, 332.
Sprage, Lt., 311.
Spurs, see Horse Equipment.
Stackhouse, Richard, 289.
Stacy, Stace, ——, 405.
  John, 454.
  Rebecca, 404, 405.
  Simon, 366.
  Thomas, 278, 280, 366.
Stainwood, Staynwood, Philip, 343, 388.
Stanian, Anthony, 407.
Stanly, Mathy, 271.
Stanwood, see Stainwood.
Staples, see Tools.
Starr, Robert, 331.
Stebines, John, 400.
Steel, see Metals.
Steelyard, see Tools.
Steers, see Animals (domestic).
Stevens, Steevens, Stephens, Stevenes, ——, 119, 172.
  Benjamin, 377.
  Elizabeth, 153, 154, 377, 378.
  Ephraim, 377.
  John, 153, 377, 378.
  Joseph, 377.
  Mary, 377.
  Nathan, 377.
  Richard, 15.
  Samuel, 153.
  Timothy, 377.
  Walter, 15.
  William, 148, 153, 359.
Stickney, Sticknah, Stickne, Andrew, 297.
  Samuel, 303.
  William, 80, 371.
Stiles, Robert, 268.
Stillman, Stileman, ——, 227.
  Elias, 159, 162, 182, 185, 186, 197, 199, 213, 227, 242, 243, 320, 390, 414, 419, 432, 454.
Stirrups, see Horse Equipment.
Stockings, see Clothing.

Stocks, 172.
Stoder, Barbara, 257.
Stomacher, *see* Clothing.
Stone, John, 333.
  Samuel, 333.
Stools, *see* Furniture.
Stow, Nathaniel, 177, 327.
Stuart, Stuward, Sarah, 449.
  William, 449.
Stuff, *see* Cloth.
Sudbury, 215.
Suet, *see* Food.
Sugar, *see* Food.
Sussex, Walter, 361.
Swan, Richard, 202, 203, 233, 301, 390, 443.
  Robert, 425.
Swaysy, John, 118.
  Katherine, 118.
Swett, Sweat, Sweett, Benjamin, 158, 246, 342.
  John, 83.
  Stephen, 216, 217, 408.
Swine, *see* Animals (domestic).
Swinerton, Swinnerton, Job, 417, 421.
Swords, *see* Weapons.
Sylvester, Silvester, Nathaniel, 318, 319.
Symonds, Simmons, Simonds, Simons, Symens, Symmons, Symons, ——, 7, 8, 79, 163.
  Harliken, 171.
  Jane, 296.
  Joanna, 285, 286.
  John, 171.
  Mark, 47, 48, 62, 63, 84-86, 125, 127, 285, 286.
  Martha, 171.
  Priscilla, 171.
  Ruth, 171.
  Samuel, 114, 122, 170, 171, 257, 275, 290, 352, 353, 381, 388, 405, 443, 455.
  William, 171, 175, 425.

Table boards, *see* Furniture.
Table linen, *see* Furnishings.
Tables, *see* Furniture.
Taffety, *see* Cloth.
Tailor, *see* Trades.
Talbey, Talby, Tarbey, Anne, 40.
  John, 39, 40, 434.
  Stephen, 40.
Tallow, *see* Manufactures.

Tally, Thomas, 119.
Tamme, *see* Cloth.
Tar, 172.
Tarbey, *see* Talbey.
Taylor, Tayler, ——, 424.
  George, 430.
Tayre, Roger, 150.
Tenney, Tene, Tenny, Ann, 207.
  Elizabeth, 333.
  Thomas, 80, 118, 352.
  William, 303.
Tewksbury, Henry, 437.
Thatcher, Thacher, Theacher, ——, 256.
  Anthony, 3.
  Thomas, 107, 108.
Thomas, Alice, 343, 344.
  Evan, 343.
  James, 50.
  John, 28.
Thompson, *see* Tompson.
Thore, John, 42.
Thorndike, John, 20, 270, 418.
Thorne, John, 50.
Thread, 13, 38, 45, 70, 78, 85, 158, 164, 180, 198, 204, 322, 344, 360, 431.
Thurston, ——, 177.
  Daniel, 176, 205, 218.
  John, 37, 38.
Tibbott, Tibbot, Walter, 132, 133.
Ticking, *see* Cloth.
Tildisleg, Francis, 94.
Tiler, ——, 59.
  Nathaniel, 33.
Tilton, Tillton, ——, 429.
  Daniel, 370, 371.
  Samuel, 370, 371, 424.
  William, 26, 56, 124, 155.
Ting, Edward, 362, 363.
Titcombe, Titcom, Tittcum, Johan, 86, 87, 187, 215.
Tobacco, 51, 65, 118, 119, 132, 282, 431.
Tod, Todd, John, 177, 232, 233, 237, 260, 272, 300, 302, 303, 312, 329, 351, 408.
Tomlins, Edward, 26.
  Timothy, 24.
Tompkins, John, 416.
  Ralph, 256.
Tompson, Tomson, Alexander, 418.
  Simon, 81, 235.

# INDEX

Tongs, *see* Tools, and Utensils.
Tools, implements, etc., 18, 20, 22, 23, 33, 39, 42, 44, 47, 49, 54, 55, 64, 80, 81, 97, 102, 107, 123, 130, 144, 146, 149, 162, 172-174, 176, 180, 192, 204, 210, 239, 243, 246, 256, 260, 263, 265-267, 269, 271, 274, 277, 282, 286, 295, 304, 316, 322, 350, 370, 377, 400, 406, 434, 455, 456.
Adze, 90, 165, 180, 198, 211, 216, 279, 341, 378, 381.
Anvils, 49, 149.
Augers, 48, 64, 70, 71, 90, 98, 102, 125, 127, 142, 176, 180, 183, 192, 198, 211, 249, 279, 312, 341, 379, 381, 388, 456.
Awls, 70, 192, 279.
Axe, cooper's, 180, 198.
Axe, mortising, 201.
Axe, pole, 383.
Axes, 14, 18, 27, 29, 30, 32, 33, 39, 42, 45, 48, 50, 54-56, 64, 71, 75, 77, 80, 85, 89, 90, 92, 95, 98, 100, 107, 121, 123, 125, 127, 131, 133, 140, 142, 148, 154, 157, 161, 162, 165-167, 169, 173-176, 180, 183, 185, 188-192, 198, 203-205, 208, 211, 214, 216, 220, 229, 233, 247, 254, 256, 262, 265, 269, 271, 276, 277, 279, 281, 282, 284, 286, 289, 302, 304, 308, 311, 316, 322, 324, 326, 335, 337, 341, 342, 352-354, 358, 368, 370, 374, 376-378, 381, 383, 393, 395, 396, 398, 403, 407, 413, 417, 419, 423, 431, 441, 445, 449, 451, 455, 456.
Axle-pin, 291, 374.
Bands, 71.
Battlelor, 128.
Beakhorn, 49.
Beam and leaden weights, 192.
Beam and scales, 70, 233, 414.
Beetle rings, 45, 64, 78, 80, 157, 167, 188, 190, 202, 218, 229, 253, 262, 280, 284, 305, 311, 337, 342, 344, 352, 353, 383, 396, 398, 449.
Beetles, 33, 48, 75, 89, 174, 176, 205, 279, 282, 286, 308, 335, 374, 379, 403, 423, 441.
Beeving bill, 14.

Tools.
Bellows, 41, 43, 45, 49, 149, 166, 212, 393.
Bill, black, 316.
Bill rings, 183.
Bills, 30, 75, 89, 90, 165, 167, 169, 180, 198, 374.
Bits, 180.
Blocks, 386.
Board irons, 152.
Bodkins, 233.
Bodkins, silver, 46, 139, 179.
Bolsters, iron, 49.
Bolts, 130, 172, 208, 302, 352, 379, 429.
Borers, 216, 247, 304.
Box iron, 275, 279, 308.
Braces, 180.
Brake, double, 379.
Brakes, 21, 125, 245, 434.
Brand irons, 85, 195, 337.
Briske, 130.
Broad axe, 48, 89, 176, 279, 311.
Brush bill, 85.
Bung borer, 198.
Burnishing steel, 49.
Cards, 57, 155, 174, 251, 254, 265, 271, 274, 277, 282, 293, 301, 308, 322, 341, 351, 352, 371, 396, 403, 449, 455, 458.
Cards, tow, 201.
Cards, wool, 214, 243, 342.
Carpenter's tools, 51, 152, 218, 288, 370, 396, 426, 429.
Cart body, 379, 449.
Cart irons, 83.
Cart ropes, 70, 90, 142, 158, 180, 206, 208, 212, 262, 277, 302, 308, 335, 352, 403, 426.
Cart, stone, 379.
Carts, 20, 22, 30, 61, 71, 80, 83, 90, 106, 109, 112, 124, 130, 131, 133, 142, 154, 157, 161, 162, 168, 170, 176, 180-183, 189, 191, 205, 208, 214, 218, 225, 229, 236, 245, 260, 267, 277, 286, 289, 302, 308, 311, 319, 322, 328, 335, 341, 351-353, 370, 372, 377, 380, 383, 388, 395, 403, 407, 409, 417, 423, 426, 431, 441, 456, 458.
Catches, 180.
Chain, brass, 49.
Chain, draft, 407.
Chain, timber, 407.

Tools.
  Chain, trammel, 14.
  Chains, 30, 56, 70, 71, 80, 85, 90, 97, 100, 106, 109, 112, 124, 130, 142, 154, 157, 158, 180, 192, 208, 211, 212, 218, 236, 279, 291, 301, 302, 308, 311, 335, 337, 341, 352, 353, 370, 374, 377, 379, 380, 395, 396, 400, 407, 409, 417, 422, 426, 456, 458.
  Chisels, 14, 36, 45, 48, 64, 70, 90, 142, 180, 211, 229, 278, 279, 322, 379.
  Cimmet, 350.
  Cleavers, 154, 186, 211, 341, 374, 383.
  Clenzer, 233.
  Clevis, 180.
  Clouts, 180.
  Collars, 181, 188.
  Collier's tools, 305.
  Colter, 32, 90, 112, 124, 180, 370, 379, 396.
  Compasses, 180, 198.
  Crackell, 125.
  Crank, 337.
  Cressets, 198.
  Crook, iron, 216.
  Crooks, 70, 112, 239.
  Crows, 89, 142, 180, 211, 229, 232, 315.
  Dibble, 89.
  Door latches, 180.
  Dovetail, 279.
  Draft, 124.
  Draft shave, 30, 70, 201, 216, 247.
  Draft yoke, 279.
  Drag, 203.
  Drag prongs, 395.
  Drawing knives, 45, 98, 125, 148, 180, 182, 198, 388.
  Drill box, 49.
  Ears, 308.
  Edge tools, 335.
  Esses, 158.
  Fans, 124, 170, 205, 286, 353, 374.
  Fetters, 180, 374, 376, 379.
  File hafts, 49.
  Files, 49, 70, 149, 180, 233.
  Foot, iron, 75, 216.
  Fork tines, 203.
  Forks, 153, 157, 180, 192, 233, 263, 271, 284, 308, 335, 352, 353, 379, 403, 407.

Tools.
  Forks, dung, 75, 208, 281, 344.
  Frows, 30, 48, 52, 64, 71, 90, 130, 180, 188, 198, 211, 214, 286, 378.
  Frows, clapboard, 249.
  Furnace, brass, 201, 243.
  Furnace, copper, 181.
  Furnace, iron, 378.
  Furnaces, 188.
  Gallow balk, 208.
  Gallows, 49.
  Gears, 80, 87.
  Gimbals, 14.
  Gimlet, 45, 70, 216, 279.
  Gins, 172.
  Gouges, 14, 45, 48, 70, 142, 216, 229, 278, 279.
  Graplin, 447.
  Grindstones, 21, 42, 64, 71, 90, 112, 128, 130, 142, 148, 149, 152, 155, 170, 183, 192, 198, 200, 212, 218, 249, 250, 279, 286, 288, 337, 378, 381, 386, 407.
  Grubaxe, 30, 216.
  Hales, 77, 112, 189.
  Hammer, hack, 49.
  Hammer, lathing, 42, 214.
  Hammer, stone, 42.
  Hammers, 30, 49, 52, 57, 64, 70, 78, 89, 142, 148, 149, 155, 161, 169, 180, 182, 183, 202, 211, 214, 216, 229, 233, 316, 341, 374, 381, 383, 388, 398, 431.
  Handbar, 71.
  Handbills, 14.
  Hand-carts, 21.
  Handhook, 216.
  Hand irons, 99, 200.
  Hand saws, 30, 45, 50, 56, 64, 70, 71, 75, 90, 98, 100, 107, 125, 165, 168, 169, 182, 192, 198, 205, 211, 216, 229, 247, 249, 265, 278, 311, 341, 342, 403, 449, 457.
  Hare, 32, 89.
  Harnesses, 216, 414.
  Harrow tines, 22, 75.
  Harrow tooth, 203, 322.
  Harrows, 20, 71, 91, 112, 124, 142, 181, 191, 205, 212, 262, 291, 456, 458.
  Hartops, 49.

INDEX 509

Tools.
  Hatchets, 5, 15, 27, 30, 45, 48, 52, 64, 71, 89, 130, 140, 161, 182, 183, 185, 192, 195, 198, 247, 281, 286, 316, 341, 376.
  Hay knife, 189, 229.
  Hearth staff, 49.
  Heckell, 249.
  Heckell, double, 249.
  Hedgebill, 341.
  Hedge hook, 71.
  Heels, 253, 302.
  Hinges, 5, 46, 176, 180.
  Hoe, broad, 54, 286, 398, 407.
  Hoe, grubbing, 188.
  Hoes, 5, 18, 22, 29, 32, 33, 42, 45, 46, 48, 50, 52, 56, 57, 71, 75, 77, 89, 90, 107, 121, 130, 140, 142, 148, 165, 174-176, 180, 188, 190-192, 198, 201, 203-205, 216, 218, 220, 229, 233, 247, 251, 257, 262, 271, 277, 279, 282, 308, 315, 335, 337, 341, 342, 344, 353, 374, 378, 381, 388, 413, 417, 423, 431, 434, 441, 449, 455, 456.
  Holdfast, 64, 80.
  Hooks, 15, 29, 46, 70, 112, 124, 125, 132, 142, 153, 183, 193, 247, 388.
  Hooks and eyes, 75.
  Hoops, 89, 180, 202, 449.
  Hoops, beetle, 302.
  Hoops, iron, 192, 250, 374.
  Hoops, scythe, 203.
  Hoops, trussing, 198.
  Horse comb, 112.
  Howels, 198.
  Husbandry tools, 426.
  Iron, 70, 85, 112, 158, 180, 250, 301, 337, 413.
  Iron beam, 95.
  Iron gears, 245.
  Iron, old, 14, 18, 27, 39, 45, 46, 57, 70, 75, 77, 85, 112, 127, 186, 189, 192, 212, 226, 249, 279, 379.
  Iron tools, 93, 183, 208, 226, 251, 316, 400, 424.
  Ironmonger's ware, 382.
  Irons, 61, 212.
  Jack, 67, 89, 112, 232, 335, 391, 432.
  Joiners, 180, 198, 357, 358.
  Joints, 90, 169.

Tools.
  Knife, currier's, 158.
  Knives, cutting, 70, 195.
  Knives, shredding, 322, 341.
  Ladders, 5, 48, 57, 71, 112, 123, 148, 165, 181, 183, 186, 214, 216, 247, 344, 378, 434.
  Lasts, 70, 87, 192.
  Linch pins, 71, 291.
  Lists, 70.
  Loom tackling, 403.
  Looms, 37, 56, 77, 216, 236, 253, 324, 372, 403, 414, 456.
  Looms, woolen, 148.
  Marking iron, 112, 180.
  Mattocks, 27, 42, 57, 64, 75, 80, 89, 90, 109, 142, 148, 165, 174, 205, 229, 233, 378, 396.
  Maule, 281, 413.
  Mill, steel, 87, 112.
  Millstones, 212.
  Millstones, malt, 391.
  Molds, 149.
  Needles, 70, 139, 180, 204.
  Nibs, 70, 202, 216.
  Nippers, 201.
  Pan bore, 49.
  Peel, 90.
  Pick, 396.
  Pickaxes, 14, 92, 180, 216, 381.
  Piercer bits, 42, 180, 198, 279.
  Piercer stocks, 279.
  Piercers, 42.
  Pincers, 75, 169, 180, 183, 189, 192, 233, 279, 302.
  Pins, 180, 250, 407, 409.
  Pitchforks, 14, 30, 45, 48, 64, 71, 75, 78, 80, 90, 113, 128, 142, 148, 165, 226, 281, 286, 381, 388, 413.
  Planes, 42, 64, 70, 130, 279.
  Plough chains, 29, 32, 133, 183, 236, 257, 274, 286, 351, 441.
  Plough gear, 162, 229, 319.
  Plough harness, 388.
  Plough irons, 61, 142, 154, 155, 188, 192, 208, 212, 257, 262, 277, 284, 286, 353, 378, 379, 408, 431.
  Ploughshares, 157, 169, 380.
  Plough tackle, 170, 265-267, 271, 383, 403, 422.
  Ploughs, 20, 30, 61, 71, 80, 83, 90, 100, 106, 112, 124, 130, 133, 142, 154, 155, 161, 162,

Tools.
  Ploughs, *continued*, 168, 170,
    176, 181, 186, 188, 191, 192,
    208, 214, 218, 225, 229, 236,
    245, 260, 262, 265-267, 271,
    277, 282, 284, 291, 302, 308,
    311, 322, 328, 335, 341, 351-
    353, 368, 372, 374, 377, 379,
    383, 395, 396, 400, 403, 407,
    417, 423, 426, 429, 456, 458.
  Poles, 350.
  Pot, dung, 456.
  Prongs, 205, 247, 342, 377.
  Punches, cold, 49.
  Punches, forging hot, 49.
  Punches, iron, 249.
  Quern, 183.
  Quern, pepper, 203.
  Rail hooks, 36.
  Rakes, 39, 64, 80, 112, 263, 381, 407.
  Rakes, garden, 70, 75, 90, 127.
  Rakes, iron, 21.
  Reap hooks, 50, 71, 185, 201, 233, 262, 293, 312, 342, 381.
  Reeds, 77.
  Reels, 57, 293.
  Reems, 242.
  Riddle, 253.
  Ring pin, 71.
  Rings, 14, 56, 70, 216, 250, 253, 279, 284, 322, 352.
  Rings, iron, 148, 172, 205.
  Roast iron, 189.
  Ropes, 48, 61, 112, 129, 172, 267, 378, 381, 386, 403, 430.
  Ropes, gin, 172.
  Round shaves, 198.
  Saws, 14, 30, 32, 33, 42, 61, 64, 80, 90, 95, 98, 112, 127, 142, 149, 180, 183, 188, 190, 208, 229, 232, 254, 277, 286, 292, 304, 311, 326, 337, 374, 377, 381, 395, 431.
  Saws, *see also* Hand saws.
  Saws, crosscut, 75, 85, 90, 192, 205, 212, 214, 218, 239, 265, 266, 279, 281, 286, 322, 341, 368, 379, 399, 407.
  Saws, frame, 64, 169.
  Saws, hack, 169.
  Saws, mill, 407.
  Saws, tennant, 192, 216.
  Saws, thwart, 50, 198, 383.
  Scake, 157.

Tools.
  Scales, 181, 188, 229, 308, 381, 383, 448.
  Scales and weights, 82, 85, 90, 93, 95, 165, 201, 212, 233, 243, 245, 286, 303, 328, 344, 379, 388, 391, 451.
  Scales, wooden, 95, 176, 448.
  Scissors, 176, 180, 203, 233, 322, 424.
  Scythes, 5, 14, 45, 46, 50, 56, 61, 70, 80, 83, 85, 90, 124, 140, 142, 154, 155, 165, 167, 170, 176, 180, 183, 192, 198, 202, 216, 247, 254, 279, 282, 284, 286, 302, 308, 335, 342, 352, 367, 374, 381, 395, 403, 407, 434, 449.
  Search, 70.
  Shackles, 130, 208, 302, 352.
  Shares, 32, 71, 90, 109, 112, 124, 180, 374, 379.
  Shaves, 48, 64, 90, 265, 279, 316, 342, 381, 431.
  Shears, 33, 46, 70, 71, 89, 98, 170, 185, 233, 272, 286, 341, 379, 428, 431, 455.
  Shoemaker's lasts, 316.
  Shoemaker's tools, 316, 447.
  Shop tools, 163, 164, 308, 400.
  Shot weight, 414.
  Shovel tip, 89.
  Shovels, 14, 30, 41, 64, 71, 75, 80, 85, 149, 153, 154, 165, 174, 205, 233, 262, 282, 286, 341, 353, 374, 381, 388, 391, 430.
  Shuttle, 253, 414.
  Sickles, 48, 75, 90, 112, 142, 165, 170, 180, 218, 220, 233, 247, 251, 262, 282, 302, 322, 335, 342, 353, 374, 396, 398, 431.
  Sleds, 22, 71, 90, 142, 154, 161, 193, 205, 208, 253, 279, 286, 302, 308, 322, 335, 352, 377, 379, 383, 396, 400, 407.
  Sleighs, 216, 253, 324, 414, 456.
  Slings, 232.
  Smith's tools, 432.
  Snaths, 45, 176, 216, 226.
  Sockets, 382.
  Soles, iron, 229.
  Span shackle, 279, 284, 407, 409.
  Spades, 14, 30, 42, 45, 48, 56, 64, 71, 75, 77, 80, 89, 90, 92,

INDEX                                                                                          511

Tools.
  Spades, *continued*, 95, 112, 123, 128, 142, 148, 149, 154, 157, 165, 169, 174, 180, 182, 185, 188-190, 192, 198, 200, 203, 205, 208, 216, 218, 233, 247, 262, 265, 266, 274, 281, 282, 311, 341, 342, 344, 353, 368, 374, 378, 381, 391, 403, 407, 413, 431, 451.
  Spigot, 180.
  Spindle, 202, 216.
  Spinning wheels, 21, 22, 36, 39, 41, 42, 50, 57, 58, 63, 79, 90, 95, 142, 154, 167, 206, 208, 212, 214, 216, 240, 247, 251, 253, 277, 282, 293, 301, 302, 305, 308, 311, 322, 324, 326, 337, 342, 351, 352, 371, 377, 379, 388, 395, 396, 403, 413, 418, 419, 423, 424, 433, 445, 455, 458.
  Spinning wheels, linen, 58, 75, 90, 100, 107, 128, 167, 174, 180, 201, 272, 295, 305, 308, 335, 341, 431, 456.
  Spinning wheels, woolen, 75, 243, 308, 335, 341, 379, 424, 458.
  Spokeshave, 39.
  Spooling wheel, 216.
  Squares, 64, 176, 182, 249, 279.
  Staples, 193, 279.
  Staples, iron, 70, 205.
  Steel, 5.
  Steel tools, 400.
  Steeling iron, 70, 140, 383.
  Steelyards, 112, 258, 383, 386, 388.
  Stock locks, 90, 128.
  Stock nail tools, 49.
  Stool trees, 316.
  Storne plates, 49.
  Swings, 326.
  Tackling, 170, 236, 378.
  Teams, 25, 93, 335.
  Tenipel, 253.
  Thimble, 179, 382.
  Tongs, forging, 49.
  Tongs, vice, 49.
  Tow combs, 21, 71, 80, 337.
  Trap, iron or steel, 85, 183, 212.
  Trestle, 286.
  Trowels, 42, 45, 56, 89, 180, 216, 388.

Tools.
  Tumbrel, 157, 282, 286, 335, 353, 374, 378, 407, 458.
  Turns, 274.
  Tuter, 21.
  Twibill, 64.
  Vice, hand, 279.
  Vice, turn, 49.
  Vices, 49, 90, 149, 229, 350.
  Wagon, 271.
  Wain, 32, 124.
  Wain body, 5.
  Warping beam, 216.
  Warping woof, 253.
  Washers, 291.
  Watchbill, 341.
  Wedges, 14, 27, 29, 33, 45, 48, 52, 56, 64, 71, 75, 80, 85, 89, 98, 109, 125, 127, 131, 133, 142, 148, 149, 157, 161, 162, 165, 167, 169, 174, 175, 180, 183, 188, 189, 202, 204, 205, 212, 216, 218, 229, 253, 262, 271, 279, 280, 282, 284, 286, 302, 305, 308, 311, 315, 316, 335, 337, 342, 344, 352, 353, 374, 379, 381, 383, 395, 396, 398, 403, 419, 423, 431, 441, 445, 449, 451.
  Weights, 14, 75.
  Weights, lead, 95, 112, 128, 181, 183, 184, 216, 353, 448.
  Wheelbarrow wheel, 344.
  Wheelbarrows, 14, 75, 154, 165, 216, 381, 424, 434.
  Wheels, 5, 61, 71, 80, 93, 97, 124, 142, 153-155, 158, 165, 172, 180, 181, 189, 192, 205, 208, 226, 236, 242, 250, 263, 267, 271, 282, 286, 311, 322, 341, 351, 352, 370, 380, 388, 403, 407, 409, 423, 429, 430, 431, 440.
  Wheels, iron bound, 378.
  Whip saw, 39, 85, 172, 211, 212, 239, 249, 265, 266, 433.
  Wimbles, 45, 216, 322.
  Wimble-trees, 14.
  Winch, 64.
  Winding blades, 179.
  Winnowing sheets, 14, 71, 201, 376.
  Winopet, 97.
  Wire, brass, 180.
  Woodpress, 70.

512 INDEX

Tools.
  Wrenches, 49.
  Yoke chains, 61, 262.
  Yoke tire, 208.
  Yokes, 22, 30, 32, 61, 71, 80, 85, 90, 97. 100, 109, 112, 124, 130, 131, 142, 154, 155, 158, 181, 192, 208, 214, 218, 262, 284, 286, 301, 302, 308, 311, 335, 341, 352, 353, 370, 374, 377, 379, 395, 396, 400, 407, 426, 441, 456, 458.
Toppan, Tappan, Tappin, Tappine, ———, 138, 408.
  Abraham, 65, 68, 139, 216, 342, 394, 395, 433.
  Peter, 139, 342.
  Susan, 65.
  Susanna, 71.
Topsfield, 239, 267, 271, 324, 367, 398.
Torrey, Tore, Josiah, 453.
  Shadrach, 453.
  William, 453.
Tow, 56, 57, 165, 174.
Towels, see Furnishings.
Town, ———, 214.
Traces, see Horse Equipment.
Trades and Occupations.
  Blacksmith, see Smith.
  Brazier, 51.
  Carpenter, 3, 51, 62, 152, 238, 288, 370, 396, 426, 429, 441.
  Collier, 305.
  Constable, 410.
  Cooper, 180, 198.
  Cow keeper, 100, 256, 289, 431.
  Currier, 193.
  Docter, ship, 444.
  Ferryman, 41.
  Fisherman, 423, 454.
  Flaxman, 134.
  Gentleman, 110, 113, 215.
  Husbandman, 82, 204, 228, 231, 251, 260.
  Husbandry, 319, 426, 442.
  Ironmonger, 382, 403, 406.
  Mariner, 419.
  Mercer, 15, 16.
  Merchant, 15, 16, 230, 278, 444.
  Physician, 175, 365, 392.
  Planter, 53.
  Schoolmaster, 46.
  Seaman, 228.
  Shoemaker, 44, 87, 100, 316, 447.

Trades.
  Smith, 119, 350, 432.
  Soapmaker, 16.
  Tailor, 44, 326, 360.
  Weaver, 37, 82, 214-216, 273, 403.
  Wheelwright, 267.
  Yeoman, 153, 215, 230, 231, 392.
Trammels, see Utensils.
Trask, Traske, ———, 89.
  Capt., 228.
  Hannah, 318.
  Henry, 229, 318.
  Mary, 318.
  Sarah, 318.
  William, 159, 269.
Travers, Traverse, Bridget, 294.
  Henry, 292-294.
  James, 292, 294.
  Sarah, 293, 294.
Trays, see Utensils.
Tredwell, ———, 163, 164.
  Mary, 164, 166.
  Thomas, 166.
Trees, 186, 188.
  Apple, 4, 96, 186, 210, 257.
  Elm, 296, 299.
  Fruit, 96, 97.
  Oak, 291, 296-299.
  Pine, 291.
  Walnut, 297.
Trees, see also Orchards.
Trenchers, see Utensils.
Tresler, Treslor, Trusler, ———, 212.
  Edward, 211.
  Elinor, 211.
  Henry, 211.
  Nicholas, 211.
  Thomas, 143, 183.
Trevett, see Utensils.
Trimman, John, 187.
Troter, William, 433.
Troughs, see Utensils.
Trowels, see Tools.
Trucking cloth, see Cloth.
True, Henry, 58, 195, 311, 401.
  Israel, 195.
Trumble, Tromble, Trumball, Trumbell, Abigail, 259.
  Ann, 254, 259, 260.
  Hannah, 259, 453.
  John, 80, 174, 236, 253, 259, 302, 373, 432.

INDEX 513

Trumble, Joseph, 259, 303, 432,
    453, 454.
  Judah, 259.
  Mary, 259.
  Ruth, 259, 312.
Trunks, *see* Furniture,
Tubs, bark, 399.
Tubs, *see* Utensils.
Tucke, Robert, 148.
Tucker, Andrew, 454.
  John, 59.
  Nicholas, 454.
  Robert, 133.
  Roger, 323.
Tumbrel, *see* Tools.
Turkey Hill, 393.
Turner, Charles, 26.
  Rachel, 26.
Tuttle, Tuttell, ——, 313.
  Joanna, 278.
  John, 4, 277, 278, 314.
  Rebecca, 60.
  Simon, 277, 278, 336.
Twine, 180, 216, 232, 233.
Tyler, *see* Tiler.

Udale, Philip, 42.
Underwood, *see* Inderwood.
University, 27.
Unkaway, 268.
Upton, John, 451.
Usher, ——, 119.
Usselton, Frances, 268.
Utensils, Household, 76, 97, 106,
    142, 257, 303, 328, 342.
  Alchemy, 424.
  Andirons, 12, 27, 63, 66, 70, 75,
    89, 95, 98, 127, 129, 144, 148,
    154, 157, 160, 166, 172, 184,
    195, 198, 212, 214, 224, 229,
    242, 243, 246, 250, 256, 274,
    280, 286, 287, 293, 303, 310,
    322, 337, 341, 379, 391, 393,
    432, 447, 455.
  Bags, 5, 14, 33, 39, 48, 50, 56,
    57, 65, 71, 75, 79, 87, 97, 129,
    130, 166, 175, 180, 189, 202-
    204, 208, 232, 233, 251, 260,
    282, 288, 302, 308, 341, 342,
    352, 377, 381, 388, 391, 403,
    414, 419, 445, 454.
  Bags, leather, 93, 165.
  Bags, meal; 46, 155.
  Baking iron, 58.
  Baking pan, brass, 75.

Utensils.
  Baking pan, copper, 95.
  Baking pans, 77, 186, 224.
  Balk, iron, 433.
  Barrel heads, 180.
  Barrels, 22, 36, 39, 41, 42, 45,
    55, 56, 61, 70, 75, 79, 80, 85,
    89, 93, 95, 97, 142, 144, 155,
    157, 172, 175, 180, 182, 183,
    186, 189, 192, 212, 230, 239,
    243, 246, 256, 267, 269, 271,
    284, 308, 311, 315, 316, 319,
    322, 324, 326, 337, 350, 360,
    363, 370, 377, 379, 389, 396,
    400, 403, 418, 419, 424, 445, 454.
  Barrels, beer, 71, 75, 100, 153,
    157, 190, 214, 224, 250, 353.
  Barrels, drink, 125.
  Basin, pewter, 77, 144, 184, 189,
    229, 388, 391.
  Basin, pewter rim, 281.
  Basins, 80, 95, 148, 151, 157,
    160, 198, 200, 224, 243, 246,
    276, 280, 287, 293, 311, 312,
    341, 363, 377, 396, 412, 414,
    419, 445, 447, 457.
  Basket, hand, 308.
  Basket, Indian, 448.
  Basket, linen, 419, 445.
  Basket, table, 224, 230, 393.
  Basket, wicker, 224.
  Baskets, 5, 45, 70, 90, 93, 95,
    128, 151, 157, 165, 175, 216,
    226, 233, 265, 266, 271, 276,
    308, 310, 326, 341, 385, 389,
    414, 418, 432, 445, 447.
  Beaker, balk, 112.
  Beaker, silver, 20, 111, 288.
  Beakers, 63, 71, 79, 80, 144, 189,
    243, 341, 363, 419, 445, 446.
  Beef pricker, 391.
  Beerstall, 64, 224.
  Beer vessels, 5, 31, 48, 64, 216,
    218, 251, 280, 286, 308, 341,
    352, 398.
  Bellows, 5, 14, 33, 36, 48, 50, 63,
    70, 75, 80, 87, 89, 90, 93, 148,
    157, 165, 169, 174, 180, 182,
    183, 185, 198, 226, 233, 254, 258,
    264, 276, 341, 365, 388, 391.
  Bin, 350.
  Bottles, 89, 125, 153, 155, 157,
    164, 175, 176, 203, 204, 218,
    230, 271, 286, 287, 341, 370,
    391, 432.

514 INDEX

Utensils.
  Bottles, case of, 5, 39, 61, 93, 105, 148, 151, 192, 210, 230, 232, 246, 258, 341, 342, 344, 385, 423, 433.
  Bottles, jug, 415, 419, 445.
  Bottles, leather, 45, 85, 127, 189.
  Bottles, pewter, 48, 290, 316, 342.
  Bottles, stone, 87, 192, 414.
  Bottles, suckling, 415.
  Bottles, vinegar, 165.
  Bottles, wooden, 182, 216, 433.
  Bowls, 58, 70, 77, 80, 85, 89, 144, 184, 190, 200, 280, 293, 315, 341, 342, 353, 419, 445.
  Bowls, beer, 396.
  Bowls, drinking, 200.
  Bowls, glass, 79.
  Bowls, pewter, 446.
  Bowls, silver, 4, 89, 179, 185, 246, 384, 385.
  Bowls, silver wine, 404.
  Bowls, wine, 110, 388.
  Bowls, wooden, 50, 71.
  Brass, 20, 22, 47, 61, 73, 89, 93, 129, 137, 142, 143, 155, 179, 182, 227, 232, 240, 249, 258, 267, 272, 287, 295, 300, 301, 303, 328, 337, 344, 350, 353, 356, 357, 374, 386, 395, 400, 406, 415, 433, 440, 455, 456.
  Brass vessels, 162, 246, 277, 335, 352, 371.
  Brewing vessels, 151.
  Broiling irons, 56, 100.
  Brush, hat, 45, 157, 201.
  Brushes, 58, 70, 148, 157, 169, 172, 233, 276, 281, 286, 287, 295, 342, 370, 419, 433, 445.
  Bucket, brass, 287.
  Bucket and chain, 181.
  Buckets, 98, 205, 246, 247, 277, 293, 311, 341, 342.
  Buckets bale, 293.
  Butts, 71, 181, 342.
  Caldron, 31.
  Candlesticks, 27, 32, 36, 66, 70, 80, 105, 127, 154, 164, 182, 200, 210, 212, 233, 243, 253, 273, 282, 287, 302, 315, 363, 379, 388, 389, 393, 396, 451.
  Candlesticks, brass, 29, 39, 42, 57, 58, 63, 70, 99, 105, 112,

Utensils.
  Candlesticks, brass, *continued*, 113, 154, 157, 172, 183, 186, 203, 218, 224, 229, 242, 246, 280, 287, 310, 341, 363, 412, 414, 415, 419, 444-446.
  Candlesticks, hanging, 132, 183, 287.
  Candlesticks, iron, 64, 70, 90, 95, 214, 415.
  Candlesticks, pewter, 48, 7 89, 160, 186, 189, 229, 23 249, 286, 293, 316.
  Candlesticks, tin, 157, 184, 220.
  Candlesticks, wire, 184.
  Cans, 315, 379, 391.
  Case, 433.
  Case and glasses, 131, 182, 370.
  Casks, 6, 33, 61, 80, 148, 151, 161, 170, 180, 182, 189, 191, 210, 225, 226, 230, 250, 258 264, 295, 308, 360, 368, 391 426, 456.
  Cellar case, 165.
  Cellar with glasses, 90.
  Chafing dish, 14, 21, 22, 46, 55, 58, 70, 85, 89, 98, 105, 127, 154, 202, 212, 224, 239, 253, 286, 293, 341, 389, 396, 432, 433, 451.
  Chafing dish, brass, 160, 174, 184, 242, 405, 412, 447.
  Charger, pewter, 212.
  Chargers, 246, 326.
  Chaser, brass, 70.
  Cheese fats, 206, 253, 341, 458.
  Cheese moats, 5, 89, 142, 279, 286, 370.
  Cheese press, 89, 97, 148, 157, 172, 181, 192, 195, 200, 224, 246, 253, 279, 286, 341, 370, 412, 448, 456.
  Cheese vats, 71, 157.
  Churns, 22, 31, 45, 55, 61, 71, 79, 85, 89, 93, 107, 109, 125, 127, 154, 155, 157, 161, 176, 180, 181, 189, 192, 203, 236, 246, 286, 311, 341, 351, 368, 393, 403, 449, 458.
  Clasp, 117.
  Cob irons, 29, 31, 43, 48, 89, 90, 105, 106, 165, 189, 223, 224, 281, 337, 377, 407.
  Conell, 42.

Utensils.
  Copper, 44, 89, 105, 112, 142, 151, 152, 181, 188, 224, 242, 310, 391, 457.
  Copper, brass, 67, 70.
  Cottrels, 28, 142, 184, 206, 246, 342.
  Covers, 33, 70, 71, 75, 189, 429.
  Cowles, 31, 48, 89, 281, 341, 342.
  Cowpery ware, 240.
  Cranes, 322, 337.
  Creeper, 225.
  Crocks, 264, 381, 388.
  Cullender, 433.
  Cullender, brass, 280.
  Cullender, pewter, 189.
  Cups, 89, 189, 233, 239, 243, 273, 310, 315, 341, 363, 412.
  Cups, beer, 66, 214.
  Cups, brass, 363.
  Cups, dram, 214, 293, 316, 388, 437.
  Cups, drinking, 70, 151, 189, 367, 377.
  Cups, earthen, 315.
  Cups, pewter, 63, 70, 92, 287, 391.
  Cups, pewter beer, 315.
  Cups, silver, 139, 160, 177.
  Cups, silver dram, 229, 243, 306, 432, 488.
  Cups, silver wine, 338, 438.
  Cups, wine, 66, 184, 189, 214, 229, 243.
  Cups, wooden, 71.
  Dairy ware, 407, 456.
  Dial case, 132.
  Dial, leaden, 279.
  Dish, straining, 220.
  Dishes, 42, 64, 77, 80, 89, 132, 153, 157, 175, 185, 189, 191, 193, 204, 205, 280, 293, 308, 317, 351, 353, 363, 370, 376, 377, 389.
  Dishes, butter, 70, 160.
  Dishes, china, 67, 341, 379.
  Dishes, earthen, 144, 247, 367, 385.
  Dishes, fruit, 75, 229, 341.
  Dishes, gally, 204, 393.
  Dishes, paint, 239.
  Dishes, painted, 388.
  Dishes, pewter, 31, 42, 44-46, 48, 63, 75, 81, 83, 107, 109, 140, 160, 182, 186, 193, 198,

Utensils.
  Dishes, pewter, *continued*, 200, 205, 214, 220, 226, 243, 265, 272, 273, 280, 282, 284, 287, 315, 316, 363, 379, 388, 389, 393, 412, 414, 419, 445.
  Dishes, skimming, 182.
  Dishes, wooden, 33, 39, 50, 58, 80, 95, 140, 144, 250, 367, 419, 431, 445, 448.
  Drink vessels, 154, 206, 247, 311, 312.
  Dripping pans, 27, 29, 70, 89, 93, 95, 98, 100, 105, 112, 128, 157, 172, 174, 189, 210, 224, 246, 269, 304, 344, 350, 388, 389, 391, 411, 412, 457, 458.
  Earthen ware, 36, 56, 92, 95, 164, 175, 176, 182, 185, 190, 198, 201, 204, 226, 240, 242, 243, 245, 253, 265, 266, 272-274, 280, 282, 286, 288, 308, 310, 311, 324, 326, 352, 386, 391, 395, 396, 398, 418, 429, 431-433, 447, 448, 456, 457.
  Ewer, 276, 287, 341.
  Faucet, 180.
  Fender, 70.
  Fire dogs, 41, 58, 70, 226, 276, 432.
  Fire forks, 71, 89, 112, 184, 224, 308.
  Fire irons, 89, 224, 276, 353.
  Fire pans, 29, 31, 43, 48, 63, 70, 80, 89, 90, 95, 105, 154, 166, 189, 198, 203, 224, 242, 246, 269, 276, 280, 286, 305, 370, 377, 388, 391, 393, 396, 448.
  Fire shovels, 5, 52, 61, 66, 67, 75, 98, 99, 107, 129, 144, 172, 184, 192, 205, 212, 214, 226, 239, 248, 273, 274, 287, 288, 293, 316, 335, 341, 350, 363, 383, 413, 419, 423, 432, 444, 445, 447, 451.
  Fire slice, 201, 337.
  Firkins, 5, 31, 52, 79, 89, 128, 140, 142, 157, 165, 176, 190, 192, 230, 231, 233, 265, 266, 308, 370, 386.
  Flagon pottle, 311.
  Flagons, 66, 70, 152, 201, 246, 341.
  Flagons, pewter, 89, 105, 157, 184, 229, 344, 391.

516　INDEX

Utensils.
　Flask, 179.
　Flasket, 70, 71, 128, 165, 250.
　Fleshal, 184.
　Frying pans, 5, 18, 23, 27, 33, 41, 42, 45, 48, 50, 55-57, 61, 70, 75, 80, 83, 85, 87, 89, 92, 95, 98, 105, 107, 109, 112, 121, 124, 132, 133, 140, 148, 149, 151, 152, 155, 161, 165, 169, 170, 172-175, 179, 182, 185, 188, 189, 192, 195, 198, 201, 204, 214, 216, 218, 220, 224, 226, 229, 233, 239, 245, 246, 247, 249, 250, 251, 253, 254, 256-258, 262, 265, 266, 271, 272, 276, 279, 281, 284, 286, 287, 293, 301, 304, 308, 310, 312, 315, 316, 335, 337, 341, 342, 349, 350, 363, 365, 376, 381-383, 388, 389, 391, 393, 396, 403, 407, 412, 414, 419, 429, 433, 442, 445, 449, 451.
　Funnels, 168, 182, 239, 391.
　Furnace, 246.
　Furs, 281.
　Gable balk, 129.
　Glass case, 98, 128, 295, 310, 358, 393.
　Glass vial, 216.
　Glasses, 36, 52, 70, 92, 179, 180, 204, 210, 224, 230, 265, 266, 331, 379, 385, 419, 445.
　Glue pot, 39.
　Grater, 70, 232, 243, 388.
　Grates, 5, 202.
　Gridirons, 5, 31, 33, 43, 45, 50, 55, 58, 63, 70, 75, 85, 89, 95, 124, 132, 140, 148, 154, 155, 158, 165, 172, 174, 184, 188, 192, 198, 200, 201, 203, 205, 211, 216, 226, 229, 232, 242, 269, 272, 279, 286, 293, 308, 315, 337, 350, 363, 379, 388, 391, 407, 411, 412, 419, 422, 432, 445, 447, 448.
　Gridiron toaster, 212.
　Hachell, 58.
　Hakes, 58, 148, 172, 200, 229, 242, 253, 256, 276, 281, 302, 316, 322, 363, 391, 415, 419, 422, 432, 445, 456.
　Hangers, 36, 67, 70, 132, 149, 157, 226, 239, 243, 262, 273, 317, 413, 433, 444.

Utensils.
　Heaters, 89, 179, 275.
　Heating irons, 316.
　Heats, 204.
　Hogsheads, 14, 22, 32, 45, 47, 48, 64, 65, 67, 70, 71, 75, 78, 85, 90, 107, 127, 140, 155, 157, 160, 168, 175, 180, 181, 192, 202, 204, 245-247, 260, 272, 315, 326, 341, 342, 350, 363, 426, 431.
　Hooks, 155, 182, 200, 239, 245, 308, 316, 326, 429.
　Hooks, flesh, 211, 337, 341, 342.
　Hooks, reck, 50, 99.
　Hour glasses, 64, 117, 157, 175, 176, 180, 183, 198, 201, 204, 210, 212, 271, 276, 341, 388.
　Husbandry utensils, 341.
　Hushellments, 100.
　Inkhorn, silver, 384.
　Inkhorns, 57, 117, 182, 216, 331, 367.
　Iron, 67, 70, 109, 132, 139, 169, 258, 276, 303, 352, 356, 357, 365, 395, 398, 406, 415, 433, 440.
　Iron, back, 245.
　Iron ware, 143, 162, 179, 240, 277, 328, 352, 358, 371, 418, 442.
　Jack, 224, 246.
　Jack, leather, 153, 157.
　Jars, 210, 316, 386.
　Jars, oil, 430.
　Jugs, 5, 59, 70, 79, 85, 89, 180, 233, 245, 254, 315.
　Jugs, Holland, 127.
　Jugs, silver tipped, 99, 139.
　Jugs, stone, 281, 287, 382.
　Jug, tipped, 393.
　Keckines, 100.
　Keelers, 55, 64, 85, 89, 98, 127, 140, 154, 161, 166, 174, 176, 189, 246, 280, 282, 293, 308, 311, 341, 393, 396, 398, 433, 440, 448.
　Kegs, 49.
　Kettles, 5, 15, 27, 31, 41, 42, 44, 45, 48, 55, 56, 58, 63, 64, 67, 79, 81, 83, 85, 87, 89, 95, 98, 99, 105, 107, 112, 124, 127, 132, 144, 151, 152, 161, 165-167, 169, 172, 176, 179, 185, 186, 190, 191, 201, 202, 205,

Utensils.
  Kettles, *continued*, 208, 211, 216, 218, 224, 226, 232, 236, 242, 245, 247, 251, 253, 254, 257, 258, 260, 262, 264, 265, 271, 273, 274, 279, 282, 286, 288-290, 293, 300, 305, 308, 310, 315, 316, 319, 322-324, 326, 342, 344, 349, 350, 365, 370, 376, 377, 379, 381-383, 389, 391, 403, 412, 414, 417, 419, 422, 423, 426, 429-433, 441, 445, 447, 457, 458.
  Kettles, bell metal, 312.
  Kettles, brass, 27, 28, 33, 36, 39, 42, 44, 52, 58, 70, 75, 81, 92, 97, 99, 100, 102, 133, 144, 148, 149, 152, 154, 157, 160, 182, 184, 185, 189, 193, 198, 201, 211, 212, 214, 220, 226, 239, 242, 243, 246, 248, 249, 256, 265, 266, 269, 271, 276, 280, 293, 302, 304, 310, 316, 324, 341, 342, 344, 349, 363, 379, 383, 389, 391, 393, 396, 398, 411, 412, 414, 419, 422, 430-433, 444, 445, 447, 448, 451, 458.
  Kettles, copper, 67, 132, 198, 211, 224, 227, 229, 241, 243, 287, 292, 407.
  Knives, 5, 70, 77, 117, 140, 180, 203, 226, 232, 271, 368.
  Knives, case of, 322, 432.
  Knives, chopping, 211, 341.
  Ladles, 45, 48, 58, 80, 95, 160, 198, 204, 224, 233, 326, 433.
  Ladles, basting, 127, 157, 189.
  Ladles, brass, 85, 89, 113, 151, 166, 175, 176, 184, 212, 220, 239, 249, 308, 341, 342, 391, 414, 419, 445.
  Ladles, iron, 5, 249.
  Lamp, latten, 316.
  Lamps, 64, 70, 77, 117, 157, 160, 165, 182, 201, 210, 282, 287, 302, 308, 341, 342, 388, 393, 396, 433.
  Lamps, brass, 49, 189, 415.
  Lamps, pewter, 67.
  Landiron, 407.
  Lantern, dark, 5.
  Lantern, latten, 160.
  Lantern, tin, 385.
  Lanterns, 22, 56, 64, 93, 128, 189, 243, 254, 271, 326, 381.

Utensils.
  Latten quart, 239.
  Latten ware, 89, 182, 271, 308, 315, 324, 391, 419, 422, 445.
  Lisbon ware, 185, 198, 350, 412, 419, 445.
  Lumber ware, 185.
  Milk vessels, 93, 151, 153, 251, 350, 352, 403, 406, 423.
  Mortar, 5, 27, 28, 59, 98, 99, 109, 172, 209, 210, 224, 308, 370, 383, 389, 457.
  Mortar, bell metal, 281.
  Mortar, brass, 87, 113, 144, 154, 161, 169, 200, 242, 282, 287, 308, 396, 444, 447.
  Mortar and pestle, 32, 36, 41, 48, 58, 63, 70, 75, 79, 89, 95, 105, 148, 151, 157, 164, 166, 174, 179, 185, 204, 214, 229, 239, 256, 271, 279, 286, 310, 322, 341, 391, 407, 414, 430, 433, 451.
  Mortar and pestle, bell metal, 276.
  Mortar and pestle, brass, 85, 93, 246, 419, 445.
  Nipples, silver, 45.
  Nips, 154.
  Pails, 31, 33, 36, 41, 42, 50, 56-58, 75, 77, 89, 121, 127, 128, 133, 142, 144, 152, 155, 157, 165, 169, 172, 185, 189, 190, 192, 198, 201, 204, 211, 212, 226, 230, 243, 256, 264, 269, 271, 279, 281, 282, 284, 302, 308, 311, 315, 322, 350, 353, 376, 396, 398, 419, 422, 431, 433, 440, 445, 448, 449, 451, 456, 458.
  Pails, water, 153, 204.
  Pans, 5, 56, 57, 89, 139, 148, 190, 250, 326.
  Pans, bed, 5, 224, 287.
  Pans, brass, 21, 29, 31, 45, 48, 63, 67, 95, 97, 105, 144, 152, 184, 195, 201, 211, 212, 229, 248, 249, 253, 257, 269, 276, 279, 280, 304, 341.
  Pans, earthen, 55, 58, 80, 447.
  Pans, latten, 189, 190, 265, 266, 316, 377.
  Pans, milk, 449, 458.
  Pans, pewter, 308.
  Pans, pudding, 151, 160, 166, 182, 204, 224, 293, 316, 433.

518                INDEX

Utensils.
  Pans, sauce, 190, 316.
  Pans, tin, 175, 412.
  Pans, tin sauce, 342.
  Pashel, 71, 189, 337, 341.
  Peel, 67, 75, 80, 95, 341.
  Peel, oven, 192.
  Pestle, brass, 27.
  Pestles, 80, 113, 154, 448.
  Pewter, 5, 20, 22, 23, 31, 36, 39,
    41, 42, 45, 47, 55-58, 61, 67,
    73, 81, 85, 89, 93, 95, 97-100,
    102, 105, 111, 121, 123, 124,
    127, 129, 132, 133, 142, 143,
    148, 149, 151, 152, 154, 155,
    160, 164, 166, 168, 169, 172,
    174, 179, 182, 184, 185, 189,
    201, 203, 204, 208, 210, 212,
    214, 218, 224, 226, 227, 232,
    236, 240, 242, 245, 249, 251,
    254, 256-258, 260, 262, 267,
    269, 271, 275, 276, 279, 286,
    287, 289, 295, 300-302, 304,
    305, 308, 322, 324, 326, 328,
    335, 337, 344, 348, 350, 352,
    353, 356-358, 367, 370, 371,
    374, 379, 381, 386, 388, 391,
    395, 396, 398, 400, 406, 407,
    411, 414, 415, 417, 418, 422,
    423, 426, 429, 430, 432-434,
    440, 444, 448, 451, 455-458.
  Pewter vessels, 162, 258, 277,
    431.
  Pipkin, 77.
  Plate, 44, 105, 110, 139, 162,
    224, 295, 303, 310, 321, 385,
    406.
  Plate, iron, 322.
  Plate, silver, 66, 111, 334.
  Plates, 66, 107, 193, 414.
  Plates, fish, 95.
  Plates, pewter, 42, 144, 229,
    287.
  Platters, 15, 58, 77, 79, 89, 144,
    148, 190, 248, 264, 311, 341,
    376, 383, 396, 412, 438.
  Platters, earthen, 151.
  Platters, pewter, 12, 21, 27, 29,
    57, 66, 70, 87, 95, 137, 144,
    152, 157, 184, 186, 189, 190,
    198, 200, 201, 211, 212, 229,
    239, 246, 248, 249, 253, 265,
    266, 293, 300, 317, 342, 344,
    365, 377, 379, 391, 396, 414,
    427, 439, 446, 447, 449, 457.

Utensils.
  Platters, Spanish, 223.
  Platters, wooden, 80, 151, 216,
    220, 391, 431.
  Porringers, 5, 12, 48, 70, 71, 77,
    79, 107, 151, 154, 157, 158,
    160, 182, 190, 198, 229, 265,
    266, 272, 282, 284, 290, 315,
    341, 342, 377, 393, 396, 415,
    419, 445, 446.
  Porringers, earthen, 286, 293.
  Porringers, pewter, 75, 184,
    189, 229, 280, 287, 365.
  Porringers, silver, 4.
  Portingale ware, 271.
  Posnet, 22, 42, 44, 50, 55, 63,
    81, 83, 89, 95, 107, 124, 128,
    132, 164, 166, 167, 169, 189,
    218, 317, 363, 377, 396.
  Posnet, brass, 21, 154, 195, 239.
  Postiron, 77.
  Pot, ele, 48.
  Pot hangers, 27, 28, 41, 42, 52,
    70, 87, 92, 98, 144, 158, 161,
    185, 198, 214, 249, 269, 277,
    287, 288, 376, 447.
  Pot hooks, 5, 18, 23, 27, 33, 42,
    45, 48, 50, 61, 64, 70, 77, 83,
    89, 92, 95, 98, 100, 142, 144,
    148, 154, 155, 157, 161, 165-
    167, 174, 184, 188, 189, 198,
    200, 201, 204, 211, 216, 218,
    220, 224, 229, 239, 246, 248,
    249, 253, 254, 262, 271, 276,
    279, 281, 286, 290, 305, 308,
    315, 337, 341, 342, 350, 367,
    377, 381, 388, 393, 407, 414,
    419, 422, 434, 441, 445, 449,
    455.
  Pot irons, 79.
  Pot lid, 89, 229.
  Pot racks, 45, 75.
  Potenshee, 363.
  Pots, 57-59, 67, 70, 89, 99, 128,
    164, 165, 172, 180, 191, 203,
    226, 232, 233, 236, 245, 251,
    254, 257, 260, 262, 264, 271,
    274, 289, 300, 317, 326, 350,
    370, 379, 386, 388, 393, 400,
    403, 412, 417, 423, 426, 429,
    430, 449.
  Pots, band, 179.
  Pots, brass, 5, 21, 22, 31, 39,
    41, 55, 57, 61, 67, 70, 83, 85,
    87, 89, 92, 93, 95, 97-99, 102,

INDEX 519

Utensils.
Pots, brass, *continued*, 105, 112, 128, 132, 148, 152, 154, 155, 166, 173, 179, 183, 185, 189, 195, 201, 205, 211, 212, 214, 216, 220, 224, 229, 239, 246, 249, 272, 273, 279, 293, 322, 341, 348, 349, 377, 412, 414, 431, 434, 441.
Pots, butter, 78, 204.
Pots, chamber, 5, 31, 33, 36, 44, 48, 63, 67, 70, 75, 80, 151, 157, 158, 169, 184, 189, 229, 246, 253, 273, 282, 286, 287, 311, 341, 344, 363, 377, 396, 398, 412, 414, 415, 447.
Pots, copper, 98.
Pots, drinking, 77, 85, 127.
Pots, earthen, 39, 45, 50, 57, 71, 155, 172, 176, 189, 190, 218, 246, 247, 287, 302, 315, 368, 419, 430, 445.
Pots, gally, 127, 180, 246, 379.
Pots, half pint, 445.
Pots, iron, 5, 18, 20, 22, 28, 31, 33, 35, 36, 42, 44, 45, 48, 55, 56, 58, 61, 64, 70, 75, 77, 79, 81, 85, 92, 93, 95, 97, 98, 105, 107, 121, 124, 129, 133, 140, 142, 144, 148, 149, 151, 152, 154, 155, 157, 160, 161, 164, 166, 167, 169, 175, 176, 182, 184, 185, 188-190, 193, 198, 200, 201, 204, 205, 208, 211, 212, 214, 218, 224, 226, 229, 242, 243, 246-249, 253, 256, 258, 265, 266, 269, 271, 272, 275, 279, 280, 282, 284, 286, 288-290, 292, 293, 295, 301, 302, 304, 305, 308, 310, 312, 315, 317, 319, 324, 335, 337, 341, 342, 344, 348, 350, 353, 363, 365, 367, 368, 370, 377, 379, 381, 383, 386, 389, 391, 393, 395, 396, 398, 407, 411, 412, 414, 419, 422, 423, 431, 433, 434, 441, 444, 445, 447, 449, 451, 455-458.
Pots, pewter, 66, 75, 89, 144, 157, 198, 202, 212, 233, 449.
Pots, pewter drinking, 246.
Pots, pewter half pint, 391.
Pots, pewter pint, 33, 75, 184, 186, 287, 363, 391.
Pots, pewter quart, 363, 391.

Utensils.
Pots, pint, 46, 63, 80, 87, 107, 154, 160, 193, 239, 282, 290, 293, 311, 316, 341, 342, 376, 388, 412, 419.
Pots, pottage, 403.
Pots, quart, 63, 80, 151, 154, 182, 184, 186, 239, 243, 311, 341, 379, 388, 419, 445, 447.
Pots, stone, 93.
Powder blue, 95, 233.
Pressing iron, 33, 98, 185, 286, 341, 431, 455.
Racks, 162, 184, 212, 233, 249, 271, 391.
Reel, 175.
Ring, silver, 85.
Runlet, 50, 51, 57, 128, 148, 176, 185, 192, 204.
Sack, mill, 344.
Sacks, 14, 42, 48, 71, 75, 79, 82, 142, 165, 180, 247, 282, 341, 374, 376, 386, 442, 449.
Safe, 246.
Salt box, 71, 216, 233.
Salt cellars, 48, 70, 77, 80, 144, 154, 157, 160, 184, 189, 200, 246, 287, 315, 341, 363, 377, 412, 419, 445.
Salt cellars, double, 12, 75.
Salt cellars, earthen, 89.
Salt cellars, pewter, 63, 89, 184, 186, 229, 239, 388.
Salt cellars, silver, 160, 229.
Saucers, 5, 48, 67, 70, 71, 75, 77, 79, 144, 184, 189, 239, 265, 266, 287, 315, 341, 388, 396, 414, 419, 445.
Saucers, pewter, 229, 363, 391.
Shoe horn, 52, 233.
Sieves, 36, 45, 48, 58, 69, 70, 79, 80, 89, 121, 125, 128, 140, 142, 151, 153, 157, 175, 176, 180, 185, 189, 192, 198, 201, 203, 204, 208, 214, 216, 218, 220, 226, 233, 245, 251, 254, 265, 275, 279, 280, 282, 286, 293, 308, 308, 315, 335, 341, 352, 381, 388, 391, 396, 403, 419, 430, 433, 440, 444, 445, 449, 455, 458.
Sieves, hair, 95, 208, 247, 250, 342.
Sieves, tiffany, 95, 247.
Sieves, wire, 250.

Utensils.
  Silver, 85, 247, 254, 334.
  Skillet frame, 189.
  Skillets, 5, 23, 27, 31, 36, 41, 45, 48, 50, 52, 57, 58, 79, 85, 98, 102, 149, 151, 155, 158, 160, 172, 174, 176, 179, 182, 185, 190, 198, 201, 203-205, 211, 212, 216, 224, 226, 242, 243, 251, 254, 256, 258, 262, 264, 269, 271-273, 275, 279, 284, 286, 287, 293, 304, 308, 310, 312, 316, 324, 326, 337, 341, 350, 365, 370, 377, 383, 389, 396, 398, 412, 423, 429, 441, 447.
  Skillets, bell metal, 28, 70, 183, 414.
  Skillets, brass, 29, 42, 58, 70, 75, 77, 99, 105, 121, 144, 154, 157, 158, 160, 175, 183, 189, 201, 211, 220, 229, 239, 242, 246, 265, 266, 282, 302, 305, 310, 342, 349, 363, 367, 393, 407, 412, 414, 419, 422, 432, 433, 444, 445, 447-449, 457.
  Skillets, iron, 42, 169, 249, 253, 265, 266, 282, 292, 302, 316, 350, 376, 379, 388, 407, 412, 419, 433, 445, 448, 457.
  Skimmers, 36, 39, 48, 55, 58, 70, 79, 85, 89, 98, 127, 148, 154, 157, 165, 169, 174, 184, 185, 205, 211, 233, 249, 258, 271, 272, 279, 286, 287, 310, 341, 365, 377, 396, 414, 433.
  Skimmers, brass, 75, 95, 160, 186, 189, 216, 229, 308, 391.
  Slice, 14, 165, 175, 204, 305, 310, 379.
  Smoothing irons, 39, 56, 75, 77, 89, 95, 149, 155, 166, 169, 175, 179, 201, 204, 226, 229, 239, 243, 251, 265, 266, 271, 281, 282, 287, 293, 312, 315, 316, 322, 337, 341, 342, 350, 365, 377, 379, 388, 393, 396, 403, 411, 412, 418, 419, 432, 445, 449.
  Snuffers, 49, 341, 388.
  Snuffers, brass, 70, 243.
  Spits, 14, 27, 29, 31, 39, 42, 45, 48, 56, 61, 63, 67, 70, 75, 85, 87, 89, 95, 98, 100, 105, 112, 127, 132, 151, 154, 157, 161,

Utensils.
  Spits, *continued*, 165, 166, 172, 174, 179, 184, 185, 188, 189, 192, 200, 201, 205, 210-212, 214, 224, 226, 229, 232, 233, 239, 242, 243, 246, 249, 256, 257, 269, 272, 274, 276, 280, 286, 288, 293, 303, 304, 308, 310, 312, 315, 322, 335, 337, 341, 344, 350, 363, 370, 377, 379, 388, 389, 391, 395, 396, 411, 419, 429, 432, 445, 447, 448.
  Spoons, 5, 12, 15, 20, 33, 42, 45, 50, 57, 77, 80, 89, 105, 107, 110, 127, 140, 149, 154, 157, 158, 160, 166, 175, 176, 193, 203-205, 233, 247, 265, 266, 271, 273, 284, 293, 301, 310, 351, 352, 367, 377, 379, 388, 415, 419, 433, 441, 445, 449.
  Spoons, alchemy, 48, 89, 169, 282, 341.
  Spoons, pewter, 75, 89, 151, 184, 189, 282, 303.
  Spoons, silver, 29, 31, 46-48, 61, 66, 79, 85, 89, 95, 99, 127, 129, 139, 160, 177, 179, 189, 227, 229, 243, 247, 275, 279, 300, 341, 357, 393, 437, 438, 441, 444.
  Stew-pan, 224, 232, 287.
  Still, 71, 93, 105.
  Sundial, 230.
  Tankard, pewter, 287.
  Taps, 5.
  Timber vessels, 102, 381, 388.
  Tin, 164, 302, 352, 353, 371, 393, 406, 455.
  Tinder box, 233.
  Toasting fork, 281.
  Toasting irons, 127, 165, 233.
  Tongs, 5, 27, 29, 31, 41, 45, 48, 56, 58, 61, 63, 64, 66, 67, 70, 75, 80, 89, 90, 95, 98-100, 105-107, 112, 127, 129, 133, 142, 144, 154, 161, 162, 165, 172, 182, 185, 189, 192, 198, 201, 205, 211, 212, 214, 216, 220, 223-226, 229, 233, 239, 242, 243, 246, 251, 254, 256, 262, 265, 266, 269, 272-274, 276, 280, 281, 286-288, 293, 308, 310, 312, 315, 316, 322, 326, 335, 337, 341, 342, 350, 352,

INDEX 521

Utensils.
　Tongs, *continued*, 363, 368, 370, 376, 377, 379, 381, 383, 388, 396, 403, 413, 419, 423, 430, 432, 444, 445, 447, 448, 451.
　Tongue, 148, 391, 440.
　Trammels, 31, 43, 48, 61, 63, 85, 89, 95, 105, 109, 133, 151, 157, 165-167, 174, 175, 192, 201, 203, 204, 216, 224, 233, 286, 293, 308, 310, 312, 337, 341, 350, 352, 377, 379, 396, 407, 431, 440, 455.
　Trays, 5, 32, 33, 36, 42, 45, 56-58, 71, 75, 77, 85, 89, 98, 121, 123, 125, 128, 132, 142, 149, 154, 157, 166, 185, 189, 193, 208, 212, 224, 226, 247, 253, 267, 272, 280, 302, 303, 308, 311, 316, 322, 326, 341, 342, 350, 353, 367, 370, 376, 377, 389, 396, 398, 407, 419, 422, 440, 445, 447, 458.
　Trays, milk, 206.
　Trays, wooden, 50, 220, 250, 287, 431.
　Trenchers, 33, 66, 71, 77, 89, 95, 140, 144, 151, 172, 175, 176, 179, 192, 198, 204, 220, 233, 279, 293, 295, 308, 315, 326, 341, 351, 377, 379, 388, 391, 419, 430, 432, 445, 449.
　Trevett, 5, 14, 48, 67, 89, 98, 169, 180, 189, 224, 242, 246, 377.
　Troughs, 33, 64, 93, 204, 233, 245.
　Troughs, kneading, 33, 64, 71, 107, 128, 165, 224, 250, 279, 286, 308, 370, 398, 455, 458.
　Troughs, meal, 201, 204, 247, 342, 367.
　Troughs, minging, 77.
　Troughs, salting, 189, 350.
　Trow, sifting, 433.
　Tubs, 15, 18, 36, 39, 42, 45, 50, 56, 61, 66, 67, 71, 85, 97, 100, 125, 127, 132, 133, 142, 144, 148, 149, 152, 164-166, 170, 172, 175, 176, 180, 182, 183, 186, 189-192, 201, 205, 208, 211, 212, 214, 218, 224, 236, 239, 243, 245-247, 251, 256, 267, 269, 277, 279, 284, 286, 302, 315, 322, 326, 341, 342, 350, 374, 377, 379, 389, 391,

Utensils.
　Tubs, *continued*, 396, 398, 399, 406, 423, 430, 445, 447, 451.
　Tubs, beer, 342.
　Tubs, brewing, 293, 311.
　Tubs, bucking, 98, 127, 176, 282, 414.
　Tubs, butter, 250, 341.
　Tubs, drink, 161.
　Tubs, meal, 144, 155, 175.
　Tubs, powdering, 48, 55, 64, 71, 95, 98, 107, 127, 157, 174, 176, 192, 204, 206, 216, 224, 246, 280, 282, 286, 308, 311, 341, 396, 398, 412.
　Tunnels, 67, 70, 71, 80, 85, 139, 189, 202, 220, 233, 342.
　Vessels, 79, 102, 396.
　Voider ware, 242.
　Warming pan cover, 293.
　Warming pans, 5, 21, 27, 29, 31, 36, 41, 43, 45, 50, 55, 56, 58, 64, 66, 70, 75, 79, 85, 87, 89, 92, 95, 97-99, 105, 107, 128, 140, 142, 148, 151, 152, 154, 155, 157, 159, 161, 165, 167, 169, 172, 174, 176, 179, 183, 185, 186, 189, 195, 198, 200, 201, 205, 208, 211, 212, 214, 218, 224, 226, 229, 236, 239, 242, 246, 249, 251, 253, 254, 256-258, 262, 264-266, 271, 272, 274, 276, 279, 281, 282, 286, 287, 301, 302, 304, 308, 310, 312, 315, 316, 326, 341, 342, 349, 350, 363, 365, 366, 370, 377, 379, 381, 383, 388, 391, 393, 396, 398, 407, 412, 419, 423, 427, 429, 430, 432, 434, 445, 447, 451, 455, 458.
　Water case, 311.
　Wine, half pint, 189.
　Wine measures, 214.
　Wine quart, 189.
　Wine quart, pewter, 391.
　Wine tap, 144.
　Wooden ware, 81, 83, 97, 100, 129, 148, 155, 164, 176, 180, 181, 189, 198, 208, 211, 226, 245, 254, 260, 263, 265, 266, 271, 273, 274, 295, 301, 302, 315, 324, 326, 335, 344, 363, 371, 379, 393, 395, 396, 398, 400, 412, 418, 429, 434, 441, 442, 449, 455-457.

Valances, *see* Furnishings.
Vane, ——, 107.
Varnam, Vernham, ——, 31.
  George, 108.
  Hannah, 109.
  Samuel, 109.
Varney, Varny, Varnye, ——, 220, 221.
  Bridget, 173.
  Thomas, 147.
  William, 120, 156, 173.
Vat, dry, 188.
Vaughan, Vaghan, George, 137, 138.
Veal, *see* Food.
Velvet, *see* Cloth.
Veren, Vearin, Verin, Vering, Hilliard, 181, 242, 257, 269, 324, 343, 345, 347, 354, 355, 376, 378, 382, 388, 390, 413, 414, 416, 449, 450, 452, 456-458.
  Nathaniel, 42.
  Philip, 123, 289.
Vernham, *see* Varnam.
Very, Verry, Alice, 289.
  Elizabeth, 289.
  John, 289.
  Samuel, 289, 290, 417.
  Sarah, 289.
  Thomas, 289, 359.
Vessels and equipments, 119, 312, 400.
  Anchor, 432.
  Bark, 65.
  Boats, 14, 102, 147, 172, 254, 288, 323, 454.
  Cabin rug, 454.
  Canoes, 5, 36, 39, 42, 97, 133, 147, 158, 218, 281, 323, 342, 388, 408, 418, 423.
  Compass, 176, 180, 198, 385.
  Cordage, 324.
  Forestaff, 385.
  Gunter's scale, 385.
  Harping iron, 342.
  Keele stem, 172.
  Ketch, 172, 331, 365, 385.
  Key (wharf), 172.
  Lighter, 172.
  Mariner's instrument, 148.
  Oakum, 288.
  Quadrant, 385.
  Rudder, 172.
  Sail canvas, 197.
  Sail cloth, 148.

Vessels and equipments.
  Sea beds, 51, 381, 419, 445.
  Sea books, 317.
  Sea chests, 4, 42, 200.
  Sea clothes, 317, 365, 454.
  Sea instruments, 317.
  Sea pillows, 51.
  Shallops, 65, 271.
  Ships, 6, 288.
  Skiff, 198.
  Stern post, 172.
  Trunnell, 172.
  Wharf, 235.

  Alligator (ketch), 147.
  Flower (ketch), 147.
  Gift (ketch), 147.
  Kettle (ship), 6.
  Mary Ann (ship), 87.
  Return (ketch), 147.
  Sarah (ship), 106.
  Seaflower (ship), 10.
  William (ketch), 288.
Vicary, George, 60.
Vinegar, *see* Food.
Vinson, William, 102.
Viol, treble, 224.
Virginia, 118, 161.
Vise, *see* Tools.

Wade, Wad, ——, 9, 271.
  John, 135.
  Jonathan, 61.
Wainewright, Francis, 440, 441.
Waistcoats, *see* Clothing.
Waite, Wayte, Thomas, 367, 369, 370.
Wake, John, 181.
  Katherine, 181.
  William, 181.
Wakefield, William, 114.
Waklye, Isaac, 359, 361.
Wal, Capt., 148.
Walcott, Alice, 43.
  William, 25.
Walderswick, Eng., 12.
Waldo, Francis, 156.
Waldridge, William, 275.
Walford, ——, 135.
Walker, ——, 119.
  Henry, 360.
  Richard, 370, 418.
Wallet, *see* Clothing.
Wallington, Walington, Nicholas, 294, 310.
  Sarah, 294.

INDEX    523

Wallis, Nicholas, 219.
  Robert, 144, 192.
Walner, John, 285.
Walton, Waltom, ——, 256.
  William, 59, 60.
Wandley, ——, 134.
  Nathaniel, 135.
  Samuel, 134, 136.
War, Abraham, 175.
  Sarah, 175.
Ward, Warde, ——, 4, 7, 8, 234, 274, 290.
  Alice, 203.
  John, 234, 235.
  Miles, 118, 119.
  Nathaniel, 234.
  Rebecca, 171.
  Sarah, 203.
Warehouse, see Buildings.
Warming pans, see Utensils.
Warner, ——, 167.
  Daniel, 167, 169.
  John, 175, 203.
  Mark, 398.
  Thomas, 172.
Warren, Thomas, 12, 149.
Watch, see Clothing.
Waters, Walters, Watters, Hannah, 317, 318.
  Richard, 49, 145, 269.
  Stephen, 254.
  William, 254, 317, 454.
Watertown, 124, 230, 392.
Wathen, Wathin, Wathing, ——, 34, 35.
  Deborah, 35, 39.
  Edmund, 148.
  Elinor, 35.
  Ezekiel, 39, 263, 384.
  Margery, 38, 39.
  Thomas, 148, 263.
Watkins, John, 13.
Watson, Wadson, Wadsson, Wattson, ——, 41, 307.
  Thomas, 40, 41, 196, 198, 199, 452.
Weapons, armor and equipments.
  Ammunition, 149, 335, 341, 356, 367.
  Armor, 162, 254, 335, 431.
  Arms, 97, 123, 129, 154, 174, 255, 257, 319, 356, 395, 434.
  Bandelier and belt, 190, 276, 277.
  Bandelier rest, 148, 226.

Weapons, armor and equipments.
  Bandeliers, 14, 18, 20, 22, 42, 50, 51, 55, 63, 68, 75, 79, 82, 83, 85, 89, 93, 102, 121, 124, 127, 142, 149, 151, 152, 155, 158, 161, 164, 168, 169, 179, 184, 192, 198, 203, 208, 209, 226, 229, 232, 242, 247, 253, 256, 260, 267, 271, 308, 344, 363, 383, 418, 422, 453.
  Birding piece, 20, 57, 188.
  Bolts, 229.
  Bowstrings, 180.
  Bullets, 5, 70, 123, 148, 180, 184, 233, 453.
  Caliver, 286.
  Carbine, 52, 112, 123, 148, 179, 192, 214, 249, 255.
  Cocks, 233.
  Corselet, 44, 89, 112, 152, 201, 228, 353, 377, 379, 399, 426.
  Crossbow, 188.
  Curtle, 184.
  Cutlass, 66, 142, 212, 377, 379, 433.
  Dagger, 180, 233.
  Drum, 232.
  Drum and sticks, 176.
  Feather, 68.
  Firelock, 75, 229.
  Fowling piece, 22, 25, 29-31, 43, 63, 75, 89, 92, 93, 97, 102, 105, 112, 124, 136, 142, 148, 161, 169, 176, 179, 184, 188, 189, 210, 212, 228, 239, 242, 255, 260, 271, 274, 311, 324, 379, 388, 399, 429, 454.
  Gun barrel, 449.
  Gun lock, 449.
  Guns, 39, 56, 61, 74, 85, 100, 124, 132, 154, 182, 220, 233, 240, 247, 255, 267, 287, 289, 292, 302, 337, 341, 353, 358, 379, 381, 386, 396, 400, 430, 433, 453.
  Halberd, 48, 89, 144, 179, 260, 377.
  Head piece, 85, 377.
  Holsters, 352, 353, 379.
  Javelin, 447.
  Knapsacks, 123, 164, 180, 233.
  Knife sheath, 149.
  Knives, 180, 388.
  Lead, 453.
  Match, 180, 205.

524                                INDEX

Weapons, armor and equipments.
  Match lock, 49.
  Molds, 164, 184.
  Molds, bullet, 30, 203.
  Molds, shot, 30, 381.
  Musket barrels, 210, 341.
  Musket rests, 77, 92, 124, 314.
  Muskets, 14, 18, 20, 22, 23, 29, 42, 43, 50, 51, 55, 57, 63, 68, 70, 75, 77, 79, 81, 83, 87, 89, 93, 97, 105, 121, 123, 124, 127, 142, 144, 148, 149, 151, 152, 155, 158, 162, 164, 168, 169, 174, 179, 182, 184, 188, 189, 192, 193, 198, 200, 202, 205, 208-210, 212, 214, 216, 218, 223, 226, 229, 236, 242, 245, 247, 255, 256, 263, 265, 266, 271, 277, 279, 284, 286, 304, 308, 311, 314, 322, 363, 367, 370, 374, 377, 379, 383, 391, 393, 403, 407, 418, 419, 422, 433, 444, 445, 447.
  Pike, 89, 308, 379, 399, 426.
  Pike, half, 229.
  Pikeheads, 229.
  Pistol, brass, 250.
  Pistol dag, 75.
  Pistolet, 81.
  Pistols, 30, 61, 68, 192, 239, 275, 295, 301, 352, 353, 358, 379, 433, 436, 442.
  Pistols, pocket, 229.
  Poniard, 68.
  Pouch, 236, 284.
  Powder, 50, 61, 63, 70, 80, 82, 123, 131, 152, 176, 180, 184, 198, 203, 205, 226, 233, 254, 353, 423.
  Powder can, 70.
  Rapier, 89, 190, 209, 276, 295, 301, 353, 383, 449, 453.
  Rapier and belt, 176, 271, 302, 353.
  Rests, 14, 18, 51, 55, 89, 164, 179, 184, 233, 284, 430.
  Scourer, 164, 202.
  Sheath, 388.
  Shot, 52, 70, 79, 131, 148, 176, 180, 423.
  Staff, 456.
  Sword and belt, 20, 50, 124, 182, 192, 203, 232, 239, 253, 282, 308, 396, 456.

Weapons, armor and equipments.
  Swords, 14, 22, 30, 31, 42, 45, 51, 61, 63, 68, 74, 75, 79, 82, 83, 89, 92, 93, 102, 112, 121, 123, 127, 142, 144, 148, 149, 151, 152, 154, 155, 161, 164, 168, 169, 174, 179, 184, 188, 189, 192, 198, 200, 205, 208, 212, 214, 220, 226, 228, 229, 236, 242, 245, 247, 249, 251, 256, 260, 265-267, 271, 277, 279, 284, 286, 287, 289, 311, 322, 324, 337, 341, 344, 352, 363, 367, 377, 383, 386, 399, 403, 407, 414, 418, 422, 426, 430, 433, 436, 444.
  Worm, 202.
Weaver, see Trades.
Webb, ——, 107, 158.
Webster, ——, 61.
  Abigail, 53.
  Elizabeth, 53.
  Hannah, 52.
  Israel, 53, 402.
  John, 52, 53, 402, 408.
  Mary, 52, 53.
  Nathan, 52, 402.
  Stephen, 52.
Wedges, see Tools.
Weed, Ephraim, 409.
  John, 400.
Weekes, Wickes, Wikes, ——, 177.
  Thomas, 49.
Weevils, 280.
Weights, see Tools.
Well, 181.
Wells, Richard, 102, 405, 406, 410, 443.
  Thomas, 6, 106, 401.
Wenham, 18, 57, 73, 76, 77, 171, 188, 189, 222, 252, 306.
Wenham, see also Enon.
West, ——, 100, 258.
  Isabel, 41.
  John, 170.
Westgate, Wesgate, Adam, 256, 289.
Wethersfield, 234.
Wethersfield, Eng., 331.
Weymouth, 453.
Wharton, Whorten, Edward, 256.
  Philip, 396.
Wharf, 235.
Wheat, see Food.

Wheelbarrows, *see* Tools.
Wheels, *see* Tools.
Wheelwright, *see* Trades.
Whipcord, 180.
Whipple, Wheeple, Whipell, Whiple, ——, 321.
  Elder, 302.
  Ann, 25.
  Anna, 88.
  Elizabeth, 88.
  John, 28, 31, 43, 88, 89, 105, 138, 169, 223, 278, 280, 321, 333, 336, 369, 370, 396, 417, 418, 440, 441.
  Joseph, 88, 418.
  Mary, 25, 88, 274, 275, 417.
  Matthew, 87-89, 274, 275, 417, 418.
  Rose, 88.
Whistle, silver, 32.
White, ——, 47.
  Capt., 342.
  Elias, 415.
  Mary, 415.
  Richard, 449.
  William, 14, 268, 274, 367, 398.
Whiting, Whightinge, Whiten, ——, 33, 100, 178, 256, 430.
  Dorothy, 55.
  Elizabeth, 55.
  Samuel, 346.
Whitlock, John, 42.
Whittingham, Whitingham,——, 62, 105.
  Elizabeth, 104.
  John, 103-105.
  Judith, 104.
  Martha, 104.
  Richard, 104.
  William, 104.
Whittle, *see* Clothing.
Whittredge, Whithredg, Whitrige, ——, 347.
  Susanna, 409.
Whittear, Whitehear, Whittyr, Whittyre, Whityare, Whityr, Abraham, 60, 428.
  John, 438.
  Richard, 438.
  Thomas, 21, 438.
Whittier, *see* Whittear.
Wickes, Wicks, Alice, 241, 242.
  Bethiah, 241.
  Elizabeth, 385.
  Hannah, 241.
  Thomas, 241, 242.

Wicome, Wickam, Wicom, Wycom, Capt., 296, 299.
  Ann, 441.
  Daniel, 237, 238, 296, 435, 441, 453.
  Richard, 441.
Wigglesworth, ——, 321.
  Mercy, 321.
Wild, Wyldes, Elizabeth, 397, 398.
  John, 175, 398.
  William, 254, 397, 398.
Wilkes, Wilks, John, 119.
  Robert, 382.
  Thomas, 171, 381, 382.
Wilkins, ——, 313.
Willcott, Jonathan, 389.
Willemore, William, 58.
Willet, Jacob, 278.
Williams, Bethiah, 196, 198, 199.
  George, 59, 195, 196, 198-200, 238.
  John, 196, 198.
  Joseph, 196, 198, 199.
  Marie, 196, 199.
  Mary, 199.
  Nathaniel, 193.
  Samuel, 196, 199, 396.
  Sarah, 196, 199.
Willix, Belshazzar, 130.
  Mary, 130, 140, 442.
Wilson, Willson, Wilsone, ——, 163-165, 221, 272, 313.
  Edward, 59.
  Elizabeth, 164, 165.
  Humphrey, 424.
  Seaborne, 165.
  Theophilus, 89, 97, 163, 164, 169, 220, 398.
  Thomas, 165.
Wilson hill, 329, 330.
Wimbles, *see* Tools.
Winbrough, ——, 158.
Winddum, 222.
Windmill hill, 346.
Windmill, *see* Buildings.
Window, Bridget, 294.
  Richard, 294.
Wine, *see* Drinks.
Winge, John, 11.
Winsley, Ann, 424.
  Samuel, 121, 130, 424.
Winter, Wenter, ——, 402.
  Hannah, 32, 33.
  Josias, 32, 33.
  William, 32, 33.

Winter Island, 147.
Wintrip, ——, 286.
Wire, see Tools.
Wise, Wisse, Ann, 11.
  Benjamin, 11.
  Em., 11.
  Humphrey, 11.
  Joseph, 11.
  Mary, 400.
  Sarah, 11.
Wiswall, John, 381.
Withars, Katherine, 110.
Witt, Wit, John, 56, 213, 277.
Witter, Annis, 350, 351.
  Josiah, 350.
  William, 350.
Wolves, see Animals (wild).
Wood, Daniel, 106.
  Mary, 106.
  Sisly, 80.
  Thomas, 219, 231, 237, 302, 330.
Wood, 39, 49, 56, 181, 204, 233, 281, 303, 304.
Woodam, Wooddam, ——, 272.
  John, 25, 177.
Woodbridge, Woodbridg, ——, 108.
  John, 15.
  N. J., 84.
Woodbury, Woodberie, Woodberry, Woodbery, Andrew, 444.
  Ann, 21.
  Annis, 263.
  Hannah, 263.
  John, 21.
  Nicholas, 270.
  William, 41, 96, 414.
Woodcocke, William, 414.
Wooden ware, see Utensils.
Woodis, Wooddes, John, 289, 290.
Wool, 155, 165, 180, 225, 230, 236, 237, 251, 277, 279, 286, 288, 302, 303, 311, 344, 363, 368, 376, 414, 423, 430.
Wool, see also Manufactures.

Wool, cotton, 79, 81, 93, 121, 130, 142, 154, 165, 182, 183, 220, 221, 245, 247, 253, 260, 263, 267, 271, 274, 282, 284, 301, 302, 308, 316, 342, 351, 353, 368, 388, 407, 426, 431, 433.
Wool, English, 182.
Wool, sheep's, 218, 236, 245, 274, 282, 302, 308, 335, 344, 399, 407, 426.
Woolen, see Cloth, Clothing, and Furnishings.
Woodman, ——, 53, 216, 247, 311, 342, 408.
  Archelaus, 205.
  Edward, 13, 17, 53, 142, 146, 230, 231, 247, 310.
  Richard, 91.
Worcester, Wooster, ——, 103, 193, 312, 406, 408.
  Moses, 404, 406, 410.
  Rebecca, 405.
  Samuel, 404, 408.
  Susanna, 404, 410.
  Timothy, 404, 405, 410.
  William, 102, 403-406, 410.
Workhouse, see Buildings.
Wormehill, Joseph, 109.
Worsted, see Cloth, and Manufactures.
Wright, John, 275.
Wyatt, Wiatt, Wiet, Wyat, ——, 82.
  John, 81, 82, 441.

Yarn, see Manufactures.
Yearlings, see Animals (domestic).
Yeoman, see Trades.
Yoe, Rebecca, 263.
  Samuel, 263.
Yokes, see Tools.
Yonge, Yongs, Christopher, 76-78.
  Joseph, 76, 77.
  Mary, 77.
  Sarah, 77.

www.ingramcontent.com/pod-product-compliance
Lightning Source LLC
Chambersburg PA
CBHW030537080526
44585CB00012B/187